READINGS IN THE STRATEGY PROCESS

—THIRD EDITION—

HENRY MINTZBERG
McGill University

JAMES BRIAN QUINN
Dartmouth College

PRENTICE HALL
Upper Saddle River, New Jersey 07458

Senior Editor: David Shafer
Assistant Editor: Lisamarie Brassini
Editor-in-Chief: Natalie Anderson
Editorial Assistant: Christopher Stogdill
Marketing Manager: Tami Wederbrand
Production Editor: Judith Leale
Managing Editor: Dee Josephson
Manufacturing Buyer: Diane Peirano
Manufacturing Supervisor: Arnold Vila
Manufacturing Manager: Vincent Scelta
Cover Design: Lorraine Castellano/John Romer

Copyright © 1998, 1992, 1988 by Prentice-Hall, Inc.
A Simon & Schuster Company
Upper Saddle River, New Jersey 07458

Mintzberg, Henry.
    Readings in the strategy process. / Henry Mintzberg, James Brian
Quinn.
        p.   cm
    Readings from: The strategy process. 3rd ed. c1996.
    Includes bibliographical references and indexes.
    ISBN 0–13–494964-1
    1. Strategic planning.   I. Quinn, James Brian.
II. Mintzberg, Henry.   Strategy process.   III. Title.
HD30.28.Q53   1998
658.4′012—dc21   97–43049
                                                            CIP

Prentice-Hall International (UK) Limited, London
Prentice-Hall of Australia Pty. Limited, Sydney
Prentice-Hall Canada, Inc., Toronto
Prentice-Hall Hispanoamericana, S.A., Mexico
Prentice-Hall of India Private Limited, New Delhi
Prentice-Hall of Japan, Inc., Tokyo
Simon & Schuster Asia Pte. Ltd., Singapore
Editora Prentice-Hall do Brasil, Ltda., Rio de Janeiro

Printed in the United States of America

10 9 8 7 6 5 4 3 2

CONTENTS

iii
▼

v

ACKNOWLEDGMENTS

We have been involved in the teaching and practice of strategy formation since the 1960s. What originally brought this book together was our firm belief that this field badly needed a new kind of text. We wanted one that looked at process issues as well as analysis; one that was built around dynamic strategy concepts and contexts instead of overworked analytical rigidities and the dichotomy of formulation and implementation— and one that accomplished these aims in an intelligent, eclectic, and lively style. We sought to combine theory and practice, description and prescription, in new ways that offered insights none could achieve alone.

In any work of this scope, there are far too many people involved to thank each one individually. We would, however, like to acknowledge the special assistance given us by those ho went especially out of their way to be helpful. In the academic community, several people deserve special mention. Deans Hennessey, Blaydon, and Fox at the Tuck School kindly arranged for time and funding support. Mr. Hiroshi Murakami and Dean Melvyn Copen of the International University of Japan generously contributed funding and contacts in Japan. While at INSEAD, Sumantra Ghoshal offered especially valuable advice on new readings to consider.

The people who really make such a major product as this happen are the competent research associates and secretaries who have undertaken the major buden of the work. At the Amos Tuck School of Business Administration, Penny C. Paquette, Suzanne Sweet, and Tammy Stebbins deserve special praise. Ms. Paquette was a researcher and oversaw the endless problems of coordinating clearances and production logistics for major portions of the book. Mrs. Sweet and Stebbins very professionally managed thousands of pages of original text and revisions with secretarial and computer skills that were invaluable. At McGill, Kate Maguire-Devlin's untold numbers of little contributions, important though they were, do not stand up to her big one—to provide a good-natured order without which the readings portion of this book could never have been finished.

At Prentice Hall, we thank David Shafer who took over this book with skill and energy, and Lisamarie Brassini who has been working on it helpfully for some time.

A special thanks must also be offered to those who worked with the book in both its preliminary stages and in the various revisions and provided invaluable feedback: the many classes of "guinea pig" McGill and Tuck MBA students and our many professional and academic colleagues who have made useful suggestions for new readings, and thoughtfully commented on how to improve this text. In particular: Bill Joyce, Rich D'Aveni, Philip Anderson, and Sydney Finkelstein at Tuck; John Voyer at University of Southern Main; Sumantra Ghoshal at LBS; Bill Davidson at the University of Southern California; Pierre Brunet and Bill Taylor at Concordia; Fritz Reiger at Windsor; Jan Jorgensen, Cynthia Hardy, and Tom Powell at McGill; Robert Burgelman at Stanford; and Franz Lohrke and Gary Castrogiovanni at Louisiana State University.

One last word; this book is not "finished." Our text, like the subject of so much of its content, is an ongoing process, not a static statement. So much of this book is different from conventional strategy textbooks, indeed from our own text last time, that there are bound to be all kinds of opportunities for improvement. We would like to ask you to help us in this regard. Please write to any of us with your suggestions on how to improve the readings and the organization of the book and its presentation. Strategy making, we believe, is a learning process; we are also engaged in a learning process. And for that we need your feedback. Thank you and enjoy what follows.

Henry Mintzberg
James Brian Quinn

INTRODUCTION

In our first edition, we set out to produce a different kind of textbook in the field of business policy or, as it is now more popularly called, strategic management. We tried to provide the reader with a richness of theory, a richness of practice, and a strong basis for linkage between the two. We rejected the strictly case study approach, which leaves theory out altogether, or soft-pedals it, and thereby denies the accumulated benefits of many years of careful research and thought about management processes. We also rejected an alternate approach that forces on readers a highly rationalistic model of how the strategy process *should* function. We collaborated on this book because we believe that in this complex world of organizations a range of concepts is needed to cut through and illuminate particular aspects of that complexity.

There is no "one best way" to create strategy, nor is there "one best form" of organization. Quite different forms work well in particular contexts. We believe that exploring a fuller variety systematically will create a deeper and more useful appreciation of the strategy process.

This text, unlike most others, is eclectic. Presenting published articles and portions of other books in their original form, rather than filtered through our minds and pens, is one way to reinforce this variety. Each author has his or her ideas and his or her own best way of expressing them (ourselves included!). Summarized by us, these readings would lose a good deal of their richness.

We do not apologize for contradictions among the ideas of leading thinkers. The world is full of contradictions. The real danger lies in using pat solutions to a nuanced reality, not in opening perspectives up to different interpretations. The effective strategist is one who can live with contradictions, learn to appreciate their causes and effects, and reconcile them sufficiently for effective action. The readings have, nonetheless, been ordered by chapter to suggest some ways in which reconciliation can be considered. Our own chapter introductions are also intended to assist in this task and to help place the readings in perspective.

ON THEORY

A word on theory is in order. We do not consider theory a dirty word, nor do we apologize for making it a major component of this book. To some people, to be theoretical is to be detached and impractical. But a bright social scientist once said, "There is nothing so practical as a good theory." And every successful doctor, engineer, and physicist would have to agree: They would be unable to practice their modern work without theories. Theories are useful because they shortcut the need to store masses of data. It is easier to remember a simple framework about some phenomenon than it is to consider every small detail you ever observed. In a sense theories are a bit like cataloging systems in libraries: The world would be impossibly confusing without them. They enable you to store and conveniently access your own experiences as well as those of others.

One can, however, suffer not just from an absence of theories but also from being dominated by them without realizing it. To paraphrase the words of John Maynard Keynes, most "practical men" are the slaves of some defunct theory . Whether we realize it or not, our behavior is guided by the systems of ideas that we have internalized over the years. Much can be learned by bringing these out in the open, examining them more carefully, and comparing them with alternative ways to view the world—including ones based on systematic study (that is, research). One of our prime intentions in this book is to expose the limitations of conventional theories and to offer alternate explanations that can be superior guides of understanding and taking action in specific contexts.

PRESCRIPTIVE THEORY VERSUS DESCRIPTIVE THEORY

Unlike many textbooks in this field, this one tries to explain the world as it is rather than as someone thinks it is *supposed* to be. Although there has sometimes been a tendency to disdain such *descriptive* theories, *prescriptive* (or normative) ones have often been the problem, rather than the solution, in the field of management. There is no one best way in management; no prescription works for all organizations. Even when a prescription seems effective in some context, it requires a sophisticated understanding of exactly what that context is and how it functions. In other words, one cannot decide reliably what should be done in a system as complicated as a contemporary organization without a genuine understanding of how that organization really works. In engineering, no student ever questions having to learn physics, in medicine, having to learn anatomy. Imagine an engineering student's hand shooting up in physics class: "Listen, prof, it's fine to tell us how the atom does work. But what we really want to know is how the atom *should* work." Why should a management student's similar demand in the realm of strategy or structure be considered any more appropriate? How can people manage complex systems they do not understand?

Nevertheless, we have not ignored prescriptive theory when it appears useful. A number of prescriptive techniques (industry analysis, experience curves, and so on) are discussed. But these are associated with other readings that will help you understand the context and limitations of their usefulness. The readings offer opportunities to pursue the full complexity of strategic situations. You will find a wide range of issues and perspectives addressed. One of our main goals is to integrate a variety of views, rather than allow strategy to be fragmented into just "human issues" and "economics issues." The text provides a basis for treating the full complexity of strategic management.

ON SOURCES

How were the readings selected and edited? Some textbooks boast about how new all their readings are. We make no such claim; indeed we would like to make a different boast; many of our readings have been around quite a while, long enough to mature, like fine wine. Our criterion for inclusion was not the newness of the article so much as the quality of its insight—that is, its ability to explain some aspect of the strategy process better than any other article. Time does not age the really good articles. Quite the opposite—it distinguishes their quality (but sometimes brings us back to the old habits of masculine gender; we apologize to our readers for this). We are, of course, not biased toward old articles—just toward good ones. Hence, the materials in this book range from classics of the 1960s to some published just before our final selection was made (as well as a few hitherto unpublished pieces). You will find articles from the most serious academic journals, the best practitioner magazines, books, and some very obscure sources. The best can sometimes be found in strange places!

We have tried to include many shorter readings rather than fewer longer ones, and we have tried to present as wide a variety of good ideas as possible while maintaining clarity. To do so we often had to cut within readings. We have, in fact, put a great deal of effort into the cutting in order to extract the key messages of each reading in as brief, concise, and clear a manner as possible. Unfortunately, our cutting sometimes forced us to eliminate interesting examples and side issues. (In the readings, dots... signify portions that have been deleted from the original, while square brackets [ ] signify our own insertions of minor clarifications into the original text). We apologize to you, the reader, as well as to the authors, for having done this, but hope that the overall result has rendered these changes worthwhile.

We have also included a number of our own works. Perhaps we are biased, having less objective standards by which to judge what we have written. But we have messages to convey, too, and our own writings do examine the basic themes that we feel are important in policy and strategy courses today.

THIS BOOK'S STRUCTURE

NOT FORMULATION, THEN IMPLEMENTATION

The first edition of this text offered a chapter format that was new to the policy or strategy field. Unlike most others, it had no specific chapter or section devoted to "implementation" per se. The assumption in other texts is that strategy is formulated and then implemented, with organizational structures, control systems, and the like following obediently behind strategy. In this text, as in reality, formulation and implementation are intertwined as complex interactive processes in which politics, values, organizational culture, and management styles determine or constrain particular strategic decisions. And strategy, structure, and systems mix together in complicated ways to influence outcomes. While strategy formulation and implementation may be separated in some situations—perhaps in crises, in some totally new ventures, as well as in organizations facing predictable futures—these events are far from typical. We certainly do not believe in building a whole book (let alone a whole field) around this conceptual distinction.

BUT CONCEPTS, THEN CONTEXTS

The readings are divided roughly into two different parts. The first deals with *concepts*, the second with *contexts*. We introduce strategy and structure as well

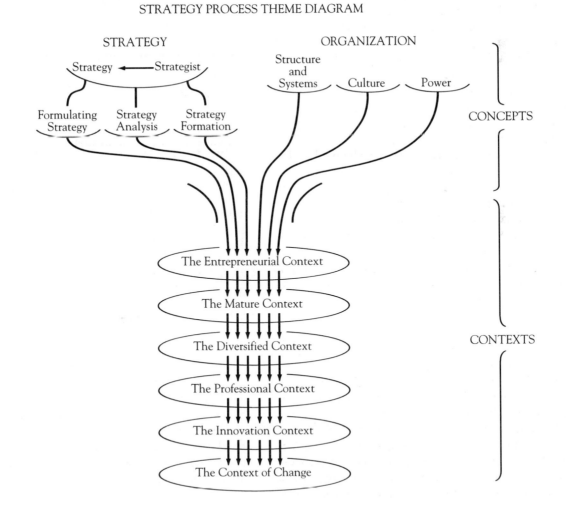

STRATEGY PROCESS THEME DIAGRAM

as power, culture, and several other concepts early in the text as equal partners in the complex web of ideas that make up what we call "the strategy process." In the second half of the text we weave these concepts together in a number of distinct situations, which we call *contexts*.

Our theme diagram illustrates this. Concepts, shown on top, are divided into two groups—strategy and organization—to represent the first two sections of the book. Contexts draw all these concepts together, in a variety of situations—covered in the third section—which we consider the key ones in the field of strategy today (though hardly the only ones). The outline of the text, chapter by chapter, proceeds as follows:

SECTION I: STRATEGY

The first section is called *Strategy*; it comprises five chapters (two introductory in nature and three on the processes by which strategy making takes place). Chapter 1 introduces *the strategy concept* and probes the meaning of this important word to broaden your view of it. Here the pattern is set of challenging you to question conventional views, especially when these act to narrow perspectives. The themes introduced in this chapter carry throughout the book and are worth care in understanding.

Chapter 2 introduces a very important character in this book, *the strategist* as general manager. This person may not be the only one who makes strategy in an organization, but he or she is clearly a key player. In examining the work of the general manager and the character of his or her job, we shall perhaps upset a number of widely accepted notions. We do this to help you understand the very real complexities and difficulties of making strategy and managing in contemporary organizations.

Chapters 3, 4, and 5 take up a theme that is treated extensively in the text—to the point of being reflected in its title: the development of an understanding of the *processes* by which strategies are made. Chapter 3 looks at *formulating strategy*, specifically at some widely accepted prescriptive models for how organizations should go about developing their strategies. Chapter 4 extends these ideas to more formal ways of doing *strategy analysis* and considering what, if any, "generic" forms a strategy can take. While readings in later chapters will challenge some of these precepts, what will not be questioned is the importance

of having to understand them. They are fundamental to appreciating the strategy process today.

Chapter 5 switches from a prescriptive to a descriptive approach. Concerned with understanding *strategy formation*, it considers how strategies actually *do* form in organizations (not necessarily by being formulated) and *why* different processes may be effective in specific circumstances. This text takes an unconventional stand by viewing planning and other formal approaches as not the only—and often indeed not even the most desirable—ways to make strategy. You will find our emphasis on the descriptive process—as an equal partner with the more traditional concerns for technical and analytical issues—to be one of the unifying themes of this book.

SECTION II: ORGANIZATION

In Section I, the readings introduced strategy, the strategist, and various ways in which strategy might be formulated and does in fact form. In Section II, entitled *Organization*, we introduce other concepts that constitute part of the strategy process.

In Chapter 6, we consider structure and systems, where particular attention is paid to the various forms that structure can take as well as the mechanisms that comprise it. In Chapter 7, we consider culture and power, especially how strong systems of beliefs, called "ideologies," impact on organizations and their strategies and so influence their effectiveness. We also view how power distributes itself among the various actors within the organization and how the organization acts as a political entity in its own right, whether or not responsibly, in the face of opposing forces in society. Both aspects will be seen to influence significantly the processes by which strategies are formulated or form. Then Chapter 8 takes a hard look at managerial styles as they impact strategy and operations, and introduces an especially important actor, the middle manager.

SECTION III: CONTEXTS

Section III is called *Contexts*. We consider how all of the elements introduced so far—strategy, the processes by which it is formulated and gets formed, the strategist, structure, systems, culture, power, and style—combine to suit particular contexts, seven in all.

Chapter 9 deals with the entrepreneurial context, where a rather simple organization comes under the close control of a strong leader, often a person with vision. Chapter 10 examines the mature context, one common to many large business and government organizations involved in the mass production or distribution of goods and services.

Chapters 11 and 12 develop the contexts of professionalism and innovation, both involving organizations of high expertise. In the professional context, the experts work relatively independently in rather stable conditions, while in the innovation context, they combine in project teams under more dynamic conditions. What these two contexts have in common, however, is that they act in ways that upset many of the widely accepted notions about how organizations should be structured and make strategy.

Chapter 13 introduces the diversified context, and deals with organizations that have diversified their product or service line and usually divisionalized their structures to deal with the greater varieties of environments they face. In Chapter 14, we take a look at an increasingly important and popular aspect of the diversified context, that of geography—namely the international or so-called global context.

In considering each of these widely different contexts we seek to discuss (where appropriate material is available) the situation in which each is most likely to be found, the structures most suited to it, the kinds of strategies that tend to be pursued, the processes by which these strategies tend to be formed and might be formulated, and the social issues associated with the context.

Chapter 15 is devoted not so much to a specific context as to managing change between contexts, or within a context (which we can, of course, characterize as the context of change). The major concerns are how organizations can cope with crises, turnarounds, revitalizations, and new stages in their own life cycles or those of their key products.

Well, there you have it. We have worked hard on this book, in both the original and revised editions, to get it right. We have tried to think things through from the basics, with a resulting text that in style, format, and content is unusual for the field of policy or strategy. Our product may not be perfect, but we believe it is good—indeed better than any other text available. Now it's your turn to find out if you agree. Have fun doing so!

Henry Mintzberg
James Brian Quinn

READINGS
— IN THE —
STRATEGY
PROCESS

STRATEGY

1

THE STRATEGY CONCEPT

We open this text on its focal point: strategy. The first section is called "Strategy," the first chapter, "The Strategy Concept." Later chapters in this section describe the role of the general manager as strategist and consider the processes by which strategies develop from three perspectives: deliberate formulation, systematic analysis, and emergent formation. But in this opening chapter, we consider the central concept—strategy itself.

What is strategy? There is no single, universally accepted definition. Different authors and managers use the term differently; for example, some include goals and objectives as part of strategy while others make firm distinctions between them. Our intention in including the following readings is not to promote any one view of strategy, but rather to suggest a number that seem useful. As will be evident throughout this text, our wish is not to narrow perspectives but to broaden them by trying to clarify issues. In pursuing these readings, it will be helpful to think about the meaning of strategy, to try to understand how different people have used the term, and later to see if certain definitions hold up better in particular contexts.

We have taken the opportunity to include in this first chapter readings by each of us, the coauthors of the book. They set the tone for the material that follows and provide an indication of our own thinking. As you will see, our views are similar but certainly not identical; indeed in places we differ somewhat (for example, on the word "tactics"). But overall, we believe you will find these views complementary.

The first reading, by James Brian Quinn of the Amos Tuck School at Dartmouth College, provides a general overview by clarifying some of the vocabulary in this field and introducing a number of the themes that will appear throughout the text. In this reading from his book *Strategies for Change: Logical Incrementalism*, Quinn places special emphasis on the military uses of the term "strategy" and draws from this domain a set of essential "dimensions" or criteria for successful strategies. To derive these, he goes back to Philip and Alexander of Macedonia for his main example; he also provides a brief kaleidoscope of how similar concepts have influenced later military and diplomatic strategists.

Discussion of the military aspects of strategy must surely be among the oldest continuous literatures in the world. In fact, the origins of the word "strategy" go back even farther than this experience in Macedonia, to the Greeks whom Alexander and his father defeated. As Quinn notes and Roger Evered, in another article, elaborates,

> Initially *strategos* referred to a role (a general in command of an army). Later it came to mean "the art of the general," which is to say the psychological and behavioral skills with which he occupied the role. By the time of Pericles (450 B.C.) it came to mean managerial skill (administration, leadership, oration, power). And by Alexander's time (330 B.C.) it referred to the skill of employing forces to overcome opposition and to create a unified system of global governance. (1980:3)

The second reading, by Henry Mintzberg who is professor of management in the Faculty of Management at McGill University in Montreal and at INSEAD in France, serves to open up the concept of strategy to a variety of views, some very different from traditional military or business writings (but suggested briefly in the Quinn reading). Mintzberg focuses on various distinct definitions of strategy—as plan (as well as ploy), pattern, position, and perspective. He uses the first two of these definitions to take us beyond deliberate strategy—beyond the traditional view of the term—to the notion of *emergent* strategy. This introduces the idea that strategies can *form* in an organization without being consciously intended, that is, without being *formulated*. This may seem to run counter to the whole thrust of the strategy literature, but Mintzberg argues that many people implicitly use the term this way even though they would not so define it.

Upon completion of these readings, we hope that you will be less sure of the use of the word "strategy" but more ready to tackle the study of the strategy process with a broadened perspective and an open mind. There are no universally right answers in this field (any more than there are in most other fields), but there are interesting and constructive orientations.

▼ READING 1.1   STRATEGIES FOR CHANGE*

by James Brian Quinn

Some Useful Definitions

Because the words *strategy, objectives, goals, policy,* and *programs* have different meanings to individual readers or to various organizational cultures, I [try] to use certain definitions consistently . . . For clarity—not pedantry—these are set forth as follows:

A **strategy** is the *pattern* or *plan* that *integrates* an organization's *major* goals, policies, and action sequences into a *cohesive* whole. A well-formulated strategy helps to *marshal* and *allocate* an organization's resources into a *unique and viable posture* based on its relative *internal competencies* and *shortcomings*, anticipated *changes in the environment*, and contingent moves by *intelligent opponents*.

Goals (or **objectives**) state *what* is to be achieved and *when* results are to be accomplished, but they do not state *how* the results are to be achieved. All organizations have multiple goals existing in a complex hierarchy (Simon, 1964): from value objectives, which express the broad value premises toward which the company is to strive; through overall organizational objectives, which establish the intended *nature* of the enterprise and the *directions* in which it should move; to a series of less permanent goals that define targets for each organizational unit, its subunits, and finally all major program activities within each subunit. Major goals—those that affect the entity's overall direction and viability—are called *strategic goals*.

* Excerpted from James Brian Quinn, *Strategies for Change: Logical Incrementalism* (copyright © Richard D. Irwin, Inc. 1980), Chaps. 1 and 5; reprinted by permission of the publisher.

Policies are rules or guidelines that express the *limits* within which action should occur. These rules often take the form of contingent decisions for resolving conflicts among specific objectives. For example: "Don't exceed three months' inventory in any item without corporate approval." Like the objectives they support, policies exist in a hierarchy throughout the organization. Major policies—those that guide the entity's overall direction and posture or determine its viability—are called *strategic policies*.

Programs specify the *step-by-step sequence of actions* necessary to achieve major objectives. They express *how* objectives will be achieved within the limits set by policy. They ensure that resources are committed to achieve goals, and they provide the dynamic track against which progress can be measured. Those major programs that determine the entity's overall thrust and viability are called *strategic programs*.

Strategic decisions are those that determine the overall direction of an enterprise and its ultimate viability in light of the predictable, the unpredictable, and the unknowable changes that may occur in its most important surrounding environments. They intimately shape the true goals of the enterprise. They help delineate the broad limits within which the enterprise operates. They dictate both the resources the enterprise will have accessible for its tasks and the principal patterns in which these resources will be allocated. And they determine the effectiveness of the enterprise—whether its major thrusts are in the right directions given its resource potentials—rather than whether individual tasks are performed efficiently. Management for efficiency, along with the myriad decisions necessary to maintain the daily life and services of the enterprise, is the domain of operations.

STRATEGIES VERSUS TACTICS

Strategies normally exist at many different levels in any large organization. For example, in government there are world trade, national economic, treasury department, military spending, investment, fiscal, monetary supply, banking, regional development, and local reemployment strategies—all related to each other somewhat hierarchically yet each having imperatives of its own. Similarly, businesses have numerous strategies from corporate levels to department levels within divisions. Yet if strategies exist at all these levels, how do strategies and tactics differ? Often the primary difference lies in the scale of action or the perspective of the leader. What appears to be a "tactic" to the chief executive officer (or general) may be a "strategy" to the marketing head (or lieutenant) if it determines the ultimate success and viability of his or her organization. In a more precise sense, tactics can occur at either level. They are the short-duration, adaptive, action-interaction realignments that opposing forces use to accomplish limited goals after their initial contact. Strategy defines a continuing basis for ordering these adaptations toward more broadly conceived purposes.

A genuine strategy is always needed when the potential actions or responses of intelligent opponents can seriously affect the endeavor's desired outcome—regardless of that endeavor's organizational level in the total enterprise. This condition almost always pertains to the important actions taken at the top level of competitive organizations. However, game theorists quickly point out that some important top-level actions—for example, sending a peacetime fleet across the Atlantic—merely require elaborate coordinative plans and programs (Von Neumann and Morgenstern, 1944; Shubik, 1975; McDonald, 1950). A whole new set of concepts, a true strategy, is needed if some people or nations decide to oppose the fleet's purposes. And it is these concepts that in large part distinguish strategic formulation from simpler programmatic planning.

Strategies may be looked at as either a priori statements to guide action or a posteriori results of actual decision behavior. In most complex organizations . . . one would be hard pressed to find a complete a priori statement of a total strategy that actually is followed. Yet often the existence of a strategy (or strategy change) may be clear to an objective observer, although it is not yet apparent to the executives making critical decisions. One, therefore, must look at the actual emerging *pattern* of the enterprise's operant goals, policies, and major programs to see what its true strategy is (Mintzberg, 1972). Whether it is consciously set forth in advance or is simply a widely held understanding resulting from a stream of decisions, this pattern becomes the real strategy of the enterprise. And it is changes in this pattern—regardless of what any formal strategic documents may say—that either analysts or strategic decision makers must address if they wish to comprehend or alter the concern's strategic posture. . . .

The Classical Approach to Strategy

Military-diplomatic strategies have existed since prehistoric times. In fact, one function of the earliest historians and poets was to collect the accumulated lore of these successful and unsuccessful life-and-death strategies and convert them into wisdom and guidance for the future. As societies grew larger and conflicts more complex, generals, statesmen, and captains studied, codified, and tested essential strategic concepts until a coherent body of principles seemed to emerge. In various forms these were ultimately distilled into the maxims of Sun Tzu (1963), Machiavelli (1950), Napoleon (1940), Von Clausewitz (1976), Foch (1970), Lenin (1927), Hart (1954), Montgomery (1958), or Mao Tse-Tung (1967). Yet with a few exceptions—largely introduced by modern technology—the most basic principles of strategy were in place and recorded long before the Christian era. More modern institutions primarily adapted and modified these to their own special environments.

Although one could choose any number of classical military-diplomatic strategies as examples, Philip and Alexander's actions at Chaeronea (in 338 B.C.) contain many currently relevant concepts (Varner and Alger, 1978; Green, 1970). . . .

A CLASSICAL STRATEGY

A Grand Strategy

Philip and his young son, Alexander, had very *clear goals*. They sought to rid Macedonia of influence by the Greek city-states and to *establish dominance* over what was then essentially northern Greece. They also wanted Athens to join a coalition with them against Persia on their eastern flank. *Assessing their resources,* they *decided to* avoid the overwhelming superiority of the Athenian fleet and *chose to forego* attack on the powerful walled cities of Athens and Thebes where their superbly trained phalanxes and cavalry would not *have distinct advantages.*

Philip and Alexander *used an indirect approach* when an invitation by the Amphictyonic Council brought their army south to punish Amphissa. In a *planned sequence of actions and deceptive maneuvers,* they cut away from a direct line of march to Amphissa, *bypassed the enemy,* and *fortified a key base,* Elatea. They then took steps to *weaken their opponents politically and morally* by pressing restoration of the Phoenician communities earlier dispersed by the Thebans and by having Philip declared a champion of the Delphic gods. Then *using misleading messages* to make the enemy believe they had moved north to Thrace and also *using developed intelligence sources,* the Macedonians in a *surprise attack* annihilated the Greeks' positions near Amphissa. This *lured their opponents away from their defensive positions* in the nearby mountain passes to *consolidate their forces* near the town of Chaeronea.

There, *assessing the relative strengths* of their opponents, the Macedonians first *attempted to negotiate* to achieve their goals. When this was unsuccessful they had a *well-developed contingency plan* on how to *attack and overwhelm* the Greeks. Prior to this time, of course, the Macedonians had *organized* their troops into the famed phalanxes, and had *developed the full logistics* needed for their field support including a longer spear, which helped the Macedonian phalanxes penetrate the solid shield wall of the heavily massed Greek formations. *Using the natural advantages* of their terrain, the Macedonians had developed cavalry support for their phalanxes' movements far beyond the Greek capability. Finally, using a *relative advantage*—the *command structure* their hierarchical *social system* allowed—against the more democratic Greeks, the Macedonian nobles had *trained their personnel* into one of the most *disciplined and highly motivated forces* in the world.

The Battle Strategy

Supporting this was the battle strategy at Chaeronea, which emerged as follows. Philip and Alexander first *analyzed their specific strengths and weaknesses and their opponents' current alignments and probable moves.* The Macedonian strength lay in their new spear technology, the *mobility* of their superbly disciplined phalanxes, and the powerful cavalry units led by Alexander. Their weaknesses were that they were badly outnumbered and faced—in the Athenians and the Theban Band—some of the finest foot troops in the world. However, their opponents had two weak points. One was the Greek left flank with lightly armed local troops placed near the Chaeronean Acropolis and next to some more heavily armed—but hastily assembled—hoplites bridging to the strong center held by the Athenians. The famed Theban Band anchored the Greek right wing near a swamp on the Cephissus River. [See Figure 1.]

Philip and Alexander *organized their leadership to command key positions,* Philip took over the right wing and Alexander the cavalry. They *aligned their forces* into *a unique posture* which *used their strengths* and *offset their weaknesses.* They decided on those spots at which they would *concentrate their forces,* what *positions to concede,* and what *key points* they *must take and hold.* Starting with their units angled back from the Greek lines (see map), they developed a *focused major thrust* against the Greek left wing and *attacked their opponents' weaknesses*—the troops near Chaeronea—with the most disciplined of the Macedonian units, the guards' brigade. After building up pressure and stretching the Greek line to its left, the guards' brigade abruptly began a *planned withdrawal.* This *feint* caused the Greek left to break ranks and rush forward, believing the Macedonians to be in full retreat. This *stretched the opponents' resources* as the Greek center moved left to *maintain contact* with its flank and to attack the "fleeing" Macedonians.

Then *with predetermined timing,* Alexander's cavalry *attacked the exposure* of the stretched line at the same moment Philip's phalanxes *re-formed as planned* on the high ground at the edge of the Heamon River. Alexander *broke through* and *formed a bridgehead* behind the Greeks. He *refocused his forces against a segment* of the opponents' line; his cavalry *surrounded and destroyed* the Theban Band

FIGURE 1
The Battle of Chaeronea
Source: Modified with permission from P. Green, *Alexander the Great,* Praeger Publishers, New York (1970).

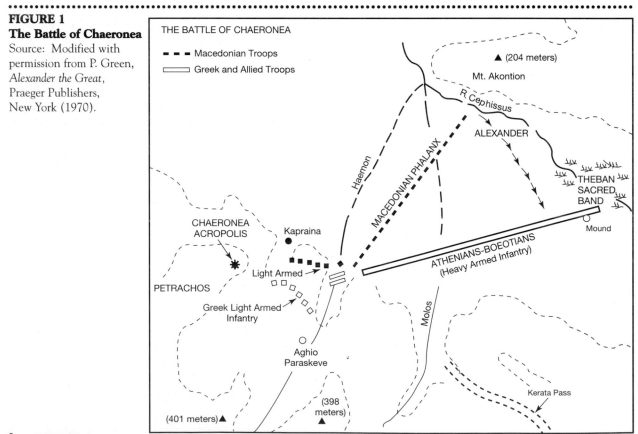

as the *overwhelming power* of the phalanxes poured through the gap he had created. From its *secured position*, the Macedonian left flank then turned and *attacked the flank* of the Athenians. With the help of Philip's *planned counterattack*, the Macedonians *expanded their dominance and overwhelmed the critical target*, i.e., the Greek center. . . .

MODERN ANALOGIES

Similar concepts have continued to dominate the modern era of formal strategic thought. As this period begins, Scharnhorst still points to the need to *analyze social forces and structures* as a basis for *understanding effective command styles* and *motivational stimuli* (Von Clausewitz, 1976:8). Frederick the Great proved this point in the field. Presumably based on such analyses, he adopted *training, discipline,* and *fast maneuvers* as the central concepts for a tightly disciplined German culture that had to be constantly ready to fight on two fronts (Phillips, 1940). Von Bülow (1806) continued to emphasize the dominant strategic roles of *geographical positioning* and *logistical support systems* in strategy. Both Jomini (1971) and Von Bülow (1806) stressed the concepts of *concentration, points of domination,* and *rapidity of movement* as central strategic themes and even tried to develop them into mathematically precise principles for their time.

Still later Von Clausewitz expounded on the paramountcy of *clear major objectives* in war and on developing war strategies as a component of the nation's *broader goals* with *time horizons* extending beyond the war itself. Within this context he postulated that an effective strategy should be focused around a relatively *few central principles* which can *create, guide,* and *maintain dominance* despite the enormous frictions that occur as one tries to position or maneuver large forces in war. Among these he included many of the concepts operant in Macedonian times: *spirit or morale, surprise, cunning, concentration in space, dominance of selected positions, use of strategic reserves, unification over time, tension and release,* and so on. He showed how these broad principles applied to a number of specific attack, defense, flanking, and retreat situations; but he always stressed the intangible of *leadership*. His basic positioning and organizational principles were to be mixed with boldness, perseverance, and genius. He constantly emphasized—as did Napoleon—the need for *planned flexibility* once the battle was joined.

Later strategic analysts adapted these classic themes for larger-scale conflicts. Von Schlieffen linked together the huge numerical and production *strengths* of Germany and the vast *maneuvering capabilities* of Flanders fields to pull the nation's might together conceptually behind a *unique alignment of forces* ("a giant hayrake"), which would *outflank* his French opponents, *attack weaknesses* (their supply lines and rear), capture and *hold key political centers* of France, and *dominate or destroy* its weakened army in the field (Tuchman, 1962). On the other side, Foch and Grandmaison saw *morale* ("élan"), *nerve* ("cran"), and continuous *concentrated attack* ("attaque à outrance") as *matching the values* of a volatile, recently defeated, and vengeful French nation, which had decided (for both moral and *coalition* reasons) to *set important limits* on its own actions in World War I—that is, not to attack first or through Belgium.

As these two strategies lost shape and became the head-on slaughter of trench warfare, Hart (1954) revitalized the *indirect approach,* and this became a central theme of British strategic thinking between the wars. Later in the United States, Matloff and Snell (1953) began to stress planning for *large-scale coalitions* as the giant forces of World War II developed. The Enigma group *moved secretly to develop the intelligence network* that was so crucial in the war's outcome (Stevenson, 1976). But once engaged in war, George Marshall still saw the only hope for Allied victory in *concentrating overwhelming forces* against one enemy (Germany) first, then after *conceding early losses* in the Pacific, *refocusing Allied forces* in a gigantic *sequential coordinated movement* against Japan. In the eastern theater, MacArthur first *fell back, consolidated a base* for operations, *built up his logistics, avoided his opponent's strengths,* bypassed Japan's established defensive positions, and in a *gigantic flanking maneuver* was ready to invade Japan after *softening its political and psychological will* through saturation bombing (James, 1970).

All these modern thinkers and practitioners utilized classical principles of strategy dating back to the Greek era, but perhaps the most startling analogies of World War II lay in Patton's and Rommel's battle strategies, which were almost carbon copies of the Macedonians' concepts of planned concentration, rapid breakthrough, encirclement, and attack on the enemy's rear (Essame, 1974; Farago, 1964; Irving, 1977; Young, 1974).

Similar concepts still pervade well-conceived strategies—whether they are government, diplomatic, military, sports, or business strategies. What could be more direct than the parallel between Chaeronea and a well-developed business strategy that first probes and withdraws to determine opponents' strengths, forces opponents to stretch their commitments, then concentrates resources, attacks a clear exposure, overwhelms a selected market segment, builds a bridgehead in that market, and then regroups and expands from that base to dominate a wider field? Many companies have followed just such strategies with great success. . . .

Dimensions of Strategy

Analysis of military-diplomatic strategies and similar analogies in other fields provides some essential insights into the basic dimensions, nature, and design of formal strategies.

First, effective formal strategies contain three essential elements: (1) the most important *goals* (or objectives) to be achieved, (2) the most significant *policies* guiding or limiting action, and (3) the major *action sequences* (or programs) that are to accomplish the defined goals within the limits set. Since strategy determines the overall direction and action focus of the organization, its formulation cannot be regarded as the mere generation and alignment of programs to meet predetermined goals. Goal development is an integral part of strategy formulation. . . .

Second, effective strategies develop around a *few key concepts and thrusts,* which give them cohesion, balance, and focus. Some thrusts are temporary; others are carried through to the end of the strategy. Some cost more per unit gain than others. Yet resources must be *allocated in patterns* that provide sufficient resources for each thrust to succeed regardless of its relative cost/gain ratio. And organizational units must be coordinated and actions controlled to support the intended thrust pattern or else the total strategy will fail. . . .

Third, strategy deals not just with the unpredictable but also with the *unknowable.* For major enterprise strategies, no analyst could predict the precise ways in which all impinging forces could interact with each other, be distorted by nature or human emotions, or be modified by the imaginations and purposeful counteractions of intelligent opponents (Braybrooke and Lindblom, 1963). Many have noted how large-scale systems can respond quite counterintuitively (Forrester, 1971) to apparently rational actions or how a seemingly bizarre series of events can conspire to prevent or assist success (White, 1978; Lindblom, 1959). . . .

Consequently, the essence of strategy—whether military, diplomatic, business, sports, (or) political . . . —is to *build a posture* that is so strong (and potentially flexible) in selective ways that the organization can achieve its goals despite the unforeseeable ways external forces may actually interact when the time comes.

Fourth, just as military organizations have multiple echelons of grand, theater, area, battle, infantry, and artillery strategies, so should other complex organizations have a number of hierarchically related and mutually supporting strategies (Vancil and Lorange, 1975; Vancil, 1976). Each such strategy must be more or less complete in itself, congruent with the level of decentralization intended. Yet each must be shaped as a cohesive element of higher-level strategies. Although, for reasons cited, achieving total cohesion among all of a major organization's strategies would be a superhuman task for any chief executive officer, it is important that there be a systematic means for testing each component strategy and seeing that it fulfills the major tenets of a well-formed strategy.

The criteria derived from military-diplomatic strategies provide an excellent framework for this, yet too often one sees purported formal strategies at all organizational levels that are not strategies at all. Because they ignore or violate even the most basic strategic principles, they are little more than aggregates of philosophies or agglomerations of programs. They lack the cohesiveness, flexibility, thrust, sense of positioning against intelligent opposition, and other criteria that historical analysis suggests effective strategies must contain. Whether formally or incrementally derived, strategies should be at least intellectually tested against the proper criteria.

CRITERIA FOR EFFECTIVE STRATEGY

In devising a strategy to deal with the unknowable, what factors should one consider? Although each strategic situation is unique, are there some common criteria that tend to define a good strategy? The fact that a strategy worked in retrospect is not a sufficient criterion for judging any strategy. Was Grant really a greater strategist than Lee? Was Foch's strategy better than Von Schlieffen's? Was Xerxes's strategy superior to that of Leonidas? Was it the Russians' strategy that allowed them to roll over the Czechoslovaks in 1968? Clearly other factors than strategy—including luck, overwhelming resources, superb or stupid implementation, and enemy errors—help determine ultimate results. Besides, at the time one formulates a strategy, one cannot use the criterion of ultimate success because the outcome is still in doubt. Yet one clearly needs some guidelines to define an effective strategic structure.

A few studies have suggested some initial criteria for evaluating a strategy (Tilles, 1963; Christensen et al., 1978). These include its clarity, motivational impact, internal consistency, compatibility with the environment, appropriateness in light of resources, degree of risk, match to the personal values of key figures, time horizon, and workability. . . . In addition, historical examples—from both business and military-diplomatic settings—suggest that effective strategies should at a minimum encompass certain other critical factors and structural elements. . . .

▼ *Clear, decisive objectives*: Are all efforts directed toward clearly understood, decisive, and attainable overall goals? Specific goals of subordinate units may change in the heat of campaigns or competition, but the overriding goals of the strategy for all units must remain clear enough to provide continuity and cohesion for tactical choices during the time horizon of the strategy. All goals need not be written down or numerically precise, but they must be understood and be decisive—that is. if they are achieved they should ensure the continued viability and vitality of the entity vis-à-vis its opponents.

▼ *Maintaining the initiative*: Does the strategy preserve freedom of action and enhance commitment? Does it set the pace and determine the course of events rather than reacting to them? A prolonged reactive posture breeds unrest, lowers morale, and surrenders the advantage of timing and intangibles to opponents. Ultimately such a posture increases costs, decreases the number of options available, and lowers the probability of achieving sufficient success to ensure independence and continuity.

▼ *Concentration*: Does the strategy concentrate superior power at the place and time likely to be decisive? Has the strategy defined precisely what will make the enterprise superior in power—that is, "best" in critical dimensions—in relation to its opponents? A distinctive competency yields greater success with fewer resources and is the essential basis for higher gains (or profits) than competitors. . . .

▼ *Flexibility:* Has the strategy purposely built in resource buffers and dimensions for flexibility and maneuver? Reserved capabilities, planned maneuverability, and repositioning allow one to use minimum resources while keeping opponents at a relative disadvantage. As corollaries of concentration and concession, they permit the strategist to reuse the same forces to overwhelm selected positions at different times. They also force less flexible opponents to use more resources to hold predetermined positions, while simultaneously requiring minimum fixed commitment of one's own resources for defensive purposes.

▼ *Coordinated and committed leadership:* Does the strategy provide responsible, committed leadership for each of its major goals? . . . [Leaders] must be so chosen and motivated that their own interests and values match the needs of their roles. Successful strategies require commitment, not just acceptance.

▼ *Surprise:* Has the strategy made use of speed, secrecy, and intelligence to attack exposed or unprepared opponents at unexpected times? With surprise and correct timing, success can be achieved out of all proportion to the energy exerted and can decisively change strategic positions. . . .

▼ *Security:* Does the strategy secure resource bases and all vital operating points for the enterprise? Does it develop an effective intelligence system sufficient to prevent surprises by opponents? Does it develop the full logistics to support each of its major thrusts? Does it use coalitions effectively to extend the resource base and zones of friendly acceptance for the enterprise? . . .

These are critical elements of strategy, whether in business, government, or warfare.

▼ READING 1.2   FIVE Ps FOR STRATEGY*

by Henry Mintzberg

Human nature insists on *a* definition for every concept. But the word *strategy* has long been used implicitly in different ways even if it has traditionally been defined in only one. Explicit recognition of multiple definitions can help people to maneuver through this difficult field. Accordingly, five definitions of strategy are presented here—as plan, ploy, pattern, position, and perspective—and some of their interrelationships are then considered.

Strategy As Plan

To almost anyone you care to ask, **strategy is a plan**—some sort of *consciously intended* course of action, a guideline (or set of guidelines) to deal with a situation. A kid has a "strategy" to get over a fence, a corporation has one to capture a market. By this definition, strategies have two essential characteristics: they are made in advance of the actions to which they apply, and they are developed consciously and purposefully. A host of definitions in a variety of fields reinforce this view. For example:

▼ in the military: Strategy is concerned with "draft[ing] the plan of war . . . shap[ing] the individual campaigns and within these, decid[ing] on the individual engagements" (Von Clausewitz, 1976:177).

▼ in game theory: Strategy is "a complete plan: a plan which specifies what choices [the player] will make in every possible situation" (von Newman and Morgenstern, 1944:79).

* Originally published in the *California Management Review* (Fall 1987), © 1987 by the Regents of the University of California. Reprinted with deletions by permission of the *California Management Review*.

▼ in management: "Strategy is a unified, comprehensive, and integrated plan . . . designed to ensure that the basic objectives of the enterprise are achieved" (Glueck, 1980:9).

As plans, strategies may be general or they can be specific. There is one use of the word in the specific sense that should be identified here. As plan, **a strategy can be a ploy,** too, really just a specific "maneuver" intended to outwit an opponent or competitor. The kid may use the fence as a ploy to draw a bully into his yard, where his Doberman pinscher awaits intruders. Likewise, a corporation may threaten to expand plant capacity to discourage a competitor from building a new plant. Here the real strategy (as plan, that is, the real intention) is the threat, not the expansion itself, and as such is a ploy.

In fact, there is a growing literature in the field of strategic management, as well as on the general process of bargaining, that views strategy in this way and so focuses attention on its most dynamic and competitive aspects. For example, in his popular book, *Competitive Strategy,* Porter (1980) devotes one chapter to "Market Signals" (including discussion of the effects of announcing moves, the use of "the fighting brand, " and the use of threats of private antitrust suits) and another to "Competitive Moves" (including actions to preempt competitive response). And Schelling (1980) devotes much of his famous book, *The Strategy of Conflict,* to the topic of ploys to outwit rivals in a competitive or bargaining situation.

Strategy As Pattern

But if strategies can be intended (whether as general plans or specific ploys), surely they can also be realized. In other words, defining strategy as a plan is not sufficient; we also need a definition that encompasses the resulting behavior. Thus a third definition is proposed: **strategy is a pattern**—specifically, a pattern in a stream of actions (Mintzberg and Waters, 1985). By this definition, when Picasso painted blue for a time, that was a strategy, just as was the behavior of the Ford Motor Company when Henry Ford offered his Model T only in black. In other words, by this definition, strategy is *consistency* in behavior, *whether or not* intended.

This may sound like a strange definition for a word that has been so bound up with free will ("strategos" in Greek, the art of the army general [Evered 1983]). But the fact of the matter is that while hardly anyone defines strategy in this way, many people seem at one time or another to so use it. Consider this quotation from a business executive: "Gradually the successful approaches merge into a pattern of action that becomes our strategy. We certainly don't have an overall strategy on this" (quoted in Quinn, 1980:35). This comment is inconsistent only if we restrict ourselves to one definition of strategy: what this man seems to be saying is that his firm has strategy as pattern, but not as plan. Or consider this comment in *Business Week* on a joint venture between General Motors and Toyota:

> The tentative Toyota deal may be most significant because it is another example of how GM's strategy boils down to doing a little bit of everything until the market decides where it is going. (*Business Week,* October 31, 1983)

A journalist has inferred a pattern in the behavior of a corporation and labeled it strategy.

The point is that every time a journalist imputes a strategy to a corporation or to a government, and every time a manager does the same thing to a competitor or even to the senior management of his own firm, they are implicitly defining strategy as pattern in action—that is, inferring consistency in behavior and labeling it strategy. They may, of course, go further and impute intention to that consistency—that is, assume there is a plan behind the pattern. But that is an assumption, which may prove false.

Thus, the definitions of strategy as plan and pattern can be quite independent of each other: plans may go unrealized, while patterns may appear without preconception. To paraphrase Hume, strategies may result from human actions but not human designs (see Majone, 1976–77). If we label the first definition *intended* strategy and the second *realized* strategy, as shown in Figure 1, then we can distinguish *deliberate* strategies, where intentions that existed previously were realized, from *emergent* strategies, where patterns developed in the absence of intentions, or despite them (which went *unrealized*).

For a strategy to be truly deliberate—that is, for a pattern to have been intended *exactly* as realized—would seem to be a tall order. Precise intentions would have had to be stated in advance by the leadership of the organization; these would have had to be accepted as is by everyone else, and then realized with no interference by market, technological, or political forces and so on. Likewise, a truly emergent strategy is again a tall order, requiring consistency in action without any hint of intention. (No consistency means *no* strategy, or at least unrealized strategy.) Yet some strategies do come close enough to either form, while others—probably most—sit on the continuum that exists between the two, reflecting deliberate as well as emergent aspects. Table 1 lists various kinds of strategies along this continuum.

STRATEGIES ABOUT WHAT?

Labeling strategies as plans or patterns still begs one basic question: *strategies about what?* Many writers respond by discussing the deployment of resources, but the question remains: which resources and for what purposes? An army may plan to reduce the number of nails in its shoes, or a corporation may realize a pattern of marketing only products painted black, but these hardly meet the lofty label "strategy." Or do they?

As the word has been handed down from the military, "strategy" refers to the important things, "tactics" to the details (more formally, "tactics teaches the use of armed forces in the engagement, strategy the use of engagements for the object of the war," von Clausewitz, 1976:128). Nails in shoes, colors of cars; these are certainly details. The problem is that in retrospect details can sometimes prove "strategic." Even in the military: "For want of a Nail, the Shoe was lost; for want of a Shoe the Horse was lost . . . ," and so on through the rider and general to the battle, "all for want of Care about a Horseshoe Nail" (Franklin, 1977:280). Indeed one of the reasons Henry Ford lost his war with General Motors was that he refused to paint his cars anything but black.

FIGURE 1
Deliberate and Emergent Strategies

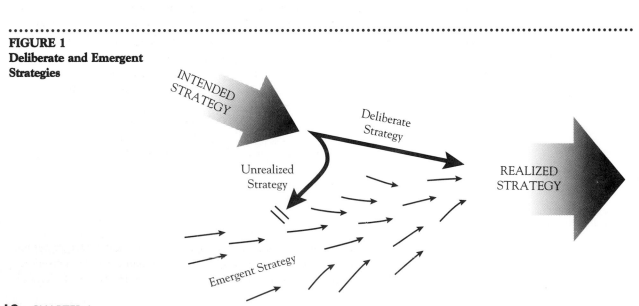

TABLE 1
Various Kinds of
Strategies, from Rather
Deliberate to Mostly
Emergent*

Planned Strategy: Precise intentions are formulated and articulated by a central leadership, and backed up by formal controls to ensure their surprise-free implementation in an environment that is benign, controllable, or predictable (to ensure no distortion of intentions); these strategies are highly deliberate.

Entrepreneurial Strategy: Intentions exist as the personal, unarticulated vision of a single leader, and so are adaptable to new opportunities; the organization is under the personal control of the leader and located in a protected niche in its environment; these strategies are relatively deliberate but can emerge too.

Ideological Strategy: Intentions exist as the collective vision of all the members of the organization, controlled through strong shared norms; the organization is often proactive vis-à-vis its environment; these strategies are rather deliberate.

Umbrella Strategy: A leadership in partial control of organizational actions defines strategic targets or boundaries within which others must act (for example, that all new products be high priced and at the technological cutting edge, although what these actual products are to be is left to emerge); as a result, strategies are partly deliberate (the boundaries) and partly emergent (the patterns within them); this strategy can also be called deliberately emergent, in that the leadership purposefully allows others the flexibility to maneuver and form patterns within the boundaries.

Process Strategy: The leadership controls the process aspects of strategy (who gets hired and so gets a chance to influence strategy, what structures they work within, etc.), leaving the actual content of strategy to others; strategies are again partly deliberate (concerning process) and partly emergent (concerning content), and deliberately emergent.

Disconnected Strategy: Members or subunits loosely coupled to the rest of the organization produce patterns in the streams of their own actions in the absence of, or in direct contradiction to the central or common intentions of the organization at large; the strategies can be deliberate for those who make them.

Consensus Strategy: Through mutual adjustment, various members converge on patterns that pervade the organization in the absence of central or common intentions; these strategies are rather emergent in nature.

Imposed Strategy: The external environment dictates patterns in actions, either through direct imposition (say, by an outside owner or by a strong customer) or through implicitly preempting or bounding organizational choice (as in a large airline that must fly jumbo jets to remain viable); these strategies are organizationally emergent, although they may be internalized and made deliberate.

*Adapted from Mintzberg and Waters (1985:270).

Rumelt (1979) notes that "one person's strategies are another's tactics—that what is strategic depends on where you sit." It also depends on *when* you sit; what seems tactical today may prove strategic tomorrow. The point is that labels should not be used to imply that some issues are *inevitably* more important than others. There are times when it pays to manage the details and let the strategies emerge for themselves. Thus there is good reason to refer to issues as more or less "strategic," in other words, more or less "important" in some context, whether as intended before acting or as realized after it. Accordingly, the answer to the question, strategy about what, is: potentially about anything. About products and processes, customers and citizens, social responsibilities and self interests, control and color.

Two aspects of the content of strategies must, however, be singled out because they are of particular importance.

Strategy As Position

The fourth definition is that **strategy is a position**—specifically, a means of locating an organization in what organization theorists like to call an "environment." By this definition, strategy becomes the mediating force—or "match," according to Hofer and Schendel

(1978:4)—between organization and environment, that is, between the internal and the external context. In ecological terms, strategy becomes a "niche"; in economic terms, a place that generates "rent" (that is "returns to [being] in a 'unique' place" (Bowman, 1974:47)); in management terms, formally, a product-market "domain" (Thompson, 1967), the place in the environment where resources are concentrated.

Note that this definition of strategy can be compatible with either (or all) of the preceding ones; a position can be preselected and aspired to through a plan (or ploy) and/or it can be reached, perhaps even found, through a pattern of behavior.

In military and game theory views of strategy, it is generally used in the context of what is called a "two-person game," better known in business as head-on competition (where ploys are especially common). The definition of strategy as position, however, implicitly allows us to open up the concept, to so-called n-person games (that is, many players), and beyond. In other words, while position can always be defined with respect to a single competitor (literally so in the military, where position becomes the site of battle), it can also be considered in the context of a number of competitors or simply with respect to markets or an environment at large. But strategy as position can extend beyond competition too, economic and otherwise. Indeed, what is the meaning of the word "niche" but a position that is occupied to *avoid* competition. Thus, we can move from the definition employed by General Ulysses Grant in the 1860s, "Strategy [is] the deployment of one's resources in a manner which is most likely to defeat the enemy," to that of Professor Richard Rumelt in the 1980s, "Strategy is creating situations for economic rents and finding ways to sustain them," (Rumelt, 1982) that is, any viable position, whether or not directly competitive.

Astley and Fombrun (1983), in fact, take the next logical step by introducing the notion of "collective" strategy, that is, strategy pursued to promote cooperation between organizations, even would-be competitors (equivalent in biology to animals herding together for protection). Such strategies can range "from informal arrangements and discussions to formal devices such as interlocking directorates, joint ventures, and mergers" (p. 577). In fact, considered from a slightly different angle, these can sometimes be described as *political* strategies, that is strategies to subvert the legitimate forces of competition.

Strategy As Perspective

While the fourth definition of strategy looks out, seeking to locate the organization in the external environment, and down to concrete positions, the fifth looks inside the organization, indeed inside the heads of the collective strategist, but up to a broader view. Here, **strategy is a perspective,** its content consisting not just of a chosen position, but of an ingrained way of perceiving the world. There are organizations that favor marketing and build a whole ideology around that (an IBM); Hewlett-Packard has developed the "H-P way," based on its engineering culture, while McDonald's has become famous for its emphasis on quality, service, and cleanliness.

Strategy in this respect is to the organization what personality is to the individual. Indeed, one of the earliest and most influential writers on strategy (at least as his ideas have been reflected in more popular writings) was Philip Selznick (1957:47), who wrote about the "character" of an organization—distinct and integrated "commitments to ways of acting and responding" that are built right into it. A variety of concepts from other fields also capture this notion; anthropologists refer to the "culture" of a society and sociologists to its "ideology"; military theorists write of the "grand strategy" of armies; while management theorists have used terms such as the "theory of the business" and its "driving force" (Drucker, 1974; Tregoe and Zimmerman, 1980); and Germans perhaps capture it best with their word "Weltanschauung, " literally "world view," meaning collective intuition about how the world works.

This fifth definition suggests above all that strategy is a *concept*. This has one important implication, namely, that all strategies are abstractions which exist only in the minds of interested parties. It is important to remember that no one has ever seen a strategy or touched one; every strategy is an invention, a figment of someone's imagination, whether conceived of as intentions to regulate behavior before it takes place or inferred as patterns to describe behavior that has already occurred.

What is of key importance about this fifth definition, however, is that the perspective is *shared*. As implied in the words Weltanschauung, culture, and ideology (with respect to a society), but not the word personality, strategy is a perspective shared by the members of an organization, through their intentions and/or by their actions. In effect, when we are talking of strategy in this context, we are entering the realm of the *collective mind*—individuals united by common thinking and/or behavior. A major issue in the study of strategy formation becomes, therefore, how to read that collective mind—to understand how intentions diffuse through the system called organization to become shared and how actions come to be exercised on a collective yet consistent basis.

Interrelating the Ps

As suggested above, strategy as both position and perspective can be compatible with strategy as plan and/or pattern. But, in fact, the relationships between these different definitions can be more involved than that. For example, while some consider perspective to *be* a plan (Lapierre, 1980, writes of strategies as "dreams in search of reality"), others describe it as *giving rise* to plans (for example, as positions and/or patterns in some kind of implicit hierarchy). But the concept of emergent strategy is that a pattern can emerge and be recognized so that it gives rise to a formal plan, perhaps within an overall perspective.

We may ask how perspective arises in the first place. Probably through earlier experiences: the organization tried various things in its formative years and gradually consolidated a perspective around what worked. In other words, organizations would appear to develop "character" much as people develop personality—by interacting with the world as they find it through the use of their innate skills and natural propensities. Thus pattern can give rise to perspective too. And so can position. Witness Perrow's (1970:161) discussion of the "wool men" and "silk men" of the textile trade, people who developed an almost religious dedication to the fibers they produced.

No matter how they appear, however, there is reason to believe that while plans and positions may be dispensable, perspectives are immutable (Brunsson, 1982). In other words, once they are established, perspectives become difficult to change. Indeed, a perspective may become so deeply ingrained in the behavior of an organization that the associated beliefs can become subconscious in the minds of its members. When that happens, perspective can come to look more like pattern than like plan—in other words, it can be found more in the consistency of behaviors than in the articulation of intentions.

Of course, if perspective is immutable, then change in plan and position within perspective is easy compared to change of perspective. In this regard, it is interesting to take up the case of Egg McMuffin. Was this product when new—the American breakfast in a bun—a strategic change for the McDonald's fast-food chain? Posed in MBA classes, this earth-shattering (or at least stomach-shattering) question inevitably evokes heated debate. Proponents (usually people sympathetic to fast food) argue that of course it was: it brought McDonald's into a new market, the breakfast one, extending the use of existing facilities. Opponents retort that this is nonsense; nothing changed but a few ingredients: this was the same old pap in a new package. Both sides are, of course, right—and wrong. It simply depends on how you define strategy. Position changed; perspective remained the same.

Indeed—and this is the point—the position could be changed easily because it was compatible with the existing perspective. Egg McMuffin is pure McDonald's, not only in product and package, but also in production and propagation. But imagine a change of position at McDonald's that would require a change of perspective—say, to introduce candlelight dining with personal service (your McDuckling à l'Orange cooked to order) to capture the late evening market. We needn't say more, except perhaps to label this the "Egg McMuffin syndrome."

The Need for Eclecticism in Definition

While various relationships exist among the different definitions, no one relationship, nor any single definition for that matter, takes precedence over the others. In some ways, these definitions compete (in that they can substitute for each other), but in perhaps more important ways, they complement. Not all plans become patterns nor are all patterns that develop planned; some ploys are less than positions, while other strategies are more than positions yet less than perspectives. Each definition adds important elements to our understanding of strategy, indeed encourages us to address fundamental questions about organizations in general.

As plan, strategy deals with how leaders try to establish direction for organizations, to set them on predetermined courses of action. Strategy as plan also raises the fundamental issue of cognition—how intentions are conceived in the human brain in the first place, indeed, what intentions really mean. The road to hell in this field can be paved with those who take all stated intentions at face value. In studying strategy as plan, we must somehow get into the mind of the strategist, to find out what is really intended.

As ploy, strategy takes us into the realm of direct competition, where threats and feints and various other maneuvers are employed to gain advantage. This places the process of strategy formation in its most dynamic setting, with moves provoking countermoves and so on. Yet ironically, strategy itself is a concept rooted not in change but in stability—in set plans and established patterns. How then to reconcile the dynamic notions of strategy as ploy with the static ones of strategy as pattern and other forms of plan?

As pattern, strategy focuses on action, reminding us that the concept is an empty one if it does not take behavior into account. Strategy as pattern also introduces the notion of convergence, the achievement of consistency in an organization's behavior. How does this consistency form, where does it come from? Realized strategy, when considered alongside intended strategy, encourages us to consider the notion that strategies can emerge as well as be deliberately imposed.

As position, strategy encourages us to look at organizations in their competitive environments—how they find their positions and protect them in order to meet competition, avoid it, or subvert it. This enables us to think of organizations in ecological terms, as organisms in niches that struggle for survival in a world of hostility and uncertainty as well as symbiosis.

And finally as perspective, strategy raises intriguing questions about intention and behavior in a collective context. If we define organization as collective action in the pursuit of common mission (a fancy way of saying that a group of people under a common label—whether a General Motors or a Luigi's Body Shop—somehow find the means to cooperate in the production of specific goods and services), then strategy as perspective raises the issue of how intentions diffuse through a group of people to become shared as norms and values, and how patterns of behavior become deeply ingrained in the group.

Thus, strategy is not just a notion of how to deal with an enemy or a set of competitors or a market, as it is treated in so much of the literature and in its popular usage. It also draws us into some of the most fundamental issues about organizations as instruments for collective perception and action.

To conclude, a good deal of the confusion in this field stems from contradictory and ill-defined uses of the term strategy. By explicating and using various definitions, we may be able to avoid some of this confusion, and thereby enrich our ability to understand and manage the processes by which strategies form.

THE STRATEGIST

Every conventional strategy or policy textbook focuses on the job of the general manager as a main ingredient in understanding the process of strategy formation. The discussion of emergent strategy in the last chapter suggests that we do not take such a narrow view of the strategist. Anyone in the organization who happens to control key or precedent-setting actions can be a strategist; the strategist can be a collection of people as well. Nevertheless, managers—especially senior general managers—are obviously prime candidates for such a role because their perspective is generally broader than any of their subordinates' and because so much power naturally resides with them. Hence, in this chapter we focus on the general manager as strategist.

We present three readings that describe the work of the manager. The one by Mintzberg challenges the conventional view of the manager. The image presented in this article is a very different one: of a job characterized by pressure, inter-ruption, orientation to action, oral rather than written communication, and work-ing with outsiders and colleagues as much as with so-called subordinates. These findings pertain to the characteristics of managerial work, described as they appeared in Mintzberg's original study of managerial work some years ago. The reading then goes on to describe the content of managerial work as Mintzberg has developed that in his more recent research. This part of the reading draws on a paper he published in the *Sloan Management Review* in 1994. Here managerial work is characterized as taking place on three levels—a rather abstract informa-tion level, an in-between people level, and a concrete action level. The roles the manager performs can be seen to fit into these levels, but, as emphasized, all man-agers must ultimately deal with all levels, in an integrated fashion, although most will favor one level or another.

While the issue is not addressed at this point in any detail, one evident and important conclusion is that managers who work in such ways cannot possibly function as traditionally depicted strategists supposedly do—as leaders directing their organizations the way conductors direct their orchestras (at least the way it looks on the podium). We shall develop this point further in Chapter 5, when we consider how strategies really are formed in organizations. The article by Edward Wrapp, of the University of Chicago, provides at least one widely referenced model illustrating how this does happen in large organizations. He depicts man-agers as somewhat political animals, providing broad guidance, but facilitating or pushing through their strategies, bit by bit, in rather unexpected ways. They rarely state specific goals. They practice "the art of imprecision," trying to "avoid policy strait-jackets," while concentrating on only a few really significant issues. They move whenever possible through "corridors of comparative indifference" to avoid undue opposition; at the same time they are trying to ensure that the organization has a cohesive sense of direction. Wrapp's observations challenge the more prescriptive views of strategy formulation.

The article by Gary Hamel and C. K. Prahalad of the University of Michigan presents a view of the management role that is consistent with the military analogy of strategy in Quinn's article in the preceding chapter. The challenge of building global leadership, according to Hamel and Prahalad, is to embed the ambitions for such leadership throughout the company and to create "an obsession with winning" which will energize the collective action of all employees. The role is to build such an ambition, to help people develop faith in their own ability to deliver on tough goals, to motivate them to do so, and to channel their energies into a step-by-step progression that they compare with "running the marathon in 400-meter sprints."

How do you reconcile these different views on the role of the strategist? At one level, perhaps you do not need a grand theory that integrates across all of them. There are different kinds of managers, different beliefs and styles, and different kinds of authors—different lenses capture different aspects of managerial work. Some of you may also observe many similarities in the roles and tasks of the strategist described in these readings, despite the very different languages the authors use. You may, for instance, think about how the advocacies of Hamel and Prahalad relate to the managerial roles Mintzberg describes.

▼ READING 2.1   THE MANAGER'S JOB*

by Henry Mintzberg

Tom Peters tells us that good managers are doers. (Wall Street says they "do deals.") Michael Porter suggests that they are thinkers. Not so, argue Abraham Zaleznik and Warren Bennis: good managers are really leaders. Yet, for the better part of this century, the classical writers—Henri Fayol and Lyndell Urwick, among others—keep telling us that good managers are essentially controllers.

It is a curiosity of the management literature that its best-known writers all seem to emphasize one particular part of the manager's job to the exclusion of the others. Together, perhaps, they cover all the parts, but even that does not describe the whole job of managing.

Moreover, the image left by all of this of the manager's job is that it is a highly systematic, carefully controlled job. That is the folklore. The facts are quite different.

We shall begin by reviewing some of the early research findings on the *characteristics* of the manager's job, comparing that folklore with the facts, as I observed them in my first study of managerial work (published in the 1970s), reinforced by other research. Then we shall present a new framework to think about the *content* of the job—what managers really do— based on some recent observations I have made of managers in very different situations.

---

* This paper combines excerpts from "The Manager's Job: Folklore and Fact" which appeared in the *Harvard Business Review* (July-August 1975) on the characteristics of the job, with the framework of the context of the job which was published as "Rounding Out the Manager's Job" in the *Sloan Management Review* (Fall 1994).

Some Folklore and Facts About Managerial Work

There are four myths about the manager's job that do not bear up under careful scrutiny of the facts.

Folklore: The manager is a reflective, systematic planner. The evidence on this issue is overwhelming, but not a shred of it supports this statement.

Fact: Study after study has shown that managers work at an unrelenting pace, that their activities are characterized by brevity, variety, and discontinuity, and that they are strongly oriented to action and dislike reflective activities. Consider this evidence:

▼ Half the activities engaged in by the five [American] chief executives [that I studied in my own research (Mintzberg, 1973a)] lasted less than nine minutes, and only 10% exceeded one hour. A study of 56 U.S. foremen found that they averaged 583 activities per eight-hour shift, an average of 1 every 48 seconds (Guest, 1956:478). The work pace for both chief executives and foremen was unrelenting. The chief executives met a steady stream of callers and mail from the moment they arrived in the morning until they left in the evening. Coffee breaks and lunches were inevitably work related, and ever-present subordinates seemed to usurp any free moment.

▼ A diary study of 160 British middle and top managers found that they worked for a half hour or more without interruption only about once every two days (Stewart, 1967).

▼ Of the verbal contacts of the chief executives in my study, 93% were arranged on an ad hoc basis. Only 1% of the executives' time was spent in open-ended observational tours. Only 1 out of 368 verbal contacts was unrelated to a specific issue and could be called general planning. Another researcher finds that "in *not one single case* did a manager report the obtaining of important external information from a general conversation or other undirected personal communication" (Aguilar, 1967:102).

▼ No study has found important patterns in the way managers schedule their time. They seem to jump from issue to issue, continually responding to the needs of the moment.

Is this the planner that the classical view describes? Hardly. How, then, can we explain this behavior? The manager is simply responding to the pressures of the job. I found that my chief executives terminated many of their own activities, often leaving meetings before the end and interrupted their desk work to call in subordinates. One president not only placed his desk so that he could look down a long hallway but also left his door open when he was alone—an invitation for subordinates to come in and interrupt him.

Clearly, these managers wanted to encourage the flow of current information. But more significantly, they seemed to be conditioned by their own work loads. They appreciated the opportunity cost of their own time, and they were continually aware of their ever-present obligations—mail to be answered, callers to attend to, and so on. It seems that no matter what he or she is doing, the manager is plagued by the possibilities of what he or she might do and must do.

When the manager must plan, he or she seems to do so implicitly in the context of daily actions, not in some abstract process reserved for two weeks in the organization's mountain retreat. The plans of the chief executives I studied seemed to exist only in their heads—as flexible, but often specific, intentions. The traditional literature notwithstanding, the job of managing does not breed reflective planners; the manager is a real-time responder to stimuli, an individual who is conditioned by his or her job to prefer live to delayed action.

Folklore: The effective manager has no regular duties to perform. Managers are constantly being told to spend more time planning and delegating, and less time on operating details. These are not, after all, the true tasks of the manager. To use the popular analogy, the good manager, like the good conductor, carefully orchestrates everything in advance, then sits back to enjoy the fruits of his or her labor, responding occasionally to an unforeseeable exception. . . .

Fact: In addition to handling exceptions, managerial work involves performing a number of regular duties, including ritual and ceremony, negotiations, and processing of soft information that links the organization with its environment. Consider some evidence from the early research studies:

▼ A study of the work of the presidents of small companies found that they engaged in routine activities because their companies could not afford staff specialists and were so thin on operating personnel that a single absence often required the president to substitute (Choran in Mintzberg, 1973a).

▼ One study of field sales managers and another of chief executives suggest that it is a natural part of both jobs to see important customers, assuming the managers wish to keep those customers (Davis, 1957; Copeman, 1963).

▼ Someone, only half in jest, once described the manager as that person who sees visitors so that everyone else can get his or her work done. In my study, I found that certain ceremonial duties—meeting visiting dignitaries, giving out gold watches, presiding at Christmas dinners—were an intrinsic part of the chief executive's job.

▼ Studies of managers' information flow suggest that managers play a key role in securing "soft" external information (much of it available only to them because of their status) and in passing it along to their subordinates.

Folklore: The senior manager needs aggregated information, which a formal management information system best provides. In keeping with the classical view of the manager as that individual perched on the apex of a regulated, hierarchical system, the literature's manager was to receive all important information from a giant, comprehensive MIS.

But this never proved true at all. A look at how managers actually process information makes the reason quite clear. Managers have five media at their command—documents, telephone calls, scheduled and unscheduled meetings, and observational tours.

Fact: Managers strongly favor the verbal media—namely, telephone calls and meetings. The evidence comes from every one of the early studies of managerial work: Consider the following:

▼ In two British studies, managers spent an average of 66% and 80% of their time in verbal (oral) communication (Stewart, 1967; Burns, 1954). In my study of five American chief executives, the figure was 78%.

▼ These five chief executives treated mail processing as a burden to be dispensed with. One came in Saturday morning to process 142 pieces of mail in just over three hours, to "get rid of all the stuff." This same manager looked at the first piece of "hard" mail he had received all week, a standard cost report, and put it aside with the comment, "I never look at this."

▼ These same five chief executives responded immediately to 2 of the 40 routine reports they received during the five weeks of my study and to four items in the 104 periodicals. They skimmed most of the periodicals in seconds, almost ritualistically. In all, these chief executives of good-sized organizations initiated on their own—that is, not in response to something else—a grand total of 25 pieces of mail during the 25 days I observed them.

An analysis of the mail the executives received reveals an interesting picture—only 13% was of specific and immediate use. So now we have another piece of the puzzle: not much of the mail provides live, current information—the action of a competitor, the mood of a government legislator, or the rating of last night's television show. Yet this is the information that drove the managers, interrupting their meetings and rescheduling their workdays.

Consider another interesting finding. Managers seem to cherish "soft" information, especially gossip, hearsay, and speculation. Why? The reason is its timeliness; today's gossip may be tomorrow's fact. The manager who is not accessible for the telephone call informing him or her that the firm's biggest customer was seen golfing with its main competitor may read about a dramatic drop in sales in the next quarterly report. But then it's too late.

Consider the words of Richard Neustadt, who studied the information-collecting habits of Presidents Roosevelt, Truman, and Eisenhower.

> It is not information of a general sort that helps a President see personal stakes; not summaries, not surveys, not the *bland amalgams*. Rather . . . it is the odds and ends of *tangible detail* that pieced together in his mind illuminate the underside of issues put before him. To help himself he must reach out as widely as he can for every scrap of fact, opinion, gossip, bearing on his interests and relationships as President. He must become his own director of his own central intelligence (1960:153–154; italics added).

The manager's emphasis on the verbal media raises two important points:

First, verbal information is stored in the brains of people. Only when people write this information down can it be stored in the files of the organization—whether in metal cabinets or computer memory—and managers apparently do not write down much of what they hear. Thus the strategic data bank of the organization is not in the memory of its computers but in the minds of its managers.

Second, the managers' extensive use of verbal media helps to explain why they are reluctant to delegate tasks. When we note that most of the managers' important information comes in verbal form and is stored in their heads, we can well appreciate their reluctance. It is not as if they can hand a dossier over to someone; they must take the time to "dump memory"—to tell that someone all they know about the subject. But this could take so long that the managers find it easier to do the task themselves. Thus the managers are damned by their own information systems to a "dilemma of delegation"—to do too much themselves or to delegate to their subordinates with inadequate briefing.

Folklore: Management is, or at least is quickly becoming, a science and a profession. By almost any definitions of *science* and *profession*, this statement is false. Brief observation of any manager will quickly lay to rest the notion that managers practice a science. A science involves the enaction of systematic, analytically determined procedures or programs. If we do not even know what procedures managers use, how can we prescribe them by scientific analysis? And how can we call management a profession if we cannot specify what managers are to learn?

Fact: The managers' programs—to schedule time, process information, make decisions, and so on—remain locked deep inside their brains. Thus, to describe these programs, we rely on words like judgment and intuition, seldom stopping to realize that they are merely labels for our ignorance.

I was struck during my study by the fact that the executives I was observing—all very competent by any standard—are fundamentally indistinguishable from their counterparts of a hundred years ago (or a thousand years ago, for that matter). The information they need differs, but they seek it in the same way—by word of mouth. Their decisions concern modern technology, but the procedures they use to make them are the same as the procedures of the nineteenth-century manager. In fact, the manager is in a kind of loop, with increasingly heavy work pressures but no aid forthcoming from management science.

Considering the facts about managerial work, we can see that the manager's job is enormously complicated and difficult. The manager is overburdened with obligations; yet he or she cannot easily delegate tasks. As a result, he or she is driven to overwork and is forced to do many tasks superficially. Brevity, fragmentation, and verbal communication characterize the work. Yet these are the very characteristics of managerial work that have imped-ed scientific attempts to improve it. As a result, the management scientists have concen-trated their efforts on the specialized functions of the organization, where they could more easily analyze the procedure and quantify the relevant information. Thus the first step in providing managers with some help is to find out what their job really is.

Toward a Basic Description of Managerial Work

Now let us try to put some of the pieces of this puzzle together. The manager can be defined as that person in charge of an organization or one of its units. Besides chief executive offi-cers, this definition would include vice presidents, head nurses, hockey coaches, and prime ministers. Can all of these people have anything in common? Indeed, they can. Our description takes the form of a model, building the image of the manager's job from the inside out, beginning at the center with the person and his or her frame and working out from there, layer by layer.

THE PERSON IN THE JOB

We begin at the center, with the person who comes to the job. People are not neutral when they take on a new managerial job, mere putty to be molded into the required shape. Figure 1 shows that an individual comes to a managerial job with a set of *values*, by this stage in life probably rather firmly set, also a body of *experience* that, on the one hand, has forged a set of skills or *competencies*, perhaps honed by training, and, on the other, has provided a base of *knowledge*. That knowledge is, of course, used directly, but it is also converted into a set of *mental models*, key means by which managers interpret the world around them—for example, how the head nurse on a hospital ward perceives the behavior of the surgeons with whom she must work. Together, all these characteristics greatly determine how any man-ager approaches a given job—his or her *style* of managing. Style will come to life as we begin to see *how* a manager carries out *what* his or her job requires.

THE FRAME OF THE JOB

Embed the person depicted in a given managerial job and you get managerial work. At the core of it is some kind of *frame* for the job, the mental set the incumbent assumes to carry it out. Frame is strategy, to be sure, possibly even vision, but it is more than that. It is pur-pose, whether to create something in the first place, maintain something that has already been created or adapt it to changes, or else recreate something. Frame is also *perspective*—the broad view of the organization and its mission—and *positions*—concerning specific products, services, and markets.

Alain Noël, who studied the relationship between the frames and the work of the chief executives of three small companies, has said that managers have "occupations" and they have "preoccupations," (Noël, 1989). Frame describes the preoccupations, while roles (dis-cussed below) describe the occupations. But frame does give rise to a first role in this model as well, which I call **conceiving**, namely thinking through the purpose, perspective, and positions of a particular unit to be managed over a particular period of time.

THE AGENDA OF THE WORK

Given a person in a particular managerial job with a particular frame, the question arises of how this is manifested in the form of specific activities. That happens through the *agenda* to carry out the work, and the associated role of **scheduling**, which has received consider-

FIGURE 1
The Person in the Job

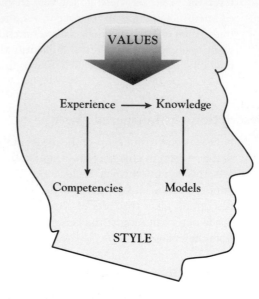

able attention in the literature of management. Agenda is considered in two respects here. First, the frame gets manifested as a set of current *issues*, in effect, whatever is of concern to the manager, broken down into manageable units—what Tom Peters likes to call "chunks." Ask any manager about his or her work, and the almost inevitable first reply will be about the "issues" of central concern, those things "on the plate," as the saying goes. Or take a look at the agendas of meetings and you will likewise see a list of issues (rather than decisions). These, in effect, operationalize the frame (as well as change it, of course, by feeding in new concerns).

The sharper the frame, the more integrated the issues. The more realizable they may be as well, since it is a vague frame that gives rise to that all-too-common phenomenon of the unattainable "wishlist" in an organization. Sometimes a frame can be so sharp, and the issues therefore so tightly integrated, that they all reduce to what Noël has called one "magnificent obsession" (Noël, 1989). In effect, all the concerns of the manager revolve around one central issue, for example, making a new merger work.

Second, the frame and the issues get manifested in the more tangible *schedule*, the specific allocations of managerial time on a day-to-day basis. Also included here, however implicitly, is the setting of priorities among the issues. The scheduling of time and the prioritization of issues are obviously of great concern to all managers, and, in fact, are themselves significant consumers of managerial time. Accordingly, a great deal of attention has been devoted to these concerns, including numerous courses on "time management."

THE CORE IN CONTEXT

If we label the person in the job with a frame manifested by an agenda, the central *core* of the manager's job (shown by the concentric circles in Figure 2), then we turn next to the context in which this core is embedded, the milieu in which the work is practiced.

The context of the job is depicted in Figure 2 by the lines that surround the core. Context can be split into three areas, labeled inside, within, and outside on Figure 2.

FIGURE 2
The Core in Context

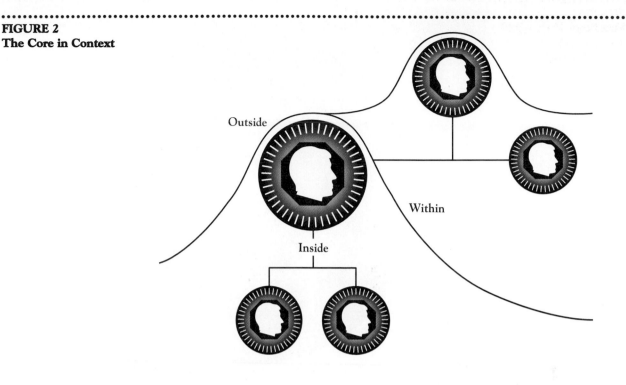

Inside refers to the unit being managed, shown below the manager to represent his or her formal authority over its people and activities—the hospital ward in the case of the head nurse, for example. *Within*, shown to the right, refers to the rest of the organization—other members and other units with which the manager must work but over which he or she has no formal authority, for example, the doctors, the kitchen, the physiotherapists in the rest of the hospital, to continue with the same example. (Of course, in the case of the chief executive, there is no inside separate from within: that person has authority over the entire organization.) And *outside* refers to the rest of the context not formally part of the organization with which the manager must work—in this example, patients' relatives, long-term care institutions to which some of the unit's patients are discharged, nursing associations, and so on. The importance of this distinction (for convenience, we shall mostly refer to inside versus outside) is that much of managerial work is clearly directed either to the unit itself, for which the manager has official responsibility, or at its various boundary contexts, through which the manager must act without that responsibility.

Managing on Three Levels

We are now ready to address the actual behaviors that managers engage in to do their jobs. The essence of the model, designed to enable us to "see" managerial work comprehensively, in one figure, is that these roles are carried out on three successive levels, each inside and outside the unit. This is depicted by concentric circles of increasing specificity, shown in Figure 3.

From the outside (or most tangible level) in, managers can manage *action* directly, they can manage *people* to encourage them to take the necessary actions, and they can manage *information* to influence the people in turn to take their necessary actions. In other words,

FIGURE 3
Three Levels of
Evoking Action

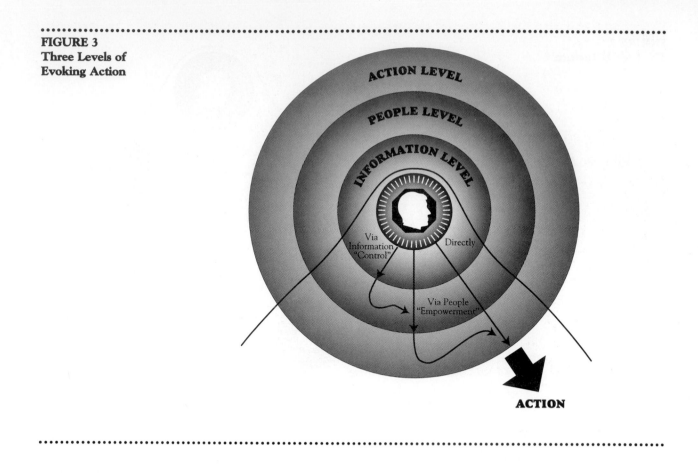

the ultimate objective of managerial work, and of the functioning of any organizational unit, the taking of action, can be managed directly, indirectly through people, or even more indirectly by information through people. The manager can thus choose to intervene at any of the three levels, but once done, he or she must work through the remaining ones. Later we shall see that the level a given manager favors becomes an important determinant of his or her managerial style, especially distinguishing so-called "doers" who prefer direct action, "leaders" who prefer working through people, and "administrators" who prefer to work by information.

MANAGING BY INFORMATION

To manage by information is to sit two steps removed from the purpose of managerial work. The manager processes information to drive other people who, in turn, are supposed to ensure that necessary actions are taken. In other words, here the managers' own activities focus neither on people nor on actions per se, but rather on information as an indirect way to make things happen. Ironically, while this was the classic perception of managerial work for the first half of this century, in recent years it has also become a newly popular, in some quarters almost obsessional, view, epitomized by the so-called "bottom line" approach to management.

The manager's various informational behaviors may be grouped into two broad roles, here labeled communicating and controlling, shown in Figure 4.

Communicating refers to the collection and dissemination of information. In Figure 4, communicating is shown by double arrows to indicate that managers devote a great deal of effort to the two-way flow of information with the people all around them—employees

FIGURE 4
The Information Roles

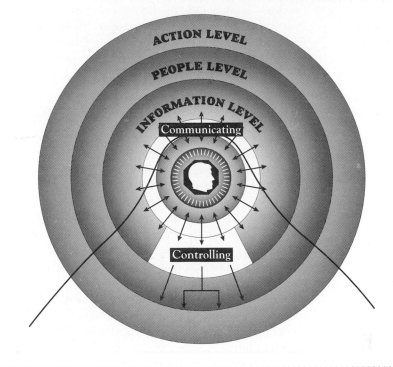

inside their own units, others in the rest of the organization, and especially, as the empirical evidence makes abundantly clear, a great number of outsiders with whom they maintain regular contact. Thus the head of one regional division of the national police force spent a good part of the day I observed him passing information back and forth between the central headquarters and the people on his staff.

Managers "scan" their environments, they monitor their own units, and they share with and disseminate to others considerable amounts of the information they pick up. Managers can be described as "nerve centers" of their units, who use their status of office to gain access to a wide variety of informational sources. Inside the unit, everyone else is a specialist who generally knows more about his or her specialty than the manager. But, because the manager is connected to all those specialists, he or she should have the broadest base of knowledge about the unit in general. This should apply to the head of a huge health care system, with regard to broad policy issues, no less than to the clinical director of one of its hospital units, with regard to the service rendered there. And externally, by virtue of their status, managers have access to other managers who are themselves nerve centers of their own units. And so they tend to be exposed to powerful sources of external information and thus emerge as external nerve centers as well. The health care chief executive can thus talk to people running health care systems in other countries and so gain access to an array of information perhaps inaccessible even to his most influential reports.

The result of all this is that a considerable amount of the manager's information turns out to be privileged, especially when we consider how much of it is oral and nonverbal. Accordingly, to function effectively with the people around them, managers have to spend considerable time sharing their information, both with outsiders (in a kind of spokesperson role) and with insiders (in a kind of disseminator role).

I found in my initial study of chief executives that perhaps 40 percent of their time was devoted almost exclusively to the communicating role—just to gaining and sharing information—leaving aside the information processing aspects of all the other roles. In other words, the job of managing is fundamentally one of processing information, notably by talking and especially listening. Thus Figure 4 shows the inner core (the person in the job, conceiving and scheduling) connected to the outer rings (the more tangible roles of managing people and action) through what can be called the membrane of information processing all around the job.

What can be called the **controlling** role describes the managers' efforts, not just to gain and share information, but to use it in a directive way inside their units: to evoke or provoke general action by the people who report to them. They do this in three broad ways: they develop systems, they design structures, and they impose directives. Each of these seeks to control how other people work, especially with regard to the allocation of resources, and so what actions they are inclined to take.

First, developing systems is the most general of these three, and the closest to conceiving. It uses information to control peoples' behaviors. Managers often take charge of establishing and even running such systems in their units, including those of planning and performance control (such as budgeting). Robert Simons has noted how chief executives tend to select one such system and make it key to their exercise of control, in a manner he calls "interactive" (Simons, 1990, 1991).

Second, managers exercise control through designing the structures of their units. By establishing responsibilities and defining hierarchical authority, they again exercise control rather passively, through the processing of information. People are informed of their duties, which in turn is expected to drive them to carry out the appropriate actions.

Third is imposing directives, which is the most direct of the three, closest to the people and action, although still informational in nature. Managers pronounce: they make specific choices and give specific orders, usually in the process of "delegating" particular responsibilities and "authorizing" particular requests. In effect, managers manage by transmitting information to people so that they can act.

If a full decision-making process can be considered in the three stages of diagnosing, designing, and deciding—in other words, identifying issues, working out possible solutions, and selecting one—then here we are dealing with a restricted view of decision making. Delegating means mostly diagnosing ("Would you please handle this problem in this context"), while authorizing means mostly deciding ("OK, you can proceed"). Either way, the richest part of the process, the stage of designing possible solutions, resides with the person being controlled rather than with the manager him or herself, whose own behavior remains rather passive. Thus the manager as controller seems less an *actor* with sleeves rolled up, digging in, than a *reviewer* who sits back in the office and passes judgment. That is why this role is characterized as informational; I will describe a richer approach to decision making in the section on action roles.

The controlling role is shown in Figure 4 propelling down into the manager's own unit, since that is where formal authority is exercised. The single-headed arrows represent the imposed directives, while the pitchfork shape symbolizes both the design of structure and the development of systems. The proximity of the controlling role in Figure 4 to the manager's agenda reflects the fact that informational control is the most direct way to operationalize the agenda, for example, by using budgets to impose priorities or delegation to assign responsibilities. The controlling role is, of course, what people have in mind when they refer to the "administrative" aspect of managerial work.

MANAGING THROUGH PEOPLE

To manage through people, instead of by information, is to move one step closer to action, but still to remain removed from it. That is because here the focus of managerial attention becomes affect instead of effect. Other people become the means to get things done, not the manager him or herself, or even the substance of the manager's thoughts.

If the information roles (and controlling in particular) dominated our early thinking about managerial work, then after that, people entered the scene, or at least they entered the textbooks, as entities to be "motivated" and later "empowered." Influencing began to replace informing, and commitment began to vie with calculation for the attention of the manager. Indeed, in the 1960s and 1970s especially, the management of people, quite independent of content—of the strategies to be realized, the information to be processed, even the actions to be taken—became a virtual obsession of the literature, whether by the label of "human relations," "Theory Y," or "participative management" (and later "quality of work life," to be replaced by "total quality management").

For a long time, however, these people remained "subordinates" in more ways than one. "Participation" kept them subordinate, for this was always considered to be granted at the behest of the managers still fully in control. So does the currently popular term "empowerment," which implies that power is being granted, thanks to the managers. (Hospital directors do not "empower" physicians!) People also remained subordinates because the whole focus was on those inside the unit, not outside it. Not until serious research on managerial work began did it become evident how important to managers were contacts with individuals outside their units. Virtually every single study of how all kinds of managers spent their time has indicated that outsiders, of an enormously wide variety, generally take as much of the managers' attention as so-called "subordinates." We shall thus describe two people roles here, shown in Figure 5, one internal, called leading, and one external, called linking.

The **leading** role has probably received more attention in the literature of management than all the other roles combined. And so we need not dwell on it here. But neither can we ignore it: managers certainly do much more than lead the people in their own units, and leading certainly infuses much else of what managers do (as, in fact, do all the roles, as we have already noted about communicating). But their work just as certainly cannot be understood without this dimension. We can describe the role of leading on three levels, as indicated in Figure 5.

First, managers lead on the *individual* level, "one on one," as the expression goes. They encourage and drive the people of their units—motivate them, inspire them, coach them, nurture them, push them, mentor them, and so on. All the managers I observed, from the chief executive of a major police force to the front-country manager in a mountain park, stopped to chat with their people informally during the day to encourage them in their work. Second, managers lead on the *group* level, especially by building and managing teams, an effort that has received considerable attention in recent years. Again, team meetings, including team building, figured in many of my observations; for example, the head of a London film company who brought film-making teams together for both effective and affective purposes. And third, they lead on the *unit* level, especially with regard to the creation and maintenance of culture, another subject of increasing attention in recent years (thanks especially to the Japanese). Managers, for example, engage in many acts of symbolic nature ("figurehead" duties) to sustain culture, as when the head of the national police force visited its officer training institute (as he did frequently) to imbue the force's norms and attitudes in its graduating class.

All managers seem to spend time on all three levels of leadership, although, again, styles do vary according to context and personality. If the communicating role describes the manager as the nerve center of the unit, then the leading role must characterize him or her as its "energy center," a concept perhaps best captured in Maeterlinck's wonderful description of the "spirit of the hive" (Maeterlinck, 1918). Given the right managerial "chemistry" (in the case of Maeterlinck's queen bee, quite literally!), it may be the manager's mere presence that somehow draws things together. By exuding that mystical substance, the leader

FIGURE 5
The People Roles

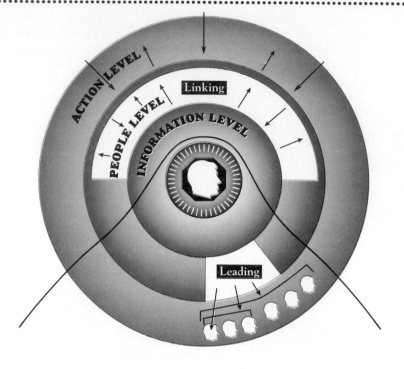

unites his or her people, galvanizing them into action to accomplish the unit's mission and adapt it to a changing world.

The excess attention to the role of leading has probably been matched by the inadequate attention to the role of **linking**. For, in their sheer allocation of time, managers have been shown to be external linkers as much as they are internal leaders, in study after study. Yet, still the point seems hardly appreciated. Indeed, now more than ever, it must be understood, given the great growth of joint ventures and other collaborating and networking relationships between organizations, as well as the gradual reconception of the "captive" employee as an autonomous "agent" who supplies labor.

Figure 5 suggests a small model of the linking role. The arrows go in and out to indicate that the manager is both an advocate of its influence outside the unit and, in turn, a recipient of much of the influence exerted on it from the outside. In the middle are two parallel lines to represent the buffering aspect of this role—that managers must regulate the receipt of external influence to protect their units. To use a popular term, they are the "gatekeepers" of influence. Or, to add a metaphor, the manager acts as a kind of valve between the unit and its environment. Nowhere was this clearer than in my observation of three levels of management in a national park system—a regional director, the head of one mountain park, and the front-country manager of that park. They sit in an immensely complex array of forces—developers who want to enhance their business opportunities, environmentalists who want to preserve the natural habitat, tourists who want to enjoy the beauty, truckers who want to drive through the park unimpeded, politicians who want to avoid negative publicity, etc. It is a delicate balancing, or buffering, act indeed!

All managers appear to spend a great deal of time "networking"—building vast arrays of contacts and intricate coalitions of supporters beyond their own units, whether within the rest of the organization or outside, in the world at large. To all these contacts, the manager represents the unit externally, promotes its needs, and lobbies for its causes. In response, these people are expected to provide a steady inflow of information to the unit as well as various means of support and specific favors for it. This networking was most evident in the case of the film company managing director I observed, who exhibited an impressive network of contracts in order to negotiate her complex contracts with various media in different countries.

In turn, people intent on influencing the behavior of an organization or one of its subunits will often exercise pressure directly on its manager, expecting that person to transmit the influence inside, as was most pointedly clear in the work of the parks manager. Here, then, the managerial job becomes one of delicate balance, a tricky act of mediation. Those managers who let external influence pass inside too freely—who act like sieves—are apt to drive their people crazy. (Of course, those who act like sponges and absorb all the influence personally are apt to drive themselves crazy!) And those who block out all influence—who act like lead to x-rays—are apt to detach their units from reality (and so dry up the sources of external support). Thus, what influence to pass on and how, bearing in mind the quid pro quo that influence exerted out is likely to be mirrored by influence coming back in, becomes another key aspect of managerial style, worthy of greatly increased attention in both the study of the job and the training of its occupants.

MANAGING ACTION

If managers manage passively by information and affectively through people, then they also manage actively and instrumentally by their own direct involvement in action. Indeed, this has been a long-established view of managerial work, although the excess attention in this century, first to controlling and then to leading, and more recently to conceiving (of planned strategy), has obscured its importance. Leonard Sayles, however, has long and steadily insisted on this, beginning with his 1964 book and culminating in *The Working Leader* (published in 1993), in which he makes his strongest statement yet, insisting that managers must be the focal points for action in and by their units (Sayles 1964, 1993). Their direct involvement must, in his view, take precedence over the pulling force of leadership and the pushing force of controllership.

I shall refer to this involvement as the **doing** role. But, in using this label—a popular one in the managerial vernacular ("Mary Ann's a doer")—it is necessary to point out that managers, in fact, hardly ever "do" anything. Many barely even dial their own telephones! Watch a manager and you will see someone whose work consists almost exclusively of talking and listening, alongside, of course, watching and "feeling." (That, incidentally, is why I show the manager at the core of the model as a head and not a full body!)

What "doing" presumably means, therefore, is getting closer to the action, ultimately being just one step removed from it. Managers as doers manage the carrying out of action directly, instead of indirectly through managing people or by processing information. In effect, a "doer" is really someone who gets it done (or, as the French put it with their expression *faire faire*, to "make" something "get made"). And the managerial vernacular is, in fact, full of expressions that reflect just this: "doing deals," "championing change," "fighting fires," "juggling projects." In the terms of decision making introduced earlier, here the manager diagnoses and designs as well as decides: he or she gets deeply and fully involved in the management of particular activities. Thus, in the day I spent with the head of the small retail chain, I saw a steady stream of all sorts of people coming and going, most involved with some aspect of store development or store operations, and there to get specific instructions on how to proceed next. He was not delegating or authorizing, but very clearly managing specific development projects step by step.

Just as they communicate all around the circle, so too do managers "do" all around it, as shown in Figure 6. *Doing inside* involves projects and problems. In other words, much "doing"

FIGURE 6
The Action Roles

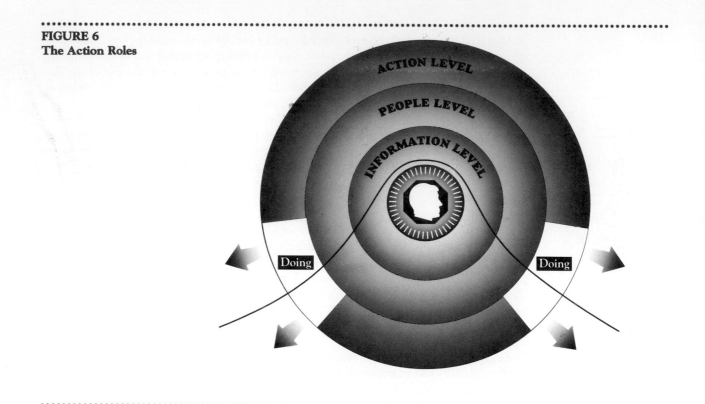

has to do with changing the unit itself, both proactively and reactively. Managers champion change to exploit opportunities for their units, and they handle its problems and resolve its crises, often with "hands on" involvement. Indeed, the president I observed of a large French systems company spent part of his day in a meeting on a very specific customer contract. Asked why he attended, he said it was a leading-edge project that could well change his company. He was being informed, to be sure, but also "doing" (more than controlling): he was an active member of the team. Here, then, the manager becomes a true designer (or, in the example above, a partner in the design), not of abstract strategies or of generalized structures, but of tangible projects of change. And the evidence, in fact, is that managers at all levels typically juggle many such projects concurrently, perhaps several dozen in the case of chief executives. Hence the popularity of the term "project management."

Some managers continue to do regular work after they have become managers as well. For example, a head nurse might see a patient, just as the Pope leads prayers, or a dean might teach a class. Done for its own sake, this might be considered separate from managerial work. But such things are often done for very managerial reasons as well. This may be an effective way of "keeping in touch" with the unit's work and finding out about its problems, in which case it falls under the role of communicating. Or it may be done to demonstrate involvement and commitment with others in the unit, in which case it falls under the role of culture building in the role of leading.

Doing outside takes place in terms of deals and negotiations. Again, there is no shortage of evidence on the importance of negotiating as well as dealing in managerial work. Most evident in my observations was the managing director of the film company, who was working on one intricate deal after another. This was a small company, and making deals was a key part of her job. But even in larger organizations, senior managers have to spend considerable time on negotiations themselves, especially when critical moments arise. After all, they are the ones who have the authority to commit the resources of their unit, and it is they who are the nerve centers of its information as well as the energy centers of its activity, not to mention the conceptual centers of its strategy. All around the circles, therefore, action connects to people who connect to information, which connects to the frame.

The Well-Rounded Job of Managing

I opened this article by noting that the best-known writers of management all seem to emphasize one aspect of the job—in the terms we now have, "doing" for Tom Peters, "conceiving" for Michael Porter, "leading" for Abraham Zaleznik and Warren Bennis, "controlling" for the classical writers. Now it can be appreciated why all may well be wrong: heeding the advice of any one of them must lead to the lopsided practice of managerial work. Like an unbalanced wheel at resonant frequency, the job risks flying out of control. That is why it is important to show all of the components of managerial work on a single integrated diagram, as in Figure 7, to remind people, at a glance, that these components form one job and cannot be separated.

Acceptance of Tom Peters' urgings—"'Don't think, do' is the phrase I favor"—could lead to the centrifugal explosion of the job, as it flies off in all directions, free of a strong frame anchoring it at the core. But acceptance of the spirit of Michael Porter's opposite writings—that what matters most is conception of the frame, especially of strategic positions—could produce a result no better: centripetal implosion, as the job closes in on itself cerebrally, free of the tangible connection to its outer actions. Thinking is heavy and can

FIGURE 7
Managerial Work
Rounded Out

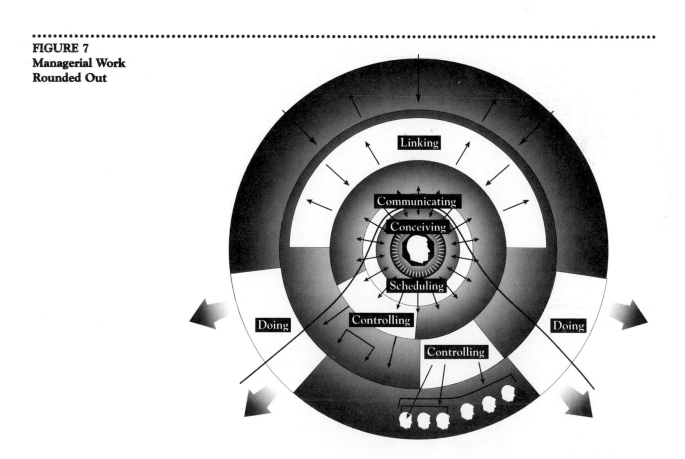

wear down the incumbent, while acting is light and cannot keep him or her in place. Only together do they provide the balance that seems so characteristic of effective management.

Too much leading produces a job free of content—aimless, frameless, and actionless— while too much linking produces a job detached from its internal roots—public relations instead of public service. The manager who only communicates or only conceives never gets anything done, while the manager who only "does" ends up doing it all alone. And, of course, we all know that happens to managers who believe their job is merely to control. A bad pun may thus make for good practice: the manager must practice a well-rounded job.

In fact, while we may be able to separate the components of this job conceptually, I maintain that they cannot be separated behaviorally. In other words, it may be useful, even necessary, to delineate the parts for purposes of design, selection, training, and support. But this job cannot be practiced as a set of independent parts. The core is a kind of magnet that holds the rest together, while the communication ring acts as a membrane that allows the flow of information between inner thinking and outer behaviors, which themselves tie people to action.

Indeed, the most interesting aspects of this job may well fall on the edges, between the component parts. For example, Andrew Grove, president of Intel, likes to describe what he does as "nudging," a perfect blend of controlling, leading, and doing (Grove, 1983). This can mean pushing people, tangibly but not aggressively, as might happen with pure doing, and not coldly, as with pure controlling, but with a sense of leading. There are similar edges between the inside and the outside, thinking and behaving, and communicating and controlling, as we shall see.

Managers who try to "do" outside without "doing" inside inevitably get themselves into trouble. Just consider all those chief executives who "did the deal," acquired the company or whatever, and then dropped it into the laps of others for execution. Likewise, it makes no more sense to conceive and then fail to lead and do (as has been the tendency in so-called "strategic planning," where controlling has often been considered sufficient for "implementation") than it makes sense to do or to lead without thinking through the frame in which to embed these activities. A single managerial job may be carried out by a small team, but only if its members are so tightly knitted together—especially by that ring of communication—that they act as a single entity. This is not to argue, of course, that different managers do not emphasize different roles or different aspects of the job. For example, we can distinguish a *conceptual* style of management, which focuses on the development of the frame, an *administrative* style, which concerns itself primarily with controlling, an *interpersonal* style, which favors leading on the inside or linking on the outside, and an *action* style, which is concerned mainly with tangible doing. And as we move out in this order, the overall style of managing can be described as less *opaque*, more *visible*.

A final aspect of managerial style has to do with the interrelationships among the various components of managerial work. For example, an important distinction can be made between *deductive* and *inductive* approaches to managerial work. The former proceeds from the core out, as the conceived frame is implemented through scheduling that uses information to drive people to get action done. We can call this a *cerebral* style of managing—highly deliberate. But there is an alternate, emergent view of the management process as well, which proceeds inductively, from the outer surface to the inner core. We might label it an *insightful* style. As Karl Weick puts it, managers act in order to think. They try things to gain experience, retain what works, and then, by interpreting the results, gradually evolve their frames (Weick, 1979).

Clearly, there is an infinity of possible contexts within which management can be practiced. But just as clearly, perhaps, a model such as the one presented here can help to order them and so come to grips with the difficult requirements of designing managerial jobs, selecting the right people to fill them, and training people accordingly.

by H. Edward Wrapp

The upper reaches of management are a land of mystery and intrigue. Very few people have ever been there, and the present inhabitants frequently send back messages that are incoherent both to other levels of management and to the world in general. This may account for the myths, illusions, and caricatures that permeate the literature of management—for example, such widely held notions as these:

▼   Life gets less complicated as a manager reaches the top of the pyramid.

▼   The manager at the top level knows everything that's going on in the organization, can command whatever resources he may need, and therefore can be more decisive.

▼   The general manager's day is taken up with making broad policy decisions and formulating precise objectives.

▼   The top executive's primary activity is conceptualizing long-range plans.

▼   In a large company, the top executive may be seen meditating about the role of his organization in society.

I suggest that none of these versions alone, or in combination, is an accurate portrayal of what a general manager does. Perhaps students of the management process have been overly eager to develop a theory and a discipline. As one executive I know puts it, "I guess I do some of the things described in the books and articles, but the descriptions are lifeless, and my job isn't."

What common characteristics, then, do successful executives exhibit *in reality?* I shall identify five skills or talents which, in my experience, seem especially significant. . . .

Keeping Well Informed

First, each of my heroes has a special talent for keeping himself informed about a wide range of operating decisions being made at different levels in the company. As he moves up the ladder, he develops a network of information sources in many different departments. He cultivates these sources and keeps them open no matter how high he climbs in the organization. When the need arises, he bypasses the lines on the organization chart to seek more than one version of a situation.

In some instances, especially when they suspect he would not be in total agreement with their decision, his subordinates will elect to inform him in advance, before they announce a decision. In these circumstances, he is in a position to defer the decision, or redirect it, or even block further action. However, he does not insist on this procedure. Ordinarily he leaves it up to the members of his organization to decide at what stage they inform him.

Top-level managers are frequently criticized by writers, consultants, and lower levels of management for continuing to enmesh themselves in operating problems, after promotion to the top, rather than withdrawing to the "big picture." Without any doubt, some managers do get lost in a welter of detail and insist on making too many decisions. Superficially, the good manager may seem to make the same mistake—but his purposes are different. He knows that only by keeping well informed about the decisions being made can he avoid the sterility so often found in those who isolate themselves from operations. If he follows the advice to free himself from operations, he may soon find himself subsisting on a diet of

* Originally published in the *Harvard Business Review* (September–October 1967) and winner of the McKinsey prize for the best article in the *Review* in 1967. Copyright © 1967 by the President and Fellows of Harvard College; all rights reserved. Reprinted with deletions by permission of the *Harvard Business Review*.

abstractions, leaving the choice of what he eats in the hands of his subordinates. As Kenneth Boulding puts it, "The very purpose of a hierarchy is to prevent information from reaching higher layers. It operates as an information filter, and there are little wastebaskets all along the way" (in *Business Week*, February 18, 1967:202). . . .

Focusing Time and Energy

The second skill of the good manager is that he knows how to save his energy and hours for those few particular issues, decisions, or problems to which he should give his personal attention. He knows the fine and subtle distinction between keeping fully informed about operating decisions and allowing the organization to force him into participating in these decisions or, even worse, making them. Recognizing that he can bring his special talents to bear on only a limited number of matters, he chooses those issues which he believes will have the greatest long-term impact on the company, and on which his special abilities can be most productive. Under ordinary circumstances he will limit himself to three or four major objectives during any single period of sustained activity.

What about the situations he elects *not* to become involved in as a decision maker? He makes sure (using the skill first mentioned) that the organization keeps him informed about them at various stages; he does not want to be accused of indifference to such issues. He trains his subordinates not to bring the matters to him for a decision. The communication to him from below is essentially one of. "Here is our sizeup, and here's what we propose to do." Reserving his hearty encouragement for those projects which hold superior promise of a contribution to total corporate strategy, he simply acknowledges receipt of information on other matters. When he sees a problem where the organization needs his help, he finds a way to transmit his know-how short of giving orders—usually by asking perceptive questions.

Playing the Power Game

To what extent do successful top executives push their ideas and proposals through the organization? The rather common notion that the "prime mover" continually creates and forces through new programs, like a powerful majority leader in a liberal Congress, is in my opinion very misleading.

The successful manager is sensitive to the power structure in the organization. In considering any major current proposal, he can plot the position of the various individuals and units in the organization of a scale ranging from complete, outspoken support down to determined, sometimes bitter, and oftentimes well cloaked opposition. In the middle of the scale is an area of comparative indifference. Usually, several aspects of a proposal will fall into this area, and *here is where he knows he can operate*. He assesses the depth and nature of the blocs in the organization. His perception permits him to move through what I call *corridors* of comparative indifference. He seldom challenges when a corridor is blocked, preferring to pause until it has opened up.

Related to this particular skill is his ability to recognize the need for a few trial-balloon launchers in the organization. He knows that the organization will tolerate only a certain number of proposals which emanate from the apex of the pyramid. No matter how sorely he may be tempted to stimulate the organization with a flow of his own ideas, he knows he must work through idea men in different parts of the organization. As he studies the reactions of key individuals and groups to the trial balloons these men send up, he is able to make a better assessment of how to limit the emasculation of the various proposals. For seldom does he find a proposal which is supported by all quarters of the organization. The emergence of strong support in certain quarters is almost sure to evoke strong opposition in others.

VALUE OF SENSE OF TIMING

Circumstances like these mean that a good sense of timing is a priceless asset for a top executive. . . . As a good manager stands at a point in time, he can identify a set of goals he is interested in, albeit the outline of them may be pretty hazy. His timetable, which is also pretty hazy, suggests that some must be accomplished sooner than others, and that some may be safely postponed for several months or years. He has a still hazier notion of how he can reach these goals. He assesses key individuals and groups. He knows that each has its own set of goals, some of which he understands rather thoroughly and others about which he can only speculate. He knows also that these individuals and groups represent blocks to certain programs or projects, and that these points of opposition must be taken into account. As the day-to-day operating decisions are made, and as proposals are responded to both by individuals and by groups, he perceives more clearly where the corridors of comparative indifference are. He takes action accordingly.

The Art of Imprecision

The fourth skill of the successful manager is knowing how to satisfy the organization that it has a sense of direction *without ever actually getting himself committed to a specific set of objectives*. This is not to say that he does not have objectives—personal and corporate, long-term and short-term. They are significant guides to his thinking, and he modifies them continually as he better understands the resources he is working with, the competition, and the changing market demands. But as the organization clamors for statements of objectives, these are samples of what they get back from him:

> "Our company aims to be number one in its industry."
> "Our objective is growth with profit."
> "We seek the maximum return on investment."
> "Management's goal is to meet its responsibilities to stockholders, employees, and the public."

In my opinion, statements such as these provide almost no guidance to the various levels of management. Yet they are quite readily accepted as objectives by large numbers of intelligent people.

MAINTAINING VIABILITY

Why does the good manager shy away from precise statements of his objectives for the organization? The main reason is that he finds it impossible to set down specific objectives which will be relevant for any reasonable period into the future. Conditions in business change continually and rapidly, and corporate strategy must be revised to take the changes into account. The more explicit the statement of strategy, the more difficult it becomes to persuade the organization to turn to different goals when needs and conditions shift.

The public and the stockholders, to be sure, must perceive the organization as having a well-defined set of objectives and clear sense of direction. But in reality the good top manager is seldom so certain of the direction which should be taken. Better than anyone else, he senses the many, many threats to his company—threats which lie in the economy, in the actions of competitors, and, not least, within his own organization.

He also knows that it is impossible to state objectives clearly enough so that everyone in the organization understands what they mean. Objectives get communicated only over time by a consistency or pattern in operating decisions. Such decisions are more meaningful than words. In instances where precise objectives are spelled out, the organization tends to interpret them so they fit its own needs.

Subordinates who keep pressing for more precise objectives are in truth working against their own best interests. Each time the objectives are stated more specifically, a subordinate's range of possibilities for operating are reduced. The narrower field means less room to roam and to accommodate the flow of ideas coming up from his part of the organization.

AVOIDING POLICY STRAITJACKETS

The successful manager's reluctance to be precise extends into the area of policy decisions. He seldom makes a forthright statement of policy. He may be aware that in some companies there are executives who spend more time in arbitrating disputes caused by stated policies than in moving the company forward. The management textbooks contend that well-defined policies are the sine qua non of a well-managed company. My research does not bear out this contention. For example,

> The president of one company with which I am familiar deliberately leaves the assignments of his top officers vague and refuses to define policies for them. He passes out new assignments with seemingly no pattern in mind and consciously sets up competitive ventures among his subordinates. His methods, though they would never be sanctioned by a classical organization planner, are deliberate—and, incidentally, quite effective.

Since able managers do not make policy decisions, does this mean that well-managed companies operate without policies? Certainly not. But the policies are those which evolve over time from an indescribable mix of operating decisions. From any single operating decision might have come a very minor dimension of the policy as the organization understands it; from a series of decisions comes a pattern of guidelines for various levels of the organization.

The skillful manager resists the urge to write a company creed or to compile a policy manual. Preoccupation with detailed statements of corporate objectives and departmental goals and with comprehensive organization charts and job descriptions is often the first symptom of an organization which is in the early stages of atrophy.

The "management by objectives" school, so widely heralded in recent years, suggests that detailed objectives be spelled out at all levels in the corporation. This method is feasible at lower levels of management, but it becomes unworkable at the upper levels. The top manager must think out objectives in detail, but ordinarily some of the objectives must be withheld, or at least communicated to the organization in modest doses. A conditioning process which may stretch over months or years is necessary in order to prepare the organization for radical departures from what it is currently striving to attain.

Suppose, for example, that a president is convinced his company must phase out of the principal business it has been in for 35 years. Although making this change of course is one of his objectives, he may well feel that he cannot disclose the idea even to his vice presidents, whose total know-how is in the present business. A blunt announcement that the company is changing horses would be too great a shock for most of them to bear. And so he begins moving toward this goal but without a full disclosure to his management group.

A detailed spelling out of objectives may only complicate the task of reaching them. Specific, detailed statements give the opposition an opportunity to organize its defenses.

The fifth, and most important, skill I shall describe bears little relation to the doctrine that management is (or should be) a comprehensive, systematic, logical, well-programmed science. Of all the heresies set forth here, this should strike doctrinaires as the rankest of all!

The successful manager, in my observation, recognizes the futility of trying to push total packages or programs through the organization. He is willing to take less than total acceptance in order to achieve modest progress toward his goals. Avoiding debates on principles, he tries to piece together particles that may appear to be incidentals into a program that moves at least part of the way toward his objectives. His attitude is based on optimism and persistence. Over and over he says to himself, "There must be some parts of this proposal on which we can capitalize."

Whenever he identifies relationships among the different proposals before him, he knows that they present opportunities for combination and restructuring. It follows that he is a man of wide-ranging interests and curiosity. The more things he knows about, the more opportunities he will have to discover parts which are related. This process does not require great intellectual brilliance or unusual creativity. The wider ranging his interests, the more likely that he will be able to tie together several unrelated proposals. He is skilled as an analyst, but even more talented as a conceptualizer.

If the manager has built or inherited a solid organization, it will be difficult for him to come up with an idea which no one in the company has ever thought of before. His most significant contribution may be that he can see relationships which no one else has seen. . . .

CONTRASTING PICTURES

It is interesting to note, in the writings of several students of management, the emergence of the concept that, rather than making decisions, the leader's principal task is maintaining operating conditions which permit the various decision-making systems to function effectively. The supporters of this theory, it seems to me, overlook the subtle turns of direction which the leader can provide. He cannot add purpose and structure to the balanced judgments of subordinates if he simply rubberstamps their decisions. He must weigh the issues and reach his own decision. . . .

Many of the articles about successful executives picture them as great thinkers who sit at their desks drafting master blueprints for their companies. The successful top executives I have seen at work do not operate this way. Rather than produce a full-grown decision tree, they start with a twig, help it grow, and ease themselves out on the limbs only after they have tested to see how much weight the limbs can stand.

In my picture, the general manager sits in the midst of a continuous stream of operating problems. His organization presents him with a flow of proposals to deal with the problems. Some of these proposals are contained in voluminous, well-documented, formal reports; some are as fleeting as the walk-in visit from a subordinate whose latest inspiration came during the morning's coffee break. Knowing how meaningless it is to say, "This is a finance problem," or, "That is a communications problem," the manager feels no compulsion to classify his problems. He is, in fact, undismayed by a problem that defies classification. As the late Gary Steiner, in one of his speeches, put it, "He has a high tolerance for ambiguity."

In considering each proposal, the general manager tests it against at least three criteria:

1. Will the total proposal—or, more often, will some part of the proposal—move the organization toward the objectives which he has in mind?

2. How will the whole or parts of the proposal be received by the various groups and sub-groups in the organization? Where will the strongest opposition come from, which group will furnish the strongest support, and which group will be neutral or indifferent?

3. How does the proposal relate to programs already in process or currently proposed? Can some parts of the proposal under consideration be added on to a program already under way, or can they be combined with all or parts of other proposals in a package which can be steered through the organization? . . .

Conclusion

To recapitulate, the general manager possesses five important skills. He knows how to:

1. *Keep open many pipelines of information*—No one will quarrel with the desirability of an early warning system which provides varied viewpoints on an issue. However, very few managers know how to practice this skill, and the books on management add precious little to our understanding of the techniques which make it practicable.

2. *Concentrate on a limited number of significant issues*—No matter how skillful the manager is in focusing his energies and talents, he is inevitably caught up in a number of inconsequential duties. Active leadership of an organization demands a high level of personal involvement, and personal involvement brings with it many time-consuming activities which have an infinitesimal impact on corporate strategy. Hence this second skill, while perhaps the most logical of the five, is by no means the easiest to apply.

3. *Identify the corridors of comparative indifference*—Are there inferences here that the good manager has no ideas of his own, that he stands by until his organization proposes solutions, that he never uses his authority to force a proposal through the organization? Such inferences are not intended. The message is that a good organization will tolerate only so much direction from the top; the good manager therefore is adept at sensing how hard he can push.

4. *Give the organization a sense of direction with open-ended objectives*—In assessing this skill, keep in mind that I am talking about top levels of management. At lower levels, the manager should be encouraged to write down his objectives, if for no other reason than to ascertain if they are consistent with corporate strategy.

5. *Spot opportunities and relationships in the stream of operating problems and decisions*—Lest it be concluded from the description of this skill that the good manager is more an improviser than a planner, let me emphasize that he is a planner and encourages planning by his subordinates. Interestingly, though, professional planners may be irritated by a good general manager. Most of them complain about his lack of vision. They devise a master plan, but the president (or other operating executive) seems to ignore it, or to give it minimum acknowledgment by borrowing bits and pieces for implementation. They seem to feel that the power of a good master plan will be obvious to everyone, and its implementation automatic. But the general manager knows that even if the plan is sound and imaginative, the job has only begun. The long, painful task of implementation will depend on his skill, not that of the planner. . . .

by Gary Hamel and
C. K. Prahalad

Today managers in many industries are working hard to match the competitive advantages of their new global rivals. They are moving manufacturing offshore in search of low labor costs, rationalizing product lines to capture global scale economies, instituting quality circles and just-in-time production, and adopting Japanese human resource practices. When competitiveness still seems out of reach, they form strategic alliances, often with the very companies that upset the competitive balance in the first place.

Important as these initiatives are, few of them go beyond mere imitation. . . .For these executives and their companies, regaining competitiveness will mean rethinking many of the basic concepts of strategy. . . . The new global competitors approach strategy from a perspective that is fundamentally different from that which underpins Western management thought. . . .

Companies that have risen to global leadership over the past 20 years invariably began with ambitions that were out of all proportion to their resources and capabilities. But they created an obsession with winning at all levels of the organization and then sustained that obsession over the 10- to 20-year quest for global leadership. We term this obsession "strategic intent."

On the one hand, strategic intent envisions a desired leadership position and establishes the criteria the organization will use to chart its progress. Komatsu set out to "Encircle Caterpillar." Canon sought to "Beat Xerox." Honda strove to become a second Ford—an automotive pioneer. All are expressions of strategic intent.

At the same time, strategic intent is more than simply unfettered ambition. (Many companies possess an ambitious strategic intent yet fall short of their goals.) The concept also encompasses an active management process that includes: focusing the organization's attention on the essence of winning; motivating people by communicating the value of the target; leaving room for individual and team contributions; sustaining enthusiasm by providing new operations definitions as circumstances change; and using intent consistently to guide resource allocations.

Strategic intent captures the essence of winning. The Apollo program—landing a man on the moon ahead of the Soviets—was as competitively focused as Komatsu's drive against Caterpillar. The space program became the scorecard for America's technology race with the USSR. . . . For Coca-Cola, strategic intent has been to put Coke within "arms reach" of every consumer in the world.

Strategic intent is stable over time. In battles for global leadership, one of the most critical tasks is to lengthen the organization's attention span. Strategic intent provides consistency to short-term action, while leaving room for reinterpretation as new opportunities emerge. . . .

Strategic intent sets a target that deserves personal effort and commitment. Ask the chairmen of many American corporations how they measure their contributions to their companies' success and you've likely to get an answer expressed in terms of shareholder wealth. In a company that possesses a strategic intent, top management is more likely to talk in terms of global market leadership. Market share leadership typically yields shareholder wealth, to be sure. But the two goals do not have the same motivational impact. It is hard to imagine middle managers, let alone blue-collar employees, waking up each day with the sole thought of creating more shareholder wealth. But mightn't they feel different given the challenge to "Beat Benz"—the rallying cry at one Japanese auto producer? Strategic intent gives employees the only goal that is worthy of commitment: to unseat the best or remain the best, worldwide. . . .

Just as you cannot plan a 10- to-20-year quest for global leadership, the chance of falling into a leadership position by accident is also remote. We don't believe that global leadership comes from an undirected process of intrapreneurship. Nor is it the product of a skunkworks or other techniques for internal venturing. Behind such programs lies a nihilistic assumption: the organization is so hide-bound, so orthodox ridden that the only way to innovate is to put a few bright people in a dark room, pour in some money, and hope that something wonderful will happen. In the "Silicon Valley" approach to innovation, the only role for top managers is to retrofit their corporate strategy to the entrepreneurial successes that emerge from below. Here the value added of top management is low indeed. . . .

In companies that overcame resource constraints to build leadership positions, we see a different relationship between means and ends. While strategic intent is clear about ends, it is flexible as to means—it leaves room for improvisation. Achieving strategic intent requires enormous creativity with respect to means. . . . But this creativity comes in the service of a clearly prescribed end. Creativity is unbridled, but not uncorraled, because top management establishes the criterion against which employees can pretest the logic of their initiatives. Middle managers must do more than deliver on promised financial targets; they must also deliver on the broad direction implicit in their organization's strategic intent.

Strategic intent implies a sizable stretch for an organization. Current capabilities and resources will not suffice. This forces the organization to be more inventive, to make the most of limited resources. Whereas the traditional view of strategy focuses on the degree of fit between existing resources and current opportunities, strategic intent creates an extreme misfit between resources and ambitions. Top management then challenges the organization to close the gap by systematically building new advantages. For Canon this meant first understanding Xerox's patents, then licensing technology to create a product that would yield early market experience, then gearing up internal R&D efforts, then licensing its own technology to other manufacturers to fund further R&D, then entering marketing segments in Japan and Europe where Xerox was weak, and so on.

In this respect, strategic intent is like a marathon run in 400-meter sprints. No one knows what the terrain will look like at mile 26, so the role of top management is to focus the organization's attention on the ground to be covered in the next 400 meters. In several companies, management did this by presenting the organization with a series of corporate challenges, each specifying the next hill in the race to achieve strategic intent. One year the challenge might be quality, the next total customer care, the next entry into new markets, the next a rejuvenated product line. As this example indicates, corporate challenges are a way to stage the acquisition of new competitive advantages, a way to identify the focal point for employees' efforts in the near to medium term. As with strategic intent, top management is specific about the ends (reducing product development times by 75%, for example) but less prescriptive about the means.

Like strategic intent, challenges stretch the organization. To preempt Xerox in the personal copier business, Canon set its engineers a target price of $1,000 for a home copier. At the time, Canon's least expensive copier sold for several thousand dollars. . . . Canon engineers were challenged to reinvent the copier—a challenge they met by substituting a disposable cartridge for the complex image-transfer mechanism used in other copiers. . . .

For a challenge to be effective, individuals and teams throughout the organization must understand it and see its implications for their own jobs. Companies that set corporate challenges to create new competitive advantages (as Ford and IBM did with quality improvement) quickly discover that engaging the entire organization requires top management to:

Create a sense of urgency, or quasi crisis, by amplifying weak signals in the environment that point up the need to improve, instead of allowing inaction to precipitate a real crisis. . . .

Develop a competitor focus at every level through widespread use of competitive intelligence. Every employee should be able to benchmark his or her efforts against best-in-class competitors so that the challenge becomes personal. . . .

Provide employees with the skills they need to work effectively—training in statistical tools, problem solving, value engineering, and team building, for example.

Give the organization time to digest one challenge before launching another. When competing initiatives overload the organization, middle managers often try to protect their people from the whipsaw of shifting priorities. But this "wait and see if they're serious this time" attitude ultimately destroys the credibility of corporate challenges.

Establish clear milestones and review mechanisms to track progress and ensure that internal recognition and rewards reinforce desired behavior. The goal is to make the challenge inescapable for everyone in the company. . . .

Reciprocal responsibility means shared gain and shared pain . . . at Nissan when the yen strengthened: top management took a big pay cut and then asked middle managers and line employees to sacrifice relatively less. In too many companies, the pain of revitalization falls almost exclusively on the employees least responsible for the enterprise's decline. . . . This one-sided approach to regaining competitiveness keeps many companies from harnessing the intellectual horsepower of their employees.

Creating a sense of reciprocal responsibility is crucial because competitiveness ultimately depends on the pace at which a company embeds new advantages deep within its organization, not on its stock of advantages at any given time. Thus we need to expand the concept of competitive advantage beyond the scorecard many managers now use: Are my costs lower? Will my product command a price premium?

Few competitive advantages are long lasting. Uncovering a new competitive advantage is a bit like getting a hot tip on a stock: the first person to act on the insight makes more money than the last. . . .

Keeping score of existing advantages is not the same as building new advantages. The essence of strategy lies in creating tomorrow's competitive advantages faster than competitors mimic the ones you possess today. In the 1960s, Japanese producers relied on labor and capital cost advantages. As Western manufacturers began to move production offshore, Japanese companies accelerated their investment in process technology and created scale and quality advantages. Then as their U.S. and European competitors rationalized manufacturing, they added another string to their bow by accelerating the rate of product development. Then they built global brands. Then they deskilled competitors through alliances and outsourcing deals. The moral? An organization's capacity to improve existing skills and learn new ones is the most defensible competitive advantage of all.

To achieve strategic intent, a company must usually take on larger, better financed competitors. That means carefully managing competitive engagements so that scarce resources are conserved. Managers cannot do that simply by playing the same game better—making marginal improvement to competitor's technology and business practices. Instead, they must fundamentally change the game in ways that disadvantage incumbents—designing novel approaches to market entry, advantage building, and competitive warfare. For smart competitors, the goal is not competitive imitation but competitive innovation, the art of containing competitive risks within manageable proportions.

Four approaches to competitive innovation are evident in the global expansion of Japanese companies. These are: building layers of advantage, searching for loose bricks, changing the terms of engagement, and competing through collaboration.

The wider a company's portfolio of advantages, the less risk it faces in competitive battles. New global competitors have built such portfolios by steadily expanding their arsenals of competitive weapons. They have moved inexorably from less defensible advantages such as low wage costs to more defensible advantages like global brands. . . .

Business schools have perpetuated the notion that a manager with new present value calculations in one hand and portfolio planning in the other can manage any business anywhere.

In many diversified companies, top management evaluates line managers on numbers alone because no other basis for dialogue exists. Managers move so many times as part of their "career development" that they often do not understand the nuances of the businesses they are managing. At GE, for example, one fast-track manager heading an important new venture had moved across five businesses in five years. His series of quick successes finally came to an end when he confronted a Japanese competitor whose managers had been plodding along in the same business for more than a decade.

Regardless of ability and effort, fast-track managers are unlikely to develop the deep business knowledge they need to discuss technology options, competitors' strategies, and global opportunities substantively. Invariably, therefore, discussions gravitate to "the numbers," while the value added of managers is limited to the financial and planning savvy they carry from job to job. Knowledge of the company's internal planning and accounting systems substitutes for substantive knowledge of the business, making competitive innovation unlikely.

When managers know that their assignments have a two- to three-year time frame, they feel great pressure to create a good track record fast. This pressure often takes on one of two forms. Either the manager does not commit to goals whose time line extends beyond his or her expected tenure. Or ambitious goals are adopted and squeezed into an unrealistically short time frame. Aiming to be number one in a business is the essence of strategic intent; but imposing a three- to four-year horizon on that effort simply invites disaster. Acquisitions are made with little attention to the problems of integration. The organization becomes overloaded with initiatives. Collaborative ventures are formed without adequate attention to competitive consequences.

Almost every strategic management theory and nearly every corporate planning system is premised on a strategy hierarchy in which corporate goals guide business unit strategies and business unit strategies guide functional tactics. In this hierarchy, senior management makes strategy and low levels execute it. The dichotomy between formulation and implementation is familiar and widely accepted. But the strategy hierarchy undermines competitiveness by fostering an elitist view of management that tends to disenfranchise most of the organization. Employees fail to identify with corporate goals or involve themselves deeply in the work of becoming more competitive.

The strategy hierarchy isn't the only explanation for an elitist view of management, of course. The myths that grow up around successful top managers. . . perpetuate it. So does the turbulent business environment. Middle managers buffeted by circumstances that seem to be beyond their control desperately want to believe that top management has all the answers. And top management, in turn, hesitates to admit it does not for fear of demoralizing lower level employees. . . .

Unfortunately, a threat that everyone perceives but no one talks about creates more anxiety that a threat that has been clearly identified and made the focal point for the problem-solving efforts of the entire company. That is one reason honesty and humility on the part of top management may be the first prerequisite of revitalization. Another reason is the need to make participation more than a buzzword.

Programs such as quality circles and total customer service often fall short of expectations because management does not recognize that successful implementation requires more than administrative structures. Difficulties in embedding new capabilities are typically put down to "communication" problems, with the unstated assumption that if only downward communication were more effective—"if only middle management would get the message straight"—the new program would quickly take root. The need for upward communication is often ignored, or assumed to mean nothing more than feedback. In contrast, Japanese companies win, not because they have smarter managers, but because they have developed ways to harness the "wisdom of the anthill." They realize the top managers are a bit like the astronauts who circle the earth in the space shuttle. It may be the astronauts who get all the glory, but everyone knows that the real intelligence behind the mission is located firmly on the ground. . . .

Developing faith in the organization's ability to deliver on tough goals, motivating it to do so, focusing its attention long enough to internalize new capabilities—this is the real challenge for top management. Only by rising to this challenge will senior managers gain the courage they need to commit themselves and their companies to global leadership.

FORMULATING STRATEGY

Most of what has been published in this field deals with how strategy *should* be designed or consciously *formulated.* On the prescription of how this should be accomplished, there has been a good deal of consensus, although, as we shall see later, this is now eroding. Perhaps we should more properly conclude that there have been two waves of consensus. The first, which developed in the 1960s, is presented in this chapter; the second, which emerged around 1980, did not challenge the first so much as build on it. This is presented in Chapter 4.

Ken Andrews of the Harvard Business School is the person most commonly associated with the first wave, although Bill Newman of Columbia wrote on some of these issues much earlier and Igor Ansoff simultaneously outlined very similar views while he was at Carnegie-Mellon. But the Andrews text became the best known, in part because it was so simply and clearly written, in part because it was embodied in a popular textbook (with cases) emanating from the Harvard Business School.

We reproduce parts of the Andrews text (as revised in its own publication in 1980, but based on the original 1965 edition). These serve to introduce the basic point that strategy ultimately requires the achievement of fit between the external situation (opportunities and threats) and internal capability (strengths and weaknesses). Note how the Andrews approach builds directly on some of the military concepts outlined earlier. Both seek to leverage the impact of resources by concentrating efforts within a defined zone of dominance while attempting to anticipate the effects of potentially damaging external forces.

As you read the Andrews text, a number of basic premises will quickly become evident. Among these are: the clear distinction made between strategy formulation and strategy implementation (in effect, between thinking and action); the belief that strategy (or at least intended strategy) should be made explicit; the notion that structure should follow strategy (in other words, be designed in accordance with it); and the assumption that strategy emanates from the formal leadership of the organization. Similar premises underlie most of the prescriptive literature of strategic management.

This model (if we can call it that) has proven very useful in many circumstances as a broad way to analyze a strategic situation and to think about making strategy. A careful strategist should certainly touch all the bases suggested in this approach. But in many circumstances the model cannot or should not be followed to the letter, as shall be discussed in Chapter 5 and later ones.

The Rumelt reading (an updated version for this text) elaborates on one element in this traditional model—the evaluation of strategies. While the Andrews text contains a similar discussion, Rumelt, a graduate of the Harvard Business School and strategy professor at UCLA, develops it in a particularly elegant way, helping to round out this chapter on the classical view of formulating strategy.

One more reading, by Quinn and Hilmer, combines two crucial concepts that have taken center stage in the strategy formation literature in recent years. One is "core competency," the idea that companies have to build, sustain, and use in their formulation of strategy fundamental competencies where they contribute unique value to customers by performing at "best in world" levels, to quote the authors. The authors develop this concept in a rich way. The second is strategic outsourcing. If companies are to focus on their core competencies, then they have to consider shedding much else, where they do not have distinct advantages. If they perform in-house activities that others could perform better, they sacrifice competitive edge. Hence, these two concepts must be linked together, as this article does elegantly, being careful to point out the pitfalls.

▼ READING 3.1   THE CONCEPT OF CORPORATE STRATEGY*

by Kenneth R. Andrews

The Strategy Concept

WHAT STRATEGY IS

Corporate strategy is the pattern of decisions in a company that determines and reveals its objectives, purposes, or goals, produces the principal policies and plans for achieving those goals, and defines the range of business the company is to pursue, the kind of economic and human organization it is or intends to be, and the nature of the economic and noneconomic contribution it intends to make to its shareholders, employees, customers, and communities. . . .

The strategic decision contributing to this pattern is one that is effective over long periods of time, affects the company in many different ways, and focuses and commits a significant portion of its resources to the expected outcomes. The pattern resulting from a series of such decisions will probably define the central character and image of a company, the individuality it has for its members and various publics, and the position it will occupy in its industry and markets. It will permit the specification of particular objectives to be attained through a timed sequence investment and implementation decisions and will govern directly the deployment or redeployment of resources to make these decisions effective.

Some aspects of such a pattern of decision may be in an established corporation unchanging over long periods of time, like a commitment to quality, or high technology, or certain raw materials or good labor relations. Other aspects of strategy must change as or before the world changes, such as product line, manufacturing process, or merchandising and styling practices. The basic determinants of company character, if purposefully institutionalized, are likely to persist through and shape the nature of substantial changes in product-market choices and allocation of resources. . . .

It is important, however, not to take the idea apart in another way, that is, to separate goals from the policies designed to achieve those goals. The essence of the definition of strategy I have just recorded is *pattern*. The interdependence of purposes, policies, and organized action is crucial to the particularity of an individual strategy and its opportunity to

* Excerpted from Kenneth R. Andrews, *The Concept of Corporate Strategy*, rev. ed. (copyright © by Richard D. Irwin, Inc., 1980), Chaps. 2 and 3; reprinted by permission of the publisher.

identify competitive advantage. It is the unity, coherence, and internal consistency of a company's strategic decisions that position the company in its environment and give the firm its identity, its power to mobilize its strengths, and its likelihood of success in the marketplace. It is the interrelationship of a set of goals and policies that crystallizes from the formless reality of a company's environment a set of problems an organization can seize upon and solve.

What you are doing, in short, is never meaningful unless you can say or imply what you are doing it for: the quality of administrative action and the motivation lending it power cannot be appraised without knowing its relationship to purpose. Breaking up the system of corporate goals and the character-determining major policies for attainment leads to narrow and mechanical conceptions of strategic management and endless logic chopping. . . .

SUMMARY STATEMENTS OF STRATEGY

Before we proceed to clarification of this concept by application, we should specify the terms in which strategy is usually expressed. A summary statement of strategy will characterize the product line and services offered or planned by the company, the markets and market segments for which products and services are now or will be designed, and the channels through which these markets will be reached. The means by which the operation is to be financed will be specified, as will the profit objectives and the emphasis to be placed on the safety of capital versus level of return. Major policy in central functions such as marketing, manufacturing, procurement, research and development, labor relations, and personnel, will be stated where they distinguish the company from others, and usually the intended size, form, and climate of the organization will be included.

Each company, if it were to construct a summary strategy from what it understands itself to be aiming at, would have a different statement with different categories of decision emphasized to indicate what it wanted to be or do. . . .

FORMULATION OF STRATEGY

Corporate strategy is an organization process, in many ways inseparable from the structure, behavior, and culture of the company in which it takes place. Nevertheless, we may abstract from the process two important aspects, interrelated in real life but separable for the purposes of analysis. The first of these we may call *formulation*, the second *implementation*. Deciding what strategy should be may be approached as a rational undertaking, even if in life emotional attachments . . . may complicate choice among future alternatives. . . .

The principal subactivities of strategy formulation as a logical activity include identifying opportunities and threats in the company's environment and attaching some estimate or risk to the discernible alternatives. Before a choice can be made, the company's strengths and weaknesses should be appraised together with the resources on hand and available. Its actual or potential capacity to take advantage of perceived market needs or to cope with attendant risks should be estimated as objectively as possible. The strategic alternative which results from matching opportunity and corporate capability at an acceptable level of risk is what we may call an *economic strategy*.

The process described thus far assumes that strategists are analytically objective in estimating the relative capacity of their company and the opportunity they see or anticipate in developing markets. The extent to which they wish to undertake low or high risk presumably depends on their profit objectives. The higher they set the latter, the more willing they must be to assume a correspondingly high risk that the market opportunity they see will not develop or that the corporate competence required to excel competition will not be forthcoming.

So far we have described the intellectual processes of ascertaining what a company *might do* in terms of environmental opportunity, of deciding what it *can do* in terms of ability and power, and of bringing these two considerations together in optimal equilibrium. The determination of strategy also requires consideration of what alternatives are preferred by the chief executive and perhaps by his or her immediate associates as well, quite apart from economic considerations. Personal values, aspirations, and ideals do, and in our judgment quite properly should, influence the final choice of purposes. Thus what the executives of a company *want to do* must be brought into the strategic decision.

Finally strategic choice has an ethical aspect—a fact much more dramatically illustrated in some industries than in others. Just as alternatives may be ordered in terms of the degree of risk that they entail, so may they be examined against the standards of responsiveness to the expectations of society that the strategist elects. Some alternatives may seem to the executive considering them more attractive than others when the public good or service to society is considered. What a company *should do* thus appears as a fourth element of the strategic decision. . . .

THE IMPLEMENTATION OF STRATEGY

Since effective implementation can make a sound strategic decision ineffective or a debatable choice successful, it is as important to examine the processes of implementation as to weigh the advantages of available strategic alternatives. The implementation of strategy is comprised of a series of subactivities which are primarily administrative. If purpose is determined, then the resources of a company can be mobilized to accomplish it. An organizational structure appropriate for the efficient performance of the required tasks must be made effective by information systems and relationships permitting coordination of subdivided activities. The organizational processes of performance measurement, compensation, management development—all of them enmeshed in systems of incentives and controls—must be directed toward the kind of behavior required by organizational purpose. The role of personal leadership is important and sometimes decisive in the accomplishment of strategy. Although we know that organization structure and processes of compensation, incentives, control, and management development influence and constrain the formulation of strategy, we should look first at the logical proposition that structure should follow strategy in order to cope later with the organizational reality that strategy also follows structure. When we have examined both tendencies, we will understand and to some extent be prepared to deal with the interdependence of the formulation and implementation of corporate purpose. Figure 1 may be useful in understanding the analysis of strategy as a pattern of interrelated decisions. . . .

Relating Opportunities to Resources

Determination of a suitable strategy for a company begins in identifying the opportunities and risks in its environment. This [discussion] is concerned with the identification of a range of strategic alternatives, the narrowing of this range by recognizing the constraints imposed by corporate capability, and the determination of one or more economic strategies at acceptable levels of risk. . . .

THE NATURE OF THE COMPANY'S ENVIRONMENT

The environment of an organization in business, like that of any other organic entity, is the pattern of all the external conditions and influences that affect its life and development. The environmental influences relevant to strategic decision operate in a company's industry, the total business community, its city, its country, and the world. They are technological, economic, physical, social, and political in kind. The corporate strategist is usually at

FIGURE 1

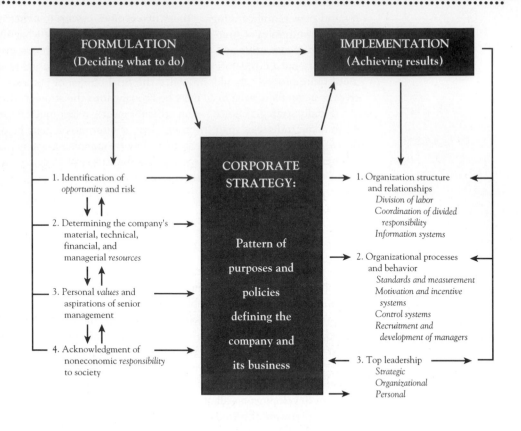

least intuitively aware of these features of the current environment. But in all these categories change is taking place at varying rates—fastest in technology, less rapidly in politics. Change in the environment of business necessitates continuous monitoring of a company's definition of its business, lest it falter, blur, or become obsolete. Since by definition the formulation of strategy is performed with the future in mind, executives who take part in the strategic planning process must be aware of those aspects of their company's environment especially susceptible to the kind of change that will affect their company's future.

TECHNOLOGY

From the point of view of the corporate strategist, technological developments are not only the fastest unfolding but the most far-reaching in extending or contracting opportunity for an established company. They include the discoveries of science, the impact of related product development, the less dramatic machinery and process improvements, and the progress of automation and data processing. . . .

ECOLOGY

It used to be possible to take for granted the physical characteristics of the environment and find them favorable to industrial development. Plant sites were chosen using criteria like availability of process and cooling water, accessibility to various forms of transportation, and stability of soil conditions. With the increase in sensitivity to the impact on the physical environment of all industrial activity, it becomes essential, often to comply with law, to consider how planned expansion and even continued operation under changing standards will affect and be perceived to affect the air, water, traffic density, and quality of life generally of any area which a company would like to enter. . . .

ECONOMICS

Because business is more accustomed to monitoring economic trends than those in other spheres, it is less likely to be taken by surprise by such massive developments as the internationalization of competition, the return of China and Russia to trade with the West, the slower than projected development of the Third World countries, the Americanization of demand and culture in the developing countries and the resulting backlash of nationalism, the increased importance of the large multinational corporations and the consequences of host-country hostility, the recurrence of recession, and the persistence of inflation in all phases of the business cycle. The consequences of world economic trends need to be monitored in much greater detail for any one industry or company.

INDUSTRY

Although the industry environment is the one most company strategists believe they know most about, the opportunities and risks that reside there are often blurred by familiarity and the uncritical acceptance of the established relative position of competitors. . . .

SOCIETY

Social developments of which strategists keep aware include such influential forces as the quest for equality for minority groups, the demand of women for opportunity and recognition, the changing patterns of work and leisure, the effects of urbanization upon the individual, family, and neighborhood, the rise of crime, the decline of conventional morality, and the changing composition of world population.

POLITICS

The political forces important to the business firm are similarly extensive and complex—the changing relations between communist and noncommunist countries (East and West) and between prosperous and poor countries (North and South), the relation between private enterprise and government, between workers and management, the impact of national planning on corporate planning, and the rise of what George Lodge (1975) calls the communitarian ideology. . . .

Although it is not possible to know or spell out here the significance of such technical, economic, social, and political trends, and possibilities for the strategist of a given business or company, some simple things are clear. Changing values will lead to different expectations of the role business should perform. Business will be expected to perform its mission not only with economy in the use of energy but with sensitivity to the ecological environment. Organizations in all walks of life will be called upon to be more explicit about their goals and to meet the needs and aspirations (for example, for education) of their membership.

In any case, change threatens all established strategies. We know that a thriving company—itself a living system—is bound up in a variety of interrelationships with larger systems comprising its technological, economic, ecological, social, and political environment. If environmental developments are destroying and creating business opportunities, advance notice of specific instances relevant to a single company is essential to intelligent planning. Risk and opportunity in the last quarter of the twentieth century require of executives a keen interest in what is going on outside their companies. More than that, a practical means of tracking developments promising good or ill, and profit or loss, needs to be devised. . . .

For the firm that has not determined what its strategy dictates it needs to know or has not embarked upon the systematic surveillance of environmental change, a few simple questions kept constantly in mind will highlight changing opportunity and risk. In examining your own company or one you are interested in, these questions should lead to an estimate of opportunity and danger in the present and predicted company setting.

1. What are the essential economic, technical, and physical characteristics of the industry in which the company participates? . . .
2. What trends suggesting future change in economic and technical characteristics are apparent? . . .
3. What is the nature of competition both within the industry and across industries? . . .
4. What are the requirements for success in competition in the company's industry? . . .
5. Given the technical, economic, social, and political developments that most directly apply, what is the range of strategy available to any company in this industry? . . .

IDENTIFYING CORPORATE COMPETENCE AND RESOURCES

The first step in validating a tentative choice among several opportunities is to determine whether the organization has the capacity to prosecute it successfully. The capability of an organization is its demonstrated and potential ability to accomplish, against the opposition of circumstance or competition, whatever it sets out to do. Every organization has actual and potential strengths and weaknesses. Since it is prudent in formulating strategy to extend or maximize the one and contain or minimize the other, it is important to try to determine what they are and to distinguish one from the other.

It is just as possible, though much more difficult, for a company to know its own strengths and limitations as it is to maintain a workable surveillance of its changing environment. Subjectivity, lack of confidence, and unwillingness to face reality may make it hard for organizations as well as for individuals to know themselves. But just as it is essential, though difficult, that a maturing person achieve reasonable self-awareness, so an organization can identify approximately its central strength and critical vulnerability. . . .

To make an effective contribution to strategic planning, the key attributes to be appraised should be identified and consistent criteria established for judging them. If attention is directed to strategies, policy commitments, and past practices in the context of discrepancy between organization goals and attainment, an outcome useful to an individual manager's strategic planning is possible. The assessment of strengths and weaknesses associated with the attainment of specific objectives becomes in Stevenson's (1976) words a "key link in a feedback loop" which allows managers to learn from the success or failures of the policies they institute.

Although [a] study by Stevenson did not find or establish a systematic way of developing or using such knowledge, members of organizations develop judgments about what the company can do particularly well—its core of competence. If consensus can be reached about this capability, no matter how subjectively arrived at, its application to identified opportunity can be estimated.

SOURCES OF CAPABILITIES

The powers of a company constituting a resource for growth and diversification accrue primarily from experience in making and marketing a product line or providing a service. They inhere as well in (1) the developing strengths and weaknesses of the individuals comprising the organization, (2) the degree to which individual capability is effectively applied to the common task, and (3) the quality of coordination of individual and group effort.

The experience gained through successful execution of a strategy centered upon one goal may unexpectedly develop capabilities which could be applied to different ends. Whether they should be so applied is another question. For example, a manufacturer of salt can strengthen his competitive position by offering his customers salt-dispensing equipment. If, in the course of making engineering improvements in this equipment, a new solenoid principle is perfected that has application to many industrial switching problems, should this patentable and marketable innovation be exploited? The answer would turn not only on whether economic analysis of the opportunity shows this to be a durable and profitable possibility, but also on whether the organization can muster the financial, manufacturing, and marketing strength to exploit the discovery and live with its success. The former question is likely to have a more positive answer than the latter. In this connection, it seems important to remember that individual and unsupported flashes of strength are not as dependable as the gradually accumulated product and market-related fruits of experience.

Even where competence to exploit an opportunity is nurtured by experience in related fields, the level of that competence may be too low for any great reliance to be placed upon it. Thus a chain of children's clothing stores might well acquire the administrative, merchandising, buying, and selling skills that would permit it to add departments in women's wear. Similarly, a sales force effective in distributing typewriters might gain proficiency in selling office machinery and supplies. But even here it would be well to ask what *distinctive* ability these companies could bring to the retailing of soft goods or office equipment to attract customers away from a plethora of competitors.

IDENTIFYING STRENGTHS

The distinctive competence of an organization is more than what it can do; it is what it can do particularly well. To identify the less obvious or by-product strengths of an organization that may well be transferable to some more profitable new opportunity, one might well begin by examining the organization's current product line and by defining the functions it serves in its markets. Almost any important consumer product has functions which are related to others into which a qualified company might move. The typewriter, for example, is more than the simple machine for mechanizing handwriting that it once appeared to be when looked at only from the point of view of its designer and manufacturer. Closely analyzed from the point of view of the potential user, the typewriter is found to contribute to a broad range of information processing functions. Any one of these might have suggested an area to be exploited by a typewriter manufacturer. Tacitly defining a typewriter as a replacement for a fountain pen as a writing instrument rather than as an input-output device for word processing is the explanation provided by hindsight for the failure of the old-line typewriter companies to develop before IBM did the electric typewriter and the computer-related input-output devices it made possible. The definition of product which would lead to identification of transferable skills must be expressed in terms of the market needs it may fill rather than the engineering specifications to which it conforms.

Besides looking at the uses or functions to which present products contribute, the would-be diversifier might profitably identify the skills that underlie whatever success has been achieved. The qualifications of an organization efficient at performing its long-accustomed tasks come to be taken for granted and considered humdrum, like the steady provision of first-class service. The insight required to identify the essential strength justifying new ventures does not come naturally. Its cultivation can probably be helped by recognition of the need for analysis. In any case, we should look beyond the company's capacity to invent new products. Product leadership is not possible for a majority of companies, so it is fortunate that patentable new products are not the only major highway to new opportunities. Other avenues include new marketing services, new methods of distribution, new values in quality-price combinations, and creative merchandising. The effort to find or to create a competence that is truly distinctive may hold the real key to a company's success or even to its future development. For example, the ability of a cement manufacturer to run a truck fleet more effectively than its competitors may constitute one of its principal competitive strengths in selling an undifferentiated product.

MATCHING OPPORTUNITY AND COMPETENCE

The way to narrow the range of alternatives, made extensive by imaginative identification of new possibilities, is to match opportunity to competence, once each has been accurately identified and its future significance estimated. It is this combination which establishes a company's economic mission and its position in its environment. The combination is designed to minimize organizational weakness and to maximize strength. In every case, risk attends it. And when opportunity seems to outrun present distinctive competence, the willingness to gamble that the latter can be built up to the required level is almost indispensable to a strategy that challenges the organization and the people in it. Figure 2 diagrams the matching of opportunity and resources that results in an economic strategy.

FIGURE 2

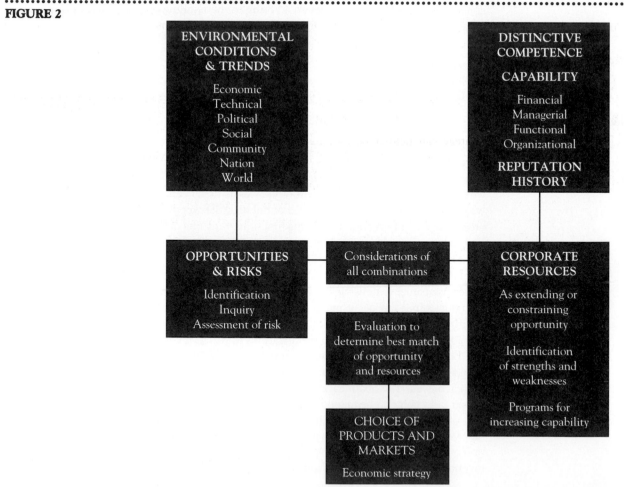

Before we leave the creative act of putting together a company's unique internal capability and opportunity evolving in the external world, we should note that—aside from distinctive competence—the principal resources found in any company are money and people—technical and managerial people. At an advanced stage of economic development, money seems less a problem than technical competence, and the latter less critical than managerial ability. Do not assume that managerial capacity can rise to any occasion. The diversification of American industry is marked by hundreds of instances in which a company strong in one endeavor lacked the ability to manage an enterprise requiring different skills. The right to make handsome profits over a long period must be earned. Opportunism without competence is a path to fairyland.

Besides equating an appraisal of market opportunity and organizational capability, the decision to make and market a particular product or service should be accompanied by an identification of the nature of the business and the kind of company its management desires. Such a guiding concept is a product of many considerations, including the managers' personal values. . . .

UNIQUENESS OF STRATEGY

In each company, the way in which distinctive competence, organizational resources, and organizational values are combined is or should be unique. Differences among companies are as numerous as differences among individuals. The combinations of opportunity to which distinctive competencies, resources, and values may be applied are equally extensive. Generalizing about how to make an effective match is less rewarding than working at it. The effort is a highly stimulating and challenging exercise. The outcome will be unique for each company and each situation.

▼ READING 3.2   EVALUATING BUSINESS STRATEGY*

by Richard R. Rumelt

Strategy can neither be formulated nor adjusted to changing circumstances without a process of strategy evaluation. Whether performed by an individual or as part of an organizational review procedure, strategy evaluation forms an essential step in the process of guiding an enterprise.

For many executives strategy evaluation is simply an appraisal of how well a business performs. Has it grown? Is the profit rate normal or better? If the answers to these questions are affirmative, it is argued that the firm's strategy must be sound. Despite its unassailable simplicity, this line of reasoning misses the whole point of strategy—that the critical factors determining the quality of current results are often not directly observable or simply measured, and that by the time strategic opportunities or threats do directly affect operating results, it may well be too late for an effective response. Thus, strategy evaluation is an attempt to look beyond the obvious facts regarding the short-term health of a business and appraise instead those more fundamental factors and trends that govern success in the chosen field of endeavor.

---

* This paper is a revised and updated version for this book. "The Evaluation of Business Strategy" was originally published in W. F. Glueck, *Strategic Management and Business Policy* (New York: McGraw-Hill, 1980). New version printed here by permission of the author.

However it is accomplished, the products of a business strategy evaluation are answers to these three questions:

▼ Are the objectives of the business appropriate?
▼ Are the major policies and plans appropriate?
▼ Do the results obtained to date confirm or refute critical assumptions on which the strategy rests?

Devising adequate answers to these questions is neither simple nor straightforward. It requires a reasonable store of situation-based knowledge and more than the usual degree of insight. In particular, the major issues which make evaluation difficult and with which the analyst must come to grips are these:

▼ Each business strategy is unique. For example, one paper manufacturer might rely on its vast timber holdings to weather almost any storm while another might place primary reliance in modern machinery and an extensive distribution system. Neither strategy is "wrong" nor "right" in any absolute sense; both may be right or wrong for the firms in question. Strategy evaluation must, then, rest on a type of situational logic that does not focus on "one best way" but which can be tailored to each problem as it is faced.
▼ Strategy is centrally concerned with the selection of goals and objectives. Many people, including seasoned executives, find it much easier to set or try to achieve goals than to evaluate them. In part this is a consequence of training in problem solving rather than in problem structuring. It also arises out of a tendency to confuse values, which are fundamental expressions of human personality, with objectives, which are devices for lending coherence to action.
▼ Formal systems of strategic review, while appealing in principal, can create explosive conflict situations. Not only are there serious questions as to who is qualified to give an objective evaluation, the whole idea of strategy evaluation implies management by "much more than results" and runs counter to much of currently popular management philosophy.

The General Principles of Strategy Evaluation

The term "strategy" has been so widely used for different purposes that it has lost any clearly defined meaning. For our purposes a strategy is a set of objectives, policies, and plans that, taken together, define the scope of the enterprise and its approach to survival and success. Alternatively, we could say that the particular policies, plans, and objectives of a business express its strategy for coping with a complex competitive environment.

One of the fundamental tenets of science is that a theory can never be proven to be absolutely true. A theory can, however, be declared absolutely false if it fails to stand up to testing. Similarly, it is impossible to demonstrate conclusively that a particular business strategy is optimal or even to guarantee that it will work. One can, nevertheless, test it for critical flaws. Of the many tests which could be justifiably applied to a business strategy, most will fit within one of these broad criteria:

▼ *Consistency*: The strategy must not present mutually inconsistent goals and policies.
▼ *Consonance*: The strategy must represent an adaptive response to the external environment and to the critical changes occurring within it.
▼ *Advantage*: The strategy must provide for the creation and/or maintenance of a competitive advantage in the selected area of activity.

▼ *Feasibility*: The strategy must neither overtax available resources nor create unsolvable sub problems.

A strategy that fails to meet one or more of these criteria is strongly suspect. It fails to perform at least one of the key functions that are necessary for the survival of the business. Experience within a particular industry or other setting will permit the analyst to sharpen these criteria and add others that are appropriate to the situation at hand.

CONSISTENCY

Gross inconsistency within a strategy seems unlikely until it is realized that many strategies have not been explicitly formulated but have evolved over time in an ad hoc fashion. Even strategies that are the result of formal procedures may easily contain compromise arrangements between opposing power groups.

Inconsistency in strategy is not simply a flaw in logic. A key function of strategy is to provide coherence to organizational action. A clear and explicit concept of strategy can foster a climate of tacit coordination that is more efficient than most administrative mechanisms. Many high-technology firms, for example, face a basic strategic choice between offering high-cost products with high custom-engineering content and lower-cost products that are more standardized and sold at higher volume. If senior management does not enunciate a clear consistent sense of where the corporation stands on these issues, there will be continuing conflict between sales, design, engineering, and manufacturing people. A clear consistent strategy, by contrast, allows a sales engineer to negotiate a contract with a minimum of coordination—the trade-offs are an explicit part of the firm's posture.

Organizational conflict and interdepartmental bickering are often symptoms of a managerial disorder but may also indicate problems of strategic inconsistency. Here are some indicators that can help sort out these two different problems:

▼ If problems in coordination and planning continue despite changes in personnel and tend to be issue- rather than people-based, they are probably due to inconsistencies in strategy.

▼ If success for one organizational department means, or is interpreted to mean, failure for another department, either the basic objective structure is inconsistent or the organizational structure is wastefully duplicative.

▼ If, despite attempts to delegate authority, operating problems continue to be brought to the top for the resolution of policy issues, the basic strategy is probably inconsistent.

A final type of consistency that must be sought in strategy is between organizational objectives and the values of the management group. Inconsistency in this area is more of a problem in strategy formulation than in the evaluation of a strategy that has already been implemented. It can still arise, however, if the future direction of the business requires changes that conflict with managerial values. The most frequent source of such conflict is growth. As a business expands beyond the scale that allows an easy informal method of operation, many executives experience a sharp sense of loss. While growth can of course be curtailed, it often will require special attention to a firm's competitive position if survival without growth is desired. The same basic issues arise when other types of personal or social values come into conflict with existing or apparently necessary policies: the resolution of the conflict will normally require an adjustment in the competitive strategy.

CONSONANCE

The way in which a business relates to its environment has two aspects: the business must both match and be adapted to its environment and it must at the same time compete with other firms that are also trying to adapt. This dual character of the relationship between the firm and its environment has its analog in two different aspects of strategic choice and two different methods of strategy evaluation.

The first aspect of fit deals with the basic mission or scope of the business and the second with its special competitive position or "edge." Analysis of the first is normally done by looking at changing economic and social conditions over time. Analysis of the second, by contrast, typically focuses on the differences across firms at a given time. We call the first the *generic* aspect of strategy and the second *competitive* strategy. Generic strategy deals with the creation of social value—with the question of whether the products and services being created are worth more than their cost. Competitive strategy, by contrast, deals with the firm's need to capture some of the social value as profit. Exhibit 1 summarizes the differences between these concepts.

The notion of consonance, or matching, therefore, invites a focus on generic strategy. The role of the evaluator in this case is to examine the basic pattern of economic relationships that characterize the business and determine whether or not sufficient value is being created to sustain the strategy. Most macroanalysis of changing economic conditions is oriented toward the formulation or evaluation of generic strategies. For example, a planning department forecasts that within six years flat-panel liquid crystal displays will replace CRT-based video displays in computers. The basic message here to makers of CRT-based video displays is that their generic strategies are becoming obsolete. Note that the threat in this case is not to a particular firm, competitive position, or individual approach to the marketplace but to the basic generic mission.

One major difficulty in evaluating consonance is that most of the critical threats to a business are those which come from without, threatening an entire group of firms. Management, however, is often so engrossed in competitive thinking that such threats are only recognized after the damage has reached considerable proportions.

Another difficulty in appraising the fit between a firm's mission and the environment is that trend analysis does not normally reveal the most critical changes—they are the result of interactions among trends. The supermarket, for example, comes into being only when home refrigeration and the widespread use of automobiles allow shoppers to buy in significantly larger volumes. The supermarket, the automobile, and the move to suburbia together form the nexus which gives rise to shopping centers. These, in turn, change the nature of retailing and, together with the decline of urban centers, create new forms of enterprise, such as the suburban film theater with four screens. Thus, while gross economic or demographic trends might appear steady for many years, there are waves of change going on at the institutional level.

EXHIBIT 1
Generic versus Competitive Strategy

	GENERIC STRATEGY	COMPETITIVE STRATEGY
Value Issue	Social value	Corporate value
Value Constraint	Customer value > Cost	Price > Cost
Success Indicator	Sales growth	Increased corporate worth
Basic Strategic Task	Adapting to change	Innovating, impeding imitation, deterring rivals
How Strategy Is Expressed	Product-market definition	Advantage, position, and policies supporting them
Basic Approach to Analysis	Study of an industry over time	Comparison across rivals

The key to evaluating consonance is an understanding of why the business, as it currently stands, exists at all and how it assumed its current pattern. Once the analyst obtains a good grasp of the basic economic foundation that supports and defines the business, it is possible to study the consequences of key trends and changes. Without such an understanding, there is no good way of deciding what kinds of changes are most crucial and the analyst can be quickly overwhelmed with data.

ADVANTAGE

It is no exaggeration to say that competitive strategy is the art of creating or exploiting those advantages that are most telling, enduring, and most difficult to duplicate.

Competitive strategy, in contrast with generic strategy, focuses on the differences among firms rather than their common missions. The problem it addresses is not so much "how can this function be performed" but "how can we perform it either better than, or at least instead of, our rivals?" The chain supermarket, for example, represents a successful generic strategy. As a way of doing business, of organizing economic transactions, it has replaced almost all the smaller owner-managed food shops of an earlier era. Yet a potential or actual participant in the retail food business must go beyond this generic strategy and find a way of competing in this business. As another illustration, IBM's early success in the PC industry was generic—other firms soon copied the basic product concept. Once this happened, IBM had to try to either forge a strong competitive strategy in this area or seek a different type of competitive arena.

Competitive advantages can normally be traced to one of three roots:

▼ Superior skills

▼ Superior resources

▼ Superior position

In examining a potential advantage, the critical question is "What sustains this advantage, keeping competitors from imitating or replicating it?" A firm's skills can be a source of advantage if they are based on its own history of learning-by-doing and if they are rooted in the coordinated behavior of many people. By contrast, skills that are based on generally understood scientific principles, on training that can be purchased by competitors, or which can be analyzed and replicated by others are not sources of sustained advantage.

The *skills* which compose advantages are usually organizational, rather than individual, skills. They involve the adept coordination or collaboration of individual specialists and are built through the interplay of investment, work, and learning. Unlike physical assets, skills are enhanced by their use. Skills that are not continually used and improved will atrophy.

Resources include patents, trademark rights, specialized physical assets, and the firm's working relationships with suppliers and distribution channels. In addition, a firm's reputation with its employees, suppliers, and customers is a resource. Resources that constitute advantages are specialized to the firm, are built up slowly over time through the accumulated exercise of superior skills, or are obtained through being an insightful first mover, or by just plain luck. For example, Nucor's special skills in mini-mill construction are embodied in superior physical plants. Goldman Sachs' reputation as the premier U.S. investment banking house has been built up over many years and is now a major resource in its own right.

A firm's *position* consists of the products or services it provides, the market segments it sells to, and the degree to which it is isolated from direct competition. In general, the best positions involve supplying very uniquely valuable products to price insensitive buyers, whereas poor positions involve being one of many firms supplying marginally valuable products to very well informed, price sensitive buyers.

Positional advantage can be gained by foresight, superior skill and/or resources, or just plain luck. Once gained, a good position is defensible. This means that it (1) returns enough value to warrant its continued maintenance and (2) would be so costly to capture that rivals are deterred from full-scale attacks on the core of the business. Position, it must be noted, tends to be self-sustaining as long as the basic environmental factors that underlie it remain stable. Thus, entrenched firms can be almost impossible to unseat, even if their raw skill levels are only average. And when a shifting environment allows position to be gained by a new entrant or innovator, the results can be spectacular.

Positional advantages are of two types: (1) first mover advantages and (2) reinforcers. The most basic *first mover advantage* occurs when the minimum scale to be efficient requires a large (sunk) investment relative to the market. Thus, the first firm to open a large discount retail store in a rural area precludes, through its relative scale, close followers. More subtle first mover advantages occur when standardization effects "lock-in" customers to the first mover's product (e.g., Lotus 1-2-3). Buyer learning and related phenomena can increase the buyer's switching costs, protecting an incumbent's customer base from attack. Frequent flyer programs are aimed in this direction. First movers may also gain advantages in building distribution channels, in tying up specialized suppliers, or in gaining the attention of customers. The first product of a class to engage in mass advertising, for example, tends to impress itself more deeply in people's minds than the second, third, or fourth. In a careful study of frequently purchased consumer products, Urban et al. (1986) found that (other things being equal) the first entrant will have a market share that is $\sqrt{n}$ times as large as that of the nth entrant.

Reinforcers are policies or practices acting to strengthen or preserve a strong market position and which are easier to carry out because of the position. The idea that certain arrangements of one's resources can enhance their combined effectiveness, and perhaps even put rival forces in a state of disarray, is at the heart of the traditional notion of strategy. It is reinforcers which provide positional advantage, the strategic quality familiar to military theorists, chess players, and diplomats.

A firm with a larger market share, due to being an early mover or to having a technological lead, can typically build a more efficient production and distribution system. Competitors with less demand simply cannot cover the fixed costs of the larger more efficient facilities, so for them larger facilities are not an economic choice. In this case, scale economies are a reinforcer of market position, not the cause of market position. The firm that has a strong brand can use it as a reinforcer in the introduction of related brands. A company that sells a specialty coating to a broader variety of users may have better data on how to adapt the coating to special conditions than a competitor with more limited sales—properly used, this information is a reinforcer. A famous brand will appear on TV and in films because it is famous, another reinforcer. An example given by Porter (1985: 145) is that of Steinway and Sons, the premier U.S. maker of fine pianos. Steinway maintains a dispersed inventory of grand pianos that approved pianists are permitted to use for concerts at very low rental rates. The policy is less expensive for a leader than for a follower and helps maintain leadership.

The positive feedback provided by reinforcers is the source of the power of position-based advantages—the policies that act to enhance position may not require unusual skills; they simply work most effectively for those who are already in the position in the first place.

While it is not true that larger businesses always have the advantages, it is true that larger businesses will tend to operate in markets and use procedures that turn their size to advantage. Large national consumer-products firms, for example, will normally have an advantage over smaller regional firms in the efficient use of mass advertising, especially network TV. The larger firm will, then, tend to deal in those products where the marginal effect of advertising is most potent, while the smaller firms will seek product/market positions that exploit other types of advantage.

Other position-based advantages follow from such factors as:

▼ The ownership of special raw material sources or advantageous long-term supply contracts
▼ Being geographically located near key customers in a business involving significant fixed investment and high transport costs
▼ Being a leader in a service field that permits or requires the building of a unique experience base while serving clients
▼ Being a full-line producer in a market with heavy trade-up phenomena
▼ Having a wide reputation for providing a needed product or service trait reliably and dependably

In each case, the position permits competitive policies to be adopted that can serve to reinforce the position. Whenever this type of positive-feedback phenomena is encountered, the particular policy mix that creates it will be found to be a defensible business position. The key factors that sparked industrial success stories such as IBM and Eastman Kodak were the early and rapid domination of strong positions opened up by new technologies.

FEASIBILITY

The final broad test of strategy is its feasibility. Can the strategy be attempted within the physical, human, and financial resources available? The financial resources of a business are the easiest to quantify and are normally the first limitations against which strategy is tested. It is sometimes forgotten, however, that innovative approaches to financing expansion can both stretch the ultimate limitations and provide a competitive advantage, even if it is only temporary. Devices such as captive finance subsidiaries, sale-leaseback arrangements, and tying plant mortgages to long-term contracts have all been used effectively to help win key positions in suddenly expanding industries.

The less quantifiable but actually more rigid limitation on strategic choice is that imposed by the individual and organization capabilities that are available.

In assessing the organization's ability to carry out a strategy, it is helpful to ask three separate questions:

1. Has the organization demonstrated that it possesses the problem-solving abilities and/or special competencies required by the strategy? A strategy, as such, does not and cannot specify in detail each action that must be carried out. Its purpose is to provide structure to the general issue of the business' goals and approaches to coping with its environment. It is up to the members and departments of the organization to carry out the tasks defined by strategy. A strategy that requires tasks to be accomplished which fall outside the realm of available or easily obtainable skill and knowledge cannot be accepted. It is either unfeasible or incomplete.

2. Has the organization demonstrated the degree of coordinative and integrative skill necessary to carry out the strategy? The key tasks required of a strategy not only require specialized skill, but often make considerable demands on the organization's ability to integrate disparate activities. A manufacturer of standard office furniture may find, for example, that its primary difficulty in entering the new market for modular office systems is a lack of sophisticated interaction between its field sales offices and its manufacturing plant. Firms that hope to span national boundaries with integrated worldwide systems of production and marketing may also find that organizational process, rather than functional skill per se or isolated competitive strength, becomes the weak link in the strategic posture.

3. Does the strategy challenge and motivate key personnel and is it acceptable to those who must lend their support? The purpose of strategy is to effectively deploy the unique

and distinctive resources of an enterprise. If key managers are unmoved by a strategy, not excited by its goals or methods, or strongly support an alternative, it fails in a major way.

The Process of Strategy Evaluation

Strategy evaluation can take place as an abstract analytic task, perhaps performed by consultants. But most often it is an integral part of an organization's processes of planning, review, and control. In some organizations, evaluation is informal, only occasional, brief, and cursory. Others have created elaborate systems containing formal periodic strategy review sessions. In either case, the quality of strategy evaluation, and ultimately, the quality of corporate performance, will be determined more by the organization's capacity for self-appraisal and learning than by the particular analytic technique employed.

In their study of organizational learning, Argyris and Schon distinguish between single-loop and double-loop learning. They argue that normal organizational learning is of the feedback-control type-deviations between expected and actual performance lead to problem solving which brings the system back under control. They note that

> [Single-loop learning] is concerned primarily with effectiveness—that is, with how best to achieve existing goals and objectives and how best to keep organizational performance within the range specified by existing norms. In some cases, however, error correction requires a learning cycle in which organizational norms themselves are modified. . . . We call this sort of learning "double-loop." There is . . . a double feedback loop which connects the detection of error not only to strategies and assumptions for effective performance but to the very norms which define effective performance. [1978:20]

These ideas parallel those of Ashby, a cyberneticist. Ashby (1954) has argued that all feedback systems require more than single-loop error control for stability; they also need a way of monitoring certain critical variables and changing the system "goals" when old control methods are no longer working.

These viewpoints help to remind us that the real strategic processes in any organization are not found by looking at those things that happen to be labeled "strategic" or "long range." Rather, the real components of the strategic process are, by definition, those activities which most strongly affect the selection and modification of objectives and which influence the irreversible commitment of important resources. They also suggest that appropriate methods of strategy evaluation cannot be specified in abstract terms. Instead, an organization's approach to evaluation must fit its strategic posture and work in conjunction with its methods of planning and control.

In most firms comprehensive strategy evaluation is infrequent and, if it occurs, is normally triggered by a change in leadership or financial performance. The fact that comprehensive strategy evaluation is neither a regular event nor part of a formal system tends to be deplored by some theorists, but there are several good reasons for this state of affairs. Most obviously, any activity that becomes an annual procedure is bound to become more automatic. While evaluating strategy on an annual basis might lead to some sorts of efficiencies in data collection and analysis, it would also tend to strongly channel the types of questions asked and inhibit broad-ranging reflection.

Second, a good strategy does not need constant reformulation. It is a framework for continuing problem solving, not the problem solving itself. One senior executive expressed it this way: "If you play from strength you don't always need to be rethinking the whole plan; you can concentrate on details. So when you see us talking about slight changes in tooling, it isn't because we forgot the big picture, it's because we took care of it."

Strategy also represents a political alignment within the firm and embodies the past convictions and commitments of key executives. Comprehensive strategy evaluation is not just an analytical exercise, it calls into question this basic pattern of commitments and policies. Most organizations would be hurt rather than helped to have their mission's validity called into question on a regular basis. Zero-base budgeting, for example, was an attempt to get agencies to re-justify their existence each time a new budget is drawn up. If this were literally true, there would be little time or energy remaining for any but political activity.

Finally, there are competitive reasons for not reviewing the validity of a strategy too freely! There are a wide range of rivalrous confrontations in which it is crucial to be able to convince others that one's position, or strategy, is fixed and unshakable. Schelling's (1963) analysis of bargaining and conflict shows that a great deal of what is involved in negotiating is finding ways to bind or commit oneself convincingly. This is the principle underlying the concept of deterrence and what lies behind the union leader's tactic of claiming that while he would go along with management's desire for moderation, he cannot control the members if the less moderate demands are not met. In business strategy, such situations occur in classic oligopoly, plant-capacity duels, new-product conflicts, and other situations in which the winner may be the party whose policies are most credibly unswayable. Japanese electronics firms, for example, have gained such strong reputations as low-cost committed players that their very entry into a market has come to induce rivals to give up. If such firms had instead the reputation of continually reviewing the advisability of continuing each product, they would be much less threatening, and thus less effective, competitors. . . .

CONCLUSIONS

Strategy evaluation is the appraisal of plans and the results of plans that centrally concern or affect the basic mission of an enterprise. Its special focus is the separation between obvious current operating results and those factors which underlie success or failure in the chosen domain of activity. Its result is the rejection, modification, or ratification of existing strategies and plans. . . .

In most medium- to large-size firms, strategy evaluation is not a purely intellectual task. The issues involved are too important and too closely associated with the distribution of power and authority for either strategy formulation or evaluation to take place in an ivory tower environment. In fact, most firms rarely engage in explicit formal strategy evaluation. Rather, the evaluation of current strategy is a continuing process and one that is difficult to separate from the normal planning, reporting, control, and reward systems of the firm. From this point of view, strategy evaluation is not so much an intellectual task as it is an organizational process.

Ultimately, a firm's ability to maintain its competitive position in a world of rivalry and change may be best served by managers who can maintain a dual view of strategy and strategy evaluation—they must be willing and able to perceive the strategy within the welter of daily activity and to build and maintain structures and systems that make strategic factors the object of current activity.

▼ READING 3.3 CORE COMPETENCIES AND STRATEGIC OUTSOURCING*

by James Brian Quinn and Frederick G. Hilmer

Two new strategic approaches, when properly combined, allow managers to leverage their companies' skills and resources well beyond levels available with other strategies:

* Originally published as "Strategic Outsourcing," reprinted from *Sloan Management Review* (Summer 1994) by permission of the publisher. Copyright by the Sloan Management.

▼ Concentrating the firm's own resources on a set "of core competencies" where it can achieve definable preeminence and provide unique value for customers (Quinn, Doorley, Paquette 1990).

▼ Strategically outsourcing other activities—including many traditionally considered integral to any company—where the firm has neither a critical strategic need nor special capabilities (Quinn, 1992).

The benefits of successfully combining the two approaches are significant. Managers can leverage their company's resources in four ways. First, they maximize returns on internal resources by concentrating investments and energies on what the enterprise does best. Second, well developed core competencies provide formidable barriers against present and future competitors seeking to expand into the company's areas of interest thus facilitating and protecting the strategic advantages of market share. Third, perhaps the greatest leverage of all is the full utilization of external suppliers' investments, innovations, and specialized professional capabilities that would be prohibitively expensive or even impossible to duplicate internally. Fourth, in rapidly changing marketplaces and technological situations, this joint strategy decreases risks, shortens cycle times, lowers investments, and creates better responsiveness to customer needs. Two examples from our studies of Australian and U.S. companies illustrate our point:

▼ Nike, Inc., is the largest supplier of athletic shoes in the world. Yet it outsources 100% of its shoe production and manufactures only key technical components of its "Nike Air" system. Athletic footwear is technology- and fashion-intensive, requiring high flexibility at both the production and marketing levels. Nike creates maximum value by concentrating on preproduction (research and development) and post production activities (marketing, distribution and sales) linked together by perhaps the best marketing information system in the industry. Using a carefully developed, on-site "expatriate" program to coordinate its foreign-based suppliers, Nike even outsourced the advertising component of its marketing program to Weiden and Kennedy, whose creative efforts drove Nike to the top of the product recognition scale. Nike grew at a compounded 20% growth rate and earned a 31% ROE for its shareholders through most of the last decade.

▼ Knowing it could not be the best at making chips, boxes, monitors, cables, keyboards, and so on for its explosively successful Apple II, Apple Computer outsourced 70% of its manufacturing costs and components. Instead of building internal bureaucracies where it had no unique skills, Apple outsourced critical items like design (to Frogdesign), printers (to Tokyo Electric), and even key elements of marketing (to Regis McKenna, which achieved a "$100 million image" for Apple when it had only a few employees and about $1 million to spend). Apple focused its internal resources on its own Apple DOS (disk operating system) and the supporting macro software to give Apple products their unique look and feel. Its open architecture policy stimulated independent developers to write the much-needed software that gave Apple II's customers uniquely high functionality. Apple thus avoided unnecessary investments, benefited from its vendors' R&D and technical expertise, kept itself flexible to adopt new technologies as they became available, and leveraged its limited capital resources to a huge extent. Operating with an extremely flat organization, Apple enjoyed three times the capital turnover and the highest market value versus fixed investment ratio among major computer producers throughout the 1980s.

How can managers combine core competency concepts and strategic outsourcing for maximum effectiveness? To achieve benefits like Nike's or Apple's requires careful attention to several difficult issues, each of which we discuss in turn:

1. What exactly is a "core competency"? Unfortunately, most of the literature on this subject is tautological—"core" equals "key" or "critical" or "fundamental." How can man-

agers analytically select and develop the core competencies that will provide the firm's uniqueness, competitive edge, and basis of value creation for the future?

2. Granting that the competencies defining the firm and its essential reasons for existence should be kept in house, should all else be outsourced? In most cases, common sense and theory suggest a clear "no." How then can managers determine strategically, rather than in a short term or *ad hoc* fashion, which activities to maintain internally and which to outsource?

3. How can managers assess the relative risks and benefits of outsourcing in particular situations? And how can they contain critical risks—especially the potential loss of crucial skills or control over the company's future directions—when outsourcing is desirable?

Core Competency Strategies

The basic ideas behind core competencies and strategic outsourcing have been well supported by research extending over a 20-year period. In 1974, Rumelt noted that neither of the then-favored strategies—unrelated diversification or vertical integration—yielded consistently high returns. Since then, other carefully structured research has indicated the effectiveness of disaggregation strategies in many industries (Rumelt 1974; D'Aveni and Illinich 1992; Batteyri 1988). Noting the failures of many conglomerates in the 1960s and 1970s, both financial theorists and investors began to support more focused company concepts. Generally this meant "sticking to your knitting" by cutting back to fewer product lines. Unfortunately, this also meant a concomitant increase in the "systematic risk" these narrower markets represented.

However, some analysts noticed that many highly successful Japanese and American companies had very wide product lines yet were not very vertically integrated (Maloney 1992; Miles and Show 1986). Japanese companies, like Sony, Mitsubishi, Matsushita, or Yamaha, had extremely diverse product offerings, as did 3M or Hewlett Packard in the United States. Yet, they were not conglomerates in the normal sense. They were first termed "related conglomerates," redeploying certain key skills from market to market. At the same time these companies also contracted out significant support activities.

The term "core competency strategies" was later used to describe these and other less diversified strategies developed around a central set of corporate skills (Prahalad and Hamel 1990). However, there has been little theory or consistency in the literature about what "core" really means. Consequently, many executives have been understandably confused about the topic. They need not be if they think in terms of the specific skills the company has or must have to create unique value for customers. However, their analyses must go well beyond looking at traditional product or functional strategies to the fundamentals of what the company can do better than anyone else.

▼   For example, after some difficult times, it was easy enough for a "beer company" like Foster's to decide that it should not be in the finance, forest products, and pastoral businesses into which it had diversified. It has now divested these peripheral businesses and is concentrating on beer. However, even within this concept, Foster's true competencies are in brewing and marketing beer. Many of its distribution, transportation, and can production activities, for example, might actually be more effectively contracted out. Within individual functions like production, Foster's could further extend its competitive advantage by outsourcing selected activities—such as maintenance or computing—where it has no unique capabilities.

THE ESSENCE OF CORE COMPETENCIES

What then is really core? And why? The concept requires that managers think much more carefully about which of the firm's activities really do—or could—create unique value and what activities could more effectively be bought externally. Careful study of both successful and unsuccessful corporate examples suggests that effective core competencies are:

1. SKILL OR KNOWLEDGE SETS, NOT PRODUCTS OR FUNCTIONS. Executives need to look beyond the company's products to the intellectual skills or management systems that actually create a maintainable competitive edge. Products, even those with valuable legal protection, can be too easily back engineered, duplicated, or replaced by substitutes. Nor is a competency typically one of the traditional functions such as production, engineering, sales, or finance around which organizations were formed in the past. Instead, competencies tend to be sets of skills which cut across traditional functions. This interaction allows the organization to consistently perform an activity better than functional competitors and to continually improve on the activity as markets, technology and competition evolve. Competencies thus involve activities such as product or service design, technology creation, customer service, or logistics—that tend to be based on knowledge rather than ownership of assets or intellectual property per se. Knowledge-based activities generate most of the value in services and manufacturing. In services, which account for 79% of all jobs and 76% of all value added in the United States, intellectual inputs create virtually all of the value added. Banking, financial services, advertising, consulting, accounting, retailing, wholesaling, education, entertainment, communications, and health care are clear examples. In manufacturing, knowledge-based activities—like R&D, product design, process design, logistics, marketing research, marketing, advertising, distribution, and customer service—also dominate the value-added chain of most companies (see Figure 1). [Editors note: See Chapter 4 of this text for discussion of the value chain.]

2. FLEXIBLE, LONG-TERM PLATFORMS—CAPABLE OF ADAPTATION OR EVOLUTION. Too many companies try to focus on the narrow areas where they currently excel, usually on some product-oriented skills. The real challenge is to consciously build dominating skills in areas that the customer will continue to value over time, as Motorola is doing with its focus on "superior quality, portable communications." The uniqueness of Toys "R" Us lies in its powerful information and distribution systems for toys; and that of State Street Boston in its developing advanced information and management systems for large custodial accounts. Problems occur when managers choose to concentrate too narrowly on products (as computer companies did on hardware) or too inflexibly on formats and skills that no longer match customer needs (as FotoMat and numerous department stores did). Flexible skill sets and constant, conscious reassessment of trends are hallmarks of successful core competency strategies.

3. LIMITED IN NUMBER. Most companies target two or three (not one or more than five) activities in the value chain most critical to future success. For example, 3M concentrates on four critical technologies in great depth and supports these with a peerless innovative system. As work becomes more complex, and the opportunities to excel in many detailed activities proliferate, managers find they cannot be best in every activity in the value chain. As they go beyond three to five activities or skill sets, they are unable to match the performance of their more focused competitors or suppliers. Each skill set requires intensity and management dedication that cannot tolerate dilution. It is hard to imagine Microsoft's top managers taking their enthusiasm and skills in software into, say, chip design or even large-

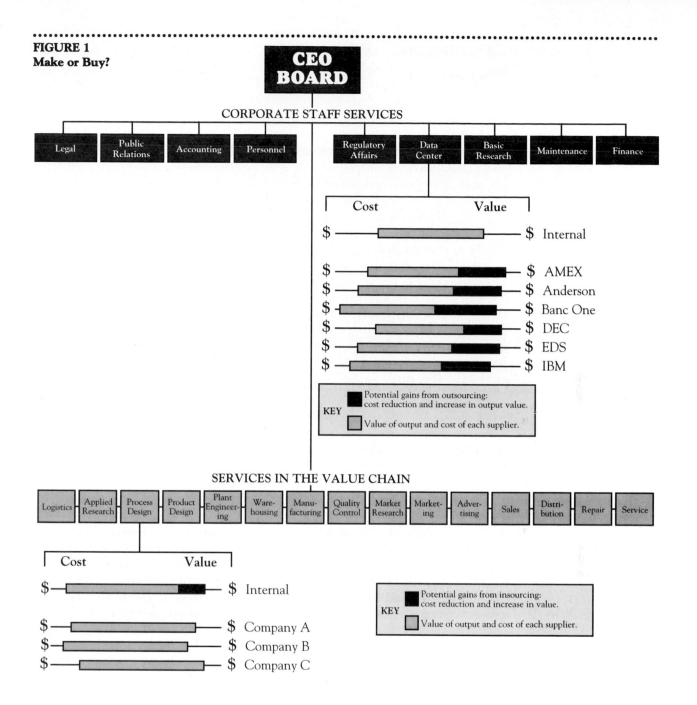

FIGURE 1
Make or Buy?

CEO BOARD

CORPORATE STAFF SERVICES

| Legal | Public Relations | Accounting | Personnel | | Regulatory Affairs | Data Center | Basic Research | Maintenance | Finance |

Cost   Value

$ ——— Internal

$ ——— AMEX
$ ——— Anderson
$ ——— Banc One
$ ——— DEC
$ ——— EDS
$ ——— IBM

KEY
■ Potential gains from outsourcing: cost reduction and increase in output value.
▢ Value of output and cost of each supplier.

SERVICES IN THE VALUE CHAIN

| Logistics | Applied Research | Process Design | Product Design | Plant Engineering | Ware-housing | Manu-facturing | Quality Control | Market Research | Marketing | Adver-tising | Sales | Distri-bution | Repair | Service |

Cost   Value

$ ——— Internal

$ ——— Company A
$ ——— Company B
$ ——— Company C

KEY
■ Potential gains from insourcing: cost reduction and increase in value.
▢ Value of output and cost of each supplier.

scale training in software usage. And if they did, what would be the cost of their loss of attention to software development?

4. UNIQUE SOURCES OF LEVERAGE IN THE VALUE CHAIN. Effective strategies seek out places where there are market imperfections or knowledge gaps that the company is uniquely qualified to fill and where investments in intellectual resources can be highly leveraged. Raychem and Intel concentrate on depth-in-design and on highly specialized test-feedback systems supporting carefully selected knowledge-based products—not on volume production of standardized products—to jump over the experience curve advantages of their larger competitors. Morgan Stanley, through its TAPS system and Bear Stearns, through its integrated bond-trading programs, have developed in-depth knowledge bases creating unique intellectual advantages in their highly competitive markets.

5. AREAS WHERE THE COMPANY CAN DOMINATE. Companies make consistently more money than their competitors only if they can perform some activities—which are important to customers—more effectively than anyone else. True focus in strategy means the capacity to bring more power to bear on a selected sector than any competitior can. Once, this meant owning and managing all the elements in the value chain supporting a specific product or service in a selected market position. Today, however, some outside supplier, by specializing on the specific skills and technologies underlying a single element in the value chain, can become more proficient at that activity than virtually any company spreading its efforts over the whole value chain. In essence, each company is in competition with all potential suppliers of each activity in its value chain. Hence, it must benchmark its selected core competencies against all other potential suppliers of that activity and continue to build these core capabilities until it is demonstrably best. Thus the basic nature of strategic analysis changes from an industry analysis perspective to a horizontal analysis of capabilities across *all potential providers of an activity* regardless of which industry the provider might be in. (See Figure 1.)

6. ELEMENTS IMPORTANT TO CUSTOMERS IN THE LONG RUN. At least one of the firm's core competencies should normally relate directly to understanding and serving its customers. High tech companies with the world's best state-of-the-art technology often fail when they ignore this caveat. . . .

7. EMBEDDED IN THE ORGANIZATION'S SYSTEMS. Maintaining competencies cannot depend on one or two talented stars—such as Steven Jobs and Stephen Wozniak at Apple or Herbert Boyer and Arthur D. Riggs at Genentech—whose departure could destroy a company's success. Instead the firm must convert these into a corporate reputation or culture that outlives the stars. Especially when a strategy is heavily dependent on creativity, personal dedication, and initiative, or on attracting top-flight professionals, core competency must be captured within the company's systems—broadly defined to include its values, organization structures, and management systems. . . (Turner and Crawford 1992).

PREEMINENCE: THE KEY STRATEGIC BARRIER. For its selected core competencies, the company must ensure that it maintains absolute preeminence. It may also need to surround these core competencies with defensive positions, both upstream and downstream. In some cases, it may have to perform some activities where it is not best-in-world, just to keep existing or potential competitors from learning, taking over, eroding, or bypassing elements of its special competencies. In fact, managers should consciously develop their core competencies to strategically block competitors and avoid outsourcing these or giving suppliers access to the knowledge bases or skills critical to their core competencies. Honda, for example, does all its engine R&D in-house and makes all the critical parts for its small motor design core competency in closely controlled facilities in Japan. It will consider outsourcing any other noncritical elements in its products, but builds a careful strategic block around this most essential element for all its businesses.

Most important, as a company's preeminence in selected fields grows, its knowledge-based core competencies become ever harder to overtake. Knowledge bases tend to grow exponentially in value with investment and experience. Intellectual leadership tends to attract the most talented people, who then work on and solve the most interesting problems. The combination in turn creates higher returns and attracts the next round of outstanding talent. . . .

Some executives regard core activities as those the company is continuously engaged in, while peripheral activities are those which are intermittent and therefore can be outsourced. From the viewpoint of outsourcing strategy, however, core competencies are the activities that offer long-term competitive advantage and thus must be rigidly controlled and protected. Peripheral activities are those not critical to the company's competitive edge.

Strategic Outsourcing

If supplier markets were totally reliable and efficient, rational companies would outsource everything except those special activities where they could achieve a unique competitive edge, i.e., their core competencies. Unfortunately, most supplier markets are imperfect and do entail some risks for both buyer and seller with respect to price, quality, time, or other key terms. Moreover, outsourcing entails unique transaction costs—searching, contracting, controlling, and recontracting—that at times may exceed the transaction costs of having the activity directly under management's in-house control.

To address these difficulties managers must answer three key questions about any activity considered for outsourcing. First, what is the potential for obtaining competitive advantage in this activity, taking account of transaction costs? Second, what is the potential vulnerability that could arise from market failure if the activity is outsourced? These two factors can be arrayed in a simple matrix (see Figure 2). Third, what can we do to alleviate our vulnerability by structuring arrangements with suppliers to provide appropriate controls yet provide for necessary flexibilities in demand?

The two extremes on the matrix are relatively straightforward. When the potentials for both competitive edge and strategic vulnerability are high, the company needs a high degree of control, usually entailing production internally, through joint ownership arrangements, or through tight long-term contracts (explicit or implicit). . . .

At each intervening point the question is not just whether to make or buy, but how to implement a desired balance between independence and incentives for the supplier versus control and security for the buyer. Most companies will benefit by extending outsourcing first in less critical areas— or parts of activities like payroll, rather than all of accounting. As they gain experience, they may increase profit opportunities greatly by outsourcing more critical activities to noncompeting firms that can perform them more effectively. In a few cases, more complex alliances with competitors may be essential to garner specialized skills that cannot be obtained in other ways. At each level, the company must isolate and rigorously control strategically critical relationships between its suppliers and its customers.

COMPETITIVE EDGE

The key strategic issue in insourcing versus outsourcing is whether a company can achieve a maintainable competitive edge by performing an activity internally—usually cheaper, better, in a more timely fashion, or with some unique capability—on a continuing basis. If one or more of these dimensions is critical to the customer and if the potential buyer can perform that function uniquely well, the activity should normally be kept in-house. Many companies unfortunately assume that because they have performed an activity internally, or because it seems integral to their business, the activity should be insourced. However, on closer investigation and with careful benchmarking, its internal capabilities may turn out

FIGURE 2
**Competitive Advantage
vs. Strategic Vulnerability**

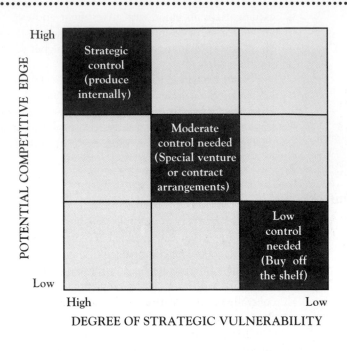

to be significantly below those of best-in-world suppliers. For example, Ford Motor Company found that many of its internal suppliers' quality practices and costs were nowhere near those of external suppliers when it began its famous "best in class" worldwide benchmarking studies on 400 subassemblies for the new Taurus-Sable line. . . . In interviews with top operating managers in both service and manufacturing companies concerning benchmarking, we frequently encountered a paraphrase of, "We thought we were best in the world at many activities. But when we benchmarked against the best external suppliers, we found we were not even up to the worst of the benchmarking cases."

TRANSACTION COSTS

In all calculations, analysts must include both internal transaction costs as well as those associated with external sourcing. If the company is to produce the item or service internally on a long-term basis, it must be prepared to back up its decision with continuing R&D, personnel development, and infrastructure investments which at least match those of the best external supplier. Otherwise, it will lose its competitive edge over time. Managers often tend to overlook such backup costs, as well as the losses from laggard innovation and nonresponsiveness from internal groups who know they have a guaranteed market. Finally, there are the headquarters and support costs of constantly managing the insourced activity. One of the great gains of outsourcing is the decrease in executive time for managing peripheral activities—freeing top management to focus more on the core of its business.

Various studies have shown that, when these internal transaction costs are thoroughly analyzed, they can be extremely high (D'Aveni and Ravenscraft, 1994). Since it is easier to identify the explicit transaction costs of dealing with external suppliers, these generally tend to be included in analyses. Harder-to-identify internal transaction costs are often not included, thus biasing results.

VULNERABILITY

When there are a large number of suppliers (with adequate but not dominating scale) and mature market standards and terms, a potential buyer is unlikely to be more efficient than the best available supplier. If, on the other hand, there is not sufficient depth in the market, overly powerful suppliers can hold the company to ransom. Conversely, if the number of suppliers is limited or individual suppliers are too weak, they may be unable to supply innovative products or services as well as a much larger buyer could by performing the activity in house. . . .

Another form of vulnerability is a lack of information available in the marketplace or from individual suppliers. For example, a supplier may secretly expect labour disruptions or raw material problems but hide these until it is too late for the customer to go elsewhere. A related problem occurs when a supplier has unique information capabilities; for example, large wholesalers or retailers, market research firms, software companies, or legal specialists may have information or fact-gathering systems that would be impossible for the buyer or any other single supplier to reproduce efficiently. Such suppliers may be able to charge essentially monopoly prices, but this could still be less costly than reproducing the service internally. In other cases, there may be many capable suppliers (e.g., of R&D or software), but the costs of adequately monitoring progress on the suppliers' premises might make outsourcing prohibitive. . . .

DEGREE OF SOURCING CONTROL

There is a full spectrum of outsourcing arrangements, depending on the buyer's control versus flexibility needs. (See Figure 3.) The issue is less whether to make or buy an activity than it is how to structure internal versus external sourcing on an optimal basis. Companies are outsourcing much more of what used to be considered either integral elements of their value chains or necessary staff activities. Because of greater complexity, higher specialization, and new technological capabilities, outside suppliers can now perform many such activities at lower cost and with higher value added than a fully integrated buying company can. . . .

STRATEGIC RISKS

Outsourcing complete or partial activities creates great opportunities but also new types of risks. Managements' main strategic concerns are: (1) loss of critical skills or developing the wrong skills, (2) loss of cross-functional skills, and (3) loss of control over a supplier.

1. LOSS OF CRITICAL SKILLS OR DEVELOPING THE WRONG SKILLS. Unfortunately, many U.S. companies have outsourced manufacture of what, at the time, seemed to be only minor componentry, like semiconductor chips or a bicycle frame, and taught suppliers how to build them to needed quality standards. Later these companies found their suppliers were unable or unwilling to supply the company as required. By then, the buying company had lost the skills it needed to reenter manufacture and could not prevent its suppliers from either assisting competitors or entering downstream markets on their own. In some cases, by outsourcing a key component, the company had lost its own strategic flexibility to introduce new designs when it wanted, rather than when the vendor permitted it. . . .

2. LOSS OF CROSS-FUNCTIONAL SKILLS. The interactions among skilled people in different functional activities often develop unexpected new insights or solutions. Companies fear outsourcing will make such cross-functional serendipity less likely. However, if the company consciously ensures that its remaining employees interact constantly and closely

FIGURE 3
Potential Contract
Relationships

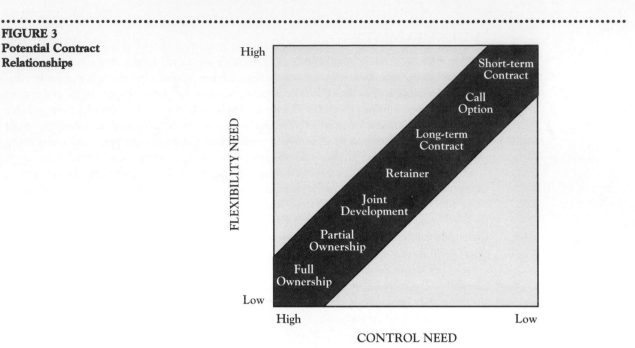

with its outsourced experts, its employees' knowledge base can be much higher than if production were in-house, and the creativity benefits can be even greater.

3. LOSS OF CONTROL OVER A SUPPLIER. Real problems can occur when the supplier's priorities do not match the buyer's. The most successful outsourcers find it absolutely essential to have both close personal contact and rapport at the floor level and political clout and understanding with the supplier's top management. For this reason, Nike both has full-time "production expatriates" on its suppliers' premises and frequently brings the suppliers' top people to Beaverton, Oregon, to exchange details about future capabilities and prospects. . . .

NEW MANAGEMENT APPROACHES

Most large companies have already developed very sophisticated techniques for traditional purchasing of parts, subassemblies, supplies, equipment, construction, or standard services. And models from the natural resources, real estate/construction, and finance/insurance industries—where joint ventures have been common for years—can provide useful guides for more complex partnering relationships. In addition to seeking out these experiences, the main management adjustments for most companies are those needed for coping with the increased scale, diversity, and service-oriented nature of the activities potentially outsourced. These center on (1) a much more professional and highly-trained purchasing and contract management group (as compared with the lowly purchasing groups of the past); and (2) a greatly enhanced logistics-information system (to track and evaluate vendors, coordinate transportation activities, and manage service transactions and materials movements from vendors' hands through to the customers'). . . .

Conclusion

Most companies can substantially leverage their resources through strategic outsourcing by: (1) developing a few well-selected core competencies of significance to customers and in which the company can be best-in-world; (2) focusing investment and management attention on them; and (3) strategically outsourcing many other activities where it cannot be or need not be best. There are always some inherent risks in outsourcing, but there are also risks and costs of insourcing. When approached with a genuinely strategic framework, using the variety of outsourcing options available and analyzing the strategic issues developed here, companies can overcome many of the costs and risks. When intelligently combined, core competency and extensive outsourcing strategies provide improved returns on capital, lowered risk, greater flexibility, and better responsiveness to customer needs at lower costs.

STRATEGY ANALYSIS

A s noted in the introduction to Chapter 3, there is a second prescriptive view of the way strategy should be formulated, which developed in the 1980s. Its contribution is less as a new conceptual model—in fact it embraces most of the premises of the traditional model—than in carefully structuring the kinds of formal analyses that should be undertaken to develop a successful strategy. One outcome of this more formal approach is that many of its adherents came to see strategies as fitting certain "generic" classifications—not being created so much individually as selected from a limited set of options based on systematic study of the firm and the industry conditions it faces. This approach has proved to be powerful and useful in specific situations.

A leader of this approach is Michael Porter of the Harvard Business School, who studied at the doctoral level in Harvard's economics department. By building intellectual bridges between the fields of management policy and industrial organization—the latter a branch of economics concerned with the performance of industries as a function of their competitive characteristics—Porter elaborated on the earlier views of Andrews, Ansoff, Newman, and the like.

We open this chapter with Porter's basic model of competitive and industry analysis, probably his best-known work in the area of strategy analysis. As presented in this award-winning *Harvard Business Review* article, it proposes a framework of five forces which in his view define the basic posture of competition in an industry—the bargaining power of existing suppliers and buyers, the threat of substitutes and new entrants, and the intensity of existing rivalry. The model is a powerful one, as you will see in references to it in subsequent readings.

Porter is known for several other frameworks as well: for example, his concept of "generic strategies," of which he argues there are three in particular—cost leadership, differentiation, and focus (or scope); his discussion of the "value chain" as a way of decomposing the activities of a business to apply strategy analyses of various kinds; his notion of strategic groups, where firms with like sets of strategies compete in subsegments of an industry; and his concept of "generic industry environments," such as "fragmented" or "mature," which reflect similar characteristics.

We shall hear from Porter again on the last of these in our context section. But his three generic strategies as well as his value chain concept will be summarized in a second reading in this chapter, by Mintzberg, that seeks to present a more comprehensive picture of the various strategies that firms commonly pursue at the so-called "business" level—that is for their individual businesses (as opposed to the "corporate" level, which concerns itself with strategies for the set of businesses a "diversified" company operates in; a companion reading in Chapter 13 discusses corporate-level generic strategies). These generic business strategies are described at three levels—strategies concerned with locating the core business, with distinguishing the core business by means of "differentiation" and "scope," and with elaborating the core business.

The literature of strategic analysis, or "positioning" as it is sometimes called, tends—like analysis itself—to be rather decomposed: more concerned with probing into parts than with combining into wholes. Accordingly, the concepts tend to come and go at a frantic pace, confusing reader and writer alike. And so Mintzberg has prepared a new integrative piece, called "A Guide to Strategic Positioning," which sets out to place into a single framework these many concepts. To do so, he uses the metaphors of a launching vehicle that projects its products and services into the terrain of markets. You should have some fun with this new contribution to the strategic management literature and an important addition to this book.

▼ READING 4.1   HOW COMPETITIVE FORCES SHAPE STRATEGY*

by Michael E. Porter

The essence of strategy formulation is coping with competition. Yet it is easy to view competition too narrowly and too pessimistically. While one sometimes hears executives complaining to the contrary, intense competition in an industry is neither coincidence nor bad luck.

Moreover, in the fight for market share, competition is not manifested only in the other players. Rather, competition in an industry is rooted in its underlying economics, and competitive forces exist that go well beyond the established combatants in a particular industry. Customers, suppliers, potential entrants, and substitute products are all competitors that may be more or less prominent or active depending on the industry.

The state of competition in an industry depends on five basic forces, which are diagrammed in Figure 1. The collective strength of these forces determines the ultimate profit potential of an industry. It ranges from *intense* in industries like tires, metal cans, and steel, where no company earns spectacular returns on investment, to *mild* in industries like oil field services and equipment, soft drinks, and toiletries, where there is room for quite high returns.

In the economists' "perfectly competitive" industry, jockeying for position is unbridled and entry to the industry very easy. This kind of industry structure, of course, offers the worst prospect for long-run profitability. The weaker the forces collectively, however, the greater the opportunity for superior performance.

Whatever their collective strength, the corporate strategist's goal is to find a position in the industry where his or her company can best defend itself against these forces or can influence them in its favor. The collective strength of the forces may be painfully apparent to all the antagonists; but to cope with them, the strategist must delve below the surface and analyze the sources of each. For example, what makes the industry vulnerable to entry? What determines the bargaining power of suppliers?

Knowledge of these underlying sources of competitive pressure provides the groundwork for a strategic agenda of action. They highlight the critical strengths and weaknesses of the company, animate the positioning of the company in its industry, clarify the areas where strategic changes may yield the greatest payoff, and highlight the places where industry trends promise to hold the greatest significance as either opportunities or threats. Understanding these sources also proves to be of help in considering areas for diversification.

FIGURE 1
Elements of
Industry Structure

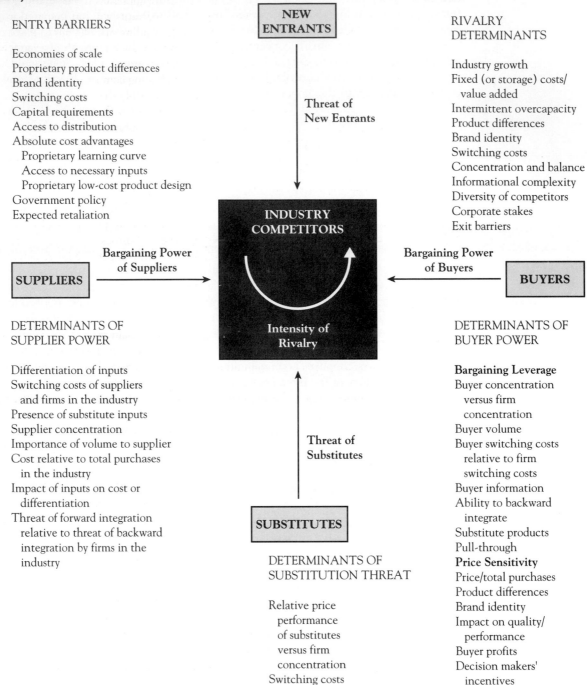

ENTRY BARRIERS

Economies of scale
Proprietary product differences
Brand identity
Switching costs
Capital requirements
Access to distribution
Absolute cost advantages
    Proprietary learning curve
    Access to necessary inputs
    Proprietary low-cost product design
Government policy
Expected retaliation

NEW
ENTRANTS

Threat of
New Entrants

RIVALRY
DETERMINANTS

Industry growth
Fixed (or storage) costs/
    value added
Intermittent overcapacity
Product differences
Brand identity
Switching costs
Concentration and balance
Informational complexity
Diversity of competitors
Corporate stakes
Exit barriers

Bargaining Power
of Suppliers

SUPPLIERS

INDUSTRY
COMPETITORS

Intensity of
Rivalry

Bargaining Power
of Buyers

BUYERS

DETERMINANTS OF
SUPPLIER POWER

Differentiation of inputs
Switching costs of suppliers
    and firms in the industry
Presence of substitute inputs
Supplier concentration
Importance of volume to supplier
Cost relative to total purchases
    in the industry
Impact of inputs on cost or
    differentiation
Threat of forward integration
    relative to threat of backward
    integration by firms in the
    industry

Threat of
Substitutes

SUBSTITUTES

DETERMINANTS OF
SUBSTITUTION THREAT

Relative price
    performance
    of substitutes
    versus firm
    concentration
Switching costs
Buyer propensity
    to substitute

DETERMINANTS OF
BUYER POWER

Bargaining Leverage
Buyer concentration
    versus firm
    concentration
Buyer volume
Buyer switching costs
    relative to firm
    switching costs
Buyer information
Ability to backward
    integrate
Substitute products
Pull-through
Price Sensitivity
Price/total purchases
Product differences
Brand identity
Impact on quality/
    performance
Buyer profits
Decision makers'
    incentives

Used with permission of the The Free Press, a Division of Macmillan, Inc., from *Competitive Strategy: Techniques for Analyzing Industries and Competitors* by Michael E. Porter. Copyright © 1980 by The Free Press. [used in place of article's Figure 1 as it contains more detail]

The strongest competitive force or forces determine the profitability of an industry and so are of greatest importance in strategy formulation. For example, even a company with a strong position in an industry unthreatened by potential entrants will earn low returns if it faces a superior or lower-cost substitute product—as the leading manufacturers of vacuum tubes and coffee percolators have learned to their sorrow. In such a situation, coping with the substitute product becomes the number one strategic priority.

Different forces take on prominence, of course, in shaping competition in each industry. In the oceangoing tanker industry the key force is probably the buyers (the major oil companies), while in tires it is powerful OEM buyers coupled with tough competitors. In the steel industry the key forces are foreign competitors and substitute materials.

Every industry has an underlying structure, or a set of fundamental economic and technical characteristics, that gives rise to these competitive forces. The strategist, wanting to position his company to cope best with its industry environment or to influence that environment in the company's favor, must learn what makes the environment tick.

This view of competition pertains equally to industries dealing in services and to those selling products. To avoid monotony in this article, I refer to both products and services as "products." The same general principles apply to all types of business.

A few characteristics are critical to the strength of each competitive force. I shall discuss them in this section.

THREAT OF ENTRY

New entrants to an industry bring new capacity, the desire to gain market share, and often substantial resources. Companies diversifying through acquisition into the industry from other markets often leverage their resources to cause a shakeup, as Philip Morris did with Miller beer.

The seriousness of the threat of entry depends on the barriers present and on the reaction from existing competitors that the entrant can expect. If barriers to entry are high and a newcomer can expect sharp retaliation from the entrenched competitors, obviously he will not pose a serious threat of entering.

There are six major sources of barriers to entry:

1. *Economies of scale*—These economies deter entry by forcing the aspirant either to come in on a large scale or to accept a cost disadvantage. Scale economies in production, research, marketing, and service are probably the key barriers to entry in the mainframe computer industry, as Xerox and GE sadly discovered. Economies of scale can also act as hurdles in distribution, utilization of the sales force, financing, and nearly any other part of a business.

2. *Product differentiation*—Brand identification creates a barrier by forcing entrants to spend heavily to overcome customer loyalty. Advertising, customer service, being first in the industry, and product differences are among the factors fostering brand identification. It is perhaps the most important entry barrier in soft drinks, over-the-counter drugs, cosmetics, investment banking, and public accounting. To create high fences around their businesses, brewers couple brand identification with economies of scale in production, distribution, and marketing.

3. *Capital requirements*—The need to invest large financial resources in order to compete creates a barrier to entry, particularly if the capital is required for unrecoverable expenditures in up-front advertising or R&D. Capital is necessary not only for fixed facilities but also for customer credit, inventories, and absorbing start-up losses. While major corporations have the financial resources to invade almost any industry, the huge cap-

ital requirements in certain fields, such as computer manufacturing and mineral extraction, limit the pool of likely entrants.

4. *Cost disadvantages independent of size*—Entrenched companies may have cost advantages not available to potential rivals, no matter what their size and attainable economies of scale. These advantages can stem from the effects of the learning curve (and of its first cousin, the experience curve), proprietary technology, access to the best raw materials sources, assets purchased at preinflation prices, government subsidies, or favorable locations. Sometimes cost advantages are legally enforceable, as they are through patents. . . .

5. *Access to distribution channels*—The new boy on the block must, of course, secure distribution of his product or service. A new food product, for example, must displace others from the supermarket shelf via price breaks, promotions, intense selling efforts, or some other means. The more limited the wholesale or retail channels are and the more that existing competitors have these tied up, obviously the tougher that entry into the industry will be. Sometimes this barrier is so high that, to surmount it, a new contestant must create its own distribution channels, as Timex did in the watch industry in the 1950s.

6. *Government policy*—The government can limit or even foreclose industries with such controls as license requirements and limits on access to raw materials. Regulated industries like trucking, liquor retailing, and freight forwarding are noticeable examples; more subtle government restrictions operate in fields like ski-area development and coal mining. The government also can play a major indirect role by affecting entry barriers through controls such as air and water pollution standards and safety regulations.

The potential rival's expectations about the reaction of existing competitors also will influence its decision on whether to enter. The company is likely to have second thoughts if incumbents have previously lashed out at new entrants or if:

▼ The incumbents possess substantial resources to fight back, including excess cash and unused borrowing power, productive capacity, or clout with distribution channels and customers.

▼ The incumbents seem likely to cut prices because of a desire to keep market shares or because of industrywide excess capacity.

▼ Industry growth is slow, affecting its ability to absorb the new arrival and probably causing the financial performance of all the parties involved to decline.

CHANGING CONDITIONS

From a strategic standpoint there are two important additional points to note about the threat of entry.

First, it changes, of course, as these conditions change. The expiration of Polaroid's basic patents on instant photography, for instance, greatly reduced its absolute cost entry barrier built by proprietary technology. It is not surprising that Kodak plunged into the market. Product differentiation in printing has all but disappeared. Conversely, in the auto industry economies of scale increased enormously with post–World War II automation and vertical integration—virtually stopping successful new entry.

Second, strategic decisions involving a large segment of an industry can have a major impact on the conditions determining the threat of entry. For example, the actions of many U.S. wine producers in the 1960s to step up product introductions, raise advertising levels, and expand distribution nationally surely strengthened the entry roadblocks by raising economies of scale and making access to distribution channels more difficult. Similarly, decisions by members of the recreational vehicle industry to vertically integrate in order to lower costs have greatly increased the economies of scale and raised the capital cost barriers.

POWERFUL SUPPLIERS AND BUYERS

Suppliers can exert bargaining power on participants in an industry by raising prices or reducing the quality of purchased goods and services. Powerful suppliers can thereby squeeze profitability out of an industry unable to recover cost increases in its own prices. By raising their prices, soft drink concentrate producers have contributed to the erosion of profitability of bottling companies because the bottlers, facing intense competition from powdered mixes, fruit drinks, and other beverages, have limited freedom to raise *their* prices accordingly. Customers likewise can force down prices, demand higher quality or more service, and play competitors off against each other—all at the expense of industry profits.

The power of each important supplier or buyer group depends on a number of characteristics of its market situation and on the relative importance of its sales or purchases to the industry compared with its overall business.

A *supplier* group is powerful if:

▼ It is dominated by a few companies and is more concentrated than the industry it sells to.

▼ Its product is unique or at least differentiated, or if it has built up switching costs. Switching costs are fixed costs buyers face in changing suppliers. These arise because, among other things, a buyer's product specifications tie it to particular suppliers, it has invested heavily in specialized ancillary equipment or in learning how to operate a supplier's equipment (as in computer software), or its production lines are connected to the supplier's manufacturing facilities (as in some manufacture of beverage containers).

▼ It is not obliged to contend with other products for sale to the industry. For instance, the competition between the steel companies and the aluminum companies to sell to the can industry checks the power of each supplier.

▼ It poses a credible threat of integrating forward into the industry's business. This provides a check against the industry's ability to improve the terms on which it purchases.

▼ The industry is not an important customer of the supplier group. If the industry *is* an important customer, suppliers' fortunes will be closely tied to the industry, and they will want to protect the industry through reasonable pricing and assistance in activities like R&D and lobbying.

A *buyer* group is powerful if:

▼ It is concentrated or purchases in large volumes. Large-volume buyers are particularly potent forces if heavy fixed costs characterize the industry—as they do in metal containers, corn refining, and bulk chemicals, for example—which raise the stakes to keep capacity filled.

▼ The products it purchases from the industry are standard or undifferentiated. The buyers, sure that they can always find alternative suppliers, may play one company against another, as they do in aluminum extrusion.

▼ The products it purchases from the industry form a component of its product and represent a significant fraction of its cost. The buyers are likely to shop for a favorable price and purchase selectively. Where the product sold by the industry in question is a small fraction of buyers' costs, buyers are usually much less price sensitive.

▼ It earns low profits, which create great incentive to lower its purchasing costs. Highly profitable buyers, however, are generally less price sensitive (that is, of course, if the item does not represent a large fraction of their costs).

▼ The industry's product is unimportant to the quality of the buyers' products or services. Where the quality of the buyers' products is very much affected by the industry's product, buyers are generally less price sensitive. Industries in which this situation includes oil field equipment, where a malfunction can lead to large losses, and enclosures for electronic medical and test instruments, where the quality of the enclosure can influence the user's impression about the quality of the equipment inside.

▼ The industry's product does not save the buyer money. Where the industry's product or service can pay for itself many times over, the buyer is rarely price sensitive; rather, he is interested in quality. This is true in services like investment banking and public accounting, where errors in judgment can be costly and embarrassing, and in businesses like the logging of oil wells, where an accurate survey can save thousands of dollars in drilling costs.

▼ The buyers pose a credible threat of integrating backward to make the industry's product. The Big Three auto producers and major buyers of cars have often used the threat of self-manufacture as a bargaining lever. But sometimes an industry engenders a threat to buyers that its members may integrate forward.

Most of these sources of buyer power can be attributed to consumers as a group as well as to industrial and commercial buyers; only a modification of the frame of reference is necessary. Consumers tend to be more price sensitive if they are purchasing products that are undifferentiated, expensive relative to their incomes, and of a sort where quality is not particularly important.

The buying power of retailers is determined by the same rules, with one important addition. Retailers can gain significant bargaining power over manufacturers when they can influence consumers' purchasing decisions, as they do in audio components, jewelry, appliances, sporting goods, and other goods.

STRATEGIC ACTION

A company's choice of suppliers to buy from or buyer groups to sell to should be viewed as a crucial strategic decision. A company can improve its strategic posture by finding suppliers or buyers who possess the least power to influence it adversely.

Most common is the situation of a company being able to choose whom it will sell to—in other words, buyer selection. Rarely do all the buyer groups a company sells to enjoy equal power. Even if a company sells to a single industry, segments usually exist within that industry that exercise less power (and that are therefore less price sensitive) than others. For example, the replacement market for most products is less price sensitive than the overall market.

As a rule, a company can sell to powerful buyers and still come away with above-average profitability only if it is a low-cost producer in its industry or if its product enjoys some unusual, if not unique, features. In supplying large customers with electric motors, Emerson Electric earns high returns because its low-cost position permits the company to meet or undercut competitors' prices.

If the company lacks a low-cost position or a unique product, selling to everyone is self-defeating because the more sales it achieves, the more vulnerable it becomes. The company may have to muster the courage to turn away business and sell only to less potent customers.

Buyer selection has been a key to the success of National Can and Crown Cork & Seal. They focus on the segments of the can industry where they can create product differentiation, minimize the threat of backward integration, and otherwise mitigate the awesome power of their customers. Of course, some industries do not enjoy the luxury of selecting "good" buyers.

As the factors creating supplier and buyer power change with time or as a result of a company's strategic decisions, naturally the power of these groups rises or declines. In the ready-to-wear clothing industry, as the buyers (department stores and clothing stores) have become more concentrated and control has passed to large chains, the industry has come under increasing pressure and suffered falling margins. The industry has been unable to differentiate its product or engender switching costs that lock in its buyers enough to neutralize these trends.

SUBSTITUTE PRODUCTS

By placing a ceiling on prices it can charge, substitute products or services limit the potential of an industry. Unless it can upgrade the quality of the product or differentiate it somehow (as via marketing), the industry will suffer in earnings and possibly in growth.

Manifestly, the more attractive the price-performance trade-off offered by substitute products, the firmer the lid placed on the industry's profit potential. Sugar producers confronted with the large-scale commercialization of high-fructose corn syrup, a sugar substitute, are learning this lesson today.

Substitutes not only limit profits in normal times; they also reduce the bonanza an industry can reap in boom times. In 1978 the producers of fiberglass insulation enjoyed unprecedented demand as a result of high energy costs and severe winter weather. But the industry's ability to raise prices was tempered by the plethora of insulation substitutes, including cellulose, rock wool, and styrofoam. These substitutes are bound to become an even stronger force once the current round of plant additions by fiberglass insulation producers has boosted capacity enough to meet demand (and then some).

Substitute products that deserve the most attention strategically are those that (1) are subject to trends improving their price-performance trade-off with the industry's product, or (2) are produced by industries earning high profits. Substitutes often come rapidly into play if some development increases competition in their industries and causes price reduction or performance improvement.

JOCKEYING FOR POSITION

Rivalry among existing competitors takes the familiar form of jockeying for position—using tactics like price competition, product introduction, and advertising slugfests. Intense rivalry is related to the presence of a number of factors:

▼ Competitors are numerous or are roughly equal in size and power. In many U.S. industries in recent years foreign contenders, of course, have become part of the competitive picture.

▼ Industry growth is slow, precipitating fights for market share that involve expansion-minded members.

▼ The product or service lacks differentiation or switching costs, which lock in buyers and protect one combatant from raids on its customers by another.

▼ Fixed costs are high or the product is perishable, creating strong temptation to cut prices. Many basic materials businesses, like paper and aluminum, suffer from this problem when demand slackens.

▼ Capacity is normally augmented in large increments. Such additions, as in the chlorine and vinyl chloride businesses, disrupt the industry's supply-demand balance and often lead to periods of overcapacity and price cutting.

▼ Exit barriers are high. Exit barriers, like very specialized assets or management's loyalty to a particular business, keep companies competing even though they may be earning low or even negative returns on investment. Excess capacity remains functioning, and the profitability of the healthy competitors suffers as the sick ones hang on. If the entire industry suffers from overcapacity, it may seek government help—particularly if foreign competition is present.

▼ The rivals are diverse in strategies, origins, and "personalities." They have different ideas about how to compete and continually run head on into each other in the process. . . .

While a company must live with many of these factors—because they are built into industry economics—it may have some latitude for improving matters through strategic shifts. For example, it may try to raise buyers' switching costs or increase product differentiation. A focus on selling efforts in the fastest-growing segments of the industry or on market areas with the lowest fixed costs can reduce the impact of industry rivalry. If it is feasible, a company can try to avoid confrontation with competitors having high exit barriers and can thus sidestep involvement in bitter price cutting.

Formulation of Strategy

Once the corporate strategist has assessed the forces affecting competition in his industry and their underlying causes, he can identify his company's strengths and weaknesses. The crucial strengths and weaknesses from a strategic standpoint are the company's posture vis-a-vis the underlying causes of each force. Where does it stand against substitutes? Against the sources of entry barriers?

Then the strategist can devise a plan of action that may include (1) positioning the company so that its capabilities provide the best defense against the competitive force; and/or (2) influencing the balance of the forces through strategic moves, thereby improving the company's position; and/or (3) anticipating shifts in the factors underlying the forces and responding to them, with the hope of exploiting change by choosing a strategy appropriate for the new competitive balance before opponents recognize it. I shall consider each strategic approach in turn.

POSITIONING THE COMPANY

The first approach takes the structure of the industry as given and matches the company's strengths and weaknesses to it. Strategy can be viewed as building defenses against the competitive forces or as finding positions in the industry where the forces are weakest.

Knowledge of the company's capabilities and of the causes of the competitive forces will highlight the areas where the company should confront competition and where avoid it. If the company is a low-cost producer, it may choose to confront powerful buyers while it takes care to sell them only products not vulnerable to competition from substitutes. . . .

INFLUENCING THE BALANCE

When dealing with the forces that drive industry competition, a company can devise a strategy that takes the offensive. This posture is designed to do more than merely cope with the forces themselves; it is meant to alter their causes.

Innovations in marketing can raise brand identification or otherwise differentiate the product. Capital investments in large-scale facilities or vertical integration affect entry barriers. The balance of forces is partly a result of external factors and partly in the company's control.

EXPLOITING INDUSTRY CHANGE

Industry evolution is important strategically because evolution, of course, brings with it changes in the sources of competition I have identified. In the familiar product life-cycle pattern, for example, growth rates change, product differentiation is said to decline as the business becomes more mature, and the companies tend to integrate vertically.

These trends are not so important in themselves; what is critical is whether they affect the sources of competition. . . .

Obviously, the trends carrying the highest priority from a strategic standpoint are those that affect the most important sources of competition in the industry and those that elevate new causes to the forefront. . . .

The framework for analyzing competition that I have described can also be used to predict the eventual profitability of an industry. In long-range planning the task is to examine each competitive force, forecast the magnitude of each underlying cause, and then construct a composite picture of the likely profit potential of the industry. . . .

The key to growth—even survival—is to stake out a position that is less vulnerable to attack from head-to-head opponents, whether established or new, and less vulnerable to erosion from the direction of buyers, suppliers, and substitute goods. Establishing such a position can take many forms—solidifying relationships with favorable customers, differentiating the product either substantively or psychologically through marketing, integrating forward or backward, establishing technological leadership.

▼ READING 4.2   GENERIC BUSINESS STRATEGIES*

by Henry Mintzberg

Almost every serious author concerned with "content" issues in strategic management, not to mention strategy consulting "boutiques," has his, her, or its own list of strategies commonly pursued by different organizations. The problem is that these lists almost always either focus narrowly on special types of strategies or else aggregate arbitrarily across all varieties of them with no real order.

In 1965, Igor Ansoff proposed a matrix of four strategies which became quite well known—market penetration, product development, market development, and diversification (1965: 109). But this was hardly comprehensive. Fifteen years later, Michael Porter (1980) introduced what became the best-known list of "generic strategies": cost leadership, differentiation, and focus. But the Porter list was also incomplete: while Ansoff focused on *extensions* of business strategy, Porter focused on *identifying* business strategy in the first place.

We believe that families of strategies may be divided into five broad groupings. These are:

1. Locating the core business.

2. Distinguishing the core business.

3. Elaborating the core business.

4. Extending the core business.

5. Reconceiving the core business.

This reading examines the first three, locating, distinguishing, and elaborating the core business, since they are more relevant for business-level strategy. A companion reading in

---

* Abbreviated version prepared for this book of an article by Henry Mintzberg, "Generic Strategies Toward a Comprehensive Framework," originally published in *Advances in Strategic Management*, Vol. 5 (Greenwich, CT: JAI Press, 1988), pp. 1–67.

Chapter 13 discusses the two more relevant for corporate-level strategy—extending and reconceiving the core business. These five groupings of strategies are presented as a logical hierarchy, although it should be emphasized that strategies do not necessarily develop that way in organizations.

Locating the Core Business

A business can be thought to exist at a junction in a network of industries that take raw materials and through selling to and buying from each other produce various finished products (or services). Figure 1, for example, shows a hypothetical canoe business in such a network. Core location strategies can be described with respect to the stage of the business in the network and the particular industry in question.

STRATEGIES OF STAGE OF OPERATIONS

Traditionally, industries have been categorized as being in the primary (raw materials extraction and conversion), secondary (manufacturing) or tertiary (delivery or other ser-

FIGURE 1
Locating a Core Business as a Junction in a Network of Industries

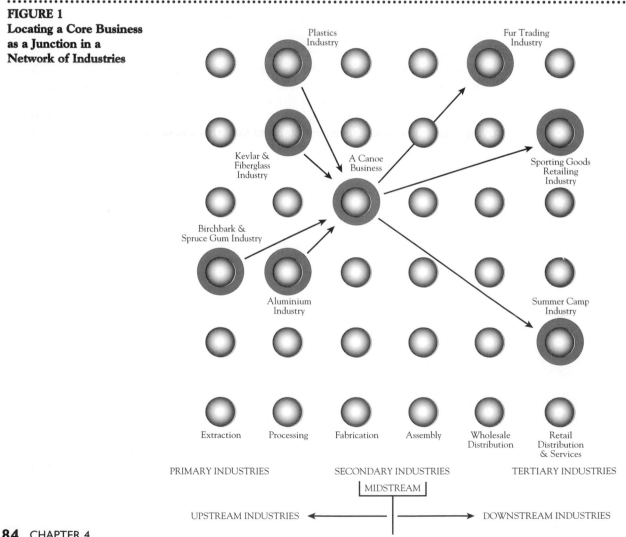

vice) stage of operations. More recently, however, state in the "stream" has been the favored form of description:

UPSTREAM BUSINESS STRATEGY

Upstream businesses function close to the raw material. The flow of product tends to be divergent, from a basic material (wood, aluminum) to a variety of uses for it. Upstream business tends to be technology- and capital-intensive rather than people-intensive, and more inclined to search for advantage through low costs than through high margins and to favor sales push over market pull (Galbraith, 1983: 65–66).

MIDSTREAM BUSINESS STRATEGY

Here the organization sits at the neck of an hour-glass, drawing a variety of inputs into a single production process out of which flows the product to a variety of users, much as the canoe business is shown in Figure 1.

DOWNSTREAM BUSINESS STRATEGY

Here a wide variety of inputs converge into a narrow funnel, as in the many products sold by a department store.

STRATEGIES OF INDUSTRY

Many factors are involved in the identification of an industry, so many that it would be difficult to develop a concise set of generic labels. Moreover, change continually renders the boundaries between "industries" arbitrary. Diverse products get bundled together so that two industries become one, while traditionally bundled products get separated so that one industry becomes two. Economists in government and elsewhere spend a great deal of time trying to pin these things down, via Standard Industrial Classification codes and the like. In effect, they try to fix what strategists try to change: competitive advantage often comes from reconceiving the definition of an industry.

Distinguishing the Core Business

Having located the circle that identifies the core business, the next step is to open it up— to distinguish the characteristics that enable an organization to achieve competitive advantage and so to survive in its own context.

THE FUNCTIONAL AREAS

This second level of strategy can encompass a whole host of strategies in the various functional areas. As shown in Figure 2, they may include input "sourcing" strategies, throughput "processing" strategies, and output "delivery" strategies, all reinforced by a set of "supporting" strategies.

It has been popular to describe organizations in this way, especially since Michael Porter built his 1985 book around the "generic value chain," shown in Figure 3. Porter presents it as "a systematic way of examining all the activities a firm performs and how they interact . . . for analyzing the sources of competitive advantage" (1985: 33). Such a chain, and how it performs individual activities, reflects a firm's "history, its strategy, its approach to implementing its strategy, and the underlying economies of the activities themselves" (p. 36). According to Porter

FIGURE 2
Functional Areas,
in Systems Terms

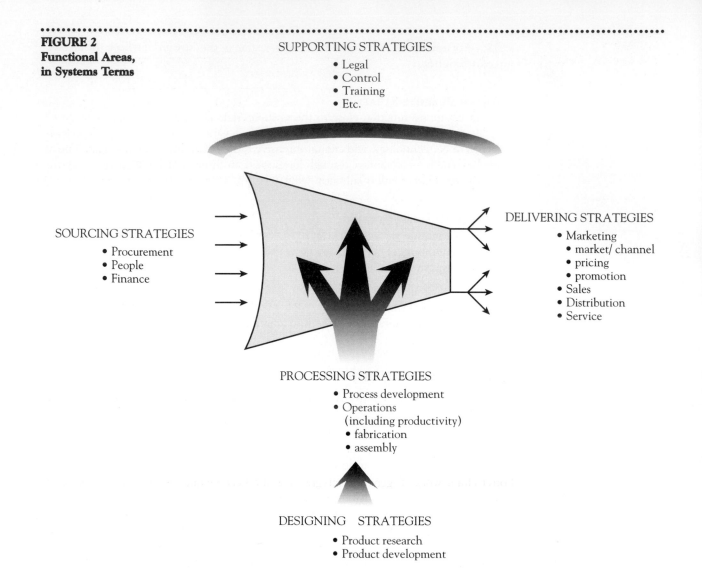

SUPPORTING STRATEGIES
- Legal
- Control
- Training
- Etc.

SOURCING STRATEGIES
- Procurement
- People
- Finance

DELIVERING STRATEGIES
- Marketing
  - market/ channel
  - pricing
  - promotion
- Sales
- Distribution
- Service

PROCESSING STRATEGIES
- Process development
- Operations
  (including productivity)
  - fabrication
  - assembly

DESIGNING   STRATEGIES
- Product research
- Product development

"the goal of any generic strategy" is to "create value for buyers" at a profit. Accordingly, the value chain displays total value, and consists of *value activities* and *margin*. Value activities are the physically and technologically distinct activities a firm performs. These are the building blocks by which a firm creates a product valuable to its buyers. Margin is the difference between total value and the collective cost of performing the value activities. . . .

Value activities can be divided into two broad types, *primary* activities and *support* activities. Primary activities, listed along the bottom of Figure 3, are the activities involved in the physical creation of the product and its sale and transfer to the buyer as well as after-sale assistance. In any firm, primary activities can be divided into the five generic categories shown in Figure 3. Support activities support the primary activities and each other by providing purchased inputs, technology, human resources, and various firmwide functions. (p. 38)*

---

* In other words, it is the differentiation of price that naturally drives the functional strategy of reducing costs just as it is the differentiation of product that naturally drives the functional strategies of enhancing quality or creating innovation. (To be consistent with the label of "cost leadership," Porter would have had to call his differentiation strategy "product leadership.") A company could, of course, cut costs while holding prices equivalent to competitors'. But often that means less service, lower quality, fewer features, etc., and so the customers would have to be attracted by lower prices. (See Mintzberg (1988: 14–17) for a fuller discussion of this point.)

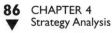

FIGURE 3
The Generic Value Chain
Source: *Porter* (1983:3)

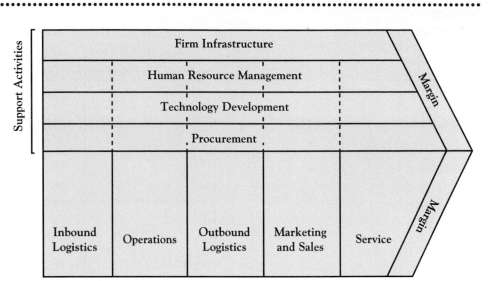

Primary Activities

PORTER'S GENERIC STRATEGIES

Porter's framework of "generic strategies" has also become quite widely used. In our terms, these constitute strategies to distinguish the core business. Porter believes there are but two "basic types of competitive advantage a firm can possess: low costs or differentiation" (1985:11). These combine with the "scope" of a firm's operation (the range of market segments targeted) to produce "three *generic strategies* for achieving above-average performance in an industry: cost leadership, differentiation, and focus" (namely, narrow scope), shown in Figure 4.

To Porter, firms that wish to gain competitive advantage must "make a choice" among these: "being 'all things to all people' is a recipe for strategic mediocrity and below-average performance" (p. 12). Or in the words that have become more controversial, "a firm that engages in each generic strategy but fails to achieve any of them is 'stuck in the middle'" (p. 16). Gilbert and Strebel (1992), however, have disagreed with this, arguing that highly successful companies, such as some of the Japanese automobile manufacturers, have adopted "outpacing strategies." First they use a low cost strategy to secure markets, and then, by "proactive" differentiation moves (say an increase in quality), they capture certain important market segments. Or else firms begin with value differentiation and follow that up with "preemptive" price cutting. In effect, the authors argue that companies can achieve both forms of Porter's competitive advantage simultaneously.

The strategies we describe in this section take their lead from Porter, but depart in some respects. We shall distinguish scope and differentiation, as Porter did in his 1980 book (focus being introduced as narrow scope in his later book), but we shall include cost leadership as a form of differentiation (namely, with regard to low price). If, as Porter argues, the intention of generic strategies is to seize and sustain competitive advantage, then it is not

FIGURE 4
Porter's Generic Strategies
Source: *Porter* (1983:3).

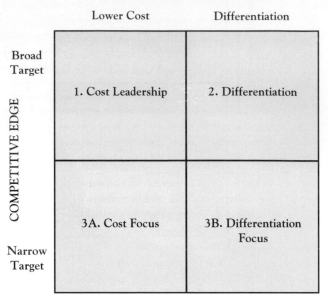

COMPETITIVE ADVANTAGE

just taking leadership on cutting costs that matters so much as using that cost leadership to underprice competitors and so to attract buyers.*

Thus two types of strategy for distinguishing a core business are presented here. First is a set of increasingly extensive strategies of *differentiation*, shown on the face of the circle. These identify what is fundamentally distinct about a business in the marketplace, in effect as perceived by its customers. Second is a set of decreasingly extensive strategies of *scope*. These identify what markets the business is after, as perceived by itself.

STRATEGIES OF DIFFERENTIATION

As is generally agreed in the literature of strategic management, an organization distinguishes itself in a competitive marketplace by differentiating its offerings in some way—by acting to distinguish its product and services from those of its competitors. Hence, differentiation fills the face of the circle used to identify the core business. An organization can differentiate its offerings in six basic ways:

---

* Our figure differs from Porter's in certain ways. Because he places his major emphasis on the flow of physical materials (for example, referring to "inbound logistics" as encompassing materials handling, warehousing, inventory control, vehicle scheduling, and returns to suppliers), he shows procurement and human resource management as support activities, whereas by taking more of a general system orientation, our Figure 2 shows them as inputs, among the sourcing strategies. Likewise, he considers technology development as support whereas Figure 2 considers it as part of processing. (Among the reasons Porter gives for doing this is that such development can pertain to "outbound logistics" or delivery as well as processing. While true, it also seems true that far more technology development pertains to operations than to delivery, especially in the manufacturing firms that are the focus of Porter's attention. Likewise, Porter describes procurement as pertaining to any of the primary activities, or other support activities for that matter. But in our terms that does not make it any less an aspect of sourcing on the inbound side.) In fact, Porter's description would relegate engineering and product design (not to mention human resources and purchasing) to staff rather than line activities, a place that would certainly be disputed in many manufacturing firms (with product design, for example, being mentioned only peripherally in his text (p. 42) alongside other "technology development" activities such as media research and servicing procedures).

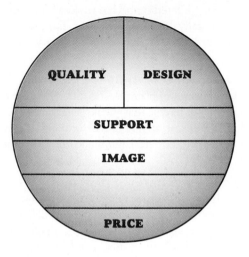

PRICE DIFFERENTIATION STRATEGY

The most basic way to differentiate a product (or service) is simply to charge a lower price for it. All things being equal, or not too unequal, some people at least will always beat a path to the door of the cheaper product. Price differentiation may be used with a product undifferentiated in any other way—in effect, a standard design, perhaps a commodity. The producer simply absorbs the lost margin, or makes it up through a higher volume of sales. But other times, backing up price differentiation is a strategy of design intended to create a product that is intrinsically cheaper.

IMAGE DIFFERENTIATION STRATEGY

Marketing is sometimes used to feign differentiation where it does not otherwise exist—an image is created for the product. This can also include cosmetic differences to a product that do not enhance its performance in any serious way, for example, putting a fancier package around yogurt. (Of course, if it is the image that is for sale, in other words if the product is intrinsically cosmetic, as, say, in "designer" jeans, then cosmetic differences would have to be described as design differentiation.)

SUPPORT DIFFERENTIATION STRATEGY

More substantial, yet still having no effect on the product itself, is to differentiate on the basis of something that goes alongside the product, some basis of support. This may have to do with selling the product (such as special credit or 24-hour delivery), servicing the product (such as exceptional after-sales service), or providing a related product or service alongside the basic one (paddling lessons with the canoe you buy). In an article entitled "Marketing Success Through Differentiation—of Anything," Theodore Levitt has argued the interesting point that "there is no such thing as a commodity" (1980: 8). His basic point is that no matter how difficult it may be to achieve differentiation by design, there is always a basis to achieve another substantial form of differentiation, especially by support.

QUALITY DIFFERENTIATION STRATEGY

Quality differentiation has to do with features of the product that make it better—not fundamentally different, just better. The product performs with (1) greater initial reliability, (2) greater long-term durability, and/or (3) superior performance.

DESIGN DIFFERENTIATION STRATEGY

Last but certainly not least is differentiation on the basis of design—offering something that is truly different, that breaks away from the "dominant design" if there is one, to provide unique features. When everyone else was making cameras whose pictures could be seen next week, Edward Land made one whose pictures could be seen in the next minute.

UNDIFFERENTIATION STRATEGY

To have no basis for differentiation is a strategy: indeed by all observation a common one, and in fact one that may be pursued deliberately. Hence there is a blank space in the circle. Given enough room in a market, and a management without the skill or the will to differentiate what it does, there can be a place for copycats.

SCOPE STRATEGIES

The second dimension to distinguish the core business is by the *scope* of the products and services offered, in effect the extent of the markets in which they are sold. Scope is essentially a demand-driven concept, taking its lead from the market for what exists out there. Differentiation, in contrast, is a supply-driven concern, rooted in the nature of the product itself—what is offered to the market (W. E. Smith, 1956). Differentiation, by concentrating on the product offered, adopts the perspective of the customer, existing only when that person perceives some characteristic of the product that adds value. And scope, by focusing on the market served, adopts the perspective of the producer, existing only in the collective mind of the organization—in terms of how it diffuses and disaggregates its markets (in other words, what marketing people call segmentation).

UNSEGMENTATION STRATEGY

"One size fits all": the Ford Model T, table salt. In fact, it is difficult to think of any product today that is not segmented in some way. What the unsegmented strategy really means then is that the organization tries to capture a wide chunk of the market with a basic configuration of the product.

SEGMENTATION STRATEGIES

The possibilities for segmentation are limitless, as are the possible degrees. We can, however, distinguish a range of this, from a simple segmentation strategy (three basic sizes of paper clips) to a hyperfine segmentation strategy (as in designer lighting). Also, some organizations seek to be *comprehensive*, to serve all segments (department stores, large cereal manufacturers), others to be *selective*, targeting carefully only certain segments (e.g., "clean" mutual funds).

NICHE STRATEGY

Niche strategies focus on a single segment. Just as the panda bear has found its biological niche in the consumption of bamboo shoots, so too is there the canoe company that has found its market niche in the fabrication of racing canoes, or the many firms which are distinguished only by the fact that they provide their highly standardized offerings in a unique place, a geographical niche—the corner grocery store, the regional cement producer, the national Red Cross office. All tend to follow "industry" recipes to the letter, providing them to their particular community. In a sense, all strategies are in some sense niche, characterized as much by what they exclude as by what they include. No organization can be all things to all people. The all-encompassing strategy is no strategy at all.

CUSTOMIZING STRATEGIES

Customization is the limiting case of segmentation: disaggregation of the market to the point where each customer constitutes a unique segment. *Pure* customization, in which the product is developed from scratch for each customer, is found in the architecturally designed house and the special purpose machine. It infiltrates the entire value chain: the product is not only delivered in a personalized way, not only assembled and even fabricated to order, but is also designed for the individual customer in the first place. Less ambitious but probably more common is *tailored* customization: a basic design is modified, usually in the fabrication stage, to the customer's needs or specifications (certain housing, prostheses modified to fit the bone joints of each customer, and so on). *Standardized customization* means that final products are assembled to individual request from standard components—as in automobiles in which the customer is allowed to choose color, engine and various accessories. Advances in computer-aided design and manufacturing (CAD, CAM) have caused a proliferation of standardized customization, as well as tailored customization.

Elaborating the Core Business

An organization can elaborate a business in a number of ways. It can develop its product offerings within that business, it can develop its market via new segments, new channels or new geographical areas, or it can simply push the same products more vigorously through the same markets. Back in 1965, Igor Ansoff showed these strategies (as well as one to be discussed in Chapter 13) as presented in Figure 5.

PENETRATION STRATEGIES

Penetration strategies work from a base of existing products and existing markets, seeking to penetrate the market by increasing the organization's share of it. This may be done by straight *expansion* or by the *takeover* of existing competitors. Trying to expand sales with no fundamental change in product or market (buying market share through more promotion, etc.) is at one and the same time the most obvious thing to do and perhaps the most difficult to succeed at, because, at least in a relatively stable market, it means extracting market share from other firms, which logically leads to increased competition. Takeover, where possible, obviously avoids this, but perhaps at a high cost. The harvesting strategy, popularized in the 1970s by the Boston Consulting Group, in some ways represents the opposite of the penetration strategies. The way to deal with "cash cows"—businesses with high market shares but low growth potential—was to harvest them, cease investment and exploit whatever potential remained. The mixing of the metaphors may have been an indication of the dubiousness of the strategy since to harvest a cow is, of course, to kill it.

MARKET DEVELOPMENT STRATEGIES

A predominant strategy here is *market elaboration*, which means promoting existing products in new markets—in effect broadening the scope of the business by finding new market segments, perhaps served by new channels. Product substitution is a particular case of market elaboration, where uses for a product are promoted which enable it to substitute for

FIGURE 5
Ways to Elaborate a
Given Business
Source: *Ansoff* (1965:109)
with minor modifications;
see also Johnson and Jones
(1957:52).

	EXISTING PRODUCT	NEW PRODUCT
EXISTING MARKET	Penetration Strategies	Product Development Strategies
NEW MARKET	Market Development Strategies	Diversification Strategies

other products. *Market consolidation* is the inverse of market elaboration, namely reducing the number of segments. But this is not just a strategy of failure. Given the common tendency to proliferate market segments, it makes sense for the healthy organization to rationalize them periodically, to purge the excesses.

GEOGRAPHIC EXPANSION STRATEGIES
An important form of market development can be geographic expansion—carrying the existing product offering to new geographical areas, anywhere from the next block to across the world. When this also involves a strategy of geographic rationalization—locating different business functions in different places—it is sometimes referred to as a "global strategy." The IKEA furniture company, for example, designs in Scandinavia, sources in Eastern Europe among other places, and markets in Western Europe and North America.

PRODUCT DEVELOPMENT STRATEGIES
Here we can distinguish a simple *product extension* strategy from a more extensive *product line proliferation* strategy, and their counterparts, *product line rationalization*. Offering new or modified products in the same basic business is another obvious way to elaborate a core business—from cornflakes to bran flakes and rice crispies, eventually offering every permutation and combination of the edible grains. This may amount to differentiation by design, if the products are new and distinctive, or else to no more than increased scope through segmentation, if standardized products are added to the line. Product line proliferation means aiming at comprehensive product segmentation—the complete coverage of a given business. Rationalization means culling products and thinning the line to get rid of overlaps or unprofitable excesses. Again we might expect cycles of product extension and rationalization, at least in businesses (such as cosmetics and textiles) predisposed to proliferation in their product lines.

We shall take this analysis beyond generic business strategies to generic corporate ones in Chapter 13.

by Henry Mintzberg

In the large literature of strategic management that deals with positioning, the concepts come and go at a frantic pace. There is thus a need to pin them down—to develop a framework to see them all, as well as to provide a "glossary" of what they are, even for experts who tend to beaver away in one area or another. There is woefully little synthesis in the world of analysis!

Thus a little model is offered here. It is visual because, in a sense, all of this needs to be seen to be believed. The model is a metaphor of sorts, consisting of a **launching** device, representing an organization, that sends **projectiles**, namely products and services, at a landscape of **targets**, meaning markets, faced with **rivals**, or competition, in the hope of attaining **fit**.

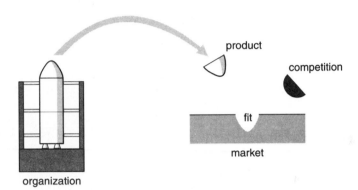

We should add that we have not chosen this metaphor casually: the hunting or military (or any other) implication very much reflects how writers of this school tend to see the world. We use the model to locate, explain, illustrate and especially link the various concepts that make up this school.

The Vehicle (Organization)

The organization is depicted as a launching device which develops, produces and distributes its products and services into markets. To do that, it performs a series of **business functions** that sequence themselves into what Michael Porter (1985) has labelled a **value chain**. As depicted in our figure, design (of product and process) and production are the basic platform, while supply and sourcing (including financing) form one tower, and administration and support (such as public relations and industrial relations) form the other. The launch vehicle has two booster rockets (which fall away during the product's voyage)—the first for sales and marketing, the second for physical distribution.

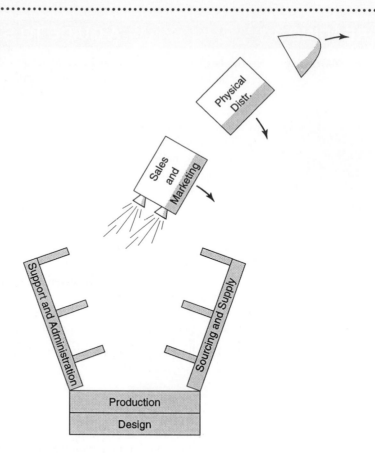

The business functions are executed by using a bundle of **competences** or **capabilities** of various kinds (such as the ability to do research or to produce products inexpensively) and supported by all sorts of **resources** or **assets** (including patents, machinery, and so on). Itami (1987) has referred to key competences as **invisible assets**, while Prahalad and Hamel (1990) have drawn attention to **core competences**, the ones that have developed deep within the organization over its history and explain its **comparative** and **competitive advantages** (as in the example of product venturing in 3M or quality design in Maytag). These can perhaps be distinguished from shallow or common competences, more tangible, codified and so **imitable** in nature (such as selling groceries in the corner shop). These are easily acquired and so easily lost too—more generic than genetic.

These core competences must be sustained and enhanced as the key to the organization's future. In part, this is done by accumulating **experience**, according to a theory popularized by the Boston Consulting Group in the 1970s (see Henderson, 1979): the more the organization produces, the more it engages in **learning**, and so the faster it reduces its costs.

Indeed, currently popular theory has it that the organization should shed as many of its non-core competences as it can, in order to become lean and flexible, and so be able to focus attention on doing what it does best. The rest should be bought from suppliers. Thus, the old strategy of **vertical integration**—encompassing your suppliers **upstream** as well as your intermediate customers **downstream** so that you can control their activities tightly—gets replaced by the new one of **outsourcing**, resulting in the **virtual organization**.

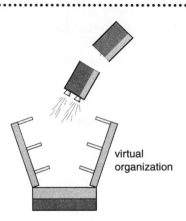

virtual
organization

Competences can be combined in various ways, for example through **joint ventures** or other forms of **alliances** with partners, **licensing** agreements, **franchising** relationships and **long-term contracts**, the extensive combinations of which result in **networks**. This can happen in parallel, as when an electronics firm combines its research capabilities with that of a mechanical products firm to develop new electromagnetic products together. Or it can happen sequentially, as when the design-capability of one firm is combined with the production-capability of another. These result in **synergy**, the $2 + 2 = 5$ effect (Ansof, 1965).

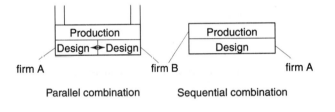

Parallel combination   Sequential combination

The Projectile (Products and Services)

Proceeding along the value chain eventually creates a product (or service) which is launched at a target market. The ways in which this can be done is described, according to the positioning school, by a set of **generic strategies** (Porter, 1980). We can use our metaphor or describe a broad array of these (based on Mintzberg, 1988), according to the nature of the projectile (size, shape, surrounding, etc.) and the sequence of projectives launched (frequency, direction, etc.). First are the generic strategies that characterize the product itself:

Low cost or **price differentiation strategy** (meaning high volume, commodity-type production)

Image differentiation strategy (e.g. nice packaging)

Support differentiation strategy (e.g. provision of after-sales service)

Quality differentiation strategy (e.g. more durable, more reliable, higher performance)

Design differentiation strategy (i.e. different in function)

Then there are the strategies that elaborate or extend the range of products offered:

Penetration strategy (targeting the same product more intensely at the same market, for example, through increased advertising)

Bundling strategy (selling two products together, such as computer software with hardware)

Market development strategy (targeting the same product at new markets)

Product development strategy (targeting new products at the same market)

Diversification strategy (targeting different products at different markets)

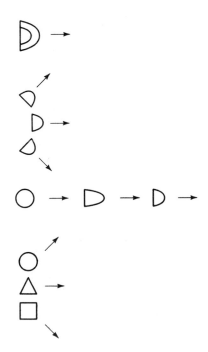

whether the different products are
unrelated or related

and whether this is done by the
acquisition of other companies

or **internal development** of the new
product/market

The Target (Markets)

Again, the metaphor can be used for purposes of illustration, but here we show the generic characteristics of markets (the targeted place), first by size and divisibility, then by location, and finally by stage of evolution or change.

Mass market
(large, homogeneous)

Fragmented market
(many small niches)

Segmented market
(differing demand segments)

Thin market
(few, occasional buyers, as in nuclear reactors)

Geographic markets
(looked at from the perspective of place)

local
regional
global

Emerging market
(young, not yet clearly defined)

Established (mature) market
(clearly defined)

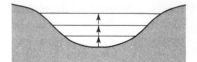

Eroding market

Erupting market
(undergoing destabilizing changes)

INDUSTRY AND GROUP

Where does one market end and another begin? In our discussion, we have spanned the concerns of various disciplines associated with strategy, from those of organization theory (the launching device) to strategic management (the projectile) and then to marketing (the target). Here, in further elaborating the target, or more exactly the nature of the targeted terrain, we move into the realm of economics, with its focus on "industry."

Economists spend a lot of time worrying about the identifying industries (through the definition of SIC codes and the like). However, much of this is arbitrary, since they often no sooner find one than a strategist destroys it (because one job of the strategist is to break up the very industries that economists identify, as in the case of a CNN that took the news program and turned it into a sub-industry, namely a television network, in its own right).

In our terms here, an industry can be defined as a landscape of associated markets, isolated from others by blockages in the terrain. In the literature of economics and strategic positioning, these are known as **barriers to entry**—for example, some kind of special know-how or close ties to the customers that keep potential new competitors out. Michael Porter (1980) elaborated on this with his notion of **strategic group**, really a kind of sub-industry, housing companies that pursue similar strategies (for example, national news magazines, as opposed to magazines targeted at specific audiences, such as amateur photographers). These are distinguished by **barriers to mobility**, in other words, difficulties of shifting into the group even though it is within the overall industry. These concepts map easily into our metaphor, with higher barriers shown for industries and lower ones for strategic groups, as follows:

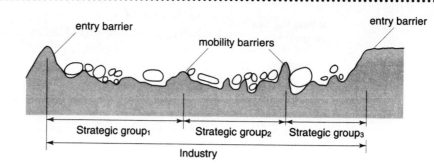

Strategic group₁ — Strategic group₂ — Strategic group₃

Industry

The Fit (Strategic Positions)

When products and markets (projectiles and targets) come together, we reach the central concept of strategic management, namely **fit**, or the strategic position itself—how the product sits in the market. Fit is logically discussed, first in terms of the match between the breadth of the products offered and markets served (which Porter calls **scope**). After this, we shall turn to the quality of the fit and ways to improve it.

Commodity strategy targets a (perceived) mass market with a single, standardized product

Segmentation strategy targets a (perceived) segmented market with a range of products, geared to each of the different segments

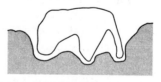

Niche strategy targets a small isolated market segment with a sharply delineated product

Customization strategy (the ultimate in both niching and segmentation) designs or tailors each specific product to one particular customer need (such as the architecturally designed home)

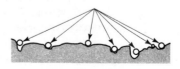

Once fit, or scope, is established, then attention turns to its strength, namely how secure it is—its durability, or **sustainability**. Here the concepts of the positioning school are less developed, so we use our metaphor to introduce some new ones that might prove useful.

First of all, we identify **natural fit**—where the product and market fit each other quite naturally, whether it was the product that created the market or the market that encouraged the development of the product. Natural fit is inherently sustainable (for example, because there is usually intrinsic customer loyalty, perhaps secured by high switching costs).

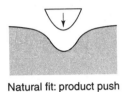

Natural fit: product push

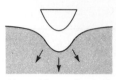

Natural fit: market pull

This can be distinguished from **forced fit**, as well as **vulnerable fit**, which is weak and so easily dislodged, whether by attack from competitors or loss of interest from customers.

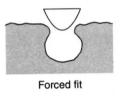

Forced fit

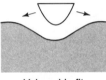

Vulnerable fit

When fit is not perfect (as is always true in an imperfect world), and so not easily sustainable, attention has to be given to what can be called **reinforcing mechanisms**, to improve it, or **isolating mechanisms**, to protect it. Inspired by the metaphor itself, we suggest three types of these:

Burrowing strategy
(driving into the market deeper, for example by using advertising to strengthen brand loyalty—but this could prove costly)

Packing strategy
(tightening the fit by adding supporting elements, such as strong after-sales services, or the use of supporting brands—but the seller can get stuck too)

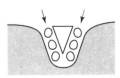

Fortifying strategy
(building up barriers or **shelters** around the fit, such as seeking tariff or patent protection, or creating long-term contracts with customers—but these can topple, or else, in fact, blind the seller to changes occurring elsewhere)

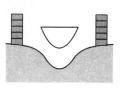

There can also be a **learning strategy** to improve fit through adaptability, for example, by riding the **experience curve** to take advantage of the steady stream of learning that comes from producing more and more of the product, or simply by coming to know better the needs of the customers, or by taking advantage of the **complementarities** that come from different parts of a strategy that reinforce each other, such as franchising and mass preparation in fast-food retailing).

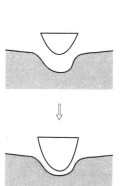

Of course, if there can be natural fit and forced fit and vulnerable fit, then there can also be **misfit**. This concept has not been much developed in the literature, but we can at least offer a few ideas here:

Capacity misfit
(what is offered exceeds what the market can take)

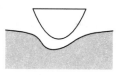

Competence misfit
(the competences of the producer do not match the needs of the market)

Design misfit
(the design is wrong for the market)

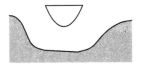

Sunk misfit
(being stuck in a market due to **exit** barriers, as in **sunk costs** such as dedicated machinery that cannot be used elsewhere)

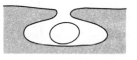

Myopic misfit
(the producer cannot see the market—perhaps because of too long concentration on other markets)

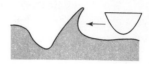

Location misfit
(the producer is in the wrong place, and cannot reach the market—perhaps because some barrier is too high)

Rivalry (Competition)

So far, almost all these relationships have been between a single seller and one or more target markets. But sellers are no more found alone than are buyers. There is **rivalry** in markets, consisting of **competitors**—capable of doing better or doing differently. So we return to economics to describe various competitive situations.

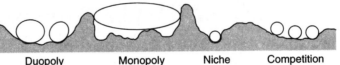

Duopoly   Monopoly   Niche   Competition

Market Leader (or **dominant firm**)

Stable Competition

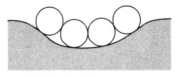

Multipoint Competition
(ability to take action in one market to influence competitor's actions in another)

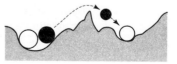

Unstable Competition
(in a mature market)

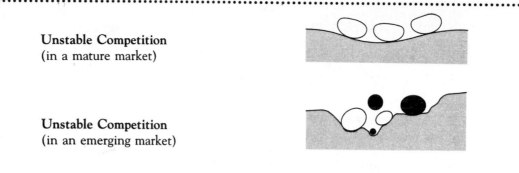

Unstable Competition
(in an emerging market)

CONTESTABILITY

Obviously, markets are **contestable**. New competitors can seek to drive themselves in. Here we draw especially on the literature of military strategy, adapted to business by such writers as Quinn (1980) and Porter (1980).

    First movers seek to position themselves in new markets to keep rivals out. But **later entrants** (including **second movers**) come along and seek a share, if not to displace their

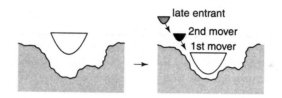

rivals altogether. (**Strategic window** refers to the period of opportunity when an initial or later move becomes possible, for example, because the rival is having trouble, such as a strike in the factory, or because customers are suddenly vulnerable to a brand change). Later entrants use various military-type strategies:

Frontal attack
(by the **concentration of forces**, e.g. cost-cutting)

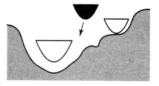

Lateral (or **indirect** or **flanking**) **attack**, perhaps by

—undermining (e.g. taking away the least loyal customers through lower prices)

—attacking a supporting brand (to dislodge the main one)

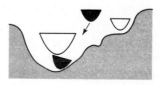

—attacking fortifications, through a **battering strategy** (e.g. lobbying for the elimination of tariff barriers)

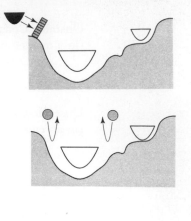

Guerrilla attack (series of small "hit and run" attacks, such as sudden moves of deep discounting)

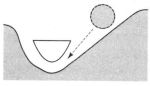

Market signalling by feint (giving the impression of doing something, such as pretending to expand the plant to scare off a potential competitor)

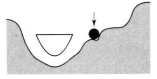

Later entrants may also seek to carve out small territories through niche strategies (sometimes called "picking up the crumbs").

Finally, rivals may reach an accord with the existing players so that all settle down to a **collaborative strategy**, perhaps in a cozy price fixing or market allocating **cartel**.

The truly creative strategist, however, shuns all of these categories, or at least recombines them in innovative ways, to develop a **novel strategy**, for which there is no diagram, since no one can tell what it might look like!

STRATEGY FORMATION

The readings of the last two chapters described how strategies are supposed to be made and thereby illustrate the *prescriptive* side of the field. This chapter presents readings that describe how strategies really do seem to be made, the *descriptive* side. We title this chapter "Strategy Formation" to emphasize the point introduced in Chapter 1 that strategies can *form* implicitly as well as be *formulated* explicitly.

The preceding chapters may seem to deal with an unreachable utopia, this one with an imperfect reality. But there may be a better conclusion: that *prescription* offers useful guidelines for thinking about ends and how to order physical resources efficiently to achieve them, while *description* provides a useful frame of reference for considering how this must be related to real-world patterns of behavior in organizations. Another way to say this is that while the analytical tools and models prescribed earlier are vital to thinking about strategy intelligently, they must also be rooted in a genuine understanding of the realities of organizations. Unfortunately, management writers, especially in traditional strategy textbooks, have often been quick to prescribe without offering enough appreciation of why managers and organizations act in the ways they do.

Brian Quinn and John Voyer (of the University of Southern Maine) open with a sharp focus on how managers really do seem to behave when they create strategy. This reading is drawn from Quinn's book *Strategies for Change: Logical Incrementalism,* and it develops a particular view of the strategy-making process based on intensive interviews in some of America's and Europe's best-known corporations. Planning does not capture the essence of strategy formation, according to Quinn and Voyer, although it does play an important role in developing new data and in confirming strategies derived in other ways. The traditional view of incrementalism does not fit observed behavioral patterns either. The processes may seem randomly incremental on the surface, but a powerful logic underlies them. And, unlike the other incremental processes, these are not so much *reactive* as subtly *proactive*. Executives use incremental approaches to deal simultaneously with the informational, motivational, and political aspects of creating a strategy.

Above all, Quinn and Voyer depict strategy formation as a managed interactive *learning* process in which the chief strategist gradually works out strategy in his or her own mind and orchestrates the organization's acceptance of it. In emphasizing the role of a central strategist—or small groups managing "subsystems" of strategy—Quinn and Voyer often seem close to Andrews' views. But the two differ markedly in other important respects. In their emphasis on the political and motivational dimensions of strategy, they may be closer to Wrapp, whose managers "don't make policy decisions." In fact, Quinn and Voyer attempt to integrate their views with the traditional one, noting that while the strategies themselves "emerge" from an incremental process, they have many of the characteristics of the highly deliberate ones of Andrews' strategists. This reading ends with practical advice on how to manage strategy making as an incremental process.

The following reading by Mintzberg complements the first one. Called "Crafting Strategy," it shows how managers mold strategies the way craftsmen mold their clay. This reading also builds on Mintzberg's reading of Chapter 1 on the different forms of strategy, developing further the concept of emergent strategy.

As you will see, the two authors of this book share a basic philosophy about how organizations must go about the difficult process of setting basic direction in a complex world. They also share a basic belief in the key role of the actual strategy-making process in organizations. Hence the title of the book, *Readings in the Strategy Process*, and the particular importance of this chapter in it.

In a chapter that challenges many of the accepted notions about how strategy should be made, the next reading may be the most upsetting of all. In it Richard Pascale, a well-known consultant, writer, and lecturer, challenges head-on not only the whole approach to strategy analysis (as represented in the last chapter), expecially as practiced by the Boston Consulting Group (one of the better-known "strategy boutiques" whose ideas will be discussed in Chapter 10), but also the very concept of strategy formulation itself.

As his point of departure, Pascale describes a BCG study carried out for the British government to explain how manufacturers in that country lost the American motorcycle market to the Japanese, and to the Honda Company in particular. The analysis seems impeccable and eminently logical: the Japanese were simply more clever, by thinking through a brilliant strategy before they acted. But then Pascale flew to Japan and interviewed those clever executives who pulled off this coup. We shall save the story for Pascale, who tells it with a great deal of color, except to note here its basic message: an openness to learning and a fierce commitment to an organization and its markets may count for more in strategy making than all the brilliant analysis one can imagine. (Ask yourself while reading these accounts how the strategic behavior of the British motorcycle manufacturers who received the BCG report might have differed if they had instead received Pascale's second story.) Pascale in effect takes the arguments for incrementalism and strategy making as a crafting and learning process to their natural conclusions (or one of them, at least).

No one who reads Pascale's account can ever feel quite so smug about rational strategy analysis again. We include this reading, however, not to encourage rejection of that type of analysis or the very solid thinking that has gone into the works of Porter, Ansoff, and others. Rather, we wish to balance the message conveyed in so much of the strategy literature with the practical lessons from the field. The point is that successful strategies can no more rely exclusively on such analysis than they can do without it. Effective strategy formation, one must conclude from all these readings, is a sometimes deceptive and multifaceted affair, its complexity never to be underestimated.

We have mentioned the complementarity of the Quinn and Mintzberg views of strategy making. But there is one difference that is worth addressing. While both view the process as one of evolution and learning, Quinn tends to place greater emphasis on the role of the chief executive, and the senior management team in general, as central strategist, while Mintzberg tends to place a little more emphasis on others who can feed strategy up the hierarchy, especially in his discussion of a "grass-roots" approach to the process. In effect, organizations may have senior managers sending their strategic visions down the hierarchy, while creative people below may be sending strategic initiatives back up.

Effective organizations seem to do both, but that raises a major problem in the strategy process: the middle managers may get caught in the middle, between these two.

How can one reconcile the two opposing pressures? In the Sayles reading of Chapter 8, we shall return to this important issue.

▼ READING 5.1 LOGICAL INCREMENTALISM: MANAGING STRATEGY FORMATION*

*by James Brian Quinn
and John Voyer*

The Logic of Logical Incrementalism

Strategy change processes in well-managed major organizations rarely resemble the rational-analytical systems touted in the literature. Instead, strategic change processes are typically fragmented, evolutionary, and intuitive. Real strategy *evolves* as internal decisions and external events flow together to create a new, widely shared consensus for action.

THE FORMAL SYSTEMS PLANNING APPROACH

There is a strong literature stating which factors *should* be included in a systematically planned strategy. This systems-planning approach focuses on quantitative factors, and underemphasizes qualitative, organizational, and power factors. Systems planning *can* make a contribution, but it should be just one building block in the continuous stream of events that creates organizational strategy.

THE POWER-BEHAVIORAL APPROACH

Another body of literature has enhanced our understanding of *multiple goal structures*, the *politics* of strategic decisions, *bargaining* and *negotiation* processes, *satisficing* in decision making, the role of *coalitions*, and the practice of *"muddling"* in public sector management. The shortcomings of this body of literature are that it has typically been far-removed from strategy making, it has ignored the contributions of useful analytical approaches, and it has offered few practical recommendations for the strategist.

SUMMARY FINDINGS FROM STUDY OF ACTUAL CHANGE PROCESSES

Recognizing the strengths and weaknesses of each of these approaches, the change processes in ten major organizations were documented. Several important findings emerged from these investigations.

  Neither approach above adequately describes strategy processes.

---

* Originally published in the collegiate edition of *The Strategy Process*, Prentice Hall, 1994. Based on James Brian Quinn, "Strategic Change: Logical Incrementalism," *Sloan Management Review*, Fall 1978, pp. 1–21, and James Brian Quinn, "Managing Strategies Incrementally," *Omega: The International Journal of Management Science*, 1982, drawn from his book *Strategies for Change: Logical Incrementalism* (Irwin, 1980).

▼ Effective strategies tend to emerge incrementally and opportunistically, as subsystems of organizational activity (e.g., acquisitions, divestitures, major reorganizations, even formal plans) are blended into a coherent pattern.

▼ The logic behind this process is so powerful that it may be the best approach to recommend for strategy formation in large companies.

▼ Because of cognitive and process limits, this approach must be managed and linked together in a way best described as "logical incrementalism."

▼ Such incrementalism is not "muddling." It is a purposeful, effective, active management technique for improving and integrating *both* the analytical and behavioral aspects of strategy formation.

CRITICAL STRATEGIC ISSUES

Though "hard data" decisions dominate the literature, there are various "soft" kinds of changes that affect strategy:

▼ The design of an organization's structure
▼ The characteristic management style in the firm
▼ A firm's external (especially government) relations
▼ Acquisitions, divestitures, or divisional control issues
▼ A firm's international posture and relationships
▼ An organization's innovative capabilities
▼ The effects of an organization's growth on the motivation of its personnel
▼ Value and expectation changes, and their effects on worker and professional relationships in the organization
▼ Technological changes that affect the organization.

Top executives made several important points about these kinds of changes. Few of these issues lend themselves to quantitative modeling or financial analysis. Most firms use different subsystems to handle different types of strategic changes, yet the subsystems were similar across firms. Lastly, no single formal analytical process could handle all strategic variables simultaneously using a planning approach.

PRECIPITATING EVENTS AND INCREMENTAL LOGIC

Executives reported that various events often resulted in interim decisions that shaped the company's future strategy. This was evident in the decisions forced on General Motors by the 1973–74 oil crisis, in the shift in posture pressed upon Exxon by the Prince William Sound oil spill, or in the dramatic opportunities allowed for Haloid Corporation and Pilkington Brothers by the unexpected inventions of xerography and float glass. No organization—no matter how brilliant, rational, or imaginative—could possibly have foreseen the timing, severity, or even the nature of all such precipitating events.

Recognizing this, top executives tried to respond incrementally. They kept early commitments broadly formative, tentative, and subject to later review. Future implications were too hard to understand, so parties wanted to test assumptions and have an opportunity to learn. Also, top executives were sensitive to social and political structures in the organization; they tried to handle things in a way that would make the change process a good one.

THE DIVERSIFICATION SUBSYSTEM

Strategies for diversification provide excellent examples of the value of proceeding incrementally. Incremental processes aid both the formal aspects of diversification (price and strategic fit, for example), and the psychological and political aspects. Most important

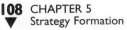

among the latter are generating a genuine, top-level psychological commitment to diversification, consciously preparing the firm to move opportunistically, building a "comfort factor" for risk taking, and developing a new ethos based on the success of new divisions.

THE MAJOR REORGANIZATION SUBSYSTEM

Large-scale organizational moves may have negative effects on organizational politics and social structure. Logical incrementalism makes it easier to avoid those negative effects. As the organization proceeds incrementally, it can assess the new roles, capabilities, and individual reactions of those involved in the restructuring. It allows new people to be trained and tested, perhaps for extended periods. Logical incrementalism allows organizational actors to modify the idea behind the reorganization as more is learned. It also gives executives the luxury of making final commitments as late as possible. Executives may move opportunistically, step-by-step, selectively moving people as developments warrant (events seldom come together at one convenient time). They may also articulate the broad organizational concept in detail only when the last pieces fit together. Lastly, logical incrementalism works well in large-scale reorganization because it allows for testing, flexibility, and feedback.

FORMAL PLANNING IN CORPORATE STRATEGY

Formal planning techniques do serve some essential functions. They discipline managers to look ahead, and to express goals and resource allocations. Long-term planning encourages longer time horizons, and eases the evaluation of short-term plans. Long-term plans create a psychological backdrop and an information framework about the future against which managers can calibrate short-term or interim decisions. Lastly, "special studies," like the white papers used at Pillsbury to inform the chicken-business divestiture decision, have a large effect at key junctures for specific decisions.

Planning may make incrementalism standard organizational practice, for two reasons. First, most planning is "bottom up," and the people at the bottom have an interest in their existing products and processes. Second, executives want most plans to be "living" or "ever green," intended to be only frameworks, providing guidance and consistency for incremental decisions. To do otherwise would be to deny that further information could have value. Thus, properly used formal planning can be part of incremental logic.

TOTAL POSTURE PLANNING

Occasionally, managements did attempt very broad assessments of their companies' total posture. But these major product thrusts were usually unsuccessful. Actual strategies *evolved*, as each company overextended, consolidated, made errors, and rebalanced various thrusts over time. The executives thought that this was both logical and expected.

LOGICAL INCREMENTALISM

Strategic decisions cannot be aggregated into a single decision matrix, with factors treated simultaneously to achieve an optimum solution. There are cognitive limits, but also "process limits"—timing and sequencing requirements, the needs to create awareness, to build comfort levels, to develop consensus, to select and train people, and so forth.

A STRATEGY EMERGES

Successful executives connect and sequentially arrange a series of strategic processes and decisions over a period of years. They attempt to build a resource base and posture that are strong enough to withstand all but the most devastating events. They constantly reconfigure corporate structure and strategy as new information suggests better—but never perfect—alignments. The process is dynamic, with no definite beginning or end.

CONCLUSIONS

Strategy deals with the unknowable, not the uncertain. It involves so many forces, most of which have great strength and the power to combine, that one cannot, in a probabilistic sense, predict events. Therefore, logic dictates that one proceed flexibly and experimentally from broad ideas toward specific commitments. Making the latter concrete as late as possible narrows the bands of uncertainty, and allows the firm to benefit from the best available information. This is the process of "logical incrementalism." It is not "muddling." Logical incrementalism is conscious, purposeful, active, good management. It allows executives to blend analysis, organizational politics, and individual needs into a cohesive new direction.

Managing Incrementally

How can one actively manage the logical incremental process? The study discussed here shows that executives tend to use similar incremental processes as they manage complex strategy shifts.

BEING AHEAD OF THE FORMAL INFORMATION SYSTEM
The earliest signals for strategy change rarely come from formal company systems. Using multiple internal and external sources, managers "sense" the need for change before the formal systems do. T. Vincent Learson at IBM drove the company to develop the 360 series of computers based on his feeling that, despite its current success, IBM was heading toward market confusion. IBM's formal intelligence system did not pick up any market signals until three years after Learson launched the development process.

BUILDING ORGANIZATIONAL AWARENESS
This is essential when key players lack information or psychological stimulation to change. At early stages, management processes are broad, tentative, formative, information-seeking, and purposely avoid irreversible commitments. They also try to avoid provoking potential opponents of an idea.

BUILDING CREDIBILITY/CHANGING SYMBOLS
Symbols may help managers signal to the organization that certain types of changes are coming, even when specific solutions are not yet in hand. Highly visible symbolic actions can communicate effectively to large numbers of people. Grapevines can amplify signals of pending change. Symbolic moves often verify the intention of a new strategy, or give it credibility in its early stages. Without such actions, people may interpret even forceful verbiage as mere rhetoric and delay their commitment to new strategic ideas.

LEGITIMIZING NEW VIEWPOINTS
Planned delays allow the organization to debate and discuss threatening issues, work out implications of new solutions, or gain an improved information base. Sometimes, strategic ideas that are initially resisted can gain acceptance and commitment simply by the passage of time and open discussion of new information. Many top executives, planners and change agents consciously arrange such "gestation periods." For example, William Spoor at

Pillsbury allowed more than a year of discussion and information-gathering before the company decided to divest its chicken business.

TACTICAL SHIFTS AND PARTIAL SOLUTIONS

These are typical steps in developing a new strategic posture, especially when early problem resolutions need to be partial, tentative or experimental. Tactical adjustments, or a series of small programs, typically encounter little opposition, while a broad strategic change could encounter much opposition. These approaches allow the continuation of ongoing strengths while shifting momentum at the margin. Experimentation can occur with minimized risk, leading to many different ways to succeed.

As events unfurl, the solutions to several problems, which may initially have seemed unrelated, tend to flow together into a new combination. When possible, strategic logic (risk minimization) dictates starting broad initiatives that can be flexibly guided in any of several possible desirable directions.

BROADENING POLITICAL SUPPORT

This is an essential and consciously-active step in major strategy changes. Committees, task forces or retreats tend to be favored mechanisms. By selecting such groups' chairpersons, membership, timing, and agenda the guiding executives can largely influence and predict a desired outcome, yet nudge other executives toward a consensus. Interactive consensus building also improves the quality of decisions, and encourages positive and innovative help when things go wrong.

OVERCOMING OPPOSITION

Unnecessary alienation of managers from an earlier era in the organization's history should be avoided; their talents may be needed. But overcoming opposition is usually necessary. Preferred methods are persuasion, co-optation, neutralization, or moving through zones of indifference (i.e., pushing those portions of a project that are non-controversial to most of the interested parties). To be sure, successful executives honor and even stimulate legitimate differences. Opponents sometimes thoughtfully shape new strategies into more effective directions; sometimes they even change their views. Occasionally, though, strong-minded executives may need to be moved to less-influential positions, or be stimulated to leave.

CONSCIOUSLY STRUCTURED FLEXIBILITY

Flexibility is essential in dealing with the many "unknowables" in the environment. Successful organizations actively create flexibility. This requires active horizon scanning, creating resource buffers, developing and positioning champions, and shortening decision lines. These are the keys to *real* contingency planning, not the usual pre-capsuled (and shelved) programs designed to respond to stimuli that never occur quite as expected.

TRIAL BALLOONS AND SYSTEMATIC WAITING

Strategists may have to wait patiently for the proper option to appear or precipitating event to occur. For example, although he wanted to divest Pillsbury's chicken business, William Spoor waited until his investment bankers found a buyer at a good price. Executives may also consciously launch trial ideas, like Spoor's "Super Box" at Pillsbury, to attract options and concrete proposals. Without making a commitment to any specific solution, the executive mobilizes the organization's creative abilities.

CREATING POCKETS OF COMMITMENT

Executives often need this tactic when they are trying to get organizations to adopt entirely new strategic directions. Small projects, deep within the organization, are used to test options, create skills, or build commitments for several possible options. The executive provides broad goals, proper climate, and flexible resource support, without public commitment. This avoids attention on, and identification with, any project. Yet executives can stimulate the good options, make life harder for the poorer options, or even kill the weakest ones.

CRYSTALLIZING THE FOCUS

At some point, this becomes vital. Early commitments are necessarily vague, but once executives develop information or consensus on desirable ways to proceed, they may use their prestige or power to push or crystallize a particular formulation. This should not be done too early, as it might inadvertently centralize the organization or preempt interesting options. Focusing too early might also provide a common target for otherwise fragmented opposition, or cause the organization to undertake undesirable actions just to carry out a stated commitment. When to crystallize viewpoints and when to maintain open options is a true art of strategic management.

FORMALIZING COMMITMENT

This is the final step in the logical incremental strategy formation process. It usually occurs after general acceptance exists, and when the timing is right. Typically, the decision is announced publicly, programs and budgets are formed, and control and reward systems are aligned to reflect intended strategic emphases.

CONTINUING THE DYNAMICS AND MUTATING THE CONSENSUS

Advocates of the "new" strategy can become as strong a source of inflexible resistance to new ideas as were the advocates of the "old" strategy. Effective strategic managers immediately introduce new ideas and stimuli at the top, to maintain the adaptability of the strategic thrusts they have just solidified. This is a most difficult, but essential, psychological task.

NOT A LINEAR PROCESS

While generation of a strategy generally flows along the sequence presented above, the stages are usually not ordered or discrete. The process is more like fermentation in biochemistry, instead of being like an industrial assembly line. Segments of major strategies are likely to be at different stages of development. They are usually integrated in the minds of top executives, each of whom may nevertheless see things differently. Lastly, the process is so continuous that it may be hard to discern the particular point in time when specific clear-cut decisions are made.

An important point to remember is that the validity of a strategy lies not in its pristine clarity or rigorously maintained structure. Its value lies in its capacity to capture the initiative, to deal with unknowable events, and to redeploy and concentrate resources as new opportunities and thrusts emerge. This allows the organization to use resources most effectively toward selected goals.

INTEGRATING THE STRATEGY

The process described above may be incremental, but it is not piecemeal. Effective executives constantly reassess the total organization, its capacities, and its needs as related to the surrounding environment.

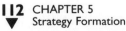

CONCENTRATING ON A FEW KEY THRUSTS

Effective strategic managers constantly seek to distill a few (six to ten) "central themes" that draw the firm's actions together. These maintain focus and consistency in the strategy. They make it easier to discuss and monitor intended directions. By contrast, formal models, designed to keep track of divisional progress toward realizing strategy, tend to become bound up in red tape, procedure, and rigid bureaucracy.

COALITION MANAGEMENT

The heart of all controlled strategy development is coalition management. Top managers act at the confluence of pressures from all stakeholders. These stakeholders will form coalitions, so managers must be active in forming their own. People selection and coalition management are the ultimate controls top executives have in guiding and coordinating their companies' strategies.

CONCLUSIONS

Many recent attempts to devise strategy using approaches that emphasize formal planning have failed because of poor implementation. This results from the classic trap of thinking about strategy formulation and implementation as separate and sequential processes. Successful managers who operate logically and actively, in an *incremental* mode, build the seeds of understanding, identity and commitment into the very processes that create their strategies. Strategy "formulation" and strategy "implementation" interact in the organization's continuing stream of events.

▼ READING 5.2   CRAFTING STRATEGY*

by Henry Mintzberg

Imagine someone planning strategy. What likely springs to mind is an image of orderly thinking: a senior manager, or a group of them, sitting in an office formulating courses of action that everyone else will implement on schedule. The keynote is reason—rational control, the systematic analysis of competitors and markets, of company strengths and weaknesses, the combination of these analyses producing clear, explicit, full-blown strategies.

Now imagine someone *crafting* strategy. A wholly different image likely results, as different from planning as craft is from mechanization. Craft evokes traditional skill, dedication, perfection through the mastery of detail. What springs to mind is not so much thinking and reason as involvement, a feeling of intimacy and harmony with the materials at hand, developed through long experience and commitment. Formulation and implementation merge into a fluid process of learning through which creative strategies evolve.

My thesis is simple: the crafting image better captures the process by which effective strategies come to be. The planning image, long popular in the literature, distorts these processes and thereby misguides organizations that embrace it unreservedly.

In developing this thesis, I shall draw on the experiences of a single craftsman, a potter, and compare them with the results of a research project that tracked the strategies of a number of corporations across several decades. Because the two contexts are so obviously different, my metaphor, like my assertion, may seem far-fetched at first. Yet if we think of a craftsman as an organization of one, we can see that he or she must also resolve one of the great challenges the corporate strategist faces: knowing the organization's capabilities well enough

---

* Originally published in the *Harvard Business Review* (July–August 1987) and winner of McKinsey prize for second best article in the *Review* 1987. Copyright © 1987 by the President and Fellows of Harvard College; all rights reserved. Reprinted with deletions by permission of the *Harvard Business Review*.

to think deeply enough about its strategic direction. By considering strategy making from the perspective of one person, free of all the paraphernalia of what has been called the strategy industry, we can learn something about the formation of strategy in the corporation. For much as our potter has to manage her craft, so too managers have to craft their strategy.

At work, the potter sits before a lump of clay on the wheel. Her mind is on the clay, but she is also aware of sitting between her past experiences and her future prospects. She knows exactly what has and has not worked for her in the past. She has an intimate knowledge of her work, her capabilities, and her markets. As a craftsman, she senses rather than analyzes these things; her knowledge is "tacit." All these things are working in her mind as her hands are working the clay. The product that emerges on the wheel is likely to be in the tradition of her past work, but she may break away and embark on a new direction. Even so, the past is no less present, projecting itself into the future.

In my metaphor, managers are craftsmen and strategy is their clay. Like the potter, they sit between the past of corporate capabilities and a future of market opportunities. And if they are truly craftsmen, they bring to their work an equally intimate knowledge of the materials at hand. That is the essence of crafting strategy.

1. Strategies Are Both Plans for the Future and Patterns from the Past

Ask almost anyone what strategy is, and they will define it as a plan of some sort, an explicit guide to future behavior. Then ask them what strategy a competitor or a government or even they themselves have actually pursued. Chances are they will describe consistency in *past* behavior—a pattern in action over time. Strategy, it turns out, is one of those words that people define in one way and often use in another, without realizing the difference.

The reason for this is simple. Strategy's formal definition and its Greek military origins not withstanding, we need the word as much to explain past actions as to describe intended behavior. After all, if strategies can be planned and intended, they can also be pursued and realized (or not realized, as the case may be). And pattern in action, or what we call realized strategy, explains that pursuit. Moreover, just as a plan need not produce a pattern (some strategies that are intended are simply not realized), so too a pattern need not result from a plan. An organization can have a pattern (or realized strategy) without knowing it, let alone making it explicit.

Patterns, like beauty, are in the mind of the beholder, of course. But finding them in organizations is not very difficult. But what about intended strategies, those formal plans and pronouncements we think of when we use the term *strategy*? Ironically, here we run into all kinds of problems. Even with a single craftsman, how can we know what her intended strategies really were? If we could go back, would we find expressions of intention? And if we could, would we be able to trust them? We often fool ourselves, as well as others, by denying our subconscious motives. And remember that intentions are cheap, at least when compared with realizations.

READING THE ORGANIZATION'S MIND

If you believe all this has more to do with the Freudian recesses of a craftsman's mind than with the practical realities of producing automobiles, then think again. For who knows what the intended strategies of an organization really mean, let alone what they are? Can we simply assume in this collective context that the company's intended strategies are represented by its formal plans or by other statements emanating from the executive suite? Might these be just vain hopes or rationalizations or ploys to fool the competition? And even if expressed intentions do exist, to what extent do various people in the organization share them? How do we read the collective mind? Who is the strategist anyway?

The traditional view of strategic management resolves these problems quite simply, by what organizational theorists call attribution. You see it all the time in the business press. When General Motors acts, it's because its CEO has made a strategy. Given realization, there must have been intention, and that is automatically attributed to the chief.

In a short magazine article, this assumption is understandable. Journalists don't have a lot of time to uncover the origins of strategy, and GM is a large, complicated organization. But just consider all the complexity and confusion that gets tucked under this assumption— all the meetings and debates, the many people, the dead ends, the folding and unfolding of ideas. Now imagine trying to build a formal strategy-making system around that assumption. Is it any wonder that formal strategic planning is often such a resounding failure?

To unravel some of the confusion—and move away from the artificial complexity we have piled around the strategy-making process—we need to get back to some basic concepts. The most basic of all is the intimate connection between thought and action. That is the key to craft, and so also to the crafting of strategy.

2. Strategies Need Not Be Deliberate—They Can Also Emerge, More or Less

Virtually everything that has been written about strategy making depicts it as a deliberate process. First we think, then we act. We formulate, then we implement. The progression seems so perfectly sensible. Why would anybody want to proceed differently?

Our potter is in the studio, rolling the clay to make a waferlike sculpture. The clay sticks to the rolling pin, and a round form appears. Why not make a cylindrical vase? One idea leads to another, until a new pattern forms. Action has driven thinking: a strategy has emerged.

Out in the field, a salesman visits a customer. The product isn't quite right, and together they work out some modifications. The salesman returns to his company and puts the changes through; after two or three more rounds, they finally get it right. A new product emerges, which eventually opens up a new market. The company has changed strategic course.

In fact, most salespeople are less fortunate than this one or than our craftsman. In an organization of one, the implementor is the formulator, so innovations can be incorporated into strategy quickly and easily. In a large organization, the innovator may be ten levels removed from the leader who is supposed to dictate strategy and may also have to sell the idea to dozens of peers doing the same job.

Some salespeople, of course, can proceed on their own, modifying products to suit their customers and convincing skunkworks in the factory to produce them. In effect, they pursue their own strategies. Maybe no one else notices or cares. Sometimes, however, their innovations do get noticed, perhaps years later, when the company's prevalent strategies have broken down and its leaders are groping for something new. Then the salesperson's strategy may be allowed to pervade the system, to become organizational.

Is this story farfetched? Certainly not. We've all heard stories like it. But since we tend to see only what we believe, if we believe that strategies have to be planned, we're unlikely to see the real meaning such stories hold.

Consider how the National Film Board of Canada (NFB) came to adopt a feature-film strategy. The NFB is a federal government agency, famous for its creativity and expert in the production of short documentaries. Some years back, it funded a filmmaker on a project that unexpectedly ran long. To distribute his film, the NFB turned to theaters and so inadvertently gained experience in marketing feature-length films. Other filmmakers caught onto the idea, and eventually the NFB found itself pursuing a feature-film strategy—a pattern of producing such films.

My point is simple, deceptively simple: strategies can *form* as well as be *formulated*. A realized strategy can emerge in response to an evolving situation, or it can be brought about deliberately, through a process of formulation followed by implementation. But when these planned intentions do not produce the desired actions, organizations are left with unrealized strategies.

Today we hear a great deal about unrealized strategies, almost always in concert with the claim that implementation has failed. Management has been lax, controls have been loose, people haven't been committed. Excuses abound. At times, indeed, they may be valid. But often these explanations prove too easy. So some people look beyond implementation to formulation. The strategists haven't been smart enough.

While it is certainly true that many intended strategies are ill conceived, I believe that the problem often lies one step beyond, in the distinction we make between formulation and implementation, the common assumption that thought must be independent of and precede action. Sure, people could be smarter—but not only by conceiving more clever strategies. Sometimes they can be smarter by allowing their strategies to develop gradually, through the organization's actions and experiences. Smart strategists appreciate that they cannot always be smart enough to think through everything in advance.

HANDS AND MINDS

No craftsman thinks some days and works others. The craftsman's mind is going constantly, in tandem with her hands. Yet large organizations try to separate the work of minds and hands. In so doing, they often sever the vital feedback linking between the two. The salesperson who finds a customer with an unmet need may possess the most strategic bit of information in the entire organization. But that information is useless if he or she cannot create a strategy in response to it or else convey the information to someone who can—because the channels are blocked or because the formulators have simply finished formulating. The notion that strategy is something that should happen way up there, far removed from the details of running an organization on a daily basis, is one of the great fallacies of conventional strategic management. And it explains a good many of the most dramatic failures in business and public policy today.

Strategies like the NFB's that appear without clear intentions—or in spite of them—can be called emergent. Actions simply converge into patterns. They may become deliberate, of course, if the pattern is recognized and then legitimated by senior management. But that's after the fact.

All this may sound rather strange, I know. Strategies that emerge? Managers who acknowledge strategies already formed? Over the years we have met with a good deal of resistance from people upset by what they perceive to be our passive definition of a word so bound up with proactive behavior and free will. After all, strategy means control—the ancient Greeks used it to describe the art of the army general.

STRATEGIC LEARNING

But we have persisted in this usage for one reason: learning. Purely deliberate strategy precludes learning once the strategy is formulated; emergent strategy fosters it. People take actions one by one and respond to them, so that patterns eventually form.

Our craftsman tries to make a freestanding sculptural form. It doesn't work, so she rounds it a bit here, flattens it a bit there. The result looks better, but still isn't quite right. She makes another and another and another. Eventually, after days or months or years, she finally has what she wants. She is off on a new strategy.

In practice, of course, all strategy making walks on two feet: one deliberate, the other emergent. For just as purely deliberate strategy making precludes learning, so purely emergent strategy making precludes control. Pushed to the limit, neither approach makes much sense. Learning must be coupled with control. That is why we use the word *strategy* for both emergent and deliberate behavior.

Likewise, there is no such thing as a purely deliberate strategy or a purely emergent one. No organization—not even the ones commanded by those ancient Greek generals—knows enough to work everything out in advance, to ignore learning en route. And no one—not even a solitary potter—can be flexible enough to leave everything to happenstance, to give up all control. Craft requires control just as it requires responsiveness to the material at hand. Thus deliberate and emergent strategy form the end points of a continuum along which the strategies that are crafted in the real world may be found. Some strategies may approach either end, but many more fall at intermediate points.

3. Effective Strategies Develop in All Kinds of Strange Ways

Effective strategies can show up in the strangest places and develop through the most unexpected means. There is no one best way to make strategy.

The form for a ceramic cat collapses on the wheel, and our potter sees a bull taking shape. Clay sticks to a rolling pin, and a line of cylinders results. Wafers come into being because of a shortage of clay and limited kiln space while visiting a studio in France. Thus errors become opportunities, and limitations stimulate creativity. The natural propensity to experiment, even boredom, likewise stimulates strategic change.

Organizations that craft their strategies have similar experiences. Recall the National Film Board with its inadvertently long film. Or consider its experiences with experimental films, which made special use of animation and sound. For 20 years, the NFB produced a bare but steady trickle of such films. In fact, every film but one in that trickle was produced by a single person, Norman McLaren, the NFB's most celebrated filmmaker. McLaren pursued a *personal strategy* of experimentation, deliberate for him perhaps (though who can know whether he had the whole stream in mind or simply planned one film at a time?) but not for the organization. Then 20 years later, others followed his lead and the trickle widened, his personal strategy becoming more broadly organizational.

While the NFB may seem like an extreme case, it highlights behavior that can be found, albeit in muted form, in all organizations. Those who doubt this might read Richard Pascale's account of how Honda stumbled into its enormous success in the American motorcycle market [the following article in this book].

GRASS-ROOTS STRATEGY MAKING

These strategies all reflect, in whole or part, what we like to call a grass-roots approach to strategic management. Strategies grow like weeds in a garden. They take root in all kinds of places, wherever people have the capacity to learn (because they are in touch with the situation) and the resources to support that capacity. These strategies become organizational when they become collective, that is, when they proliferate to guide the behavior of the organization at large.

Of course, this view is overstated. But it is no less extreme than the conventional view of strategic management, which might be labeled the hothouse approach. Neither is right. Reality falls between the two. Some of the most effective strategies we uncovered in our research combined deliberation and control with flexibility and organizational learning.

Consider first what we call the *umbrella strategy*. Here senior management sets out broad guidelines (say, to produce only high-margin products at the cutting edge of technology or to favor products using bonding technology) and leaves the specifics (such as what these products will be) to others lower down in the organization. This strategy is not only deliberate (in its guidelines) and emergent (in its specifics), but it is also deliberately emergent, in that the process is consciously managed to allow strategies to emerge en route. IBM used the umbrella strategy in the early 1960s with the impending 360 series, when its senior management approved a set of broad criteria for the design of a family of computers later developed in detail throughout the organization. [See the IBM case in this section.]

Deliberately emergent, too, is what we call the *process strategy*. Here management controls the process of strategy formation—concerning itself with the design of the structure, its staffing, procedures, and so on—while, leaving the actual content to others.

Both process and umbrella strategies seem to be especially prevalent in businesses that require great expertise and creativity—a 3M, a Hewlett-Packard, a National Film Board. Such organizations can be effective only if their implementors are allowed to be formulators, because it is people way down in the hierarchy who are in touch with the situation at hand and have the requisite technical expertise. In a sense, these are organizations peopled with craftsmen, all of whom must be strategists.

4. Strategic Reorientations Happen in Brief, Quantum Leaps

The conventional view of strategic management, especially in the planning literature, claims that change must be continuous: the organization should be adapting all the time. Yet this view proves to be ironic because the very concept of strategy is rooted in stability, not change. As this same literature makes clear, organizations pursue strategies to set direction, to lay out courses of action, and to elicit cooperation from their members around common, established guidelines. By any definition, strategy imposes stability on an organization. No stability means no strategy (no course to the future, no pattern from the past). Indeed, the very fact of having a strategy, and especially of making it explicit (as the conventional literature implores managers to do), creates resistance to strategic change!

What the conventional view fails to come to grips with, then, is how and when to promote change. A fundamental dilemma of strategy making is the need to reconcile the forces for stability and for change—to focus efforts and gain operating efficiencies on the one hand, yet adapt and maintain currency with a changing external environment on the other.

QUANTUM LEAPS

Our own research and that of colleagues suggest that organizations resolve these opposing forces by attending first to one and then to the other. Clear periods of stability and change can usually be distinguished in any organization: while it is true that particular strategies may always be changing marginally, it seems equally true that major shifts in strategic orientation occur only rarely.

In our study of Steinberg, Inc., a large Quebec supermarket chain headquartered in Montreal, we found only two important reorientations in the 60 years from its founding to the mid-1970s: a shift to self-service in 1933 and the introduction of shopping centers and public financing in 1953. At Volkswagenwerk, we saw only one between the late 1940s and the 1970s, the tumultuous shift from the traditional Beetle to the Audi-type design. And at Air Canada, we found none over the airline's first four decades, following its initial positioning.

Our colleagues at McGill, Danny Miller and Peter Friesen (1984), found this pattern of change so common in their studies of large numbers of companies (especially the high-performance ones) that they built a theory around it, which they labeled the quantum theory of strategic change. Their basic point is that organizations adopt two distinctly different modes of behavior at different times.

Most of the time they pursue a given strategic orientation. Change may seem continuous, but it occurs in the context of that orientation (perfecting a given retailing formula, for example) and usually amounts to doing more of the same, perhaps better as well. Most organizations favor these periods of stability because they achieve success not by changing strategies but by exploiting the ones they have. They, like craftsmen, seek continuous improvement by using their distinctive competencies on established courses.

While this goes on, however, the world continues to change, sometimes slowly, occasionally in dramatic shifts. Thus gradually or suddenly, the organization's strategic orientation moves out of sync with its environment. Then what Miller and Friesen call a strategic revolution must take place. That long period of evolutionary change is suddenly punctuated by a brief bout of revolutionary turmoil in which the organization quickly alters many of its established patterns. In effect, it tries to leap to a new stability quickly to reestablish an integrated posture among a new set of strategies, structures, and culture.

But what about all those emergent strategies, growing like weeds around the organization? What the quantum theory suggests is that the really novel ones are generally held in check in some corner of the organization until a strategic revolution becomes necessary. Then, as an alternative to having to develop new strategies from scratch or having to import generic strategies from competitors, the organization can turn to its own emerging patterns to find its new orientation. As the old, established strategy disintegrates, the seeds of the new one begin to spread.

This quantum theory of change seems to apply particularly well to large established, mass-production companies, like a Volkswagenwerk. Because they are especially reliant on standardized procedures, their resistance to strategic reorientation tends to be especially fierce. So we find long periods of stability broken by short disruptive periods of revolutionary change. Strategic reorientations really are cultural revolutions.

In more creative organizations we see a somewhat different pattern of change and stability, one that is more balanced. Companies in the business of producing novel outputs apparently need to run off in all directions from time to time to sustain their creativity. Yet they also need to settle down after such periods to find some order in the resulting chaos—convergence following divergence.

Whether through quantum revolutions or cycles of convergence and divergence, however, organizations seem to need to separate in time the basic forces for change and stability, reconciling them by attending to each in turn. Many strategic failures can be attributed either to mixing the two or to an obsession with one of these forces at the expense of the other.

The problems are evident in the work of many craftsmen. On the one hand, there are those who seize on the perfection of a single theme and never change. Eventually the creativity disappears from their work and the world passes them by—much as it did Volkswagenwerk until the company was shocked into its strategic revolution. And then there are those who are always changing, who flit from one idea to another and never settle down. Because no theme or strategy ever emerges in their work, they cannot exploit or even develop any distinctive competence. And because their work lacks definition, identity crises are likely to develop, with neither the craftsmen nor their clientele knowing what to make of it. Miller and Friesen (1978: 921) found this behavior in conventional business too; they label it "the impulsive firm running blind." How often have we seen it in companies that go on acquisition sprees?

5. To Manage Strategy, Then, Is to Craft Thought and Action, Control and Learning, Stability and Change

The popular view sees the strategist as a planner or as a visionary, someone sitting on a pedestal dictating brilliant strategies for everyone else to implement While recognizing the importance of thinking ahead and especially of the need for creative vision in this pedantic world, I wish to propose an additional view of the strategist—as a pattern recognizer, a learner if you will—who manages a process in which strategies (and visions) can emerge as well as be deliberately conceived. I also wish to redefine that strategist, to extend that someone into the collective entity made up of the many actors whose interplay speaks an organization's mind. This strategist *finds* strategies no less than creates them, often in patterns that form inadvertently in his or her own behavior.

What, then, does it mean to craft strategy? Let us return to the words associated with craft: dedication, experience, involvement with the material, the personal touch, mastery of detail, a sense of harmony and integration. Managers who craft strategy do not spend much time in executive suites reading MIS reports or industry analyses. They are involved, responsive to their materials, learning about their organizations and industries through personal touch. They are also sensitive to experience, recognizing that while individual vision may be important, other factors must help determine strategy as well.

MANAGE STABILITY

Managing strategy is mostly managing stability, not change. Indeed, most of the time senior managers should not be formulating strategy at all; they should be getting on with making their organizations as effective as possible in pursuing the strategies they already have. Like distinguished craftsmen, organizations become distinguished because they master the details.

To manage strategy, then, at least in the first instance, is not so much to promote change as to know *when* to do so. Advocates of strategic planning often urge managers to plan for perpetual instability in the environment (for example, by rolling over five-year plans annually). But this obsession with change is dysfunctional. Organizations that reassess their strategies continuously are like individuals who reassess their jobs or their marriages continuously—in both cases, they will drive themselves crazy or else reduce themselves to inaction. The formal planning process repeats itself so often and so mechanically that it desensitizes the organization to real change, programs it more and more deeply into set patterns, and thereby encourages it to make only minor adaptations.

So-called strategic planning must be recognized for what it is: a means, not to create strategy, but to program a strategy already created—to work out its implications formally. It is essentially analytic in nature, based on decomposition, while strategy creation is essentially a process of synthesis. That is why trying to create strategies through formal planning most often leads to extrapolating existing ones or copying those of competitors.

This is not to say that planners have no role to play in strategy formation. In addition to programming strategies created by other means, they can feed ad hoc analyses into the strategy-making process at the front end to be sure that the hard data are taken into consideration. They can also stimulate others to think strategically. And of course people called planners can be strategists too, so long as they are creative thinkers who are in touch with what is relevant. But that has nothing to do with the technology of formal planning.

DETECT DISCONTINUITY

Environments don't change on any regular or orderly basis. And they seldom undergo continuous dramatic change, claims about our "age of discontinuity" and environmental "turbulence" notwithstanding. (Go tell people who lived through the Great Depression or survivors of the siege of Leningrad during World War II that ours are turbulent times.) Much of the time, change is minor and even temporary and requires no strategic response. Once in a while there is a truly significant discontinuity or, even less often, a gestalt shift in the environment, where everything important seems to change at once. But these events, while critical, are also easy to recognize.

The real challenge in crafting strategy lies in detecting the subtle discontinuities that may undermine a business in the future. And for that, there is no technique, no program, just a sharp mind in touch with the situation. Such discontinuities are unexpected and irregular, essentially unprecedented. They can be dealt with only by minds that are attuned to existing patterns yet able to perceive important breaks in them. Unfortunately, this form of strategic thinking tends to atrophy during the long periods of stability that most organizations experience. So the trick is to manage within a given strategic orientation most of the time yet be able to pick out the occasional discontinuity that really matters. The ability to make that kind of switch in thinking is the essence of strategic management. And it has more to do with vision and involvement than it does with analytic technique.

KNOW THE BUSINESS

Note the kind of knowledge involved in strategic thinking: not intellectual knowledge, not analytical reports or abstracted facts and figures (though these can certainly help), but personal knowledge, intimate understanding, equivalent to the craftsman's feel for the clay. Facts are available to anyone; this kind of knowledge is not. Wisdom is the word that captures it best. But wisdom is a word that has been lost in the bureaucracies we have built for ourselves, systems designed to distance leaders from operating details. Show me managers who think they can rely on formal planning to create their strategies, and I'll show you managers who lack intimate knowledge of their businesses or the creativity to do something with it.

Craftsmen have to train themselves to see, to pick up things other people miss. The same holds true for managers of strategy. It is those with a kind of peripheral vision who are best able to detect and take advantage of events as they unfold.

MANAGE PATTERNS

Whether in an executive suite in Manhattan or a pottery studio in Montreal, a key to managing strategy is the ability to detect emerging patterns and help them take shape. The job of the manager is not just to preconceive specific strategies but also to recognize their emergence elsewhere in the organization and intervene when appropriate.

Like weeds that appear unexpectedly in a garden, some emergent strategies may need to be uprooted immediately. But management cannot be too quick to cut off the unexpected, for tomorrow's vision may grow out of today's aberration. (Europeans, after all, enjoy salads made from the leaves of the dandelion, America's most notorious weed.) Thus some patterns are worth watching until their effects have more clearly manifested themselves. Then those that prove useful can be made deliberate and be incorporated into the formal strategy, even if that means shifting the strategic umbrella to cover them.

To manage in this context, then, is to create the climate within which a wide variety of strategies can grow. In more complex organizations, this may mean building flexible structures, hiring creative people, defining broad umbrella strategies and watching for the patterns that emerge.

RECONCILE CHANGE AND CONTINUITY

Finally, managers considering radical departures need to keep the quantum theory of change in mind. As Ecclesiastes reminds us, there is a time to sow and a time to reap. Some new patterns must be held in check until the organization is ready for a strategic revolution, or at least a period of divergence. Managers who are obsessed with either change or stability are bound eventually to harm their organizations. As pattern recognizer, the manager has to be able to sense when to exploit an established crop of strategies and when to encourage new strains to displace the old.

While strategy is a word that is usually associated with the future, its link to the past is no less central. As Kierkegaard once observed, life is lived forward but understood backward. Managers may have to live strategy in the future, but they must understand it through the past.

Like potters at the wheel, organizations must make sense of the past if they hope to manage the future. Only by coming to understand the patterns that form in their own behavior do they get to know their capabilities and their potential. Thus crafting strategy, like managing craft, requires a natural synthesis of the future, present, and past.

▼ READING 5.3   THE HONDA EFFECT*

by Richard T.
Pascale

At face value, "strategy" is an innocent noun. Webster defines it as the large-scale planning and direction of operations. In the business context, it pertains to a process by which a firm searches and analyzes its environment and resources in order to (1) select opportunities defined in terms of markets to be served and products to serve them and (2) make discrete decisions to invest resources in order to achieve identified objectives. (Bower, 1970: 7–8).

But for a vast and influential population of executives, planners, academics, and consultants, strategy is more than a conventional English noun. It embodies an implicit model of how organizations should be guided and consequently, preconfigures our way of thinking. Strategy formulation (1) is generally assumed to be driven by senior management whom we expect to set strategic direction, (2) has been extensively influenced by empirical models and concepts, and (3) is often associated with a laborious strategic planning process that, in some companies, has produced more paper than insight.

A $500-million-a-year "strategy" industry has emerged in the United States and Europe comprised of management consultants, strategic planning staffs, and business school academics. It caters to the unique emphasis that American and European companies place upon this particular aspect of managing and directing corporations.

Words often derive meaning from their cultural context. *Strategy* is one such word and nowhere is the contrast of meanings more pronounced than between Japan and the United States. The Japanese view the emphasis we place on "strategy" as we might regard their enthusiasm for Kabuki or sumo wrestling. They note our interests not with an intent of acquiring similar ones but for insight into our peculiarities. The Japanese are somewhat distrustful of a single "strategy" for in their view any idea that focuses attention does so at the expense of peripheral vision. They strongly believe that *peripheral vision* is essential to discerning changes in the customer, the technology or competition, and is the key to corporate survival over the long haul. They regard any propensity to be driven by a single-minded strategy as a weakness.

The Japanese have particular discomfort with strategic concepts. While they do not reject ideas such as the experience curve or portfolio theory outright they regard them as a stimulus to perception. They have often ferreted out the "formula" of their concept-driven American competitors and exploited their inflexibility. In musical instruments, for example (a mature industry facing stagnation as birthrates in the United States and Japan declined), Yamaha might have classified its products as "cash cows" and gone on to better things (as its chief U.S. competitor, Baldwin United, had done). Instead, beginning with a negligible share of the U.S. market, Yamaha plowed ahead and destroyed Baldwin's seemingly unchallengeable dominance. YKK's success in zippers against Talon (a Textron division) and Honda's outflanking of Harley-Davidson (a former AMF subsidiary) in the motorcycle field provide parallel illustrations. All three cases involved American conglomerates,

*Excerpted from an article originally entitled "Perspectives on Strategy: The Real Story Behind Honda's Success," *California Management Review* XXVI, no. 3, pp. 47–72. Copyright © 1994 by the Regents of the University of California. Reprinted by permission of the Regents.

wedded to the portfolio concept, that had classified pianos, zippers, and motorcycles as mature businesses to be harvested rather than nourished and defended. Of course, those who developed portfolio theory and other strategic concepts protest that they were never intended to be mindlessly applied in setting strategic direction. But most would also agree that there is a widespread tendency in American corporations to misapply concepts and to otherwise become strategically myopic—ignoring the marketplace, the customer, and the problems of execution. This tendency toward misapplication, being both pervasive and persistent over several decades, is a phenomenon that the literature has largely ignored [for exceptions, see Hayes and Abernathy, 1980:67; Hayes and Garvin, 1982:71]. There is a need to identify explicitly the factors that influence how we conceptualize strategy—and which foster its misuse.

Honda: The Strategy Model

In 1975, Boston Consulting Group (BCG) presented the British government its final report: *Strategy Alternatives for the British Motorcycle Industry*. This 120-page document identified two key factors leading to the British demise in the world's motorcycle industry:

▼ Market share loss and profitability declines
▼ Scale economy disadvantages in technology, distribution, and manufacturing

During the period 1959 to 1973, the British share of the U.S. motorcycle industry had dropped from 49% to 9%. Introducing BCG's recommended strategy (of targeting market segments where sufficient production volumes could be attained to be price competitive) the report states:

> The success of the Japanese manufacturers originated with the growth of their domestic market during the 1950s. As recently as 1960, only 4 percent of Japanese motorcycle production was exported. By this time, however, the Japanese had developed huge production volumes in small motorcycles in their domestic market, and volume-related cost reductions had followed. This resulted in a highly competitive cost position which the Japanese used as a springboard for penetration of world markets with small motorcycles in the early 1960s (BCG, 1975:xiv).

The BCG study was made public by the British government and rapidly disseminated in the United States. It exemplifies the necessary (and, I argue, insufficient) strategist's perspective of:

▼ examining competition primarily from an intercompany perspective,
▼ at a high level of abstraction,
▼ with heavy reliance on macroeconomic concepts (such as the experience curve).

Case writers at Harvard Business School, UCLA, and the University of Virginia quickly condensed the BCG report for classroom use in case discussions. It currently enjoys extensive use in first-term courses in business policy.

Of particular note in the BCG study, and in the subsequent Harvard Business School rendition, is the historical treatment of Honda.

> The mix of competitors in the U.S. motorcycle market underwent a major shift in the 1960s. Motorcycle registrations increased from 575,000 in 1960 to 1,382,000 in 1965. Prior to 1960 the U.S. market was served mainly by Harley-Davidson of U.S.A., BSA, Triumph and Norton of U.K. and Moto-Guzzi of Italy. Harley was the market leader with total 1959 sales of $16.6 million. After the second world war, motorcycles in the U.S.A. attracted a very limited group of people other than police and army personnel who used motorcycles on the job. While most motorcyclists were no doubt decent people, groups of rowdies who went around on motorcycles and called themselves by such names as "Hell's Angels," "Satan's Slaves" gave motorcycling a

bad image. Even leather jackets which were worn by motorcyclists as a protective device acquired an unsavory image. A 1953 movie called "The Wild Ones" starring a 650cc Triumph, a black leather jacket and Marlon Brando gave the rowdy motorcyclists wide media coverage. The stereotype of the motorcyclist was a leather-jacketed, teenage troublemaker.

Honda established an American subsidiary in 1959—American Honda Motor Company. This was in sharp contrast to other foreign producers who relied on distributors. Honda's marketing strategy was described in the 1963 annual report as "With its policy of selling, not primarily to confirmed motorcyclists but rather to members of the general public who had never before given a second thought to a motorcycle. . . ." Honda started its push in the U.S. market with the smallest, lightweight motorcycles. It had a three-speed transmisson, an automatic clutch, five horsepower (the American cycle only had two and a half), an electric starter and step through frame for female riders. And it was easier to handle. The Honda machines sold for under $250 in retail compared with $1,000–$1,500 for the bigger American or British machines. Even at that early date Honda was probably superior to other competitors in productivity.

By June 1960 Honda's Research and Development effort was staffed with 700 designers/engineers. This might be contrasted with 100 engineers/draftsmen employed by . . . (European and American competitors). In 1962 production per man-year was running at 159 units, (a figure not matched by Harley-Davidson until 1974). Honda's net fixed asset investment was $8170 per employee . . . (more than twice its European and American competitors). With 1959 sales of $55 million Honda was already the largest motorcycle producer in the world.

Honda followed a policy of developing the market region by region. They started on the West Coast and moved eastward over a period of four–five years. Honda sold 2,500 machines in the U.S. in 1960. In 1961 they lined up 125 distributors and spent $150,000 on regional advertising. Their advertising was directed to the young families, their advertising theme was "You Meet the Nicest People on a Honda." This was a deliberate attempt to dissociate motorcycles from rowdy, Hell's Angels type people.

Honda's success in creating demand for lightweight motorcycles was phenomenal. American Honda's sales went from $500,000 in 1960 to $77 million in 1965. By 1966 the market share data showed the ascendancy of Japanese producers and their success in selling lightweight motorcycles. [Honda had 63% of the market] . . . Starting from virtually nothing in 1960, the lightweight motorcycles had clearly established their lead (Purkayastha, 1981: 5, 10, 11, 12).

Quoting from the BCG report:

The Japanese motorcycle industry, and in particular Honda, the market leader, present a [consistent] picture. The basic philosophy of the Japanese manufacturers is that high volumes per model provide the potential for high productivity as a result of using capital intensive and highly automated techniques. Their marketing strategies are therefore directed towards developing these high model volumes, hence the careful attention that we have observed them giving to growth and market share.

The overall result of this philosophy over time has been that the Japanese have now developed an entrenched and leading position in terms of technology and production methods. . . . The major factors which appear to account for the Japanese superiority in both these areas are . . . (specialized production systems, balancing engineering and market requirements, and the cost efficiency and reliability of suppliers) (BCG, pp. 59, 40).

As evidence of Honda's strategy of taking position as low cost producer and exploiting economies of scale, other sources cite Honda's construction in 1959 of a plant to manufacture 30,000 motorcycles per month well ahead of existing demand at the time. (Up until then Honda's most popular models sold 2,000–3,000 units per month.) (Sakiya, 1982:119)

The overall picture as depicted by the quotes exemplifies the "strategy model." Honda is portrayed as a firm dedicated to being the low price producer, utilizing its dominant market position in Japan to force entry into the U.S. market, expanding that market by redefining a leisure class ("Nicest People") segment, and exploiting its comparative advantage via aggressive pricing and advertising. Richard Rumelt, writing the teaching note for the UCLA adaptation of the case states: "The fundamental contribution of BCG is not the

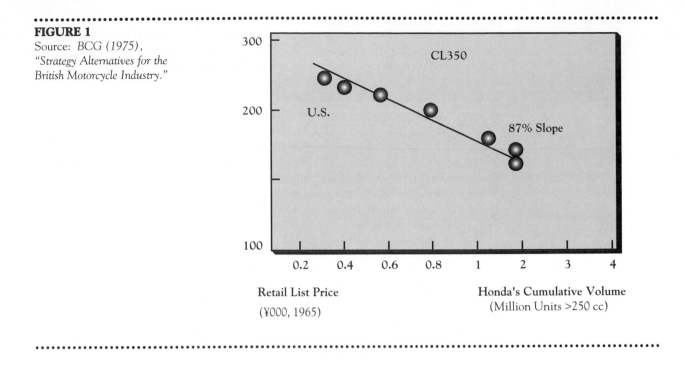

FIGURE 1
Source: BCG (1975),
"Strategy Alternatives for the
British Motorcycle Industry."

CL350

U.S.

87% Slope

300

200

100

0.2   0.4   0.6   0.8   1   2   3   4

Retail List Price
(¥000, 1965)

Honda's Cumulative Volume
(Million Units >250 cc)

experience curve per se but the ever-present assumption that differences in cost (or efficiency) are the fundamental components of strategy." (Rumelt, 1980:2).

The Organizational Process Perspective

On September 10, 1982, the six Japanese executives responsible for Honda's entry into the U.S. motorcycle market in 1959 assembled in Honda's Tokyo headquarters. They had gathered at my request to describe in fine grain detail the sequence of events that had led to Honda's ultimate position of dominance in the U.S. market. All were in their sixties; three were retired. The story that unfolded, greatly abbreviated below, highlights miscalculation, serendipity, and organizational learning—counterpoints to the streamlined "strategy" version related earlier. . . .

Any account of Honda's successes must grasp at the outset the unusual character of its founder, Sochiro Honda, and his partner, Takeo Fujisawa. Honda was an inventive genius with a large ego and mercurial temperament, given to bouts of "philandering" (to use his expression) (Sakiya, 1979). . . .

Postwar Japan was in desperate need of transportation. Motorcycle manufacturers proliferated, producing clip-on engines that converted bicycles into makeshift "mopeds." Honda was among these but it was not until he teamed up with Fujisawa in 1949 that the elements of a successful enterprise began to take shape. Fujisawa provided money as well as financial and marketing strengths. In 1950 their first D-type motorcycle was introduced. They were, at that juncture, participating in a fragmented industry along with 247 other manufacturers. Other than its sturdy frame, this introductory product was unnoteworthy and did not enjoy great commercial success. (Sakiya, 1979, 1982).

Honda embodied a rare combination of inventive ability and ultimate self-confidence. His motivation was not primarily commercial. Rather, the company served as a vehicle to give expression to his inventive abilities. A successful company would provide a resource base to pursue, in Fujisawa's words, his "grandiose dream." Fujisawa continues, "There was no end to his pursuit of technology." (Sakiya, 1982).

Fujisawa, in an effort to save the faltering company, pressed Honda to abandon their noisy two-stroke engine and pursue a four-stroke design. The quieter four-stroke engines were appearing on competitive motorcycles, therefore threatening Honda with extinction. Mr. Honda balked. But a year later, Honda stunned Fujisawa with a breakthrough design that doubled the horsepower of competitive four-stroke engines. With this innovation, the firm was off and putting, and by 1951 demand was brisk. There was no organization, however, and the plant was chaotic (Sakiya, 1982). Strong demand, however, required early investment in a simplified mass production process. As a result, *primarily* due to design advantages, and secondarily to production methods, Honda became one of the four or five industry leaders by 1954 with 15 percent market share (data provided by company). . . .

For Fujisawa, the engine innovation meant increased sales and easier access to financing. For Mr. Honda, the higher horsepower engine opened the possibility of pursuing one of his central ambitions in life—to race his motorcycle and win. . . .

Fujisawa, throughout the fifties, sought to turn Honda's attention from his enthusiasm with racing to the more mundane requirements of running an enterprise. By 1956, as the innovations gained from racing had begun to pay off in vastly more efficient engines, Fujisawa pressed Honda to adapt this technology for a commercial motorcycle (Sakiya, 1979, 1982). Fujisawa had a particular segment in mind. Most motorcyclists in Japan were male and the machines were used primarily as an alternative form of transportation to trains and buses. There were, however, a vast number of small commercial establishments in Japan that still delivered goods and ran errands on bicycles. Trains and buses were inconvenient for these activities. The pursestrings of these small enterprises were controlled by the Japanese wife—who resisted buying conventional motorcycles because they were expensive, dangerous, and hard to handle. Fujisawa challenged Honda: Can you use what you've learned from racing to come up with an inexpensive, safe-looking motorcycle that can be driven with one hand (to facilitate carrying packages).

In 1958, the Honda 50cc Supercub was introduced—with an automatic clutch, three-speed transmission, automatic starter, and the safe, friendly look of a bicycle (without the stigma of the outmoded mopeds). Owing almost entirely to its high horsepower but *lightweight 50cc engine* (not to production efficiencies), it was affordable. Overnight, the firm was overwhelmed with orders. Engulfed by demand, they sought financing to build a new plant with a 30,000 unit per month capacity. "It wasn't a speculative investment," recalls one executive. "We had the proprietary technology, we had the market and the demand was enormous." (The plant was completed in mid-1960.) Prior to its opening, demand was met through makeshift, high cost, company-owned assembly and farmed-out assembly through subcontractors. By the end of 1959, Honda had skyrocketed into first place among Japanese motorcycle manufacturers. Of its total sales that year of 285,000 units, 168,000 were Supercubs.

Fujisawa utilized the Supercub to restructure Honda's channels of distribution. For many years, Honda had rankled under the two-tier distribution system that prevailed in the industry. These problems had been exacerbated by the fact that Honda was a late entry and had been carried as secondary line by distributors whose loyalties lay with their older manufacturers. Further weakening Honda's leverage, all manufacturer sales were on a consignment basis.

Deftly, Fujisawa had characterized the Supercub to Honda's distributors as "something much more like a bicycle than a motorcycle." The traditional channels, to their later regret, agreed. Under amicable terms Fujisawa began selling the Supercub directly to retailers—and primarily through bicycle shops. Since these shops were small and numerous (approximately 12,000 in Japan), sales on consignment were unthinkable. A cash-on-delivery system was installed, giving Honda significantly more leverage over its dealerships than the other motorcycle manufacturers enjoyed.

The stage was now set for exploration of the U.S. market. Mr. Honda's racing conquests in the late 1950s had given substance to his convictions about his abilities. . . .

Two Honda executives—the soon-to-be-named president of American Honda, Kihachiro Kawashima, and his assistant—arrived in the United States in late 1958. Their itinerary: San Francisco, Los Angeles, Dallas, New York, and Columbus. Mr. Kawashima recounts his impressions:

My first reaction after travelling across the United States was: how could we have been so stupid as to start a war with such a vast and wealthy country! My second reaction was discomfort. I spoke poor English. We dropped in on motorcycle dealers who treated us discourteously and in addition, gave the general impression of being motorcycle enthusiasts who, secondarily, were in business. There were only 3,000 motorcycle dealers in the United States at the time and only 1,000 of them were open five days a week. The remainder were open on nights and weekends. Inventory was poor, manufacturers sold motorcycles to dealers on consignment, the retailers provided consumer financing; after-sales service was poor. It was discouraging.

My other impression was that everyone in the United States drove an automobile—making it doubtful that motorcycles could ever do very well in the market. However, with 450,000 motorcycle registrations in the U.S. and 60,000 motorcycles imported from Europe each year it didn't seem unreasonable to shoot for 10 percent of the import market. I returned to Japan with that report.

In truth, we had no strategy other than the idea of seeing if we could sell something in the United States. It was a new frontier, a new challenge and it fit the "success against all odds" culture that Mr. Honda had cultivated. I reported my impressions to Fujisawa—including the seat-of-the-pants target of trying, over several years, to attain a 10 percent share of U.S. imports. He didn't probe that target quantitatively. We did not discuss profits or deadlines for breakeven. Fujisawa told me if anyone could succeed, I could and authorized $1 million for the venture.

The next hurdle was to obtain a currency allocation from the Ministry of Finance. They were extraordinarily skeptical. Toyota had launched the Toyopet in the U.S. in 1958 and had failed miserably. "How could Honda succeed?" they asked. Months went by. We put the project on hold. Suddenly, five months after our application, we were given the go-ahead—but at only a fraction of our expected level of commitment. "You can invest $250,000 in the U.S. market." they said, "but only $110,000 in cash." The remainder of our assets had to be in parts and motorcycle inventory.

We moved into frantic activity as the government, hoping we would give up on the idea, continued to hold us to the July 1959 start-up timetable. Our focus, as mentioned earlier, was to compete with the European exports. We knew our products at the time were good but not far superior. Mr. Honda was especially confident of the 250cc and 305cc machines. The shape of the handlebar on these larger machines looked like the eyebrow of Buddha, which he felt was a strong selling point. Thus, after some discussion and with no compelling criteria for selection, we configured our start-up inventory with 25 percent of each of our four products—the 50cc Supercub and the 125cc, 250cc, and 305cc machines. In dollar value terms, of course, the inventory was heavily weighted toward the larger bikes.

The stringent monetary controls of the Japanese government together with the unfriendly reception we had received during our 1958 visit caused us to start small. We chose Los Angeles where there was a large second and third generation Japanese community, a climate suitable for motorcycle use, and a growing population. We were so strapped for cash that the three of us shared a furnished apartment that rented for $80 per month. Two of us slept on the floor. We obtained a warehouse in a run-down section of the city and waited for the ship to arrive. Not daring to spare our funds for equipment, the three of us stacked the motorcycle crates three high—by hand, swept the floors, and built and maintained the parts bin.

We were entirely in the dark the first year. We were not aware the motorcycle business in the United States occurs during a seasonable April-to-August window—and our timing coincided with the closing of the 1959 season. Our hard-learned experiences with distributorships in Japan convinced us to try to go to the retailers direct. We ran ads in the motorcycle trade magazine for dealers. A few responded. By spring of 1960, we had forty dealers and some of our inventory in their stores—mostly larger bikes. A few of the 250cc and 305cc bikes began to sell. Then disaster struck.

By the first week of April 1960, reports were coming in that our machines were leaking oil and encountering clutch failure. This was our lowest moment. Honda's fragile reputation was being destroyed before it could be established. As it turned out, motorcycles in the United States are driven much farther and much faster than in Japan. We dug deeply into our precious cash reserves to air freight our motorcycles to the Honda testing lab in Japan. Through the dark month of April, Pan Am was the only enterprise in the U.S. that was nice to us. Our testing lab worked twenty-four-hour days bench testing the bikes to try to replicate the failure. Within a month, a redesigned head gasket and clutch spring solved the problem. But in the meantime, events had taken a surprising turn.

Throughout our first eight months, following Mr. Honda's and our own instincts, we had not attempted to move the 50cc Supercubs. While they were a smash success in Japan (and manufacturing couldn't keep up with demand there), they seemed wholly unsuitable for the U.S. market where everything was bigger and more luxurious. As a clincher, we had our sights on the import market—and the Europeans, like the American manufacturers, emphasized the larger machines.

We used the Honda 50s ourselves to ride around Los Angeles on errands. They attracted a lot of attention. One day we had a call from a Sears buyer. While persisting in our refusal to sell through an intermediary, we took note of Sears' interest. But we still hesitated to push the 50cc bikes out of fear they might harm our image in a heavily macho market. But when the larger bikes started breaking, we had no choice. We let the 50cc bikes move. And surprisingly, the retailers who wanted to sell them weren't motorcycle dealers, they were sporting goods stores.

The excitement created by the Honda Supercub began to gain momentum. Under restrictions from the Japanese government, we were still on a cash basis. Working with our initial cash and inventory, we sold machines, reinvested in inventory, and sunk the profits into additional inventory and advertising. Our advertising tried to straddle the market. While retailers continued to inform us that our Supercub customers were normal everyday Americans, we hesitated to target toward this segment out of fear of alienating the high margin end of our business—sold through the traditional motorcycle dealers to a more traditional "black leather jacket" customer.

Honda's phenomenal sales and share gains over the ensuing years have been previously reported. History has it that Honda *"redefined"* the U.S. motorcycle industry. In the view of American Honda's start-up team, this was an innovation they backed into—and reluctantly. It was certainly not the strategy they embarked on in 1959. As late as 1963, Honda was still working with its original Los Angeles advertising agency, its ad campaigns straddling all customers so as not to antagonize one market in pursuit of another.

In the spring of 1963, an undergraduate advertising major at UCLA submitted, in fulfillment of a routine course assignment, an ad campaign for Honda. Its theme: You Meet the Nicest People on a Honda. Encouraged by his instructor, the student passed his work on to a friend at Grey Advertising. Grey had been soliciting the Honda account—which with a $5 million a year budget was becoming an attractive potential client. Grey purchased the student's idea—on a tightly kept nondisclosure basis. Grey attempted to sell the idea to Honda.

Interestingly, the Honda management team, which by 1963 had grown to five Japanese executives, was badly split on this advertising decision. The president and treasurer favored another proposal from another agency. The director of sales, however, felt strongly that the Nicest People campaign was the right one—and his commitment eventually held sway. Thus, in 1963, through an inadvertent sequence of events, Honda came to adopt a strategy that directly identified and targeted that large untapped segment of the marketplace that has since become inseparable from the Honda legend.

The Nicest People campaign drove Honda's sales at an even greater rate. By 1964, nearly one out of every two motorcycles sold was a Honda. As a result of the influx of medium income leisure class consumers, banks and other consumer credit companies began to finance motorcycles—shifting away from dealer credit, which had been the traditional pur-

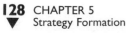

chasing mechanism available. Honda, seizing the opportunity of soaring demand for its products, took a courageous and seemingly risky position. Late in 1964, they announced that thereafter, they would cease to ship on a consignment basis but would require cash on delivery. Honda braced itself for revolt. While nearly every dealer questioned, appealed, or complained, none relinquished his franchise. In one fell swoop, Honda shifted the power relationship from the dealer to the manufacturer. Within three years, this would become the pattern for the industry.

The "Honda Effect"

The preceding account of Honda's inroads in the U.S. motorcycle industry provides more than a second perspective on reality. It focuses our attention on different issues and raises different questions. What factors permitted two men as unlike one another as Honda and Fujisawa to function effectively as a team? What incentives and understandings permitted the Japanese executives at American Honda to respond to the market as it emerged rather than doggedly pursue the 250cc and 305 cc strategy that Mr. Honda favored? What decision process permitted the relatively junior sales director to overturn the bosses' preferences and choose the Nicest People campaign? What values or commitment drove Honda to take the enormous risk of alienating its dealers in 1964 in shifting from a consignment to cash? In hindsight, these pivotal events all seem ho-hum common sense. But each day, as organizations live out their lives without the benefit of hindsight, few choose so well and so consistently.

The juxtaposed perspectives reveal what I shall call the "Honda Effect." Western consultants, academics, and executives express a preference for oversimplifications of reality and cognitively linear explanations of events. To be sure, they have always acknowledged that the "human factor" must be taken into account. But extensive reading of strategy cases at business schools, consultants' reports, strategic planning documents as well as the coverage of the popular press, reveals a widespread tendency to overlook the process through which organizations experiment, adapt, and learn. We tend to impute coherence and purposive rationality to events when the opposite may be closer to the truth. How an organization deals with miscalculation, mistakes, and serendipitous events *outside its field of vision is often crucial to success over time*. It is this realm that requires better understanding and further research if we are to enhance our ability to guide an organization's destiny. . . .

An earlier section has addressed the shortcomings of the narrowly defined macroeconomic strategy model. The Japanese avoid this pitfall by adopting a broader notion of "strategy." In our recent awe of things Japanese, most Americans forget that the original products of the Japanese automotive manufacturers badly missed the mark. Toyota's Toyopet was square, sexless, and mechanically defective. It failed miserably, as did Datsun's first several entries into the U.S. market. More recently, Mazda miscalculated badly with its first rotary engine and nearly went bankrupt. Contrary to myth, the Japanese did not from the onset embark on a strategy to seize the high-quality small-car market. They manufactured what they were accustomed to building in Japan and tried to sell it abroad. Their success, as any Japanese automotive executive will readily agree, did not result from a bold insight by a few big brains at the top. On the contrary, success was achieved by senior managers humble enough not to take their initial strategic positions too seriously. What saved Japan's near-failures was the cumulative impact of "little brains" in the form of salesmen and dealers and production workers, all contributing incrementally to the quality and market position these companies enjoy today. Middle and upper management saw their primary task as guiding and orchestrating this input from below rather than steering the organization from above along a predetermined strategic course.

The Japanese don't use the term "strategy" to describe a crisp business definition or competitive master plan. They think more in terms of "strategic accommodation," or "adaptive persistence," underscoring their belief that corporate direction evolves from an incremental adjustment to unfolding events. Rarely, in their view, does one leader (or a strategic planning group) produce a bold strategy that guides a firm unerringly. Far more frequently, the input is from below. It is this ability of an organization to move information and ideas from the bottom to the top and back again in continuous dialogue that the Japanese value above all things. As this dialogue is pursued, what in hindsight may be "strategy" evolves. In sum, "strategy" is defined as "all the things necessary for the successful functioning of organization as an adaptive mechanism." . . .

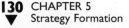

II ORGANIZATION

DEALING WITH STRUCTURE AND SYSTEMS

Chapter 5 has completed Section I, which introduced the concepts related to our central theme, strategy—what it is, how it should and does get made, and the nature of the work of one of its key makers, the general manager. Chapter 6 begins Section II, which deals with another set of concepts that every student of general management must come to understand. We group these under the title Organization because they all pertain to the basic design and running of the organization.

In this chapter we examine the design of organizational *structure* and the development of *systems* for coordination and control. In Chapter 7, we consider *culture,* that ideological glue that holds organizations together, enhancing their ability to pursue strategies on one hand, but sometimes impeding strategic change on the other. And then we turn to the questions of *power*—how it flows within the organization and how the organization uses it in its external environment. Finally, we close this section with a chapter on the styles of managers in making all this happen.

Structure, in our view, no more follows strategy than the left foot follows the right in walking. The two exist *inter*dependently, each influencing the other. There are certainly times when a structure is redesigned to carry out a new strategy. But the choice of any new strategy is likewise influenced by the realities and potentials of the existing structure. Indeed, the classical model of strategy formulation (discussed in Chapter 3) implicitly recognizes this by showing the strengths and weaknesses of the organization as an input to the creation of strategies. Surely these strengths and weaknesses are deeply rooted within the existing structure, indeed often part and parcel of it. Hence, we introduce here structure and the associated administrative systems which make it work as essential factors to consider in the strategy process. Later when we present the various contexts within which organizations function, we shall consider the different ways in which strategy and structure interact.

All of the readings of this chapter reinforce these points. In his article "Strategy and Organization Planning," Jay Galbraith, a former MIT and Wharton Business School professor who worked as an independent management consultant for several years and now teaches at IMD in Lausarne, Switzerland, also views structure broadly as encompassing support systems of various kinds. Building on concepts such as "driving force" and "center of gravity," Galbraith links various strategies (of vertical integration and diversification) to forms of structure, ranging from the functional to the increasingly diversified. Galbraith covers a wide body of important literature in the field and uses visual imagery to make his points. The result is one of the best articles in print on the relationship between the strategy of diversification and the structure of divisionalization.

The second reading, excerpted originally from Mintzberg's book, *The Structuring of Organizations,* comprehensively probes the design of organizational structures, including their formal systems. It seeks to do two things: first to delineate the basic dimensions or organizations and then to combine these to identify various basic types of organizations, called "configurations." The dimensions introduced include mechanisms used to coordinate work in organizations, parameters to consider in designing structures, and situational factors which influence choices among these design parameters. This reading also introduces a somewhat novel diagram to depict organizations, not as the usual organizational chart or cybernetic flow process, but as a visual combination of the critical parts of an organization. This reading then clusters all these dimensions into a set of configurations each introduced briefly here and discussed at length in later chapters. In fact, the choice of the chapters on context — entrepreneurial, mature, professional, innovative, and diversified (leaving aside the international one and that on change) — was really based on five of these types, so that reading the conclusion to this article will help to introduce you to Section III.

There has been a great deal of attention in recent years to new forms of organizing. This has released a colorful new vocabulary — downsizing (or rightsizing!), the virtual corporation, or the hollow corporation, and so forth. Along with it has come a great deal of confusion. Quinn, Anderson, and Finkelstein, all of the Amos Tuck School at Dartmouth, in the third reading of this chapter (based on an unpublished monograph) sort out much of the confusion and clarify what really seems to be going on. They explain the "network organization" and delineate five new forms to deal with what their colleague Richard D'Aveni has termed "hypercompetition." These are called the infinitely flat organization, the inverted organization, the spider's web organization, the cluster organization, and the starburst organization and are very different from the matrix, extended hierarchical, or cross-functional team organizations often called "networks." The authors' major contributions are to provide insights about the differences among the emerging organization forms and to explain how to organize in terms of desired intellectual or knowledge flows instead of authority flows. They provide guidelines for the emerging "knowledge industries", which provide about 80 percent of all employment today and will account for even more in the future.

Other forms of organization, hardly new but having risen to great prominence recently, are "alliances" among various companies (which may or may not be linked by ownership ties). These have proved especially powerful for competing across borders or in serving the varied demands of markets in very different parts of the world. Our final reading of this chapter, called "Collaborating to Compete," reviews such alliances. The article is adapted from the recent book of that title by two McKinsey & Co. consultants, Joel Bleeke and David Ernst, who sought to capture the company's experiences with such activities. The old style of competition is out, they argue, replaced by a more collaborative style. And to succeed at it, companies must arbitrage their skills, market access, and capital, and they must see this as a flexible sequence of actions.

by Jay R. Galbraith

. . . There has been a great deal of progress in the knowledge base supporting organization planning in the last twenty-five years. Modern research on corporate structures probably started with Chandler's *Strategy and Structure*. Subsequent research has been aimed at expanding the number of attributes of an organization beyond that of just structure. I have used the model shown in Figure 1 to indicate that organization consists of structure, processes that cut the structural lines like budgeting, planning, teams, and so on, reward systems like promotions and compensation, and finally people practices like selection and development (Galbraith, 1977). The trend. . . is to expand to more attributes like the 7-Ss (Waterman, 1980) comprising structure, strategy, systems, skills, style, staff, and superordinate goals and to "softer" attributes like culture.

All of these models are intended to convey the same ideas. First, organization is more than just structure. And, second, all of the elements must "fit" to be in "harmony" with each other. The effective organization is one that has blended its structure, management practices, rewards, and people into a package that in turn fits with its strategy. However, strategies change and therefore the organization must change.

The research of the past few years is creating some evidence by which organizations and strategies are matched. Some of the strategies are proving more successful than others. One of the explanations is organizational in nature. Also the evidence shows that for any strategy, the high performers are those who have achieved a fit between their strategy and their organization.

These findings give organization planning a base from which to work. The organization planner should become a member of the strategic team in order to guide management to choose the appropriate strategies for which the organization is developed or to choose the appropriate organization for the new strategy.

In the sections that follow, the strategic changes that are made by organizations are described. Then the strategy and organization evidence is presented. Finally the data on economic performance and fit is discussed.

---

*Originally published in *Human Resource Management* (Spring-Summer 1983). Copyright © 1983 John Wiley & Sons, Inc. Reprinted with deletions by permission of John Wiley & Sons, Inc.

FIGURE 1
Model of Organization Structure

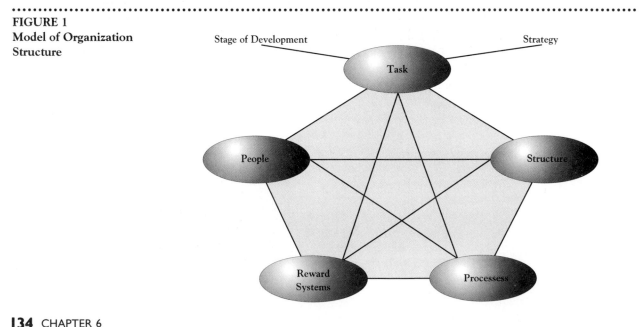

Strategy and Organization

There has been a good deal of recent attention given to the match between strategy and organization. Much of this work consists of empirical tests of Chandler's ideas presented in *Strategy and Structure* (1962). Most of this material is reviewed elsewhere (Galbraith and Nathanson, 1978). However, some recent work and ideas hold out considerable potential for understanding how different patterns of strategic change lead to different organization structures, management systems, and company cultures. In addition, some good relationships with economic performance are also attained.

The ideas rest on the concept of an organization having a center of gravity or driving force. (Tregoe and Zimmerman, 1980). This center of gravity arises from the firm's initial success in the industry in which it grew up. Let us first explore the concept of center of gravity, then the patterns of strategic change that have been followed by American enterprises.

The center of gravity of a company depends on where in the industry supply chain the company started. In order to explain the concept, manufacturing industries will be used. Figure 2 depicts the stages of supply in an industry chain. Six stages are shown here. Each industry may have more or fewer stages. Service industries typically have fewer stages.

The chain begins with a raw material extraction stage which supplies crude oil, iron ore, logs, or bauxite to the second stage of primary manufacturing. The second stage is a variety-reducing stage to produce a standardized output (petrochemicals, steel, paper pulp, or aluminum ingots). The next stage fabricates commodity products from this primary material. Fabricators produce polyethylene, cans, sheet steel, cardboard cartons, and semi-conductor components. The next stage is the product producers who add value, usually through product development, patents, and proprietary products. The next stage is the marketer and distributors. These are the consumer branded product manufacturers and various distributors. Finally, there are the retailers who have the direct contact with the ultimate consumer.

The line splitting the chain into two segments divides the industry into upstream and downstream halves. While there are differences between each of the stages, the differences between the upstream and downstream stages are striking. The upstream stages add value by reducing the variety of raw materials found on the earth's surface to a few standard commodities. The purpose is to produce flexible, predictable raw materials and intermediate products from which an increasing variety of downstream products are made. The downstream stages add value through producing a variety of products to meet varying customer needs. The downstream value is added through advertising, product positioning, marketing channels, and R&D. Thus, the upstream and downstream companies face very different business problems and tasks.

FIGURE 2
Supply Stages in an Industry Chain

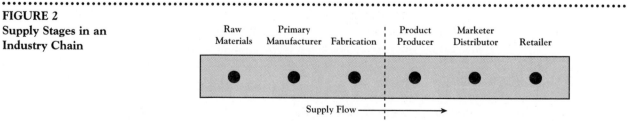

The reason for distinguishing between upstream and downstream companies is that the factors for success, the lessons learned by managers, and the organizations used are fundamentally different. The successful, experienced manager has been shaped and formed in fundamentally different ways in the different stages. The management processes are different, as are the dominant functions. In short, the company's culture is shaped by where it began in the industry chain. Listed are some fundamental differences that illustrate the contrast:

Upstream	Downstream
Standardize/homogenize	Customize/segment
Low-cost producer	High margins/proprietary positions
Process innovation	Product innovation
Capital budget	R&D/advertising budget
Technology/capital intensive	People intensive
Supply/trader/engineering	R&D/marketing dominated
Line driven	Line/staff
Maximize end users	Target end users
⋮	⋮
Sales push	Market pull

The mind set of the upstream manager is geared toward standardization and efficiency. They are the producers of standardized commodity products. In contrast, downstream managers try to customize and tailor output to diverse customer needs. They segment markets and target individual users. The upstream company wants to standardize in order to maximize the number of end users and get volume to lower costs. The downstream company wants to target particular sets of end users. Therefore, the upstreamers have a divergent view of the world based on their commodity. For example, the cover of the 1981 annual report of Intel (a fabricator of commodity semiconductors) is a listing of the 10,000 uses to which microprocessors have been put. The downstreamers have a convergent view of the world based on customer needs and will select whatever commodity will best serve that need. In the electronics industry there is always a conflict between the upstream component types and the downstream systems types because of this contrast in mind sets.

The basis of competition is different in the two stages. Commodities compete on price since the products are the same. Therefore, it is essential that the successful upstreamer be the low-cost producer. Their organizations are the lean and mean ones with a minimum of overheads. Low cost is also important for the downstreamer, but it is proprietary features that generate high margins. That feature may be a brand image, such as Maxwell House, a patented technology, an endorsement (such as the American Dental Association's endorsement of Crest toothpaste), customer service policy, and so on. Competition revolves around product features and product positioning and less on price. This means that marketing and product management sets prices. Products move by marketing pull. In contrast, the upstream company pushes the product through a strong sales force. Often salespeople negotiate prices within limits set by top management.

The organizations are different as well. The upstream companies are functional and line driven. They seek a minimum of staff, and even those staffs that are used are in supporting roles. The downstream company with multiple products and multiple markets learns to manage diversity early. Profit centers emerge and resources need to be allocated across products and markets. Larger staffs arise to assist top management in priority setting across competing product/market advocates. Higher margins permit the overhead to exist.

Both upstream and downstream companies use research and development. However, the upstream company invests in process development in order to lower costs. The downstream company invests primarily in product development in order to achieve proprietary positions.

The key managerial processes also vary. The upstream companies are driven by the capital budget and have various capital appropriations controls. The downstream companies also have a capital budget but are driven by the R&D budget (product producers) or the advertising budget (marketers). Further downstream it is working capital that becomes paramount. Managers learn to control the business by managing the turnover of inventory and accounts receivable. Thus, the upstream company is capital intensive and technological "know-how" is critical. Downstream companies are more people intensive. Therefore, the critical skills revolve around human resources management.

The dominant functions also vary with stages. The raw material processor is dominated by geologists, petroleum engineers, and traders. The supply and distribution function which searches for the most economical end use is powerful. The manufacturers of commodities are dominated by engineers who come up through manufacturing. The downstream companies are dominated first by technologists in research and product development. Farther downstream, it is marketing and then merchandising that emerge as the power centers. The line of succession to the CEO usually runs through this dominant function.

In summary, the upstream and downstream companies are very different entities. The differences, a bit exaggerated here because of the dichotomy, lead to differences in organization structure, management processes, dominant functions, succession paths, management beliefs and values or, in short, the management way of life. Thus, companies can be in the same industry but be very different because they developed from a beginning at a particular stage of the industry. This beginning, and the initial successes, teaches management the lessons of that stage. The firm develops an integrated organization (structure, processes, rewards, and people) which is peculiar to that stage and forms the center of gravity.

Strategic Change

The first strategic change that an organization makes is to vertically integrate within its industry. At a certain size, the organization can move backward to prior stages to guarantee sources of supply and secure bargaining leverage on vendors. And/or it can move forward to guarantee markets and volume for capital investments and become a customer to feed back data for new products. This initial strategic move does not change the center of gravity because the prior and subsequent stages are usually operated for the benefit of the center-of-gravity stage.

The paper industry is used to illustrate the concepts of center of gravity and vertical integration. Figure 3 depicts five paper companies which operate from different centers of gravity. The first is Weyerhauser. Its center of gravity is at the land and timber stage of the industry. Weyerhauser seeks the highest return use for a log. They make pulp and paper rolls. They make containers and milk cartons. But they are a timber company. If the returns are better in lumber, the pulp mills get fed with sawdust and chips. International Paper (the name of the company tells it all), by contrast, is a primary manufacturer of paper. It also has timber lands, container plants, and works on new products around aseptic packaging. However, if the pulp mills ran out of logs, the manager of the woodlands used to be fired. The raw material stage is to supply the manufacturing stage, not seek the highest return for its timber. The Container Corporation (again, the name describes the company) is the example of the fabricator. It also has woodlands and pulp mills, but they are to supply the container making operations. The product producer is Appleton. It makes specialty paper

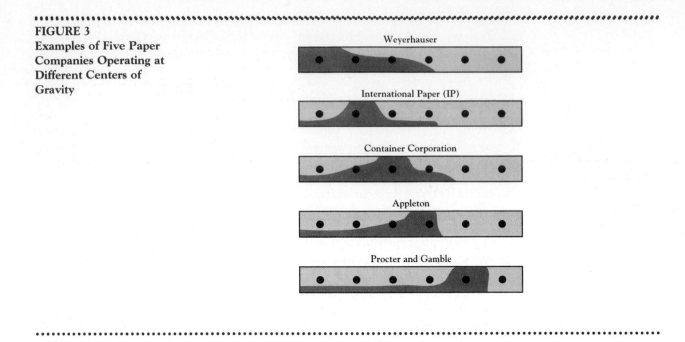

products. For example, Appleton produces a paper with globules of ink imbedded in it. The globules burst and form a letter or number when struck with an impact printer.

The last company is Procter & Gamble. P&G is a consumer products company. And, like the other companies, it operates pulp mills and owns timber lands. However, it is driven by the advertising or marketing function. If one wanted to be CEO of P&G, one would not run a pulp mill or the woodlands. The path to CEO is through the brand manager for Charmin or Pampers.

Thus, each of these companies is in the paper industry. Each operates at a number of stages in the industry. Yet each is a very different company because it has its center of gravity at a different stage. The center of gravity establishes a base from which subsequent strategic changes take place. That is, as a company's industry matures, the company feels a need to change its center of gravity in order to move to a place in the industry where better returns can be obtained, or move to a new industry but use its same center of gravity and skills in that industry, or make some combination of industry and center of gravity change. These options lead to different patterns of corporate developments.

BY-PRODUCTS DIVERSIFICATION

One of the first diversification moves that a vertically integrated company makes is to sell by-products from points along the industry chain. Figure 4 depicts this strategy. These companies appear to be diversified if one attributes revenue to the various industries in which the company operates. But the company has changed neither its industry nor its center of gravity. The company is behaving intelligently by seeking additional sources of revenue and profit. However, it is still psychologically committed to its center of gravity and to its industry. Alcoa is such a firm. Even though they operate in several industries, their output varies directly with the aluminum cycle. They have not reduced their dependence on a single industry, as one would with real diversification.

FIGURE 4
By-product
Diversification

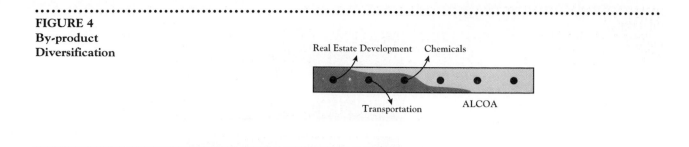

RELATED DIVERSIFICATION

Another strategic change is the diversification into new industries but at the same center of gravity. This is called "related diversification." The firm diversifies into new businesses, but they are all related. The relationship revolves around the company's center of gravity. Figure 5 depicts the diversification moves of Procter & Gamble. After beginning in the soap industry, P&G vertically integrated back into doing its own chemical processing (fatty acids) and seed crushing. Then, in order to pursue new growth opportunities, it has been diversifying into paper, food, beverages, pharmaceuticals, coffee, and so on. But each move into a new industry is made at the company's center of gravity. The new businesses are all consumer products which are driven out of advertising by brand managers. The 3M Company also follows a related diversification strategy, but theirs is based on technology. They have 40,000 different products which are produced by some seventy divisions. However, 95% of the products are based on coating and bonding technologies. Its center of gravity is a product producer, and it adds value through R&D.

LINKED DIVERSIFICATION

A third type of diversification involves moving into new industries and operating at different centers of gravity in those new industries. However, there is a linkage of some type among various businesses. Figure 6 depicts Union Camp as following this pattern of corporate development. Union Camp is a primary producer of paper products. As such, it vertically integrated backwards to own woodlands. From there, it moved downstream within the wood products industry by running sawmills and fabricating plants. However, they recently purchased a retail lumber business.

They also moved into the chemical business by selling by-products from the pulping process. This business was successful and expanded. Recently, Union Camp was bidding for

FIGURE 5
Related
Diversification

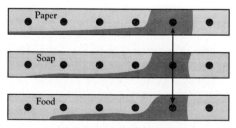

PROCTER AND GAMBLE

FIGURE 6
Linked
Diversification

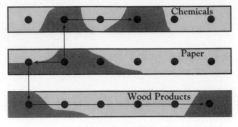

UNION CAMP

a flavors and fragrances (F&F) company. The F&F company is a product producer which adds value through creating flavors and fragrances for mostly consumer products companies.

Thus, Union Camp is an upstream company that is acquiring downstream companies. However, these new companies are in industries in which the company already diversified from its upstream center of gravity. But these new acquisitions are not operated for the benefit of the center of gravity but are stand-alone profit centers.

UNRELATED DIVERSIFICATION

The final type of strategic change is to diversify into unrelated businesses. Like the linked diversifiers, unrelated diversifiers move into new industries often at different centers of gravity. They almost always use acquisition, while related and linked companies will use some acquisitions but rely heavily on internal development. There is often very little relation between the industries into which the unrelated company diversifies. Textron and Teledyne have been the paradigm examples. They operate in industrial equipment, aerospace, consumer products, insurance, and so on. Others have spread into retailing, services, and entertainment. The purpose is to insulate the company's earnings from the uncertainties of any one industry, or from the business cycle.

CENTER OF GRAVITY CHANGE

Another possibility is for an organization to stay in the same industry but change its center of gravity in that industry. Recent articles describe the attempts of chemical companies to move downstream into higher margin, proprietary products. They went to move away from the overcapacity/undercapacity cycles of commodity businesses with their low margins and high capital intensity. In aerospace, some of the system integration houses are moving backward into making electronic components. For example, there are going to be fewer airplanes and more effort on the avionics, radars, weapons, and so on that go into airplanes. In either case, it means a shift in the center of gravity of the company.

In summary, several patterns of strategic change can occur in a company. These involve changes to the company's industry of origination, changes to the center of gravity of the company, or some combination of the two. For some of the strategic changes there are appropriate organizations and measures of their economic performance.

Strategy, Organization, and Performance

For a number of years now, studies have been made of strategy and structure of the *Fortune* 500. Most of these were conducted by the Harvard Business School. These studies were reviewed in previous work (Galbraith and Nathanson, 1978). The current view is illustrated in Table 1. If one samples the *Fortune* 500 and categorizes them by strategy and structure, the following relationships hold.

One can still find organizations staying in their same original business. Such a single business is Wrigley Chewing Gum. These organizations are run by centralized functional organizations. The next strategic type is the vertically integrated by-product seller. Again, these companies have some diversification but remain committed to their industry and center of gravity. The companies are also functional, but the sequential stages are often operated as profit and loss divisions. The companies are usually quite centralized and run by collegial management groups. The profit centers are not true ones in being independent to run their own businesses. These are almost all upstream companies.

The related businesses are those that move into new industries at their center of gravity. Usually these are downstream companies. They adopt the decentralized profit center divisions. However, the divisions are not completely decentralized. There are usually strong corporate staffs and some centralized marketing, manufacturing, and R&D. There may be several thousand people on the corporate payroll.

The clearest contrast to the related diversifier is the unrelated business company. These companies enter a variety of businesses at several centers of gravity. The organization they adopt is the very decentralized holding company. Their outstanding feature is the small corporate staff. Depending on their size, the numbers range between fifty and two hundred. Usually these are support staffs. All of the marketing, manufacturing, and R&D is decentralized to the divisions. Group executives have no staffs and are generally corporate oriented.

The linked companies are neither of these extremes. Often linked forms are transitory. The organizations that they utilize are usually mixed forms that are not easily classified. Some divisions are autonomous, while others are managed out of the corporate HQ. Still others have strong group executives with group staffs. Some work has been done on classifying these structures (Allen, 1978).

There has been virtually no work done on center of gravity changes and their changes in structure. Likewise, there has been nothing done on comparisons for economic performance. But for the other categories and structures, there is emerging some good data on relative economic performance.

The studies of economic performance have compared the various strategic patterns and the concept of fit between strategy and organization. Both sets of results have organization design implications. The economic studies use return on equity as the performance measure. If one compares the strategic categories listed in Table 1, there are distinct performance differences. The high performers are consistently the related diversifiers (Rumelt, 1974; Galbraith and Nathanson, 1978; Nathanson and Cassano, 1982; Bettis, 1981; Rumelt, 1982).

TABLE 1

STRATEGY	STRUCTURE
Single business	Functional
Vertical by-products	Functional with P&Ls
Related businesses	Divisional
Linked businesses	Mixed structures
Unrelated businesses	Holding company

There are several explanations for this performance difference. One explanation is that the related diversifiers are all downstream companies in businesses with high R&D and advertising expenditures. These businesses have higher margins and returns than other businesses. Thus, it may not be the strategy but the businesses the relateds happen to be in. However, if the unrelateds are good acquirers, why do they not enter the high-return businesses?

The other explanation is that the relateds learn a set of core skills and design an organization to perform at a particular center of gravity. Then, when they diversify, they take on the task of learning a new business, but at the same center of gravity. Therefore, they get a diversified portfolio of businesses but each with a system of management and an organization that is understood by everyone. The management understands the business and is not spread thin.

The unrelateds, however, have to learn new industries and also how to operate to a different center of gravity. This latter change is the most difficult to accomplish. One upstream company diversified via acquisition into downstream companies. It consistently encountered control troubles. It instituted a capital appropriation process for each investment of $50,000 or more. It still had problems, however. The retail division opened a couple of stores with leases for $40,000. It didn't use the capital process. The company got blindsided because the stores required $40 million in working capital for inventory and receivables. Thus, the management systems did not fit the new downstream business. It appears that organizational fit makes a difference. . . .

One additional piece of evidence results from the studies of economic performance. This result is that the poorest performer of the strategic categories is the vertically integrated by-product seller. Recall these companies are all upstream, raw material, and primary manufacturers. They make up a good portion of "Smokestack America." In some respects, these companies made their money early in the century, and their value added is shifting to lesser developed countries in the natural course of industrial development. However, what is significant here is their inability to change. It is no secret to anyone that they have been under-performers, yet they have continued to put money back into the same business.

My explanation revolves around the center of gravity. These previously successful companies put together an organization that fit their industry and stage. When the industry declined, they were unable to change as well as the downstream companies. The reason is that upstream companies were functional organizations with few general managers. Their resource allocation was within a single business, not across multiple products. The management skill is partly technological knowhow. This technology does not transfer across industries at the primary manufacturing center of gravity. The knowledge of paper making does not help very much in glass making. Yet both might be combined in a package company. Also, the capital intensity of these industries limits the diversification. Usually one industry must be chosen and capital invested to be the low-cost producer. So there are a number of reasons why these companies have been notoriously poor diversifiers.

In addition, it appears to be very difficult to change centers of gravity no matter where an organization is along the industry chain. The reason is that a center of gravity shift requires a dismantling of the current power structure, rejection of parts of the old culture, and establishing all new management systems. The related diversification works for exactly the opposite reasons. They can move into new businesses with minimal change to the power structure and accepted ways of doing things. Changes in the center of gravity usually occur by new start-ups at a new center of gravity rather than a shift in the center of established firms. . . .

There are some exceptions that prove the rule. Some organizations have shifted from upstream commodity producers to downstream product producers and consumer product firms. General Mills moved from a flour miller to a related diversified provider of products for the homemaker. Over a long period of time they shifted downstream into consumer food products from their cake mix product beginnings. From there, they diversified into related areas after selling off the milling operations, the old core of the company. . . . [In these cases], however, new management was brought in and acquisition and divestment used to make the transition. So, even though vestiges of the old name remain, these are substantially different companies. . . .

The vast majority of our research has examined one kind of strategic change—diversification. The far more difficult one, the change in center of gravity, has received far less [attention]. For the most part, the concept is difficult to measure and not publicly reported like the number of industries in which a company operates. Case studies will have to be used. But there is a need for more systematic knowledge around this kind of strategic change.

▼ READING 6.2   THE STRUCTURING OF ORGANIZATIONS*

by Henry Mintzberg

The "one best way" approach has dominated our thinking about organizational structure since the turn of the century. There is a right way and a wrong way to design an organization. A variety of failures, however, has made it clear that organizations differ, that, for example, long-range planning systems or organizational development programs are good for some but not others. And so recent management theory has moved away from the "one best way" approach, toward an "it all depends" approach, formally known as "contingency theory." Structure should reflect the organization's situation—for example, its age, size, type of production system, the extent to which its environment is complex and dynamic.

This reading argues that the "it all depends" approach does not go far enough, that structures are rightfully designed on the basis of a third approach, which might be called the "getting it all together" or "configuration" approach. Spans of control, types of formalization and decentralization, planning systems, and matrix structures should not be picked and chosen independently, the way a shopper picks vegetables at the market. Rather, these and other elements of organizational design should logically configure into internally consistent groupings.

When the enormous amount of research that has been done on organizational structure is looked at in the light of this conclusion, much of its confusion falls away, and a convergence is evident around several configurations, which are distinct in their structural designs, in the situations in which they are found, and even in the periods of history in which they first developed.

To understand these configurations, we must first understand each of the elements that make them up. Accordingly, the first four sections of this reading discuss the basic parts of organizations, the mechanisms by which organizations coordinate their activities, the parameters they use to design their structures, and their contingency, or situational, factors. The final section introduces the structural configurations, each of which will be discussed at length in Section III of this text.

Six Basic Parts of the Organization

At the base of any organization can be found its operators, those people who perform the basic work of producing the products and rendering the services. They form the *operating core*. All but the simplest organizations also require at least one full-time manager who

---

* Excerpted originally from *The Structuring of Organizations* (Prentice Hall, 1979), with added sections from *Power in and Around Organizations* (Prentice Hall, 1983). This chapter was rewritten for this edition of the text, based on two other excerpts: "A Typology of Organizational Structure," published as Chapter 3 in Danny Miller and Peter Friesen, *Organizations: A Quantum View*, (Prentice Hall, 1984) and "Deriving Configurations," Chapter 6 in *Mintzberg on Management: Inside Our Strange World of Organizations* (Free Press, 1989).

occupies what we shall call the *strategic apex,* where the whole system is overseen. And as the organization grows, more managers are needed—not only managers of operators but also managers of managers. A *middle line* is created, a hierarchy of authority between the operating core and the strategic apex.

As the organization becomes still more complex, it generally requires another group of people, whom we shall call the analysts. They, too, perform administrative duties—to plan and control formally the work of others—but of a different nature, often labeled "staff." These analysts form what we shall call the *technostructure,* outside the hierarchy of line authority. Most organizations also add staff units of a different kind, to provide various internal services, from a cafeteria or mailroom to a legal counsel or public relations office. We shall call these units and the part of the organization they form the *support staff.*

Finally, every active organization has a sixth part, which we call its *ideology* (by which is meant a strong "culture"). Ideology encompasses the traditions and beliefs of an organization that distinguish it from other organizations and infuse a certain life into the skeleton of its structure.

This gives us six basic parts of an organization. As shown in Figure 1, we have a small strategic apex connected by a flaring middle line to a large, flat operating core at the base. These three parts of the organization are drawn in one uninterrupted sequence to indicate that they are typically connected through a single chain of formal authority. The technostructure and the support staff are shown off to either side to indicate that they are separate from this main line of authority, influencing the operating core only indirectly. The ideology is shown as a kind of halo that surrounds the entire system.

These people, all of whom work inside the organization to make its decisions and take its actions—full-time employees or, in some cases, committed volunteers—may be thought of as *influencers* who form a kind of internal coalition. By this term, we mean a system within which people vie among themselves to determine the distribution of power.

In addition, various outside people also try to exert influence on the organization, seeking to affect the decisions and actions taken inside. These external influencers, who create a field of forces around the organization, can include owners, unions and other employee

FIGURE 1
The Six Basic Parts of the Organization

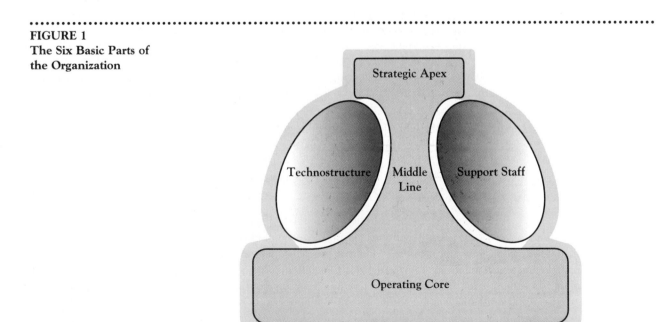

associations, suppliers, clients, partners, competitors, and all kinds of publics, in the form of governments, special interest groups, and so forth. Together they can all be thought to form an *external coalition*.

Sometimes the external coalition is relatively *passive* (as in the typical behavior of the shareholders of a widely held corporation or the members of a large union). Other times it is *dominated* by one active influencer or some group of them acting in concert (such as an outside owner of a business firm or a community intent on imposing a certain philosophy on its school system). And in still other cases, the external coalition may be *divided*, as different groups seek to impose contradictory pressures on the organization (as in a prison buffeted between two community groups, one favoring custody, the other rehabilitation).

Six Basic Coordinating Mechanisms

Every organized human activity—from the making of pottery to the placing of a man on the moon—gives rise to two fundamental and opposing requirements: the *division of labor* into various tasks to be performed and the *coordination* of those tasks to accomplish the activity. The structure of an organization can be defined simply as the total of the ways in which its labor is divided into distinct tasks and then its coordination achieved among those tasks.

1. *Mutual adjustment* achieves coordination of work by the simple process of informal communication. The people who do the work interact with one another to coordinate, much as two canoeists in the rapids adjust to one another's actions. Figure 2a shows mutual adjustment in terms of an arrow between two operators. Mutual adjustment is obviously used in the simplest of organizations—it is the most obvious way to coordinate. But, paradoxically, it is also used in the most complex, because it is the only means that can be relied upon under extremely difficult circumstances, such as trying to figure out how to put a man on the moon for the first time.
2. *Direct supervision* in which one person coordinates by giving orders to others, tends to come into play after a certain number of people must work together. Thus, fifteen people in a war canoe cannot coordinate by mutual adjustment; they need a leader who, by virtue of instructions, coordinates their work, much as a football team requires a quarterback to call the plays. Figure 2b shows the leader as a manager with the instructions as arrows to the operators.

Coordination can also be achieved by *standardization*—in effect, automatically, by virtue of standards that predetermine what people do and so ensure that their work is coordinated. We can consider four forms—the standardization of the work processes themselves, of the outputs of the work, of the knowledge and skills that serve as inputs to the work, or of the norms that more generally guide the work.

3. *Standardization of work processes* means the specification—that is, the programming—of the content of the work directly, the procedures to be followed, as in the case of the assembly instructions that come with many children's toys. As shown in Figure 2c, it is typically the job of the analysts to so program the work of different people in order to coordinate it tightly.
4. *Standardization of outputs* means the specification not of what is to be done but of its results. In that way, the interfaces between jobs is predetermined, as when a machinist is told to drill holes in a certain place on a fender so that they will fit the bolts being welded by someone else, or a division manager is told to achieve a sales growth of 10% so that the corporation can meet some overall sales target. Again, such standards generally emanate from the analysts, as shown in Figure 2d.

FIGURE 2
The Basic Mechanisms
of Coordination

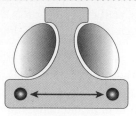

a) Mutual Adjustment

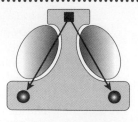

b) Direct Supervision

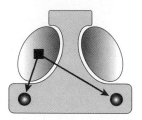

c) Standardization of Work

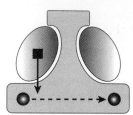

d) Standardization of Outputs

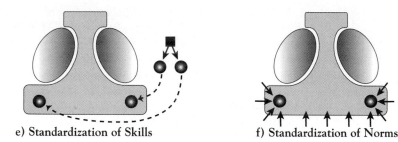

e) Standardization of Skills

f) Standardization of Norms

5. *Standardization of skills,* as well as knowledge, is another, though looser way to achieve coordination. Here, it is the worker rather than the work or the outputs that is standardized. He or she is taught a body of knowledge and a set of skills which are subsequently applied to the work. Such standardization typically takes place outside the organization—for example in a professional school of a university before the worker takes his or her first job—indicated in Figure 2e. In effect, the standards do not come from the analyst; they are internalized by the operator as inputs to the job he or she takes. Coordination is then achieved by virtue of various operators' having learned what to expect of each other. When an anesthetist and a surgeon meet in the operating room to remove an appendix, they need hardly communicate (that is, use mutual adjustment, let alone direct supervision); each knows exactly what the other will do and can coordinate accordingly.

6. *Standardization of norms* means that the workers share a common set of beliefs and can achieve coordination based on it, as implied in Figure 2f. For example, if every member of a religious order shares a belief in the importance of attracting converts, then all will work together to achieve this aim.

These coordinating mechanisms can be considered the most basic elements of structure, the glue that holds organizations together. They seem to fall into a rough order: As organizational work becomes more complicated, the favored means of coordination seems to shift from mutual adjustment (the simplest mechanism) to direct supervision, then to standardization, preferably of work processes or norms, otherwise of outputs or of skills, finally reverting back to mutual adjustment. But no organization can rely on a single one of those mechanisms; all will typically be found in every reasonably developed organization.

Still, the important point for us here is that many organizations do favor one mechanism over the others, at least at certain stages of their lives. In fact, organizations that favor none seem most prone to becoming politicized, simply because of the conflicts that naturally arise when people have to vie for influence in a relative vacuum of power.

The Essential Parameters of Design

The essence of organizational design is the manipulation of a series of parameters that determine the division of labor and the achievement of coordination. Some of these concern the design of individual positions, others the design of the superstructure (the overall network of subunits, reflected in the organizational chart), some the design of lateral linkages to flesh out that superstructure, and a final group concerns the design of the decision-making system of the organization. Listed as follows are the main parameters of structural design, with links to the coordinating mechanisms.

▼ **Job specialization** refers to the number of tasks in a given job and the workers' control over these tasks. A job is *horizontally* specialized to the extent that it encompasses a few narrowly defined tasks, *vertically* specialized to the extent that the worker lacks control of the tasks performed. *Unskilled* jobs are typically highly specialized in both dimensions; skilled or *professional* jobs are typically specialized horizontally but not vertically. "Job enrichment" refers to the enlargement of jobs in both the vertical and horizontal dimension.

▼ **Behavior formalization** refers to the standardization of work processes by the imposition of operating instructions, job descriptions, rules, regulations, and the like. Structures that rely on any form of standardization for coordination may be defined as *bureaucratic*, those that do not as *organic*.

▼ **Training** refers to the use of formal instructional programs to establish and standardize in people the requisite skills and knowledge to do particular jobs in organizations. Training is a key design parameter in all work we call professional. Training and formalization are basically substitutes for achieving the standardization (in effect, the bureaucratization) of behavior. In one, the standards are learned as skills, in the other they are imposed on the job as rules.

▼ **Indoctrination** refers to programs and techniques by which the norms of the members of an organization are standardized, so that they become responsive to its ideological needs and can thereby be trusted to make its decisions and take its actions. Indoctrination too is a substitute for formalization, as well as for skill training, in this case the standards being internalized as deeply rooted beliefs.

▼ **Unit grouping** refers to the choice of the bases by which positions are grouped together into units, and those units into higher-order units (typically shown on the organization chart). Grouping encourages coordination by putting different jobs under common supervision, by requiring them to share common resources and achieve common measures of performance, and by using proximity to facilitate mutual adjustment among them. The various bases for grouping—by work process, product, client, place, and so on—can be reduced to two fundamental ones—the *function* performed and the *market* served. The former (illustrated in Fig. 3) refers to means, that is to a single link

FIGURE 3
**Grouping by Function:
A Cultural Center**

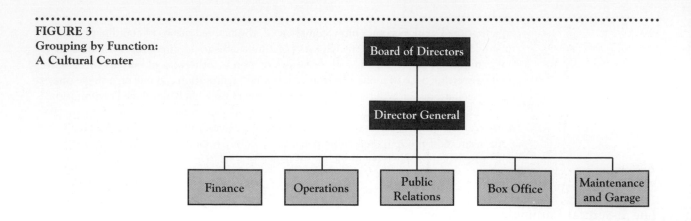

in the chain of processes by which products or services are produced; the latter (in Fig. 4) to ends, that is, the whole chain for specific end products, services, or markets. On what criteria should the choice of a basis for grouping be made? First, there is the consideration of workflow linkages, or "interdependencies." Obviously, the more tightly linked are positions or units in the workflow, the more desirable that they be grouped together to facilitate their coordination. Second is the consideration of process interdependencies—for example, across people doing the same kind of work but in different workflows (such as maintenance men working on different machines). It sometimes makes sense to group them together to facilitate their sharing of equipment or ideas, to encourage the improvement of their skills, and so on. Third is the question of scale interdependencies. For example, all maintenance people in a factory may have to be grouped together because no single department has enough maintenance work for one person. Finally, there are the social interdependencies, the need to group people together for social reasons, as in coal mines where mutual support under dangerous working conditions can be a factor in deciding how to group people. Clearly, grouping by function is favored by process and scale interdependencies. and to a lesser extent by social interdependencies (in the sense that people who do the same kind of job often tend to get along better). Grouping by function also encourages specialization, for example, by allowing specialists to come together under the supervision of one of their own kind. The problem with functional grouping, however, is that it narrows perspectives, encouraging a focus on means instead of ends—the way to do the job instead of the reason for doing the job in the first place. Thus grouping by market is used to favor coordination in the workflow at the expense of process and scale specialization. In general, market grouping reduces the ability to do specialized or repetitive tasks well and is more wasteful, being less able to take advantage of economies of scale and often requiring the duplication of resources. But it enables the organization to accomplish a wider variety of tasks and to change its tasks more easily to serve the organization's end markets. And so if the workflow interdependencies are the important ones and if the organization cannot easily handle them by standardization, then it will tend to favor the market bases for grouping in order to encourage mutual adjustment and direct supervision. But if the workflow is irregular (as in a "job shop"), if standardization can easily contain the important workflow interdependencies, or if the process or scale interdependencies are the important ones, then the organization will be inclined to seek the advantages of specialization and group on the basis of function instead. Of

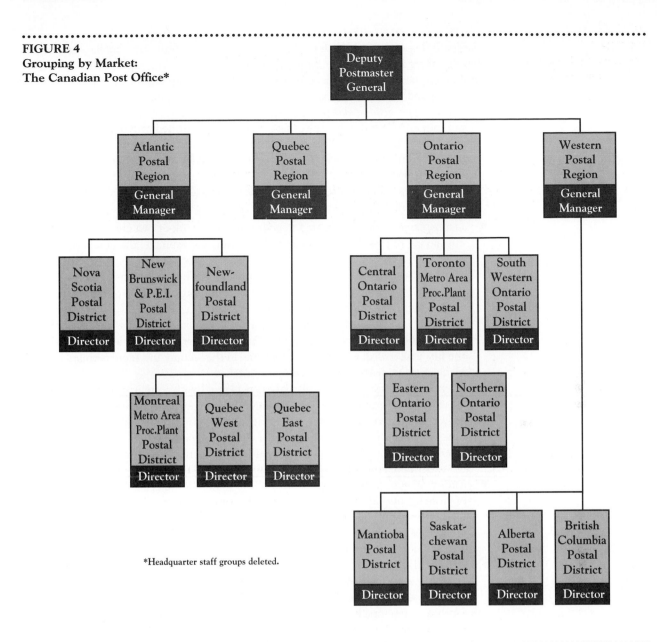

FIGURE 4
Grouping by Market:
The Canadian Post Office*

*Headquarter staff groups deleted.

course in all but the smallest organizations, the question is not so much *which* basis of grouping, but in what *order*. Much as fires are built by stacking logs first one way and then the other, so too are organizations built by varying the different bases for grouping to take care of various interdependencies.

▼ **Unit size** refers to the number of positions (or units) contained in a single unit. The equivalent term, *span of control*, is not used here, because sometimes units are kept small despite an absence of close supervisory control. For example, when experts coordinate extensively by mutual adjustment, as in an engineering team in a space agency, they will form into small units. In this case, unit size is small and span of control is low despite a relative absence of direct supervision. In contrast, when work is highly standardized (because of either formalization or training), unit size can be very large, because there is little need for direct supervision. One foreman can supervise dozens of assemblers, because they work according to very tight instructions.

▼ **Planning and control systems** are used to standardize outputs. They may be divided into two types: *action planning* systems, which specify the results of specific actions before they are taken (for example, that holes should be drilled with diameters of 3 centimeters); and *performance control* systems, which specify the desired results of whole ranges of actions after the fact (for example, that sales of a division should grow by 10% in a given year).

▼ **Liaison devices** refer to a whole series of mechanisms used to encourage mutual adjustment within and between units. Four are of particular importance:

    ▼ *Liaison positions* are jobs created to coordinate the work of two units directly, without having to pass through managerial channels, for example, the purchasing engineer who sits between purchasing and engineering or the sales liaison person who mediates between the sales force and the factory. These positions carry no formal authority per se; rather, those who serve in them must use their powers of persuasion, negotiation, and so on to bring the two sides together.

    ▼ *Task forces and standing committees* are institutionalized forms of meetings which bring members of a number of different units together on a more intensive basis, in the first case to deal with a temporary issue, in the second, in a more permanent and regular way to discuss issues of common interest.

    ▼ *Integrating managers*—essentially liaison personnel with formal authority—provide for stronger coordination. These "managers" are given authority not over the units they link, but over something important to those units, for example, their budgets. One example is the brand manager in a consumer goods firm who is responsible for a certain product but who must negotiate its production and marketing with different functional departments.

    ▼ *Matrix structure* carries liaison to its natural conclusion. No matter what the bases of grouping at one level in an organization, some interdependencies always remain. Figure 5 suggests various ways to deal with these "residual interdependencies": a different type of grouping can be used at the next level in the hierarchy; staff units can be formed next to line units to advise on the problems; or one of the liaison devices already discussed can be overlaid on the grouping. But in each case, one basis of grouping is favored over the others. The concept of matrix structure is balance between two (or more) bases of grouping, for example functional with market (or for that matter, one kind of market with another—say, regional with product). This is done by the creation of a dual authority structure—two (or more) managers, units, or individuals are made jointly and equally responsible for the same decisions. We can distinguish a *permanent* form of matrix structure, where the units and the people in them remain more or less in place, as shown in the example of a whimsical multinational firm in Figure 6, and a *shifting* form, suited to project work, where the units and the people in them move around frequently. Shifting matrix structures are common in high-technology industries, which group specialists in functional departments for housekeeping purposes (process interdependencies, etc.) but deploy them from various departments in project teams to do the work, as shown for NASA in Figure 7.

▼ **Decentralization** refers to the diffusion of decision-making power. When all the power rests at a single point in an organization, we call its structure centralized; to the extent that the power is dispersed among many individuals, we call it relatively decentralized. We can distinguish *vertical decentralization*—the delegation of formal power down the

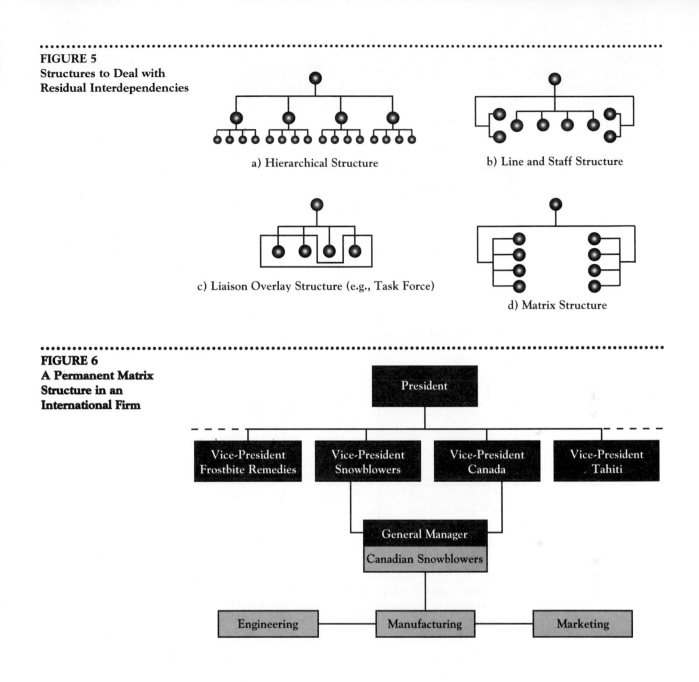

FIGURE 5
Structures to Deal with Residual Interdependencies

a) Hierarchical Structure

b) Line and Staff Structure

c) Liaison Overlay Structure (e.g., Task Force)

d) Matrix Structure

FIGURE 6
A Permanent Matrix Structure in an International Firm

President

Vice-President Frostbite Remedies

Vice-President Snowblowers

Vice-President Canada

Vice-President Tahiti

General Manager
Canadian Snowblowers

Engineering

Manufacturing

Marketing

hierarchy to line managers—from *horizontal decentralization*—the extent to which formal or informal power is dispersed out of the line hierarchy to nonmanagers (operators, analysts, and support staffers). We can also distinguish *selective* decentralization—the dispersal of power over different decisions to different places in the organization—from *parallel* decentralization—where the power over various kinds of decisions is delegated to the same place. Six forms of decentralization may thus be described: (1) vertical and horizontal centralization, where all the power rests at the strategic apex; (2) limited horizontal decentralization (selective), where the strategic apex shares some power with the technostructure that standardizes everybody else's work; (3) limited vertical

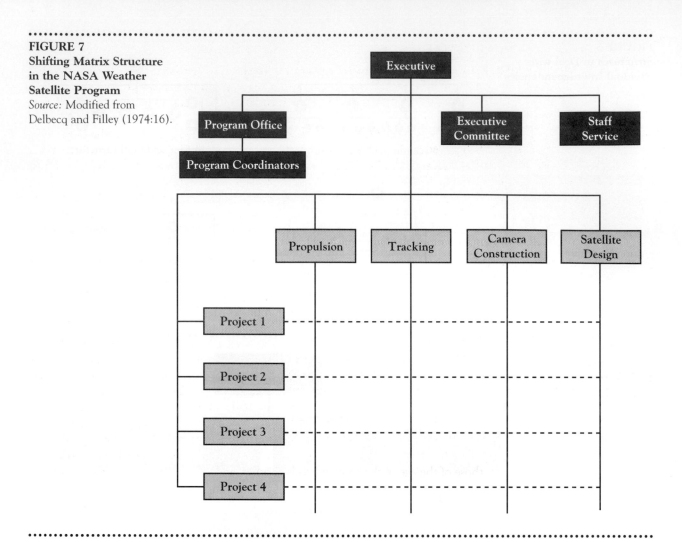

FIGURE 7
Shifting Matrix Structure in the NASA Weather Satellite Program
Source: Modified from Delbecq and Filley (1974:16).

decentralization (parallel), where managers of market-based units are delegated the power to control most of the decisions concerning their line units; (4) vertical and horizontal decentralization, where most of the power rests in the operating core, at the bottom of the structure; (5) selective vertical and horizontal decentralization, where the power over different decisions is dispersed to various places in the organization, among managers, staff experts, and operators who work in teams at various levels in the hierarchy; and (6) pure decentralization, where power is shared more or less equally by all members of the organization.

The Situational Factors

A number of "contingency" or "situational" factors influence the choice of these design parameters, and vice versa. They include the age and size of the organization; its technical system of production; various characteristics of its environment, such as stability and complexity; and its power system, for example, whether or not it is tightly controlled by outside influencers. Some of the effects of these factors, as found in an extensive body of research literature, are summarized below as hypotheses.

AGE AND SIZE

▼ **The older an organization, the more formalized its behavior.** What we have here is the "we've-seen-it-all-before" syndrome. As organizations age, they tend to repeat their behaviors: as a result, these become more predictable and so more amenable to formalization.

▼ **The larger an organization, the more formalized its behavior.** Just as the older organization formalizes what it has seen before, so the larger organization formalizes what it sees often. ("Listen mister, I've heard that story at least five times today. Just fill in the form like it says.")

▼ **The larger an organization, the more elaborate its structure; that is, the more specialized its jobs and units and the more developed its administrative components.** As organizations grow in size, they are able to specialize their jobs more finely. (The big barbershop can afford a specialist to cut children's hair; the small one cannot.) As a result, they can also specialize—or "differentiate"—the work of their units more extensively. This requires more effort at coordination. And so the larger organization tends also to enlarge its hierarchy to effect direct supervision and to make greater use of its technostructure to achieve coordination by standardization, or else to encourage more coordination by mutual adjustment.

▼ **The larger the organization, the larger the size of its average unit.** This finding relates to the previous two, the size of units growing larger as organizations themselves grow larger because (1) as behavior becomes more formalized, and (2) as the work of each unit becomes more homogeneous, managers are able to supervise more employees.

▼ **Structure reflects the age of the industry from its founding.** This is a curious finding, but one that we shall see holds up remarkably well. An organization's structure seems to reflect the age of the industry in which it operates, no matter what its own age. Industries that predate the industrial revolution seem to favor one kind of structure, those of the age of the early railroads another, and so on. We should obviously expect different structures in different periods; the surprising thing is that these structures seem to carry through to new periods, old industries remaining relatively true to earlier structures.

TECHNICAL SYSTEM

Technical system refers to the instruments used in the operating core to produce the outputs. (This should be distinguished from "technology," which refers to the knowledge base of an organization.)

▼ **The more regulating the technical system—that is, the more it controls the work of the operators—the more formalized the operating work and the more bureaucratic the structure of the operating core.** Technical systems that regulate the work of the operators—for example, mass production assembly lines—render that work highly routine and predictable, and so encourage its specialization and formalization, which in turn create the conditions for bureaucracy in the operating core.

▼ **The more complex the technical system, the more elaborate and professional the support staff.** Essentially, if an organization is to use complex machinery, it must hire staff experts who can understand that machinery—who have the capability to design, select, and modify it. And then it must give them considerable power to make decisions concerning that machinery, and encourage them to use the liaison devices to ensure mutual adjustment among them.

▼ **The automation of the operating core forms a bureaucratic administrative structure into an organic one.** When unskilled work is coordinated by the standardization of work processes, we tend to get bureaucratic structure throughout the organization, because a control mentality pervades the whole system. But when the work of the operating core becomes automated, social relationships tend to change. Now it is machines, not people, that are regulated. So the obsession with control tends to disappear—machines do not need to be watched over—and with it go many of the managers and analysts who were needed to control the operators. In their place come the support specialists to look after the machinery, coordinating their own work by mutual adjustment. Thus, automation reduces line authority in favor of staff expertise and reduces the tendency to rely on standardization for coordination.

ENVIRONMENT

Environment refers to various characteristics of the organization's outside context, related to markets, political climate, economic conditions, and so on.

▼ **The more dynamic an organization's environment, the more organic its structure.** It stands to reason that in a stable environment—where nothing changes—an organization can predict its future conditions and so, all other things being equal, can easily rely on standardization for coordination. But when conditions become dynamic—when the need for product change is frequent, labor turnover is high, and political conditions are unstable—the organization cannot standardize but must instead remain flexible through the use of direct supervision or mutual adjustment for coordination, and so it must use a more organic structure. Thus, for example, armies, which tend to be highly bureaucratic institutions in peacetime, can become rather organic when engaged in highly dynamic, guerilla-type warfare.

▼ **The more complex an organization's environment, the more decentralized its structure.** The prime reason to decentralize a structure is that all the information needed to make decisions cannot be comprehended in one head. Thus, when the operations of an organization are based on a complex body of knowledge, there is usually a need to decentralize decision-making power. Note that a simple environment can be stable or dynamic (the manufacturer of dresses faces a simple environment yet cannot predict style from one season to another), as can a complex one (the specialist in perfected open heart surgery faces a complex task, yet knows what to expect).

▼ **The more diversified an organization's markets, the greater the propensity to split it into market-based units, or divisions, given favorable economies of scale.** When an organization can identify distinct markets—geographical regions, clients, but especially products and services—it will be predisposed to split itself into high level units on that basis, and to give each a good deal of control over its own operations (that is, to use what we called "limited vertical decentralization"). In simple terms, diversification breeds divisionalization. Each unit can be given all the functions associated with its own markets. But this assumes favorable economies of scale: If the operating core cannot be divided, as in the case of an aluminum smelter, also if some critical function must be centrally coordinated, as in purchasing in a retail chain, then full divisionalization may not be possible.

▼ **Extreme hostility in its environment drives any organization to centralize its structure temporarily.** When threatened by extreme hostility in its environment, the tendency for an organization is to centralize power, in other words, to fall back on its tightest coordinating mechanism, direct supervision. Here a single leader can ensure fast and tightly coordinated response to the threat (at least temporarily).

POWER

▼ **The greater the external control of an organization, the more centralized and formalized its structure.** This important hypothesis claims that to the extent that an organization is controlled externally, for example by a parent firm or a government that dominates its external coalition—it tends to centralize power at the strategic apex and to formalize its behavior. The reason is that the two most effective ways to control an organization from the outside are to hold its chief executive officer responsible for its actions and to impose clearly defined standards on it. Moreover, external control forces the organization to be especially careful about its actions.

▼ **A divided external coalition will tend to give rise to a politicized internal coalition, and vice versa.** In effect, conflict in one of the coalitions tends to spill over to the other, as one set of influencers seeks to enlist the support of the others.

▼ **Fashion favors the structure of the day (and of the culture), sometimes even when inappropriate.** Ideally, the design parameters are chosen according to the dictates of age, size, technical system, and environment. In fact, however, fashion seems to play a role too, encouraging many organizations to adopt currently popular design parameters that are inappropriate for themselves. Paris has its salons of haute couture; likewise New York has its offices of "haute structure," the consulting firms that sometimes tend to oversell the latest in structural fashion.

The Configurations

We have now introduced various attributes of organizations—parts, coordinating mechanisms, design parameters, situational factors, How do they all combine?

We proceed here on the assumption that a limited number of configurations can help explain much of what is observed in organizations. We have introduced in our discussion six basic parts of the organization, six basic mechanisms of coordination. as well as six basic types of decentralization. In fact, there seems to be a fundamental correspondence between all of these sixes, which can be explained by a set of pulls exerted on the organization by each of its six parts, as shown in Figure 8. When conditions favor one of these pulls, the associated part of the organization becomes key, the coordinating mechanism appropriate to itself becomes prime, and the form of decentralization that passes power to itself emerges. The organization is thus drawn to design itself as a particular configuration. We list here (see Table 1) and then introduce briefly the six resulting configurations, together with a seventh that tends to appear when no one pull or part dominates.

TABLE 1

CONFIGURATION	PRIME COORDINATING MECHANISM	KEY PART OF ORGANIZATION	TYPE OF DECENTRALIZATION
Entrepreneurial organization	Direct Supervision	Strategic apex	Vertical and horizontal centralization
Machine organization	Standardization of work processes	Technostructure	Limited horizontal decentralization
Professional organization	Standardization of skills	Operating core	Horizontal decentralization
Diversified organization	Standardization of outputs	Middle line	Limited vertical decentralization
Innovative organization	Mutual adjustment	Support staff	Selected decentralization
Missionary organization	Standardization of norms	Ideology	Decentralization
Political organization	None	None	Varies

FIGURE 8
Basic Pulls on the
Organization

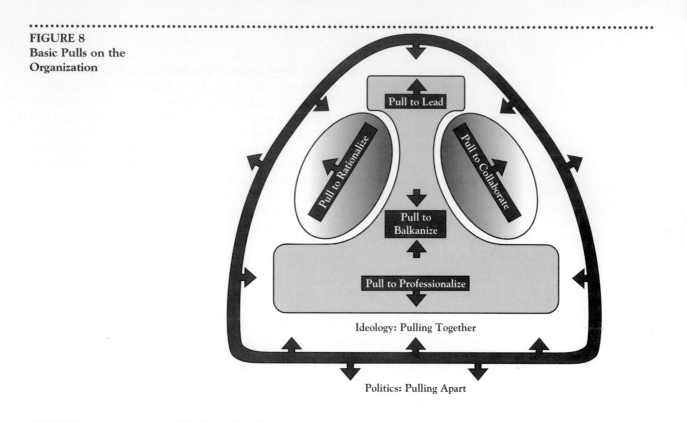

The name tells it all. And the figure above shows it all. The structure is simple, not much more than one large unit consisting of one or a few top managers, one of whom dominates by the pull to lead, and a group of operators who do the basic work. Little of the behavior in the organization is formalized and minimal use is made of planning, training, or the liaison devices. The absence of standardization means that the structure is organic and has little need for staff analysts. Likewise there are few middle line managers because so much of the coordination is handled at the top. Even the support staff is minimized, in order to keep the structure lean, the organization flexible.

The organization must be flexible because it operates in a dynamic environment, often by choice since that is the only place where it can outsmart the bureaucracies. But that environment must be simple, as must the production system, or else the chief executive could not for long hold on to the lion's share of the power. The organization is often young, in part because time drives it toward bureaucracy, in part because the vulnerability of its simple structure often causes it to fail. And many of these organizations are often small,

THE ENTREPRENEURIAL ORGANIZATION

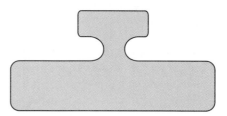

since size too drives the structure toward bureaucracy. Not infrequently the chief executive purposely keeps the organization small in order to retain his or her personal control.

The classic case is of course the small entrepreneurial firm, controlled tightly and personally by its owner. Sometimes, however, under the control of a strong leader the organization can grow to large. Likewise, entrepreneurial organizations can be found in other sectors too, like government, where strong leaders personally control particular agencies, often ones they have founded. Sometimes under crisis conditions, large organizations also revert temporarily to the entrepreneurial form to allow forceful leaders to try to save them.

THE MACHINE ORGANIZATION

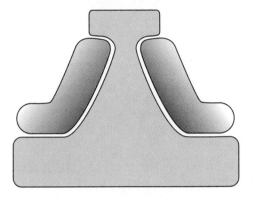

The machine organization is the offspring of the Industrial Revolution, when jobs became highly specialized and work became highly standardized. As can be seen in the figure above, in contrast to entrepreneurial organizations, the machine one elaborates its administration. First, it requires a large technostructure to design and maintain its systems of standardization, notably those that formalize its behaviors and plan its actions. And by virtue of the organization's dependence on these systems, the technostructure gains a good deal of informal power, resulting in a limited amount of horizontal decentralization reflecting the pull to rationalize. A large hierarchy of middle-line managers emerges to control the highly specialized work of the operating core. But the middle line hierarchy is usually structured on a functional basis all the way up to the top, where the real power of coordination lies. So the structure tends to be rather centralized in the vertical sense.

To enable the top managers to maintain centralized control, both the environment and the production system of the machine organization must be fairly simple, the latter regulating the work of the operators but not itself automated. In fact, machine organizations fit most naturally with mass production. Indeed it is interesting that this structure is most prevalent in industries that date back to the period from the Industrial Revolution to the early part of this century.

THE PROFESSIONAL ORGANIZATION

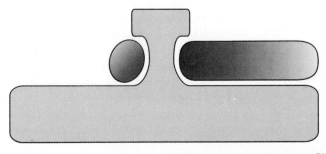

There is another bureaucratic configuration, but because this one relies on the standardization of skills rather than of work processes or outputs for its coordination, it emerges as dramatically different from the machine one. Here the pull to professionalize dominates. In having to rely on trained professionals—people highly specialized, but with considerable control over their work, as in hospitals or universities—to do its operating tasks, the organization surrenders a good deal of its power not only to the professionals themselves but also to the associations and institutions that select and train them in the first place. So the structure emerges as highly decentralized horizontally; power over many decisions, both operating and strategic, flows all the way down the hierarchy, to the professionals of the operating core.

Above the operating core we find a rather unique structure. There is little need for a technostructure, since the main standardization occurs as a result of training that takes place outside the organization. Because the professionals work so independently, the size of operating units can be very large, and few first line managers are needed. The support staff is typically very large too, in order to back up the high-priced professionals.

The professional organization is called for whenever an organization finds itself in an environment that is stable yet complex. Complexity requires decentralization to highly trained individuals, and stability enables them to apply standardized skills and so to work with a good deal of autonomy. To ensure that autonomy, the production system must be neither highly regulating, complex, nor automated.

THE DIVERSIFIED ORGANIZATION

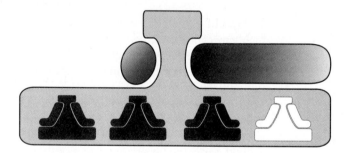

Like the professional organization, the diversified one is not so much an integrated organization as a set of rather independent entities coupled together by a loose administrative structure. But whereas those entities of the professional organization are individuals, in the diversified one they are units in the middle line, generally called "divisions," exerting a dominant pull to Balkanize. This configuration differs from the others in one major respect: it is not a complete structure, but a partial one superimposed on the others. Each division has its own structure.

An organization divisionalizes for one reason above all, because its product lines are diversified. And that tends to happen most often in the largest and most mature organizations, the ones that have run out of opportunities—or have become bored—in their traditional markets. Such diversification encourages the organization to replace functional by market-based units, one for each distinct product line (as shown in the diversified organization figure), and to grant considerable autonomy to each to run its own business. The result is a limited form of decentralization down the chain of command.

How does the central headquarters maintain a semblance of control over the divisions? Some direction supervision is used. But too much of that interferes with the necessary divisional autonomy. So the headquarters relies on performance control systems, in other words, the standardization of outputs. To design these control systems, headquarters creates a small technostructure. This is shown in the figure, across from the small central support staff that headquarters sets up to provide certain services common to the divisions such as legal counsel and public relations. And because headquarters' control constitutes external control, as discussed in the first hypothesis on power, the structure of the divisions tend to be drawn toward the machine form.

THE INNOVATIVE ORGANIZATION

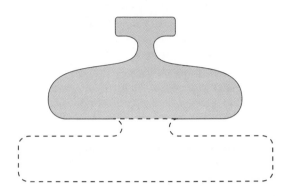

None of the structures so far discussed suits the industries of our age, industries such as aerospace, petrochemicals, think-tank consulting, and film making. These organizations need above all to innovate in very complex ways. The bureaucratic structures are too inflexible, and the entrepreneurial one too centralized. These industries require "project structures," ones that can fuse experts drawn from different specialties into smoothly functioning creative teams. That is the role of our fifth configuration, the innovative organization, which we shall also call "adhocracy," dominated by the experts' pull to collaborate.

Adhocracy is an organic structure that relies for coordination on mutual adjustment among its highly trained and highly specialized experts, which it encourages by the extensive use of the liaison devices—integrating managers, standing committees, and above all task forces and matrix structure. Typically the experts are grouped in functional units for housekeeping purposes but deployed in small market based project teams to do their work. To these teams, located all over the structure in accordance with the decisions to be made, is delegated power over different kinds of decisions. So the structure becomes decentralized selectively in the vertical and horizontal dimensions, that is, power is distributed unevenly, all over the structure, according to expertise and need.

All the distinctions of conventional structure disappear in the innovative organization, as can be seen in the figure above. With power based on expertise, the line-staff distinction evaporates. With power distributed throughout the structure, the distinction between the strategic apex and the rest of the structure blurs.

These organizations are found in environments that are both complex and dynamic, because those are the ones that require sophisticated innovation, the type that calls for the cooperative efforts of many different kinds of experts. One type of adhocracy is often associated with a production system that is very complex, sometimes automated, and so requires a highly skilled and influential support staff to design and maintain the technical system of the operating core. (The dashed lines of the figure designate the separation of the operating core from the adhocratic administrative structure.) Here the projects take place in the administration to bring new operating facilities on line (as when a new complex is designed in a petrochemicals firm). Another type of adhocracy produces its projects directly for its clients (as in a think tank consulting firm or manufacturer of engineering prototypes). Here, as a result, the operators also take part in the projects, bringing their expertise to bear on them; hence the operating core blends into the administrative structure (as indicated in the figure above the dashed line). This second type of adhocracy tends to be young on average, because with no standard products or services, many tend to fail while others escape their vulnerability by standardizing some products or services and so converting themselves to a form of bureaucracy.[1]

THE MISSIONARY ORGANIZATION

Our sixth configuration forms another rather distinct combination of the elements we have been discussing. When an organization is dominated by its ideology, its members are encouraged to pull together, and so there tends to be a loose division of labor, little job specialization, as well as a reduction of the various forms of differentiation found in the other configurations—of the strategic apex from the rest, of staff from line or administration from operations, between operators, between divisions, and so on.

What holds the missionary together—that is, provides for its coordination—is the standardization of norms, the sharing of values and beliefs among all its members. And the key to ensuring this is their socialization, effected through the design parameter of indoctrination. Once the new member has been indoctrinated into the organization—once he or she identifies strongly with the common beliefs—then he or she can be given considerable freedom to make decisions. Thus the result of effective indoctrination is the most complete form of decentralization. And because other forms of coordination need not be relied upon, the missionary organization formalizes little of its behavior as such and makes minimal use of planning and control systems. As a result, it has little technostructure. Likewise, external professional training is not relied upon, because that would force the organization to surrender a certain control to external agencies.

Hence, the missionary organization ends up as an amorphous mass of members, with little specialization as to job, differentiation as to part, division as to status.

Missionaries tend not to be very young organizations—it takes time for a set of beliefs to become institutionalized as an ideology. Many missionaries do not get a chance to grow very old either (with notable exceptions, such as certain long standing religious orders). Missionary organizations cannot grow very large per se—they rely on personal contacts among their members—although some tend to spin off other enclaves in the form of relatively independent units sharing the same ideology. Neither the environment nor the technical system of the missionary organization can be very complex, because that would require the use of highly skilled specialists, who would hold a certain power and status over others and thereby serve to differentiate the structure. Thus we would expect to find the simplest

---

[1] We shall clarify in a later reading these two basic types of adhocracies. Toffler employed the term adhocracy in his popular book *Future Shock*, but it can be found in print at least as far back as 1964.

technical systems in these organizations, usually hardly any at all, as in religious orders or in the primitive farm cooperatives.

THE POLITICAL ORGANIZATION

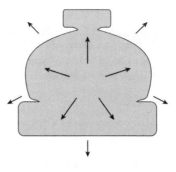

Finally, we come to a form of organization characterized, structurally at least, by what it lacks. When an organization has no dominate part, no dominant mechanism of coordination, and no stable form of centralization or decentralization, it may have difficulty tempering the conflicts within its midst, and a form of organization called the *political* may result. What characterizes its behavior is the pulling apart of its different parts, as shown in the figure above.

Political organizations can take on different forms. Some are temporary, reflecting difficult transitions in strategy or structure that evoke conflict. Others are more permanent, perhaps because the organization must face competing internal forces (say, between necessarily strong marketing and production departments), perhaps because a kind of political rot has set in but the organization is sufficiently entrenched to support it (being, for example, a monopoly or a protected government unit).

Together, all these configurations seem to encompass and integrate a good deal of what we know about organizations. It should be emphasized however, that as presented, each configuration is idealized—a simplification, really a caricature of reality. No real organization is ever exactly like any one of them, although some do come remarkably close, while others seem to reflect combinations of them, sometimes in transition from one to another.

The first five represent what seem to be the most common forms of organizations; thus these will form the basis for the "context" section of this book—labeled entrepreneurial, mature, diversified, innovation, and professional. There, a reading in each chapter will be devoted to each of these configurations, describing its structure, functioning, conditions, strategy-making process, and the issues that surround it. Other readings in these chapters will look at specific strategies in each of these contexts, industry conditions, strategy techniques, and so on.

The other two configurations—the missionary and the political—seem to be less common, represented more by the forces of culture and conflict that exist in all organizations than by distinct forms as such. Hence they will be discussed in the chapter that immediately follows this one, on "Dealing with Culture and Power." But because all these configurations themselves must not be taken as hard and fast, indeed because ideology and politics work within different configurations in all kinds of interesting ways, a final chapter in the context section, on managing change, will include a reading called "Beyond Configuration: Forces and Forms in Effective Organizations," that seeks to broaden this view of organizations.

by James Brian Quinn, Philip Anderson, and Sydney Finkelstein

Many forces are combining to compel the end of static competitive advantage strategies. In today's hypercompetitive environments, firms face a continually shifting competitive landscape in which traditional sources of dominance—cost and quality, timing and know-how, the creation of competitive strongholds, and deep pockets—are constantly eroded. The key message of the hypercompetition concept is that the only enduring advantage results from the ability to generate new advantages: for example, while no cost or quality advantage is sustainable, the skill of generating new cost and quality advantages is sustainable. Furthermore, firms must keep pace with rivals in many different arenas; failure to keep up is not met with leniency (D'Aveni, 1994).

HYPERCOMPETITION AND ORGANIZATION FORMS

It is natural to conclude that organization forms designed for and adapted to a different era will not suffice in hypercompetitive environments. Indeed, it is quite widely accepted that new organization forms are emerging in response to such environmental trends as customization, globalization, rapid technological change, deregulation, and shifting work force demographics (Miles Snow, and Coleman, 1992). The dynamic driving the appearance of new forms appears to be a transformation from command and control to information-based organization (Drucker, 1988).

The term "network organization" has become a popular catch-all category, and is frequently used to describe any new organizational form that will supersede the multidivisional form as the dominant way of structuring a modern firm. Although the term "network organization" has been used in so many different ways that it is difficult to pin down the concept, a common theme of those describing networks as a new form of organization is debureaucratization. In the network organization, lateral relations are more important than vertical relations, and hierarchies are either very flat or disappear altogether. A central theme of this paper is that no one "network organizational form" will prevail as the dominant structure adapted to hypercompetitive environments.

We suggest these forms seldom occur in pure form across the entire entity, integrating all aspects of a major enterprise, and their evolution is not being driven by their emergence in totally new enterprises. Rather they are forms of organizing, not forms of organization, and they are typically embedded in larger organizational structures that are still at least partly bureaucratic. Because these forms are building blocks, with several typically co-existing inside larger organizations, a key challenge for top management is integrating these different forms of organizing into a coherent whole. The organization of the future will not be a hybrid, but will be polymorphic, containing within itself subunits whose fundamental ways of bringing intellect to bear upon problems are vastly different from one another

Five very different network configurations—adapted to different purposes and confronting managers with different challenges—will, however, be among the key building blocks. The fundamental difference between these forms is that they represent different models for deploying intellect, the key to hypercompetitive survival. Since the inception of administrative theory, organizational structure has been defined primarily by functional specialization, power relationships, and hierarchy. We suggest that today managers must focus instead upon how the enterprise develops and deploys intellect.

---

* Unpublished monograph, Amos Tuck School, Dartmouth College; used with the permission of the authors.

The Network Organization

At least since Burns and Stalker (1961), it has been widely agreed that organic organizational forms are better suited to turbulent environments than are mechanistic forms. However, hypercompetition is not simply turbulence. In hypercompetitive environments, firms cannot compete solely by emphasizing one advantage (e.g., cost, flexibility, or quality), and they cannot fall very far behind world-class standards on any key competitive dimension (D'Aveni, 1994). Firms must simultaneously be both efficient and flexible. In such environments, successful firms are unlikely to be purely organic—rather, they must combine both mechanistic and organic properties. This is precisely why network organizations are of such interest to scholars exploring what structures will thrive under hypercompetitive conditions. Networks seem able to achieve both efficiency and flexibility.

One group of scholars and practitioners conceives of network organizations as entities in which lateral ties are substituted for vertical ones. In this view, the formal structure will come to look more like the informal structure—employees at all levels will ignore boundaries, using information technology to locate and contact directly those individuals whose knowledge or cooperation they require. McKinsey & Co. popularized the use of the term "horizontal corporation" for such flat, boundary-less forms (Byrne, 1993), but scholars have been predicting for decades that future organizations will be much flatter than simple extrapolation from the past would suggest (e.g., Bennis and Slater, 1968).

In this view, what will replace the hierarchical department as the building block of organizations? There is no consensus answer, but many writers who conceive of the network organization in terms of lateral ties argue that cross-functional teams are emerging as the basic structural unit. . . . Another group of scholars takes a different view of network organization, stressing the replacement of command relationships by quasi-market mechanisms. . . . Both perspectives provide interesting insights. However, we contend that extremely flat designs are but one form of organization enabled by new information technologies, and we question whether cross-functional teams will serve as the universal building block of network organizations. Although quasi-market relationships lie at the core of one organizing form we analyze, we do not identify the "network organization" with a single control mechanism. We further contend that: (1) bureaucracy will not disappear; (2) hierarchy in the broadest sense—systems consisting of stably interrelated sub-assemblies—will continue to be the dominant mode of organizing; and (3) the core problem that network organization must address is the effective deployment of intellect. These contentions then lead us to an exploration of five emerging forms of network organizing that we suggest will serve as fundamental building blocks for organizations designed to cope with hypercompetition.

BUREAUCRACY

It is entirely likely that many, perhaps most, organizations will contain some highly bureaucratic subunits for the foreseeable future. The basic reason why bureaucracy will continue to prove indispensable is that under modern capitalism, goals of flexibility and efficiency must co-exist with demands for reliability, independence, or compliance. . . . Bureaucracy is an effective design for stable units whose paramount concern is consistency, accountability, and relative incrementalism. . . .We expect that organizations in hypercompetitive environments will often require some loosely coupled subunits whose bureaucratic design responds to such institutional needs.

HIERARCHY

It may well be that classic bureaucratic structure will be limited to those subunits whose principal mission is adapting the organization to institutional pressures. What then of the organizational core, charged with achieving simultaneous efficiency and flexibility? Will it consist of a flat web of teams with direct ties criss-crossing to all other teams in the organization? In hypercompetitive environments, organizations are likely to have to deal with more complex, not simpler events. Complex systems—those made up of a large number of parts that interact in a non-simple way (Simon, 1962)—are far more capable of adapting to environments which place multiple, simultaneous demands on the firm. As Simon notes, complexity very often takes the form of hierarchy, which he defines as a structure composed of interrelated subsystems that ultimately rest on a small number of fundamental building blocks. It is in this sense that we contend organizations in hypercompetitive environments will be hierarchical. Some hierarchy will clearly be necessary to resolve disputes and to allocate limited resources. Hierarchy will also survive because evolution and learning are accelerated by the existence of relatively stable organizational subassemblies containing high expertise (Simon, 1962). Learning is the fundamental challenge facing organizations under hypercompetition—the methodology for continually generating new advantages while old ones are eroded away.

NETWORKS, SPEED, AND INTELLECT

Generally, the emergence of network organization is attributed to contemporary pressures for speed and responsiveness without sacrificing efficiency. Network organizations, by combining the advantages of centralization with decentralization, are thought to overcome the classic mechanistic vs. organic dilemma. We contend that there is a more fundamental reason why some network forms of organizing hold the key to surviving in hypercompetitive environments. The basic challenge confronting the modern enterprise is the need to develop and deploy intellectual assets. The "intelligent enterprise" (Quinn, 1992) uses various network forms to bring its intellect to bear on critical problems. . . .

Driving the shift to network organizing forms is an epochal change in the nature of capitalism, from a mass-production system—where the principal source of value was capital and labor transforming materials into useful products—*toward* innovation-mediated production, where the principal component of value creation is knowledge and intellectual capabilities. Central to this transformation is the emergence of services as the critical links in a firm's value chain (Quinn, 1992). The creation and distribution of services and intangibles now accounts for over three-fourths of all economic activity, and much of this value added depends on capturing and distributing intellectual outputs to the point of their consumption or use. Even "manufacturing" firms find that service activities—like research, product design, logistics, marketing, or information management—account for most of the value added between raw materials and finished goods. . . . The shift toward services and innovation-mediated production means that firms must re-think what dominance is. Dominance is not simply a function of market share for a particular product class. In service-based enterprises, dominance means being able to bring more talent to bear on an activity critical to customers than any rival can. This occurs when (1) a company has the most effective presence in the specific service activities its segment of the market most desires, and (2) it can capture and defend some special experience or specialization benefits accruing to that activity share.

Different Organizations for Different Purposes

A complex organization often contains different units organized for different purposes with different sets of strengths and weaknesses. We suggest that "the network organization" (as that term has been used) is not a single form of organization, but embraces a complex variety of fundamentally different forms of organizing. Each represents a different model of how the firm brings intellect to bear on the challenges it faces. The firm "mixes and matches" these forms as necessary, depending on the problems with which it must cope.

TABLE 1
**Outline of Five Forms
of Organizing**

	Infinitely Flat	Inverted	Spider's Web	Cluster	Starburst
Definition of node	Individual	Individual	Individual	Cluster	Business units
Locus of intellect	Center	Nodes	Nodes	Cluster	Center and nodes
Locus of novelty	Nodes	Nodes	Project	Project	Nodes
Mode of linkage	Center to nodes	None	Node to node	Cluster to project	Center to nodes
Source of leverage	Multiplicative	Distributive	Exponential	Additive	Synthetic
Management problems and challenges	• Lack of career path. • Need for pay based on individual performance. • Dependent on isolated professional management • Need to maintain system flexibility.	• Loss of formal authority for line managers. • Need to simultaneously empower and and control contact people at nodes.	• Need to foster communication without overloading the system. • Managing competition across nodes.	• Individuals face dual pressures from clusters and cross-cluster teams. • Dependent on quality of leadership, breadth of training, and motivation of participants.	• Need to balance autonomy and control. • Need to generate significant resources.
Example	Brokerage firms	Hospitals	Internet	Corporate staff	Major movie studio

In the following section, we focus on five forms of organizing that have emerged from an intensive study of firms in service industries. We do not suggest that these five structures exhaust the range of possibilities. Rather, we hope to move the field beyond thinking of "the network organization" as a unitary structural form, perhaps the successor to the multi-divisional form as the dominant way of organizing an enterprise. In delineating these five forms, we first focus on what distinguishes one form from the others, what favors use of that particular form, and what the distinctive management problems are in each. Table 1 summarizes this analysis. Four intellectual dimensions most distinguish each form. These are:

▼ *Locus of intellect*, the principal domain(s) within the organization where deep knowledge of its fundamental disciplines reside(s).

▼ *Locus of novelty*, the principal location(s) at which intellect is converted to novel solutions.

▼ *Mode of linkage*, the direction of flow of information and how the locus of intellect and the locus of novelty are connected.

▼ *Source of leverage*, how the enterprise leverages its know-how base.

THE "INFINITELY" FLAT ORGANIZATION

In infinitely flat organizations—so called because there is no inherent limit to their span—the primary locus of intellect is the center of the organization. The central point of the network contains a highly specialized form of intellect; for example, the operations knowledge of a fast food franchising organization or the huge body of data and analysis possessed by a brokerage firm. Each node becomes the locus of novelty, the point at which the center's know-how is applied to customer problems. Know-how flows principally in a one-way direction, from the center to the nodes. Here, the source of leverage is multiplicative. There appears to be virtually no limit to the number of nodes that can be linked directly to a center, through which an organization can effectively make analyzed knowledge about the outside world useful and the *cumulative* experience curve of its many nodes available to each individual node. Single centers in such organizations have been observed to coordinate

FIGURE 1
The Infinitely Flat
Organization

20 ⟶ 40 ⟶ 100 ⟶ 400 ⟶ ∞

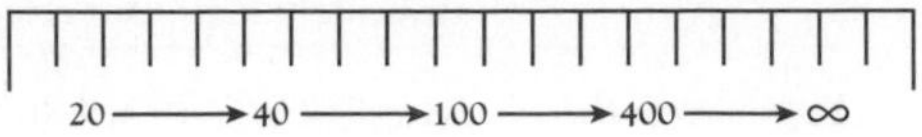

anywhere from 20 to 18,000 individual nodes. Common examples could include highly dispersed fast food, brokerage, airlines, shipping, or mail order operations.

In this organizing form, few orders for direct action are given by the line organization to those below. The nodes themselves rarely need to communicate with one another and can operate quite independently. Instead, the central authority usually becomes an information source, a communications coordinator, or a reference desk for unusual inquiries. Lower organizational levels generally connect into it to obtain information for the purpose of performing better, rather than for instructions or specific guidance. Rules are often programmed into the system and changed automatically by software, and many operations are monitored electronically.

For example, Merrill Lynch's more than 450 domestic brokerage offices each connect directly into their parents' central information offices for routine needs, yet can bypass the electronic system to gain personal access to individual experts in headquarters. Merrill Lynch has a PC-based workstation for each of its "financial consultants" (brokers) linked through local area networks and SNA connections to its central mainframe computers. Although regional marketing structures exist, business is conducted as if each of Merrill Lynch's 17,000-odd branch office contact people reported directly to headquarters, with their only personal oversight being at the local level. Computers extend Merrill Lynch's system capabilities to the level of individual customers, printing 400 million pages of output a year, largely customer reports captured directly from on-line transaction data. In effect, technology permits the company to compete in a coordinated fashion with the full power and scale economies of a major financial enterprise, yet local brokers can manage their own small units and accounts as independently as if they alone provided the total service on a local basis. From an operations viewpoint, the organization is absolutely flat; 17,000 brokers connect directly into headquarters for all their needs.

Infinitely flat organizations operate best when the activity at the node can be broken down and measured to the level of its minimum repeatable transaction elements; for example, cooking and operations procedures in fast food chains or the basic components of a financial transaction in a widely dispersed brokerage network. Response times can be nearly instantaneous, and within the programmed rules such organizations can accommodate high levels of empowerment and personalized sales behavior. Infinitely flat organizations can be established to support any degree of decentralized authority or responsibility desired. . . .

Infinitely flat organizations function well when each node is totally independent of other nodes. Managers residing at the center are often the most highly skilled professionals—e.g., investment analysts or logistics planners. The value they add stems from their ability to collect information from all internal and external sources, and to analyze and present relevant information to the nodes. Under proper circumstances, the electronic systems of infinitely flat organizations capture the experience curve of the organization, allowing less-trained people quickly to achieve levels of performance ordinarily associated with much more experienced personnel. Because quality and productivity can be monitored at the point of customer contact, well-designed systems simultaneously offer *both* highest responsiveness and maximum efficiencies. This allows firms to function in hypercompetitive environments, where firms configured to follow a single "generic" strategy (e.g., low cost or differentiation) would fail.

The infinitely flat organization presents certain inherent management problems. Perhaps the most severe is that in the absence of hierarchy, lower-level personnel wonder how to advance in a career path. In addition, under infinitely flat conditions traditional (e.g., "Hay point") systems of compensation break down, and new compensation systems based upon individual performance become extremely important. Reward systems may include a great variety of titles and intangible rewards, in addition to financial rewards for people at the nodes.

A second problem is that it is very difficult to train management coordinators in these systems. There is little opportunity to transfer personnel from the nodes to the center because the tasks are too different; indeed, the professionalism and analytical depth characteristic of the center may be incompatible with the more personalized service demands placed on people at the nodes.

Third, the information system must achieve a series of delicate balances. Measurement systems must capture both the quantitative and the intangible aspects of operations, or work at the nodes can become dehumanized. This usually means that electronic systems must be supplemented by customer sampling or personal observation systems. There is a tendency for systems to rigidify with time, if companies continue to use the same measurement and control systems over long periods. Consequently, internal systems must typically be bolstered by an external scanning system that forces the entire organization to adapt to environmental changes. In addition to the structured "hard information" linkages of the infinitely flat line organization, there frequently needs to be a team or cluster organization that conveys intangible information (e.g., values) from the center to the nodes, trains individuals in new tasks, and provides a level of professionalism the nodes lack when confronted with challenges such as public relations crises or the installation of new marketing concepts—as the specialized technology training or marketing teams of Merrill Lynch do.

THE INVERTED ORGANIZATION

In this form, the major locus of intellect is the nodes contacting customers, not the center. Hospitals or medical clinics, therapeutic care-giving units, or consulting engineering firms provide examples of such situations. The point of novelty creation is also at the node, typically because this is where a service is uniquely adapted and delivered to a customer. The nodes tend to be professional and self-sufficient. Accordingly, there is no direct linkage for routinely moving intellect from one point to another. The loci of intellect and novelty creation are the same points. When critical know-how diffuses, it usually does so informally from node to node—or formally from node to center—the opposite of the infinitely flat organization. The leverage of this form of organization is distributive. The role of the support structure is to provide logistics or specially requested support to the nodes and to relieve them of administrative detail. The center can also serve as a repository accessing new information from the outside and facilitating the acquisition of know-how from a limited number of other nodes through special interconnections, such as seminars or similar updating techniques.

In inverted organizations, the line hierarchy becomes a "support" structure instead of an "order-giving" structure. For example, the hospital CEO does not give orders to doctors, nor does the chief pilot give orders to airline pilots except in extreme emergencies. Hierarchy continues to exist because neither the CEO (in the hospital example) nor the chief pilot (in the airline example) can work for each individual contact person at the same time. The function of line managers becomes bottleneck breaking, culture development, communication of values, developing special studies and consulting upon request, expediting resource movements, and providing service economies of scale. Division of labor and hierarchy facilitate the ability of different managers to support contact personnel as needed—what was line management now performs essentially "staff" activities.

FIGURE 2
The Inverted
Organization

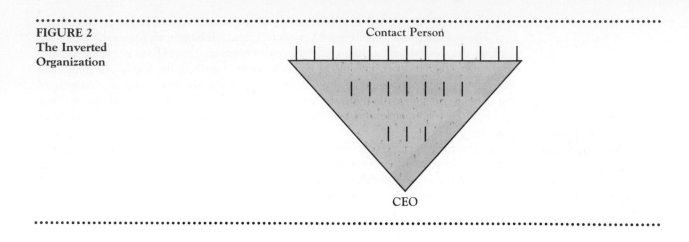

Contact Person

CEO

A well known example of the inverted organization is NovaCare, the largest provider of rehabilitation care in the U.S. and one of the fastest growing health care companies of the last decade. Its central resource—well trained physical, occupational, and speech therapists—are in short supply. NovaCare provides the business infrastructure for over 4,000 therapists, arranging contracts with nursing homes and chains, handling accounting and credit activities, providing training updates, and stabilizing and enhancing the therapists' earnings. The key to the business is the therapists and the quality of their service. The rest of the organization is consciously set up to support them and to solve problems for them. Executives, including the CEO, refer to therapists as "my bosses" and are judged on how well they respond to orders from the therapists, who—though well trained as caregivers— were not trained for and often disliked the business side of their activities. Electronic planning and monitoring systems allow the therapists to perform efficiently in very dispersed locations and accurately meet the constantly changing requirements of regulatory bodies, the profession, and payer groups.

The inverted organization works well when servicing the customer at the point of contact is the most important activity in the enterprise, *and* the person at the point of contact has more information about the individual customer's problem and its potential solutions than anyone else. Quite often this form is restricted to only certain units in direct contact with customers; however, in some intellectual aristocracies, such as law firms, medical clinics, or colleges, the inverted organization may pervade virtually all departments. Experience suggests that because they present unique problems, inverted organizations should be used sparingly, and not as "gimmicks" to improve empowerment. Their proper functioning depends on the genuinely superior knowledge of the contact people. Nevertheless, members of the line hierarchy retain substantive roles, particularly as analysts of special issues and arbiters of last resort. They also often enjoy greatly expanded opportunities to perform more influential long term activities (such as resource building or public policy participation) once freed of traditional routing burdens.

The inverted organization presents management with both people and systems challenges. The loss of formal authority can be very traumatic for line managers. Additionally, this form depends on continuous professional training for contact people, great attention to personnel selection, and reinforcement of consistent organizational values. Given acknowledged formal power, point people may tend to act ever more like specialists with strictly "professional" outlooks, and resist any set of organization rules or business norms. It is difficult for contact people—particularly those who must serve a diverse customer mix—to internalize or stay current with sufficient details concerning the firm's own complex internal systems. Empowerment of contact personnel without adequate control can be extremely dangerous (consider, for instance, the case of People Express). Therefore, very powerful information systems and constant reinforcement of operating norms are required to support inverted organizations.

THE "SPIDER'S WEB" ORGANIZATION

This form of organization is a true network; to avoid confusion with other "network-like" forms (particularly those which are more akin to matrix organizations), we use the term "spider's web" as its descriptor. Often there is no intervening hierarchy or order giving center between the nodes of these organizations. The locus of intellect is highly dispersed, residing largely at the contact nodes as in the inverted organization. However, the point of novelty is a project or a problem that requires nodes to interact intimately or to seek others who happen to have knowledge or special capabilities they need. The organization's know-how is essentially latent, until a project forces it to materialize through connections people make with each other. Information linkages are quite complex; know-how is moved from many nodes to many other nodes, which typically collaborate temporarily in delivering a service as part of a project. The source of leverage is exponential—as defined by interactive learning theory or network theory. With even a modest number of collaborating nodes (8 to 10), the number of connections through which knowledge may be created rapidly mounts into the hundreds or thousands.

Spider's web organizations emerge when highly dispersed nodes each contain a high level of specialized intellect, yet for client effectiveness must interact with each other directly and frequently. The nodes may have no hierarchical relationship to each other, and linkages are often activated solely on a voluntary basis. Individual nodes would operate independently if it were not essential to capture information economies of scale or scope. If there is a decision center, authority interactions tend to occur through ad hoc committees or task forces. Occasionally, individual nodes may need to operate in such a highly coordinated fashion that they delegate temporary authority to a project leader—as when widely dispersed researchers present a contract proposal or an investment banking consortium services a multinational client. The purest example of a spider's web organization is the Internet, the use of which is managed by no one. Using Internet, researchers may interact with other scientists around the world as collaborators working on particular segments of a problem, with little more than a goal, personal integrity, and professional discipline to provide cohesion. Other common examples include most open markets, security exchanges, library consortia, and political action groups.

Although spider's web networks have existed for centuries (among universities or scientists, and within trading groups), they enjoy selective advantages in hypercompetitive

FIGURE 3
The "Spider's Web"
Organization

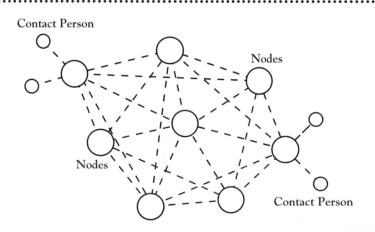

Contact Person

Nodes

Nodes

Contact Person

environments because they can simultaneously accommodate high specialization, multiple geographic locations, and a disciplined focus on a single problem or customer set. They are particularly useful in identifying or analyzing problems where customer sets are dispersed and highly diverse specialties need to be tapped. . . .Despite their many benefits, spider's webs present important challenges to managers. The dominant necessity is creating a culture for communication and willing sharing, since how one communicates and what one is willing to communicate are as important as the knowledge the nodes contain. Unfortunately, clearing these hurdles may bring on a host of other problems. Extreme overload can emerge as networks become jammed with trivia, but resist screening and sorting mechanisms. Dawdling is common, as nodes work on refining their specialist solutions instead of solving the complete problem together. Assigning credit for intellectual contributions is difficult, and cross-competition among nodes can inhibit the sharing upon which such networks depend. Appropriate incentives at both the network and local levels are essential.

THE CLUSTER ORGANIZATION

The cluster organization superficially resembles the spider's web, because the mode of know-how transport is once again from node to node. However, the locus of intellect lies in loosely formed clusters, which normally carry out some relatively permanent activity (such as staff analyses, long-term technical innovation, or customer relationships) requiring deep competence in specific disciplines (Mills, 1991). Within clusters people may form and reform into smaller teams to solve specific problems that are central to the cluster's own success. Members of clusters tend to be in close proximity most of the time, working on related problems. Occasionally, when the enterprise encounters tasks that call for a mix of skills, temporary teams are pulled together from the specialized clusters. The team is not a permanent unit; it is a temporary overlay on other organizing processes. However, the existence of cross-functional teams is not itself the defining characteristic of a cluster organization. Its essence lies in the fact that team members are cross-trained to help with enterprise-wide tasks, but spend most of their time in clusters of people who handle useful daily problems for the enterprise while they continue to build depth in their particular specialty.

In the spider's web network organization, projects generate knowledge via interaction. In the cluster organization, specialized units create knowledge; teams tend to assemble pre-existing expertise into a larger package—e.g., to acquire a company or create an alliance of interest to the whole enterprise. The point of novelty occurs when a cross-cluster team must be formed to address a problem, and the mode of transport is from cluster to team. Unlike many spider's webs organizations, there is usually a clear decision making authority designated by the enterprise to head the task group. The source of leverage for clusters is additive; teams generally package together the sum of the clusters' know-how. When the packaging and delivery are complete, team members return to their primary tasks of building specialized know-how within a cluster and performing the routine tasks of that cluster, which also may involve some teaming of specialists within the cluster.

Clusters are effective when tasks that affect the whole enterprise (e.g., mergers, acquisitions, or new ventures) temporarily require deep knowledge beyond the bounds of any individual's or group's know-how. Specialization is required, but problems are so diverse that no one functional specialty can cope with them alone. Such organizations exploit scale economies when clusters are stably occupied with a base load of common activity; the effect is greater when skills for certain problem classes can be centralized geographically. Functional organization proves inadequate because the incidence of novel, cross-specialty problem solving is high both within and across clusters. Clusters do not function as well when activities are geographically dispersed or are routinized.

FIGURE 4
The Cluster Organization
(adapted from Mills, 1991)

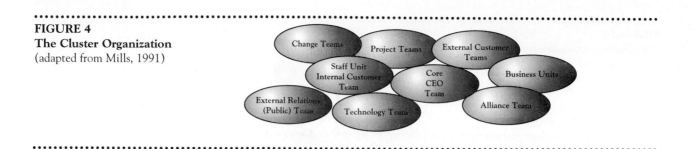

NovaCare is a case in point. When NovaCare is acquiring or building a new hospital or therapeutic care system, it pulls together a task force of therapists, planners, software, accounting and finance, marketing, regional, facilities, and general management personnel who have worked together on similar projects in the past. When the project is over, team members return to their home base, where they both diffuse specific knowledge from the project and work on smaller teams developing some aspect of therapy management in depth.

The characteristic management problem of a cluster organization is that members perceive a tension between demands to build deep, cluster-specific competence to serve their normal clientele and pressures to contribute to cross-cluster teams. The effectiveness of these organizations is dependent on breadth of training and their ability to motivate team contributions external to the cluster. Assignment, not voluntarism, is common for cross-cluster teams—posing the usual problems of equity, identity, and reentry to the cluster. Commonly, employees take several years to become acculturated to the dual pressures cluster organizations create.

THE STARBURST ORGANIZATION

The four organizing forms described above tend to function well as long as they are not required to address standing, yet very diverse sets of external customer needs. Where markets are very diverse, one may observe a special kind of network organizing form, the starburst. The starburst organization is technically an inter-organizational network, but for special reasons the organizational units are under some shared ownership. Starburst organizations are usually creative organizations that constantly peel off more permanent, but separate, units from the core competencies of their parents, like shooting stars. Spin-off subsidiaries remain partially or wholly owned by the parent, usually can raise external resources independently, and are controlled primarily via market mechanisms. Examples of different forms of starburst organizations and their ownership relationships include movie studios, Raychem, Nypro, TechComm Group (TCG), Thermo Electron, Vanguard (mutual funds), and venture capitalists. Starburst forms are associated with strong internal corporate venturing strategies (Block and MacMillan, 1993).

In this form of organization, the locus of intellect is divided. Typically, the center retains deep knowledge of some common technology or knowledge base (e.g., specialized plastic molding technology for Nypro, managing no-load funds for Vanguard). The center is a core of intellectual competency, not simply a corporate bank as in the case of holding companies. The nodes—which are essentially separate business units, not individuals or temporary clusters—are the locus of specialized market and production knowledge. They are also the locus of novelty—as either the center or a developed node organization encounters a promising new domain, it establishes a subsidiary to apply that parent's core competencies to the new set of market opportunities. The movement of intellect is typically from the center outward toward the nodes—each node draws upon the core technical know-how of the more central units, but the center does not attempt to amalgamate the diverse market knowledge of its subsidiaries. The organization rarely transfers market

FIGURE 5
The Starburst Organization

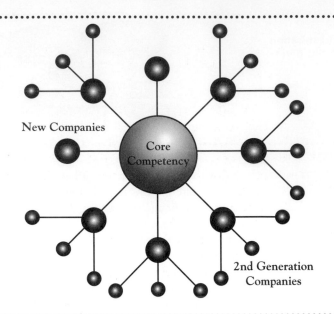

knowledge from one node laterally to another, since each node faces such different market needs. The primary source of leverage is synthetic—the firm uses local application knowledge to amplify effects from its "core competency" knowledge base. In many cases, it further leverages through outside groups the special financial or expertise access the nodes can enjoy as independent bodies.

Starburst organizations differ from conglomerates because they maintain a cohesive intellectual competency center—usually some technological or high professional skills. The center is maintained, and recharged to develop new pulses, by charging the market units a fee. In return the nodes enjoy the economies of scale and new opportunities that a large, integrated knowledge base can provide. The corporate center primarily helps raise resources, invests in maintaining the core competency, manages the culture, and sets priorities by selecting people and letting them bid for resources.

Starburst organizations work well when the core is dominated by a few knowledgeable risk-takers who know they cannot micro-manage the diverse entities in the nodes. The appropriate environment for this sort of firm is one in which entrepreneurship, not merely flexible response, is critical. For example, venture capital firms and movie studios typically operate as starbursts because they need a continuing core of creative financial and management skills, supplemented by the capacity to attract and employ a combination of risk-taking and specialized talent for each venture. The starburst organization works well in very ambiguous environments where it is difficult to associate actions with outcomes in the absence of a market test.

The classic problem of this organizational form is that management often loses faith in free-standing "shooting stars" after some time and tries to consolidate functions in the name of efficiency—as Hewlett Packard did to its regret (but later solved by reversing its policies). However, the nodes are so different that even sophisticated computer systems cannot provide or coordinate all the information needed to run such firms from the center; rather than try, managers must either live with quasi-market control or spin off the subsidiary entirely. A second difficulty faced by starburst organizations is that when heavy investment is required to achieve mass production, the starburst may find it difficult to assemble the requisite resources without over-taxing its core or some of its units. For this reason, starburst organizations tend to work best for smaller scale, lower investment, opportunities.

Polymorphism

In emphasizing that these are forms of organizing instead of organizational forms, we suggest that organizations in the face of hypercompetition will typically be polymorphic. Like NovaCare, they will include as basic building blocks some very disparate ways of organizing networks. Additionally, at least some of their components are likely to be organized bureaucratically, in response to institutional pressures or a need to provide deeply knowledgeable centers of specialized professional skills. . . .

Although NovaCare has an inverted structure for delivering its physical, occupational, and speech therapies through its 4000 professional therapists nationwide, it supports these therapists through NovaNet, which keeps track of all therapists' activities in 15 minute "units" of detail. Detailed data from within those units are used for scheduling, compensation, billing, and follow up for all therapies. Through these data NovaCare can ensure that all its customers (patients, nursing homes, hospitals, hospital directors, doctors, nursing directors, payers, and regulating bodies) are properly served, charged, and compensated in appropriate fashion. Yet within the company there are centralized functional (accounting), cluster (acquisitions), geographical hierarchical (hospital), inverted (therapy), and spider's web (professional knowledge exchange) structures. . . .

Since polymorphic organizations are likely to include several of these new forms of organizing as subassemblies, a key challenge for top management will be integrating these disparate structures into an intelligent enterprise. Software systems predicated on traditional programming principles point toward some ways in which such integration is likely to be achieved, but only hint at the power that a new paradigm is bringing to the problem of deploying the firm's accumulated know-how. The increasing power of information technology does much more than flatten organizations. It also permits organizations to integrate polymorphic forms in ways that would not have been possible a few years ago. As environments become more hypercompetitive, we expect firms to move along a continuum whose endpoints range from no central coordination (spider's web) to total coordination through software (as automated order processing systems now do). A key supporting force in this evolution is the emergence of a new paradigm in software design, "object orientation." Since the concept of programming was invented by Von Neumann and his associates, the fundamental unit of a program has been a line of code. However, in the future the fundamental building blocks of programs will probably be "objects," integrated packets of data with built-in instructions for manipulating them.

The hallmark of the object approach is that it moves away from the notion that the organization's intellect consists of a body of data that are manipulated through various algorithms. Under the object-oriented approach, managers model real-world business processes in terms of pre-packaged data "objects" which can then be used ubiquitously in many specialized operating models. The impact of object-oriented programming techniques—and their rapidly developing companion, parallel processing—upon the intelligent enterprise is significant. First, more than ever an organization's intellect will be embodied in its information systems, particularly its software. Until recently, the organization's collective knowledge and experience constituted a pool of objects with their associated rules for manipulation and the interacting models governing each of its operations. The organization's data systems will contain the essence of its way of viewing the world and its competitive capabilities. Second, object-oriented systems will not only facilitate but render imperative the process of learning from highly decentralized experience. The essence of the new paradigm is flexible re-usability, continuously creating new programs from the basic building blocks of previous ones. Those firms which develop the most effective data collection systems and dynamic models about what they know will be able to outpace firms whose data and models are less robust and less representative of their experience.

CONCLUSION

We wish to close by emphasizing that our purpose is to stimulate debate, not to foreclose it. We do not contend that what we have presented are the only five forms of organizing that exist, or that we have captured all the richness of how these forms operate. Both managers and scholars will benefit from research that tells us more about the alternatives to traditional organizations that are emerging under hypercompetitive conditions.

▼ READING 6.4   COLLABORATING TO COMPETE*

by Joel Bleeke and David Ernst

For most global businesses, the days of flat-out, predatory competition are over. The traditional drive to pit one company against the rest of an industry, to pit supplier against supplier, distributor against distributor, on and on through every aspect of a business no longer guarantees the lowest cost, best products or services, or highest profits for winners of this Darwinian game. In businesses as diverse as pharmaceuticals, jet engines, banking, and computers, managers have learned that fighting long, head-to-head battles leaves their companies financially exhausted, intellectually depleted, and vulnerable to the next wave of competition and innovation.

In place of predation, many multinational companies are learning that they must collaborate to compete. Multinationals can create highest value for customers and stakeholders by selectively sharing and trading control, costs, capital, access to markets, information, and technology with competitors and suppliers alike. Competition does not vanish. The computer and commercial aircraft markets are still brutally competitive.

Instead of competing blindly, companies should increasingly compete only in those precise areas where they have a durable advantage or where participation is necessary to preserve industry power or capture value. In packaged goods, that power comes from controlling distribution; in pharmaceuticals, having blockbuster drugs and access to doctors. Managers are beginning to see that many necessary elements of a global business are so costly (like R&D in semiconductors), so generic (like assembly), or so impenetrable (like some of the Asian markets) that it makes no sense to have a traditional competitive stance. The best approach is to find partners that already have the cash, scale, skills, or access you seek.

When a company reaches across borders, its ability and willingness to collaborate is the best predictor of success. The more equal the partnership, the brighter its future. This means that both partners must be strong financially and in the product or function that they bring to the venture. Of 49 alliances that we examined in detail, two thirds of those between equally matched strong partners succeeded, while about 60% of those involving unequal partners failed. So, too, with ownership. Fifty-fifty partnerships had the highest rate of success of any deal structure that we have examined.

THREE THEMES

The need for better understanding of cross-border alliances and acquisitions is increasingly clear. Cross-border linkages are booming, driven by globalization, Europe 1992, the opening of Eastern European and Asian markets, and an increased need for foreign sales to cover the large fixed costs of playing in high-technology businesses. Go-it-alone strategies often take too long, cost too much, or fail to provide insider access to markets. Yet, large numbers of strategic alliances and cross-border acquisitions are failing. When we examined the cross-

---

* Excerpted from "Collaborating to Compete," *Directors and Boards* (Winter, 1994); used with the permission of McKinsey & Company.

border alliances and acquisitions of the largest 150 companies in the United States, Europe, and Japan, we found that only half of these linkages succeed. The average life expectancy for most alliances is approximately seven years. Common lessons from the wide experience of many companies in cross-border strategies are beginning to emerge.

In general, three themes emerge from our studies of alliances:

▼ First, as we have mentioned, companies are learning that they must collaborate to compete. This requires different measurements of "success" from those used for traditional competition.

▼ Second, alliances between companies that are potential competitors represent an arbitrage of skills, market access, and capital between the companies. Maintaining a fair balance in this arbitrage is essential for success.

▼ Third, it is important for managers to develop a vision of international strategy and to see cross-border acquisitions and alliances as a flexible sequence of actions—not one-off deals driven by temporary competitive or financial benefit. The remainder of this article discusses each of these three themes in more detail. . . .

Old measures such as financial hurdles and strategic goals only have meaning in the new context of collaboration. As markets become increasingly competitive, managers are beginning to measure success based on the scarcest resources, including skills and access, not only capital. In the global marketplace, maximizing the value of skills and access can often be achieved only if managers are willing to share ownership with and learn from companies much *different* from their own. Success increasingly comes in proportion to a company's willingness to accept differences.

Successful collaboration also requires flexibility. Most alliances that endure are redefined in terms of geographic or product scope. The success rate for alliances that have changed their scope over time is more than twice that of alliances where the scope has not evolved. Alliances with legal or financial structures that do not permit change are nearly certain to fail. (See Figure 1 which gives Kenichi Ohmae's Tips for Collaboration.)

ALLIANCES AS ARBITRAGE

If all markets were equally accessible, all management equally skilled, all information readily available, and all balance sheets equally solid, there would be little need for collaboration among competitors. But they are not, so companies increasingly benefit by trading these "chips" across borders.

The global arbitrage reflected in cross-border alliances and acquisitions takes place at a slower pace than in capital markets, but the mechanism is similar. Each player uses the quirks, irrational differences, and inefficiencies in the marketplace as well as each company's advantages to mutual benefit. This concept applies mostly to alliances, but cross-border acquisitions can also be viewed as an extreme example of arbitrage: all cash or shares from the buyer, for all the skills, products, and access of the other company. . . .

Successful alliance partners follow several patterns in handling the inherent tensions of arbitrating with potential competitors. To begin with, they approach the negotiation phase with a win-win situation. As one executive said, "Do not sit down to negotiate a deal—build links between the companies."

Successful partners also build in conflict-resolution mechanisms such as powerful boards of directors (for joint ventures) and frequent communication between top management of the parent companies and the alliance. The CEOs of the parent companies need to be absolutely clear on where cooperation is expected and where the "old rules" of competition will apply.

FIGURE 1
Kenichi Ohmae's Tips for Collaboration

1. Treat the collaboration as a personal commitment. It's people that make partnerships work.

2. Anticipate that it will take up management time. If you can't spare the time, don't start it.

3. Mutual respect and trust are essential. If you don't trust the people you are negotiating with, forget it.

4. Remember that both partners must get something out of it (money, eventually). Mutual benefit is vital. This will probably mean you've got to give something up. Recognize this from the outset.

5. Make sure you tie up a tight legal contract. Don't put off resolving unpleasant or contentious issues until "later." Once signed, however, the contract should be put away. If you refer to it, something is wrong with the relationship.

6. Recognize that during the course of a collaboration, circumstances and markets change. Recognize your partner's problems and be flexible.

7. Make sure that you and your partner have mutual expectations of the collaboration and its time scale. One happy and one unhappy partner is a formula for failure.

8. Get to know your opposite numbers at all levels socially. Friends take longer to fall out.

9. Appreciate that cultures — both geographic and corporate — are different. Don't expect a partner to act or respond identically to you. Find out the true reason for a particular response.

10. Recognize your partner's interests and independence.

11. Even if the arrangement is tactical in your eyes, make sure you have corporate approval. Your tactical activity may be a key piece in an overall strategic jigsaw puzzle. With corporate commitment to the partnership, you can act with the positive authority needed in these relationships.

12. Celebrate achievement together. It's a shared elation, and you'll have earned it!

Postscript

Two further things to bear in mind:

1. If you're negotiating a product original equipment manufacturer (OEM) deal, look for a quid pro quo. Remember that another product may offer more in return.

2. Joint development agreements must include joint marketing arrangements. You need the largest market possible to recover development costs and to get volume/margin benefits.

— *Kenichi Ohmae*

Kenichi Ohmae is Chairman of McKinsey & Co.'s offices in Japan.

In approaching alliances as arbitrage, managers should recognize that the value of "chips" is likely to change over time. The key is to maximize your bargaining power—that is, the value of your company's contribution to the alliance—while also being ready to renegotiate the alliance as necessary. Some of the best alliances have had built-in timetables for assessing partner contributions and clear rules for valuing the contributions going forward.

A SEQUENCE OF ACTIONS

Beyond the themes of collaboration and arbitrage involved in individual deals, cross-border alliances and acquisitions need to be viewed as a *sequence* of actions in the context of overall international strategy—not as one-off transactions. Companies that take a purely financial, deal-driven approach to cross-border alliances and acquisitions usually wind up in trouble.

Looking at cross-border M&A [mergers and acquisitions], the most successful companies make a series of acquisitions that build presence in core businesses over time in the target country. One consumer goods company, for example, made an "anchor" acquisition of a leading brand to establish a solid presence in an important European market, then used its enhanced distribution clout to ensure the acceptance of several brands that were subsequently acquired.

In our study of the cross-border acquisition programs of the largest Triad companies [Asia, Europe, North America], successful acquirers had nearly twice the average and median number of purchases as unsuccessful companies. Through initial acquisitions, the acquirer refines M&A skills and becomes more comfortable with, and proficient at, using M&A for international expansion. And by completing a sequence of transactions, particularly in the same geography, it is possible to gain economies through integrating operations and eliminating overlapping functions.

WILLINGNESS TO RETHINK

It is important to think about cross-border alliances, as well as acquisitions, as a part of a sequence of actions. Most alliances evolve over time, so the initial charter and contract often are not meaningful within a few years. Since trouble is the rule, not the exception, and since two thirds of all cross-border alliances run into management trouble during the first few years, alliances require a willingness by partners to rethink their situation on a constant basis—and renegotiate as necessary.

Alliances should usually be considered as an intermediate strategic device that needs other transactions surrounding it. Approximately half of all cross-border alliances terminate within seven years, so it is critical that managers have a point of view early on of "what's next?"

Most terminating alliances are purchased by one of the partners, and termination need not mean failure. But the high rate of termination suggests that both parties should think hard early on about likely roles as a buyer or seller—the probabilities are high that alliance partners eventually will be one or the other.

The companies that can bring the largest short-term synergies to an alliance are often those companies that will most likely be direct competitors in the long term. So, if the desired sequence of management action does not include selling the business, a different, more complementary partner may need to be found at the outset. Understanding the probable sequence of transactions is therefore important in selecting even early alliance of acquisition partners. As our colleagues in Japan remind us, nothing is worse in cross-border alliances or acquisitions than to have "partners in the same bed with different dreams."

POSTSCRIPT: A LOOK AHEAD

Global corporations of the future will be rather like amoebas. This single-celled aquatic animal is among the most ancient life-forms on earth. It gets all its nourishment directly from its environment through its permeable outer walls. These walls define the creature as distinct from its environment, but allow much of what is inside to flow out and much of what is outside to come in. The amoeba is always changing shape, taking and giving with the surroundings, yet it always retains its integrity and identity as a unique creature.

To be truly global and not merely "big," organizations of the future must hold this permeability as one of their highest values. When managers enter a new market, they should first ask these questions: "How is business here different? What do I need to learn?" They have to seek partners that can share costs and swap skills and access to markets. In the fluid global marketplace, it is no longer possible or desirable for single organizations to be entirely self-sufficient. Collaboration is the value of the future. Alliances are the structure of the future.

This has enormous impact on corporate strategy. It makes the world very complex, because there is no single valid rule book for all markets. As our studies have demonstrated, alliances are based on arbitrating the unique differences between markets and partners. And so it is impossible to standardize an approach to the topic. Managers at the corporate center must be able to tolerate and in fact encourage variation: 10 different markets, 10 different partners, 10 different organization charts, 10 reporting systems, and so on. Policies and procedures must be fluid. The word *schizophrenia* has negative connotations, but it captures this idea that truly global organization must entertain two seemingly contradictory aspects—a strong identity, along with an openness to different ways of doing business, to the values of different cultures and localities.

This duality is going to be very difficult for many of the "global" companies of today. Companies with a sales-based culture, where senior executives all come from a sales background, will have a particularly hard time adapting to this new collaborative world. Such companies see the world as "us and them." They reject ideas from the outside world, even if the concept is helpful. They find it hard to live without standardization. They find it hard to collaborate with partners. Deep down, they are trying to convert everyone to their own way of doing things.

This makes them inflexible and confrontational. They don't know how to communicate and work with the outside world on its own terms. They cannot be like the amoeba, with its permeable walls and changing shape, its openness to take from every environment. These companies may survive because they are large and powerful, but they will cease to be leaders.

DEALING WITH
CULTURE AND POWER

Culture arrived on the management scene in the 1980s like a typhoon blowing from the Far East. It suddenly became fashionable in consulting circles to sell culture like some article of organizational clothing, much as "management by objectives" or "total information systems" were once sold. Power, in contrast, was always there, lurking in the background if not driving itself into the foreground. Yet the two represent different sides of the same coin in some respect—the centripetal forces that draw organizations together and the centrifugal force that can drive them apart. While power focuses on self-interest and the building of one's power base through individual initiative, culture concentrates on the collective interest and the building of a unified organization, through shared systems, beliefs, habits, and traditions. Hence, we combine culture and power in this chapter.

What gave culture its impetus was Peters and Waterman's book *In Search of Excellence* (1982). This depicted successful organizations as being rich in culture— permeated with strong and sustaining systems of beliefs. In our view—as in theirs—culture is not an article of fashion, but an intrinsic part of a deeper organizational "character." To draw on definitions introduced earlier, strategy is not just an arbitrarily chosen *position*, nor an analytically developed *plan*, but a deeply entrenched *perspective* which influences the way an organization develops new ideas, considers and weighs options, and responds to changes in its environment.

Culture thus permeates many critical aspects of strategy making. But perhaps the most crucial realm is the way people are chosen, developed, nurtured, interrelated, and rewarded in the organization. The kinds of people attracted to an organization and the way they can most effectively deal with problems and each other are largely a function of the culture a place builds—and the practices and systems which support it.

In some organizations, the culture may become so strong that it is best referred to as an "ideology" that dominates all else—as in the "missionary" configuration introduced in the Mintzberg reading on structure in Chapter 6. But culture is generally an influencing force in all organizations, and so it is appropriately considered in this book as an element of organization, alongside structure, systems, and power.

The first reading, drawn originally from two chapters of Mintzberg's book, *Power in and Around Organizations*, focuses on rich cultures—ideologies—and how these may promote "excellence" in certain situations. (Later we shall consider how culture and ideology can discourage excellence by making organizations resistant to strategic change.) It traces how ideologies evolve through three stages: their rooting in a sense of mission, their development through tradition and sagas, and their reinforcement through various forms of identifications. Mintzberg then briefly considers the missionary type organization and shows how other organizations, for example, regular business firms, sometimes overlay rich cultures on their more conventional ways of operating.

Our second reading, by Christopher Bartlett of the Harvard Business School and Sumantra Ghoshal of the London Business School, takes structure and considers it in a human sense—how to build it into the minds of managers. In that sense, the reading is really about culture—in their terms, about "building a shared vision" and developing people through recruitment and selection, training and development, and career-path management. These authors present a biological metaphor in which formal structure represents the organization's anatomy, while the interpersonal relationships and management processes are its physiology, and a shared vision together with a set of common norms and values are its psychology. They argue that to build organizational capability, large global firms must look beyond structure to vision, values, and processes.

Up to this point, the ideas and concepts we have presented in the book, for the most part, have a functionalist orientation in which organizations are viewed as rather rational and cooperative instruments. Strategies, whether formulated analytically or allowed to emerge in some kind of a learning process, nonetheless serve the good of the organization at large, as do the associated structures, systems, and cultures. True Quinn and Wrapp managers, for example, have consciously considered and dealt with potential resistance in creating and implanting their strategies. In doing so, they may have been forced to think in political terms. But the overt use of power and organized political action has largely been absent from our discussion.

An important group of thinkers in the field, however, have come to view the strategy process as an interplay of the forces of power, sometimes highly politicized. Rather than assuming that organizations are consistent, coherent, and cooperative systems, tightly integrated to pursue certain traditional ends (namely the delivery of their products and services in the pursuit of profit, at least in the private sector), these writers start with quite different premises. They believe that organizations' goals and directions are determined primarily by the power needs of those who populate them. Their analyses raise all kinds of interesting and unsettled questions, such as: For whom does the organization really exist? For what purposes? If the organization is truly a political entity, how does one manage effectively in it? And so on.

One work in the literature that sets this into perspective is the famous study of the United States' response to the Cuban Missile Crisis by Graham Allison (1971) of Harvard's Kennedy School of Government. Allison believed that our conception of how decision making proceeds in organizations can be considered from three perspectives: a "rational actor" model (which is the concept he believed the American leaders had of the Soviets), an "organizations process" model, and a "bureaucratic politics" model (both of which Allison thought could have been used as well to improve America's understanding of the Soviets' behavior). In the first model, power is embedded in a relatively rational and calculating center of strategy making as was described in Chapters 3 and 4. In the second, it is entrenched in various organizational departments, each using power to further its own particular purposes. In the third model, "politics" comes into full play as individuals and groups exercise their influence to determine outcomes for their own benefits.

Our third reading focuses especially on the third model, also incorporating aspects of the second. In parallel with Mintzberg's earlier reading in this chapter (and likewise based on two related chapters of his *Power In and Around Organizations* book), it considers first the general force of politics in organizations, what it is and what political "games" people play in organizations, and the various forms taken by organizations that are dominated by such politics, the extreme one labeled the "political arena." This reading concludes with a discussion of when and why politics sometimes plays a functional role in organizations.

The fourth reading of the chapter brings us back to strategy, but in a kind of political way. You may recall one of the definitions of strategy introduced in Chapter 1 that was not heard from since—that of ploy. In this fourth reading, ploy comes to life in the context of "competitive maneuvering," various means strategists use to outwit competitors. This reading is based on two short articles entitled "Brinkmanship in Business" and "The Nonlogical Strategy" by Bruce Henderson, drawn from his book, *Henderson on Corporate Strategy*, a collection of short, pithy, and rather opinionated views on management issues. Henderson founded the Boston Consulting Group and built it into a major international force in management consulting.

While the Mintzberg reading considers power and politics inside the organization in terms of the maneuverings of various actors to gain influence, the Henderson one looks at the maneuverings of organizations at large, vis-à-vis the competitors. This second theme is pursued in the last reading of this chapter, except that the context is extended beyond competitors to all of an organization's influencers (sometimes called "stakeholders," in contrast to only "shareholders"). To some observers, organizations are not merely instruments to produce goods and services but also political systems that seek to enhance their own power. We will refer to this as *macro* politics, in contrast to the *micro* politics that takes place within organizations.

This final reading of the chapter introduces another major theme about macro power. For whom does or should the large business corporation exist? Mintzberg proposes a whole portfolio of answers around a "conceptual horseshoe." In so doing, he perhaps helps to reconcile some of the basic differences between those who view organizations as agents of economic competition and those who consider them to be instruments of the public will, or else as political systems in their own right. This reading also discusses the concept of *social responsibility,* one of the traditional topics covered in policy or strategy courses. But here the subject is treated not in a philanthropic or ethical sense, but as a managerial or organizational one. This reading also reviews the issues of corporate democracy, of regulation and pressure campaigns, and of "free enterprise" as described by Milton Friedman.

▼ READING 7.1 IDEOLOGY AND THE MISSIONARY ORGANIZATION*

by Henry Mintzberg

We all know that 2 + 2 = 4. But general systems theory, through the concept of synergy, suggests that it can also equal 5, that the parts of a system may produce more working together than they can apart. A flashlight and a battery add up to just so many pieces of hardware; together they form a working system. Likewise an organization is a working system that can entice from its members more than they would produce apart—more effort, more creativity, more output (or, of course, less). This may be "strategic"—deriving from the way components have been combined in the organization. Or it may be motivational: The group is said to develop a "mood," an "atmosphere," to have some kind of "chemistry." In organizations, we talk of a "style," a "culture," a "character." One senses something unique when one walks

---

*Adapted from Henry Mintzberg *Power in and Around Organizations* (copyright © Prentice Hall 1983). Chaps. 11 and 21 used by permission of the publisher; based on a summary that appeared in *Mintzberg on Management: Inside Our Strange World of Organizations* (New York: Free Press, 1989).

into the offices of IBM; the chemistry of Hewlett-Packard just doesn't feel the same as that of Texas Instruments, even though the two have operated in some similar businesses.

All these words are used to describe something—intangible yet very real, over and above the concrete components of an organization—that we refer to as its *ideology*. Specifically, an ideology is taken here to mean a rich system of values and beliefs about an organization, shared by its members, that distinguishes it from other organizations. For our purposes, the key feature of such an ideology is its unifying power: It ties the individual to the organization, generating an "esprit de corps," a "sense of mission," in effect, an integration of individual and organizational goals that can produce synergy.

The Development of an Organizational Ideology

The development of an ideology in an organization will be discussed here in three stages. The roots of the ideology are planted when a group of individuals band together around a leader and, through a sense of mission, found a vigorous organization, or invigorate an existing one. The ideology then develops over time through the establishment of traditions. Finally, the existing ideology is reinforced when new members enter the organization and identify with its system of beliefs.

STAGE 1: THE ROOTING OF IDEOLOGY IN A SENSE OF MISSION

Typically, an organization is founded when a single prime mover identifies a mission—some product to be produced, service to be rendered—and collects a group around him or her to accomplish it. Some organizations are, of course, founded by other means, as when a new agency is created by a government or a subsidiary by a corporation. But a prime mover often can still be identified behind the founding of the organization.

The individuals who come together don't do so at random, but coalesce because they share some values associated with the fledgling organization. At the very least they see something in it for themselves. But in some cases, in addition to the mission per se there is a "sense of mission," that is, a feeling that the group has banded together to create something unusual and exciting. This is common in new organizations for a number of reasons.

First, unconstrained by procedure and tradition, new organizations offer wide latitude for maneuver. Second, they tend to be small, enabling the members to establish personal relationships. Third, the founding members frequently share a set of strong basic beliefs, sometimes including a sense that they wish to work together. Fourth, the founders of new organizations are often "charismatic" individuals, and so energize the followers and knit them together. Charisma, as Weber (1969:12) used the term, means a sense of "personal devotion" to the leader for the sake of his or her personal qualities rather than formal position. People join and remain with the organization because of dedication to the leader and his or her mission. Thus the roots of strong ideologies tend to be planted in the founding of organizations.

Of course, such ideologies can also develop in existing organizations. But a review of the preceding points suggests why this should be much more difficult to accomplish. Existing organizations *are* constrained by procedures and traditions, many are *already* large and impersonal, and their *existing* beliefs tend to impede the establishment of new ones. Nonetheless, with the introduction of strong charismatic leadership reinforced by a strong new sense of mission, an existing organization can sometimes be invigorated by the creation of a new ideology.

A key to the development of an organizational ideology, in a new or existing organization, is a leadership with a genuine belief in mission and an honest dedication to the people who must carry it out. Mouthing the right words might create the veneer of an organizational ideology, but it is only an authentic feeling on the part of the leadership—which followers somehow sense—that sets the roots of the ideology deep enough to sustain it when other forces, such as impersonal administration (bureaucracy) or politics, challenge it.

STAGE 2: THE DEVELOPMENT OF IDEOLOGY THROUGH TRADITIONS AND SAGAS

As a new organization establishes itself or an existing one establishes a new set of beliefs, it makes decisions and takes actions that serve as commitments and establish precedents. Behaviors reinforce themselves over time, and actions become infused with value. When those forces are strong, ideology begins to emerge in its own right. That ideology is strengthened by stories—sometimes called "myths"—that develop around important events in the organization's past. Gradually the organization establishes its own unique sense of history. All of this—the precedents, habits, myths, history—form a common base of tradition, which the members of the organization share, thus solidifying the ideology. Gradually, in Selznick's (1957) terms, the organization is converted from an expendable "instrument" for the accomplishment of externally imposed goals into an "institution," a system with a life of its own. It "acquires a self, a distinctive identity."

Thus Clark described the "distinctive college," with reference particularly to Reed, Antioch, and Swarthmore (1972:178). Such institutions develop, in his words, an "organizational saga," "a collective understanding of a unique accomplishment based on historical exploits," which links the organization's present with its past and "turns a formal place into a beloved institution." The saga captures allegiance, committing people to the institution (Clark 1970:235).

STAGE 3: THE REINFORCEMENT OF IDEOLOGY THROUGH IDENTIFICATIONS

Our description to this point makes it clear that an individual entering an organization does not join a random collection of individuals, but rather a living system with its own culture. He or she may come with a certain set of values and beliefs, but there is little doubt that the culture of the organization can weigh heavily on the behavior he or she will exhibit once inside it. This is especially true when the culture is rich—when the organization has an emerging or fully developed ideology. Then the individual's *identification* with and *loyalty* to the organization can be especially strong. Such identification can develop in a number of ways:

▼ Most simply, identification occurs *naturally* because the new member is attracted to the organization's system of beliefs.
▼ Identification may also be *selected*. New members are chosen to "fit in" with the existing beliefs, and positions of authority are likewise filled from among the members exhibiting the strongest loyalty to those beliefs.
▼ Identification may also be *evoked*. When the need for loyalty is especially great, the organization may use informal processes of *socialization* and formal programs of *indoctrination* to reinforce natural or selected commitment to its system of beliefs.

▼   Finally, and most weakly, identification can be *calculated*. In effect, individuals conform to the beliefs not because they identify naturally with them nor because they even necessarily fit in with them, not because they have been socialized or indoctrinated into them, but skimpy because it pays them to identify with the beliefs. They may enjoy the work or the social group, may like the remuneration, may work to get ahead through promotion and the like. Of course, such identification is fragile. It disappears as soon as an opportunity calculated to be better appears.

Clearly, the higher up this list an organization's members identifications tend to be, the more likely it is to sustain a strong ideology, or even to have such an ideology in the first place. Thus, strong organizational belief systems can be recognized above all by the presence of much natural identification. Attention to selected identification indicates the presence of an ideology, since it reflects an organization's efforts to sustain its ideology, as do efforts at socialization and indoctrination. Some organizations require a good deal of the latter two, because of the need to instill in their new members a complex system of beliefs. When the informal processes of socialization tend to function naturally, perhaps reinforced by more formal programs of indoctrination, then the ideology would seem to be strong. But when an organization is forced to rely almost exclusively on indoctrination, or worse to fall back on forms of calculated identification, then its ideology would appear to be weakening, if not absent to begin with.

The Missionary Organization

While some degree of ideology can be found in virtually every organization, that degree can vary considerably. At one extreme are those organizations, such as religious orders or radical political movements, whose ideologies tend to be strong and whose identifications are primarily natural and selected. Edwards (1977) refers to organizations with strong ideologies as "stylistically rich," Selznick (1957) as "institutions." It is the presence of such an ideology that enables an organization to have "a life of its own," to emerge as "a living social institution" (Selznick 1949: 10). At the other extreme are those organizations with relatively weak ideologies, "stylistically barren," in some cases business organizations with strongly utilitarian reward systems. History and tradition have no special value in these organizations. In the absence of natural forms of identification on the part of their members, these organizations sometimes try to rely on the process of indoctrination to integrate individual and organizational goals. But usually they have to fall back on calculated identifications and especially formal controls.

We can refer to "stylistically rich" organizations as *missionaries*, because they are somewhat akin in their beliefs to the religious organizations by that name. Mission counts above all—to preserve it, extend it, or perfect it. That mission is typically (1) clear and focused, so that its members are easily able to identify with it; (2) inspiring, so that the members do, in fact, develop such identifications; and (3) distinctive, so that the organization and its members are deposited into a unique niche where the ideology can flourish. As a result of their attachment to its mission, the members of the organization resist strongly any attempt to change it, to interfere with tradition. The mission and the rest of the ideology must be preserved at all costs.

The missionary organization is a distinct configuration of the attributes of structure, internally highly integrated yet different from other configurations. What holds this organization together—that is, provides for its coordination—is the standardization of its norms, in other words, the sharing of values and beliefs among its members. As was noted, that can happen informally, either through natural selection or else the informal process of socialization. But from the perspective of structural design the key attribute is indoctrination, meaning formalized programs to develop or reinforce identification with the ideology. And once the new member has been selected, socialized, and indoctrinated, he or she is accepted into the system as an equal partner, able to participate in decision making alongside everyone else. Thus, at the limit, the missionary organization can achieve the purest form of decentralization: All who are accepted into the system share its power.

But that does not mean an absence of control. Quite the contrary. No matter how subtle, control tends to be very powerful in this organization. For here, the organization controls not just people's behavior but their very souls. The machine organization buys the "workers'" attention through imposed rules; the missionary organization captures the "members'" hearts through shared values. As Jay noted in his book *Management and Machiavelli* (1970), teaching new Jesuit recruits to "love God and do what you like" is not to do what they like at all but to act in strict conformance with the order's beliefs (1970:70).

Thus, the missionary organization tends to end up as an amorphous mass of members all pulling together within the common ideology, with minimum specialization as to job, differentiation as to part, division as to status. At the limit, managers, staffers, and operators, once selected, socialized, and indoctrinated, all seem rather alike and may, in fact, rotate into each other's positions.

The traditional Israeli kibbutz is a classic example of the missionary organization. In certain seasons, everyone pitches in and picks fruit in the fields by day and then attends the meetings to decide administrative issues by night. Managerial positions exist but are generally filled on a rotating basis so that no one emerges with the status of office for long. Likewise, staff support positions exist, but they too tend to be filled on a rotating basis from the same pool of members, as are the operating positions in the fields. (Kitchen duty is, for example, considered drudgery that everyone must do periodically.) Conversion to industry has, however, threatened that ideology. As suggested, it was relatively easy to sustain the egalitarian ideology when the work was agricultural. Industry, in contrast, generally called for greater levels of technology, specialization, and expertise, with a resulting increase in the need for administrative hierarchy and functional differentiation, all a threat to the missionary orientation. The kibbutzim continue to struggle with this problem.

A number of our points about the traditional kibbutz are summarized in a table developed by Rosner (1969), which contrasts the "principles of kibbutz organization"—classic missionary—with those of "bureaucratic organization," in our terms, the classic machine.

Principles of Bureaucratic Organization	Principles of Kibbutz Organization
1. Permanency of office.	Impermanency of office.
2. The office carries with it impersonal, fixed privileges and duties.	The definition of office is flexible—privileges and duties are not formally fixed and often depend on the personality of the official.
3. A hierarchy of functional authorities expressed in the authority of the officials.	A basic assumption of the equal value of all functions without a formal hierarchy of authority.

4. Nomination of officials is based on formal objective qualifications.

Officials are elected, not nominated. Objective qualifications are not decisive, personal qualities are more important in election.

5. The office is a full-time occupation.

The office is usually supplementary to the full-time occupation of the official.

We can distinguish several forms of the pure missionary organization. Some are *reformers* that set out to change the world directly—anything from overthrowing a government to ensuring that all domestic animals are "decently" clothed. Other missionaries can be called *converters*, their mission being to change the world indirectly, by attracting members and changing them. The difference between the first two types of missionaries is the difference between the Women's Christian Temperance Union and Alcoholics Anonymous. Their ends were similar, but their means differed, seeking to reduce alcoholism in one case by promoting a general ban on liquor sales, in the other by discouraging certain individuals, namely joined members, from drinking. Third are the *cloister* missionaries that seek not to change things so much as to allow their members to pursue a unique style of life. The monasteries that close themselves off from the outside world are good examples, as are groups that go off to found new isolated colonies.

Of course, no organization can completely seal itself off from the world. All missionary organizations, in fact, face the twin opposing pressures of isolation and assimilation. Together these make them vulnerable. On one side is the threat of *isolation*, of growing ever inward in order to protect the unique ideology from the pressures of the ordinary world until the organization eventually dies for lack of renewal. On the other side is the threat of *assimilation*, of reaching out so far to promote the ideology that it eventually gets compromised. When this happens, the organization may survive but the ideology dies, and so the configuration changes (typically to the machine form).

Ideology as an Overlay on Conventional Organizations

So far we have discussed what amounts to the extreme form of ideological organization, the missionary. But more organizations have strong ideologies than can afford to structure themselves in this way. The structure may work for an Israeli kibbutz in a remote corner of the Negev desert, but this is hardly a way to run a Hewlett-Packard or a McDonald's, let alone a kibbutz closer to the worldly pressures of Tel Aviv.

What such organizations tend to do is overlay ideological characteristics on a more conventional structure—perhaps machinelike in the case of McDonald's and that second kibbutz, innovative in the case of Hewlett-Packard. The mission may sometimes seem ordinary—serving hamburgers, producing instruments and computers—but it is carried out with a good dose of ideological fervor by employees firmly committed to it.

Best known for this are, of course, certain of the Japanese corporations, Toyota being a prime example. Ouchi and Jaeger (1978:308) contrast in the table reproduced below the typical large American corporation (Type A) with its Japanese counterpart (Type J):

Type A (for American)	Type J (for Japanese)
Short-term employment	Lifetime employment
Individual decision making	Consensual decision making
Individual responsibility	Collective responsibility
Rapid evaluation and promotion	Slow evaluation and promotion
Explicit, formalized control	Implicit, informal control

Specialized career path   Nonspecialized career path
Segmented concern   Holistic concern

Ouchi and Jaeger (1978) in fact make their point best with an example in which a classic Japanese ideological orientation confronts a conventional American bureaucratic one:

[D]uring one of the author's visits to a Japanese bank in California, both the Japanese president and the American vice-presidents of the bank accused the other of being unable to formulate objectives. The Americans meant that the Japanese president could not or would not give them explicit, quantified targets to attain over the next three or six months, while the Japanese meant that the Americans could not see that once they understood the company's philosophy, they would be able to deduce for themselves the proper objective for any conceivable situation. (p. 309)

In another study, however, Ouchi together with Johnson (1978) discussed a native American corporation that does resemble the Type J firm (labeled "Type Z"; Ouchi (1981) later published a best seller about such organizations). In it, they found greater loyalty, a strong collective orientation, less specialization, and a greater reliance on informal controls. For example, "a new manager will be useless for at least four or five years. It takes that long for most people to decide whether the new person really fits in, whether they can really trust him." That was in sharp contrast to the "auction market" atmosphere of a typical American firm: It "is almost as if you could open up the doors each day with 100 executives and engineers who had been randomly selected from the country, and the organization would work just as well as it does now" (1978:302).

The trends in American business over several decades—"professional" management, emphasis on technique and rationalization, "bottom-line" mentality—have worked against the development of organizational ideologies. Certainly the missionary configuration has hardly been fashionable in the West, especially the United States. But ideology may have an important role to play there, given the enormous success many Japanese firms have had in head-on competition with American corporations organized in machine and diversified ways, with barren cultures. At the very least, we might expect more ideological overlays on the conventional forms of organizations in the West. But this, as we hope our discussion has made clear, may be both for better and for worse.

▼ READING 7.2   BUILDING STRUCTURE IN MANAGERS' MINDS*

by Christopher A. Bartlett and Sumantra Ghoshal

Top-level managers in many of today's leading corporations are losing control of their companies. The problem is not that they have misjudged the demands created by an increasingly complex environment and an accelerating rate of environmental change, nor even that they have failed to develop strategies appropriate to the new challenges. The problem is that their companies are organizationally incapable of carrying out the sophisticated strategies they have developed. Over the past 20 years, strategic thinking has far outdistanced organizational capabilities. . . .

In recent years, as more and more managers recognized oversimplification as a strategic trap, they began to accept the need to manage complexity rather than seek to minimize it. This realization, however, led many into an equally threatening organizational trap when they concluded that the best response to increasingly complex strategic requirements was increasingly complex organizational structures.

---

*Originally published as "Matrix Management: Not a Structure, a Frame of Mind," in the *Harvard Business Review*, (July-August 1990). Copyright © 1990 by the President and Fellows of Harvard College; all rights reserved. Reprinted with deletions by permission of the *Harvard Business Review*.

The obvious organizational solution to strategies that required multiple, simultaneous management capabilities was the matrix structure that became so fashionable in the late 1970s and the early 1980s. Its parallel reporting relationships acknowledged the diverse, conflicting needs of functional, product, and geographic management groups and provided a formal mechanism for resolving them. Its multiple information channels allowed the organization to capture and analyze external complexity. And its overlapping responsibilities were designed to combat parochialism and build flexibility into the company's response to change.

In practice, however, the matrix proved all but unmanageable—especially in an international context. Dual reporting led to conflict and confusion; the proliferation of channels created informational logjams as a proliferation of committees and reports bogged down the organization; and overlapping responsibilities produced turf battles and a loss of accountability. Separated by barriers of distance, language, time, and culture, managers found it virtually impossible to clarify the confusion and resolve the conflicts.

. . . For decades, we have seen the general manager as chief strategic guru and principal organizational architect. But as the competitive climate grows less stable and less predictable, it is harder for one person alone to succeed in that great visionary role. Similarly, as formal, hierarchical structure gives way to networks of personal relationships that work through informal, horizontal communication channels, the image of top management in an isolated corner office moving boxes and lines on an organization chart becomes increasingly anachronistic.

Paradoxically, as strategies and organizations become more complex and sophisticated, top-level general managers are beginning to replace their historical concentration on the grand issues of strategy and structure with a focus on the details of managing people and processes. The critical strategic requirement is not to devise the most ingenious and well coordinated plan but to build the most viable and flexible strategic process; the key organizational task is not to design the most elegant structure but to capture individual capabilities and motivate the entire organization to respond cooperatively to a complicated and dynamic environment.

BUILDING AN ORGANIZATION

While business thinkers have written a great deal about strategic innovation, they have paid far less attention to the accompanying organizational challenges. Yet many companies remain caught in the structural-complexity trap that paralyzes their ability to respond quickly or flexibly to the new strategic imperatives.

For those companies that adopted matrix structures, the problem was not in the way they defined the goal. They correctly recognized the need for multidimensional organization to respond to growing external complexity. The problem was that they defined their organizational objectives in purely structural terms. Yet formal structure describes only the organization's basic anatomy. Companies must also concern themselves with organizational physiology—the systems and relationships that allow the lifeblood of information to flow through the organization. And they need to develop a healthy organizational psychology—the shared norms, values, and beliefs that shape the way individual managers think and act.

The companies that fell into the organizational trap assumed that changing their formal structure (anatomy) would force changes in interpersonal relationships and decision processes (physiology), which in turn would reshape the individual attitudes and actions of managers (psychology).

But as many companies have discovered, reconfiguring the formal structure is a blunt and sometimes brutal instrument of change. A new structure creates new and presumably more useful managerial ties, but these can take months and often years to evolve into effective knowledge-generating and decision-making relationships. And since the new job requirements will frustrate, alienate, or simply overwhelm so many managers, changes in individual attitudes and behavior will likely take even longer.

As companies struggle to create organizational capabilities that reflect rather than diminish environmental complexity, good managers gradually stop searching for the ideal structural template to impose on the company from the top down. Instead, they focus on the challenge of building up an appropriate set of employee attitudes and skills and linking them together with carefully developed processes and relationships. In other words, they begin to focus on building the organization rather than simply on installing a new structure.

Indeed, the companies that are most successful at developing multidimensional organizations begin at the far end of the anatomy-physiology-psychology sequence. Their first objective is to alter the organizational psychology—the broad corporate beliefs and norms that shape managers' perceptions and actions. Then, by enriching and clarifying communication and decision processes, companies reinforce these psychological changes with improvements in organizational physiology. Only later do they consolidate and confirm their progress by realigning organizational anatomy through changes in the formal structure.

No company we know of has discovered a quick or easy way to change its organizational psychology to reshape the understanding, identification, and commitment of its employees. But we found three principal characteristics common to those that managed the task most effectively:

1. The development and communication of a clear and consistent corporate vision.
2. The effective management of human resource tools to broaden individual perspectives and develop identification with corporate goals.
3. The integration of individual thinking and activities into the broad corporate agenda by means of a process we call co-option.

BUILDING A SHARED VISION

Perhaps the main reason managers in large, complex companies cling to parochial attitudes is that their frame of reference is bounded by their specific responsibilities. The surest way to break down such insularity is to develop and communicate a clear sense of corporate purpose that extends into every corner of the company and gives context and meaning to each manager's particular roles and responsibilities. We are not talking about a slogan, however catchy and pointed. We are talking about a company vision, which must be crafted and articulated with clarity, continuity, and consistency: clarity of expression that makes company objectives understandable and meaningful; continuity of purpose that underscores their enduring importance; and consistency of application across business units and geographical boundaries that ensures uniformity throughout the organization.

CLARITY

There are three keys to clarity in a corporate vision: simplicity, relevance, and reinforcement. NEC's integration of computers and communications—C&C—is probably the best single example of how simplicity can make a vision more powerful. Top management has applied the C&C concept so effectively that it describes the company's business focus, defines its distinctive source of competitive advantage over large companies like IBM and AT&T, and summarizes its strategic and organizational imperatives.

The second key, relevance, means linking broad objectives to concrete agendas. When Wisse Dekker became CEO at Philips, his principal strategic concern was the problem of competing with Japan. He stated this challenge in martial terms—the U.S. had abandoned the battlefield; Philips was now Europe's last defense against insurgent Japanese electronics companies. . . .

The third key to clarity is top management's continual reinforcement, elaboration, and interpretation of the core vision to keep it from becoming obsolete or abstract. Founder

Konosuke Matsushita developed a grand, 250-year vision for his company, but he also managed to give it immediate relevance. He summed up its overall message in the "Seven Spirits of Matsushita," to which he referred constantly in his policy statements. Each January he wove the company's one-year operational objectives into his overarching concept to produce an annual theme that he then captured in a slogan. For all the loftiness of his concept of corporate purpose, he gave his managers immediate, concrete guidance in implementing Matsushita's goals.

CONTINUITY

Despite shifts in leadership and continual adjustments in short-term business priorities, companies must remain committed to the same core set of strategic objectives and organizational values. Without such continuity, unifying vision might as well be expressed in terms of quarterly goals.

It was General Electric's lack of this kind of continuity that led to the erosion of its once formidable position in electrical appliances in many countries. Over a period of 20 years and under successive CEOs, the company's international consumer-product strategy never stayed the same for long. . . . The Brazilian subsidiary, for example, built its TV business in the 1960s until it was told to stop; in the early 1970s, it emphasized large appliances until it was denied funding; then it focused on housewares until the parent company sold off that business. In two decades, GE utterly dissipated its dominant franchise in Brazil's electrical products markets.

Unilever, by contrast, made an enduring commitment to its Brazilian subsidiary, despite volatile swings in Brazil's business climate. Company chairman Floris Maljers emphasized the importance of looking past the latest political crisis or economic downturn to the long-term business potential. . . .

CONSISTENCY

The third task for top management in communicating strategic purpose is to ensure that everyone in the company shares the same vision. The cost of inconsistency can be horrendous. It always produces confusion and, in extreme cases, can lead to total chaos, with different units of the organization pursuing agendas that are mutually debilitating.

Philips is a good example of a company that, for a time, lost its consistency of corporate purpose. As a legacy of its wartime decision to give some overseas units legal autonomy, management had long experienced difficulty persuading North American Philips (NAP) to play a supportive role in the parent company's global strategies. The problem came to a head with the introduction of Philips's technologically first-rate videocassette recording system, the V2000. Despite considerable pressure from world headquarters in the Netherlands, NAP refused to launch the system, arguing that Sony's Beta system and Matsushita's VHS format were too well established and had cost, feature, and system-support advantages Philips couldn't match. Relying on its legal independence and managerial autonomy, NAP management decided instead to source products from its Japanese competitors and market them under its Magnavox brand name. As a result, Philips was unable to build the efficiency and credibility it needed to challenge Japanese dominance of the VCR business. . . .

But formulating and communicating a vision—no matter how clear, enduring, and consistent—cannot succeed unless individual employees understand and accept the company's stated goals and objectives. Problems at this level are more often related to receptivity than to communication. The development of individual understanding and acceptance is a challenge for a company's human resource practices.

DEVELOPING HUMAN RESOURCES

While top managers universally recognize their responsibility for developing and allocating a company's scarce assets and resources, their focus on finance and technology often overshadows the task of developing the scarcest resource of all—capable managers. But if there is one key to regaining control of companies that operate in fast-changing environments, it is the ability of top management to turn the perceptions, capabilities, and relationships of individual managers into the building blocks of the organization.

One pervasive problem in companies whose leaders lack this ability—or fail to exercise it—is getting managers to see how their specific responsibilities relate to the broad corporate vision. Growing external complexity and strategic sophistication have accelerated the growth of a cadre of specialists who are physically and organizationally isolated from each other, and the task of dealing with their consequent parochialism should not be delegated to the clerical staff that administers salary structures and benefit programs. Top managers inside and outside the human resource function must be leaders in the recruitment, development, and assignment of the company's vital human talent.

RECRUITMENT AND SELECTION

The first step in successfully managing complexity is to tap the full range of available talent. It is a serious mistake to permit historical imbalances in the nationality or functional background of the management group to constrain hiring or subsequent promotion. In today's global marketplace, domestically oriented recruiting limits a company's ability to capitalize on its worldwide pool of management skill and biases its decision-making processes.

Not only must companies enlarge the pool of people available for key positions, they must also develop new criteria for choosing those most likely to succeed. Because past success is no longer a sufficient qualification for increasingly subtle, sensitive, and unpredictable senior-level tasks, top management must become involved in a more discriminating selection process. At Matsushita, top management selects candidates for international assignment on the basis of a comprehensive set of personal characteristics, expressed for simplicity in the acronym SMILE: specialty (the needed skill, capability, or knowledge); management ability (particularly motivational ability); international flexibility (willingness to learn and ability to adapt); language facility; and endeavor (vitality, perseverance in the face of difficulty). These attributes are remarkably similar to those targeted by NEC and Philips, where top executives also are involved in the senior-level selection process.

TRAINING AND DEVELOPMENT

Once the appropriate top-level candidates have been identified, the next challenge is to develop their potential. The most successful development efforts have three aims that take them well beyond the skill-building objectives of classic training programs: to inculcate a common vision and shared values; to broaden management perspectives and capabilities; and to develop contacts and shape management relationships.

To build common vision and values, white-collar employees at Matsushita spend a good part of their first six months in what the company calls "cultural and spiritual training." They study the company credo, the "Seven Spirits of Matsushita," and the philosophy of Konosuke Matsushita. Then they learn how to translate these internalized lessons into daily behavior and even operational decisions. Culture-building exercises as intensive as Matsushita's are sometimes dismissed as the kind of Japanese mumbo jumbo that would not work in other societies, but in fact, Philips has a similar entry-level training practice (called "organization cohesion training"), as does Unilever (called, straightforwardly, "indoctrination").

The second objective—broadening management perspectives—is essentially a matter of teaching people how to manage complexity instead of merely to make room for it. To reverse a long and unwieldy tradition of running its operations with two- and three-headed management teams of separate technical, commercial, and sometimes administrative specialists, Philips asked its training and development group to de-specialize top management trainees. By supplementing its traditional menu of specialist courses and functional programs with more intensive general management training, Philips was able to begin replacing the ubiquitous teams with single business heads who also appreciated and respected specialist points of view.

The final aim—developing contacts and relationships—is much more than an incidental by-product of good management development, as the comments of a senior personnel manager at Unilever suggest: "By bringing managers from different countries and businesses together at Four Acres [Unilever's international management training college], we build contacts and create bonds that we could never achieve by other means. The company spends as much on training as it does on R&D not only because of the direct effect it has on upgrading skills and knowledge but also because it plays a central role in indoctrinating managers into a Unilever club where personal relationships and informal contacts are much more powerful than the formal systems and structures."

CAREER-PATH MANAGEMENT

Although recruitment and training are critically important, the most effective companies recognize that the best way to develop new perspectives and thwart parochialism in their managers is through personal experience. By moving selected managers across functions, businesses, and geographic units, a company encourages cross-fertilization of ideas as well as the flexibility and breadth of experience that enable managers to grapple with complexity and come out on top.

Unilever has long been committed to the development of its human resources as a means of attaining durable competitive advantage. As early as the 1930s, the company was recruiting and developing local employees to replace the parent-company managers who had been running most of its overseas subsidiaries. In a practice that came to be known as "-ization," the company committed itself to the Indianization of its Indian company, the Australization of its Australian company, and so on.

Although delighted with the new talent that began working its way up through the organization, management soon realized that by reducing the transfer of parent-company managers abroad, it had diluted the powerful glue that bound diverse organizational groups together and linked dispersed operations. The answer lay in formalizing a second phase of the -ization process. While continuing with Indianization, for example, Unilever added programs aimed at the Unileverization of its Indian managers.

In addition to bringing 300 to 400 managers to Four Acres each year, Unilever typically has 100 to 150 of its most promising overseas managers on short- and long-term job assignments at corporate headquarters. This policy not only brings fresh, close-to-the-market perspectives into corporate decision making but also gives the visiting managers a strong sense of Unilever's strategic vision and organizational values. In the words of one of the expatriates in the corporate offices, "The experience initiates you into the Unilever Club and the clear norms, values, and behaviors that distinguish our people—so much so that we really believe we can spot another Unilever manager anywhere in the world."

Furthermore, the company carefully transfers most of these high-potential individuals through a variety of different functional, product, and geographic positions, often rotating every two or three years. Most important, top management tracks about 1,000 of these people—some 5% of Unilever's total management group—who, as they move through the company, forge an informal network of contacts and relationships that is central to Unilever's decision-making and information-exchange processes.

Widening the perspectives and relationships of key managers as Unilever has done is a good way of developing identification with the broader corporate mission. But a broad sense of identity is not enough. To maintain control of its global strategies, Unilever must secure a strong and lasting individual commitment to corporate visions and objectives. In effect, it must co-opt individual energies and ambitions into the service of corporate goals.

CO-OPTING MANAGEMENT EFFORTS

As organizational complexity grows, managers and management groups tend to become so specialized and isolated and to focus so intently on their own immediate operating responsibilities that they are apt to respond parochially to intrusions on their organizational turf, even when the overall corporate interest is at stake. A classic example, described earlier, was the decision by North American's Philips's consumer electronics group to reject the parent company's VCR system.

At about the same time, Philips, like many other companies, began experimenting with ways to convert managers' intellectual understanding of the corporate vision—in Philips's case, an almost evangelical determination to defend Western electronics against the Japanese—into a binding personal commitment. Philips concluded that it could co-opt individuals and organizational groups into the broader vision by inviting them to contribute to the corporate agenda and then giving them direct responsibility for implementation.

In the face of intensifying Japanese competition, Philips knew it had to improve coordination in its consumer electronics among its fiercely independent national organizations. In strengthening the central product divisions, however, Philips did not want to deplete the enterprise or commitment of its capable national management teams.

The company met these conflicting needs with two cross-border initiatives. First, it created a top-level World Policy Council for its video business that included key managers from strategic markets—Germany, France, the United Kingdom, the United States, and Japan. Philips knew that its national companies' long history of independence made local managers reluctant to take orders from Dutch headquarters in Eindhoven—often for good reason, since much of the company's best market knowledge and technological expertise resided in its offshore units. Through the Council, Philips co-opted their support for company decisions about product policy and manufacturing location.

Second, and more powerful, Philips allocated global responsibilities to units that had previously been purely national in focus. Eindhoven gave NAP the leading role in the development of Philips's projection television and asked it to coordinate development and manufacture of all Philips television sets for North America and Asia. The change in the attitude of NAP managers was dramatic.

A senior manager in NAP's consumer electronics business summed up the feelings of U.S. managers: "At last, we are moving out of the dependency relationship with Eindhoven and that was so frustrating to us." Co-option had transformed the defensive, territorial attitude of NAP managers into a more collaborative mind-set. They were making important contributions to global corporate strategy instead of looking for ways to subvert it. . . .

THE MATRIX IN THE MANAGER'S MIND

Since the end of World War II, corporate strategy has survived several generations of painful transformation and has grown appropriately agile and athletic. Unfortunately, organizational development has not kept pace, and managerial attitudes lag even further behind. As a result, corporations now commonly design strategies that seem impossible to implement, for the simple reason that no one can effectively implement third-generation strategies through second-generation organizations run by first-generation managers.

Today the most successful companies are those where top executives recognize the need to manage the new environmental and competitive demands by focusing less on the quest for an ideal structure and more on developing the abilities, behavior, and performance of individual managers. . . .

▼ READING 7.3   POLITICS AND THE POLITICAL ORGANIZATION*

by Henry Mintzberg

How does conflict arise in an organization, why, and with what consequences? Years ago, the literature of organizations avoided such questions. But in the last decade or so, conflict and politics that go along with it have become not just acceptable topics but fashionable ones. Yet these topics, like most others in the field, have generally been discussed in fragments. Here we seek to consider them somewhat more comprehensively, first by themselves and then in the context of what will be called the political organization—the organization that comes to be dominated by politics and conflict.

Politics in Organizations

What do we mean by "politics" in organizations? An organization may be described as functioning on the basis of a number of systems of influence: authority, ideology, expertise, politics. The first three can be considered legitimate in some sense: Authority is based on legally sanctioned power, ideology on widely accepted beliefs, expertise on power that is officially certified. The system of politics, in contrast, reflects power that is technically illegitimate (or, perhaps more accurately, *a*legitimate), in the means it uses, and sometimes also in the ends it promotes. In other words, political power in the organization (unlike government) is not formally authorized, widely accepted, or officially certified. The result is that political activity is usually divisive and conflictive, pitting individuals or groups against the more legitimate systems of influence and, when those systems are weak, against each other.

Political Games in Organizations

Political activity in organizations is sometimes described in terms of various "games." The political scientist Graham Allison, for example, has described political games in organizations and government as "intricate and subtle, simultaneous, overlapping," but nevertheless guided by rules: "some rules are explicit, others implicit, some rules are quite clear, others fuzzy. Some are very stable; others are ever changing. But the collection of rules, in effect, defines the game" (1971:170). 1 have identified thirteen political games in particular, listed here together with their main players, the main reasons they seem to be played, and how they relate to the other systems of influence.

▼ *Insurgency game:* usually played to resist authority, although can be played to resist expertise or established ideology or even to effect change in the organization; ranges "from protest to rebellion" (Zaid and Berger, 1978:841), and is usually played by "lower participants" (Mechanic, 1962), those who feel the greatest weight of formal authority

---

*Adapted from Henry Mintzberg, *Power in and Around Organizations* (Copyright © Prentice-Hall, 1983), Chaps. 13 and 23, used by permission of the publisher; based on a summary that appeared in *Mintzberg on Management: Inside Our Strange World of Organizations* (Free Press 1989).

▼ *Counterinsurgency game*: played by those with legitimate power who fight back with political means, perhaps with legitimate means as well (e.g., excommunication in the church)

▼ *Sponsorship game*: played to build power base, in this case by using superiors; individual attaches self to someone with more status, professing loyalty in return for power

▼ *Alliance-building game*: played among peers—often line managers, sometimes experts—who negotiate implicit contracts of support for each other in order to build power base to advance selves in the organization

▼ *Empire-building game*: played by line managers, in particular, to build power bases, not cooperatively with peers but individually with subordinates

▼ *Budgeting game*: played overtly and with rather clearly defined rules to build power base; similar to last game, but less divisive, since prize is resources, not positions or units per se, at least not those of rivals

▼ *Expertise game.*: nonsanctioned use of expertise to build power base, either by flaunting it or by feigning it; true experts play by exploiting technical skills and knowledge, emphasizing the uniqueness, criticality, and irreplaceability of the expertise (Hickson et al., 1971), also by seeking to keep skills from being programmed, by keeping knowledge to selves; nonexperts play by attempting to have their work viewed as expert, ideally to have it declared professional so they alone can control it

▼ *Lording game*: played to build power base by "lording" legitimate power over those without it or with less of it (i.e., using legitimate power in illegitimate ways); manager can lord formal authority over subordinate or civil servant over a citizen; members of missionary configuration can lord its ideology over outsiders; experts can lord technical skills over the unskilled

▼ *Line versus staff game*: a game of sibling-type rivalry, played not just to enhance personal power but to defeat a rival; pits line managers with formal decision-making authority against staff advisers with specialized expertise; each side tends to exploit legitimate power in illegitimate ways

▼ *Rival camps game*: again played to defeat a rival; typically occurs when alliance or empire-building games result in two major power blocs, giving rise to two-person, zero-sum game in place of n-person game; can be most divisive game of all; conflict can be between units (e.g., between marketing and production in manufacturing firm), between rival personalities, or between two competing missions (as in prisons split between custody and rehabilitation orientations)

▼ *Strategic candidates game*: played to effect change in an organization; individuals or groups seek to promote through political means their own favored changes of a strategic nature; many play—analysts, operating personnel, lower-level managers, even senior managers and chief executives (especially in the professional configurations), who must promote own candidates politically before they can do so formally; often combines elements of other games—empire-building (as purpose of game), alliance-building (to win game), rival camps, line versus staff, expertise, and lording (evoked during game), insurgency (following game), and so on

▼ *Whistle-blowing game*: a typically brief and simple game, also played to effect organizational change; privileged information is used by an insider, usually a lower participant, to "blow the whistle" to an influential outsider on questionable or illegal behavior by the organization

▼ *Young Turks game*: played for highest stakes of all, not to effect simple change or to resist legitimate power per se, but to throw the latter into question, perhaps even to overthrow it, and institute major shift; small group of "young Turks," close to but not at center of power, seeks to reorient organization's basic strategy, displace a major body of its expertise, replace its ideology, or rid it of its leadership; Zald and Berger discuss a form of this game they call "organizational coup d'état," where the object is "to effect an unexpected succession"—to replace *holders* of authority while maintaining *system* of authority intact (1978:833).

Some of these games, such as sponsorship and lording, while themselves technically illegitimate, can nevertheless *coexist with* strong legitimate systems of influence, as found for example in the machine and missionary type organizations; indeed, they could not exist without these systems of influence. Other political games, such as insurgency and young Turks—usually highly divisive games—arise in the presence of legitimate power but are *antagonistic to it*, designed to destroy or at least weaken it. And still others, such as rival camps, often arise when legitimate power is weak and *substitute for* it, for example in the professional and innovative type organizations.

The implication of this is that politics and conflict may exist at two levels in an organization. They may be present but not dominant, existing as an overlay in a more conventional organization, perhaps a kind of fifth column acting on behalf of some challenging power. Or else politics may be the dominant system of influence, and conflict strong, having weakened the legitimate systems of influence or having arisen in their weakness. It is this second level that gives rise to the type of organization we call *political*.

Forms of Political Organizations

What characterizes the organization dominated by politics is a lack of any of the forms of order found in conventional organizations. In other words, the organization is best described in terms of power, not structure, and that power is exercised in ways not legitimate in conventional organizations. Thus, there is no preferred method of coordination, no single dominant part of the organization, no clear type of decentralization. Everything depends on the fluidity of informal power, marshaled to win individual issues.

How does such an organization come to be? There is little published research on the question. But some ideas can be advanced tentatively. First, conflict would seem to arise in a circumscribed way in an organization, say between two units (such as marketing and production) or between an influential outside group and a powerful insider (such as between a part owner and the CEO). That conflict may develop gradually or it may flare up suddenly. It may eventually be resolved, but when it becomes intense, it may tend to spread, as other influencers get drawn in on one side or the other. But since few organizations can sustain intense political activity for long, that kind of conflict must eventually moderate itself (unless it kills off the organization first). In moderated form, however, the conflict may endure, even when it pervades the whole system, so long as the organization can make up for its losses, perhaps by being in a privileged position (as in the case of a conflict-ridden regulatory agency that is sustained by a government budget, or a politicized corporation that operates in a secure cartel).

What we end up with are two dimensions of conflict, first moderate or intense and second confined or pervasive. A third dimension—enduring or brief—really combines with the first (intense conflict having to be typically brief, moderate conflict possibly enduring). Combining these dimensions, we end up with four forms of the political organization:

▼ *Confrontation*, characterized by conflict that is *intense, confined,* and *brief* (unstable)
▼ *Shaky alliance*, characterized by conflict that is *moderate, confined,* and possibly *enduring* (relatively stable)
▼ *Politicized organization*, characterized by conflict that is *moderate, pervasive,* and possibly *enduring* (relatively stable, so long as it is sustained by privileged position)

▼ *Complete political arena*, characterized by conflict that is *intense, pervasive,* and *brief* (unstable)*

One of these forms is called *complete* because its conflict is both intense and pervasive. In this form, the external influencers disagree among themselves, they try to form alliances with some insiders, while clashing with others. The internal activities are likewise conflictive, permeated by divisive political games. Authority, ideology, and expertise are all subordinated to the play of political power. An organization so politicized can pursue no goal with any consistency. At best, it attends to a number of goals inconsistently over time, at worst it consumes all its energy in disputes and never accomplishes anything. In essence, the complete political arena is less a coherent organization than a free-for-all of individuals. As such, it is probably the form of political organization least commonly found in practice, or, at least, the most unstable when it does appear.

In contrast, the other three forms of political organization manage to remain partial, one by moderating its conflict, a second by containing it, and the third by doing both. As a result, these forms are more stable than the complete form and so are probably more common, with two of them in particular appearing to be far more viable.

In the *confrontational* form, conflict may be intense, but it is also contained, focusing on two parties. Typical of this is the takeover situation, where, for example, an outside stockholder tries to seize control of a closed system corporation from its management. Another example is the situation, mentioned earlier, of two rival camps in and around a prison, one promoting the mission of custody, the other that of rehabilitation.

The *shaky alliance* commonly emerges when two or more major systems of influence or centers of power must coexist in roughly equal balance. The symphony orchestra, for example, must typically combine the strong personal authority of the conductor (entrepreneurial orientation) with the extensive expertise of the musicians (professional orientation). As Fellini demonstrated so well in his film *Orchestra Rehearsal*, this alliance, however uncomfortable (experts never being happy in the face of strong authority), is nevertheless a necessary one. Common today is the professional organization operating in the public sector, which must somehow sustain an alliance of experts and government officials, one group pushing upward for professional autonomy, the other downward for technocratic control.

Our final form, the *politicized organization*, is characterized by moderate conflict that pervades the entire system of power. This would appear to describe a number of today's largest organizations, especially ones in the public sector whose mandates are visible and controversial—many regulatory agencies, for example, and some public utilities. Here it is government protection, or monopoly power, that sustains organizations captured by conflict. This form seems to be increasingly common in the private sector too, among some of the largest corporations that are able to sustain the inefficiencies of conflict through their market power and sometimes by their ability to gain government support as well.

The Functional Role of Politics in Organizations

Little space need be devoted to the dysfunctional influence of politics in organizations. Politics is divisive and costly; it burns up energies that could instead go into the operations. It can also lead to all kinds of aberrations. Politics is often used to sustain outmoded systems of power, and sometimes to introduce new ones that are not justified. Politics can also paralyze an organization to the point where its effective functioning comes to a halt and nobody benefits. The purpose of an organization, after all, is to produce goods and services, not to provide an arena in which people can fight with one another.

---

* I do not consider conflict that is moderate, confined, and brief to merit inclusion under the label of political organization.

What does deserve space, however, because they are less widely appreciated, are those conditions in which politics and the political organization serve a functional role.

In general, the system of politics is necessary in an organization to correct certain deficiencies in its other, legitimate systems of influence—above all to provide for certain forms of flexibility discouraged by those other systems. The other systems of influence were labeled legitimate because their *means*—authority, ideology, or expertise—have some basis of legitimacy. But sometimes those means are used to pursue *ends* that are illegitimate (as in the example of the lording game, where legitimate power is flaunted unreasonably). In contrast, the system of politics, whose *means* are (by definition) illegitimate, can sometimes be used to pursue *ends* that are in fact legitimate (as in certain of the whistle-blowing and young Turks games, where political pressures are used against formal authority to correct irresponsible or ineffective behaviors). We can elaborate on this in terms of four specific points.

First, politics as a system of influence can act in a Darwinian way to ensure that the strongest members of an organization are brought into positions of leadership. Authority favors a single chain of command; weak leaders can suppress strong subordinates. Politics, on the other hand, can provide alternate channels of information and promotion, as when the sponsorship game enables someone to leap over a weak superior (McClelland, 1970). Moreover, since effective leaders have been shown to exhibit a need for power, the political games can serve as tests to demonstrate the potential for leadership. The second-string players may suffice for the scrimmages, but only the stars can be allowed to meet the competition. Political games not only suggest who those players are but also help to remove their weak rivals from contention.

Second, politics can also ensure that all sides of an issue are fully debated, whereas the other systems of influence may promote only one. The system of authority, by aggregating information up a central hierarchy, tends to advance only a single point of view, often the one already known to be favored above. So, too, does the system of ideology, since every issue is interpreted in terms of "the word," the prevailing set of beliefs. As for the system of expertise, people tend to defer to the expert on any particular issue. But experts are often closed to new ideas, ones that developed after they received their training. Politics, however, by obliging "responsible men ... to fight for what they are convinced is right" (Allison, 1971:145) encourages a variety of voices to be heard on any issue. And, because of attacks by its opponents, each voice is forced to justify its conclusions in terms of the broader good. That means it must marshal arguments and support proposals that can at least be justified in terms of the interests of the organization at large rather than the parochial needs of a particular group. As Bums has noted in an amusing footnote:

> It is impossible to avoid some reference from the observations made here to F. M. Cornford's well known "Guide for the Young Academic Politician." Jobs "fall into two classes, My Jobs and Your Jobs. My Jobs are public-spirited proposals, which happen (much to my regret) to involve the advancement of a personal friend, or (still more to my regret) of myself. Your Jobs are insidious intrigues for the advancement of yourself and your friends, spuriously disguised as public-spirited proposals." (1961-62:260)

Third, the system of politics is often required to stimulate necessary change that is blocked by the legitimate systems of influence. Internal change is generally threatening to the "vested interest" of an organization. The system of authority concentrates power up the hierarchy, often in the hands of those who were responsible for initiating the existing strategies in the first place. It also contains the established controls, which are designed to sustain the status quo. Similarly, the system of expertise concentrates power in the hands of senior and established experts, not junior ones who may possess newer, more necessary skills. Likewise, the system of ideology, because it is rooted in the past, in tradition, acts as a deterrent to change. In the face of these resistances, it is politics that is able to work as a kind of "invisible hand"—"invisible underhand" would be a better term—to promote necessary change, through such games as strategic candidates, whistle-blowing, and young Turks.

Fourth and finally, the system of politics can ease the path for the execution of decisions. Senior managers, for example, often use politics to gain acceptance for their decisions, playing the strategic candidates game early in promoting proposals to avoid having to play the more decisive and risky counterinsurgency game later in the face of resistance to them. They persuade, negotiate, and build alliances to smooth the path for the decisions they wish to make.

To conclude our discussion, while I am not personally enthusiastic about organizational politics and have no desire to live in a political organization, I do accept, and hope I have persuaded the reader to accept, that politics does have useful roles to play in a society of organizations. Organizational politics may irritate us, but it can also serve us.

▼ READING 7.4   COMPETITIVE MANEUVERING*

by Bruce Henderson

Brinkmanship in Business

A businessman often convinces himself that he is completely logical in his behavior when in fact the critical factor is his emotional bias compared to the emotional bias of his opposition. Unfortunately, some businessmen and students perceive competition as some kind of impersonal, objective, colorless affair, with a company competing against the field as a golfer competes in medal play. A better case can be made that business competition is a major battle in which there are many contenders, each of whom must be dealt with individually. Victory, if achieved, is more often won in the mind of a competitor than in the economic arena.

I shall emphasize two points. The first is that the management of a company must persuade each competitor voluntarily to stop short of a maximum effort to acquire customers and profits. The second point is that persuasion depends on emotional and intuitive factors rather than on analysis or deduction.

The negotiator's skill lies in being as arbitrary as necessary to obtain the best possible compromise without actually destroying the basis for voluntary mutual cooperation of self-restraint. There are some commonsense rules for success in such an endeavor:

1. Be sure that your rival is fully aware of what he can gain if he cooperates and what it will cost him if he does not.
2. Avoid any action which will arouse your competitor's emotions, since it is essential that he behave in a logical, reasonable fashion.
3. Convince your opponent that you are emotionally dedicated to your position and are completely convinced that it is reasonable.

It is worth emphasizing that your competitor is under the maximum handicap if he acts in a completely rational, objective, and logical fashion. For then he will cooperate as long

---

* "Brinkmanship in Business" and "The Nonlogical Strategy," in *Henderson on Corporate Strategy* (Cambridge, MA, Abt Books, 1979), pp. 27-33, title selected for this book; section on "Rules for the Strategist" originally at the end of "Brinkmanship in Business" moved to the end of "The Nonlogical Strategy," reprinted by permission of publisher.

as he thinks he can benefit. In fact, if he is completely logical, he will not forgo the profit of cooperation as long as there is *any* net benefit.

FRIENDLY COMPETITORS

It may strike most businessmen as strange to talk about cooperation with competitors. But it is hard to visualize a situation in which it would be worthwhile to pursue competition to the utter destruction of a competitor. In every case there is a greater advantage to reducing the competition on the condition that the competitor does likewise. Such mutual restraint is cooperation, whether recognized as such or not.

Without cooperation on the part of competitors, there can be no stability. We see this most clearly in international relationships during times of peace. There are constant encroachments and aggressive acts. And the eventual consequence is always either voluntarily imposed self-restraint or mutual destruction. Thus, international diplomacy has only one purpose: to stabilize cooperation between independent nations on the most favorable basis possible. Diplomacy can be described as the art of being stubborn, arbitrary, and unreasonable without arousing emotional responses.

Businessmen should notice the similarity between economic competition and the peacetime behavior of nations. The object in both cases is to achieve a voluntary, cooperative restraint on the part of otherwise aggressive competitors. Complete elimination of competition is almost inconceivable. The goal of the hottest economic war is an agreement for coexistence, not annihilation. The competition and mutual encroachment do not stop; they go on forever. But they do so under some measure of mutual restraint.

"COLD WAR" TACTICS

A breakdown in negotiations is inevitable if both parties persist in arbitrary positions which are incompatible. Yet there are major areas in business where some degree of arbitrary behavior is essential for protecting a company's self-interest. In effect, a type of brinkmanship is necessary. The term was coined to describe cold war international diplomacy, but it describes a normal pattern in business, too.

In a confrontation between parties who are in part competitors and in part cooperators, deciding what to accept is essentially emotional or arbitrary. Deciding what is attainable requires an evaluation of the other party's degree of intransigence. The purpose is to convince him that you are arbitrary and emotionally committed while trying to discover what he would really accept in settlement. The competitor known to be coldly logical is at a great disadvantage. Logically, he can afford to compromise until there is no advantage left in cooperation. If, instead, he is emotional, irrational, and arbitrary, he has a great advantage.

CONSEQUENCE

The heart of business strategy for a company is to promote attitudes on the part of its competitors that will cause them either to restrain themselves or to act in a fashion which management deems advantageous. In diplomacy and military strategy the key to success is very much the same.

The most easily recognized way of enforcing cooperation is to exhibit obvious willingness to use irresistible or overwhelming force. This requires little strategic skill, but there is the problem of convincing the competing organization that the force will be used without actually resorting to it (which would be expensive and inconvenient).

In industry, however, the available force is usually not overwhelming, although one company may be able to inflict major punishment on another. In the classic case, each party can inflict such punishment on the other. If there were open conflict, then both parties would lose. If they cooperate, both parties are better off, but not necessarily equally so—particularly if one is trying to change the status quo.

When each party can punish the other, the prospects of agreement depend on three things:

1. Each party's willingness to accept the risk of punishment
2. Each party's belief that the other party is willing to accept the risk of punishment
3. The degree of rationality in the behavior of each party

If these conclusions are correct, what can we deduce about how advantages are gained and lost in business competition?

First, management's unwillingness to accept the risk of punishment is almost certain to produce either the punishment or progressively more onerous conditions for cooperation—provided the competition recognized the attitude.

Second, beliefs about a competitor's future behavior or response are all that determine competitive cooperation. In other words, it is the judgment not of actual capability but of probable use of capability that counts.

Third, the less rational or less predictable the behavior of a competitor appears to be, the greater the advantage he possesses in establishing a favorable competitive balance. This advantage is limited only by his need to avoid forcing his competitors into an untenable position or creating an emotional antagonism that will lead them to be unreasonable and irrational (as he is).

THE NONLOGICAL STRATEGY

The goal of strategy in business, diplomacy, and war is to produce a stable relationship favorable to you with the consent of your competitors. By definition, restraint by a competitor is cooperation. Such cooperation from a competitor must seem to be profitable to him. *Any competition which does not eventually eliminate a competitor requires his cooperation to stabilize the situation.* The agreement is usually that of tacit nonaggression; the alternative is death for all but one competitor. A stable competitive situation requires an agreement between competing parties to maintain self-restraint. Such agreement cannot be arrived at by logic. It must be achieved by an emotional balance of forces. This is why it is necessary to appear irrational to competitors. For the same reason, you must seem unreasonable and arbitrary in negotiations with customers and suppliers.

Competition and cooperation go hand in hand in all real-life situations. Otherwise, conflict could only end in extermination of the competitor. There is a point in all situations of conflict where both parties gain more or lose less from peace than they can hope to gain from any foreseeable victory. Beyond that point cooperation is more profitable than conflict. But how will the benefits be shared?

In negotiated conflict situations, the participant who is coldly logical is at a great disadvantage. Logically, he can afford to compromise until there is no advantage left in cooperation. The negotiator/competitor whose behavior is irrational or arbitrary has a great advantage if he can depend upon his opponent being logical and unemotional. The arbitrary or irrational competitor can demand far more than a reasonable share and yet his logical opponent can still gain by compromise rather than breaking off the cooperation.

Absence of monopoly in business requires voluntary restraint of competition. At some point there must be a tacit agreement not to compete. Unless this restraint of trade were acceptable to all competitors, the resulting aggression would inevitably eliminate the less efficient competitors leaving only one. Antitrust laws represent a formal attempt to limit competition. All antimonopoly and fair trade laws constitute restraint of competition.

Utter destruction of a competitor is almost never profitable unless the competitor is unwilling to accept peace. In our daily social contacts, in our international affairs, and in our business affairs, we have far more ability to damage those around us than we ever dare use. Others have the same power to damage us. The implied agreement to restrain our potential aggression is all that stands between us and eventual elimination of one by the other. Both war and diplomacy are mechanisms for establishing or maintaining this self-imposed restraint on all competitors. The conflict continues, but within the implied area of cooperative agreement.

There is a definite limit to the range within which competitors can expect to achieve an equilibrium or negotiate a shift in equilibrium even by implication. Arbitrary, uncooperative, or aggressive attitudes will produce equally emotional reactions. These emotional reactions are in turn the basis for nonlogical and arbitrary responses. Thus, nonlogical behavior is self-limiting.

This is why the art of diplomacy can be described as the ability to be unreasonable without arousing resentment. It is worth remembering that the objective of diplomacy is to induce cooperation on terms that are relatively more favorable to you than to your protagonist without actual force being used.

More business victories are won in the minds of competitors than in the laboratory, the factory or the marketplace. The competitor's conviction that you are emotional, dogmatic, or otherwise nonlogical in your business strategy can be a great asset. This conviction on his part can result in an acceptance of your actions without retaliation, which would otherwise be unthinkable. More important, the anticipation of nonlogical or unrestrained reactions on your part can inhibit his competitive aggression.

RULES FOR THE STRATEGIST

If I were asked to distill the conditions and forces described into advice for the business-strategist, I would suggest five rules:

1. You must know as accurately as possible just what your competition has at stake in his contact with you. It is not what you gain or lose, but what he gains or loses that sets the limit on his ability to compromise with you.
2. The less the competition knows about your stakes, the less advantage he has. Without a reference point, he does not even know whether you are being unreasonable.
3. It is absolutely essential to know the character, attitudes, motives, and habitual behavior of a competitor if you wish to have a negotiating advantage.
4. The more arbitrary your demands are, the better your relative competitive position—provided you do not arouse an emotional reaction.
5. The less arbitrary you seem, the more arbitrary you can in fact be.

These rules make up the art of business brinkmanship. They are guidelines for winning a strategic victory in the minds of competitors. Once this victory has been won, it can be converted into a competitive victory in terms of sales volume, costs, and profits.

by Henry Mintzberg

Who should control the corporation? How? And for the pursuit of what goals? Historically, the corporation was controlled by its owners—through direct control of the managers if not through direct management—for the pursuit of economic goals. But as shareholding became dispersed, owner control weakened; and as the corporation grew to very large size, its economic actions came to have increasing social consequences. The giant, widely held corporation came increasingly under the implicit control of its managers, and the concept of social responsibility—the voluntary consideration of public social goals alongside the private economic ones—arose to provide a basis of legitimacy for their actions.

To some, including those closest to the managers themselves, this was accepted as a satisfactory arrangement for the large corporation. "Trust it" to the goodwill of the managers was their credo; these people will be able to achieve an appropriate balance between social and economic goals.

But others viewed this basis of control as fundamentally illegitimate. The corporation was too large, too influential, its actions too pervasive to be left free of the direct and concerted influence of outsiders. At the extreme were those who believed that legitimacy could be achieved only by subjecting managerial authority to formal and direct external control. "Nationalize it," said those at one end of the political spectrum, to put ultimate control in the hands of the government so that it will pursue public social goals. No, said those at the other end, "restore it" to direct shareholder control, so that it will not waiver from the pursuit of private economic goals.

Other people took less extreme positions. "Democratize it" became the rallying cry for some, to open up the governance of the large, widely held corporation to a variety of affected groups—if not the workers, then the customers, or conservation interests, or minorities. "Regulate it" was also a popular position, with its implicit premise that only by sharing their control with government would the corporation's managers attend to certain social goals. Then there were those who accepted direct management control so long as it was tempered by other, less formal types of influence. "Pressure it," said a generation of social activists, to ensure that social goals are taken into consideration. But others argued that because the corporation is an economic instrument, you must "induce it" by providing economic incentives to encourage the resolution of social problems.

Finally, there were those who argued that this whole debate was unnecessary, that a kind of invisible hand ensures that the economic corporation acts in a socially responsible manner. "Ignore it" was their implicit conclusion.

This article is written to clarify what has become a major debate of our era, *the* major debate revolving around the private sector: Who should control the corporation, specifically the large, widely held corporation, how, and for the pursuit of what goals? The answers that are eventually accepted will determine what kind of society we and our children shall live in. . . .

As implied earlier, the various positions of who should control the corporation, and how, can be laid out along a political spectrum, from nationalization at one end to the restoration of shareholder power at the other. From the managerial perspective, however, those two extremes are not so far apart. Both call for direct control of the corporation's managers by specific outsiders, in one case the government to ensure the pursuit of social goals, in the other case the shareholders to ensure the pursuit of economic ones. It is the moderate positions—notably, trusting the corporation to the social responsibility of its managers—that are farthest from the extremes. Hence, we can fold our spectrum around so that it takes the shape of a horseshoe.

* Originally published in the *California Management Review* (Fall 1984), pp. 90-115, based on a section of Henry Mintzberg, *Power in and Around Organizations* (Prentice-Hall, 1983). Copyright © 1984 by The Regents of the University of California. Reprinted with deletions by permission of The Regents.

FIGURE 1
The Conceptual
Horseshoe

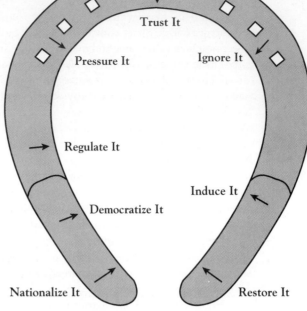

Figure 1 shows our "conceptual horseshoe," with "nationalize it" and "restore it" at the two ends. "Trust it" is at the center, because it postulates a natural balance of social and economic goals. "Democratize it," "regulate it," and "pressure it" are shown on the left side of the horseshoe, because all seek to temper economic goals with social ones. "Induce it" and "ignore it," both of which favor the exclusive pursuit of economic goals, are shown on the right side.

This conceptual horseshoe provides a basic framework to help clarify the issues in this important debate. We begin by discussing each of these positions in turn, circling the horseshoe from left to right. Finding that each (with one exception) has a logical context, we conclude—in keeping with our managerial perspective—that they should be thought of as forming a portfolio from which society can draw to deal with the issue of who should control the corporation and how.

"Nationalize It"

Nationalization of the corporation is a taboo subject in the United States—in general, but not in particular. Whenever a major corporation runs into serious difficulty (i.e., faces bankruptcy with possible loss of many jobs), mass government intervention, often including direct nationalization, inevitably comes up as an option. This option has been exercised: U.S. travelers now ride on Amtrak; Tennessee residents have for years been getting their power from a government utility; indeed, the Post Office was once a private enterprise. Other nations have, of course, been much more ambitious in this regard.

From a managerial and organizational perspective, the question is not whether nationalization is legitimate, but whether it works—at least in particular, limited circumstances.

As a response to concerns about the social responsibility of large corporations, the answer seems to be no. The evidence suggests that social difficulties arise more from the size of an organization and its degree of bureaucratization than from its form of ownership (Epstein, 1977; Jenkins, 1976). On the other hand, contrary to popular belief in the United States, nationalization does not necessarily harm economic efficiency. Over the years, Renault has been one of the most successful automobile companies outside Japan; it was nationalized by the French government shortly after World War II.... When people believe that government ownership leads to interference, politicization, and inefficiency, that may be exactly what happens. However, when they believe that nationalization *has* to work, then state-owned enterprises may be able to attract the very best talent in the country and thereby work well.

But economic efficiency is no reason to favor nationalization any more than is concern about social responsibility. Nationalization does, however, seem to make sense in at least two particular circumstances. The first is when a mission deemed necessary in a society will not be provided adequately by the private sector. That is presumably why America has its Amtrak [and why Third World nations often create state enterprises]. . . . The second is when the activities of an organization must be so intricately tied to government policy that it is best managed as a direct arm of the state. The Canadian government created Petrocan to act as a "window" and a source of expertise on the sensitive oil industry.

Thus, it is not rhetoric but requirement that should determine the role of this position as a solution to who should control the corporation. "Nationalize it" should certainly not be embraced as a panacea, but neither should it be rejected as totally inapplicable.

"Democratize It"

A less extreme position—at least in the context of the American debate—is one that calls for formal devices to broaden the governance of the corporation. The proponents of this position either accept the legal fiction of shareholder control and argue that the corporation's power base is too narrow, or else they respond to the emergent reality and question the legitimacy of managerial control. Why, they ask, do stockholders or self-selected managers have any greater right to control the profound decisions of these major institutions than do workers or customers or the neighbors downstream.

This stand is not to be confused with what is known as "participative management." The call to "democratize it" is a legal, rather than ethical one and is based on power, not generosity. Management is not asked to share its power voluntarily; rather, that power is to be reallocated constitutionally. That makes this position a fundamental and important one, *especially* in the United States with its strong tradition of pluralist control of its institutions.

The debate over democratization of the corporation has been confusing in part because many of the proposals have been so vague. We can bring some order to it by considering, in organizational terms, two basic means of democratization and two basic constituencies that can be involved. As shown in Figure 2, they suggest four possible forms of corporate democracy. One means is through the election of representatives to the board of directors, which we call *representative democracy*. The other is through formal but direct involvement in internal decision making processes, which we call *participatory democracy*. Either can focus on the *workers* . . . or else on a host of outside interest groups, the latter giving rise to a *pluralistic* form of democracy. These are basic forms of corporate democracy in theory. With one exception, they have hardly been approached—let alone achieved—in practice. But they suggest where the "democratize it" debate may be headed.

The European debate has focused on worker representative democracy. This has, in some sense, been achieved in Yugoslavia, where the workers of all but the smallest firms

FIGURE 2
Four Basic Forms of
Corporate Democracy

GROUPS INVOLVED

	Internal Employees	External Interest Groups
Board of Directors	Worker Representative Democracy **(European style, e.g., "co-determination" or worker ownership)**	Pluralistic Representative Democracy **(American style, e.g., "public interest" directors)**
Internal Decision-Making Process	Worker Participatory Democracy **(e.g., works councils)**	Pluralistic Participatory Democracy **(e.g., outsiders on new product committees)**

FOCUS OF ATTENTION

elect the members of what is the equivalent of the American board of directors. In Germany, under the so-called *Mitbestimmung* ("codetermination"), the workers and the shareholders each elect half of the directors.

The evidence on this form of corporate democracy has been consistent, and it supports neither its proponents nor its detractors. Workers' representation on the board seems to make relatively little difference one way or the other. The worker representatives concern themselves with wage and welfare issues but leave most other questions to management. Worker-controlled firms (not unlike the state-owned ones) appear to be no more socially responsible than private ones. . . .

On the other hand, worker representative democracy may have certain positive benefits. German Chancellor Helmut Schmidt is reported to have said that "the key to [his] country's postwar economic miracle was its sophisticated system of workers' participations" (in Garson, 1977:63). While no one can prove this statement, codetermination certainly does not seem to have done the German economy much harm. By providing an aura of legitimacy to the German corporation and by involving the workers (at least officially) in its governance, codetermination may perhaps have enhanced the spirit of enterprise in Germany (while having little real effect on how decisions are actually made). More significantly, codetermination may have fostered greater understanding and cooperation between the managers and the union members who fill most of the worker seats on the boards . . . .

. . . the embryonic debate over representative democracy in the United States has shown signs of moving in a different direction. Consistent with the tradition of pluralism in America's democratic institutions, there has been increasing pressure to elect outside directors who represent a wide variety of special interest groups—that is, consumers, minorities, environmentalists, and so on . . . .

Critics . . . have pointed out the problems of defining constituencies and finding the means to hold elections. "One-person, one-vote" may be easily applied to electing representatives of the workers, but no such simple rule can be found in the case of the consumer or environmental representatives, let alone ones of the public interest." Yet it is amazing how quickly things become workable in the United States when Americans decide to put their collective mind to it. Indeed, the one case of public directors that I came across is telling in this regard. According to a Conference Board report, the selection by the Chief Justice of the Supreme Court of New Jersey of 6 of the 24 members of the board of Prudential Insurance as public directors has been found by the company to be "quite workable" (Bacon and Brown, 1975:48). . . . [Note—see the associated box on "The Power of the Board."]

Despite its problems, representative democracy is crystal clear compared with participatory democracy. What the French call "autogestion" (as opposed to "cogestion," or codetermination) seems to describe a kind of bottom-up, grass-roots democracy in which the

---

THE POWER OF THE BOARD

Proposals for representative democracy, indeed those for nationalization and the restoration of shareholder control as well, rest on assumptions about the power of the board of directors. It may, therefore, be worth considering at this point the roles that boards of directors play in organizations and the board's resulting powers.

In law, traditionally, the business of a corporation was to be "managed" by its board. But of course, the board does no such thing. Managers manage, although some may happen to sit on the board. What, then, are the roles of the board, particularly of its "outside" directors?

The most tangible role of the board, and clearly provided for in law, is to name, and of course to dismiss as well, the chief executive officer, that person who in turn names the rest of the management. A second role may be to exercise direct control during periods of crisis, for example when the management has failed to provide leadership. And a third is to review the major decisions of the management as well as its overall performance.

These three constitute the board's roles of control, in principal at least because there is no shortage of evidence that boards have difficulty doing even these effectively, especially outside directors. Their job is, after all, part time, and in a brief meeting once in a while they face a complex organization led by a highly organized management that deals with it every day. The result is that board control tends to reduce to naming and replacing the chief executive, and that person's knowledge of that fact, nothing more. Indeed, even that power is circumscribed, because a management cannot be replaced very often. In a sense, the board is like a bee hovering near a person picking flowers. The person must proceed carefully, so as to not provoke the bee, but can proceed with the task. But if the bee does happen to be provoked, it only gets to sting once. Thus many boards try to know only enough to know when the management is not doing its job properly, so that they can replace it.

But if boards tend to be weaker than expected in exercising *control over* the organization, they also tend perhaps to be stronger than expected in providing *service to* the organization. Here board membership plays at least four other roles. First, it "co-opts" influential outsiders: The organization uses the status of a seat on its board to gain the support of people important to it (as in the case of the big donors who sit on university boards). Second, board membership may be used to establish contacts for the organization (as when retired military officers sit on the boards of weapons manufacturing firms). This may be done to help in such things as the securing of contracts and the raising of funds. Third, seats on the board can be used to enhance an organization's reputation (as when an astronaut or some other type of celebrity is given a seat). And fourth, the board can be used to provide advice for the organization (as in the case of many of the bankers and lawyers who sit on the boards of corporations).

How much do boards serve organizations, and how much do they control them? Some boards do, of course, exercise control, particularly when their members represent a well-defined constituency, such as the substantial owner of a corporation. But, as noted, this tends to be a loose control at best. And other boards hardly do even that, especially when their constituencies are widely dispersed.

To represent everyone is ultimately to represent no one, especially when faced with a highly organized management that knows exactly what it wants. (Or from the elector's point of view, having some distant representative sitting on a board somewhere hardly brings him or her closer to control over the things that impinge on daily life—the work performed, the products consumed, the rivers polluted.) In corporations, this has been shown to be true of the directors who represent many small shareholders no less than those who represent many workers or many customers, perhaps even those who represent government, since that can be just a confusing array of pressure groups. These boards become, at best, tools of the organization, providing it with the variety of the services discussed above, at worst mere façades of formal authority.

workers participate directly in decision making (instead of overseeing management's decisions from the board of directors) and also elect their own managers (who then become more administrators than bosses). Yet such proposals are inevitably vague, and I have heard of no large mass production or mass service firm—not even one owned by workers or a union—that comes close to this. . . .

What has impeded worker participatory democracy? In my opinion, something rather obvious has stood in its way; namely, the structure required by the very organizations in which the attempts have been made to apply it. Worker participatory democracy—and worker representative democracy too, for that matter—has been attempted primarily in organizations containing large numbers of workers who do highly routine, rather unskilled jobs that are typical of most mass production and service—what I have elsewhere called Machine Bureaucracies. The overriding requirement in Machine Bureaucracy is for tight coordination, the kind that can only be achieved by central administrators. For example, the myriad of decisions associated with producing an automobile at Volvo's Kalmar works in Sweden cannot be made by autonomous groups, each doing as it pleases. The whole car must fit together in a particular way at the end of the assembly process. These decisions require a highly sophisticated system of bureaucratic coordination. That is why automobile companies are structured into rigid hierarchies of authority. . . .

Participatory democracy *is* approached in other kinds of organizations . . . the autonomous professional institutions such as universities and hospitals, which have very different needs for central coordination. . . . But the proponents of democracy in organizations are not lobbying for changes in hospitals or universities. It is the giant, mass producers they are after, and unless the operating work in these corporations becomes largely skilled and professional in nature, nothing approaching participative democracy can be expected.

In principal, the pluralistic form of participatory democracy means that a variety of groups external to the corporation can somehow control its decision-making processes directly. In practice, of course, this concept is even more elusive than the worker form of participatory democracy. To fully open up the internal decision-making processes of the corporation to outsiders would mean chaos. Yet certain very limited forms of outside participation would seem to be not only feasible but perhaps even desirable. . . . Imagine telephone company executives resolving rate conflicts with consumer groups in quiet offices instead of having to face them in noisy public hearings.

To conclude, corporate democracy—whether representative or participatory in form—may be an elusive and difficult concept, but it cannot be dismissed. It is not just another social issue, like conservation or equal opportunity, but one that strikes at the most fundamental of values. Ours has become a society of organizations. Democracy will have decreasing meaning to most citizens if it cannot be extended beyond political and judicial processes to those institutions that impinge upon them in their daily lives—as workers, as consumers, as neighbors. This is why we shall be hearing a great deal more of "democratize it."

"Regulate It"

In theory, regulating the corporation is about as simple as democratizing it is complex. In practice, it is, of course, another matter. To the proponents of "regulate it," the corporation can be made responsive to social needs by having its actions subjected to the controls of a higher authority—typically government, in the form of a regulatory agency or legislation backed up by the courts. Under regulation, constraints are imposed externally on the corporation while its internal governance is left to its managers.

Regulation of business is at least as old as the Code of Hammurabi. In America, it has tended to come in waves. . . .

To some, regulation is a clumsy instrument that should never be relied upon; to others, it is a panacea for the problems of social responsibility. At best, regulation sets minimum and usually crude standards of acceptable behavior, when it works, it does not make any firm socially responsible so much as stop some from being grossly irresponsible. Because it is inflexible, regulation tends to be applied slowly and conservatively, usually lagging public sentiment. Regulation often does not work because of difficulties in enforcement. The problems of the regulatory agencies are legendary—limited resources and information compared with the industries they are supposed to regulate, the cooptation of the regulators by industries, and so on. When applied indiscriminately, regulation either fails dramatically or else succeeds and creates havoc.

Yet there are obvious places for regulation. A prime one is to control tangible "externalities"—costs incurred by corporations that are passed on to the public at large. When, for example, costly pollution or worker health problems can be attributed directly to a corporation, then there seems to be every reason to force it (and its customers) to incur these costs directly, or else to terminate the actions that generate them. Likewise, regulation may have a place where competition encourages the unscrupulous to pull all firms down to a base level of behavior, forcing even the well-intentioned manager to ignore the social consequences of his actions. Indeed, in such cases, the socially responsible behavior is to encourage sensible regulation. "Help us to help others," businessmen should be telling the government. . . .

Most discouraging, however, is Theodore Levitt's revelation some years ago that business has fought every piece of proposed regulatory or social legislation throughout this century, from the Child Labor Acts on up. In Levitt's opinion, much of that legislation has been good for business—dissolving the giant trusts, creating a more honest and effective stock market, and so on. Yet, "the computer is programmed to cry wolf " (Levitt, 1968:83). . . .

In summary, regulation is a clumsy instrument but not a useless one. Were the business community to take a more enlightened view of it, regulation could be applied more appropriately, and we would not need these periodic housecleanings to eliminate the excesses.

"Pressure It"

"Pressure it" is designed to do what "regulate it" fails to do: provoke corporations to act beyond some base level of behavior, usually in an area that regulation misses entirely. Here, activists bring ad hoc campaigns of pressure to bear on one or a group of corporations to keep them responsive to the activists' interpretation of social needs. . . .

"Pressure it" is a distinctively American position. While Europeans debate the theories of nationalization and corporate democracy in their cafes, Americans read about the exploits of Ralph Nader et al. in their morning newspapers. Note that "pressure it," unlike "regulate it," implicitly accepts management's right to make the final decisions. Perhaps this is one reason why it is favored in America.

While less radical than the other positions so far discussed, "pressure it" has nevertheless proved far more effective in eliciting behavior sensitive to social needs . . . [activist groups] have pressured for everything from the dismemberment of diversified corporations to the development of day care centers. Of special note is the class action suit, which has opened up a whole new realm of corporate social issues. But the effective use of the pressure campaign has not been restricted to the traditional activist. President Kennedy used it to roll back U.S. Steel price increases in the early 1960s, and business leaders in Pittsburgh used it in the late 1940s by threatening to take their freight-haulage business elsewhere if the Pennsylvania Railroad did not replace its coal burning locomotives to help clean up their city's air.

"Pressure it" as a means to change corporate behavior is informal, flexible, and focused; hence, it has been highly successful. Yet it is irregular and ad hoc, with different pressure campaigns sometimes making contradictory demands on management. Compared to the positions to its right on the horseshoe, "pressure it," like the other positions to its left, is based on confrontation rather than cooperation.

To a large and vocal contingent, which parades under the banner of "social responsibility," the corporation has no need to act irresponsibly, and therefore there is no reason for it to either be nationalized by the state, democratized by its different constituencies, regulated by the government, or pressured by activists. This contingent believes that the corporation's leaders can be trusted to attend to social goals for their own sake, simply because it is the noble thing to do. (Once this position was known as *nobelesse oblige*, literally "nobility obliges.")

We call this position "trust it," or, more exactly, "trust the corporation to the goodwill of its managers," although looking from the outside in, it might just as well be called "socialize it." We place it in the center of our conceptual horseshoe because it alone postulates a natural balance between social and economic goals—a balance which is to be attained in the heads (or perhaps the hearts) of responsible businessmen. And, as a not necessarily incidental consequence, power can be left in the hands of the managers; the corporation can be trusted to those who reconcile social and economic goals.

The attacks on social responsibility, from the right as well as the left, boil down to whether corporate managers should be trusted when they claim to pursue social goals; if so, whether they are capable of pursuing such goals; and finally, whether they have any right to pursue such goals.

The simplest attack is that social responsibility is all rhetoric, no action. E. F. Cheit refers to the "Gospel of Social Responsibility" as "designed to justify the power of managers over an ownerless system" (1964:172). . . .

Others argue that businessmen lack the personal capabilities required to pursue social goals. Levitt claims that the professional manager reaches the top of the hierarchy by dedication to his firm and his industry; as a result, his knowledge of social issues is highly restricted (Levitt, 1968:83). Others argue that an orientation to efficiency renders business leaders inadept at handling complex social problems (which require flexibility and political finesse, and sometimes involve solutions that are uneconomic). . . .

The most far reaching criticism is that businessmen have no right to pursue social goals. "Who authorized them to do that?" asks Braybrooke (1967:224), attacking from the left. What business have they—self-selected or at best appointed by shareholders—to impose *their* interpretation of the public good on society? Let the elected politicians, directly responsible to the population, look after the social goals.

But this attack comes from the right, too. Milton Friedman writes that social responsibility amounts to spending other people's money—if not that of shareholders, then of customers or employees. Drawing on all the pejorative terms of right-wing ideology, Friedman concludes that social responsibility is a "fundamentally subversive doctrine," representing "pure and unadulterated socialism," supported by businessmen who are "unwitting puppets of the intellectual forces that have been undermining the basis of a free society these past decades." To Friedman, "there is one and only one social responsibility of business—to use its resources and engage in activities designed to increase its profits so long as it stays within the rules of the game" (1970). Let businessmen, in other words, stick to their own business, which is business itself.

The empirical evidence on social responsibility is hardly more encouraging. Brenner and Molander, comparing their 1977 survey of *Harvard Business Review* readers with one conducted fifteen years earlier, concluded that the "respondents are somewhat more cynical about the ethical conduct of their peers" than they were previously (1977:59). Close to half the respondents agreed with the statement that "the American business executive tends not to apply the great ethical laws immediately to work. He is preoccupied chiefly with gain" (p. 62). Only 5% listed social responsibility as a factor "influencing ethical standards" whereas 31 % and 20% listed different factors related to pressure campaigns and 10% listed regulation. . . .

The modern corporation has been described as a rational, amoral institution—its professional managers "hired guns" who pursue "efficiently" any goals asked of them. The problem is that efficiency really means measurable efficiency, so that the guns load only with goals that can be quantified. Social goals, unlike economic ones, just don't lend themselves to quantification. As a result, the performance control systems—on which modern corporations so heavily depend—tend to drive out social goals in favor of economic ones (Ackerman, 1975). . . .

In the contemporary large corporation, professional amorality turns into economic morality. When the screws of the performance control systems are turned tight . . . economic morality can turn into social immorality. And it happens often: A *Fortune* writer found that "a surprising number of [big companies] have been involved in blatant illegalities" in the 1970s, at least 117 of 1,043 firms studied (Ross, 1980:57). . . .

How, then, is anyone to "trust it"?

The fact is that we have to trust it, for two reasons. First, the strategic decisions of large organizations inevitably involve social as well as economic consequences that are inextricably intertwined. The neat distinction between economic goals in the private sector and social goals in the public sector just doesn't hold up in practice. Every important decision of the large corporation—to introduce a new product line, to close an old plant, whatever—generates all kinds of social consequences. There is no such thing as purely economic decisions in big business. Only a conceptual ostrich, with his head deeply buried in the abstractions of economic theory, could possibly use the distinction between economic and social goals to dismiss social responsibility.

The second reason we have to "trust it" is that there is always some degree of discretion involved in corporate decision making, discretion to thwart social needs or to attend to them. Things could be a lot better in today's corporation, but they could also be an awful lot worse. It is primarily our ethics that keep us where we are. If the performance control systems favored by diversified corporations cut too deeply into our ethical standards, then our choice is clear; to reduce these standards or call into question the whole trend toward diversification.

To dismiss social responsibility is to allow corporate behavior to drop to the lowest level, propped up only by external controls such as regulation and pressure campaigns. Solzhenitsyn, who has experienced the natural conclusion of unrestrained bureaucratization, warns us (in sharp contrast to Friedman) that "a society with no other scale but the legal one is not quite worthy of man. . . . A society which is based on the letter of the law and never reaches any higher is scarcely taking advantage of the high level of human possibilities" (1978:B1).

This is not to suggest that we must trust it completely. We certainly cannot trust it unconditionally by accepting the claim popular in some quarters that only business can solve the social ills of society. Business has no business using its resources without constraint in the social sphere—whether to support political candidates or to dictate implicitly through donations how nonprofit institutions should allocate their efforts. But where business is inherently involved, where its decisions have social consequences, that is where social responsibility has a role to play: where business creates externalities that cannot be measured and attributed to it (in other words, where regulation is ineffective); where regulation would work if only business would cooperate with it; where the corporation can fool its customers, or suppliers, or government through superior knowledge; where useful products can be marketed instead of wasteful or destructive ones. In other words, we have to realize that in many spheres we must trust it, or at least socialize it (and perhaps change it) so that we can trust it. Without responsible and ethical people in important places, our society is not worth very much.

"Ignore It"

"Ignore it" differs from the other positions on the horseshoe in that explicitly or implicitly it calls for no change in corporate behavior. It assumes that social needs are met in the course of pursuing economic goals. We include this position in our horseshoe because it is held by many influential people and also because its validity would preempt support for the other positions. We must therefore, investigate it alongside the others.

It should be noted at the outset the "ignore it" is not the same position as "trust it." In the latter, to be good is the right thing to do, in the present case, "it pays to be good." The distinction is subtle but important, for now it is economics, not ethics, that elicits the desired behavior. One need not strive to be ethical; economic forces will ensure that social needs fall conveniently into place. Here we have moved one notch to the right on our horseshoe, into the realm where the economic goals dominate. . . .

"Ignore it" is sometimes referred to as "enlightened self-interest," although some of its proponents are more enlightened than others. Many a true believer in social responsibility has used the argument that it pays to be good to ward off the attacks from the right that corporations have no business pursuing social goals. Even Milton Friedman must admit that they have every right to do so if it pays them economically. The danger of such arguments, however—and a prime reason "ignore it" differs from "trust it"—is that they tend to support the status quo: corporations need not change their behavior because it already pays to be good.

Sometimes the case for "ignore it" is made in terms of corporations at large, that the whole business community will benefit from socially responsible behavior. Other times the case is made in terms of the individual corporation, that it will benefit directly from its own socially responsible actions. . . . Others make the case for "ignore it" in "social investment" terms, claiming that socially responsible behavior pays off in a better image for the firm, a more positive relationship with customers, and ultimately a healthier and more stable society in which to do business.

Then, there is what I like to call the "them" argument: "If we're not good, they will move in"—"they" being Ralph Nader, the government, whoever. In other words, "Be good or else." The trouble with this argument is that by reducing social responsibility to simply a political tool for sustaining managerial control of the corporation in the face of outside threats, it tends to encourage general pronouncements instead of concrete actions (unless of course, "they" actually deliver with pressure campaigns). . . .

The "ignore it" position rests on some shaky ground. It seems to encourage average behavior at best; and where the average does not seem to be good enough, it encourages the status quo. In fact, ironically, "ignore it" makes a strong case for "pressure it," since the whole argument collapses in the absence of pressure campaigns. Thus while many influential people take this position, we question whether in the realities of corporate behavior it can really stand alone.

"Induce It"

Continuing around to the right, our next position drops all concern with social responsibility per se and argues, simply, "pay it to be good," or, from the corporation's point of view, "be good only where it pays." Here, the corporation does not actively pursue social goals at all, whether as ends in themselves or as means to economic ends. Rather, it undertakes socially desirable programs only when induced economically to do so—usually through government incentives. If society wishes to clean up urban blight, then let its government provide subsidies for corporations that renovate buildings; if pollution is the problem, then let corporations be rewarded for reducing it.

"Induce it" faces "regulate it" on the opposite side of the horseshoe for good reason. While one penalizes the corporation for what it does do, the other rewards it for doing what it might not otherwise do. Hence these two positions can be direct substitutes: pollution can be alleviated by introducing penalties for the damage done or by offering incentives for the improvements rendered.

Logic would, however, dictate a specific role for each of these positions. Where a corporation is doing society a specific, attributable harm—as in the case of pollution—then paying it to stop hardly seems to make a lot of sense. If society does not wish to outlaw the harmful behavior altogether, then surely it must charge those responsible for it—the corporation and, ultimately, its customers. Offering financial incentives to stop causing harm would be to invite a kind of blackmail—for example, encouraging corporations to pollute so as to get paid to stop. And every citizen would be charged for the harm done by only a few.

On the other hand, where social problems exist which cannot be attributed to specific corporations, yet require the skills of certain corporations for solution, then financial incentives clearly make sense (so long, of course, as solutions can be clearly defined and tied to tangible economic rewards). Here, and not under "trust it," is where the "only business can do it" argument belongs. When it is true that only business can do it (and business has not done it to us in the first place), then business should be encouraged to do it. . . .

"Restore It"

Our last position on the horseshoe tends to be highly ideological, the first since "democratize it" to seek a fundamental change in the governance and the goals of the corporation. Like the proponents of "nationalize it," those of this position believe that managerial control is illegitimate and must be replaced by a more valid form of external control. The corporation should be restored to its former status, that is, returned to its "rightful" owners, the shareholders. The only way to ensure the relentless pursuit of economic goals—and that means the maximization of profit, free of the "subversive doctrine" of social responsibility—is to put control directly into the hands of those to whom profit means the most.

A few years ago this may have seemed to be an obsolete position. But thanks to its patron saint Milton Friedman . . . . it has recently come into prominence. Also, other forms of restoring it, including the "small is beautiful" theme, have also become popular in recent years.

Friedman has written,

> In a free-enterprise, private-property system, a corporate executive is an employee of the owners of the business. He has direct responsibility to his employers. That responsibility is to conduct the business in accordance with their desires, which generally will be to make as much money as possible while conforming to the basic rules of the society, both those embodied in law and those embodied in ethical custom. (1970:33)

Interestingly, what seems to drive Friedman is a belief that the shift over the course of this century from owner to manager control, with its concerns about social responsibility, represents an unstoppable skid around our horseshoe. In the opening chapter of his book *Capitalism and Freedom*, Friedman seems to accept only two possibilities—traditional capitalism and socialism as practiced in Eastern Europe. The absence of the former must inevitably lead to the latter:

> The preservation and expansion of freedom are today threatened from two directions. The one threat is obvious and clear. It is the external threat coming from the evil men in the Kremlin who promised to bury us. The other threat is far more subtle. It is the internal threat coming from men of good intentions and good will who wish to reform us. (1962:20)

The problem of who should control the corporation thus reduces to a war between two ideologies—in Friedman's terms, "subversive" socialism and "free" enterprise. In this world of black and white, there can be no middle ground, no moderate position between the black of "nationalize it" and the white of "restore it," none of the gray of "trust it." Either the owners will control the corporation of else the government will. Hence: " 'restore it' or else." Anchor the corporation on the right side of the horseshoe, Friedman seems to be telling us, the only place where "free" enterprise and "freedom" are safe.

All of this, in my view, rests on a series of assumptions—technical, economic, and political—which contain a number of fallacies. First is the fallacy of the technical assumption of shareholder control. Every trend in ownership during this century seems to refute the assumption that small shareholders are either willing or able to control the large, widely held corporation. The one place where free markets clearly still exist is in stock ownership, and that has served to detach ownership from control. When power is widely dispersed—among stockholders no less than workers or customers—those who share it tend to remain passive. It pays no one of them to invest the effort to exercise their power. Hence, even if serious shareholders did control the boards of widely held corporations (and one survey of all the directors of the *Fortune* 500 in 1977 found that only 1.6% of them represented significant shareholder interests, [Smith, 1978]), the question remains open as to whether they would actually try to control the management. (This is obviously not true of closely held corporations, but these—probably a decreasing minority of the *Fortune* 500—are "restored" in any event.)

The economic assumptions of free markets have been discussed at length in the literature. Whether there exists vibrant competition, unlimited entry, open information, consumer sovereignty, and labor mobility is debatable. Less debatable is the conclusion that the larger the corporation, the greater is its ability to interfere with these processes. The issues we are discussing center on the giant corporation. It is not Luigi's Body Shop that Ralph Nader is after, but General Motors, a corporation that employs more than half a million people and earns greater revenues than many national governments.

Those who laid the foundation for conventional economic theory—such as Adam Smith and Alfred Marshall—never dreamed of the massive amounts now spent for advertising campaigns, most of them designed as much for affect as for effect; of the waves of conglomeration that have combined all kinds of diverse businesses into single corporate entities; of chemical complexes that cost more than a billion dollars; and of the intimate relationships that now exist between giant corporations and government, as customer and partner not to mention subsidizer. The concept of arm's length relationships in such conditions is, at best, nostalgic. What happens to consumer sovereignty when Ford knows more about its gas tanks than do its customers? And what does labor mobility mean in the presence of an inflexible pension plan, or commitment to a special skill, or a one-factory town? It is an ironic twist of conventional economic theory that the worker is the one who typically stays put, thus rendering false the assumption of labor mobility, while the shareholder is the mobile one, thus spoiling the case for owner control.

The political assumptions are more ideological in nature, although usually implicit. These assumptions are that the corporation is essentially amoral, society's instrument for producing goods and services, and, more broadly, that a society is "free" and "democratic" so long as its governmental leaders are elected by universal suffrage and do not interfere with the legal activities of businessmen. But many people—a large majority of the general public, if polls are to be believed—seem to subscribe to one or more assumptions that contradict these "free enterprise" assumptions.

One assumption is that the large corporation is a social and political institution as much as an economic instrument. Economic activities, as noted previously, produce all kinds of social consequences. Jobs get created and rivers get polluted, cities get built and workers get injured. These social consequences cannot be factored out of corporate strategic decisions and assigned to government.

Another assumption is that society cannot achieve the necessary balance between social and economic needs so long as the private sector attends only to economic goals. Given the pervasiveness of business in society, the acceptance of Friedman's prescriptions would drive us toward a one-dimensional society—a society that is too utilitarian and too materialistic. Economic morality, as noted earlier, can amount to a social immorality.

Finally, the question is asked: Why the owners? In a democratic society, what justifies owner control of the corporation any more than worker control, or consumer control, or pluralistic control? Ours is not Adam Smith's society of small proprietors and shopkeepers. His butcher, brewer, and baker have become Iowa Beef Packers, Anheuser-Bush, and ITT Continental Baking. What was once a case for individual democracy now becomes a case for oligarchy. . . .

I see Friedman's form of "restore it" as a rather quaint position in a society of giant corporations, managed economies, and dispersed shareholders—a society in which the collective power of corporations is coming under increasing scrutiny and in which the distribution between economic and social goals is being readdressed.

Of course, there are other ways [than Friedman's] to "restore it." "Divest it" could return the corporation to the business or central theme it knows best, restoring the role of allocating funds between different businesses to capital markets instead of central headquarters. Also, boards could be restored to positions of influence by holding directors legally responsible for their actions and by making them more independent of managers (for example, by providing them with personal staffs and by precluding full-time managers from their ranks, especially the position of chairman). We might even wish to extend use of "reduce it" where possible, to decrease the size of those corporations that have grown excessively large on the basis of market or political power rather than economies of scale, and perhaps to eliminate certain forms of vertical integration. In many cases it may prove advantageous, economically as well as socially, to have the corporation trade with its suppliers and customers instead of being allowed to ingest them indiscriminately.*

I personally doubt that these proposals could be any more easily realized in today's society than those of Friedman, even though I believe them to be more desirable. "Restore it" is the nostalgic position on our horseshoe, a return to our fantasies of a glorious past. In this, society of giant organizations, it flies in the face of powerful economic and political forces.

Conclusion: If the Shoe Fits . . .

I believe that today's corporation cannot ride on any one position any more than a horse can ride on part of a shoe. In other words, we need to treat the conceptual horseshoe as a portfolio of positions from which we can draw, depending on circumstances. Exclusive

---

*A number of these proposals would be worthwhile to pursue in the public and parapublic sectors as well, to divide up overgrown hospitals, school systems, social agencies and all kinds of government departments.

reliance on one position will lead to a narrow and dogmatic society, with an excess concentration of power . . . the use of a variety of positions can encourage the pluralism I believe most of us feel is necessary to sustain democracy. If the shoe fits, then let the corporation wear it.

I do not mean to imply that the eight positions do not represent fundamentally different values and, in some cases, ideologies as well. Clearly they do. But I also believe that anyone who makes an honest assessment of the realities of power in and around today's large corporations must conclude that a variety of positions have to be relied upon [even if they themselves might tilt to the left, right or center of our horseshoe]. . . .

I tilt to the left of center, as has no doubt been obvious in my comments to this point. Let me summarize my own prescriptions as follows, and in the process provide some basis for evaluating the relevant roles of each of the eight positions.

First "trust it," or at least "socialize it." Despite my suspicions about much of the rhetoric that passes for social responsibility and the discouraging evidence about the behavior of large contemporary organizations (not only corporations), I remain firmly convinced that without honest and responsible people in important places, we are in deep trouble. We need to trust it because, no matter how much we rely on the other positions, managers will always retain a great deal of power. And that power necessarily has social no less than economic consequences. The positions on the right side of our horseshoe ignore these social consequences while some of those on the left fail to recognize the difficulties of influencing these consequences in large, hierarchical organizations. Sitting between these two sets of positions, managers can use their discretion to satisfy or to subvert the wishes of the public. Ultimately, what managers do is determined by their sense of responsibility as individual members of society.

Although we must "trust it," we cannot *only* "trust it." As I have argued, there is an appropriate and limited place for social responsibility—essentially to get the corporation's own house in order and to encourage it to act responsibly in its own sphere of operations. Beyond that, social responsibility needs to be tempered by other positions around our horseshoe.

Then "pressure it," ceaselessly. As we have seen, too many forces interfere with social responsibility. The best antidote to these forces is the ad hoc pressure campaign, designed to pinpoint unethical behavior and raise social consciousness about issues. The existence of the "pressure it" position is what most clearly distinguishes the western from the eastern "democracies." Give me one Ralph Nader to all those banks of government accountants.

In fact, "pressure it" underlies the success of most of the other positions. Pressure campaigns have brought about necessary new regulations and have highlighted the case for corporate democracy. As we have seen, the "ignore it" position collapses without "pressure it". . . .

After that, try to "democratize it." A somewhat distant third in my portfolio is "democratize it," a position I view as radical only in terms of the current U.S. debate, not in terms of fundamental American values. Democracy matters most where it affects us directly—in the water we drink, the jobs we perform, the products we consume. How can we call our society democratic when many of its most powerful institutions are closed to governance from the outside and are run as hierarchies of authority from within?

As noted earlier, I have no illusions about having found the means to achieve corporate democracy. But I do know that Americans can be very resourceful when they decide to resolve a problem—and this is a problem that badly needs resolving. Somehow, ways must be found to open the corporation up to the formal influence of the constituencies most affected by it—employees, customers, neighbors, and so on—without weakening it as an economic institution. At stake is nothing less than the maintenance of basic freedoms in our society.

Then, only where specifically appropriate, "regulate it" and "induce it." Facing each other on the horseshoe are two positions that have useful if limited roles to play. Regulation is neither a panacea nor a menace. It belongs where the corporation can abuse the power it has and can be penalized for that abuse—notably where externalities can be identified with specific corporations. Financial inducements belong, not where a corporation has created a problem, but where it has the capability to solve a problem created by someone else.

Occasionally, selectively, "nationalize it" and "restore it," but not in Friedman's way. The extreme positions should be reserved for extreme problems. If "pressure it" is a scalpel and "regulate it" a cleaver, then "nationalize it" and "restore it" are guillotines.

Both these positions are implicitly proposed as alternatives to "democratize it." One offers public control, the other "shareholder democracy." The trouble is that control by everyone often turns out to be control by no one, while control by the owners—even if attainable—would remove the corporation even further from the influence of those most influenced by it.

Yet, as noted earlier, nationalization sometimes makes sense—when private enterprise cannot provide a necessary mission, at least in a sufficient or appropriate way, and when the activities of a corporation must be intricately tied in to government policy.

As for "restore it," I believe Friedman's particular proposals will aggravate the problems of political control and social responsibility, strengthening oligarchical tendencies in society and further tilting what I see as the current imbalance between social and economic goals. In response to Friedman's choice between "subversive" socialism and "free" enterprise, I say "a pox on both your houses." Let us concentrate our efforts on the intermediate positions around the horseshoe. However, other forms of "restore it" are worth considering—to "divest it" where diversification has interfered with capital markets, competition, and economic efficiency; to "*dis*integrate it" vertically where a trading network is preferable to a managerial hierarchy; to strengthen its board so that directors can assess managers objectively; and to "reduce it" where size represents a power game rather than a means to provide better and more efficient service to the public. I stand with Friedman in wishing to see competitive markets strengthened; it is just that I believe his proposals lead in exactly the opposite direction.

Finally above all, don't "ignore it." I leave one position out of my portfolio altogether, because it contradicts the others. The one thing we must not do is ignore the large, widely held corporation. It is too influential a force in our lives. Our challenge is to find ways to distribute the power in and around our large organizations so that they will remain responsive, vital, and effective.

MANAGERIAL STYLES

This chapter on "managerial styles" is included in this book to reflect increasing attention to the importance of the "softer" aspect of style at the expense of the "harder" aspects of structure and systems. Three readings make up this chapter, each colorful in its own right.

The article by Pat Pitcher, of Montreal's École des Hautes Études Commerciales, summarizes her fascinating doctoral thesis, which focused on managerial style over the history of one large financial institution in particular. Pitcher contrasts artists, craftsmen, and technocrats—if you like, creative visionaries, sympathetic leaders, and systematic analysts. She is no friend of the technocrats, as you shall see, believing that artists and craftsmen have to take the lead in today's organizations.

The second article, by Peter Senge of the MIT Sloan School of Management and based on his highly successful book, *The Fifth Discipline*, characterizes the "leader's new work" as being to build the learning organization. Senge views the ability to learn as the primary source of a company's competitive advantage and argues that facilitating organizational learning is the principal task of the strategist. Like Hamel and Prahalad, Senge sees a long-term vision as the key source of tension in the organization and, therefore, of energy in the learning process. The manager must be the designer, the teacher, and the steward of the learning organization and to play these roles, he must develop a new set of skills, which Senge describes in the article. Above all, he promotes systems thinking. On balance, Senge's new leader may well be Pitcher's craftsman (see especially the quote he uses to end his discussion—hardly the technocrat or even the artist), in which case this reading fleshes out that style in an interesting way.

The third reading, by Leonard Sayles, who spent most of his career at the Columbia University business school, focuses on a much neglected but critical player in the organization, the middle manager. Sayles points out that if organizations want "to do things right," and not just "do the right things" (the concern of so much of the strategy literature), then they had better get smart about the role of middle managers, especially to hold things together and facilitate innovative and even strategic processes themselves. Sayles is perhaps most sympathetic to the craftsman style, too, but he also emphasizes the action level of management (as discussed in the Mintzberg reading of Chapter 2), in contrast to Pitcher and Senge, who put their attention more on the people level. Since most of you who use this book will be (or are) middle managers long before you may become senior managers, you would do well to give very careful attention to this reading. It is the superb statement of a man who has dedicated much of his career to the study of middle managers.

by Patricia Pitcher

. . .If you want to change corporate North America, you have to change its managers—not the culture, not the structure, but the people. All else is abstraction.

In my 20 years as an executive, a board member of multi-billion dollar corporations and, recently, an academic, one lesson stands out. Give a technocrat ultimate authority and he or she will drive out everything else: vision and its carriers—artists—will be replaced; experience and its carriers—craftsmen—will follow. Dissent will be driven from the board. The organization will ossify, turn inward and short-term. . . .

HOW TO IDENTIFY A TECHNOCRAT

Technocrats are never at a loss for words, charts, or graphs. They always have a plan of action in three parts. They rarely laugh out loud, except maybe at baseball games; never at work. When they explain to you why Jim or George had to be let go, they use expressions like, "He just wasn't tough, professional, modern, rigorous, serious, hard-working enough." If they go on to mention "too emotional," watch out! You have a technocrat on your hands. This person will be described by peers and colleagues as controlled, conservative, serious, analytical, no-nonsense, intense, determined, cerebral, methodical, and meticulous. Individually, any of these words might be a compliment; together, they represent a syndrome. Here is an example of how a technocrat thinks:

> Mirroring a world-wide trend . . . , we initiated in 1989 and continued in 1990 an extensive program under which operations were regrouped, assets sold, and activities rationalized. New chief executives have been appointed and our strategy is profitability.

In this one paragraph from an annual report, we notice three things. First, the technocrat loves conventional wisdom and thus the first phase, "Mirroring a world-wide trend"; if everyone else is doing it, it must be right. Second, we see the word "rationalized"; this is the watchword. Third, we are told that all the bad guys have been fired and replaced by serious folk. When things go wrong it is always the fault of someone else.

RECOGNIZING AN ARTIST

How do you recognize artists? Well, pretty much by the opposite. What is your strategic plan for the future? Answer: "to get big," "to hit $5 billion in sales," "to beat the pants off the competition," "to be a world leader by 2020." Artists may be a little short on the details, on the how. Board presentations are sometimes a little loose—unless they are done by the chief financial officer. The artist CEO might get overtly angry or euphoric at board meetings. How does the artist CEO talk? Listen to one.

> What is strategy anyway? Grand plan? No. You try to instill a vision you have and get people to buy in. The strategy comes from astrology; quirks, dreams, love affairs, science fiction, perception of society, some madness probably, ability to guess. It is clear but fluid. Action brings precision. Very vague, but becomes clear in the act of transformation. Creation is the storm.

When CEOs like this talk to their boards about "astrology; quirks, dreams," boards have a tendency to get a little uneasy. This person's peers and colleagues describe him or her as bold, daring, exciting, volatile, intuitive, entrepreneurial, inspiring, imaginative, unpredictable, and funny. Technocrats will apply labels like "star-trekky," or more simply, nuts. The artist makes both fast friends and abiding enemies. Very few have a neutral reac-

---

*Reprinted with deletions from the article originally titled "Balancing Personality Types at the Top" with permission of *Business Quarterly* (Winter 1993) published by the Western Business School, University of Western Ontario, London, Canada.

tion. The organization as a whole is an exciting place to be; confusing maybe, dizzying maybe, but exciting nonetheless.

AND NOW, THE CRAFTSMAN

Rosabeth Moss Kanter insists, and I think she is dead right, that people take the long view when they perceive their leaders as trustworthy, and that the sacrifices they are called upon to make are genuinely for the collective future and not to line someone else's pockets today. The organizational craftsmen embody these values. People trust them. They see the organization as an enduring institution, one that has a life of its own, a past and a future, one of which he or she is but a custodian. They tend to stay in one organization and are therefore intimately familiar with its past and infinitely careful about preserving its identity in the midst of change. The craftsman provides continuity and organizational glue, and stimulates loyalty and commitment.

Craft is fundamentally conservative, rooted in tradition. Samuel Johnson, the great British satirist, wrote, "You cannot with all the talk in the world, enable a man to make a shoe." Experience and practice are essential to judgment. What happens if you do not have experience in the firm, in the industry, in the organization? As one CEO once said, referring to a famous bright, young, professional, "He'll get hit by every blue-suede shoes man in the country." What he meant was that this brilliant young man would fall prey to idea salesmen peddling old ideas in new packages, and he would buy because he has no experience. He could not possibly know that the idea had been tried—and rejected—20 years ago. Craft demands submission to authority. Apprenticeship is long, frustrating and sometimes arduous. There are no short cuts. Polanyi argues:

> To learn by example is to submit to authority. You follow your master because you trust his manner of doing things even when you cannot analyze or account in detail for its effectiveness. A society which wants to preserve a kind of personal knowledge must submit to tradition.

Imagine the frustration of a brilliant young executive when his or her craftsman boss cannot answer the question, "Why?" Craft is inarticulate. The answer to the young manager's question is locked away in the tricks of the trade, in tacit knowledge. So, he or she thinks the boss a fool. If he or she is the boss, the employee is condemned as an old-fashioned fool and fired.

What does this tell us about craftsmen? First of all, craftsmen are patient, both with themselves and with others; they know that it took them a long time to acquire their skills and that it will be true for others. They regularly exhibit that much-sought-after commodity, judgement; judgment flows out of long experience. Young people rarely exhibit it. Their colleagues will describe them as wise, amiable, humane, honest, straightforward, responsible, trustworthy, reasonable, open-minded, and realistic. Here is a craftsman speaking about technocrats:

> Even if they had a vision, how would they get it done? There's no managerial continuity. At this year's planning meeting, there were four out of 14 people left over from two years ago. Every two years there's a new chief executive. There's no opportunity to fail, so there's no continuity. They focus directly on profit but they'll never get it because profit comes from the vision and the people and they won't invest in people. If you look after the people, the profit follows. You can't drive at it directly. Twelve and a half percent ROI is a joke; we'll be dead [in five years]. They refuse to see this. You can't correct a problem unless you see it exists. It's like me. I look in the mirror and I see a young fullback, not a balding, middle-aged man with his chest on his belly. You have to see reality to change it.

Craftsmen believe that technocrats do not have vision, and even if they did it would not do any good because they "won't invest in people." The craftsman speaking above objects to trend-line projections; "Twelve and a half percent ROI is a joke; we'll be dead [in

five years]." His credo is, "If you look after the people, the profit follows.". . . (See Figure 1 for a summary of these three types of managerial stereotypes.)

TEAMWORK AND THE TYPES

When serious looks at funny what does it see? Red. It sees cavalier; it sees irresponsible; it sees childish. When analytical looks at intuitive, it sees dreamer, head-in-the-clouds. When wise stares at cerebral, it sees a head without a heart, it sees brilliance devoid of judgment. And so on down the list. In short, the three types of people cannot communicate. They live in different worlds, with different values and different goals. They frame different questions and different answers to all issues confronting the corporation. They believe that their conflicts center on ideas, whereas, in fact, they center on character.

For example, recently, a major international corporation experienced pronounced difficulty with its stock price. No matter what it did, its stock traded at a 50% discount from book value. Why? Listen in on the dialogue of the deaf that goes on between senior officers and the CEO inside that corporation. They are all talking about the same subject, but you would not know it.

An *artist*: "Of course the stock price is low! (He always talks with exclamation points.) We're not doing anything to create interest, magic! We haven't bought anything, launched anything, dreamt up anything in months! Nobody believes we have an exciting future ahead of us! The stock will go up when people believe in our dream!"

A *technocrat* (firmly): "It's all the so-called dreams which have turned into cost-nightmares. We haven't showed consistent quarterly earnings over the last three years. For two quarters, our earnings have reflected some marginal improvement. As soon as the street begins to have some faith in our capacity to control costs they'll turn into believers and start to recommend our stock."

A *craftsman*: "The people on the street are not stupid. They know that we've had so much managerial turnover that we have no continuity. They know we've fallen out of touch with our traditional markets. The guy brought in to run our main widgets division

---

FIGURE 1
Mangerial Sterotypes

THE ARTIST	THE CRAFTSMAN	THE TECHNOCRAT
Bold	Responsible	Conservative
Daring	Wise	Methodical
Exciting	Humane	No-nonsense
Volatile	Straightforward	Controlled
Intuitive	Open-minded	Cerebral
Entrepreneurial	Realistic	Analytical
Inspiring	Trustworthy	Determined
Imaginative	Reasonable	Meticulous
Unpredictable	Honest	Intense
Funny	Amiable	Serious

wouldn't know a widget if he fell over one. The whole sales force is disillusioned. What we need is to get back in touch with what we do best."

Sticking to your knitting is not some new theoretical concept to craftsmen; it is their life. They have always done it. It comes as naturally as breathing. The cost-cutting program inevitably proposed by the technocrat, strikes at the core of what the craftsman considers to be the answer to the problem. The technocrat wants to cut out the fat: inflated marketing budgets, sales training conferences, and staff development expenses. The craftsman sees the profitability problem as a symptom, a reflection of the demotivation of staff, as a diminished sense of loyalty and therefore of effort—a legacy of the last round of staff cuts and the replacement of leaders that they trusted. The technocrat is dangerous because, to the craftsman, he or she is too theoretical, "too distant from the coalface" to understand the real issues. . . .

In a major multinational I have studied for the last 10 years, the technocrats have truly triumphed. Figure 2 shows the ten-year evolution of the management team. Beginning with a healthy mix of artists, craftsmen and technocrats, by 1990 the structure had tilted irrevocably to the technocrat. The two remaining craftsmen were in the power structure only nominally; both were looking for jobs.

The result of this shift has been parallel changes in strategy and in structure. Under the aegis of the artist, the corporation had been outward-looking, increasingly internationally-oriented. Fueled both by internal growth and acquisitions, assets climbed. Subsidiaries were left pretty much on their own—the power structure was decentralized—and the atmosphere, prevailing ethic, or culture if you will, was of teamwork, growth and excitement. Out of insecurity or a simple error in judgment, the artist chose as his successor his opposite. Promoted into the number one spot, the technocrat began to install others and to rationalize, organize and control. The by-product of rationalization, systematization and control was centralization. The by-production of centralization was demoralization. The strategy became, in the words of the annual reports, profitability. Profitability was not and is not a strategy and it can certainly not inspire anyone as an ultimate goal: "What do you do for a living?" "I make profit." Losing the artists, the company lost vision. Losing the craftsmen, it lost its humanity. Although profitability became the watchword, profits did not go up. Nor did share prices. The group was eventually absorbed by a more ambitious rival.

THE TRIUMPH OF THE TECHNOCRAT

. . .Technocrats have a way of making us feel secure. With their ready answers, their charts and their graphs, they give us the feeling that everything will be all right if we just follow the rules: the rules of logic, the rules of good business practice, matrix management, participatory management, total quality management and the new rules of globalization and strategic alliances. They make everything sound so straightforward, so rational, so comforting, so reassuring—sort of like Betty Crocker.

. . .What does a manager look like, I ask my students. "He's calm, rational, well-balanced, measured, analytical, methodological, skilled, trained, serious," they say. It occurs to me that I am listening to a liturgy—a liturgy from the gospel of the technocratic school. The person they describe is one kind of manager, and he or she is now firmly anchored as the only kind. It has become definitional.

THE LEARNING ORGANIZATION

If we concede for a moment the narcissistic presumption that ours is an age of discontinuity, then the old ways of doing things no longer work. Organizations need to learn—rapidly and continuously. How does learning take place? At the turn of the century, American philosopher George Santayana wrote, "Man's progress has a poetic phase in which he imag-

FIGURE 2
The Technocratic Transformation

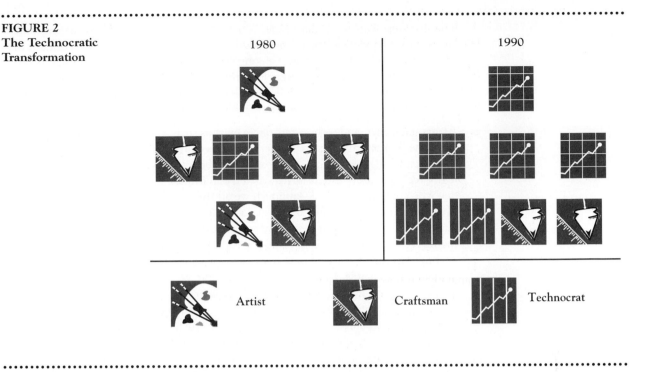

ines the world, then a scientific phase in which he sifts and tests what he has imagined." Culturally, we have always relied on our visionaries to point us toward the new way. In science, we call a visionary a genius; in letters, a poet; in politics, a statesman; in business, a leader; generically, an artist. What all these labels have in common is the idea of someone who breaks radically with conventional wisdom, someone who sees what others do not, someone who imagines a new order. This is discontinuous learning. We call it imaginative.

Then, there is continuous learning, daily learning. What is found in art comes into use and is transformed, concretized, shaped and sculpted by experience. A great idea, usually quite vague, is refined by practice over time. The bugs are worked out. Flesh is added to the skeleton. The slow accumulation of talent in its application is the domain of craft. We call its carrier, skilled.

Finally, there is a third form of learning. It comes from the codification of old knowledge; it comes from books and scientific papers. It comes from studying and diligence, and requires neither insight nor practice to make it our own. We call the person who possesses it knowledgeable, and if he or she possesses it to a very fine degree, brilliant.

With our religion we have eliminated both the poetic and the craft phase of learning, and tried to reduce everything to the scientific. (We are sons and daughters of the Enlightenment, after all.) We have come to believe that managers who have an MBA, can read a balance sheet and can talk knowledgeably about strategic alliances must make good CEOs. This is nonsense. If they have no imagination, they will only mimic the competition—strategy as paint-by-numbers art. If they have no skill, they will not understand their markets. If they have no wisdom, they will tear at the fabric of the organization.

VISION, CONTINUITY AND CONTROL

There are three ways of learning, each equally necessary. Leadership consists of knowing how to put the package together and make it work. It consists of integrating vision, continuity and control in the managerial team.

The first step is obviously diagnostic. What does my organization look like currently? How many artists, craftsmen and technocrats do I have, and how are they functionally distributed? What is the balance of power among them? What is the dominant ethic? Is there the freedom to fail, which is indispensable to the possibility to succeed? Is there sufficient pride of place given to emotion, to skill, to brilliance? This diagnosis is of course easier proposed than accomplished, and this for three main reasons:

1. Artists, craftsmen and technocrats rarely exist as such; they are archetypes. Real people come in more complex packages. We may see artists, for example, with an admixture of craft. We may see conservative, cerebral craftsmen and we may see emotionally hot technocrats, or highly analytical and determined artists. Rarely do we see someone who combines all three—although we all think we do.

2. The task is made more difficult by masquerades. Faced with an artistic type, we are rarely fooled. And, with their straightforwardness and frankness, craftsmen usually give themselves away. But the technocrat, particularly of the brilliant variety, is hard to see. Technocrats revere conventional wisdom—not wisdom of a traditional sort, but new wisdom. For example, I recently had the pleasure of listening to a discourse on total quality management and empowerment from an archetypal technocratic CEO. He had systematically eliminated all artists and craftsmen from his organization. Experimentation and loyalty were dead because one false step meant being fired. Now he wanted to graft onto this moribund organization new energies of empowerment. And, what is worse, he was sincere. He really could not know that these managerial recipes, conceived procedurally, will not work. The graft will not take. But, to his board and to other observers, this man was saying all the right things. He was masquerading as a craftsman. Others, again of the brilliant variety, will masquerade as artists; knowledgeable and well-read in a superficial sort of way, they will seem to know the future. Here, we can be radically mislead.

3. Finally, there is a third reason why the diagnosis is so fraught with uncertainty. It is us. What we see depends on where we sit. If I am a technocrat, I will have a tendency to see other, more brilliant technocrats as artists. I will think of them as visionary and entrepreneurial, far-sighted and bold. If I am a pure craftsman, I will have no use for any technocrats. As one craftsman CEO put it to me recently, "They make good consultants." To him, a brilliant technocrat is dangerous as a manager because he or she is intellectually disconnected from reality. And artists too, have their blind spots, not so much about people as about suitable objects of attention. Built into the diagnostic process, therefore, must be an element of collective judgment—judgment that does not rely too exclusively on the point of view of one or another of the archetypes. . . .

Growing frustration with formal managerial models coupled with increasing recognition of the difficulty of planning in a turbulent world, has led to the call for charismatic leadership, as though the presence of a charismatic leader could somehow take all the hard work out of managing a business. Certainly, the artists described here are charismatic and their presence is vital for success. But, they are not alone. You need artists, craftsmen and technocrats in the right dose and in the right places. You need someone with vision, but you also need someone who can develop the people, the structures and the systems to make the dream a reality. If you have the right people, they will do the job that comes naturally to them; you do not have to teach a fish how to swim. [The] key managerial task [of the CEO] is not to know everything but to build an executive team that can get the whole job done.

by Peter M. Senge

Human beings are designed for learning. No one has to teach an infant to walk, or talk, or master the spatial relationships needed to stack eight building blocks that don't topple. Children come fully equipped with an insatiable drive to explore and experiment. Unfortunately, the primary institutions of our society are oriented predominantly toward controlling rather than learning, rewarding individuals for performing for others rather than for cultivating their natural curiosity and impulse to learn. The young child entering school discovers quickly that the name of the game is getting the right answer and avoiding mistakes—a mandate no less compelling to the aspiring manager.

"Our prevailing system of management has destroyed our people," writes W. Edwards Deming, leader in the quality movement (Senge, 1990). "People are born with intrinsic motivation, self-esteem, dignity, curiosity to learn, joy in learning. The forces of destruction begin with toddlers—a prize for the best Halloween costume, grades in school, gold stars, and on up through the university. On the job, people, teams, divisions are ranked—reward for the one at the top, punishment at the bottom. MBO, quotas, incentive pay, business plans, put together separately, division by division, cause further loss, unknown and unknowable."

Ironically, by focusing on performing for someone else's approval, corporations create the very conditions that predestine them to mediocre performance. Over the long run, superior performance depends on superior learning. A Shell study showed. . . that "the key to the long term survival of the large industrial enterprise was the ability to run "experiments in the margin," to continually explore new business and organizational opportunities that create potential new sources of growth (deGues, 1988, pp. 70-74).

If anything, the need for understanding how organizations learn and accelerating that learning is greater today than ever before. The old days when a Henry Ford, Alfred Sloan, or Tom Watson *learned for the organization* are gone. In an increasingly dynamic, interdependent, and unpredictable world, it is simply no longer possible for anyone to "figure it all out at the top." The old model, "the top thinks and the local acts," must now give way to integrative thinking and acting at all levels. . . .

ADAPTIVE LEARNING AND GENERATIVE LEARNING

The prevailing view of learning organizations emphasizes increased adaptability. . . . But increasing adaptiveness is only the first stage in moving toward learning organizations. The impulse to learn in children goes deeper than desires to respond and adapt more effectively to environmental change. The impulse to learn, at its heart, is an impulse to be generative, to expand our capability. This is why leading corporations are focusing on *generative* learning, which is about creating, as well as *adaptive* learning, which is about coping. . . .

Generative learning, unlike adaptive learning, requires new ways of looking at the world, whether in understanding customers or in understanding how to better manage a business. For years, U.S. manufacturers sought competitive advantage in aggressive controls on inventories, incentives against overproduction, and rigid adherence to production forecasts. Despite these incentives, their performance was eventually eclipsed by Japanese firms who saw the challenges of manufacturing differently. They realized that eliminating delays in the production process was the key to reducing instability and improving cost, productivity, and service. They worked to build networks of relationships with trusted suppliers and to redesign physical production processes so as to reduce delays in materials procurement, production set up, and in-process inventory—a much higher-leverage approach to improving both cost and customer loyalty.

As Boston Consulting Group's George Stalk has observed, the Japanese saw the significance of delays because they saw the process of order entry, production scheduling, materials procurement, production, and distribution *as an integrated system*. "What distorts the system so badly is time," observed Stalk—the multiple delays between events and responses. "These distortions reverberate throughout the system, producing disruptions, waste, and inefficiency" (Stalk, 1988 pp. 41-51). Generative learning requires seeing the systems that control events. When we fail to grasp the systemic source of problems, we are left to "push on" symptoms rather than eliminate underlying causes. The best we can ever do is adaptive learning.

THE LEADER'S NEW WORK

. . . Our traditional view of leaders—as special people who set the direction, make the key decisions, and energize the troops—is deeply rooted in an individualistic and nonsystemic worldview. Especially in the West, leaders are *heroes*—great men (and occasionally women) who rise to the fore in times of crisis. So long as such myths prevail, they reinforce a focus on short-term events and charismatic heroes rather than on systemic forces and collective learning.

Leadership in learning organizations centers on subtler and ultimately more important work. In a learning organization, leaders' roles differ dramatically from that of the charismatic decision maker. Leaders are designers, teachers, and stewards. These roles require new skills: the ability to build shared vision, to bring to the surface and challenge prevailing mental models, and to foster more systemic patterns of thinking. In short, leaders in learning organizations are responsible for *building organizations* where people are continually expanding their capabilities to shape their future—that is, leaders are responsible for learning.

Creative Tension: The Integrating Principle

Leadership in a learning organization starts with the principle of creative tension (Fritz, 1989, 1990). Creative tension comes from seeing clearly where we want to be, our "vision," and telling the truth about where we are, our "current reality." The gap between the two generates a natural tension. . . .

Creative tension can be resolved in two basic ways: by raising current reality toward the vision, or by lowering the vision toward current reality. Individuals, groups, and organizations who learn how to work with creative tension learn how to use the energy it generates to move reality more reliably toward their visions. . . .

Without vision there is no creative tension. Creative tension cannot be generated from current reality alone. All the analysis in the world will never generate a vision. Many who are otherwise qualified to lead fail to do so because they try to substitute analysis for vision. They believe that, if only people understood current reality, they would surely feel the motivation to change. They are then disappointed to discover that people "resist" the personal and organizational changes that must be made to alter reality. What they never grasp is that the natural energy for changing reality comes from holding a picture of what might be that is more important to people than what is.

But creative tension cannot be generated from vision alone; it demands an accurate picture of current reality as well. Just as Martin Luther King had a dream, so too did he continually strive to "dramatize the shameful conditions" of racism and prejudice so that they could no longer be ignored. Vision without an understanding of current reality will more likely foster cynicism than creativity. The principle of creative tension teaches that *an accurate picture of current reality is just as important as a compelling picture of a desired future*.

Leading through creative tension is different than solving problems. In problem solving, the energy for change comes from attempting to get away from an aspect of current reality that is undesirable. With creative tension, the energy for change comes from the vision, from what we want to create, juxtaposed with current reality. While the distinction may seem small, the consequences are not. Many people and organizations find themselves motivated to change only when their problems are bad enough to cause them to change. This works for a while, but the change process runs out of steam as soon as the problems driving the change become less pressing. With problem solving, the motivation for change is extrinsic. With creative tension, the motivation is intrinsic. This distinction mirrors the distinction between adaptive and generative learning.

New Roles

The traditional authoritarian image of the leader as "the boss calling the shots" has been recognized as oversimplified and inadequate for some time. According to Edgar Schein (1985), "Leadership is intertwined with culture formation." Building an organization's culture and shaping its evolution is the "unique and essential function" of leadership. In a learning organization, the critical roles of leadership—designer, teacher, and steward—have antecedents in the ways leaders have contributed to building organizations in the past. But each role takes on new meaning in the learning organization and, as will be seen in the following sections, demands new skills and tools.

LEADER AS DESIGNER

Imagine that your organization is an ocean liner and that you are "the leader." What is your role?

I have asked this question of groups of managers many times. The most common answer, not surprisingly, is "the captain." Others say, "The navigator, setting the direction." Still others say, "The helmsman, actually controlling the direction," or "The engineer down there stoking the fire, providing energy," or "The social director, making sure everybody's enrolled, involved, and communicating." While these are legitimate leadership roles, there is another which, in many ways, eclipses them in all in importance. Yet rarely does anyone mention it.

The neglected leadership role is the *designer* of the ship. No one has a more sweeping influence than the designer. What good does it do for the captain to say, "Turn starboard 30 degrees," when the designer has build a rudder that will only turn to port, or which takes six hours to turn to starboard? It's fruitless to be the leader in an organization that is poorly designed.

The functions of design, or what some have called "social architecture," are rarely visible; they take place behind the scenes. The consequences that appear today are the result of work done long in the past, and work today will show its benefits far in the future. Those who aspire to lead out of a desire to control, or gain fame, or simply to be at the center of the action, will find little to attract them to the quiet design work of leadership.

But what, specifically, is involved in organizational design? "Organizational design is widely misconstrued as moving around boxes and lines," says Hanover Insurance Company's CEO William O'Brien. "The first task of organization design concerns designing the governing ideas of purpose, vision, and core values by which people will live." Few acts of leadership have a more enduring impact on an organization than building a foundation of purpose and core values. . . .

If governing ideas constitute the first design task of leadership, the second design task involves the policies, strategies, and structures that translate guiding ideas into business decisions. Leadership theorist Philip Selznick (1957) calls policy and structure the "institutional embodiment of purpose." "Policy making (the rules that guide decisions) ought to be separated from decision making," says Jay Forrester (1965 pp. 5-17). "Otherwise, short-term pressures will usurp time from policy creation."

Traditionally, writers like Selznick and Forrester have tended to see policy making and implementation as the work of a small number of senior managers. But that view is changing. Both the dynamic business environment and the mandate of the learning organization to engage people at all levels now make it clear that this second design task is more subtle. Henry Mintzberg has argued that strategy is less a rational plan arrived at in the abstract and implemented throughout the organization than an "emergent phenomenon." Successful organizations "craft strategy" according to Mintzberg, (1987 pp. 66-75) as they continually learn about shifting business conditions and balance what is desired and what is possible. The key is not getting the right strategy but fostering strategic thinking. "The choice of individual action is only part of . . . the policymaker's need," according to Mason and Mitroff (1981 p. 16). "More important is the need to achieve insight into the nature of the complexity and to formulate concepts and world views for coping with it."

Behind appropriate policies, strategies, and structures are effective learning processes: their creation is the third key design responsibility in learning organizations. This does not absolve senior managers of their strategic responsibilities. Actually, it deepens and extends those responsibilities. Now, they are not only responsible for ensuring that an organization have well-developed strategies and policies, but also for ensuring that processes exist whereby these are continually improved.

In the early 1970s, Shell was the weakest of the big seven oil companies. Today, Shell and Exxon are arguably the strongest, both in size and financial health. Shell's ascendance began with frustration. Around 1971 members of Shell's "Group Planning" in London began to foresee dramatic change and unpredictability in world oil markets. However, it proved impossible to persuade managers that the stable world of steady growth in oil demand and supply they had known for twenty years was about to change. Despite brilliant analysis and artful presentation, Shell's planners realized, in the words of Pierre Wack (1985 pp. 73-89), that they "had failed to change behavior in much of the Shell organization." Progress would probably have ended there, had the frustration not given way to a radically new view of corporate thinking.

As they pondered this failure, the planners' view of their basic task shifted: "We no longer saw our task as producing a documented view of the future business environment five or ten years ahead. Our real target was the microcosm (the 'mental model') of our decision makers." Only when the planners reconceptualized their basic task as fostering learning rather than devising plans did their insights begin to have impact. The initial tool used was "scenario analysis," through which planners encouraged operating managers to think through how they would manage in the future under different possible scenarios. It mattered not that the managers believed the planners' scenarios absolutely, only that they became engaged in ferreting out the implications. In this way, Shell's planners conditioned managers to be mentally prepared for a shift from low prices to high prices and from stability to instability. The results were significant. When OPEC became a reality, Shell quickly responded by increasing local operating company control (to enhance maneuverability in the new political environment), building buffer stocks, and accelerating development of non-OPEC sources—actions that its competitors took much more slowly or not at all.

Somewhat inadvertently, Shell planners had discovered the leverage of designing institutional learning processes, whereby, in the words of former planning director de Geus (1988), "Management teams change their shared mental models of their company, their markets, and their competitors." Since then, "planning as learning" has become a byword at Shell, and Group Planning has continually sought out new learning tools that can be integrated into the planning process. Some of these are described below.

LEADER AS TEACHER

"The first responsibility of a leader," writes retired Herman Miller CEO Max de Pree (1989 p. 9), "is to define reality." Much of the leverage leaders can actually exert lies in helping people achieve more accurate, more insightful, and more *empowering* views of reality.

Leader as teacher does *not* mean leader as authoritarian expert whose job it is to teach people the "correct" view of reality. Rather, it is about helping everyone in the organization, oneself included, to gain more insightful views of current reality. This is in line with a pop-ular emerging view of leaders as coaches, guides, or facilitators. . . . In learning organizations, this teaching role is developed further by virtue of explicit attention to people's mental models and by the influence of the systems perspective.

The role of leader as teacher starts with bringing to the surface people's mental models of important issues. No one carries an organization, a market, or a state of technology in his or her head. What we carry in our heads are assumptions. These mental pictures of how the world works have a significant influence on how we perceive problems and opportunities, identify courses of action, and make choices.

One reason that mental models are so deeply entrenched is that they are largely tacit. Ian Mitroff, in his study of General Motors, argues that an assumption that prevailed for years was that, in the United States, "Cars are status symbols. Styling is therefore more important than quality" (Mitroff, 1988 pp. 66-67). The Detroit automakers didn't say, "We have a *mental model* that all people care about is styling." Few actual managers would even say publicly that all people care about is styling. So long as the view remained unexpressed, there was little possibility of challenging its validity or forming more accurate assumptions.

But working with mental models goes beyond revealing hidden assumptions. "Reality," as perceived by most people in most organizations, means pressures that must be borne, crises that must be reacted to, and limitations that must be accepted. Leaders as teachers help people *restructure their views of reality* to see beyond the superficial conditions and events into the underlying causes of problems—and therefore to see new possibilities for shaping the future.

Specifically, leaders can influence people to view reality at three distinct levels: events, patterns of behavior, and systemic structure.

Systemic Structure
(Generative)

▼

Patterns of Behavior
(Responsive)

▼

Events
(Reactive)

The key question becomes *where do leaders predominantly focus their own and their orga-nization's attention?*

Contemporary society focuses predominantly on events. The media reinforces this per-spective, with almost exclusive attention to short-term, dramatic events. This focus leads naturally to explaining what happens in terms of those events: "The Dow Jones average went up sixteen points because high fourth-quarter profits were announced yesterday."

Pattern-of-behavior explanations are rarer, in contemporary culture, than event expla-nations, but they do occur. "Trend analysis" is an example of seeing patterns of behavior. A good editorial that interprets a set of current events in the context of long-term historical changes is another example. Systemic, structural explanations go even further by addressing the question, "What causes the patterns of behavior?"

In some sense, all three levels of explanation are equally true. But their usefulness is quite different. Event explanations—who did what to whom—doom their holders to a reactive stance toward change. Pattern-of-behavior explanations focus on identifying long-term trends and assessing their implications. They at least suggest how, over time, we can respond to shifting conditions. Structural explanations are the most powerful. Only they address the underlying causes of behavior at a level such that patterns of behavior can be changed.

By and large, leaders of our current institutions focus their attention on events and patterns of behavior, and, under their influence, their organizations do likewise. That is why contemporary organizations are predominantly reactive, or at best responsive—rarely generative. On the other hand, leaders in learning organizations pay attention to all three levels, but focus especially on systemic structure; largely by example, they teach people throughout the organization to do likewise.

LEADER AS STEWARD

This is the subtlest role of leadership. Unlike the roles of designer and teacher, it is almost solely a matter of attitude. It is an attitude critical to learning organizations.

While stewardship has long been recognized as an aspect of leadership, its source is still not widely understood. I believe Robert Greenleaf (1977) came closest to explaining real stewardship, in his seminal book *Servant Leadership*. There, Greenleaf argues that "The servant leader *is* servant first . . . . It begins with the natural feeling that one wants to serve, to serve *first*. This conscious choice brings one to aspire to lead. That person is sharply different from one who is leader first, perhaps because of the need to assuage an unusual power drive or to acquire material possessions."

Leaders' sense of stewardship operates on two levels: stewardship for the people they lead and stewardship for the larger purpose or mission that underlies the enterprise. The first type arises from a keen appreciation of the impact one's leadership can have on others. People can suffer economically, emotionally, and spiritually under inept leadership. If anything, people in a learning organization are more vulnerable because of their commitment and sense of shared ownership. Appreciating this naturally instills a sense of responsibility in leaders. The second type of stewardship arises from a leader's sense of personal purpose and commitment to the organization's larger mission. People's natural impulse to learn is unleashed when they are engaged in an endeavor they consider worthy of their fullest commitment. Or, as Lawrence Miller (1984) puts it, "Achieving return on equity does not, as a goal, mobilize the most noble forces of our soul."

Leaders engaged in building learning organizations naturally feel part of a larger purpose that goes beyond their organization. They are part of changing the way businesses operate, not from a vague philanthropic urge, but from a conviction that their efforts will produce more productive organizations, capable of achieving higher levels of organizational success and personal satisfaction than more traditional organizations. . . .

New Skills

New leadership roles require new leadership skills. These skills can only be developed, in my judgment, through a lifelong commitment. It is not enough for one or two individuals to develop these skills. They must be distributed widely throughout the organization. This is one reason that understanding the *disciplines* of a learning organization is so important. These disciplines embody the principles and practice that can widely foster leadership development.

Three critical areas of skills (disciplines) are building shared vision, surfacing and challenging mental models, and engaging in systems thinking.*

BUILDING SHARED VISION

How do individual visions come together to create shared visions? A useful metaphor is the hologram, the three-dimensional image created by interacting light sources.

If you cut a photograph in half, each half shows only part of the whole image. But if you divide a hologram, each part, no matter how small, shows the whole image intact. Likewise, when a group of people come to share a vision for an organization, each person sees an individual picture of the organization at its best. Each shares responsibility for the whole, not just for one piece. But the component pieces of the holograms are not identical. Each represents the whole image from a different point of view. It's something like poking holes in a window shade; each hole offers a unique angle for viewing the whole image. So, too, is each individual's vision unique.

When you add up the pieces of a hologram, something interesting happens. The image becomes more intense, more lifelike. When more people come to share a vision, the vision becomes more real in the sense of a mental reality that people can truly imagine achieving. They now have partners, co-creators; the vision no longer rests on their shoulders alone. Early on, when they are nurturing an individual vision, people may say it is "my vision." But, as the shared vision develops, it becomes both "my vision" and "our vision."

The skills involved in building shared vision include the following:

▼ *Encouraging Personal Vision.* Shared visions emerge from personal visions. It is not that people only care about their own self-interest—in fact, people's values usually include dimensions that concern family, organization, community, and even the world. Rather, it is that people's capacity for caring is *personal*.

▼ *Communicating and Asking for Support.* Leaders must be willing to continually share their own vision, rather than being the official representative of the corporate vision. They also must be prepared to ask, "Is this vision worthy of your commitment?" This can be difficult for a person used to setting goals and presuming compliance.

▼ *Visioning as an Ongoing Process.* Building shared vision is a never-ending process. At any one point there will be a particular image of the future that is predominant, but that image will evolve. Today, too many managers want to dispense with the "vision business" by going off and writing the Official Vision Statement. Such statements almost always lack the vitality, freshness, and excitement of a genuine vision that comes from people asking, "What do we really want to achieve?"

▼ *Blending Extrinsic and Intrinsic Visions.* Many energizing visions are extrinsic—that is, they focus on achieving something relative to an outsider, such as a competitor. But a goal that is limited to defeating an opponent can, once the vision is achieved, easily become a defensive posture. In contrast, intrinsic goals like creating a new type of product, taking an established product to a new level, or setting a new standard for customer satisfaction can call forth a new level of creativity and innovation. Intrinsic and extrinsic visions need to coexist; a vision solely predicated on defeating an adversary will eventually weaken an organization.

▼ *Distinguishing Positive from Negative Visions.* Many organizations only truly pull together when their survival is threatened. Similarly, most social movements aim at eliminating what people don't want: for example, anti-drugs, anti-smoking, or anti-nuclear arms movements. Negative visions carry a subtle message of powerlessness: people will only pull together when there is sufficient threat. Negative visions also tend to be short

---

* These points are condensed from the practices of the five disciplines examined in Senge (1990).

term. Two fundamental sources of energy can motivate organizations: fear and aspiration. Fear, the energy source behind negative visions, can produce extraordinary changes in shorter periods, but aspiration endures as a continuing source of learning and growth.

SURFACING AND TESTING MENTAL MODELS

Many of the best ideas in organizations never get put into practice. One reason is that new insights and initiatives often conflict with established mental models. The leadership task of challenging assumptions without invoking defensiveness requires reflection and inquiry skills possessed by few leaders in traditional controlling organizations.*

▼ *Seeing Leaps of Abstraction.* Our minds literally move at lightning speed. Ironically, this often slows our learning, because we leap to generalizations so quickly that we never think to test them. We then confuse our generalizations with the observable data upon which they are based, treating the generalizations *as if they were data.* . . .

▼ *Balancing Inquiry and Advocacy.* Most managers are skilled at articulating their views and presenting them persuasively. While important, advocacy skills can become counterproductive as managers rise in responsibility and confront increasingly complex issues that require collaborative learning among different, equally knowledgeable people. Leaders in learning organizations need to have both inquiry *and* advocacy skills. . . .

▼ *Distinguished Espoused Theory from Theory in Use.* We all like to think that we hold certain views, but often our actions reveal deeper views. For example, I may proclaim that people are trustworthy, but never lend friends money and jealously guard my possessions. Obviously, my deeper mental model (my theory in use), differs from my espoused theory. Recognizing gaps between espoused views and theories in use (which often requires the help of others) can be pivotal to deeper learning.

▼ *Recognizing and Defusing Defensive Routines.* As one CEO in our research program puts it, "Nobody ever talks about an issue at the 8:00 business meeting exactly the same way they talk about it at home that evening or over drinks at the end of the day." The reason is what Chris Argyris calls "defensive routines," entrenched habits used to protect ourselves from the embarrassment and threat that come with exposing our thinking. For most of us, such defenses began to build early in life in response to pressures to have the right answers in school or at home. Organizations add new levels of performance anxiety and thereby amplify and exacerbate this defensiveness. Ironically, this makes it even more difficult to expose hidden mental models, and thereby lessens learning.

The first challenge is to recognize defensive routines, then to inquire into their operation. Those who are best at revealing and defusing defensive routines operate with a high degree of self-disclosure regarding their own defensiveness (e.g., I notice that I am feeling uneasy about how this conversation is going. Perhaps I don't understand it or it is threatening to me in ways I don't yet see. Can you help me see this better?).

SYSTEMS THINKING

We all know that leaders should help people see the big picture. But the actual skills whereby leaders are supposed to achieve this are not well understood. In my experience, successful leaders often are "systems thinkers" to a considerable extent. They focus less on day-to-day events and more on underlying trends and forces of change. But they do this almost

---

*The ideas below are based to considerable extent on the work of Chris Argyris, Donald Schon, and their Action Science colleagues. C. Argyris and D. Schon, *Organizational Learning: A Theory-in-Action Perspective* (1978); C. Argyris, R. Putman, and D. Smith, *Action Science* (1985); C. Argyris, *Strategy, Change, and Defensive Routines* (1985); and C. Argyris, *Overcoming Organizational Defenses* (1990).

completely intuitively. The consequence is that they are often unable to explain their intuitions to others and feel frustrated that others cannot see the world the way they do.

One of the most significant developments in management science today is the gradual coalescence of managerial systems thinking as a field of study and practice. This field suggests some key skills for future leaders:

▼ *Seeing Interrelationships, Not Things, and Processes, Not Snapshots.* Most of us have been conditioned throughout our lives to focus on things and to see the world in static images. This leads us to linear explanations of systemic phenomenon. For instance, in an arms race each party is convinced that the other is *the cause* of problems. They react to each new move as an isolated event, not as part of a process. So long as they fail to see the interrelationships of these actions, they are trapped.

▼ *Moving Beyond Blame.* We tend to blame each other or outside circumstances for our problems. But it is poorly designed systems, not incompetent or unmotivated individuals, that cause most organizational problems. Systems thinking shows us that there is no outside—that you and the cause of your problems are part of a single system.

▼ *Distinguishing Detail Complexity from Dynamic Complexity.* Some types of complexity are more important strategically than others. Detail complexity arises when there are many variables. Dynamic complexity arises when cause and effect are distant in time and space, and when the consequences over time of interventions are subtle and not obvious to many participants in the system. The leverage in most management situations lies in understanding dynamic complexity, not detail complexity.

▼ *Focusing on Areas of High Leverage.* Some have called systems thinking the "new dismal science" because it teaches that most obvious solutions don't work—at best, they improve matters in the short run, only to make things worse in the long run. But there is another side to the story. Systems thinking also shows that small, well-focused actions can produce significant, enduring improvements, if they are in the right place. Systems thinkers refer to this idea as the principle of "leverage." Tackling a difficult problem is often a matter of seeing where the high leverage lies, where a change—with a minimum of effort—would lead to lasting, significant improvement.

▼ *Avoiding Symptomatic Solutions.* The pressures to intervene in management systems that are going awry can be overwhelming. Unfortunately, given the linear thinking that predominates in most organizations, interventions usually focus on symptomatic fixes, not underlying causes. This results in only temporary relief, and it tends to create still more pressures later on for further, low-leverage intervention. If leaders acquiesce to these pressures, they can be sucked into an endless spiral of increasing intervention. Sometimes the most difficult leadership acts are to refrain from intervening through popular quick fixes and to keep the pressure on everyone to identify more enduring solutions.

While leaders who can articulate systemic explanations are not rare, those who *can* will leave their stamp on an organization. . . . The consequence of leaders who lack systems thinking skills can be devastating. Many charismatic leaders manage almost exclusively at the level of events. They deal in visions and in crises, and little in between. Under their leadership, an organization hurtles from crisis to crisis. Eventually, the worldview of people in the organization becomes dominated by events and reactiveness. Many, especially those who are deeply committed, become burned out. Eventually, cynicism comes to pervade the organization. People have no control over their time, let alone their destiny.

Similar problems arise with the "visionary strategist," the leader with vision who sees both patterns of change and events. This leader is better prepared to manage change. He or she can explain strategies in terms of emerging trends, and thereby fosters a climate that is less reactive. But such leaders impart a responsive orientation rather than a generative one.

Many talented leaders have rich, highly systemic intuitions but cannot explain those intuitions to others. Ironically, they often end up being authoritarian leaders, even if they don't want to, because only they see the decisions that need to be made. They are unable to conceptualize their strategic insights so that these can become public knowledge, open to challenge and further improvement. . . .

I believe that [a] new sort of management development will focus on the roles, skills, and tools for leadership in learning organizations. Undoubtedly, the ideas offered above are only a rough approximation of this new territory. The sooner we begin seriously exploring the territory, the sooner the initial map can be improved—and the sooner we will realize an age-old vision of leadership:

The wicked leader is he who the people despise.

The good leader is he who the people revere.

The great leader is he who the people say, "We did it ourselves."

- Lao Tsu

▼ READING 8.3   MIDDLE MANAGERS TO "DO THINGS RIGHT"*

by Leonard R. Sayles

Recent strides by U.S. companies to become more competitive—by downsizing, restructuring, shedding extraneous businesses, or introducing new management techniques—fail to mask the fact that American industry allowed itself to become seriously weakened in the 70s and 80s. What went wrong? The talk in executive suites puts the blame on slothful workers, management hubris, corporate debt, leveraged buyouts, and deceptive financial readings caused by inflation, among other such culprits. But evidence suggests that the real problem was management's preoccupation with strategic issues, and its failure to concentrate on everyday performance.

Actually, it was only recently that managerial excellence was defined as the ability to make astute strategic decisions and handle hierarchical relationships effectively. But now, it seems, a fundamental and necessary shift in management priorities is taking place. A few years ago, popular wisdom told us, "The important thing is not whether you're doing something right, but whether you're doing the right thing." Now, astute managers are saying that what is really important is doing things right.

The following discussion is intended to reveal why this major shift in managerial focus is occurring, and what its implications are for middle-level managers. The conclusions are based on my own observation and interview studies, as well as on major field studies of day-to-day management issues in three multinational companies. . . .

THE SHIFT TO OPERATING CAPABILITIES

Amar Bhide, a consultant who works with large commercial banks, has observed that some companies do not have long-term strategic plans; instead, "they concentrate on operating details and doing things well." More recent studies of companies like Wal-Mart and Toyota come to the same conclusion: that operational capabilities are replacing strategic brilliance as the source of competitive advantage. Why? One clear reason is that it is easier for a competitor to copy a strategic decision (or product design or marketing campaign) than duplicate a finely tuned, highly effective day-to-day business operation.

* Originally published as "Doing Things Right: A New Imperative for Middle Managers," in *Organizational Dynamics* (Spring 1993), pp. 5-14; based on his book *The Working Leader* (Free Press, 1993); used with permission.

Closely related to the term "operational capabilities" is the relatively new, Japanese-developed management concept known as *core competencies*. Generally, core competencies can be defined as exquisitely developed operating capabilities. As a group, these capabilities form a body of accumulated organizational learning on how to integrate dispersed and diffuse technology and activities into a perfectly functioning work system.

To some, it may be surprising that companies are now turning their attention to these concepts. After all, isn't it true that nearly all modern companies already understand and can manage the everyday matters of getting things done? Industrial engineering and related fields matured decades ago, and production management is considered a strength that has propelled American companies into world prominence. Isn't "production" a core competency of almost every reasonably well-managed company? And aren't operations simply the dull routines that any good supervisor can maintain?

Not necessarily.

THE NEW MEANINGS OF "OPERATING" AND "PRODUCTION"

. . . In fact, many companies we studied had allowed themselves the luxury of higher production costs (and, presumably, lower profitability) until external pressures forced them to improve their operations. Ironically, external pressures to decrease pollution and increase quality often led to lower total operating costs, as managers were forced to improve their understanding and management of operations in order to accomplish these goals.

Clearly, operations is a difficult area for U.S. companies to master today. Why? Four major reasons stand out:

THERE ARE NO SIMPLE INTERFACES.
American industry became efficient, in part, by having jobs that interlocked easily. To oversimplify, if "A" made the screw the right size, it would fit perfectly in the hole that "B" drilled. But contemporary organizations have jobs with dozens or hundreds of elements—an "A" to "Z"—that need to "match," or be integrated with, those of other jobs. Without integration, performance will suffer. . . .

TASKS CANNOT BE PRECISELY PRESCRIBED.
Outside of mechanical assembly lines and other basic production and clerical operations, most functions defy simple prescription. There is simply a lot of "play," or leeway, when it comes to getting a job done. The technician or professional, for example, has no fixed template to match; therefore, his or her training, interests, and habits determine how work actually gets done. . . . What is useful or optimal for those who do a particular task may be incompatible with what others in the work flow need.

CHANGE IS ALMOST CONSTANT.
Again, unlike traditional production and white collar factories, where work might have remained fixed for years, most technologies we've observed are evolving constantly. Of course, many of the changes are small—a shortcut here, an elaboration there. But even small changes can have major repercussions in tightly interlocked systems. For example, in one company we studied, a programmer, in an effort to improve the software for making new credit cards, made one minor change in the program. However, this change in effect limited to 14 the number of spaces for customer names. Some weeks later, after many cards had been produced with contracted customer names, service management was deluged with complaints and canceled accounts.

ORGANIZATIONAL COHERENCE IS DIFFICULT TO ACHIEVE.
When management calls for change to provide better customer service, it is really asking for certain internal groups to be more adaptable and responsible to the outside world and to each other. Shorter product-development cycles require the same thing: more responsiveness on the part of one group to the work done at an earlier stage in the work flow. Higher efficiency, for the most part, means better coordination and integration, too—after all, what A does should fit neatly into B's work.

It is only through what Burlington Northern's CEO Gerald Grinstein calls "seamless service" that business can meet market requirements and implement its never-ending list of necessary technological changes and modifications. Even well-coordinated systems tend to degenerate over time, as the interdependent work groups initiate autonomous initiatives. Thus, contemporary organizations have the continuing challenge of coherence—of getting the parts to fit together and stay together.

THE PIVOTAL POSITION OF THE MIDDLE MANAGER

For many years, we were taught that "good" managers were "hands off" managers. They stood back, only rarely getting involved in work matters. The reasons managers behaved this way were compelling, or so they seemed:

1. Managers needed to focus on the future, on planning and bigger decisions. By practicing "management by exception," or attending only to those areas that were failing in one way or another, they could economize on their time.
2. By delegating and managing by results, managers could help motivate their workers, and provide them with a sense of responsibility.

Thus, middle managers have traditionally focused on developing a strategic vision and gaining the commitment and loyalty of subordinates. Managing operations has been the province of lower level supervisors and (in sophisticated companies) empowered, semiautonomous groups.

Ironically, however, senior executives have not perceived middle managers as occupying a critical strategic niche. When it came time to "trim the fat," many organizations made the middle ranks bear more than their share of the cuts. The implication seems to be that these individuals were "useless overhead."

To be sure, many organizations have been over-layered, and their middle-management levels needed to be trimmed. Historically, many middle managers have spent most of their time granting or withholding permission, and massaging data before sending it up the line. But excesses in these activities should not cause senior management to ignore the critical role that middle managers need to play.

What critical role is that? The middle manager should bear many of the burdens of building operating competencies. As mentioned above, the various parts of work systems are not programmed to fit together in a way that will ensure that the service department is responsive to customers, that work progresses "seamlessly," and that development projects are well coordinated. It is almost the rule, not the exception, that Department A, for good reason, will develop a way of doing things that makes Department B's work more difficult—or, in the case of a development project, even impossible.

Middle managers often become the players who can facilitate necessary trade-offs among the diverse parts of any work system. While project groups and teams and first-line supervisors can help, managerial intervention is often needed to resolve many of the contradictions and inconsistencies that exist in a large system. It is middle managers who must "massage" the parts and continuously "rejiggle" and reconfigure the interfaces. Without their initiatives, under conditions of modern technology, the real work of the organization will never be performed effectively.

To illustrate this point, we can look at some practical examples. Rebecca Henderson, a professor at M.I.T., conducted a meticulous research project of U.S. and Japanese firms in the photolithographic alignment equipment industry (machines used in semiconductor "chip" manufacturing). The study concluded, persuasively, that market leaders consistently lost their preeminent positions when a competitor introduced an improved product. Although the technology for the improvement was both obvious and available, other firms failed to integrate the improvement into their operations. Essentially the firms seeking to catch up simply "tacked" the improved feature onto their existing machine, but failed to introduce the resulting requisite changes into all the ancillary components. For the improvement to work properly, each ancillary component had to be reconfigured so that its interfaces with other components along the work flow would be effective.

My observation of this research leads to the conclusion that the "copy cat" companies had no middle managers available to renegotiate all the interfaces. Each company saw the improvement as a simple change in specifications. It is easier to make this kind of naive assumption than it is to delve into established routines, entrenched communications, and steady patterns.

On the other hand, in our own field work, we observed many energetic middle managers who recognized that nothing fit together easily. They took the initiative, painstakingly working through the necessary changes in both staff and line functions to produce an improved product or process.

For example, in one company we studied, a prestigious support group had established a standard for acquiring certain automation equipment. One division that intended to use the equipment, however, argued that the standard was unrealistic and dated. The middle manager of this division conducted an extended and risky series of negotiations, both with the management of the support group and with senior management. The effort paid off, and the support group granted an exception. . . .

WHY MIDDLE MANAGERS?

Many of the trade-offs that are necessary to make a work system effective involve tough decisions. These are not the benign "win-win" negotiations that are often emphasized in discussions of lateral relations. Rather, they are tough decisions requiring significant managerial intervention. The final choices will force well-entrenched staff groups to modify longstanding procedures, decision criteria, or routines. . . .

Of course, many problems require the input of senior management, which can approve a capital appropriation, a shift away from a previously approved technology, or some other shift in resources or jurisdiction. *But it takes a middle manager to get senior management's attention and make the case for change.*

Obviously, some fortunate general managers oversee truly decentralized operations and products. They pull all the strings and can function as entrepreneurs who run small businesses. They can make nearly all the necessary trade-offs—such as deciding what manufacturing must do to support a new marketing initiative—in their own heads. But for the foreseeable future, large organizations, consisting of some centralized and some decentralized activities, will remain critical contributors to our economic well-being. As long as some parts of the work system remain outside the span of control of a general manager, product manager, or service manager, substantial systems-leadership skills will be needed to maintain operational effectiveness.

WORKING LEADERS

We call effective middle managers "working leaders." They focus as much on operations—on getting things done effectively—as they do on maintaining the linkages between top management and supervisors. They act as hands-on, working managers. Instead of simply waiting for and evaluating results, they seek to intervene.

And the interventions they undertake require a more intimate knowledge of operations, and more involvement in the work, than those of traditional middle managers, who have historically relied more on delegation. Working leaders make real choices between the demands and apparent requirements of interdependent groups. They make persuasive arguments—supported by systematically presented, factual material—to convince senior managers to change established practices, appropriations, or jurisdictions. . . .

[One] middle manager we observed, Manager C, was responsible for a profitable product that needed continuous upgrading. That product was a component in a larger and potentially more profitable hardware system that the company was developing, which was controlled by Manager D. Since D needed to be sure that future generations of the profitable product would be compatible with her large, complex system, the software people responsible for the component also worked for her.

Thus, C and D were vendors (and customers) of one another, and since their needs were not compatible—at least not in the short run—they had numerous battles. Their mutual boss, a middle-level manager, needed an in-depth understanding of the technology to assure that the trade-offs between these two subordinate managers would support the overall financial and technological health of his department, and would properly balance short- and long-run interests.

THE WORK OF WORKING LEADERS

The work of the new breed of middle managers has at least four dimensions.

MAKING SURE THE TECHNOLOGY IS UNDERSTOOD

Middle managers today need to understand the key parameters that shape the performance of the systems for which they are responsible. It is easy to assume that this requirement is spelled out in company documents. In our research, however, we have often observed managers discovering new technical interrelationships even after they had been in their departments for several years. When managers are less-than-informed about their operations, serious problems can result. . . .

CONTINUOUS IMPROVEMENT

These same middle managers demanded that contradictions and flaws be reworked so that the frequency of problems would be reduced. And the excellent ones kept looking for additional ways of fine tuning their systems. At times, they had to be willing to take career risks by disagreeing openly with bosses and peers in order to "fix" the system. In short, they were proactive, high-initiative managers who were focused on work.

EVALUATING TRADE-OFFS

Today's middle managers also need to be close enough to actual operations to evaluate the technical quality of their subordinates' decisions. Weaker employees generally seek to maximize results by concentrating on the most obvious "target." (As one informant told us, "My people always want a clear stake in the ground that they can see and hit.") But a reality of modern business is that necessary trade-offs may, in the short run, result in inconsistent standards and requirements. . . .

PEOPLE MANAGEMENT

Finally, it is inaccurate to conclude that the middle manager's need for operational knowledge outweighs his or her need for people skills. Middle managers need finely developed interpersonal skills so they can obtain information and negotiate changes successfully. Highly involved middle managers cannot be "technocrats" or technicians who love to do things by themselves. They have to work closely with other people, most of whom have divergent interests and perspectives.

MAKING THE SYSTEM WORK

. . . The conventional view that good managers need to remove themselves from the details of work and, instead, manage by results may need revision. It worked well during that bygone era of long, fixed manufacturing runs and undifferentiated services, when customers, mesmerized by powerful advertising campaigns, took what was offered by comfortable dominant firms. It works less well in our world of constant product and market change.

We can now interpret the many observational studies of actual managerial behavior showing peripatetic managers engaging in never-ending lateral negotiations with more insight. Those managers are trying to make things work right. In our research, we observed middle managers who created core competencies and excellence in operations. They were indeed peripatetic: engaging in a never-ending series of negotiations to mediate the legitimate contradictions of supervisory-level subordinates; to encourage peers and staff to modify their demands and/or interfaces; and to persuade upper management to change policies or procedures that hampered the work flow. Most of all, they saw and appreciated larger system requirements, and while they were demanding of others, they were also able to make sacrifices in their own units to improve systems effectiveness.

Of course, we also observed traditional middle managers, who managed by results, massaged data, shifted blame and costs to adjacent departments when problems arose, and devoted their attention primarily to looking good and pleasing the boss. They had little understanding of their role as prime movers seeking to build self-maintaining work systems. Their focus was not on work, but on plans and results. They often appeared to meet their budgeted performance requirement, but their part of the organization never attained high effectiveness or achieved anything resembling core competencies.

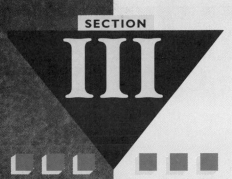

CONTEXTS

THE ENTREPRENEURIAL CONTEXT

The text of this book really divides into two basic parts, although there are three sections. The first, encompassing Chapters 1 through 8 and Sections I and II, introduces a variety of important *concepts* of organizations—strategy, the strategist, process, structure, systems, culture, power, style. The second, beginning here with Section III and Chapter 9, considers how these concepts combine to form major *contexts* of organizations. In effect, a context is a type of situation wherein can be found particular structures, power relationships, processes, competitive settings, and so on.

Traditionally, policy and strategy textbooks are divided into two very different parts—a first on the "formulation" of strategy, a second on its "implementation" (including discussion of structure, systems, culture, etc.). As some of the readings of Chapter 5 have already made clear, we believe this is often a false dichotomy: In many situations (that is, contexts), formulation and implementation can be so intertwined that it makes no sense to separate them. To build a textbook around a questionable dichotomy likewise makes no sense to us, and so we have instead proceeded by introducing all the concepts related to the strategy process first and then considering the various ways in which they might interact in specific situations.

There is no "one best way" to manage the strategy process. The notion that there are several possible "good ways" however—various contexts appropriate to strategic management—was first developed in the Mintzberg reading in Chapter 6. In fact, his *configurations* of structure serve as the basis for determining the set of contexts we include here. These are as follows:

We begin here in Chapter 9 with what seems to be the simplest context, certainly one that has had much good press in America since Horatio Alger first went into business—the *entrepreneurial* context. Here a single leader takes personal charge in a highly dynamic situation, as in a new firm or a small one operating in a growing market, or even sometimes in a large organization facing crisis.

We next consider in Chapter 10 a contrasting context that often dominates large business as well as big government. We label it the *mature* context, although it might equally be referred to as the stable context or the mass-production or mass-service context. Here, rather formal structures combine with strategy-making processes that are heavily planning and technique oriented.

Our third and fourth contexts are those of organizations largely dependent on specialists and experts. These contexts are called *professional* when the environment is stable, *innovation* when it is dynamic. Here responsibility for strategy making tends to diffuse throughout the organization, sometimes even lodging itself at the bottom of the hierarchy. The strategy process tends to become rather emergent in nature.

Fifth, we consider the context of the *diversified* organization, which has become increasingly important as waves of mergers have swept across various Western economies. Because product-market strategies are diversified, the structures tend to get divisionalized, and the focus of strategy shifts to two levels: the corporate or portfolio level and the divisional or business level. Following this, we consider the *international* context, really a form of diversification (i.e., geographical), but important enough in its own right to merit a separate chapter.

We complete our discussion of contexts with consideration of the problems of managing *change* from one of these contexts to another (often "cultural revolution") or from one major strategy and structure to another within a particular context.

In the chapter on each context, our intention is to include material that would describe all the basic concepts as they take shape in that context. We wish to describe the form of organizational structure and of strategic leadership found there, the nature of its strategy-making process, including its favored forms of strategy analysis and its most appropriate types of strategies (generic and otherwise), its natural power relationships and preferred culture, and the nature of its competition and industry structure as well as the social issues that surround it. Unfortunately, appropriate readings on all this are not available—in part we do not yet know all that we must about each context. But we believe that the readings that we have included in this section do cover a good deal of ground, enough to give a real sense of each different context.

Before beginning, we should warn you of one danger in focusing this discussion on contexts such as these: It may make the world of organizations appear to be more pat and ordered than it really is. Many organizations certainly seem to fit one context or another, as numerous examples will make clear. But none ever does so quite perfectly—the world is too nuanced for that. And then there are the many organizations that do not fit any single context at all. We believe, and have included arguments in a concluding chapter to this section, that in fact the set of contexts altogether form a framework by which to understand better all kinds of organizations. But until we get there, you should bear in mind that much of this material caricatures reality as much as it mirrors it. Of course, such caricaturing is a necessary part of formal learning and of acting. Managers, for example, would never get anything done if they could not use simplified frameworks to comprehend their experiences in order to act on them. As Miller and Mintzberg have argued in a paper called "The Case for Configuration," managers are attracted to a particular, well-defined context because that allows them to achieve a certain consistency and coherence in the design of their organization and so to facilitate its effective performance. Each context, as you will see, has its own logic—its own integrated way of dealing with its part of the world—that makes things more manageable.

This chapter of Section III discusses the entrepreneurial context. At least in its traditional form, this encompasses situations in which a single individual, typically with a clear and distinct vision of purpose, directs an organization that is structured to be as responsive as possible to his or her personal wishes. Strategy making thus revolves around a single brain, unconstrained by the forces of bureaucratic momentum.

Such entrepreneurship is typically found in young organizations, especially ones in new or emerging industries. Entrepreneurial vision tends to have a high potential payoff in these situations and may indeed be essential when there are long delays between the conception of an idea and its commercial success. In addition, in crisis situations a similar type of strong and visionary leadership may offer the only hope for successful turnaround. And it can thrive as well in highly fragmented industries, where small flexible organizations can move quickly into and out of specialized market niches, and so outmaneuver the big bureaucracies.

The word "entrepreneurship" has also been associated recently with change and innovation inside of larger, more bureaucratic organizations—sometimes under the label "intrapreneurship." In these situations, it is often not the boss, but someone in an odd corner of the organization—a "champion" for some technology or strategic issue—who takes on the entrepreneurial role. We believe, however, for reasons that will later become evident, that intrapreneurship better fits into our chapter on the innovation context.

To describe the structure that seems to be most logically associated with the traditional form of entrepreneurship, we open with material on the simple structure in Mintzberg's book *The Structuring of Organizations*. Combined with this is a discussion of strategy making in the entrepreneurial context, especially with regard to strategic vision, based on two sets of research projects carried out at McGill University. In one, strategies of visionary leadership were studied through biographies and autobiographies; in the other, the strategies of entrepreneurial firms were tracked across several decades of their histories.

Then, to investigate the external situation that seems to be most commonly (although not exclusively) associated with the entrepreneurial context, we present excerpts from a chapter on emerging industries from Michael Porter's book *Competitive Strategy*. The final reading of this chapter, by Amar Bhide of the Harvard Business School, tells how entrepreneurs go about crafting their strategies, based on his and his associates' research. Entrepreneurs select carefully but are also careful not to be too analytical (recall Pitcher's artists versus the technocrats of Chapter 8), and they maintain their ability to maneuver and to "hustle." Action must be integrated with analysis.

▼ READING 9.1   THE ENTREPRENEURIAL ORGANIZATION*

by Henry Mintzberg

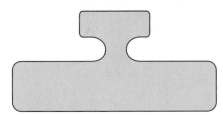

Consider an automobile dealership with a flamboyant owner, a brand-new government department, a corporation or even a nation run by an autocratic leader, or a school system in a state of crisis. In many respects, those are vastly different organizations. But the evidence suggests that they share a number of basic characteristics. They form a configuration we shall call the *entrepreneurial organization*.

* Adapted from *The Structuring of Organizations* (Prentice Hall, 1979, Chap. 17 on "The Simple Structure"), *Power In and Around Organizations* (Prentice Hall, 1983, Chap. 20 on "The Autocracy"), and the material on strategy formation from "Visionary Leadership and Strategic Management," *Strategic Management Journal* (1989) coauthored with Frances Westley); see also, "Tracking Strategy in an Entrepreneurial Firm," *Academy of Management Journal* (1982), and "Researching the Formation of Strategies: The History of a Canadian Lady, 1939–1976," in R. B. Lamb, ed., *Competitive Strategic Management* (Prentice Hall, 1984), the last two coauthored with James A. Waters. A chapter similar to this appeared in *Mintzberg on Management: Inside Our Strange World of Organizations* (Free Press, 1989).

The Basic Structure

The structure of the entrepreneurial organization is often very simple, characterized above all by what it is not: elaborated. As shown in the opening figure, typically it has little or no staff, a loose division of labor, and a small managerial hierarchy. Little of its activity is formalized, and it makes minimal use of planning procedures or training routines. In a sense, it is nonstructure; in my "structuring" book, I called it *simple structure*.

Power tends to focus on the chief executive, who exercises a high personal profile. Formal controls are discouraged as a threat to the chief's flexibility. He or she drives the organization by sheer force of personality or by more direct interventions. Under the leader's watchful eye, politics cannot easily arise. Should outsiders, such as particular customers or suppliers, seek to exert influence, such leaders are as likely as not to take the organizations to a less exposed niche in the marketplace.

Thus, it is not uncommon in small entrepreneurial organizations for everyone to report to the chief. Even in ones not so small, communication flows informally, much of it between the chief executive and others. As one group of McGill MBA students commented in their study of a small manufacturer of pumps: "It is not unusual to see the president of the company engaged in casual conversation with a machine shop mechanic. [That way he is] informed of a machine breakdown even before the shop superintendent is advised."

Decision making is likewise flexible, with a highly centralized power system allowing for rapid response. The creation of strategy is, of course, the responsibility of the chief executive, the process tending to be highly intuitive, often oriented to the aggressive search for opportunities. It is not surprising, therefore, that the resulting strategy tends to reflect the chief executive's implicit vision of the world, often an extrapolation of his or her own personality.

Handling disturbances and innovating in an entrepreneurial way are perhaps the most important aspects of the chief executive's work. In contrast, the more formal aspects of managerial work—figurehead duties, for example, receive less attention, as does the need to disseminate information and allocate resources internally, since knowledge and power remain at the top.

Conditions of the Entrepreneurial Organization

A centrist entrepreneurial configuration is fostered by an external context that is both simple and dynamic. Simpler environments (say, retailing food as opposed to designing computer systems) enable one person at the top to retain so much influence, while it is a dynamic environment that requires flexible structure, which in turn enables the organization to outmaneuver the bureaucracies. Entrepreneurial leaders are naturally attracted to such conditions.

The classic case of this is, of course, the entrepreneurial firm, where the leader is the owner. Entrepreneurs often found their own firms to escape the procedures and control of the bureaucracies where they previously worked. At the helm of their own enterprises, they continue to loathe the ways of bureaucracy, and the staff analysts that accompany them, and so they keep their organizations lean and flexible. Figure 1 shows the organigram for Steinberg's, a supermarket chain we shall be discussing shortly, during its most classically entrepreneurial years. Notice the identification of people above positions, the simplicity of the structure (the firm's sales by this time were on the order of $27 million), and the focus on the chief executive (not to mention the obvious family connections).

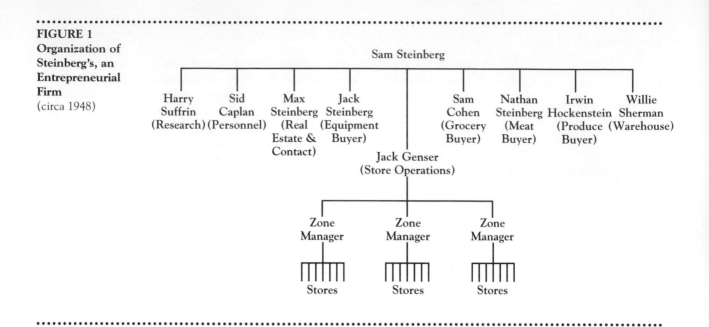

FIGURE 1
**Organization of
Steinberg's, an
Entrepreneurial
Firm**
(circa 1948)

Entrepreneurial firms are often young and aggressive, continually searching for the risky markets that scare off the bigger bureaucracies. But they are also careful to avoid the complex markets, preferring to remain in niches that their leaders can comprehend. Their small size and focused strategies allow their structures to remain simple, so that the leaders can retain tight control and maneuver flexibly. Moreover, business entrepreneurs are often visionary, sometimes charismatic or autocratic as well (sometimes both, in sequence!). Of course, not all "entrepreneurs" are so aggressive or visionary; many settle down to pursue common strategies in small geographic niches. Labeled the *local producers*, these firms can include the corner restaurant, the town bakery, the regional supermarket chain.

But an organization need not be owned by an entrepreneur, indeed need not even operate in the profit sector, to adopt the configuration we call entrepreneurial. In fact, most new organizations seem to adopt this configuration, whatever their sector, because they generally have to rely on personalized leadership to get themselves going—to establish their basic direction, or *strategic vision*, to hire their first people and set up their initial procedures. Of course, strong leaders are likewise attracted to new organizations, where they can put their own stamp on things. Thus, we can conclude that most organizations in business, government, and not-for-profit areas pass through the entrepreneurial configuration in their formative years, during *start-up*.

Moreover, while new organizations that quickly grow large or that require specialized forms of expertise may make a relatively quick transition to another configuration, many others seem to remain in the entrepreneurial form, more or less, as long as their founding leaders remain in office. This reflects the fact that the structure has often been built around the personal needs and orientation of the leader and has been staffed with people loyal to him or her.

This last comment suggests that the personal power needs of a leader can also, by themselves, give rise to this configuration in an existing organization. When a chief executive hoards power and avoids or destroys the formalization of activity as an infringement on his or her right to rule by fiat, then an autocratic form of the entrepreneurial organization will tend to appear. This can been seen in the cult of personality of the leader, in business (the last days of Henry Ford) no less than in government (the leadership of Stalin in the Soviet Union). Charisma can have a similar effect, though different consequences, when the leader gains personal power not because he or she hoards it but because the followers lavish it on the leader.

The entrepreneurial configuration also tends to arise in any other type of organization that faces severe crisis. Backed up against a wall, with its survival at stake, an organization will typically turn to a strong leader for salvation. The structure thus becomes effectively (if not formally) simple, as the normal powers of existing groups—whether staff analysts, line managers, or professional operators, and so on, with their perhaps more standardized forms of control—are suspended to allow the chief to impose a new integrated vision through his or her personalized control. The leader may cut costs and expenses in an attempt to effect what is known in the strategic management literature as an *operating turnaround*, or else reconceive the basic product and service orientation, to achieve *strategic turnaround*. Of course, once the turnaround is realized, the organization may revert to its traditional operations, and, in the bargain, spew out its entrepreneurial leader, now viewed as an impediment to its smooth functioning.

Strategy Formation in the Entrepreneurial Organization

How does strategy develop in the entrepreneurial organization? And what role does that mysterious concept known as "strategic vision" play? We know something of the entrepreneurial mode of strategy making, but less of strategic vision itself, since it is locked in the head of the individual. But some studies we have done at McGill do shed some light on both these questions. Let us consider strategic vision first.

VISIONARY LEADERSHIP

In a paper she coauthored with me, my McGill colleague Frances Westley contrasted two views of visionary leadership. One she likened to a hypodermic needle, in which the active ingredient (vision) is loaded into a syringe (words) which is injected into the employees to stimulate all kinds of energy. There is surely some truth to this, but Frances prefers another image, that of drama. Drawing from a book on theater by Peter Brook (1968), the legendary director of the Royal Shakespeare Company, she conceives strategic vision, like drama, as becoming magical in that moment when fiction and life blend together. In drama, this moment is the result of endless "rehearsal," the "performance" itself, and the "attendance" of the audience. But Brook prefers the more dynamic equivalent words in French, all of which have English meanings—"repetition," "representation," and "assistance." Frances likewise applies these words to strategic vision.

"Repetition" suggests that success comes from deep knowledge of the subject at hand. Just as Sir Laurence Olivier would repeat his lines again and again until he had trained his tongue muscles to say them effortlessly (Brook, p. 154), so too Lee Iacocca "grew up" in the automobile business, going to Chrysler after Ford because cars were "in his blood" (Iacocca, 1984:141). The visionary's inspiration stems not from luck, although chance encounters can play a role, but from endless experience in a particular context.

"Representation" means not just to perform but to make the past live again, giving it immediacy, vitality. To the strategist, that is vision articulated, in words and actions. What distinguishes visionary leaders is their profound ability with language, often in symbolic form, as metaphor. It is not just that they "see" things from a new perspective but that they get others to so see them.

Edwin Land, who built a great company around the Polaroid camera he invented, has written of the duty of "the inventor to build a new gestalt for the old one in the framework of society" (1975:50). He himself described photography as helping "to focus some aspect of [your] life"; as you look through the viewfinder, "it's not merely the camera you are focusing: you are focusing yourself . . . when you touch the button, what is inside of you comes out. It's the most basic form of creativity. Part of you is now permanent" (*Time*, 1972:84). Lofty words for 50 tourists filing out of a bus to record some pat scene, but powerful imagery for someone trying to build an organization to promote a novel camera. Steve Jobs, visionary (for a time) in his promotion, if not invention, of the personal computer, placed a grand piano and a BMW in Apple's central foyer, with the claim that "I believe people get great ideas from seeing great products" (in Wise, 1984:146).

"Assistance" means that the audience for drama, whether in the theater or in the organization, empowers the actor no less than the actor empowers the audience. Leaders become visionary because they appeal powerfully to specific constituencies at specific periods of time. That is why leaders once perceived as visionary can fall so dramatically from grace—a Steve Jobs, a Winston Churchill. Or to take a more dramatic example, here is how Albert Speer, arriving skeptical, reacted to the first lecture he heard by his future leader: "Hitler no longer seemed to be speaking to convince; rather, he seemed to feel that he was experiencing what the audience, by now transformed into a single mass, expected of him" (1970:16).

Of course, management is not theater; the leader who becomes a stage actor, playing a part he or she does not live, is destined to fall from grace. It is integrity—a genuine feeling behind what the leader says and does—that makes leadership truly visionary, and that is what makes impossible the transition of such leadership into any formula.

This visionary leadership is style and strategy, coupled together. It is drama, but not playacting. The strategic visionary is born and made, the product of a historical moment. Brook closes his book with the following quotation:

> In everyday life, "if" is a fiction, in the theatre "if" is an experiment.
> In everyday life, "if" is an evasion, in the theatre "if" is the truth.
> When we are persuaded to believe in this truth, then the theatre and life are one.
> This is a high aim. It sounds like hard work.
> To play needs much work. But when we experience the work as play, then it is not work any more.
> A play is play. (p. 157)

In the entrepreneurial organization, at best, "theater," namely strategic vision, becomes one with "life," namely organization. That way leadership creates drama; it turns work into play.

Let us now consider the entrepreneurial approach to strategy formation in terms of two specific studies we have done, one of a supermarket chain, the other of a manufacturer of women's undergarments.

THE ENTREPRENEURIAL APPROACH TO STRATEGY FORMATION IN A SUPERMARKET CHAIN

Steinberg's is a Canadian retail chain that began with a tiny food store in Montreal in 1917 and grew to sales in the billion-dollar range during the almost 60-year reign of its leader. Most of that growth came from supermarket operations. In many ways, Steinberg's fits the entrepreneurial model rather well. Sam Steinberg, who joined his mother in the first store at the age of 11 and personally made a quick decision to expand it 2 years later, maintained complete formal control of the firm (including every single voting share) to the day of his death in 1978. He also exercised close managerial control over all its major decisions, at least until the firm began to diversify after 1960, primarily into other forms of retailing.

It has been popular to describe the "bold stroke" of the entrepreneur (Cole, 1959). In Steinberg's we saw only two major reorientations of strategy in the sixty years, moves into self-service in the 1930s and into the shopping center business in the 1950s. But the stroke was not bold so much as tested. The story of the move into self-service is indicative. In 1933 one of the company's eight stores "struck it bad," in the chief executive's words, incurring "unacceptable" losses ($125 a week). Sam Steinberg closed the store one Friday evening, converted it to self-service, changed its name from "Steinberg's Service Stores" to "Wholesale Groceteria," slashed its prices by 15–20%, printed handbills, stuffed them into neighborhood mailboxes, and reopened on Monday morning. That's strategic change! But only once these changes proved successful did he convert the other stores. Then, in his words, "We grew like Topsy."

This anecdote tells us something about the bold stroke of the entrepreneur—"controlled boldness" is a better expression. The ideas were bold, the execution careful. Sam Steinberg could have simply closed the one unprofitable store. Instead he used it to create a new vision, but he tested that vision, however ambitiously, before leaping into it. Notice the interplay here of problems and opportunities. Steinberg took what most businessmen would probably have perceived as a *problem* (how to cut the losses in one store) and by treating it as a *crisis* (what is wrong with our *general* operation that produces these losses) turned it into an *opportunity* (we can grow more effectively with a new concept of retailing). That was how he got energy behind actions and kept ahead of his competitors. He "oversolved" his problem and thereby remade his company, a characteristic of some of the most effective forms of entrepreneurship.

But absolutely central to this form of entrepreneurship is intimate, detailed knowledge of the business or of analogous business situations, the "repetition" discussed earlier. The leader as conventional strategic "planner"—the so-called architect of strategy—sits on a pedestal and is fed aggregate data that he or she uses to "formulate" strategies that are "implemented" by others. But the history of Steinberg's belies that image. It suggests that clear, imaginative, integrated strategic vision depends on an involvement with detail, an intimate knowledge of specifics. And by closely controlling "implementation" personally, the leader is able to reformulate en route, to adapt the evolving vision through his or her own process of learning. That is why Steinberg tried his new ideas in one store first. And that is why, in discussing his firm's competitive advantage, he told us: "Nobody knew the grocery business like we did. Everything has to do with your knowledge." He added: "I knew merchandise, I knew cost. I knew selling, I knew customers. I knew everything . . . and I passed on all my knowledge; I kept teaching my people. That's the advantage we had. They couldn't touch us."

Such knowledge can be incredibly effective when concentrated in one individual who is fully in charge (having no need to convince others, not subordinates below, not superiors at some distant headquarters, nor market analysts looking for superficial pronouncements) and who retains a strong, long-term commitment to the organization. So long as the business is simple and focused enough to be comprehended in one brain, the entrepreneurial approach is powerful, indeed unexcelled. Nothing else can provide so clear and complete a vision, yet also allow the flexibility to elaborate and rework that vision when necessary. The conception of a new strategy is an exercise in synthesis, which is typically best carried out in a single, informed brain. That is why the entrepreneurial approach is at the center of the most glorious corporate successes.

But in its strength lies entrepreneurship's weakness. Bear in mind that strategy for the entrepreneurial leader is not a formal, detailed plan on paper. It is a personal vision, a concept of the business, locked in a single brain. It may need to get "represented," in words and metaphors, but that must remain general if the leader is to maintain the richness and flexibility of his or her concept. But success breeds a large organization, public financing, and the need for formal planning. The vision must be articulated to drive others and gain their support, and that threatens the personal nature of the vision. At the limit, as we shall see later in the case of Steinberg's, the leader can get captured by his or her very success.

In Steinberg's, moreover, when success in the traditional business encouraged diversification into new ones (new regions, new forms of retailing, new industries), the organization moved beyond the realm of its leader's personal comprehension, and the entrepreneurial mode of strategy formation lost its viability. Strategy making became more decentralized, more analytic, in some ways more careful, but at the same time less visionary, less integrated, less flexible, and ironically, less deliberate.

CONCEIVING A NEW VISION IN A GARMENT FIRM

The genius of an entrepreneur like Sam Steinberg was his ability to pursue one vision (self-service and everything that entailed) faithfully for decades and then, based on a weak signal in the environment (the building of the first small shopping center in Montreal), to realize the need to shift that vision. The planning literature makes a big issue of forecasting such discontinuities, but as far as I know there are no formal techniques to do so effectively (claims about "scenario analysis" notwithstanding). The ability to perceive a sudden shift in an established pattern and then to conceive a new vision to deal with it appears to remain largely in the realm of informed intuition, generally the purview of the wise, experienced, and energetic leader. Again, the literature is largely silent on this. But another of our studies, also concerning entrepreneurship, did reveal some aspects of this process.

Canadelle produces women's undergarments, primarily brassieres. It too was a highly successful organization, although not on the same scale as Steinberg's. Things were going well for the company in the late 1960s, under the personal leadership of Larry Nadler, the son of its founder, when suddenly everything changed. A sexual revolution of sorts was accompanying broader social manifestations, with bra burning a symbol of its resistance. For a manufacturer of brassieres the threat was obvious. For many other women the miniskirt had come to dominate the fashion scene, obsoleting the girdle and giving rise to pantyhose. As the executives of Canadelle put it, "the bottom fell out of the girdle business." The whole environment—long so receptive to the company's strategies—seemed to turn on it all at once.

At the time, a French company had entered the Quebec market with a light, sexy, molded garment called "Huit," using the theme, "just like not wearing a bra." Their target market was 15–20-year-olds. Though the product was expensive when it landed in Quebec and did not fit well in Nadler's opinion, it sold well. Nadler flew to France in an attempt to license the product for manufacture in Canada. The French firm refused, but, in Nadler's words, what he learned in "that one hour in their offices made the trip worthwhile." He realized that what women wanted was a more natural look, not no bra but less bra. Another trip shortly afterward, to a sister American firm, convinced him of the importance of market segmentation by age and life-style. That led him to the realization that the firm had two markets, one for the more mature customer, for whom the brassiere was a cosmetic to look and feel more attractive, and another for the younger customer who wanted to look and feel more natural.

Those two events led to a major shift in strategic vision. The CEO described it as sudden, the confluence of different ideas to create a new mental set. In his words, "all of a sudden the idea forms." Canadelle reconfirmed its commitment to the brassiere business, seeking greater market share while its competitors were cutting back. It introduced a new line of more natural brassieres for the younger customers, for which the firm had to work out the molding technology as well as a new approach to promotion.

We can draw on Kurt Lewin's (1951) three-stage model of unfreezing, changing, and refreezing to explain such a gestalt shift in vision. The process of *unfreezing* is essentially one of overcoming the natural defense mechanisms, the established "mental set" of how an industry is supposed to operate, to realize that things have changed fundamentally. The old assumptions no longer hold. Effective managers, especially effective strategic managers, are supposed to scan their environments continually, looking for such changes. But doing so continuously, or worse, trying to use technique to do so, may have exactly the opposite effect. So much attention may be given to strategic monitoring when nothing important is happening that when something really does, it may not even be noticed. The trick, of course, is to pick out the discontinuities that matter, and as noted earlier that seems to have more to do with informed intuition than anything else.

A second step in unfreezing is the willingness to step into the void, so to speak, for the leader to shed his or her conventional notions of how a business is supposed to function. The leader must above all avoid premature closure—seizing on a new thrust before it has become clear what its signals really mean. That takes a special kind of management, one able to live with a good deal of uncertainty and discomfort. "There is a period of confusion," Nadler told us, "you sleep on it . . . start looking for patterns . . . become an information hound, searching for [explanations] everywhere."

Strategic *change* of this magnitude seems to require a shift in mind-set before a new strategy can be conceived. And the thinking is fundamentally conceptual and inductive, probably stimulated (as in this case) by just one or two key insights. Continuous bombardment of facts, opinions, problems, and so on may prepare the mind for the shift, but it is the sudden *insight* that is likely to drive the synthesis—to bring all the disparate elements together in one "eureka"-type flash.

Once the strategist's mind is set, assuming he or she has read the new situation correctly and has not closed prematurely, then the *refreezing* process begins. Here the object is not to read the situation, at least not in a global sense, but in effect to block it out. It is a time to work out the consequences of the new strategic vision.

It has been claimed that obsession is an ingredient in effective organizations (Peters, 1980). Only for the period of refreezing would we agree, when the organization must focus on the pursuit of the new orientation—the new mind-set—with full vigor. A management that was open and divergent in its thinking must now become closed and convergent. But that means that the uncomfortable period of uncertainty has passed, and people can now get down to the exciting task of accomplishing something new. Now the organization knows where it is going; the object of the exercise is to get there using all the skills at its command, many of them formal and analytic. Of course, not everyone accepts the new vision. For those steeped in old strategies, *this* is the period of discomfort, and they can put up considerable resistance, forcing the leader to make greater use of his or her formal powers and political skills. Thus, refreezing of the leader's mind-set often involves the unfreezing, changing, and refreezing of the organization itself! But when the structure is simple, as it is in the entrepreneurial organization, that problem is relatively minor.

LEADERSHIP TAKING PRECEDENCE IN THE ENTREPRENEURIAL CONFIGURATION

To conclude, entrepreneurship is very much tied up with the creation of strategic vision, often with the attainment of a new concept. Strategies can be characterized as largely deliberate, since they reside in the intentions of a single leader. But being largely personal as well, the details of those strategies can emerge as they develop. In fact, the vision can change too. The leader can adapt en route, can learn, which means new visions can emerge too, sometimes, as we have seen, rather quickly.

In the entrepreneurial organization, as shown in Figure 2, the focus of attention is on the leader. The organization is malleable and responsive to that person's initiatives, while the environment remains benign for the most part, the result of the leader's selecting (or "enacting") the correct niche for his or her organization. The environment can, of course,

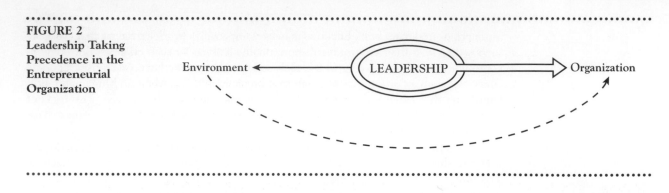

flare up occasionally to challenge the organization, and then the leader must adapt, perhaps seeking out a new and more appropriate niche in which to operate.

Some Issues Associated with the Entrepreneurial Organization

We conclude briefly with some broad issues associated with the entrepreneurial organization. In this configuration, decisions concerning both strategy and operations tend to be centralized in the office of the chief executive. This centralization has the important advantage of rooting strategic response in deep knowledge of the operations. It also allows for flexibility and adaptability: Only one person need act. But this same executive can get so enmeshed in operating problems that he or she loses sight of strategy; alternatively, he or she may become so enthusiastic about strategic opportunities that the more routine operations can wither for lack of attention and eventually pull down the whole organization. Both are frequent occurrences in entrepreneurial organizations.

This is also the riskiest of organizations, hinging on the activities of one individual. One heart attack can literally wipe out the organization's prime means of coordination. Even a leader in place can be risky. When change becomes necessary, everything hinges on the chief's response to it. If he or she resists, as is not uncommon where that person developed the existing strategy in the first place, then the organization may have no means to adapt. Then the great strength of the entrepreneurial organization—the vision of its leader plus its capacity to respond quickly—becomes its chief liability.

Another great advantage of the entrepreneurial organization is its sense of mission. Many people enjoy working in a small, intimate organization where the leader—often charismatic—knows where he or she is taking it. As a result, the organization tends to grow rapidly, with great enthusiasm. Employees can develop a solid identification with such an organization.

But other people perceive this configuration as highly restrictive. Because one person calls all the shots, they feel not like the participants on an exciting journey, but like cattle being led to market for someone else's benefit. In fact, the broadening of democratic norms into the sphere of organizations has rendered the entrepreneurial organization unfashionable in some quarters of contemporary society. It has been described as paternalistic and sometimes autocratic, and accused of concentrating too much power at the top. Certainly, without countervailing powers in the organization the chief executive can easily abuse his or her authority.

Perhaps the entrepreneurial organization is an anachronism in societies that call themselves democratic. Yet there have always been such organizations, and there always will be. This was probably the only structure known to those who first discovered the benefits of coordinating their activities in some formal way. And it probably reached its heyday in the era of the great American trusts of the late nineteenth century, when powerful entrepreneurs personally controlled huge empires. Since then, at least in Western society, the entrepreneurial organization has been on the decline. Nonetheless, it remains a prevalent and important configuration, and will continue to be so as long as society faces the conditions that require it: the prizing of entrepreneurial initiative and the resultant encouragement of new organizations, the need for small and informal organizations in some spheres and of strong personalized leadership despite larger size in others, and the need periodically to turn around ailing organizations of all types.

▼ READING 9.2 COMPETITIVE STRATEGY IN EMERGING INDUSTRIES*

*by Michael E.
Porter*

Emerging industries are newly formed or reformed industries that have been created by technological innovations, shifts in relative cost relationships, emergence of new consumer needs, or other economic and sociological changes that elevate a new product or service to the level of a potentially viable business opportunity. . . .

The essential characteristic of an emerging industry from the viewpoint of formulating strategy is that there are no rules of the game. The competitive problem in an emerging industry is that all the rules must be established such that the firm can cope with and prosper under them.

The Structural Environment

Although emerging industries can differ a great deal in their structures, there are some common structural factors that seem to characterize many industries in this stage of their development. Most of them relate either to the absence of established bases for competition or other rules of the game or to the initial small size and newness of the industry.

COMMON STRUCTURAL CHARACTERISTICS

TECHNOLOGICAL UNCERTAINTY
There is usually a great deal of uncertainty about the technology in an emerging industry: What product configuration will ultimately prove to be the best? Which production technology will prove to be the most efficient? . . .

STRATEGIC UNCERTAINTY
. . . No "right" strategy has been clearly identified, and different firms are groping with different approaches to product/market positioning, marketing, servicing, and so on, as well as betting on different product configurations or production technologies . . . . Closely related to this problem, firms often have poor information about competitors, characteristics of customers, and industry conditions in the emerging phase. No one knows who all the competitors are, and reliable industry sales and market share data are often simply unavailable, for example.

High Initial Costs but Steep Cost Reduction

Small production volume and newness usually combine to produce high costs in the emerging industry relative to those the industry can potentially achieve. . . . Ideas come rapidly in terms of improved procedures, plant layout, and so on, and employees achieve major gains in productivity as job familiarity increases. Increasing sales make major additions to the scale and total accumulated volume of output produced by firms . . . .

Embryonic Companies and Spin-Offs

The emerging phase of the industry is usually accompanied by the presence of the greatest proportion of newly formed companies (to be contrasted with newly formed units of established firms) that the industry will ever experience. . . .

First-Time Buyers

Buyers of the emerging industry's product or service are inherently first-time buyers. The marketing task is thus one of inducing substitution, or getting the buyer to purchase the new product or service instead of something else. . . .

Short Time Horizon

In many emerging industries the pressure to develop customers or produce products to meet demand is so great that bottlenecks and problems are dealt with expediently rather than as a result of an analysis of future conditions. At the same time, industry conventions are often born out of pure chance. . . .

Subsidy

In many emerging industries, especially those with radical new technology or that address areas of societal concern, there may be subsidization of early entrants. Subsidy may come from a variety of government and nongovernment sources. . . . Subsidies often add a great degree of instability to an industry, which is made dependent on political decisions that can be quickly reversed or modified. . . .

EARLY MOBILITY BARRIERS

In an emerging industry, the configuration of mobility barriers is often predictably different from that which will characterize the industry later in its development. Common early barriers are the following:

▼ proprietary technology
▼ access to distribution channels
▼ access to raw materials and other inputs (skilled labor) of appropriate cost and quality
▼ cost advantages due to experience, made more significant by the technological and competitive uncertainties
▼ risk, which raises the effective opportunity cost of capital and thereby effective capital barriers

. . . The nature of the early barriers is a key reason why we observe newly created companies in emerging industries. The typical early barriers stem less from the need to command massive resources than from the ability to bear risk, be creative technologically, and make forward-looking decisions to garner input supplies and distribution channels. . . . There may be some advantages to late entry, however. . . .

STRATEGIC CHOICES

Formulation of strategy in emerging industries must cope with the uncertainty and risk of this period of an industry's development. The rules of the competitive game are largely undefined, the structure of the industry unsettled and probably changing, and competitors hard to diagnose. Yet all these factors have another side—the emerging phase of an industry's development is probably the period when the strategic degrees of freedom are the greatest and when the leverage from good strategic choices is the highest in determining performance.

SHAPING INDUSTRY STRUCTURE

The overriding strategic issue in emerging industries is the ability of the firm to shape industry structure. Through its choices, the firm can try to set the rules of the game in areas like product policy, marketing approach, and pricing strategy. . . .

EXTERNALITIES IN INDUSTRY DEVELOPMENT

In an emerging industry, a key strategic issue is the balance the firm strikes between industry advocacy and pursuing its own narrow self-interest. Because of potential problems with industry image, credibility, and confusion of buyers . . . in the emerging phase the firm is in part dependent on others in the industry for its own success. The overriding problem for the industry is inducing substitution and attracting first-time buyers, and it is usually in the firm's interest during this phase to help promote standardization, police substandard quality and fly-by-night producers, and present a consistent front to suppliers, customers, government, and the financial community. . . .

It is probably a valid generalization that the balance between industry outlook and firm outlook must shift in the direction of the firm as the industry begins to achieve significant penetration. Sometimes firms who have taken very high profiles as industry spokespersons, much to their and the industry's benefit, fail to recognize that they must shift their orientation. As a result, they can be left behind as the industry matures. . . .

CHANGING ROLE OF SUPPLIERS AND CHANNELS

Strategically, the firm in an emerging industry must be prepared for a possible shift in the orientation of its suppliers and distribution channels as the industry grows in size and proves itself. Suppliers may become increasingly willing (or can be forced) to respond to the industry's special needs in terms of varieties, service, and delivery. Similarly, distribution channels may become more receptive to investing in facilities, advertising, and so forth in partnership with the firms. Early exploitation of these changes in orientation can give the firm strategic leverage.

SHIFTING MOBILITY BARRIERS

As outlined earlier . . . the early mobility barriers may erode quickly in an emerging industry, often to be replaced by very different ones as the industry grows in size and as the technology matures. This factor has a number of implications. The most obvious is that the firm must be prepared to find new ways to defend its position and must not rely solely on things like proprietary technology and a unique product variety on which it has succeeded in the past. Responding to shifting mobility barriers may involve commitments of capital that far exceed those that have been necessary in the early phases.

Another implication is that the *nature of entrants* into the industry may shift to more established firms attracted to the larger and increasingly proven (less risky) industry, often competing on the basis of the newer forms of mobility barriers, like scale and marketing clout. . . .

TIMING ENTRY

A crucial strategic choice for competing in emerging industries is the appropriate timing of entry. Early entry (or pioneering) involves high risk but may involve otherwise low entry barriers and can offer a large return. Early entry is appropriate when the following general circumstances hold:

▼ Image and reputation of the firm are important to the buyer, and the firm can develop an enhanced reputation by being a pioneer.

▼ Early entry can initiate the learning process in a business in which the learning curve is important, experience is difficult to imitate, and it will not be nullified by successive technological generations.

▼ Customer loyalty will be great, so that benefits will accrue to the firm that sells to the customer first.

▼ Absolute cost advantages can be gained by early commitment to supplies of raw materials, distribution channels, and so on. . . .

TACTICAL MOVES

The problems limiting development of an emerging industry suggest some tactical moves that may improve the firm's strategic position:

▼ Early commitments to suppliers of raw materials will yield favorable priorities in times of shortages.

▼ Financing can be timed to take advantage of a Wall Street love affair with the industry if it happens, even if financing is ahead of actual needs. This step lowers the firm's cost of capital. . . .

The choice of which emerging industry to enter is dependent on the outcome of a predictive exercise such as the one described above. An emerging industry is attractive if its ultimate structure (not its *initial* structure) is one that is consistent with above-average returns and if the firm can create a defendable position in the industry in the long run. The latter will depend on its resources relative to the mobility barriers that will evolve.

Too often firms enter emerging industries because they are growing rapidly, because incumbents are currently very profitable, or because ultimate industry size promises to be large. These may be contributing reasons, but the decision to enter must ultimately depend on a structural analysis. . . .

▼ READING 9.3 HOW ENTREPRENEURS CRAFT STRATEGIES THAT WORK*

by Amar Bhide

However popular it may be in the corporate world, a comprehensive analytical approach to planning doesn't suit most start-ups. Entrepreneurs typically lack the time and money to interview a representative cross section of potential customers, let alone analyze substitutes, reconstruct competitors' cost structures, or project alternative technology scenarios. In fact, too much analysis can be harmful; by the time an opportunity is investigated fully, it may no longer exist. A city map and restaurant guide on a CD may be a winner in January but worthless if delayed until December.

Interviews with the founders of 100 companies on the 1989 Inc. "500" list of the fastest growing private companies in the United States and recent research on more than 100

* Originally published as "How Entrepreneurs Craft Strategies that Work," in the *Harvard Business Review*, March–April 1994, pp. 150–161. Copyright © 1994 by the President and Fellows of Harvard College; all rights reserved. Reprinted with deletions by permission of the *Harvard Business Review*.

other thriving ventures by my MBA students suggest that many successful entrepreneurs spend little time researching and analyzing. . . . And those who do often have to scrap their strategies and start over. Furthermore, a 1990 National Federation of Independent Business study of 2,994 start-ups showed that founders who spent a long time in study, reflection, and planning were no more likely to survive their first three years than people who seized opportunities without planning. In fact, many corporations that revere comprehensive analysis develop a refined incapacity for seizing opportunities. Analysis can delay entry until it's too late or kill ideas by identifying numerous problems.

Yet all ventures merit some analysis and planning. Appearances to the contrary, successful entrepreneurs don't take risks blindly. Rather, they use a quick, cheap approach that represents a middle ground between planning paralysis and no planning at all. They don't expect perfection—even the most astute entrepreneurs have their share of false starts. Compared to typical corporate practice, however, the entrepreneurial approach is more economical and timely.

What are the critical elements of winning entrepreneurial approaches? Our evidence suggests three general guidelines for aspiring founders:

1. Screen opportunities quickly to weed out unpromising ventures.
2. Analyze ideas parsimoniously. Focus on a few important ideas.
3. Integrate action and analysis. Don't wait for all the answers, and be ready to change course.

SCREENING OUT LOSERS

Individuals who seek entrepreneurial opportunities usually generate lots of ideas. Quickly discarding those that have low potential frees aspirants to concentrate on the few ideas that merit refinement and study.

Screening out unpromising ventures requires judgment and reflection, not new data. The entrepreneur should already be familiar with the facts needed to determine whether an idea has prima facie merit. Our evidence suggests that new ventures are usually started to solve problems the founders have grappled with personally as customers or employees. . . . Companies like Federal Express, which grew out of a paper its founder wrote in college, are rare.

Profitable survival requires an edge derived from some combination of a creative idea and a superior capacity for execution. . . . The entrepreneur's creativity may involve an innovative product or a process that changes the existing order. Or the entrepreneur may have a unique insight about the course or consequence of an external change: the California gold rush, for example, made paupers of the thousands caught in the frenzy, but Levi Strauss started a company—and a legend—by recognizing the opportunity to supply rugged canvas and later denim trousers to prospectors.

But entrepreneurs cannot rely on just inventing new products or anticipating a trend. They must also execute well, especially if their concepts can be copied easily. For example, if an innovation cannot be patented or kept secret, entrepreneurs must acquire and manage the resource needed to build a brand name or other barrier that will deter imitators. Superior execution can also compensate for a me-too concept in emerging or rapidly growing industries where doing it quickly and doing it right are more important than brilliant strategy.

Ventures that obviously lack a creative concept or any special capacity to execute—the ex-consultant's scheme to exploit grandmother's cookie recipe, for instance—can be discarded without much thought. In other cases, entrepreneurs must reflect on the adequacy of their ideas and their capacities to execute them.

Successful start-ups don't need an edge on every front. The creativity of successful entrepreneurs varies considerably. Some implement a radical idea, some modify, and some show no originality. Capacity for execution also varies among entrepreneurs. Selling an industrial niche product doesn't call for the charisma that's required to pitch trinkets through infomercials. Our evidence suggests that there is no ideal entrepreneurial profile either: successful founders can be gregarious or taciturn, analytical or intuitive, good or terrible with details, risk averse or thrill seeking. They can be delegators or control freaks, pillars of the community or outsiders. In assessing the viability of a potential venture, therefore, each aspiring entrepreneur should consider three interacting factors:

1. OBJECTIVES OF THE VENTURE

Is the entrepreneur's goal to build a large, enduring enterprise, carve out a niche, or merely turn a quick profit? Ambitious goals require great creativity. Building a large enterprise quickly, either by seizing a significant share of an existing market or by creating a large new market, usually calls for a revolutionary idea. . . .

Requirements for execution are also stiff. Big ideas often necessitate big money and strong organizations. Successful entrepreneurs, therefore, require an evangelical ability to attract, retain, and balance the interests of investors, customers, employees, and suppliers for a seemingly outlandish vision, as well as the organizational and leadership skills to build a large, complex company quickly. In addition, the entrepreneur may require considerable technical know-how in deal making, strategic planning, managing overhead, and other business skills. The revolutionary entrepreneur, in other words, would appear to require almost superhuman qualities: ordinary mortals need not apply.

Consider Federal Express founder Fred Smith. His creativity lay in recognizing that customers would pay a significant premium for reliable overnight delivery and in figuring out a way to provide the service for them. Smith ruled out using existing commercial flights, whose schedules were designed to serve passenger traffic. Instead, he had the audacious idea of acquiring a dedicated fleet of jets and shipping all packages through a central hub that was located in Memphis.

As with most big ideas, the concept was difficult to execute. Smith, 28 years old at the time, had to raise $91 million in venture funding. The jets, the hub, operations in 25 states, and several hundred trained employees had to be in place before the company could open for business. And Smith needed great fortitude and skill to prevent the fledgling enterprise from going under: Federal Express lost over $40 million in its first three years. Some investors tried to remove Smith, and creditors tried to seize assets. Yet Smith somehow preserved morale and mollified investors and lenders while the company expanded its operations and launched national advertising and direct-mail campaigns to build market share.

In contrast, ventures that seek to capture a market niche, not transform or create an industry, don't need extraordinary ideas. Some ingenuity is necessary to design a product that will draw customers away from mainstream offerings and overcome the cost penalty of serving a small market. But features that are too novel can be a hindrance; a niche market will rarely justify the investment required to educate customers and distributors about the benefits of a radically new product. Similarly, a niche venture cannot support too much production or distribution innovation; unlike Federal Express, the Cape Cod Potato Company, for example, must work within the limits of its distributors and truckers.

And since niche markets cannot support much investment or overhead, entrepreneurs do not need the revolutionary's ability to raise capital and build large organizations. Rather, the entrepreneur must be able to secure others' resources on favorable terms and make do with less, building brand awareness through guerrilla marketing and word of mouth instead of national advertising, for example.

Jay Boberg and Miles Copeland, who launched International Record Syndicate (IRS) in 1979, used a niche strategy, my students Elisabeth Bentel and Victoria Hackett found, to create one of the most successful new music labels in North America. Lacking the funds or a great innovation to compete against the major labels, Boberg and Miles promoted "alternative" music—undiscovered British groups like the buzzcocks and Skafish—which the major labels were ignoring because their potential sales were too small. And IRS used low-cost, alternative marketing methods to promote their alternative music. At the time, the major record labels had not yet realized that music videos on television could be used effectively to promote their products. Boberg, however, jumped at the opportunity to produce a rock show, "The Cutting Edge," for MTV. The show proved to be a hit with fans and an effective promotional tool for IRS. Before "The Cutting Edge," Boberg had to plead with radio stations to play his songs. Afterward, the MTV audience demanded that disc jockeys play the songs they had heard on the show.

2. Leverage Provided by External Change

Exploiting opportunities in a new or changing industry is generally easier than making waves in a mature industry. Enormous creativity, experience, and contacts are needed to take business away from competitors in a mature industry, where market forces have long shaken out weak technologies, strategies, and organizations.

But new markets are different. There start-ups often face rough-around-the-edges rivals, customers who tolerate inexperienced vendors and imperfect products, and opportunities to profit from shortages. Small insights and marginal innovations, a little skill or expertise (in the land of the blind, the one-eyed person is king), and the willingness to act quickly can go a long way. In fact, with great external uncertainty, customers and investors may be hesitant to back a radical product and technology until the environment settles down. Strategic choices in a new industry are often very limited; entrepreneurs have to adhere to the emerging standards for product features, components, or distribution channels.

The leverage provided by external change is illustrated by the success of numerous start-ups in hardware, software, training, retailing, and systems integration that emerged from the personal computer revolution of the 1980s. Installing or fixing a computer system is probably easier than repairing a car; but because people with the initiative or foresight to acquire the skill were scarce, entrepreneurs like Bohdan's Peter Zacharkiw built successful dealerships by providing what customers saw as exceptional service. . . . As one Midwestern dealer told me, "We have a joke slogan around here: We aren't as incompetent as our competitors!"

Bill Gates turned Microsoft into a multibillion-dollar company without a breakthrough product by showing up in the industry early and capitalizing on the opportunities that came his way. Gates, then 19, and his partner Paul Allen, 21, launched Microsoft in 1975 to sell software they had created. By 1979, Microsoft had grown to 25 employees and $2.5 million in sales. Then in November 1980, IBM chose Microsoft to provide an operating system for its personal computer. Microsoft thereupon bought an operating system from Seattle Computer Products, which it modified into the now ubiquitous MS-DOS. The IBM name and the huge success of the 1-2-3 spreadsheet, which only ran on DOS computers, soon helped make Microsoft the dominant supplier of operating systems.

3. Basis of Competition: Proprietary Assets versus Hustle

In some industries, such as pharmaceuticals, luxury hotels, and consumer goods, a company's profitability depends significantly on the assets it owns or controls—patents, location, or brands, for example. Good management practices like listening to customers, maintaining quality, and paying attention to costs, which can improve the profits of a going business, cannot propel a start-up over such structural barriers. Here a creative new technology, product, or strategy is a must.

Companies in fragmented service industries, such as investment management, investment banking, head hunting, or consulting cannot establish proprietary advantages easily but can nonetheless enjoy high profits by providing exceptional service tailored to client demands. Start-ups in those fields rely mainly on their hustle (Bhide, 1986). Successful entrepreneurs depend on personal selling skills, contacts, their reputations for expertise, and their ability to convince clients of the value of the services rendered. They also have the capacity for institution building—skills such as recruiting and motivating stellar professionals and articulating and reinforcing company values. Where there are few natural economies of scale, an entrepreneur cannot create a going concern out of a one-man-band or ad hoc ensemble without a lot of expertise in organizational development. . . .

GAUGING ATTRACTIVENESS

Entrepreneurs should also screen potential ventures for their attractiveness—their risks and rewards—compared to other opportunities. Several factors should be considered. Capital requirements, for example, matter to the entrepreneur who lacks easy access to financial markets. An unexpected need for cash because, say, one large customer is unable to make a timely payment may shut down a venture or force a fire sale of the founder's equity. Therefore, entrepreneurs should favor ventures that aren't capital intensive and have the profit margins to sustain rapid growth with internally generated funds. In a similar fashion, entrepreneurs should look for a high margin for error, ventures with simple operations and low fixed costs that are less likely to face a cash crunch because of factors such as technical delays, cost overruns, and slow buildup of sales.

Other criteria reflect the typical entrepreneur's inability to undertake multiple projects: an attractive venture should provide a substantial enough reward to compensate the entrepreneur's exclusive commitment to it. Shut-down costs should be low: the payback should be quick, or failure soon recognized so that the venture can be terminated without a significant loss of time, money, or reputation. And the entrepreneur should have the option to cash in, for example, by selling all or part of the equity. An entrepreneur locked into an illiquid business cannot easily pursue other opportunities and risks fatigue and burnout. . . .

Ventures must also fit what the individual entrepreneur values and wants to do. Surviving the inevitable disappointments and near disasters one encounters on the rough road to success requires a passion for the chosen business. . . .

Surprisingly, small endeavors often hold more financial promise than large ones. Often the founders can keep a larger share of the profits because they don't dilute their equity interest through multiple rounds of financings. But entrepreneurs must be willing to prosper in a backwater; dominating a neglected market segment is sometimes more profitable than intellectually stimulating or glamorous. Niche enterprises can also enter the "land of the living dead" because their market is too small for the business to thrive but the entrepreneur has invested too much effort to be willing to quit. . . .

PARSIMONIOUS PLANNING AND ANALYSIS

To conserve time and money, successful entrepreneurs minimize the resources they devote to researching their ideas. Unlike the corporate world, where foil mastery and completed staff work can make a career, the entrepreneur only does as much planning and analysis as seems useful and makes subjective judgment calls when necessary. . . .

In setting their analytical priorities, entrepreneurs must recognize that some critical uncertainties cannot be resolved through more research. For example, focus groups and surveys often have little value in predicting demand for products that are truly novel. At first, consumers had dismissed the need for copiers, for instance, and told researchers they were satisfied with using carbon paper. With issues like this, entrepreneurs have to resist the temptation of endless investigation and trust their judgment. . . .

Revenues are notoriously difficult to predict. At best, entrepreneurs may satisfy themselves that their novel product or service delivers considerably greater value than current offerings do; how quickly the product catches on is a blind guess. Leverage may be obtained, however, from analyzing how customers might buy and use the product or service. Understanding the purchase process can help identify the right decision makers for the new offering. With Federal Express, for instance, it was important to go beyond the mailroom managers who traditionally bought delivery services. Understanding how products are used can also help by revealing obstacles that must be overcome before consumers can benefit from a new offering.

Visionary entrepreneurs must guard against making competitors rich from their work. Many concepts are difficult to prove but, once proven, easy to imitate. Unless the pioneer is protected by sustainable barriers to entry, the benefits of a hard-fought revolution can become a public good rather than a boon to the innovator. . . .

Entrepreneurs who hope to secure a niche face different problems: they often fail because the costs of serving a specialized segment exceed the benefits to customers. Entrepreneurs should therefore analyze carefully the incremental costs of serving a niche and take into account their lack of scale and the difficulty of marketing to a small, diffused segment. And especially if the cost disadvantage is significant, entrepreneurs should determine whether their offering provides a significant performance benefit. Whereas established companies can vie for share through line extensions or marginal tailoring of their products and services, the start-up must really wow its target customers. A marginally tastier cereal won't knock Kellogg's Cornflakes off supermarket shelves.

Inadequate payoffs also pose a risk for ventures that address small markets. For example, a niche venture that can't support a direct sales force may not generate enough commissions to attract an independent broker or manufacturers' rep. Entrepreneurs will eventually lose interest too if the rewards aren't commensurate with their efforts. Therefore, the entrepreneur should make sure that everyone who contributes can expect a high, quick, or sustainable return even if the venture's total profits are small.

Entrepreneurs who seek to leverage factors like changing technologies, customer preferences, or regulations should avoid extensive analysis. Research conducted under conditions of such turbulence isn't reliable, and the importance of a quick response precludes spending the time to make sure every detail is covered. . . .

Analyzing whether or not the rewards for winning are commensurate with the risks, however, can be a more feasible and worthwhile exercise. In some technology races, success is predictably short-lived. In the disk-drive industry, for example, companies that succeed with one generation of products are often leap-frogged when the next generation arrives. In engineering workstations, however, Sun enjoyed long-term gains from its early success because it established a durable architectural standard. If success is unlikely to be sustained, entrepreneurs should have a plan for making a good return while it lasts. . . .

INTEGRATING ACTION AND ANALYSIS

Standard operating procedure in large corporations usually makes a clear distinction between analysis and execution. In contemplating a new venture, managers in established companies face issues about its fit with ongoing activities: Does the proposed venture leverage corporate strengths? Will the resources and attention it requires reduce the company's ability to build customer loyalty and improve quality in core markets? These concerns dictate a deliberate, "trustee" approach: before they can launch a venture, managers must investigate an opportunity extensively, seek the counsel of people higher up, submit a formal plan, respond to criticisms by bosses and corporate staff, and secure a headcount and capital allocation.

Entrepreneurs who start with a clean slate, however, don't have to know all the answers before they act. In fact, they often can't easily separate action and analysis. The attractiveness of a new restaurant, for example, may depend on the terms of the lease; low rents can change the venture from a mediocre proposition into a money machine. But an entrepreneur's ability to negotiate a good lease cannot be easily determined from a general prior analysis; he or she must enter into a serious negotiation with a specific landlord for a specific property.

Acting before an opportunity is fully analyzed has many benefits. Doing something concrete builds confidence in oneself and in others. Key employees and investors will often follow the individual who has committed to action, for instance, by quitting a job, incorporating, or signing a lease. By taking a personal risk, the entrepreneur convinces other people that the venture *will* proceed, and they may believe that if they don't sign up, they could be left behind.

Early action can generate more robust, better informed strategies too. Extensive surveys and focus-group research about a concept can produce misleading evidence: slippage can arise between research and reality because the potential customers interviewed are not representative of the market, their enthusiasm for the concept wanes when they see the actual product, or they lack the authority to sign purchase orders. More robust strategies may be developed by first building a working prototype and asking customers to use it before conducting extensive market research.

The ability of individual entrepreneurs to execute quickly will naturally vary. Trial and error is less feasible with large-scale, capital-intensive ventures like Orbital Sciences, which had to raise over $50 million to build rockets for NASA, than with a consulting firm start-up. Nevertheless, some characteristics are common to an approach that integrates action and analysis:

HANDLING ANALYTICAL TASKS IN STAGES

Rather than resolve all issues at once, the entrepreneur does only enough research to justify the next action or investment. For example, an individual who has developed a new medical technology may first obtain crude estimates of market demand to determine whether it's worth seeing a patent lawyer. If the estimates and lawyer are encouraging, the individual may do more analysis to investigate the wisdom of spending money to obtain a patent. Several more iterations of analysis and action will follow before the entrepreneur prepares and circulates a formal business plan to venture capitalists.

PLUGGING HOLES QUICKLY

As soon as any problems or risks show up, the entrepreneur begins looking for solutions. For example, suppose that an entrepreneur sees it will be difficult to raise capital. Rather than kill the idea, he or she thinks creatively about solving the problem. Perhaps the investment can be reduced by modifying technology to use more standard equipment that can be rented instead of bought. Or under the right terms, a customer might underwrite the risk by providing a large initial order. Or expectations and goals for growth might be scaled down, and a niche market could be tackled first. Except with obviously unviable ideas that can be ruled out through elementary logic, the purpose of analysis is not to find fault with new ventures or find reasons for abandoning them. Analysis is an exercise in what to do next more than what not to do.

EVANGELICAL INVESTIGATION

Entrepreneurs often blur the line between research and selling. As one founder recalls, "My market research consisted of taking a prototype to a trade show and seeing if I could write orders." Software industry "beta sites" provide another example of simultaneous research and selling; customers actually pay to help vendors test early versions of their software and will often place larger orders if they are satisfied with the product.

From the beginning, entrepreneurs don't just seek opinions and information, they also look for commitment from other people. Entrepreneurs treat everyone whom they talk to as a potential customer, investor, employee, or supplier, or at least as a possible source of leads down the road. Even if they don't actually ask for an order, they take the time to build enough interest and rapport so they can come back later. This simultaneous listening and selling approach may not produce truly objective market research and statistically significant results. But the resource-constrained entrepreneur doesn't have much choice in the matter. Besides, in the initial stages, the deep knowledge and support of a few is often more valuable than broad, impersonal data.

SMART ARROGANCE

An entrepreneur's willingness to act on sketchy plans and inconclusive data is often sustained by an almost arrogant self-confidence. One successful high-tech entrepreneur likens his kind to "gamblers in a casino who know they are good at craps and are therefore likely to win. They believe: 'I'm smarter, more creative, and harder working than most people. With my unique and rare skills, I'm doing investors a favor by taking their money.'" Moreover, the entrepreneur's arrogance must stand the test of adversity. Entrepreneurs must have great confidence in their talent and ideas to persevere as customers stay away in droves, the product doesn't work, or the business runs out of cash.

But entrepreneurs who believe they are more capable or venturesome than others must also have the smarts to recognize their mistakes and to change their strategies as events unfold. Successful ventures don't always proceed in the direction on which they initially set out. A significant proportion develop entirely new markets, products, and sources of competitive advantage. Therefore, although perseverance and tenacity are valuable entrepreneurial traits, they must be complemented with flexibility and a willingness to learn. If prospects who were expected to place orders don't, the entrepreneur should consider reworking the concept. Similarly, the entrepreneur should also be prepared to exploit opportunities that didn't figure in the initial plan. . . .

The apparently sketchy planning and haphazard evolution of many successful ventures . . . doesn't mean that entrepreneurs should follow a ready-fire-aim approach. Despite appearances, astute entrepreneurs do analyze and strategize extensively. They realize, however, that businesses cannot be launched like space shuttles, with every detail of the mission planned in advance. Initial analyses only provide plausible hypotheses, which must be tested and modified. Entrepreneurs should play with and explore ideas, letting their strategies evolve through a seamless process of guesswork, analysis, and action.

THE MATURE CONTEXT

In this chapter, we focus on what has historically been one of the more common contexts for organizations. Whether we refer to this by its form of operations (usually mass production or the mass provision of services), by the form of structure adopted (machine-like bureaucracy), by the type of environment it prefers (a stable one in a mature industry), or by the specific generic strategy often found there (low cost), the context tends to give rise to certain relatively well-defined configurations. This context has received bad press of late, but don't think that it has gone away. Amidst all the talk of change, turbulence, and hypercompetition, this context remains common, indeed quite possibly still the most common of contexts an executive is likely to encounter. Bureaucracy has not left large organizations, private or public, we assure you!

The readings on what we shall refer to as the *mature* context cover these different aspects and examine some of the problems and opportunities of functioning in this realm. The first reading, on the machine organization, from Mintzberg's work, describes the structure for this context as well as the environment in which it tends to be found, and also investigates some of the social issues surrounding this particular form of organization. This reading also probes the nature of the strategy-making process in this context. Here we can see what happens when large organizations accustomed to stability suddenly have to change their strategies dramatically. The careful formal planning, on which they tend to rely so heavily in easier times, seems ill suited to dealing with changes that may require virtual revolutions in their functioning. A section of this reading thus considers what can be the role of planners when their formal procedures fail to come to grips with the needs of strategy making.

A particular technique designed for use with this strategy, and the mature context in general, is the subject of the second reading. Called "Cost Dynamics: Scale and Experience Effects" and written by Derek Abell and John Hammond for a marketing textbook, it probes the "experience curve." Developed by the Boston Consulting Group some years ago, this technique became quite popular in the 1970s. Although its limitations are now widely recognized, it still has certain applications to firms operating in the mature context.

by Henry Mintzberg

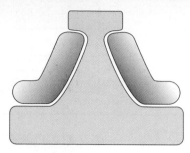

A national post office, a custodial prison, an airline, a giant automobile company, even a small security agency—all these organizations appear to have a number of characteristics in common. Above all, their operating work is routine, the greatest part of it rather simple and repetitive; as a result, their work processes are highly standardized. These characteristics give rise to the machine organizations of our society, structures fine-tuned to run as integrated, regulated, highly bureaucratic machines.

The Basic Structure

A clear configuration of the attributes has appeared consistently in the research: highly specialized, routine operating tasks; very formalized communication throughout the organization; large-size operating units; reliance on the functional basis for grouping tasks; relatively centralized power for decision making; and an elaborate administrative structure with a sharp distinction between line and staff.

THE OPERATING CORE AND ADMINISTRATION

The obvious starting point is the operating core, with its highly rationalized work flow. This means that the operating tasks are made simple and repetitive, generally requiring a minimum of skill and training, the latter often taking only hours, seldom more than a few weeks, and usually in-house. This in turn results in narrowly defined jobs and an emphasis on the standardization of work processes for coordination. with activities highly formalized. The workers are left with little discretion, as are their supervisors, who can therefore handle very large spans of control.

To achieve such high regulation of the operating work, the organization has need for an elaborate administrative structure—fully developed middle-line hierarchy and technostructure—but the two clearly distinguished.

The managers of the middle line have three prime tasks. One is to handle the disturbances that arise in the operating core. The work is so standardized that when things fall through the cracks, conflict flares, because the problems cannot be worked out informally.

* Adapted from *The Structure of Organizations* (Prentice Hall, 1979), Chap. 18 on "The Machine Bureaucracy"; also *Power In and Around Organizations* (Prentice Hall, 1983), Chaps. 18 and 19 on "The Instrument" and "The Closed System"; the material on strategy formation from "Patterns in Strategy Formation," *Management Science* (1978); "Does Planning Impede Strategic Thinking? Tracking the Strategies of Air Canada, from 1937–1976" (coauthored with Pierre Brunet and Jim Waters), in R. B. Lamb and P. Shrivastava, eds., *Advances in Strategic Management*, Volume IV (JAI press, 1986); and "The Mind of the Strategist(s)" (coauthored with Jim Waters), in S. Srivastva, ed., *The Executive Mind* (Jossey-Bass, 1983); the section on the role of planning, plans, and planners is drawn from a book in process on strategic planning. A chapter similar to this appeared in *Mintzberg on Management: Inside Our Strange World of Organizations* (Free Press, 1989).

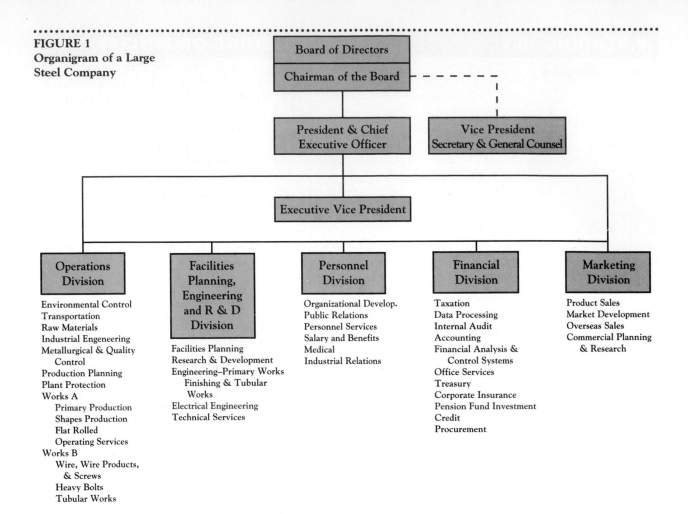

FIGURE 1
Organigram of a Large Steel Company

Board of Directors

Chairman of the Board

President & Chief Executive Officer

Vice President
Secretary & General Counsel

Executive Vice President

Operations Division

Environmental Control
Transportation
Raw Materials
Industrial Engeneering
Metallurgical & Quality
   Control
Production Planning
Plant Protection
Works A
   Primary Production
   Shapes Production
   Flat Rolled
   Operating Services
Works B
   Wire, Wire Products,
     & Screws
   Heavy Bolts
   Tubular Works

Facilities Planning, Engineering and R & D Division

Facilities Planning
Research & Development
Engineering–Primary Works
   Finishing & Tubular
    Works
Electrical Engineering
Technical Services

Personnel Division

Organizational Develop.
Public Relations
Personnel Services
Salary and Benefits
Medical
Industrial Relations

Financial Division

Taxation
Data Processing
Internal Audit
Accounting
Financial Analysis &
   Control Systems
Office Services
Treasury
Corporate Insurance
Pension Fund Investment
Credit
Procurement

Marketing Division

Product Sales
Market Development
Overseas Sales
Commercial Planning
   & Research

So it falls to managers to resolve them by direct supervision. Indeed, many problems get bumped up successive steps in the hierarchy until they reach a level of common supervision where they can be resolved by authority (as with a dispute in a company between manufacturing and marketing that may have to be resolved by the chief executive). A second task of the middle-line managers is to work with the staff analysts to incorporate their standards down into the operating units. And a third task is to support the vertical flows in the organization—the elaboration of action plans flowing down the hierarchy and the communication of feedback information back up.

The technostructure must also be highly elaborated. In fact this structure was first identified with the rise of technocratic personnel in early-nineteenth-century industries such as textiles and banking. Because the machine organization depends primarily on the standardization of its operating work for coordination, the technostructure—which houses the staff analysts who do the standardizing—emerges as the key part of the structure. To the line managers may be delegated the formal authority for the operating units, but without the standardizers—the cadre of work-study analysts, schedulers, quality control engineers, planners, budgeters, accountants, operations researchers, and many more—these structures simply could not function. Hence, despite their lack of formal authority, considerable informal power rests with these staff analysts, who standardize everyone else's work. Rules and regulations permeate the entire system: The emphasis on standardization extends well beyond the operating core of the machine organization, and with it follows the analysts' influence.

A further reflection of this formalization of behavior are the sharp divisions of labor all over the machine organization. Job specialization in the operating core and the pronounced formal distinction between line and staff have already been mentioned. In addition, the administrative structure is clearly distinguished from the operating core; unlike the entre-preneurial organization, here managers seldom work alongside operators. And they them-selves tend to be organized along functional lines, meaning that each runs a unit that per-forms a single function in the chain that produces the final outputs. Figure 1 shows this, for example, in the organigram of a large steel company, traditionally machinelike in structure.

All this suggests that the machine organization is a structure with an obsession—name-ly, control. A control mentality pervades it from top to bottom. At the bottom, consider how a Ford Assembly Division general foreman described his work:

> I refer to my watch all the time. I check different items. About every hour I tour my line. About six thirty, I'll tour labor relations to find out who is absent. At seven, I hit the end of the line. I'll check paint, check my scratches and damage. Around ten I'll start talking to all the fore-men. I make sure they're all awake. We can't have no holes, no nothing.

And at the top, consider the words of a chief executive:

> When I was president of this big corporation, we lived in a small Ohio town, where the main plant was located. The corporation specified who you could socialize with, and on what level. (His wife interjects: "Who were the wives you could play bridge with.") In a small town they didn't have to keep check on you. Everybody knew. There are certain sets of rules. (Terkel, 1972:186, 406)

The obsession with control reflects two central facts about these organizations. First, attempts are made to eliminate all possible uncertainty, so that the bureaucratic machine can run smoothly, without interruption, the operating core perfectly sealed off from exter-nal influence. Second, these are structures ridden with conflict; the control systems are required to contain it. The problem in the machine organization is not to develop an open atmosphere where people can talk the conflicts out, but to enforce a closed, tightly con-trolled one where the work can get done despite them.

The obsession with control also helps to explain the frequent proliferation of support staff in these organizations. Many of the staff services could be purchased from outside sup-pliers. But that would expose the machine organization to the uncertainties of the open market. So it "makes" rather than "buys," that is, it envelops as many of the support services as it can within its own structure in order to control them, everything from the cafeteria in the factory to the law office at headquarters.

THE STRATEGIC APEX

The managers at the strategic apex of these organizations are concerned in large part with the fine-tuning of their bureaucratic machines. Theirs is a perpetual search for more effi-cient ways to produce the given outputs.

But not all is strictly improvement of performance. Just keeping the structure together in the face of its conflicts also consumes a good deal of the energy of top management. As noted, conflict is not resolved in the machine organization; rather it is bottled up so that the work can get done. And as in the case of a bottle, the cork is applied at the top: Ultimately, it is the top managers who must keep the lid on the conflicts through their role of handling disturbances. Moreover, the managers of the strategic apex must intervene fre-quently in the activities of the middle line to ensure that coordination is achieved there. The top managers are the only generalists in the structure, the only managers with a per-spective broad enough to see all the functions.

All this leads us to the conclusion that considerable power in the machine organization rests with the managers of the strategic apex. These are, in other words, rather centralized structures: The formal power clearly rests at the top; hierarchy and chain of authority are paramount concepts. But so also does much of the informal power, since that resides in knowledge, and only at the top of the hierarchy does the formally segmented knowledge of the organization come together.

Thus, our introductory figure shows the machine organization with a fully elaborated administrative and support structure—both parts of the staff component being focused on the operating core—together with large units in the operating core but narrower ones in the middle line to reflect the tall hierarchy of authority.

Conditions of the Machine Organization

Work of a machine bureaucratic nature is found, above all, in environments that are simple and stable. The work associated with complex environments cannot be rationalized into simple tasks, and that associated with dynamic environments cannot be predicted, made repetitive, and so standardized.

In addition, the machine configuration is typically found in mature organizations, large enough to have the volume of operating work needed for repetition and standardization, and old enough to have been able to settle on the standards they wish to use. These are the organizations that have seen it all before and have established standard procedures to deal with it. Likewise, machine organizations tend to be identified with technical systems that regulate the operating work, so that it can easily be programmed. Such technical systems cannot be very sophisticated or automated (for reasons that will be discussed later).

Mass production firms are perhaps the best-known machine organizations. Their operating work flows through an integrated chain, open at one end to accept raw materials, and after that functioning as a sealed system that processes them through sequences of standardized operations. Thus, the environment may be stable because the organization has acted aggressively to stabilize it. Giant firms in such industries as transportation, tobacco, and metals are well known for their attempts to influence the forces of supply and demand by the use of advertising, the development of long-term supply contacts, sometimes the establishment of cartels. They also tend to adopt strategies of "vertical integration," that is, extend their production chains at both ends, becoming both their own suppliers and their own customers. In that way they can bring some of the forces of supply and demand within their own planning processes.

Of course, the machine organization is not restricted to large, or manufacturing, or even private enterprise organizations. Small manufacturers—for example producers of discount furniture or paper products—may sometimes prefer this structure because their operating work is simple and repetitive. Many service firms use it for the same reason, such as banks or insurance companies in their retailing activities. Another condition often found with machine organizations is external control. Many government departments, such as post offices and tax collection agencies, are machine bureaucratic not only because their operating work is routine but also because they must be accountable to the public for their actions. Everything they do—treating clients, hiring employees, and so on—must be seen to be fair, and so they proliferate regulations.

Since control is the forte of the machine bureaucracy, it stands to reason that organizations in the business of control—regulatory agencies, custodial prisons, police forces—are drawn to this configuration, sometimes in spite of contradictory conditions. The same is true for the special need for safety. Organizations that fly airplanes or put out fires must minimize the risks they take. Hence they formalize their procedures extensively to ensure that they are carried out to the letter. A fire crew cannot arrive at a burning house and then turn to the chief for orders or discuss informally who will connect the hose and who will go up the ladder.

Machine Organizations as Instruments and Closed Systems

Control raises another issue about machine organizations. Being so pervasively regulated, they themselves can easily be controlled externally, as the *instruments* of outside influencers. In contrast, however, their obsession with control runs not only up the hierarchy but beyond, to control of their own environments, so that they can become *closed systems* immune to external influence. From the perspective of power, the instrument and the closed system constitute two main types of machine organizations.

In our terms, the instrument form of machine organization is dominated by one external influencer or by a group of them acting in concert. In the "closely held" corporation, the dominant influencer is the outside owner; in some prisons, it is a community concerned with the custody rather than the rehabilitation of prisoners.

Outside influencers render an organization their instrument by appointing the chief executive, charging that person with the pursuit of clear goals (ideally quantifiable, such as return on investment or prisoner escape measures), and then holding the chief responsible for performance. That way outsiders can control an organization without actually having to manage it. And such control, by virtue of the power put in the hands of the chief executive and the numerical nature of the goals, acts to centralize and bureaucratize the internal structure, in other words, to drive it to the machine form.

In contrast to this, Charles Perrow, the colorful and outspoken organizational sociologist, does not quite see the machine organization as anyone's instrument:

> Society is adaptive to organizations, to the large, powerful organizations controlled by a few, often overlapping, leaders. To see these organizations as adaptive to a "turbulent," dynamic, very changing environment is to indulge in fantasy. The environment of most powerful organizations is well controlled by them, quite stable, and made up of other organizations with similar interests, or ones they control. (1972:199)

Perrow is, of course, describing the closed system form of machine organization, the one that uses its bureaucratic procedures to seal itself off from external control and control others instead. It controls not only its own people but its environment as well: perhaps its suppliers, customers, competitors, even government and owners too.

Of course, autonomy can be achieved not only by controlling others (for example, buying up customers and suppliers in so-called vertical integration) but simply by avoiding the control of others. Thus, for example, closed system organizations sometimes form cartels with ostensible competitors or, less blatantly, diversify markets to avoid dependence on particular customers, finance internally to avoid dependence on particular financial groups, and even buy back their own shares to weaken the influence of their own owners. Key to being a closed system is to ensure wide dispersal, and therefore pacification, of all groups of potential external influence.

What goals does the closed system organization pursue? Remember that to sustain centralized bureaucracy the goals should be operational, ideally quantifiable. What operational goals enable an organization to serve itself, as a system closed to external influence? The most obvious answer is growth. Survival may be an indispensable goal and efficiency a necessary one, but beyond those what really matters here is making the system larger. Growth serves the system by providing greater rewards for its insiders—bigger empires for managers to run or fancier private jets to fly, greater programs for analysts to design, even more power for unions to wield by virtue of having more members. (The unions may be external influencers, but the management can keep them passive by allowing them more of the spoils of the closed system.) Thus the classic closed system machine organization, the large, widely held industrial corporation, has long been described as oriented far more to growth than to the maximization of profit per se (Galbraith, 1967).

Of course, the closed system form of machine organization can exist outside the private sector too, for example in the fundraising agency that, relatively free to external control, becomes increasingly charitable to itself (as indicated by the plushness of its managers' offices), the agricultural or retail cooperative that ignores those who collectively own it, even government that becomes more intent on serving itself than the citizens for which it supposedly exists.

The communist state, at least up until very recently, seemed to fit all the characteristics of the closed system bureaucracy. It had no dominant external influencer (at least in the case of the Soviet Union, if not the other East European states, which were its "instruments"). And the population to which it is ostensibly responsible had to respond to its own plethora of rules and regulations. Its election procedures, traditionally offering a choice of one, were similar to those for the directors of the "widely held" Western corporation. The government's own structure was heavily bureaucratic, with a single hierarchy of authority and a very elaborate technostructure, ranging from state planners to KGB agents. (As James Worthy [1959:77] noted, Frederick Taylor's "Scientific Management had its fullest flowering not in America but in Soviet Russia.") All significant resources were the property of the state—the collective system—not the individual. And, as in other closed systems, the administrators tend to take the lion's share of the benefits.

Some Issues Associated with the Machine Organization

No structure has evoked more heated debate than the machine organization. As Michel Crozier, one of its most eminent students, has noted,

> On the one hand, most authors consider the bureaucratic organization to be the embodiment of rationality in the modern world, and, as such, to be intrinsically superior to all other possible forms of organizations. On the other hand, many authors—often the same ones—consider it a sort of Leviathan, preparing the enslavement of the human race. (1964:176)

Max Weber, who first wrote about this form of organization, emphasized its rationality; in fact, the word *machine* comes directly from his writings (see Gerth and Mills, 1958). A machine is certainly precise; it is also reliable and easy to control; and it is efficient—at least when restricted to the job it has been designed to do. Those are the reasons many organizations are structured as machine bureaucracies. When an integrated set of simple, repetitive tasks must be performed precisely and consistently by human beings, this is the most efficient structure—indeed, the only conceivable one.

But in these same advantages of machinelike efficiency lie all the disadvantages of this configuration. Machines consist of mechanical parts; organizational structures also include human beings—and that is where the analogy breaks down.

HUMAN PROBLEMS IN THE OPERATING CORE

James Worthy, when he was an executive of Sears, wrote a penetrating and scathing criticism of the machine organization in his book *Big Business and Free Men*. Worthy traced the root of the human problems in these structures to the "scientific management" movement led by Frederick Taylor that swept America early in this century. Worthy acknowledged Taylor's contribution to efficiency, narrowly defined. Worker initiative did not, however, enter into his efficiency equation. Taylor's pleas to remove "all possible brain work" from the shop floor also removed all possible initiative from the people who worked there: the "machine has no will of its own. Its parts have no urge to independent action. Thinking, direction—even purpose—must be provided from outside or above." This had the "consequence of destroying the meaning of work itself," which has been "fantastically wasteful for industry and society," resulting in excessive absenteeism, high worker turnover, sloppy workmanship, costly strikes, and even outright sabotage (1959:67, 79, 70). Of course, there are people who like to work in highly structured situations. But increasing numbers do not, at least not *that* highly structured.

Taylor was fond of saying, "In the past the man has been first; in the future the system must be first" (in Worthy 1959:73). Prophetic words, indeed. Modern man seems to exist for his systems; many of the organizations he created to serve him have come to enslave him. The result is that several of what Victor Thompson (1961) has called "bureau-pathologies"—dysfunctional behaviors of these structures—reinforce each other to form a vicious circle in the machine organization. The concentration on means at the expense of ends, the mistreatment of clients, the various manifestations of worker alienation—all lead to the tightening of controls on behavior. The implicit motto of the machine organization seems to be, "When in doubt, control." All problems have to be solved by the turning of the technocratic screws. But since that is what caused the bureaupathologies in the first place, increasing the controls serves only to magnify the problems, leading to the imposition of further controls, and so on.

COORDINATION PROBLEMS IN THE ADMINISTRATIVE CENTER

Since the operating core of the machine organization is not designed to handle conflict, many of the human problems that arise there spill up and over, into the administrative structure.

It is one of the ironies of the machine configuration that to achieve the control it requires, it must mirror the narrow specialization of its operating core in its administrative structure (for example, differentiating marketing managers from manufacturing managers, much as salesmen are differentiated from factory workers). This, in turn, means problems of communication and coordination. The fact is that the administrative structure of the machine organization is also ill suited to the resolution of problems through mutual adjustment. All the communication barriers in these structures—horizontal, vertical, status, line/staff—impede informal communication among managers and with staff people. "Each unit becomes jealous of its own prerogatives and finds ways to protect itself against the pressure or encroachments of others" (Worthy, 1950:176). Thus narrow functionalism not only impedes coordination; it also encourages the building of private empires, which tends to produce top-heavy organizations that can be more concerned with the political games to be won than with the clients to be served.

ADAPTATION PROBLEMS IN THE STRATEGIC APEX

But if mutual adjustment does not work in the administrative center—generating more political heat than cooperative light—how does the machine organization resolve its coordination problems? Instinctively, it tries standardization, for example, by tightening job descriptions or proliferating rules. But standardization is not suited to handling the nonroutine problems of the administrative center. Indeed, it only aggravates them, undermining the influence of the line managers and increasing the conflict. So to reconcile these coordination problems, the machine organization is left with only one coordinating mechanism, direct supervision from above. Specifically, nonroutine coordination problems between units are "bumped" up the line hierarchy until they reach a common level of supervision, often at the top of the structure. The result can be excessive centralization of power, which in turn produces a host of other problems. In effect, just as the human problems in the operating core become coordination problems in the administrative center, so too do the coordination problems in the administrative center become adaptation problems at the strategic apex. Let us take a closer look at these by concluding with a discussion of strategic change in the machine configuration.

Strategy Formation in the Machine Organization

Strategy in the machine organization is supposed to emanate from the top of the hierarchy, where the perspective is broadest and the power most focused. All the relevant information is to be sent up the hierarchy, in aggregated, MIS-type form, there to be formulated into integrated strategy (with the aid of the technostructure). Implementation then follows, with the intended strategies sent down the hierarchy to be turned into successively more elaborated programs and action plans. Notice the clear division of labor assumed between the formulators at the top and the implementors down below, based on the assumption of perfectly deliberate strategy produced through a process of planning.

That is the theory. The practice has been shown to be another matter. Drawing on our strategy research at McGill University, we shall consider first what planning really proved to be in one machinelike organization, how it may in fact have impeded strategic thinking in a second, and how a third really did change its strategy. From there we shall consider the problems of strategic change in machine organizations and their possible resolution.

PLANNING AS PROGRAMMING IN A SUPERMARKET CHAIN

What really is the role of formal planning? Does it produce original strategies? Let us return to the case of Steinberg's in the later years of its founder, as large size drove this retailing chain toward the machine form, and as is common in that form, toward a planning mode of management at the expense of entrepreneurship.

One event in particular encouraged the start of planning at Steinberg's: the company's entry into capital markets in 1953. Months before it floated its first bond issue (stock, always nonvoting, came later), Sam Steinberg boasted to a newspaper reporter that "not a cent of any money outside the family is invested in the company." And asked about future plans, he replied: "Who knows? We will try to go everywhere there seems to be a need for us." A few months later he announced a $5 million debt issue and with it a $15 million five-year expansion program, one new store every two months for a total of thirty, the doubling of sales, new stores to average double the size of existing ones.

What happened in those ensuing months was Sam Steinberg's realization, after the opening of Montreal's first shopping center, that he needed to enter the shopping center business himself to protect his supermarket chain and that he could not do so with the company's traditional methods of short-term and internal financing. And, of course, no company is allowed to go to capital markets without a plan. You can't just say: "I'm Sam Steinberg and I'm good," though that was really the issue. In a "rational" society, you have to plan (or at least appear to do so).

But what exactly was that planning? One thing for certain: It did not formulate a strategy. Sam Steinberg already had that. What planning did was justify, elaborate, and articulate the strategy that already existed in Sam Steinberg's mind. Planning operationalized his strategic vision, programmed it. It gave order to that vision, imposing form on it to comply with the needs of the organization and its environment. Thus, planning followed the strategy-making process, which had been essentially entrepreneurial.

But its effect on that process was not incidental. By specifying and articulating the vision, planning constrained it and rendered it less flexible. Sam Steinberg retained formal control of the company to the day of his death. But his control over strategy did not remain so absolute. The entrepreneur, by keeping his vision personal, is able to adapt it at will to a changing environment. But by being forced to program it, the leader loses that flexibility. The danger, ultimately, is that the planning mode forces out the entrepreneurial one; procedure replaces vision. As its structure became more machinelike, Steinberg's required planning in the form of strategic programming. But that planning also accelerated the firm's transition toward the machine form of organization.

Is there, then, such a thing as "strategic planning"? I suspect not. To be more explicit, I do not find that major new strategies are formulated through any formal procedure. Organizations that rely on formal planning procedures to formulate strategies seem to extrapolate existing strategies, perhaps with marginal changes in them, or else copy the strategies of other organizations. This came out most clearly in another of our McGill studies.

PLANNING AS AN IMPEDIMENT TO STRATEGIC THINKING IN AN AIRLINE

From about the mid-1950s, Air Canada engaged heavily in planning. Once the airline was established, particularly once it developed its basic route structure, a number of factors drove it strongly to the planning mode. Above all was the need for coordination, both of flight schedules with aircraft, crews, and maintenance, and of the purchase of expensive aircraft with the structure of the route system. (Imagine someone calling out in the hangar: "Hey, Fred, this guy says he has two 747s for us; do you know who ordered them?") Safety was another factor. The intense need for safety in the air breeds a mentality of being very careful about what the organization does on the ground, too. This is the airlines' obsession with control. Other factors included the lead times inherent in key decisions, such as ordering new airplanes or introducing new routes, the sheer cost of the capital equipment, and the size of the organization. You don't run an intricate system like an airline, necessarily very machinelike, without a great deal of formal planning.

But what we found to be the consequence of planning at Air Canada was the absence of a major reorientation of strategy during our study period (up to the mid-1970s). Aircraft certainly changed—they became larger and faster—but the basic route system did not, nor did markets. Air Canada gave only marginal attention, for example, to cargo, charter, and shuttle operations. Formal planning, in our view, impeded strategic thinking.

The problem is that planning, too, proceeds from the machine perspective, much as an assembly line or a conventional machine produces a product. It all depends on the decomposition of analysis: You split the process into a series of steps or component parts, specify each, and then by following the specifications in sequence you get the desired product. There is a fallacy in this, however. Assembly lines and conventional machines produce standardized products, while planning is supposed to produce a novel strategy. It is as if the machine is supposed to design the machine; the planning machine is expected to create the original blueprint—the strategy. To put this another way, planning is analysis oriented to decomposition, while strategy making depends on synthesis oriented to integration. That is why the term "strategic planning" has proved to be an oxymoron.

ROLES OF PLANNING, PLANS, PLANNERS

If planning does not create strategy, then what purpose does it serve? We have suggested a role above, which has to do with the programming of strategies already created in other ways. This is shown in Figure 2, coming out of a box labeled strategy formation—meant to represent what is to planning a mysterious "black box." But if planning is restricted to programming strategy, plans and planners nonetheless have other roles in play, shown in Figure 2 and discussed alongside that of planning itself.

FIGURE 2
Specific Roles of Planners

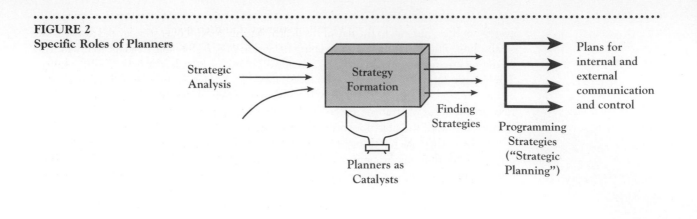

ROLE OF PLANNING

Why do organizations engage in formal planning? The answer seems to be: not to create strategies, but to program the strategies they already have, that is, to elaborate and operationalize the consequences of those strategies formally. We should really say that *effective* organizations so engage in planning, at least when they require the formalized implementation of their strategies. Thus strategy is not the *consequence* of planning but its starting point. Planning helps to translate the intended strategies into realized ones, taking the first step that leads ultimately to implementation.

This *strategic programming,* as it might properly be labeled, can be considered to involve a series of steps, namely the *codification* of given strategy, including its clarification and articulation, the *elaboration* of that strategy into substrategies, ad hoc action programs, and plans of various kinds, and the *translation* of those substrategies, programs, and plans into routine budgets and objectives. In these steps, we see planning as an analytical process that takes over after the synthesis of strategic formation is completed.

Thus formal planning properly belongs in the *implementation* of strategy, not in its formulation. But it should be emphasized that strategic programming makes sense when viable intended strategies are available, in other words when the world is expected to hold still while these strategies unfold, so that formulation can logically precede implementation, and when the organization that does the implementing in fact requires clearly codified and elaborated strategies. In other circumstances, strategic programming can do organizations harm by preempting the flexibility that managers and others may need to respond to changes in the environment, or to their own internal processes of learning.

ROLES OF PLANS

If planning is programming, then plans clearly serve two roles. They are a medium for communication and a device for control. Both roles draw on the analytical character of plans, namely, that they represent strategies in decomposed and articulated form, if not quantified then often at least quantifiable.

Why program strategy? Most obviously for coordination, to ensure that everyone in the organization pulls in the same direction, a direction that may have to be specified as precisely as possible. In Air Canada, to use our earlier example, that means linking the acquisition of new aircraft with the particular routes that are to be flown, and scheduling crews and planes to show up when the flights are to take off, and so on. Plans, as they emerge from strategic programming as programs, schedules, budgets, and so on, can be prime media to communicate not just strategic intention but also the role each individual must play to realize it.

Plans, as communication media, inform people of intended strategy and its consequences. But as control devices they can go further, specifying what role departments and

individuals must play in helping to realize strategy and then comparing that with performance in order to feed control information back into the strategy-making process.

Plans can help to effect control in a number of ways. The most obvious is control of the strategy itself. Indeed what has long paraded under the label of "strategy planning" has probably had more to do with "strategic control" than many people may realize. Strategic control has to do with keeping organizations on their strategic tracks: to ensure the realization of intended strategy, its implementation as expected, with resources appropriately allocated. But there is more to strategic control than this. Another aspect includes the assessment of the realization of strategies in the first place, namely, whether the patterns realized corresponded to the intentions specified beforehand. In other words, strategic control must assess behavior as well as performance. Then the more routine and traditional form of control can come in to consider whether the strategies that were in fact realized proved effective.

ROLES OF PLANNERS

Planners, of course, play key roles in planning (namely, strategic programming), and in using the resulting plans for purposes of communication and control. But many of the most important things planners do have little to do with planning or even plans per se. Three roles seem key here.

First, planners can play a role in finding strategies. This may seem curious, but if strategies really do emerge in organizations, then planners can help to identify the patterns that are becoming strategies, so that consideration can be given to formalizing them, that is, making them deliberate. Of course, finding the strategies of competitors—for assessment and possible modified adoption—is also important here.

Second, planners play the roles of analysts, carrying out ad hoc studies to feed into the black box of strategy making. Indeed, one could argue that this is precisely what Michael Porter proposes with his emphasis on industry and competitive analysis. The ad hoc nature of such studies should, however, be emphasized because they feed into a strategy-making process that is itself irregular, proceeding on no schedule and following no standard sequence of steps. Indeed, regularity in the planning process can interfere with strategic thinking, which must be flexible, responsive, and creative.

The third role of the planner is as a catalyst. This refers not to the traditional role long promoted in the literature of selling formal planning as some kind of religion, but to encourage strategic *thinking* throughout the organization. Here the planner encourages *informal* strategy making, trying to get others to think about the future in a creative way. He or she does not enter the black box of strategy making so much as ensure that the box is occupied with active line managers.

A PLANNER FOR EACH SIDE OF THE BRAIN

We have discussed various roles for planning, plans, and planners, summarized around the black box of strategy formation in Figure 2. These roles suggest two different orientations for planners.

On one hand (so to speak), the planner must be a highly analytic, convergent type of thinker, dedicated to bringing order to the organization. Above all, this planner programs intended strategies and sees to it that they are communicated clearly and used for purposes of control. He or she also carries out studies to ensure that the managers concerned with strategy formation take into account the necessary hard data that they may be inclined to miss and that the strategies they formulate are carefully and systematically evaluated before they are implemented.

On the other hand, there is another type of planner, less conventional a creative, divergent thinker, rather intuitive, who seeks to open up the strategy-making process. As a "soft analyst," he or she tends to conduct "quick and dirty" studies, to find strategies in strange places, and to encourage others to think strategically. This planner is inclined toward the intuitive processes identified with the brain's right hemisphere. We might call him or her a *left-handed planner*. Some organizations need to emphasize one type of planner, others the other type. But most complex organizations probably need some of both.

STRATEGIC CHANGE IN AN AUTOMOBILE FIRM

Given planning itself is not strategic, how does the planning-oriented machine bureaucracy change its strategy when it has to? Volkswagenwerk was an organization that had to. We interpreted its history from 1934 to 1974 as one long cycle of a single strategic perspective. The original "people's car," the famous "Beetle," was conceived by Ferdinand Porsche: the factory to produce it was built just before the war but did not go into civilian automobile production until after. In 1948, a man named Heinrich Nordhoff was given control of the devastated plant and began the rebuilding of it, as well as of the organization and the strategy itself, rounding out Porsche's original conception. The firm's success was dramatic.

By the late 1950s, however, problems began to appear. Demand in Germany was moving away from the Beetle. The typically machine-bureaucratic response was not to rethink the basic strategy—"it's okay" was the reaction—but rather to graft another piece onto it. A new automobile model was added, larger than the Beetle but with a similar no-nonsense approach to motoring, again air-cooled with the engine in the back. Volkswagenwerk added position but did not change perspective.

But that did not solve the basic problem, and by the mid-1960s the company was in crisis. Nordhoff, who had resisted strategic change, died in office and was replaced by a lawyer from outside the business. The company then underwent a frantic search for new models, designing, developing, or acquiring a whole host of them with engines in the front, middle, and rear; air and water cooled; front- and rear-wheel drive. To paraphrase the humorist Stephen Leacock, Volkswagenwerk leaped onto its strategic horse and rode off in all directions. Only when another leader came in, a man steeped in the company and the automobile business, did the firm consolidate itself around a new strategic perspective, based on the stylish front-wheel drive, water-cooled designs of one of its acquired firms, and thereby turn its fortunes around.

What this story suggests, first of all, is the great force of bureaucratic momentum in the machine organization. Even leaving planning aside, the immense effort of producing and marketing a new line of automobiles locks a company into a certain posture. But here the momentum was psychological, too. Nordhoff, who had been the driving force behind the great success of the organization, became a major liability when the environment demanded change. Over the years, he too had been captured by bureaucratic momentum. Moreover, the uniqueness and tight integration of Volkswagenwerk's strategy—we labeled it *gestalt*—impeded strategic change. Change an element of a tightly integrated gestalt and it *dis*integrates. Thus does success eventually breed failure.

BOTTLENECK AT THE TOP

Why the great difficulty in changing strategy in the machine organization? Here we take up that question and show how changes generally have to be achieved in a different configuration, if at all.

As discussed earlier, unanticipated problems in the machine organization tend to get bumped up the hierarchy. When these are few, which mean conditions are relatively stable, things work smoothly enough. But in times of rapid change, just when new strategies are called for, the number of such problems magnifies, resulting in a bottleneck at the top, where senior managers get overloaded. And that tends either to impede strategic change or else to render it ill considered.

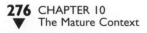

A major part of the problem is information. Senior managers face an organization decomposed into parts, like a machine itself. Marketing information comes up one channel, manufacturing information up another, and so on. Somehow it is the senior managers themselves who must integrate all that information. But the very machine bureaucratic premise of separating the administration of work from the doing of it means that the top managers often lack the intimate, detailed knowledge of issues necessary to effect such an integration. In essence, the necessary power is at the top of the structure, but the necessary knowledge is often at the bottom.

Of course, there is a machinelike solution to that problem too—not surprisingly in the form of a system. It is called a management information system, or MIS, and what it does is combine all the necessary information and package it neatly so that top managers can be informed about what is going on—the perfect solution for the overloaded executive. At least in theory.

Unfortunately, a number of real-world problems arise in the MIS. For one thing, in the tall administrative hierarchy of the machine organization, information must pass through many levels before it reaches the top. Losses take place at each one. Good news gets highlighted while bad news gets blocked on the way up. And "soft" information, so necessary for strategy information, cannot easily pass through, while much of the hard MIS-type information arrives only slowly. In a stable environment, the manager may be able to wait; in a rapidly changing one, he or she cannot. The president wants to be told right away that the firm's most important customer was seen playing golf yesterday with a main competitor, not to find out six months later in the form of a drop in a sales report. Gossip, hearsay, speculation—the softest kinds of information—warn the manager of impeding problems; the MIS all too often records for posterity ones that have already been felt. The manager who depends on an MIS in a changing environment generally finds himself or herself out of touch.

The obvious solution for top managers is to bypass the MIS and set up their own informal information systems, networks of contacts that bring them the rich, tangible, instant information they need. But that violates the machine organization's presuppositions of formality and respect for the chain of authority. Also, that takes the managers' time, the lack of which caused the bottleneck in the first place. So a fundamental dilemma faces the top managers of the machine organization as a result of its very own design: in times of change, when they most need the time to inform themselves, the system overburdens them with other pressures. They are thus reduced to acting superficially, with inadequate, abstract information.

THE FORMULATION/IMPLEMENTATION DICHOTOMY

The essential problem lies in one of the chief tenets of the machine organization, that strategy formation must be sharply separated from strategy implementation. One is thought out at the top, the other then acted out lower down. For this to work assume two conditions: first, that the formulator has full and sufficient information, and second, that the world will hold still, or at least change in predictable ways, during the implementation, so that there is no need for reformulation.

Now consider why the organization needs a new strategy in the first place. It is because its world has changed in an unpredictable way, indeed may continue to do so. We have just seen how the machine bureaucratic structure tends to violate the first condition—it misinforms the senior manager during such times of change. And when change continues in an unpredictable way (or at least the world unfolds in a way not yet predicted by an ill-informed management), then the second condition is violated too—it hardly makes sense to lock in by implementation a strategy that does not reflect changes in the world around it.

What all this amounts to is a need to collapse the formulation/implementation dichotomy precisely when the strategy of machine bureaucracy must be changed. This can be done in one of two ways.

In one case, the formulator implements. In other words, power is concentrated at the top, not only for creating the strategy but also for implementing it, step by step, in a personalized way. The strategist is put in close personal touch with the situation at hand (more commonly a strategist is appointed who has or can develop that touch) so that he or she can, on one hand, be properly informed and, on the other, control the implementation en route in order to reformulate when necessary. This, of course describes the entrepreneurial configuration, at least at the strategic apex.

In the other case, the implementers formulate. In other words, power is concentrated lower down, where the necessary information resides. As people who are naturally in touch with the specific situations at hand take individual actions—approach new customers, develop new products, et cetera—patterns form, in other words, strategies emerge. And this describes the innovative configuration, where strategic initiatives often originate in the grass roots of the organization, and then are championed by managers at middle levels who integrate them with one another or with existing strategies in order to gain their acceptance by senior management.

We conclude, therefore, that the machine configuration is ill suited to change its fundamental strategy, that the organization must in effect change configuration temporarily in order to change strategy. Either it reverts to the entrepreneurial form, to allow a single leader to develop vision (or proceed with one developed earlier), or else it overlays an innovative form on its conventional structure (for example, creates an informed network of lateral teams and task forces) so that the necessary strategies can emerge. The former can obviously function faster than the latter; that is why it tends to be used for drastic *turnaround,* while the latter tends to proceed by the slower process of *revitalization.* (Of course, quick turnaround may be necessary because there has been no slow revitalization.) In any event, both are characterized by a capacity to *learn*—that is the essence of the entrepreneurial and innovative configurations, in one case learning centralized for the simpler context, in the other, decentralized for the more complex one. The machine configuration is not so characterized.

This, however, should come as no surprise. After all, machines are specialized instruments, designed for productivity, not for adaptation. In Hunt's (1970) words, machine bureaucracies are performance systems, not problem-solving ones. Efficiency is their forte, not innovation. An organization cannot put blinders on its personnel and then expect peripheral vision. Managers here are rewarded for cutting costs and improving standards, not for taking risks and ignoring procedures. Change makes a mess of the operating systems: change one link in a carefully coupled system, and the whole chain must be reconceived. Why, then, should we be surprised when our bureaucratic machines fail to adapt?

Of course, it is fair to ask why we spend so much time trying to make them adapt. After all, when an ordinary machine becomes redundant, we simply scrap it, happy that it served us for as long and as well as it did. Converting it to another use generally proves more expensive than simply starting over. I suspect the same is often true for bureaucratic machines. But here, of course, the context is social and political. Mechanical parts don't protest, nor do displaced raw materials. Workers, suppliers, and customers do, however, protest the scrapping of organizations, for obvious reasons. But that the cost of this is awfully high in a society of giant machine organizations will be the subject of the final chapter of this book.

STRATEGIC REVOLUTIONS IN MACHINE ORGANIZATIONS

Machine organizations do sometimes change, however, at times effectively but more often it would seem at great cost and pain. The lucky ones are able to overlay an innovative structure for periodic revitalization, while many of the other survivors somehow manage to get turned around in entrepreneurial fashion.

Overall, the machine organizations seem to follow what my colleagues Danny Miller and Peter Friesen (1984) call a "quantum theory" of organization change. They pursue their

FIGURE 3
Organization Takes
Precedence

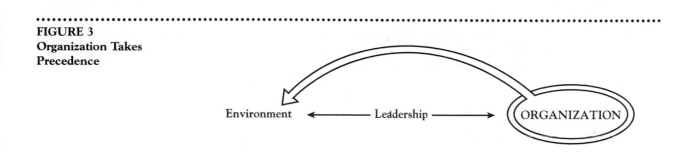

set strategies through long periods of stability (naturally occurring or created by themselves as closed systems), using planning and other procedures to do so efficiently. Periodically these are interrupted by short bursts of change, which Miller and Friesen characterize as "strategic revolutions" (although another colleague, Mihaela Firsirotu [1985], perhaps better labels it "strategic turnaround as cultural revolution").

ORGANIZATION TAKING PRECEDENCE IN THE MACHINE ORGANIZATION

To conclude, as shown in Figure 3, it is organization—with its systems and procedures, its planning and its bureaucratic momentum—that takes precedence over leadership and environment in the machine configuration. Environment fits organization, either because the organization has slotted itself into a context that matches its procedures, or else because it has forced the environment to do so. And leadership generally falls into place too, supporting the organization, indeed often becoming part of its bureaucratic momentum.

This generally works effectively, though hardly nonproblematically, at least in times of stability. But in times of change, efficiency becomes ineffective and the organization will falter unless it can find a different way to organize for adaptation.

All of this is another way of saying that the machine organization is a configuration, a species, like the others, suited to its own context but ill suited to others. But unlike the others, it is the dominant configuration in our specialized societies. As long as we demand inexpensive and so necessarily standardized goods and services, and as long as people continue to be more efficient than real machines at providing them, and remain willing to do so, then the machine organization will remain with us—and so will all its problems.

▼ READING 10.2 COST DYNAMICS: SCALE AND EXPERIENCE EFFECTS*

by Derek F. Abell and John S. Hammond

Market share is one of the primary determinants of business profitability; other things being equal, businesses with a larger share of a market are more profitable than their smaller-share competitors. For instance, a study by the PIMS Program (Buzzell, Gale and Sultan, 1975) . . . found that, on average, a difference of 10 percentage points in market share is accompanied by a difference of about 5 points in pretax ROI ("pretax operating profits" divided by "long-term debt plus equity"). Additional evidence is that companies having large market shares in their primary product markets—such as General Motors, IBM, Gillette, Eastman Kodak, and Xerox—tend to be highly profitable.

---

* Originally published in *Strategic Market Planning: Problems and Analytical Approaches* (Prentice Hall, 1979), Chap. 3. Copyright © Prentice Hall, 1979; reprinted with deletions by permission of the publisher.

An important reason for the increase in profitability with market share is that large-share firms usually have *lower costs*. The lower costs are due in part to economies of scale; for instance, very large plants cost less per unit of production to build and are often more efficient than smaller plants. Lower costs are also due in part to the so-called *experience effect*, whereby the cost of many (if not most) products declines by 10–30 percent each time a company's experience at producing and selling them doubles. In this context *experience* has a precise meaning: it is the cumulative number of units produced to date. Since at any point in time, businesses with large market shares typically (but not always) have more experience than their smaller-share competitors, they would be expected to have lower cost. . . .

This [reading] considers how costs decline due to scale and to experience, practical problems in analyzing the experience effect, strategic implications of scale and experience, and limitations of strategies based on cost reduction. . . .

Scale Effect

As mentioned earlier, scale effect refers to the fact that large businesses have the potential to operate at lower unit costs than their smaller counterparts. The increased efficiency due to size is often referred to as "economy of scale"; it could equally be called "economy of size."

Most people think of economy of scale as a manufacturing phenomenon because large manufacturing facilities can be constructed at a lower cost per unit of capacity and can be operated more efficiently than smaller ones. . . .

Just as they cost less to build, large-scale plants have lower *operating* costs per unit of output. . . . While substantial in manufacturing, scale effect is also significant in other cost elements, such as marketing, sales, distribution, administration, R&D, and service. For instance, a chain with 30 supermarkets in a metropolitan area needs much less than three times as much advertising as a chain of 10 stores. . . . Economies of scale are also achieved with purchased items such as raw material and shipping. . . .

Although scale economies potentially exist in all cost elements of a business in both the short and long run, large size alone doesn't assure the benefits of scale. It is evident from the above illustrations that size provides an *opportunity* for scale economies; to achieve them requires strategies and actions consciously designed to seize the opportunity, especially with operating costs. . . .

Experience Effect

The experience effect, whereby costs fall with cumulative production, is measurable and predictable; it has been observed in a wide range of products including automobiles, semiconductors, petrochemicals, long-distance telephone calls, synthetic fibers, airline transportation, the cost of administering life insurance, and crushed limestone, to mention a few. Note that this list ranges from high technology to low technology products, service to manufacturing industries, consumer to industrial products, new to mature products. and process to assembly oriented products, indicating the wide range of applicability. . . .

. . . it is only comparatively recently that this phenomenon has been carefully measured and quantified; at first it was thought to apply only to the labor portion of *manufacturing* costs. . . . In the 1960s evidence mounted that the phenomenon was broader. Personnel from the Boston Consulting Group and others showed that each time cumulative volume of a product doubled, total value added costs—including administration, sales, marketing, distribution, and so on in addition to manufacturing—fell by a constant and predictable percentage. In addition, the costs of purchased items usually fell as suppliers reduced prices

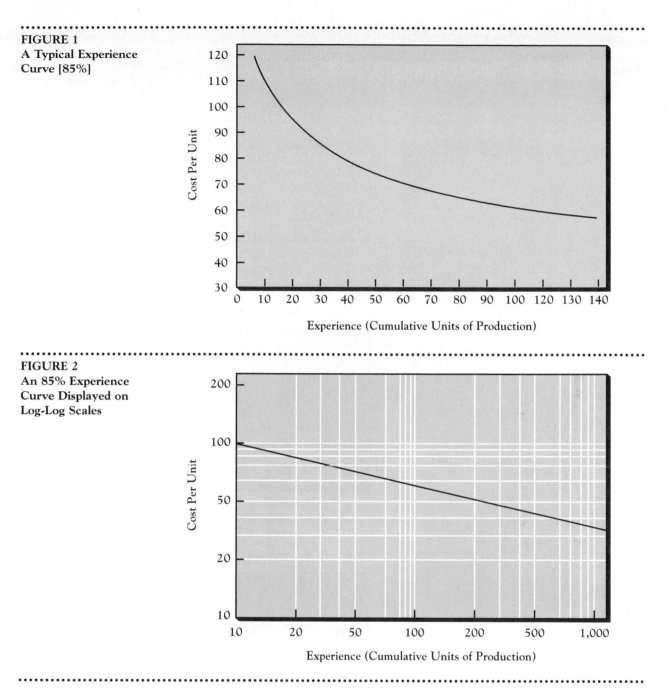

FIGURE 1
A Typical Experience Curve [85%]

Cost Per Unit

Experience (Cumulative Units of Production)

FIGURE 2
An 85% Experience Curve Displayed on Log-Log Scales

Cost Per Unit

Experience (Cumulative Units of Production)

as their costs fell, due also to the experience effect. The relationship between costs and experience was called the *experience curve* (Boston Consulting Group, 1972).

An experience curve is plotted with the cumulative units produced on the horizontal axis, and cost per unit on the vertical axis. An "85%" experience curve is shown in Figure 1. The "85%" means that every time experience doubles, costs per unit drop to 85% of the original level. It is known as the *learning rate*. Stated differently, costs per unit decrease 15 percent for every doubling of cumulative production. For example, the cost of the 20th unit produced is about 85% of the cost of the 10th unit. . . .

An experience curve appears as a straight line when plotted on a double log paper (logarithmic scale for both the horizontal and vertical axes). Figure 2 shows the "85 percent"

FIGURE 3
Some Sample Experience
Curves

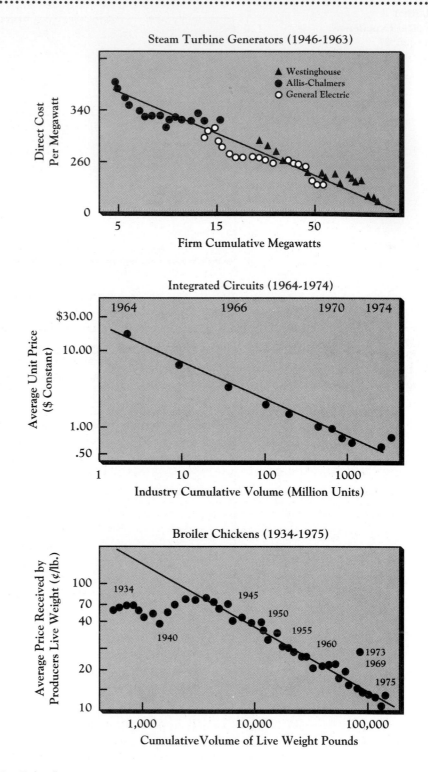

Note: *Technically an experience curve shows the relationship between cost and experience. However, cost figures are seldom pubicly available; therefore most of the above experience curves show industry price (in constant dollars) vs. experience.*
Source: The Boston Consulting Group.

experience curve from Figure 1 on the double logarithmic scale. . . . Figure 3 provides illustrations for [some specific] products.

Sources of the Experience Effect

The experience effect has a variety of sources; to capitalize on it requires knowledge of why it occurs. Sources of the experience effect are outlined as follows:

1. *Labor efficiency.* . . . As workers repeat a particular production task, they become more dextrous and learn improvements and shortcuts which increase their collective efficiency. The greater the number of worker-paced operations, the greater the amount of learning which can accrue with experience. . . .

2. *Work specialization and methods improvements.* Specialization increases worker proficiency at a given task. . . .

3. *New production processes.* Process innovations and improvements can be an important source of cost reductions, especially in capital-intensive industries. . . .

4. *Getting better performance from production equipment.* When first designed, a piece of production equipment may have a conservatively rated output. Experience may reveal innovative ways of increasing its output. . . .

5. *Changes in the resource mix.* As experience accumulates, a producer can often incorporate different or less expensive resources in the operation. . . .

6. *Product standardization.* Standardization allows the replication of tasks necessary for worker learning. Production of the Ford Model T, for example, followed a strategy of deliberate standardization; as a result, from 1909 to 1923 its price was repeatedly reduced, following an 85 percent experience curve (Abernathy and Wayne, 1974). . . .

7. *Product redesign.* As experience is gained with a product, both the manufacturer and customers gain a clearer understanding of its performance requirements. This understanding allows the product to be redesigned to conserve material, allows greater efficiency in manufacture, and substitutes less costly materials and resources, while at the same time improving performance on relevant dimensions. . . .

The foregoing list of sources dramatizes the observation that cost reductions due to experience don't occur by natural inclination; they are the result of substantial, concerted effort and pressure to lower costs. In fact, left unmanaged, costs rise. Thus, experience does not cause reductions but rather provides an opportunity that alert managements can exploit. . . .

The list of reasons for the experience effect raises perplexing questions on the difference between experience and scale effects. For instance, isn't it true that work specialization and project standardization, mentioned in the experience list, become possible because of the *size* of an operation? Therefore, aren't they each really scale effects? The answer is that they are probably both.

The confusion arises because growth in experience usually coincides with growth in size of an operation. We consider the experience effect to arise primarily due to ingenuity, cleverness, skill, and dexterity derived from experience as embodied in the adages "practice makes perfect" or "experience is the best teacher." On the other hand, scale effect comes from capitalizing on the size of an operation. . . .

Usually the overlap between the two effects is so great that it is difficult (and not too important) to separate them. This is the practice we will adopt from here on. . . .

Prices and Experience

In stable competitive markets, one would expect that as costs decrease due to experience, prices will decrease similarly. (The price-experience curves in Figure 3 are examples of prices falling with experience.) If profit margins remain at a constant percentage of price, average industry costs and prices should follow identically sloped experience curves (on double logarithmic scales). The constant gap separating them will equal the profit margin percentage; Figure 4 illustrates such an idealized situation.

In many cases, however, prices and costs exhibit a relationship similar to the one shown in Figure 5, where prices start briefly below cost, then cost reductions exceed price reductions until prices suddenly tumble. Ultimately the price and cost curves parallel, as they do in Figure 4. Specifically, in the development phase, new product prices are below average industry costs due to pricing based on anticipated costs. In the price umbrella phase, when demand exceeds supply, prices remain firm under a price umbrella supported by the market leader. This is unstable. At some point a shakeout phase starts; one producer will almost certainly reduce prices to gain share. If this does not precipitate a price decline, the high profit margins will attract enough new entrants to produce temporary overcapacity, causing prices to tumble faster than costs, and marginal producers to be forced out of the market. The stability phase starts when profit margins return to normal levels and prices begin to follow industry costs down the experience curve. . . .

Strategic Implications

In industries where a significant portion of total cost can be reduced due to scale or experience, important cost advantages can usually be achieved by pursuing a strategy geared to accumulating experience faster than competitors. (Such a strategy will ultimately require that the firm acquire the largest market share relative to competition.)

The dominant producer can greatly influence industry profitability. The rate of decline of competitors' costs must at least keep pace with the leader if they are to maintain profitability. If their costs decrease more slowly, either because they are pursuing cost reductions less aggressively or are growing more slowly than the leader, then their profits will eventually disappear, thus eliminating them from the market.

FIGURE 4
An Idealized Price-Cost Relationship When Profit Margin Is Constant

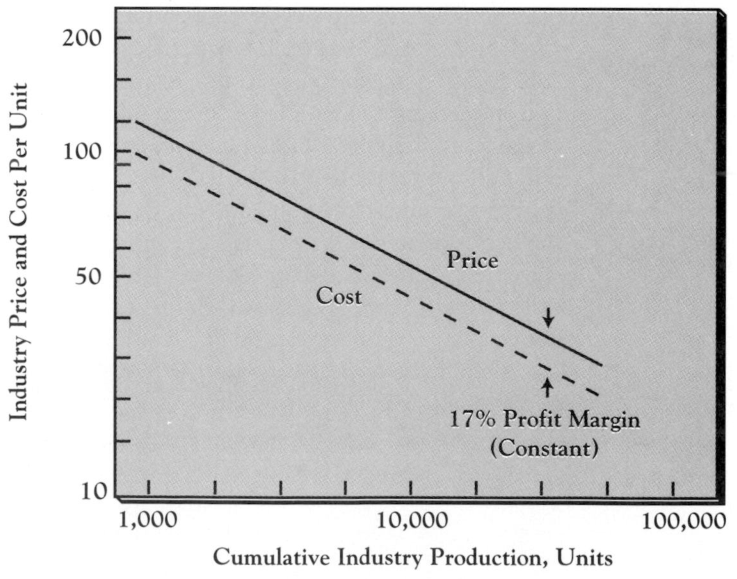

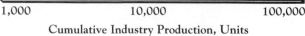

FIGURE 5
Typical Price-Cost Relationship
Source: Adapted from *Perspectives on Experience* (Boston: The Boston Consulting Group, 1972), p. 21

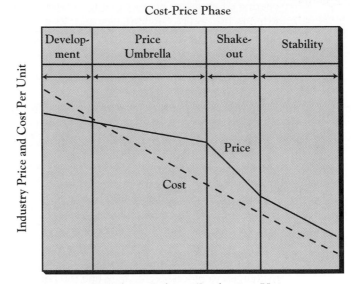

. . . the advantage of being the leader is obvious. Leadership is usually best seized at the start when experience doubles quickly (e.g., experience increases tenfold as you move from the 20th to the 2,000th unit, but only doubles as you move from the 2,000th to the 4,000th unit). Then a firm can build an unassailable cost advantage and at the same time gain price leadership. The best course of action for a product depends on a number of factors, one of the most important being the market growth rate. In fast-growing markets, experience can be gained by taking a disproportionate share of new sales, thereby avoiding taking sales away from competitors (which would be vigorously resisted). Therefore, with high rates of growth, aggressive action may be called for. But, share-gaining tactics are usually costly in the short run, due to reduced margins from lower prices, added advertising and marketing expense, new product development costs, and the like. This means that if it lacks the resources (product, financial, and other) for leadership and in particular if it is opposed by a very aggressive competitor, a firm may find it wise to abandon the market entirely or focus on a segment it can dominate. On the other hand, in no-growth or slowly growing markets it is hard to take share from competitors and the time it takes to acquire superior experience is usually too long and the cost too great to favor aggressive strategies.

In stable competitive markets, usually the firm with the largest share of market has the greatest experience and it is often the case that each firm's experience is roughly proportional to market share. A notable exception occurs when a late entrant to a market quickly obtains a commanding market share. It may have less experience than some early entrants. . . .

Efficiency versus Effectiveness: Limitations to Strategies Based on Experience or Scale

The selection of a competitive strategy based on cost reduction due to experience or scale often involves a fundamental choice. It is the selection of cost-price *efficiency* over noncost-price marketing *effectiveness*. However, when the market is more concerned with product and service features and up-to-date technology, a firm pursuing efficiency can find itself offering a low-priced product that few customers want. Thus two basic questions arise: (1) when to use an efficiency strategy and (2) if used, how far to push it before running into dangers of losing effectiveness. . . .

Whether to pursue an efficiency strategy depends on answers to questions such as,

1. Does the industry offer significant cost advantages from experience or scale (as in semi-conductors or chemicals)?
2. Are there significant market segments that will reward competitors with low prices?
3. Is the firm well equipped (financially, managerially, technologically, etc.) for or already geared up for strategies relying heavily on having the lowest cost . . . ?

If the answer is "yes" to all these questions, then "efficiency" strategies should probably be pursued.

Once it decided to pursue an "efficiency" strategy a firm must guard against going so far that it loses effectiveness, primarily through inability to respond to changes. For instance, experience-based strategies frequently require a highly specialized work force, facilities and organization, making it difficult to respond to changes in consumer demand, to respond to competitors' innovations, or to initiate them. In addition, large-scale plants are vulnerable to changes in process technology, and the heavy cost of operation below capacity.

For example, Ford's Motel T automobile ultimately suffered the consequences of inflexibility due to overemphasizing "efficiency" (Abernathy and Wayne, 1974). Ford followed a classic experience-based strategy; over time it slashed its product line to a single model (the Model T), built modern plants, pushed division of labor, introduced the continuous assembly line, obtained economies in purchased parts through high volume, backward integrated, increased mechanization, and cut prices as costs fell. The lower prices increased Ford's share of a growing market to a high of 55.4% by 1921.

In the meantime, consumer demand began shifting to heavier, closed-body cars and to more comfort. Ford's chief rival, General Motors, had the flexibility to respond quickly with new designs. Ford responded by adding features to its existing standard design. While the features softened the inroads of GM, the basic Model T design, upon which Ford's "efficiency" strategy was based, inadequately met the market's new performance standards. To make matters worse, the turmoil in production due to constant design changes slowed experience-based efficiency gains. Finally Ford was forced, at enormous cost, to close for a whole year beginning May 1927 while it retooled to introduce its Model A. Hence experience or scale-based *efficiency* was carried too far and thus it ultimately limited *effectiveness* to meet consumer needs, to innovate, and to respond.

Thus the challenge is to decide when to emphasize efficiency and when to emphasize effectiveness, and further to design efficiency strategies that maintain effectiveness and vice versa. . . .

11

THE PROFESSIONAL CONTEXT

While most large organizations draw on a variety of experts to get their jobs done, there has been a growing interest in recent years in those organizations whose work, because it is highly complex, is organized primarily around experts. These range from hospitals, universities, and research centers to consulting firms, space agencies, and biomedical companies.

This context is a rather unusual one, at least when judged against the more traditional contexts discussed in previous chapters. Both its strategic processes and its structures tend to take on forms quite different from those presented earlier. Organizations of experts, in fact, seem to divide themselves into two somewhat different contexts. In one, the experts work in rapidly changing situations that demand a good deal of collaborative innovation (as in the biotechnology or semiconductor fields); in the other, experts work more or less alone in more stable situations involving slower-changing bodies of skill or knowledge (as in law, university teaching, and accounting). This chapter takes up the latter, under the label of the "professional" context; the next chapter discusses the former under the label of "innovation."

We open this chapter with a description of the type of organization that seems best suited to the context of the more stable application of expertise. Drawn from Mintzberg's work, primarily his original description of "professional bureaucracy," it looks at the structure of the professional organization, including its important characteristic of "pigeonholing" work, the management of professionals, the unusual nature of strategy in such organizations (drawing from a paper Mintzberg coauthored with Cynthia Hardy, Ann Langley, and Janet Rose), and some issues associated with these organizations.

The second reading in this chapter, written by David Maister and originally published in the *Sloan Management Review,* focuses on one particular instance of the professional context, but one that has become an increasingly important career option for management students: the professional service firm. Maister describes how companies in businesses like consulting, investment banking, accounting, architecture, and law manage the interactions between revenue generation, compensation, and staffing to ensure long-term balanced growth.

Overall, these two readings suggest that the traditional concepts of managing and organization simply do not work as we move away from conventional mass production—which has long served as the model for "one best way" concepts in management. Whether it be highly expert work in general or service work subjected to new technologies and skills in particular, our thinking has to be opened up to some very different needs. Peter Drucker has, in a widely discussed article ("The Coming of the New Organization," *Harvard Business Review,* January–February 1988), argued the case that work in general is becoming more skilled and so structures of organizations in general are moving toward what we would call the professional form. While we would not go that far—we maintain our "contingency" view of different needs for different contexts—we do believe this is becoming a much more important form of organization.

by Henry Mintzberg

The Basic Structure

An organization can be bureaucratic without being centralized. This happens when its work is complex, requiring that it be carried out and controlled by professionals, yet at the same time remains stable, so that the skills of those professionals can be perfected through standardized operating programs. The structure takes on the form of professional bureaucracy, which is common in universities, general hospitals, public accounting firms, social work agencies, and firms doing fairly routine engineering or craft work. All rely on the skills and knowledge of their operating professionals to function; all produce standardized products or services.

THE WORK OF THE PROFESSIONAL OPERATORS

Here again we have a tightly knit configuration of the attributes of structure. Most important, the professional organization relies for coordination on the standardization of skills, which is achieved primarily through formal training. It hires duly trained specialists—professionals—for the operating core, then gives them considerable control over their own work.

Control over their work means that professionals work relatively independently of their colleagues but closely with the clients they serve—doctors treating their own patients and accountants who maintain personal contact with the companies whose books they audit. Most of the necessary coordination among the operating professionals is then handled automatically by their set skills and knowledge—in effect, by what they have learned to expect from each other. During an operation as long and as complex as open-heart surgery, "very little needs to be said [between the anesthesiologist and the surgeon] preced-

---

* Adapted from *The Structuring of Organizations* (Prentice Hall, 1979), Chap. 19 on "The Professional Bureaucracy"; also *Power In and Around Organizations* (Prentice Hall, 1983), Chap. 22 on "The Meritocracy"; the material on strategy formation from "Strategy Formation in the University Setting," coauthored with Cynthia Hardy, Ann Langley, and Janet Rose, in J. L. Bess (ed.) *College and University Organization* (New York University Press, 1984). A chapter similar to this one appeared in *Mintzberg on Management: Inside Our Strange World of Organizations* (Free Press, 1989).

ing chest opening and during the procedure on the heart itself . . . [most of the operation is] performed in absolute silence" (Gosselin, 1978). The point is perhaps best made in reverse by the cartoon that shows six surgeons standing around a patient on an operating table with one saying, "Who opens?"

Just how standardized the complex work of professionals can be is illustrated in a paper read by Spencer before a meeting of the International Cardiovascular Society. Spencer notes that an important feature of surgical training is "repetitive practice" to evoke "an automatic reflex." So automatic, in fact, that this doctor keeps a series of surgical "cookbooks" in which he lists, even for "complex" operations, the essential steps as chains of thirty to forty symbols on a single sheet, to "be reviewed mentally in sixty to 120 seconds at some time during the day preceding the operation" (1976:1179, 1182).

But no matter how standardized the knowledge and skills, their complexity ensures that considerable discretion remains in their application. No two professionals—no two surgeons or engineers or social workers—ever apply them in exactly the same way. Many judgments are required.

Training, reinforced by indoctrination, is a complicated affair in the professional organization. The initial training typically takes place over a period of years in a university or special institution, during which the skills and knowledge of the profession are formally programmed into the students. There typically follows a long period of on-the-job training, such as internship in medicine or articling in accounting, where the formal knowledge is applied and the practice of skills perfected. On-the-job training also completes the process of indoctrination, which began during the formal education. As new knowledge is generated and new skills develop, of course (so it is hoped) the professional upgrades his or her expertise.

All that training is geared to one goal, the internalization of the set procedures, which is what makes the structure technically bureaucratic (structure defined earlier as relying on standardization for coordination). But the professional bureaucracy differs markedly from the machine bureaucracy. Whereas the latter generates its own standards—through its technostructure, enforced by its line managers—many of the standards of the professional bureaucracy originate outside its own structure, in the self-governing associations its professionals belong to with their colleagues from other institutions. These associations set universal standards, which they ensure are taught by the universities and are used by all the organizations practicing the profession. So whereas the machine bureaucracy relies on authority of a hierarchical nature—the power of office—the professional bureaucracy emphasizes authority of a professional nature—the power of expertise.

Other forms of standardization are, in fact, difficult to rely on in the professional organization. The work processes themselves are too complex to be standardized directly by analysts. One need only try to imagine a work-study analyst following a cardiologist on rounds or timing the activities of a teacher in a classroom. Similarly, the outputs of professional work cannot easily be measured and so do not lend themselves to standardization. Imagine a planner trying to define a cure in psychiatry, the amount of learning that takes place in a classroom, or the quality of an accountant's audit. Likewise, direct supervision and mutual adjustment cannot be relied upon for coordination, for both impede professional autonomy.

THE PIGEONHOLING PROCESS

To understand how the professional organization functions at the operating level, it is helpful to think of it as a set of standard programs—in effect, the repertoire of skills the professionals stand ready to use—that are applied to known situations, called contingencies, also standardized. As Weick notes of one case in point, "schools are in the business of building and maintaining categories (1976:8). The process is sometimes known as *pigeonholing*. In this regard, the professional has two basic tasks: (1) to categorize, or "diagnose," the client's need in terms of one of the contingencies, which indicates which standard program to apply, and (2) to apply, or execute, that program. For example, the management consultant carries a bag of standard acronymic tricks: MBO, MIS, LRP, OD. The client with information needs gets MIS; the one with managerial conflicts, OD. Such pigeonholing, of course, simplifies matters enormously; it is also what enables each professional to work in a relatively autonomous manner.

It is in the pigeonholing process that the fundamental differences among the machine organization, the professional organization, and the innovative organization (to be discussed next) can best be seen. The machine organization is a single-purpose structure. Presented with a stimulus, it executes its one standard sequence of programs, just as we kick when tapped on the knee. No diagnosis is involved. In the professional organization, diagnosis is a fundamental task, but one highly circumscribed. The organization seeks to match a predetermined contingency to a standardized program. Fully open-ended diagnosis—that which seeks a creative solution to a unique problem—requires the innovative form of organization. No standard contingencies or programs can be relied upon there.

THE ADMINISTRATIVE STRUCTURE

Everything we have discussed so far suggests that the operating core is the key part of the professional organization. The only other part that is fully elaborated is the support staff, but that is focused very much on serving the activities of the operating core. Given the high cost of the professionals, it makes sense to back them up with as much support as possible. Thus, universities have printing facilities, faculty clubs, alma mater funds, publishing houses, archives, libraries, computer facilities, and many, many other support units.

The technostructure and middle-line management are not highly elaborated in the professional organization. They can do little to coordinate the professional work. Moreover, with so little need for direct supervision of, or mutual adjustment among, the professionals, the operating units can be very large. For example, the McGill Faculty of Management functions effectively with 50 professors under a single manager, its dean, and the rest of the university's academic hierarchy is likewise thin.

Thus, the diagram at the beginning of this chapter shows the professional organization, in terms of our logo, as a flat structure with a thin middle line, a tiny technostructure, but a fully elaborated support staff. All these characteristics are reflected in the organigram of a university hospital, shown in Figure 1.

Coordination within the administrative structure is another matter, however. Because these configurations are so decentralized, the professionals not only control their own work but they also gain much collective control over the administrative decisions that affect them—decisions, for example, to hire colleagues, to promote them, and to distribute resources. This they do partly by doing some of the administrative work themselves (most university professors, for example, sit on various administrative committees) and partly by ensuring that important administrative posts are staffed by professionals or at least sympathetic people appointed with the professionals' blessing. What emerges, therefore, is a rather democratic administrative structure. But because the administrative work requires mutual adjustment for coordination among the various people involved, task forces and especially standing committees abound at this level, as is in fact suggested in Figure 1.

Because of the power of their professional operators, these organizations are sometimes described as inverse pyramids, with the professional operators on top and the administrators down below to serve them—to ensure that the surgical facilities are kept clean and the

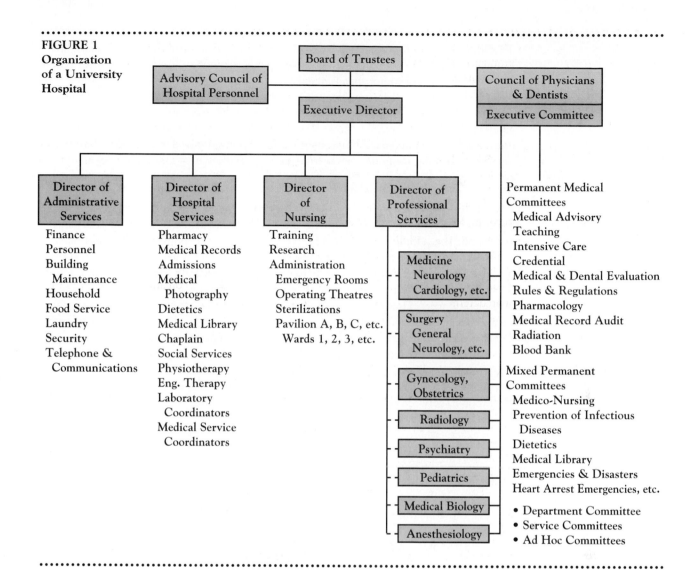

**FIGURE 1
Organization
of a University
Hospital**

Board of Trustees

Advisory Council of
Hospital Personnel

Executive Director

Council of Physicians
& Dentists

Executive Committee

**Director of
Administrative
Services**

Finance
Personnel
Building
  Maintenance
Household
Food Service
Laundry
Security
Telephone &
  Communications

**Director of
Hospital
Services**

Pharmacy
Medical Records
Admissions
Medical
  Photography
Dietetics
Medical Library
Chaplain
Social Services
Physiotherapy
Eng. Therapy
Laboratory
  Coordinators
Medical Service
  Coordinators

**Director
of
Nursing**

Training
Research
Administration
  Emergency Rooms
  Operating Theatres
  Sterilizations
  Pavilion A, B, C, etc.
    Wards 1, 2, 3, etc.

**Director of
Professional
Services**

Medicine
Neurology
Cardiology, etc.

Surgery
General
Neurology, etc.

Gynecology,
Obstetrics

Radiology

Psychiatry

Pediatrics

Medical Biology

Anesthesiology

Permanent Medical
Committees
  Medical Advisory
  Teaching
  Intensive Care
  Credential
  Medical & Dental Evaluation
  Rules & Regulations
  Pharmacology
  Medical Record Audit
  Radiation
  Blood Bank

Mixed Permanent
Committees
  Medico-Nursing
  Prevention of Infectious
    Diseases
  Dietetics
  Medical Library
  Emergencies & Disasters
  Heart Arrest Emergencies, etc.

• Department Committee
• Service Committees
• Ad Hoc Committees

classrooms well supplied with chalk. Such a description slights the power of the administrators of professional work, however, although it may be an accurate description of those who manage the support units. For the support staff—often more numerous than the professional staff, but generally less skilled—there is no democracy in the professional organization, only the oligarchy of the professionals. Such support units as housekeeping in the hospital or printing in the university are likely to be managed tightly from the top, in effect as machinelike enclaves within the professional configuration. Thus, what frequently emerges in the professional organization are parallel and separate administrative hierarchies, one democratic and bottom-up for the professionals, a second machinelike and top-down for the support staff.

THE ROLES OF THE ADMINISTRATORS
OF PROFESSIONAL WORK

Where does all this leave the administrators of the professional hierarchy, the executive directors and chiefs of the hospitals and the presidents and deans of the universities? Are they powerless? Compared with their counterparts in the entrepreneurial and machine organizations, they certainly lack a good deal of power. But that is far from the whole story.

The administrator of professional work may not be able to control the professionals directly, but he or she does perform a series of roles that can provide considerable indirect power.

First, this administrator spends much time handling disturbances in the structure. The pigeonholing process is an imperfect one at best, leading to all kinds of jurisdictional disputes between the professionals. Who should perform mastectomies in the hospitals, surgeons who look after cutting or gynecologists who look after women? Seldom, however, can one administrator impose a solution on the professionals involved in a dispute. Rather, various administrators must often sit down together and negotiate a solution on behalf of their constituencies.

Second, the administrators of professional work—especially those at higher levels—serve in key roles at the boundary of the organization, between the professionals inside and the influencers outside: governments, client associations, benefactors, and so on. On the one hand, the administrators are expected to protect the professionals' autonomy, to "buffer" them from external pressures. On the other hand, they are expected to woo those outsiders to support the organization, both morally and financially. And that often leads the outsiders to expect these administrators, in turn, to control the professionals, in machine bureaucratic ways. Thus, the external roles of the manager—maintaining liaison contacts, acting as figurehead and spokesman in a public relations capacity, negotiating with outside agencies—emerge as primary ones in the administration of professional work.

Some view the roles these administrators are called upon to perform as signs of weakness. They see these people as the errand boys of the professionals, or else as pawns caught in various tugs of war—between one professional and another, between support staffer and professional, between outsider and professional. In fact, however, these roles are the very sources of administrators' power. Power is, after all, gained at the locus of uncertainty, and that is exactly where the administrators of professionals sit. The administrator who succeeds in raising extra funds for his or her organization gains a say in how they are distributed; the one who can reconcile conflicts in favor of his or her unit or who can effectively buffer the professionals from external influence becomes a valued, and therefore powerful, member of the organization.

We can conclude that power in these structures does flow to those professionals who care to devote effort to doing administrative instead of professional work, so long as they do it well. But that, it should be stressed, is not laissez-faire power; the professional administrator maintains power only as long as the professionals perceive him or her to be serving their interests effectively.

Conditions of the Professional Organization

The professional form of organization appears wherever the operating work of an organization is dominated by skilled workers who use procedures that are difficult to learn yet are well defined. This means a situation that is both complex and stable—complex enough to require procedures that can be learned only through extensive training yet stable enough so that their use can become standardized.

Note that an elaborate technical system can work against this configuration. If highly regulating or automated, the professionals' skills might be amenable to rationalization, in other words, to be divided into simple, highly programmed steps that would destroy the basis for professional autonomy and thereby drive the structure to the machine form. And if highly complicated, the technical system would reduce the professionals' autonomy by forcing them to work in multidisciplinary teams, thereby driving the organization toward the innovative form. Thus the surgeon uses a scalpel, and the accountant a pencil. Both must be sharp, but both are otherwise simple and commonplace instruments. Yet both allow their users to perform independently what can be exceedingly complex functions.

The prime example of the professional configuration is the personal-service organization, at least the one with complex, stable work not reliant on a fancy technical system. Schools and universities, consulting firms, law and accounting offices, and social work agencies all rely on this form of organization, more or less, so long as they concentrate not on innovating in the solution of new problems but on applying standard programs to well-defined ones. The same seems to be true of hospitals, at least to the extent that their technical systems are simple. (In those areas that call for more sophisticated equipment—apparently a growing number, especially in teaching institutions—the hospital is driven toward a hybrid structure, with characteristics of the innovative form. But this tendency is mitigated by the hospital's overriding concern with safety. Only the tried and true can be relied upon, which produces a natural aversion to the looser innovative configuration.)

So far, our examples have come from the service sector. But the professional form can be found in manufacturing too, where the above conditions hold up. Such is the case of the craft enterprise, for example, the factory using skilled workers to produce ceramic products. The very term *craftsman* implies a kind of professional who learns traditional skills through long apprentice training and then is allowed to practice them free of direct supervision. Craft enterprises seem typically to have few administrators, who tend to work, in any event, alongside the operating personnel. The same would seem to be true for engineering work oriented not to creative design so much as to modification of existing dominant designs.

Strategy Formation in the Professional Organization

It is commonly assumed that strategies are formulated before they are implemented, that planning is the central process of formulation, and that structures must be designed to implement these strategies. At least this is what one reads in the conventional literature of strategic management. In the professional organization, these imperatives stand almost totally at odds with what really happens, leading to the conclusion either that such organizations are confused about how to make strategy, or else that the strategy writers are confused about how professional organizations must function. I subscribe to the latter explanation.

Using the definition of strategy as pattern in action, strategy formation in the professional organization takes on a new meaning. Rather than simply throwing up our hands at its resistance to formal strategic planning, or, at the other extreme, dismissing professional organizations as "organized anarchies" with strategy-making processes as mere "garbage cans" (March and Olsen, 1976) we can focus on how decisions and actions in such organizations order themselves into patterns over time.

Taking strategy as pattern in action, the obvious question becomes, which actions? The key area of strategy making in most organizations concerns the elaboration of the basic mission (the products or services offered to the public); in professional organizations, we shall argue, this is significantly controlled by individual professionals. Other important areas of strategy here include the inputs to the system (notably the choice of professional staff, the determination of clients, and the raising of external funds), the means to perform the mission (the construction of buildings and facilities, the purchase of research equipment, and so on), the structure and forms of governance (design of the committee system, the hierarchies, and so on), and the various means to support the mission.

Were professional organizations to formulate strategies in the conventional ways, central administrators would develop detailed and integrated plans about these issues. This sometimes happens, but in a very limited number of cases. Many strategic issues come under the direct control of individual professionals, while others can be decided neither by individual professionals nor by central administrators, but instead require the participation of a variety of people in a complex collective process. As illustrated in Figure 2, we examine in turn the decisions controlled by individual professionals, by central administrators, and by the collectivity.

DECISIONS MADE BY PROFESSIONAL JUDGMENT

Professional organizations are distinguished by the fact that the determination of the basic mission—the specific services to be offered and to whom—is in good part left to the judgment of professionals as individuals. In the university, for example, each professor has a good deal of control over what is taught and how, as well as what is researched and how. Thus the overall product-market strategy of McGill University must be seen as the composite of the individual teaching and research postures of its 1,200 professors.

That, however, does not quite constitute full autonomy, because there is a subtle but not insignificant constraint on that power. Professionals are left to decide on their own only because years of training have ensured that they will decide in ways generally accepted in their professions. Thus professors choose course contents and adopt teaching methods highly regarded by their colleagues, sometimes even formally sanctioned by their disciplines; they research subjects that will be funded by the granting agencies (which usually come under professional controls); and they publish articles acceptable to the journals refereed by their peers. Pushed to the limit, then, individual freedom becomes professional control. It may be explicit freedom from administrators, even from peers in other disciplines, but it is not implicit freedom from colleagues in their own discipline. Thus we use the label "professional judgment" to imply that while judgment may be the mode of choice, it is informed judgment, mightily influenced by professional training and affiliation.

DECISIONS MADE BY ADMINISTRATIVE FIAT

Professional expertise and autonomy, reinforced by the pigeonholing process, sharply circumscribe the capacity of central administrators to manage the professionals in the ways of conventional bureaucracy—through direct supervision and the designation of internal standards (rules, job descriptions, policies). Even the designation of standards of output or

FIGURE 2
Three Levels of Decision Making in the Professional Organization

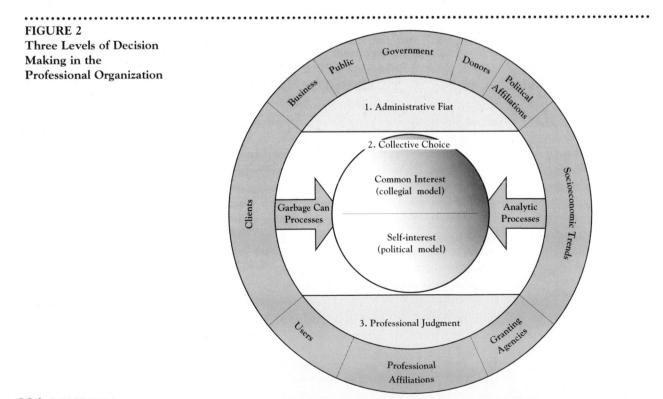

performance is discouraged by the intractable problem of operationalizing the goals of professional work.

Certain types of decisions, less related to the professional work per se, do however fall into the realm of what can be called administrative fiat, in other words, become the exclusive prerogative of the administrators. They include some financial decisions, for example, to buy and sell property and embark on fund-raising campaigns. Because many of the support services are organized in a conventional top-down hierarchy, they too tend to fall under the control of the central administration. Support services more critical to professional matters, however, such as libraries or computers in the universities, tend to fall into the realm of collective decision making, where the central administrators join the professionals in the making of choices.

Central administrators may also play a prominent role in determining the procedures by which the collective process functions: what committees exist, who gets nominated to them, and so on. It is the administrators, after all, who have the time to devote to administration. This role can give skillful administrators considerable influence, however indirect, over the decisions made by others. In addition, in times of crisis administrators may acquire more extensive powers, as the professionals become more inclined to defer to leadership to resolve the issues.

DECISIONS MADE BY COLLECTIVE CHOICE

Many decisions are, however, determined neither by administrators nor by individual professionals. Instead they are handled in interactive processes that combine professionals with administrators from a variety of levels and units. Among the most important of these decisions seem to be ones related to the definition, creation, design, and discontinuation of the pigeonholes, that is, the programs and departments of various kinds. Other important decisions here include the hiring and promotion of professionals and, in some cases, budgeting and the establishment and design of the interactive procedures themselves (if they do not fall under administrative fiat).

Decision making may be considered to involve the three phases of *identification* of the need for a decision, *development* of solutions, and *selection* of one of them. Identification seems to depend largely on individual initiative. Given the complexities of professional work and the rigidities of pigeonholing, change in this configuration is difficult to imagine without an initiating "sponsor" or "champion." Development may involve the same individual but often requires the efforts of collective task forces as well. And selection tends to be a fully interactive process, involving several layers of standing committees composed of professionals and administrators, and sometimes outsiders as well (such as government representatives). It is in this last phase that we find the full impact and complexity of mutual adjustment in the administration of professional organizations.

MODELS OF COLLECTIVE CHOICE

How do these interactive processes in fact work? Some writers have traditionally associated professional organizations with a *collegial* model, where decisions are made by a "community of individuals and groups, all of whom may have different roles and specialties, but who share common goals and objectives for the organization" (Taylor, 1983:18). *Common interest* is the guiding force, and decision making is therefore by consensus. Other writers instead propose a political model, in which the differences of interest groups are irreconcilable. Participants thus seek to serve their *self-interest*, and political factors become instrumental in determining outcomes.

Clearly, neither common interest nor self-interest will dominate decision processes all the time; some combination is naturally to be expected. Professionals may agree on goals yet conflict over how they should be achieved; alternatively, consensus can sometimes be achieved even where goals differ—Democrats do, after all, sometimes vote with Republicans in the U.S. Congress. In fact, we need to consider motivation, not just behavior, in order to distinguish collegiality from politics. Political success sometimes requires a collegial posture—one must cloak self-interest in the mantle of the common good. Likewise, collegial ends sometimes require political means. Thus, we should take as collegial any behavior that is *motivated* by a genuine concern for the good of the institution, and politics as any behavior driven fundamentally by self-interest (of the individual or his or her unit).

A third model that has been used to explain decision making in universities is the *garbage can*. Here decision making is characterized by "collections of choices looking for problems, issues and feelings looking for decision situations in which they may be aired, solutions looking for issues to which they might be an answer, and decision makers looking for work" (Cohen, March, and Olsen, 1972:1). Behavior is, in other words, nonpurposeful and often random, because goals are unclear and the means to achieve them problematic. Furthermore, participation is fluid because of the cost of time and energy. Thus, in place of the common interest of the collegial model and the self-interest of the political model, the garbage can model suggests a kind of *disinterest*.

The important question is not whether garbage can processes exist—we have all experienced them—but whether they matter. Do they apply to key issues or only to incidental ones? Of course, decisions that are not significant to anyone may well end up in the garbage can, so to speak. There is always someone with free time willing to challenge a proposal for the sake of so doing. But I have difficulty accepting that individuals to whom decisions are important do not invest the effort necessary to influence them. Thus, like common interest and self-interest, I conclude that disinterest neither dominates decision processes nor is absent from them.

Finally, *analysis* may be considered a fourth model of decision making. Here calculation is used, if not to select the best alternative, then at least to assess the acceptability of different ones. Such an approach seems consistent with the machine configuration, where a technostructure stands ready to calculate the costs and benefits of every proposal. But, in fact, analysis figures prominently in the professional configuration too, but here carried out mostly by professional operators themselves. Rational analysis structures arguments for communication and debate and enables champions and their opponents to support their respective positions. In fact, as each side seeks to pick holes in the position of the other, the real issues are more likely to emerge.

Thus, as indicated in Figure 2, the important collective decisions of the professional organization seem to be most influenced by collegial and political processes, with garbage can pressures encouraging a kind of haphazardness on one side (especially for less important decisions) and analytical interventions on the other side encouraging a certain rationality (serving as an invisible hand to keep the lid on the garbage can, so to speak!).

STRATEGIES IN THE PROFESSIONAL ORGANIZATION

Thus, we find here a very different process of strategy making, and very different resulting strategies, compared with conventional (especially machine) organizations. While it may seem difficult to create strategies in these organizations, due to the fragmentation of activity, the politics, and the garbage can phenomenon, in fact the professional organization is inundated with strategies (meaning patterning in its actions). The standardization of skills encourages patterning, as do the pigeonholing process and the professional affiliations. Collegiality promotes consistency of behavior; even politics works to resist changing existing patterns. As for the garbage can model, perhaps it just represents the unexplained variance in the system; that is, whatever is not understood looks to the outside observer like organized anarchy.

Many different people get involved in the strategy-making process here, including administrators and the various professionals, individually and collectively, so that the resulting strategies can be very fragmented (at the limit, each professional pursues his or her own product-market strategy). There are, of course, forces that encourage some overall cohesion in strategy too: the common forces of administrative fiat, the broad negotiations that take place in the collective process (for example, on new tenure regulations in a university), even the forces of habit and tradition, at the limit ideology, that can pervade a professional organization (such as hiring certain kinds of people or favoring certain styles of teaching or of surgery).

Overall, the strategies of the professional organization tend to exhibit a remarkable degree of stability. Major reorientations in strategy—"strategic revolutions"—are discouraged by the fragmentation of activity and the influence of the individual professionals and their outside associates. But at a narrower level, change is ubiquitous. Inside tiny pigeonholes, services are continually being altered, procedure redesigned, and clientele shifted, while in the collective process, pigeonholes are constantly being added and rearranged. Thus, the professional organization is, paradoxically, extremely stable at the broadest level and in a state of perpetual change at the narrowest one.

Some Issues Associated with the Professional Organization

The professional organization is unique among the different configurations in answering two of the paramount needs of contemporary men and women. It is democratic, disseminating its power directly to its workers (at least those lucky enough to be professional). And it provides them with extensive autonomy, freeing them even from the need to coordinate closely with their colleagues. Thus, the professional has the best of both worlds. He or she is attached to an organization yet is free to serve clients in his or her own way constrained only by the established standards of the profession.

The result is that professionals tend to emerge as highly motivated individuals, dedicated to their work and to the clients they serve. Unlike the machine organization, which places barriers between the operator and the client, this configuration removes them, allowing a personal relationship to develop. Moreover, autonomy enables the professionals to perfect their skills free of interference, as they repeat the same complex programs time after time.

But in these same characteristics, democracy and autonomy, lie the chief problems of the professional organization. For there is no evident way to control the work, outside of that exercised by the profession itself, no way, to correct deficiencies that the professionals choose to overlook. What they tend to overlook are the problems of coordination, of discretion, and of innovation that arise in these configurations.

PROBLEMS OF COORDINATION

The professional organization can coordinate effectively in its operating core only by relying on the standardization of skills. But that is a loose coordinating mechanism at best; it fails to cope with many of the needs that arise in these organizations. One need is to coordinate the work of professionals with that of support staffers. The professionals want to give the orders. But that can catch the support staffers between the vertical power of line authority and the horizontal power of professional expertise. Another need is to achieve overriding coordination among the professionals themselves. Professional organizations, at the limit, may be viewed as collections of independent individuals who come together only to draw on common resources and support services. Though the pigeonholing process facilitates this, some things inevitably fall through the cracks between the pigeonholes. But because the professional organization lacks any obvious coordinating mechanism to deal with these, they inevitably provoke a great deal of conflict. Much political blood is spilled in the continual reassessment of contingencies and programs that are either imperfectly conceived or artificially distinguished.

PROBLEMS OF DISCRETION

Pigeonholing raises another serious problem. It focuses most of the discretion in the hands of single professionals, whose complex skills, no matter how standardized, require the exercise of considerable judgment. Such discretion works fine when professionals are competent and conscientious. But it plays havoc when they are not. Inevitably, some professionals are simply lazy or incompetent. Others confuse the needs of their clients with the skills of their trade. They thus concentrate on a favored program to the exclusion of all others (like the psychiatrist who thinks that all patients, indeed all people, need psychoanalysis). Clients incorrectly sent their way get mistreated (in both senses of that word).

Various factors confound efforts to deal with this inversion of means and ends. One is that professionals are notoriously reluctant to act against their own, for example, to censure irresponsible behavior through their professional associations. Another (which perhaps helps to explain the first) is the intrinsic difficulty of measuring the outputs of professional work. When psychiatrists cannot even define the word *cure* or *healthy*, how are they to prove that psychoanalysis is better for schizophrenics than is chemical therapy?

Discretion allows professionals to ignore not only the needs of their clients but also those of the organization itself. Many professionals focus their loyalty on their profession, not on the place where they happen to practice it. But professional organizations have needs for loyalty too—to support their overall strategies, to staff their administrative committees, to see them through conflicts with the professional associations. Cooperation is crucial to the functioning of the administrative structure, yet many professionals resist it furiously.

PROBLEMS OF INNOVATION

In the professional organization, major innovation also depends on cooperation. Existing programs may be perfected by the single professional, but new ones usually cut across the established specialties—in essence, they require a rearrangement of the pigeonholes—and so call for collective action. As a result, the reluctance of the professionals to cooperate with each other and the complexity of the collective processes can produce resistance to innovation. These are, after all, professional *bureaucracies*, in essence, performance structures designed to perfect given programs in stable environments, not problem-solving structures to create new programs for unanticipated needs.

The problems of innovation in the professional organization find their roots in convergent thinking, in the deductive reasoning of the professional who sees the specific situation in terms of the general concept. That means new problems are forced into old pigeonholes, as is excellently illustrated in Spencer's comments: "All patients developing significant complications or death among our three hospitals . . . are reported to a central office with a narrative description of the sequence of events, with reports varying in length from a third to an entire page." And six to eight of these cases are discussed in the one-hour weekly "mortality-morbidity" conferences, including presentation of it by the surgeon and "questions and comments" by the audience (978:118). An "entire" page and ten minutes of discussion for a case with "significant complications"! Maybe that is enough to list the symptoms and slot them into pigeonholes. But it is hardly enough even to begin to think about creative solutions. As Lucy once told Charlie Brown, great art cannot be done in half an hour; it takes at least 45 minutes!

The fact is that great art and innovative problem solving require *inductive* reasoning—that is, the inference of the new general solution from the particular experience. And that kind of thinking is *divergent*; it breaks away from old routines or standards rather than perfecting existing ones. And that flies in the face of everything the professional organization is designed to do.

PUBLIC RESPONSES TO THESE PROBLEMS

What responses do the problems of coordination, discretion, and innovation evoke? Most commonly, those outside the profession see the problems as resulting from a lack of external control of the professional and the profession. So they do the obvious: try to control the work through other, more traditional means. One is direct supervision, which typically means imposing an intermediate level of supervision to watch over the professionals. But we already discussed why this cannot work for jobs that are complex. Another is to try to standardize the work or its outputs. But we also discussed why complex work cannot be formalized by rules, regulations, or measures of performance. All these types of controls really do, by transferring the responsibility for the service from the professional to the administrative structure, is destroy the effectiveness of the work. It is not the government that educates the student, not even the school system or the school itself; it is not the hospital that delivers the baby. These things are done by the individual professional. If that professional is incompetent, no plan or rule fashioned in the technostructure, no order from any administrator or government official, can ever make him or her competent. But such plans, rules, and orders can impede the competent professional from providing his or her service effectively.

Are there then no solutions for a society concerned about the performance of its professional organizations? Financial control of them and legislation against irresponsible professional behavior are obviously in order. But beyond that solutions must grow from a recognition of professional work for what it is. Change in the professional organization does not *sweep* in from new administrators taking office to announce wide reforms, or from government officials intent on bringing the professionals under technocratic control. Rather, change *seeps* in through the slow process of changing the professionals—changing who enters the profession in the first place, what they learn in its professional schools (norms as well as skills and knowledge), and thereafter how they upgrade their skills. Where desired changes are resisted, society may be best off to call on its professionals' sense of public responsibility or, failing that, to bring pressure on the professional associations rather than on the professional bureaucracies.

▼ READING 11.2 BALANCING THE PROFESSIONAL SERVICE FIRM*

by David H. Maister

The topic of managing professional service firms (PSF) (including law, consulting, investment banking, accountancy, architecture, engineering, and others) has been relatively neglected by management researchers. . . . Yet in recent years large (if not giant) PSFs have emerged in most of the professional service industries. . . .

The professional service firm is the ultimate embodiment of that familiar phrase "Our assets are our people." Frequently, a PSF tends to sell to its clients the services of particular individuals (or a team of such individuals) more than the services of the firm. Professional services usually involve a high degree of interaction with the client, together with a high degree of customization. Both of these characteristics demand that the firm attract (and retain) highly skilled individuals. The PSF, therefore, competes in two markets simultaneously: the "output" market for its services and the "input" market for its productive resources —the professional work force. It is the need to balance the often conflicting demands and constraints imposed by these two markets that constitutes the special challenge for managers of the professional service firm.

This article explores the interaction of these forces inside the professional service firm, and examines some of the major variables that firm management can attempt to manipulate in order to bring these forces into balance. The framework employed for this examination is shown in Figure 1, which illustrates the proposition that balancing the demands of the two markets is accomplished through the firm's economic and organizational structures. All four of these elements—the two markets and the two structures—are tightly interrelated. By examining each in turn, we shall attempt to identify the major variables which form the links shown in Figure 1. First, the article will examine the typical organizational structure of the firm; second, it will explore the economic structure and its relation to other elements. It shall then consider the market for professional labor, and finally discuss the market for the firm's services. As we shall see, successful PSF management is a question of balance among the four elements of Figure 1.

THE ORGANIZATIONAL STRUCTURE OF THE PSF

The archetypal structure of the professional service firm is an organization containing three professional levels which serve as a normal or expected career path. In a consulting organization, these levels might be labeled junior consultant, manager, and vice-president. In a CPA firm they might be referred to as staff accountant, manager, and partner. Law firms

FIGURE 1
Framework for Analyzing the PSF

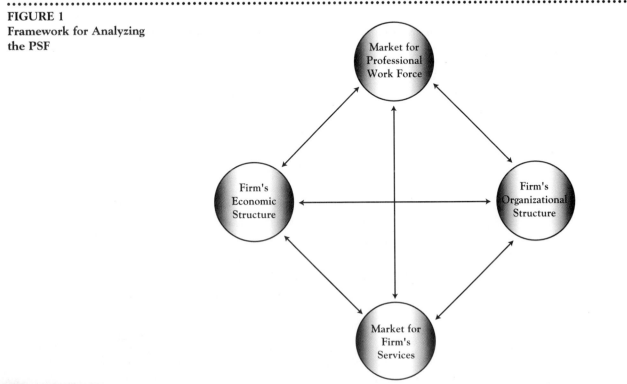

tend to have only two levels, associate and partner, although there is an increasing tendency in large law firms to formally recognize what has long been an informal distinction between junior and senior partners. Whatever the precise structure, nearly all PSFs have the pyramid form shown in Figure 2.

There is nothing magical about the common occurrence of three levels (a greater or lesser number may be found), but it is instructive to consider other organizations that have this pattern. One example is the university which has assistant professors, associate professors, and full professors. These ranks may be signs of status as well as function (reminding us of another three-level status structure: the common people, the peerage, and royalty). Another analogy is found in the organization of the medieval craftsman's shop which had apprentices, journeymen, and master craftsmen. Indeed, the early years of an individual's association with a PSF are usually viewed as an apprenticeship: the senior craftsmen repay the hard work and assistance of the juniors by teaching them their craft.

PROJECT TEAM STRUCTURE

What determines the shape or architecture of the organization—the relative mix of juniors, managers, and seniors that the organization requires? Fundamentally, this depends on the nature of the professional services that the firm provides, and how these services are delivered. Because of their customized nature, most professional activities are organized on a project basis: the professional service firms are the job shops of the service sector. The project nature of the work means that there are basically three major activities in the delivery of professional services: client relations, project management, and the performance of the detailed professional tasks.

In most PSFs, primary responsibility for these three tasks is allocated to the three levels of the organization: seniors (partners or vice-presidents) are responsible for client relations; managers, for the day-to-day supervision and coordination of projects; and juniors, for the many technical tasks necessary to complete the study. In the vernacular, the three levels are "the finders, the minders and the grinders" of the business.* Naturally, such an allocation of

FIGURE 2
The Professional Pyramid

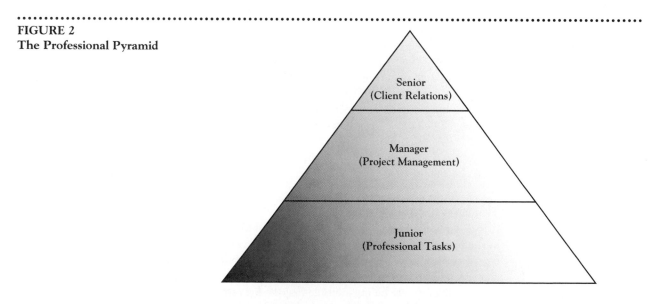

* This characteristic is, of course, simplified. Additional "levels" or functions can be identified at both the top and the bottom of the pyramid. To the top we can add those individuals responsible for managing the firm (rather than managing projects). At the bottom of the pyramid lie both "nonprofessional" support staff and trainees.

tasks need not (indeed, should not) be as rigid as this suggests. In a well-run PSF, juniors are increasingly given "manager" tasks to perform (in order to test their competence and worthiness to be promoted to the manager level), and managers are gradually given tasks that enable them to develop client-relations skills to prepare for promotion to the senior level. Nevertheless, it is still meaningful to talk of "senior tasks," "manager tasks," and "junior tasks."

CAPACITY PLANNING

The required shape of the PSF is thus primarily influenced by the mix of client relations, project management, and professional tasks involved in the firm's projects. If the PSF is a job shop, then its professional staff members are its "machines" (productive resources). As with any job shop, a balance must be established between the types of work performed and the number of different types of "machines" (people) that are required. The PSF is a "factory," and the firm must plan its capacity. . . .

THE ECONOMICS OF THE PSF

Most professional service firms are partnerships; some are corporations. Regardless of the precise form, however, certain regularities in the economic structure are observable. For example, since most PSFs have few fixed assets, they only require capital to fund accounts receivable and other working capital items. Consequently, the vast majority of revenues are disbursed in the form of salaries, bonuses, and net partnership profits. A typical division of revenues might be 33 percent for professional salaries, 33 percent for support staff and overhead, and 33 percent for senior (or shareholder) salary compensation. However, in some PSFs, partnership salary and profits might rise to 50 percent or more, usually corresponding to lower support staff and overhead costs.

GENERATING REVENUES

If revenues are typically disbursed in this way, how are they generated? . . . The relevant variable is, of course, the billing rate—the hourly charge to clients for the services of individuals at different levels of the hierarchy. The ratio between the lowest and highest rates in some firms can exceed 3 or 4 to 1. The "rewards of partnership" come only in part from the high rates that top professionals can charge their clients. Partners' rewards are also derived, in large part, from the firm's ability, through its project team structure, to *leverage* the professional skills of the seniors with the efforts of juniors. As the managing senior of a top consulting firm observed, "How is it that a young MBA, straight from graduate school, can give advice to top corporate officers?" The answer lies in the synergy of the PSF's project team. Acting independently, the juniors could not "bill out" the results of their efforts at the rates that can be charged by the PSF. The firm can obtain higher rates for the juniors' efforts because they are combined with the expertise and guidance of the seniors. . . .

THE BILLING MULTIPLE

It is also instructive to compare the net weighted billing rate to compensation levels within the firm. This (conventional) calculation is known as the billing multiple, and is calculated (for either the firm or an individual) as the billing rate per hour divided by the total compensation per hour. . . . The average multiple for most firms is between 2.5 and 4.

The appropriate billing multiple that the firm can achieve will, of course, be influenced by the added value that the firm provides and by the relative supply and demand conditions for the firm's services. The market for the firm's services will determine the fees it can command for a given project. The firm's costs will be determined by its ability to deliver the service with a "profitable" mix of junior, manager, and senior time. If the firm . . . can find a way to deliver the service with a higher proportion of juniors to seniors, it will be able to achieve lower costs and hence a higher multiple. The project team structure of the firm is, therefore, an important component of firm profitability.

The billing multiple is intimately related to the breakeven economics of the firm. If total professional salaries are taken as an amount $Y, and support staff and overhead cost approximate, say, an equivalent amount $Y, then breakeven will be attained when the firm bills $2Y. This could be attained by charging clients a multiple of 2 for professional services, but only if all available time was billed out. If the firm wishes to break even at 50 percent target utilization (a common figure in many PSFs), then the required net billing multiple will be 4. . . .

THE PSF AND THE MARKET FOR PROFESSIONAL LABOR

One of the key characteristics of the PSF is that the three levels (junior, manager, senior) constitute a well-defined career path. Individuals joining the organization normally begin at the bottom, with strong expectations of progressing through the organization at some pace agreed to (explicitly or implicitly) in advance. While this pace may not be a rigid one ("up or out in the X years"), both the individual and the organization usually share strong expectations about what constitutes a reasonable period of time. Individuals that are not promoted within this period will seek greener pastures elsewhere, either by their own choice or career ambitions or at the strong suggestion of those who do not consider them promotable. Intermediate levels in the hierarchy are not considered by the individual or the organization as career positions. It is this characteristic, perhaps more than any other, that distinguishes the PSF from other types of organizations.

PROMOTION POLICY

While there are many considerations that attract young professionals to a particular firm, career opportunities within the firm usually play a large role. Two dimensions of this rate of progress are important: the normal amount of time spent at each level before being considered for promotion and the "odds of making it" (the proportion promoted). These promotion policy variables perform an important screening function. Not all young professionals are able to develop the managerial and client-relations skills required at the higher levels. While good recruiting procedures may reduce the degree of screening required through the promotion process, they can rarely eliminate the need for the promotion process to serve this important function. The "risk of not making it" also serves the firm by placing pressure on junior personnel to work hard and succeed. This pressure can be an important motivating tool in light of the discretion which many PSF professionals have over their working schedules. . . .

ACCOMMODATING RAPID GROWTH

. . . What adjustments can be made to allow faster growth? Basically, there are four strategies. First, the firm can devote more attention and resources to its hiring process so that a higher proportion of juniors can be routinely promoted to managers. (In effect, this shifts the quality-of-personnel screen from the promotion system to the hiring system, where it is often more difficult and speculative.) Second, the firm can attempt to hasten the "apprenticeship" process through more formal training and professional development programs, rather than the "learn by example" and mentoring relationships commonly found in smaller firms and those growing at a more leisurely pace. In fact, it is the rate of growth, rather than the size of the firm, which necessitates formal development programs. . . .*

---

* Speeding the development of individuals so that the firm can grow faster is, of course, not the only role for formal training programs. They can also be a device to allow the firm to hire less (initially) qualified and hence lower wage individuals, thereby reducing its cost for juniors.

The third mechanism that the firm can adopt to accelerate its target growth rate is to make use of "lateral hires": bringing in experienced professionals at other than the junior level. In most PSFs, this strategy is avoided because of its adverse effect upon the morale of junior personnel, who tend to view such actions as reducing their own chances for promotion. Even if these have been accelerated by the fast growth rate, juniors will still tend to feel that they have been less than fairly dealt with.

Modifying the project team structure is the final strategy for accommodating rapid growth without throwing out of balance the relationships between organizational structure, promotion incentives, and economic structure. In effect, the firm would alter the mix of senior, manager, and junior time devoted to a project. This strategy will be discussed in a later section.

TURNOVER

. . . In most PSF industries, one or more firms can be identified that have a high target rate of turnover (or alternatively, choose to grow at less than their optimal rate). Yet individuals routinely join these organizations knowing that the odds of "making it" are very low. Such "churning" strategies have some clear disadvantages *and* benefits for the PSF itself. One of the benefits is that the firm's partners (or shareholders) can routinely earn the surplus value of the juniors without having to repay them in the form of promotion. The high turnover rate also allows a significant degree of screening so that only the "best" stay in the organization. Not surprisingly, firms following this strategy tend to be among the most prestigious in their industry.

This last comment gives us a clue as to why such firms are able to maintain this strategy over time. For many recruits, the experience, training, and association with a prestigious firm compensate for poor promotion opportunities. Young professionals view a short period of time at such a firm as a form of "post-postgraduate" degree, and often leave for prime positions they could not have achieved (as quickly) by another route. Indeed, most of the prestigious PSFs following this strategy not only encourage this, but also provide active "outplacement" assistance. Apart from the beneficial effects that such activities provide in recruiting the next generation of juniors, such "alumni/ae" are often the source of future business for the PSF when they recommend that their corporate employers hire their old firm (which they know and understand) over other competitors. The ability to place ex-staff in prestigious positions is one of the prerequisites of a successful churning strategy. . . .

THE MARKET FOR THE FIRM'S SERVICES

The final element in our model is the market for the firm's services. We have already explored some of the ways in which this market is linked to the firm's economic structure (through the billing rates the firm charges) and to the organizational structure (through the project team structure and target growth rate).

We must add to our model one of the most basic linkages in the dynamics of the PSF: the direct link between the market for professional labor and the market for the firm's services. The key variable that links these two markets is the quality of professional labor that the firm requires and can attract. Earlier, when we considered the factors that attract professionals to a given PSF, we omitted a major variable that often enters into the decision process: the types of projects undertaken by the firm. Top professionals are likely to be attracted to the firm that engages in exciting or challenging projects, or that provides opportunities for professional fulfillment and development. In turn, firms engaged in such projects *need* to attract the best professionals. It is, therefore, necessary to consider different types of professional service activity.

PROJECT TYPES

While there are many dimensions which may distinguish one type of professional service activity from another, one in particular is crucial: the degree of customization required in the delivery of the service. To explore this, we will characterize professional service projects into three types: "Brains," "Grey Hair," and "Procedure."

In the first type (Brains), the client's problem is likely to be extremely complex, perhaps at the forefront of professional or technical knowledge. The PSF that targets this market will be attempting to sell its services on the basis of the high professional craft of its staff. In essence, this firm's appeal to its market is "hire us because we're smart." The key elements of this type of professional service are creativity, innovation, and the pioneering of new approaches, concepts, or techniques—in effect, new solutions to new problems. [See next chapter on the innovative context.]

Grey Hair projects may require highly customized "output," but they usually involve a lesser degree of innovation and creativity than a Brains' project. The general nature of the problem is familiar, and the activities necessary to complete the project may be similar to those performed on other projects. Clients with Grey Hair problems seek out PSFs with experience in their particular type of problem. The PSF sells its knowledge, its experience, and its judgment. In effect, it is saying: "Hire us because we have been through this before. We have practice in solving this type of problem."

The third type of project (Procedure) usually involves a well-recognized and familiar type of problem, at least within the professional community. While some customization is still required, the steps necessary to accomplish this are somewhat programmatic. Although clients may have the ability and resources to perform the work themselves, they may turn to the PSF because it can perform the service more efficiently; because it is an outsider; or because the clients' staff capabilities may be employed better elsewhere. In essence, the PSF is selling its procedures, its efficiency, and its availability: "Hire us because we know how to do this and can deliver it effectively."

PROJECT TEAM STRUCTURE

One of the most significant differences between the three types of projects is the project team structure required to deliver the firm's services. Brains projects are usually denoted by an extreme job-shop operation, involving highly skilled and highly paid professionals. Few procedures are routinizable: each project is a "one-off." Accordingly, the opportunities for leveraging the top professionals with juniors are relatively limited. Even though such projects may involve significant data collection and analysis (usually done by juniors), even these activities cannot be clearly specified in advance and require the involvement of at least middle-level (project management) professionals on a continuous basis. Consequently, the ratio of junior time to middle-level and senior time on Brains projects tends to be low. The project team structure of a firm with a high proportion of Brains projects will tend to have a relatively low emphasis on juniors, with a corresponding impact on the shape of the organization.

Since the problems to be addressed in Grey Hair projects are somewhat familiar, some of the tasks to be performed (particularly the early ones) are known in advance and can be specified and delegated. More juniors can be employed to accomplish these tasks, which are then assembled and jointly evaluated at some middle stage of the process. Unlike the "pure job-shop" nature of Brains projects, the appropriate process to create and deliver a Grey Hair project more closely resembles a disconnected assembly line.

Procedure projects usually involve the highest proportion of junior time relative to senior time, and hence imply a different organizational shape for firms that specialize in such projects. The problems to be addressed in such projects, and the steps necessary to complete the analysis, diagnosis, and conclusions, are usually sufficiently well established so that they can be easily delegated to junior staff (with supervision). Whereas in Grey Hair projects senior or middle-level staff must evaluate the results of one stage of the project before deciding how to proceed, in Procedure projects the range of possible outcomes for some steps may be so well known that the appropriate responses can be "programmed." The operating procedure takes on even more of the characteristics of an assembly line.

While the three categories described are only points along a spectrum of project types, it is a simple task in any PSF industry to identify types of problems that fit these categories. The choice that the firm makes in its mix of project types is one of the most important variables available to balance the firm. As we have shown, this choice determines the firm's project team structure, thereby influencing significantly the economic and organizational structures of the firm.

CONCLUSIONS: BALANCING THE PROFESSIONAL SERVICE FIRM

Figure 3 summarizes our review of the four major elements involved in balancing the PSF and the major variables linking these elements. What may we conclude from this review? Our discussion has shown that the four elements are, indeed, tightly linked. The firm cannot change one element without making corresponding changes in one or more of the other three. . . .

In performing these balance analyses, the firm must distinguish between the "levers" (variables that it controls) and the "rocks" (variables substantially constrained by the forces of the market). . . .

Perhaps the most significant management variable is the mix of projects undertaken and the implications this has for the project team structure. This variable is a significant force in influencing the economics of the firm, its organizational structure, and both markets. The project team structure as defined in this article (i.e., the *average* or typical pro-

FIGURE 3
Balancing the PSF

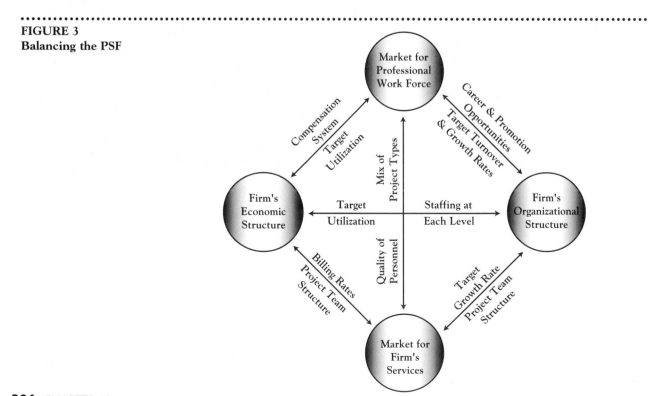

portion of time required from professionals at different levels) has not been a variable that is routinely monitored by PSF management. However, as we have shown, its role in balancing the firm is critical.

It is possible, and not uncommon, for the firm's project team structure to change over time. If it is possible to deliver the firm's services with a greater proportion of juniors, this will reduce the costs of the project. Competition in the market will, over time, require the firm to seek lower costs for projects, thus creating opportunities for more juniors to be used on projects that required a high proportion of senior time in the past. Projects that, in the past, had Brains or Grey Hair characteristics may be accomplished as Procedure projects in future years.*

When considering new projects to undertake, it is usually more profitable for the firm to engage in a project similar to one recently performed for a previous client. The knowledge, expertise, and basic approaches to the problem that were developed (often through significant personal and financial investment) can be capitalized upon by applying them to a similar or related problem. Frequently, the second project can be billed out to the client at a similar (or only slightly lower) rate, since the client perceives (and receives) something equally custom-tailored: the solution to his or her problem. However, the savings in PSF costs in delivering this customization are not all shared with the client (if, indeed, any are). The firm thus makes its most money by "leading the market": selling a service with reproducible, standardizable elements as a fully customized service at a fully customized price.

Unfortunately, even before the market catches up and refuses to bear the fully customized price, the firm may encounter an internal behavior problem. While it is in the best interest of the *firm* to undertake similar or repetitive engagements, often this does not coincide with the desires of the *individuals* involved. Apart from any reasons of status, financial rewards, or fulfillment derived from serving the clients' needs, most individuals join PSFs to experience the professional challenge and variety and to avoid routine repetition. While individuals may be content to undertake a similar project for the second or third time, they will not be for the fourth, sixth, or eighth. Yet it is in the interest of the firm (particularly if the market has not yet caught up) to take advantage of the experience and expertise that it has acquired. One solution, of course, is to convert the past experience and expertise of the individual into the expertise of the firm by accepting a similar project, but utilizing a greater proportion of juniors on it. Besides requiring a lesser commitment of time from the experienced seniors, this device serves to train the juniors.

For all these reasons, we might suspect that the proportion of juniors to seniors required by the firm *in a particular practice area* will tend to increase over time. If this is allowed to proceed without corresponding adjustments in the range of practice areas, the project team structure of the firms will be altered, causing significant impacts on the economics and organization of the firm. The dangers of failing to monitor the project team structure are thus clearly revealed. Examples of this failure abound in many PSF industries. One consulting firm that learned how to increasingly utilize junior professionals began to aggressively hire new junior staff. After a reasonable period of time for the promotion decision, the firm realized that, at its current growth rate, it could not promote its "normal" proportion of promotion candidates: it did not need as many partners and managers in relation to the number of juniors it now had. Morale and productivity in the junior ranks suffered. . . . Successful PSF management is a question of balance.

---

*This argument suggests that there is a "life-cycle" to professional "products" in the same way that such cycles exist for tangible products.

THE INNOVATION CONTEXT

Although often seen as a high-technology event involving inventor-entrepreneurs, innovation may, of course, occur in high- or low-technology, product or service, large or small organizational situations. Innovation may be thought of as the *first reduction to practice* of an idea in a culture. The more radical the idea, the more traumatic and profound its impact will tend to be. But there are no absolutes. Whatever is newest and most difficult to understand becomes the "high technology" of its age. As Jim Utterback of MIT is fond of pointing out, the delivery of ice was high technology at the turn of the century, later it was the production of automobiles. By the same token, fifty years from now, electronics may be considered mundane.

Our focus here, however, is not on innovation per se, but on the innovation *context;* that is, the situation in which steady or frequent innovation of a complex nature is an intrinsic part of the organization and the industry segment in which it chooses to operate. Such organizations depend, not just on a single entrepreneurial individual, but on teams of experts molded together.

The innovation context is one in which the organization often must deal with complex technologies or systems under conditions of dynamic change. Typically, major innovations require that a variety of experts work toward a common goal, often led by a single champion or a small group of committed individuals. Much has been learned from research in recent years on such organizations. While this knowledge may seem less structured than that of previous chapters, several dominant themes have emerged.

This chapter opens with a description of the fifth of Mintzberg's structures, here titled the innovative organization, but also referred to as "adhocracy." This is the structure that, as noted, achieves its effectiveness by being inefficient. This reading probes into the unusual ways in which strategies evolve in the context of work that is both highly complex and highly dynamic. Here we see the full flowering of the notion of emergent strategy, culminating in a description of a "grass-roots" model of the process. We also see here a strategic leadership less concerned with formulating and then implementing strategies than with managing a process through which strategies almost seem to *form* by themselves.

The second reading of this chapter, James Brian Quinn's "Managing Innovation: Controlled Chaos" (another winner of a McKinsey prize for the best *Harvard Business Review* article), suggests how the spirit of adhocracy and strategy formation as a learning process can be integrated with some of the formal strategic processes of large organizations. To achieve innovativeness, other authors have advocated adhocracy with little or no reliance on planning. Quinn suggests that blending broad strategy planning with a consciously structured adhocracy gives better results. This reading also brings back the notion of "intrapreneurship," mentioned in the introduction to Chapter 9 on the entrepreneurial context.

When it is successful, intrapreneurship—implying the stimulation and diffusion of innovative capacity throughout a larger organization, with many champions of innovations—tends to follow most of Quinn's precepts. As such, it seems to belong more to this context than the entrepreneurial one, which focuses on organizations highly centralized around the initiatives of their single leaders, whether or not innovative.

▼ READING 12.1   THE INNOVATIVE ORGANIZATION*

by Henry Mintzberg

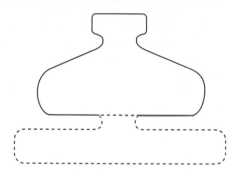

None of the organization forms so far discussed is capable of sophisticated innovation, the kind required of a high-technology research organization, an avant-garde film company, or a factory manufacturing complex prototypes. The entrepreneurial organization can certainly innovate, but only in relatively simple ways. The machine and professional organizations are performance, not problem-solving types, designed to perfect standardized programs, not to invent new ones. And although the diversified organization resolves some problem of strategic inflexibility found in the machine organization, as noted earlier it too is not a true innovator. A focus on control by standardizing outputs does not encourage innovation.

Sophisticated innovation requires a very different configuration, one that is able to fuse experts drawn from different disciplines into smoothly functioning ad hoc project teams. To borrow the word coined by Bennis and Slator in 1964 and later popularized in Alvin Toffler's *Future Shock* (1970), these are the *adhocracies* of our society.

*Adapted from *The Structuring of Organizations* (Prentice Hall, 1979), Chap. 21 on the adhocracy; on strategy formation from "Strategy Formation in an Adhocracy," coauthored with Alexandra McHugh, *Administrative Science Quarterly* (1985: 160–197), and "Strategy of Design: A Study of Architects in Co-Partnership," coauthored with Suzanne Otis, Jamal Shamsie, and James A. Waters, in J. Grant (ed.), *Strategic Management Frontiers* (JAI Press, 1988). A chapter similar to this one appeared in *Mintzberg on Management: Inside Our Strange World of Organizations* (Free Press, 1989).

The Basic Structure

Here again we have a distinct configuration of the attributes of design: highly organic structure, with little formalization of behavior; specialized jobs based on expert training; a tendency to group the specialists in functional units for housekeeping purposes but to deploy them in small project teams to do their work; a reliance on teams, on task forces, and on integrating managers of various sorts in order to encourage mutual adjustment, the key mechanism of coordination, within and between these teams; and considerable decentralization to and within these teams, which are located at various places in the organization and involve various mixtures of line managers and staff and operating experts.

To innovate means to break away from established patterns. Thus the innovative organization cannot rely on any form of standardization for coordination. In other words, it must avoid all the trappings of bureaucratic structure, notably sharp divisions of labor, extensive unit differentiation, highly formalized behaviors, and an emphasis on planning and control systems. Above all, it must remain flexible. A search for organigrams to illustrate this description elicited the following response from one corporation thought to have an adhocracy structure: "[We] would prefer not to supply an organization chart, since it would change too quickly to serve any useful purpose." Of all the configurations, this one shows the least reverence for the classical principles of management, especially unity of command. Information and decision processes flow flexibly and informally, wherever they must, to promote innovation. And that means overriding the chain of authority if need be.

The entrepreneurial configuration also retains a flexible, organic structure, and so is likewise able to innovate. But that innovation is restricted to simple situations, ones easily comprehended by a single leader. Innovation of the sophisticated variety requires another kind of flexible structure, one that can draw together different forms of expertise. Thus the adhocracy must hire and give power to experts, people whose knowledge and skills have been highly developed in training programs. But unlike the professional organization, the adhocracy cannot rely on the standardized skills of its experts to achieve coordination, because that would discourage innovation. Rather, it must treat existing knowledge and skills as bases on which to combine and build new ones. Thus the adhocracy must break through the boundaries of conventional specialization and differentiation, which it does by assigning problems not to individual experts in preestablished pigeonholes but to multidisciplinary teams that merge their efforts. Each team forms around one specific project.

Despite organizing around market-based projects, the organization must still support and encourage particular types of specialized expertise. And so the adhocracy tends to use a matrix structure: Its experts are grouped in functional units for specialized housekeeping purposes—hiring, training, professional communication, and the like—but are then deployed in the project teams to carry out the basic work of innovation.

As for coordination in and between these project teams, as noted earlier standardization is precluded as a significant coordinating mechanism. The efforts must be innovative, not routine. So, too, is direct supervision precluded because of the complexity of the work: Coordination must be accomplished by those with the knowledge, namely the experts themselves, not those with just authority. That leaves just one of our coordinating mechanisms, mutual adjustment, which we consider foremost in adhocracy. And, to encourage this, the organization makes use of a whole set of liaison devices, liaison personnel and integrating managers of all kinds, in addition to the various teams and task forces.

The result is that managers abound in the adhocracy: functional managers, integrating managers, project managers. The last-named are particularly numerous, since the project teams must be small to encourage mutual adjustment among their members, and each, of course, needs a designated manager. The consequence is that "spans of control" found in adhocracy tend to be small. But the implication of this is misleading, because the term is suited to the machine, not the innovative configuration: The managers of adhocracy seldom "manage" in the usual sense of giving orders; instead, they spend a good deal of time acting in a liaison capacity, to coordinate the work laterally among the various teams and units.

With its reliance on highly trained experts the adhocracy emerges as highly decentralized, in the "selective" sense. That means power over its decisions and actions is distributed to various places and at various levels according to the needs of the particular issue. In effect, power flows to wherever the relevant expertise happens to reside—among managers or specialists (or teams of those) in the line structure, the staff units, and the operating core.

To proceed with our discussion and to elaborate on how the innovative organization makes decisions and forms strategies, we need to distinguish two basic forms that it takes.

THE OPERATING ADHOCRACY

The *operating adhocracy* innovates and solves problems directly on behalf of its clients. Its multidisciplinary teams of experts often work under contract, as in the think-tank consulting firm, creative advertising agency, or manufacturer of engineering prototypes.

In fact, for every operating adhocracy, there is a corresponding professional bureaucracy, one that does similar work but with a narrower orientation. Faced with a client problem, the operating adhocracy engages in creative efforts to find a novel solution; the professional bureaucracy pigeonholes it into a known contingency to which it can apply a standard program. One engages in divergent thinking aimed at innovation, the other in convergent thinking aimed at perfection. Thus, one theater company might seek out new avant-garde plays to perform, while another might perfect its performance of Shakespeare year after year.

A key feature of the operating adhocracy is that its administrative and operating work tend to blend into a single effort. That is, in ad hoc project work it is difficult to separate the planning and design of the work from its execution. Both require the same specialized skills, on a project-by-project basis. Thus it can be difficult to distinguish the middle levels of the organization from its operating core, since line managers and staff specialists may take their place alongside operating specialists on the project teams.

Figure 1 shows the organigram of the National Film Board of Canada, a classic operating adhocracy (even though it does produce a chart—one that changes frequently it might be added). The Board is an agency of the Canadian federal government and produces mostly short films, many of them documentaries. At the time of this organigram, the characteristics of adhocracy were particularly in evidence: It shows a large number of support units as well as liaison positions (for example, research, technical, and production coordinators), with the operating core containing loose concurrent functional and market groupings, the latter by region as well as by type of film produced and, as can be seen, some not even connected to the line hierarchy!

THE ADMINISTRATIVE ADHOCRACY

The second type of adhocracy also functions with project teams, but toward a different end. Whereas the operating adhocracy undertakes projects to serve its clients, the *administrative adhocracy* undertakes projects to serve itself, to bring new facilities or activities on line, as in the administrative structure of a highly automated company. And in sharp contrast to the operating adhocracy, the administrative adhocracy makes a clear distinction between

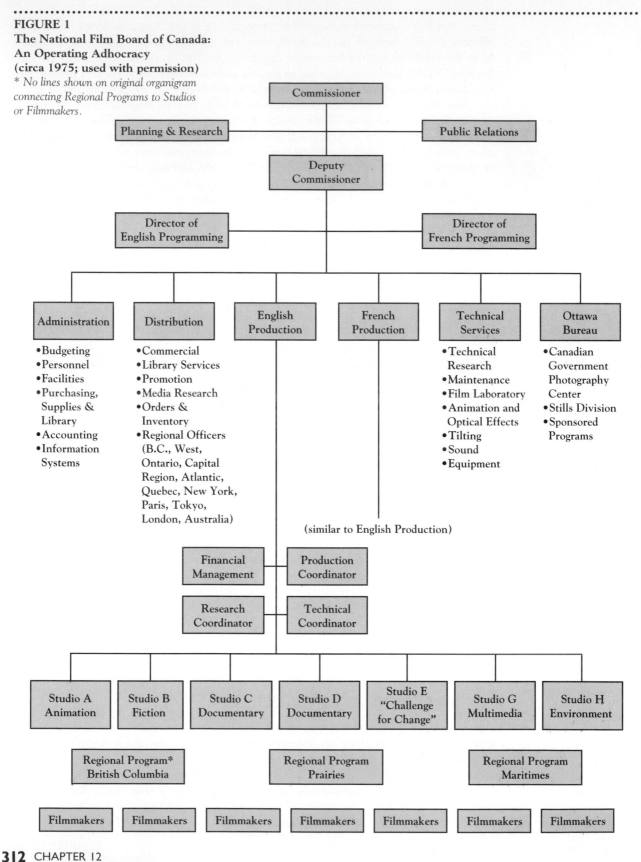

FIGURE 1
The National Film Board of Canada:
An Operating Adhocracy
(circa 1975; used with permission)
* *No lines shown on original organigram*
connecting Regional Programs to Studios
or Filmmakers.

Commissioner

Planning & Research

Public Relations

Deputy Commissioner

Director of English Programming

Director of French Programming

Administration
- Budgeting
- Personnel
- Facilities
- Purchasing, Supplies & Library
- Accounting
- Information Systems

Distribution
- Commercial
- Library Services
- Promotion
- Media Research
- Orders & Inventory
- Regional Officers (B.C., West, Ontario, Capital Region, Atlantic, Quebec, New York, Paris, Tokyo, London, Australia)

English Production

French Production

Technical Services
- Technical Research
- Maintenance
- Film Laboratory
- Animation and Optical Effects
- Tilting
- Sound
- Equipment

Ottawa Bureau
- Canadian Government Photography Center
- Stills Division
- Sponsored Programs

(similar to English Production)

Financial Management

Production Coordinator

Research Coordinator

Technical Coordinator

Studio A Animation

Studio B Fiction

Studio C Documentary

Studio D Documentary

Studio E "Challenge for Change"

Studio G Multimedia

Studio H Environment

Regional Program* British Columbia

Regional Program Prairies

Regional Program Maritimes

Filmmakers Filmmakers Filmmakers Filmmakers Filmmakers Filmmakers Filmmakers its administrative component and its operating core. That core is *truncated*—cut right off from the rest of the organization—so that the administrative component that remains can be structured as an adhocracy.

This truncation may take place in a number of ways. First, when the operations have to be machinelike and so could impede innovation in the administration (because of the associated need for control), it may be established as an independent organization. Second, the operating core may be done away with altogether—in effect, contracted out to other organizations. That leaves the organization free to concentrate on the development work, as did NASA during the Apollo project. A third form of truncation arises when the operating core becomes automated. This enables it to run itself, largely independent of the need for direct controls from the administrative component, leaving the latter free to structure itself as an adhocracy to bring new facilities on line or to modify old ones.

Oil companies, because of the high degree of automation of their production process, are in part at least drawn toward administrative adhocracy. Figure 2 shows the organigram for one oil company, reproduced exactly as presented by the company (except for modifications to mask its identity, done at the company's request). Note the domination of "Administration and Services," shown at the bottom of the chart; the operating functions, particularly "Production," are lost by comparison. Note also the description of the strategic apex in terms of standing committees instead of individual executives.

THE ADMINISTRATIVE COMPONENT OF THE ADHOCRACIES

The important conclusion to be drawn from this discussion is that in both types of adhocracy the relation between the operating core and the administrative component is unlike that in any other configuration. In the administrative adhocracy, the operating core is truncated and becomes a relatively unimportant part of the organization; in the operating adhocracy, the two merge into a single entity. Either way, the need for traditional direct supervision is diminished, so managers derive their influence more from their expertise and interpersonal skills than from formal position. And that means the distinction between line and staff blurs. It no longer makes sense to distinguish those who have the formal power to decide from those who have only the informal right to advise. Power over decision making in the adhocracy flows to anyone with the required expertise, regardless of position.

In fact, the support staff plays a key role in adhocracy, because that is where many of the experts reside (especially in administrative adhocracy). As suggested, however, that staff is not sharply differentiated from the other parts of the organization, not off to one side, to speak only when spoken to, as in the bureaucratic configurations. The other type of staff, however, the technostructure, is less important here, because the adhocracy does not rely for coordination on standards that it develops. Technostructure analysts may, of course, be used for some action planning and other forms of analysis—marketing research and economic forecasting, for example—but these analysts are as likely to take their place alongside the other specialists on the project teams as to stand back and design systems to control them.

To summarize, the administrative component of the adhocracy emerges as an organic mass of line managers and staff experts, combined with operators in the operating adhocracy, working together in ever-shifting relationships on ad hoc projects. Our logo figure at the start of this chapter shows adhocracy with its parts mingled together in one amorphous mass in the middle. In the operating adhocracy, that mass includes the middle line, support staff, technostructure, and operating core. Of these, the administrative adhocracy excludes just the operating core, which is truncated, as shown by the dotted section below the central mass. The reader will also note that the strategic apex of the figure is shown partly merged into the central mass as well, for reasons we shall present in our discussion of strategy formation.

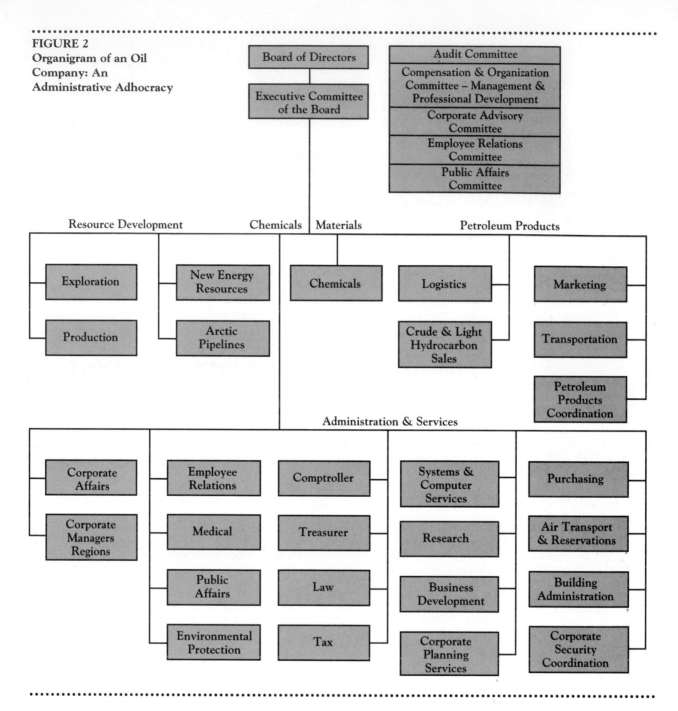

FIGURE 2
Organigram of an Oil Company: An Administrative Adhocracy

Board of Directors

Executive Committee of the Board

Audit Committee

Compensation & Organization Committee – Management & Professional Development

Corporate Advisory Committee

Employee Relations Committee

Public Affairs Committee

Resource Development

Chemicals | Materials

Petroleum Products

Exploration

Production

New Energy Resources

Arctic Pipelines

Chemicals

Logistics

Crude & Light Hydrocarbon Sales

Marketing

Transportation

Petroleum Products Coordination

Administration & Services

Corporate Affairs

Corporate Managers Regions

Employee Relations

Medical

Public Affairs

Environmental Protection

Comptroller

Treasurer

Law

Tax

Systems & Computer Services

Research

Business Development

Corporate Planning Services

Purchasing

Air Transport & Reservations

Building Administration

Corporate Security Coordination

THE ROLES OF THE STRATEGIC APEX

The top managers of the strategic apex of this configuration do not spend much time formulating explicit strategies (as we shall see). But they must spend a good deal of their time in the battles that ensue over strategic choices and in handling the many other disturbances that arise all over these fluid structures. The innovative configuration combines fluid working arrangements with power based on expertise, not authority. Together those breed aggressiveness and conflict. But the job of the managers here, at all levels, is not to bottle up that aggression and conflict so much as to channel them to productive ends. Thus, the managers of adhocracy must be masters of human relations, able to use persuasion, negotiation, coalition, reputation, and rapport to fuse the individualistic experts into smoothly functioning teams.

Top managers must also devote a good deal of time to monitoring the projects. Innovative project work is notoriously difficult to control. No MIS can be relied upon to provide complete, unambiguous results. So there must be careful personal monitoring of projects to ensure that they are completed according to specifications, on schedule and within budget (or, more likely, not excessively late and not too far in excess of cost estimates).

Perhaps the most important single role of the top management of this configuration (especially the operating adhocracy form) is liaison with the external environment. The other configurations tend to focus their attention on clearly defined markets and so are more or less assured of a steady flow of work. Not so the operating adhocracy, which lives from project to project and disappears when it can find no more. Since each project is different, the organization can never be sure where the next one will come from. So the top managers must devote a great deal of their time to ensuring a steady and balanced stream of incoming projects. That means developing liaison contacts with potential customers and negotiating contracts with them. Nowhere is this more clearly illustrated than in the consulting business, particularly where the approach is innovative. When a consultant becomes a partner in one of these firms, he or she normally hangs up the calculator and becomes virtually a full-time salesperson. It is a distinguishing characteristic of many an operating adhocracy that the selling function literally takes place at the strategic apex.

Project work poses related problems in the administrative adhocracy. Reeser asked a group of managers in three aerospace companies, "What are some of the human problems of project management?" Among the common answers: "[M]embers of the organization who are displaced because of the phasing out of [their] work . . . may have to wait a long time before they get another assignment at as high a level of responsibility" and "the temporary nature of the organization often necessitates 'make work' assignments for [these] displaced members." (1969:463) Thus senior managers must again concern themselves with a steady flow of projects, although in this case, internally generated.

Conditions of the Innovative Organization

This configuration is found in environments that are both dynamic and complex. A dynamic environment, being unpredictable, calls for organic structure; a complex one calls for decentralized structure. This configuration is the only type that provides both. Thus we tend to find the innovative organization wherever these conditions prevail, ranging from guerrilla warfare to space agencies. There appears to be no other way to fight a war in the jungle or to put the first man on the moon.

As we have noted for all the configurations, organizations that prefer particular structures also try to "choose" environments appropriate to them. This is especially clear in the case of the operating adhocracy. Advertising agencies and consulting firms that prefer to structure themselves as professional bureaucracies seek out stable environments; those that prefer the innovative form find environments that are dynamic, where the client needs are difficult and unpredictable.*

---

*I like to tell a story of the hospital patient with an appendix about to burst who presents himself to a hospital organized as an adhocracy: "Who wants to do another appendectomy? We're into livers now," as they go about exploring new procedures. But the patient returning from a trip to the jungle with a rare tropical disease had better beware of the hospital organized as a professional bureaucracy. A student came up to me after I once said this and explained how hospital doctors puzzled by her bloated stomach and not knowing what to do took out her appendix. Luckily, her problem resolved itself, some time later. Another time, a surgeon told me that his hospital no longer does appendectomies!

A number of organizations are drawn toward this configuration because of the dynamic conditions that result from very frequent product change. The extreme case is the unit producer, the manufacturing firm that custom-makes each of its products to order, as in the engineering company that produces prototypes or the fabricator of extremely expensive machinery. Because each customer order constitutes a new project, the organization is encouraged to structure itself as an operating adhocracy.

Some manufacturers of consumer goods operate in markets so competitive that they must be constantly changing their product offerings, even though each product may itself be mass produced. A company that records rock music would be a prime example, as would some cosmetic and pharmaceutical companies. Here again, dynamic conditions, when coupled with some complexity, drive the organization toward the innovative configuration, with the mass production operations truncated to allow for adhocracy in product development.

Youth is another condition often associated with this type of organization. That is because it is difficult to sustain any structure in a state of adhocracy for a long period—to keep behaviors from formalizing and thereby discouraging innovation. All kinds of forces drive the innovative configuration to bureaucratize itself as it ages. On the other hand, young organizations prefer naturally organic structures, since they must find their own ways and tend to be eager to innovate. Unless they are entrepreneurial, they tend to become intrapreneurial.

The operating adhocracy is particularly prone to a short life, since it faces a risky market which can quickly destroy it. The loss of one major contract can literally close it down overnight. But if some operating adhocracies have short lives because they fail, others have short lives because they succeed. Success over time encourages metamorphosis, driving the organization toward a more stable environment and a more bureaucratic structure. As it ages, the successful organization develops a reputation for what it does best. That encourages it to repeat certain activities, which may suit the employees who, themselves aging, may welcome more stability in their work. So operating adhocracy is driven over time toward professional bureaucracy to perfect the activities it does best, perhaps even toward the machine bureaucracy to exploit a single invention. The organization survives, but the configuration dies.

Administrative adhocracies typically live longer. They, too, feel the pressures to bureaucratize as they age, which can lead them to stop innovating or else to innovate in stereotyped ways and thereby to adopt bureaucratic structure. But this will not work if the organization functions in an industry that requires sophisticated innovation from all its participants. Since many of the industries where administrative adhocracies are found do, organizations that survive in them tend to retain this configuration for long periods.

In recognition of the tendency for organizations to bureaucratize as they age, a variant of the innovative configuration has emerged—"the organizational equivalent of paper dresses or throw-away tissues" (Toffler, 1970:133)—which might be called the "temporary adhocracy." It draws together specialists from various organizations to carry out a project, and then it disbands. Temporary adhocracies are becoming increasingly common in modern society: the production group that performs a single play, the election campaign committee that promotes a single candidate, the guerrilla group that overthrows a single government, the Olympic committee that plans a single game. Related is what can be called the "mammoth project adhocracy," a giant temporary adhocracy that draws on thousands of experts for a number of years to carry out a single major task, the Manhattan Project of World War II being one famous example.

Sophisticated and automated technical systems also tend to drive organizations toward the administrative adhocracy. When an organization's technical system is sophisticated, it requires an elaborate, highly trained support staff, working in teams, to design or purchase, modify, and maintain the equipment. In other words, complex machinery requires specialists who have the knowledge, power, and flexible working arrangements to cope with it, which generally requires the organization to structure itself as an adhocracy.

Automation of a technical system can evoke even stronger forces in the same direction. That is why a machine organization that succeeds in automating its operating core tends to undergo a dramatic metamorphosis. The problem of motivating bored workers disappears, and with it goes the control mentality that permeates the structure; the distinction between line and staff blurs (machines being indifferent to who turns their knobs), which leads to another important reduction in conflict; the technostructure loses its influence, since control is built into the machinery by its own designers rather than having to be imposed on workers by the standards of the analysts. Overall, then, the administrative structure becomes more decentralized and organic, emerging as an adhocracy. Of course, for automated organizations with simple technical systems (as in the production of hand creams), the entrepreneurial configuration may suffice instead of the innovative one.

Fashion is most decidedly another condition of the innovative configuration. Every one of its characteristics is very much in vogue today: emphasis on expertise, organic structure, project teams, task forces, decentralization of power, matrix structure, sophisticated technical systems, automation, and young organizations. Thus, if the entrepreneurial and machine forms were earlier configurations, and the professional and the diversified forms yesterday's, then the innovative is clearly today's. This is the configuration for a population growing ever better educated and more specialized, yet under constant encouragement to adopt the "systems" approach—to view the world as an integrated whole instead of a collection of loosely coupled parts. It is the configuration for environments that are becoming more complex and more insistent on innovation, and for technical systems that are growing more sophisticated and more highly automated. It is the only configuration among our types appropriate for those who believe organizations must become at the same time more democratic and less bureaucratic.

Yet despite our current infatuation with it, adhocracy is not the structure for all organizations. Like all the others, it too has its place. And that place, as our examples make clear, seems to be in the new industries of our age—aerospace, electronics, think-tank consulting, research, advertising, filmmaking, petrochemicals—virtually all of which experienced their greatest development since World War II. The innovative adhocracy appears to be the configuration for the industries of the last half of the twentieth century.

Strategy Formation in the Innovative Organization

The structure of the innovative organization may seem unconventional, but its strategy making is even more so, upsetting virtually everything we have been taught to believe about that process.

Because the innovative organization must respond continuously to a complex, unpredictable environment, it cannot rely on deliberate strategy. In other words, it cannot predetermine precise patterns in its activities and then impose them on its work through some kind of formal planning process. Rather, many of its actions must be decided upon individually, according to the needs of the moment. It proceeds incrementally; to use Charles Lindblom's words, it prefers "continual nibbling" to a "good bite" (1968:25).

Here, then, the process is best thought of as strategy *formation*, because strategy is not formulated consciously in one place so much as formed implicitly by the specific actions taken in many places. That is why action planning cannot be extensively relied upon in these organizations: Any process that separates thinking from action—planning from execution, formalization from implementation—would impede the flexibility of the organization to respond creatively to its dynamic environment.

STRATEGY FORMATION IN THE OPERATING ADHOCRACY

In the operating adhocracy, a project organization never quite sure what it will do next, the strategy never really stabilizes totally but is responsive to new projects, which themselves involve the activities of a whole host of people. Take the example of the National Film Board. Among its most important strategies are those related to the content of the hundred or so mostly short, documentary-type films that it makes each year. Were the Board structured as a machine bureaucracy, the word on what films to make would come down from on high. Instead, when we studied it some years ago, proposals for new films were submitted to a standing committee, which included elected filmmakers, marketing people, and the heads of production and programming—in other words, operators, line managers, and staff specialists. The chief executive had to approve the committee's choices, and usually did, but the vast majority of the proposals were initiated by the filmmakers and the executive producers lower down. Strategies formed as themes developed among these individual proposals. The operating adhocracy's strategy thus evolves continuously as all kinds of such decisions are made, each leaving its imprint on the strategy by creating a precedent or reinforcing an existing one.

STRATEGY FORMATION IN THE ADMINISTRATIVE ADHOCRACY

Similar things can be said about the administrative adhocracy, although the strategy-making process is slightly neater there. That is because the organization tends to concentrate its attention on fewer projects, which involve more people. NASA's Apollo project, for example, involved most of its personnel for almost ten years.

Administrative adhocracies also need to give more attention to action planning, but of a loose kind—to specify perhaps the ends to be reached while leaving flexibility to work out the means en route. Again, therefore, it is only through the making of specific decisions— namely, those that determine which projects are undertaken and how these projects unfold—that strategies can evolve.

STRATEGIES NONETHELESS

With their activities so disjointed, one might wonder whether adhocracies (of either type) can form strategies (that is, patterns) at all. In fact, they do, at least at certain times.

At the Film Board, despite the little direction from the management, the content of films did converge on certain clear themes periodically and then diverge, in remarkably regular cycles. In the early 1940s, there was a focus on films related to the war effort. After the war, having lost that raison d'être as well as its founding leader, the Board's films went off in all directions. They converged again in the mid-1950s around series of films for television, but by the late 1950s were again diverging widely. And in the mid-1960s and again in the early 1970s (with a brief period of divergence in between), the Board again showed a certain degree of convergence, this time on the themes of social commentary and experimentation.

This habit of cycling in and out of focus is quite unlike what takes place in the other configurations. In the machine organization especially, and somewhat in the entrepreneurial one, convergence proves much stronger and much longer (recall Volkswagenwerk's concentration on the Beetle for twenty years), while divergence tends to be very brief. The machine organization, in particular, cannot tolerate the ambiguity of change and so tries to leap from one strategic orientation to another. The innovative organization, in contrast, seems not only able to function at times without strategic focus, but positively to thrive on it. Perhaps that is the way it keeps itself innovative—by periodically cleansing itself of some of its existing strategic baggage.

THE VARIED STRATEGIES OF ADHOCRACY

Where do the strategies of adhocracy come from? While some may be imposed deliberately by the central management (as in staff cuts at the Film Board), most seem to emerge in a variety of other ways.

In some cases, a single ad hoc decision sets a precedent which evokes a pattern. That is how the National Film Board got into making series of films for television. While a debate raged over the issue, with management hesitant, one filmmaker slipped out and made one such series, and when many of his colleagues quickly followed suit, the organization suddenly found itself deeply, if unintentionally, committed to a major new strategy. It was, in effect, a strategy of spontaneous but implicit consensus on the part of its operating employees. In another case, even the initial precedent-setting decision wasn't deliberate. One film inadvertently ran longer than expected, it had to be distributed as a feature, the first for the organization, and as some other filmmakers took advantage of the precedent, a feature film strategy emerged.

Sometimes a strategy will be pursued in a pocket of an organization (perhaps in a clandestine manner, in a so-called "skunkworks"), which then later becomes more broadly organizational when the organization, in need of change and casting about for new strategies, seizes upon it. Some salesman has been pursuing a new market, or some engineer has developed a new product, and is ignored until the organization has need for some fresh strategic thinking. Then it finds it, not in the vision of its leaders or the procedures of its planners, not elsewhere in its industry, but hidden in the bowels of its own operations, developed through the learning of its workers.

What then becomes the role of the leadership of the innovative configuration in making strategy? If it cannot impose deliberate strategies, what does it do? The answer is that it manages patterns, seeking partial control over strategies but otherwise attempting to influence what happens to those strategies that do emerge lower down.

These are the organizations in which trying to manage strategy is a little like trying to drive an automobile without having your hands on the steering wheel. You can accelerate and brake but cannot determine direction. But there do remain important forms of control. First the leaders can manage the *process* of strategy-making if not the content of strategy. In other words, they can set up the structures to encourage certain kinds of activities and hire the people who themselves will carry out these activities. Second, they can provide general guidelines for strategy—what we have called *umbrella* strategies—seeking to define certain boundaries outside of which the specific patterns developed below should not stray. Then they can watch the patterns that do emerge and use the umbrella to decide which to encourage and which to discourage, remembering, however, that the umbrella can be shifted too.

A GRASS-ROOTS MODEL OF STRATEGY FORMATION

We can summarize this discussion in terms of a "grass-roots" model of strategy formation, comprising six points.

1. *Strategies grow initially like weeds in a garden, they are not cultivated like tomatoes in a hothouse.* In other words, the process of strategy formation can be overmanaged; sometimes it is more important to let patterns emerge than to force an artificial consistency upon an organization prematurely. The hothouse. if needed, can come later.

2. *These strategies can take root in all kinds of places, virtually anywhere people have the capacity to learn and the resources to support that capacity.* Sometimes an individual or unit in touch with a particular opportunity creates his, her, or its own pattern. This may happen inadvertently, when an initial action sets a precedent. Even senior managers can fall into strategies by experimenting with ideas until they converge on something that

works (though the final result may appear to the observer to have been deliberately designed). At other times, a variety of actions converge on a strategic theme through the mutual adjustment of various people, whether gradually or spontaneously. And then the external environment can impose a pattern on an unsuspecting organization. The point is that organizations cannot always plan where their strategies will emerge, let alone plan the strategies themselves.

3. *Such strategies become organizational when they become collective, that is, when the patterns proliferate to pervade the behavior of the organization at large.* Weeds can proliferate and encompass a whole garden; then the conventional plants may look out of place. Likewise, emergent strategies can sometimes displace the existing deliberate ones. But, of course, what is a weed but a plant that wasn't expected? With a change of perspective, the emergent strategy, like the weed, can become what is valued (just as Europeans enjoy salads of the leaves of America's most notorious weed, the dandelion!).

4. *The processes of proliferation may be conscious but need not be; likewise they may be managed but need not be.* The processes by which the initial patterns work their way through the organization need not be consciously intended, by formal leaders or even informal ones. Patterns may simply spread by collective action, much as plants proliferate themselves. Of course, once strategies are recognized as valuable, the processes by which they proliferate can be managed, just as plants can be selectively propagated.

5. *New strategies, which may be emerging continuously, tend to pervade the organization during periods of change, which punctuate periods of more integrated continuity.* Put more simply, organizations, like gardens, may accept the biblical maxim of a time to sow and a time to reap (even though they can sometimes reap what they did not mean to sow). Periods of convergence, during which the organization exploits its prevalent, established strategies, tend to be interrupted periodically by periods of divergence, during which the organization experiments with and subsequently accepts new strategic themes. The blurring of the separation between these two types of periods may have the same effect on an organization that the blurring of the separation between sowing and reaping has on a garden—the destruction of the system's productive capacity.

6. *To manage this process is not to preconceive strategies but to recognize their emergence and intervene when appropriate.* A destructive weed, once noticed, is best uprooted immediately. But one that seems capable of bearing fruit is worth watching, indeed sometimes even worth building a hothouse around. To manage in this context is to create the climate within which a wide variety of strategies can grow (to establish flexible structures, develop appropriate processes, encourage supporting ideologies, and define guiding "umbrella" strategies) and then to watch what does in fact come up. The strategic initiatives that do come "up" may in fact originate anywhere, although often low down in the organization, where the detailed knowledge of products and markets resides. (In fact, to be successful in some organizations, these initiatives must be recognized by middle-level managers and "championed" by combining them with each other or with existing strategies before promoting them to the senior management.) In effect, the management encourages those initiatives that appear to have potential, otherwise it discourages them. But it must not be too quick to cut off the unexpected: Sometimes it is better to pretend not to notice an emerging pattern to allow it more time to unfold. Likewise, there are times when it makes sense to shift or enlarge an umbrella to encompass a new pattern—in other words, to let the organization adapt to the initiative rather than vice versa. Moreover, a management must know when to resist change for the sake of internal efficiency and when to promote it for the sake of external adaptation. In other words, it must sense when to exploit an established crop of strategies and when to encourage new strains to displace them. It is the excesses of either—failure to focus (running blind) or failure to change (bureaucratic momentum)—that most harms organizations.

I call this a "grass-roots" model because the strategies grow up from the base of the organization, rooted in the solid earth of its operations rather than the ethereal abstractions of its administration. (Even the strategic initiatives of the senior management itself are in this model rooted in its tangible involvement with the operations.)

Of course, the model is overstated. But no more so than the more widely accepted deliberate one, which we might call the "hothouse" model of strategy form*u*lation. Management theory must encompass both, perhaps more broadly labeled the *learning* model and the *planning* model, as well as a third, the *visionary* model.

I have discussed the learning model under the innovative configuration, the planning model under the machine configuration, and the visionary model under the entrepreneurial configuration. But in truth, all organizations need to mix these approaches in various ways at different times in their development. For example, our discussion of strategic change in the machine organization concluded, in effect, that they had to revert to the learning model for revitalization and the visionary model for turnaround. Of course, the visionary leader must learn, as must the learning organization evolve a kind of strategic vision, and both sometimes need planning to program the strategies they develop. And overall, no organization can function with strategies that are always and purely emergent; that would amount to a complete abdication of will and leadership, not to mention conscious thought. But none can function either with strategies that are always and purely deliberate; that would amount to an unwillingness to learn, a blindness to whatever is unexpected.

ENVIRONMENT TAKING PRECEDENCE IN THE INNOVATIVE ORGANIZATION

To conclude our discussion of strategy formation, as shown in Figure 3, in the innovative configuration it is the environment that takes precedence. It drives the organization, which responds continuously and eclectically, but does nevertheless achieve convergence during certain periods.* The formal leadership seeks somehow to influence both sides in this relationship, negotiating with the environment for support and attempting to impose some broad general (umbrella) guidelines on the organization.

If the strategist of the entrepreneurial organization is largely a concept attainer and that of the machine organization largely a planner, then the strategist of the innovative organization is largely a *pattern recognizer*, seeking to detect emerging patterns within and outside the strategic umbrella. Then strategies deemed unsuitable can be discouraged while those that seem appropriate can be encouraged, even if that means moving the umbrella. Here, then, we may find the curious situation of leadership changing its intentions to fit the realized behavior of its organization. But that is curious only in the perspective of traditional management theory.

FIGURE 3
Environment Taking the Lead in Adhocracy

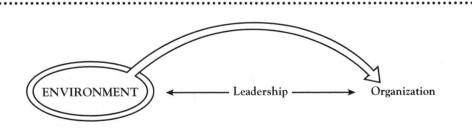

---

*We might take this convergence as the expression of an "organization's mind"—the focusing on a strategic theme as a result of the mutual adjustments among its many actors.

Some Issues Associated with the Innovative Organization

Three issues associated with the innovative configuration merit attention here: its ambiguities and the reactions of people who must live with them, its inefficiencies, and its propensity to make inappropriate transitions to other configurations.

HUMAN REACTIONS TO AMBIGUITY

Many people, especially creative ones, dislike both structural rigidity and the concentration of power. That leaves them only one configuration, the innovative, which is both organic and decentralized. Thus they find it a great place to work. In essence, adhocracy is the only structure for people who believe in more democracy with less bureaucracy.

But not everyone shares those values (not even everyone who professes to). Many people need order, and so prefer the machine or professional type of organization. They see adhocracy as a nice place to visit but no place to spend a career. Even dedicated members of adhocracies periodically get frustrated with this structure's fluidity, confusion, and ambiguity. "In these situations, all managers some of the time and many managers all the time yearn for more definition and structure" (Bums and Stalker, 1966:122–123). The managers of innovative organizations report anxiety related to the eventual phaseout of projects; confusion as to who their boss is, whom to impress to get promoted; a lack of clarity in job definitions, authority relationships, and lines of communication; and intense competition for resources, recognition, and rewards (Reeser, 1969). This last point suggests another serious problem of ambiguity here, the politicization of these configurations. Combining its ambiguities with its interdependencies, the innovative form can emerge as a rather politicized and ruthless organization—supportive of the fit, as long as they remain fit, but destructive of the weak.

PROBLEMS OF EFFICIENCY

No configuration is better suited to solving complex, ill-structured problems than this one. None can match it for sophisticated innovation. Or, unfortunately, for the costs of that innovation. This is simply not an efficient way to function. Although it is ideally suited for the one-of-a-kind project, the innovative configuration is not competent at doing *ordinary* things. It is designed for the *extra*ordinary. The bureaucracies are all mass producers; they gain efficiency through standardization. The adhocracy is a custom producer, unable to standardize and so be efficient. It gains its effectiveness (innovation) at the price of efficiency.

One source of inefficiency lies in the unbalanced workload, mentioned earlier. It is almost impossible to keep the personnel of a project structure—high-priced specialists, it should be noted—busy on a steady basis. In January they may be working overtime with no hope of completing the new project on time; by May they may be playing cards for want of work.

But the real root of inefficiency is the high cost of communication. People talk a lot in these organizations; that is how they combine their knowledge to develop new ideas. But that takes time, a great deal of time. Faced with the need to make a decision in the machine organization, someone up above gives an order and that is that. Not so in the innovative one, where everyone must get into the act—managers of all kinds (functional, project, liaison), as well as all the specialists who believe their point of view should be represented. A meeting is called, probably to schedule another meeting, eventually to decide who should participate in the decision. The problem then gets defined and redefined, ideas for its solution get generated and debated, alliances build and fall around different solutions, until eventually everyone settles down to the hard bargaining over which one to adopt. Finally a decision emerges—that in itself is an accomplishment—although it is typically late and will probably be modified later.

THE DANGERS OF INAPPROPRIATE TRANSITION

Of course, one solution to the problems of ambiguity and inefficiency is to change the configuration. Employees no longer able to tolerate the ambiguity and customers fed up with the inefficiency may try to drive the organization to a more stable, bureaucratic form.

That is relatively easily done in the operating adhocracy, as noted earlier. The organization simply selects the set of standard programs it does best, reverting to the professional configuration, or else innovates one last time to find a lucrative market niche in which to mass produce, and then becomes a machine configuration. But those transitions, however easily effected, are not always appropriate. The organization came into being to solve problems imaginatively, not to apply standards indiscriminately, In many spheres, society has more mass producers than it needs; what it lacks are true problem solvers—the consulting firm that can handle a unique problem instead of applying a pat solution, the advertising agency that can come up with a novel campaign instead of the common imitation, the research laboratory that can make the really serious breakthrough instead of just modifying an existing design. The television networks seem to be classic examples of bureaucracies that provide largely standardized fare when the creativity of adhocracy is called for (except, perhaps, for the newsrooms and the specials, where an ad hoc orientation encourages more creativity).

The administrative adhocracy can run into more serious difficulties when it succumbs to the pressures to bureaucratize. It exists to innovate for itself, in its own industry. Unlike the operating adhocracy, it often cannot change orientation while remaining in the same industry. And so its conversion to the machine configuration (the natural transition for administrative adhocracy tired of perpetual change), by destroying the organization's ability to innovate, can eventually destroy the organization itself.

▼ READING 12.2 MANAGING INNOVATION: CONTROLLED CHAOS*

by James Brian Quinn

Management observers frequently claim that small organizations are more innovative than large ones. But is this commonplace necessarily true? Some large enterprises are highly innovative. How do they do it? . . . This article [reports on a] 2½ year worldwide study . . . [of] both well-documented small ventures and large U.S., Japanese, and European companies and programs selected for their innovation records. . . . More striking than the cultural differences among these companies are the similarities between innovative small and large organizations and among innovative organizations in different countries. Effective management of innovation seems much the same, regardless of national boundaries or scale of operations.

There are . . . many reasons why small companies appear to produce a disproportionate number of innovations. First, innovation occurs in a probabilistic setting. A company never knows whether a particular technical result can be achieved and whether it will succeed in the marketplace. For every new solution that succeeds, tens to hundreds fail. The sheer number of attempts—most by small-scale entrepreneurs—means that some ventures will survive. The 90% to 99% that fail are distributed widely throughout society and receive little notice.

On the other hand, a big company that wishes to move a concept from invention to the marketplace must absorb all potential failure costs itself. This risk may be socially or managerially intolerable, jeopardizing the many other products, projects, jobs, and communities the company supports. Even if its innovation is successful, a big company may face

*Originally published in the *Harvard Business Review* (May–June, 1985); winner of the McKinsey prize for the best article in the *Review* in 1985.

costs that newcomers do not bear, like converting existing operations and customer bases to the new solution.

By contrast, a new enterprise does not risk losing an existing investment base or cannibalizing customer franchises built at great expense. It does not have to change an internal culture that has successfully supported doing things another way or that has developed intellectual depth and belief in the technologies that led to past successes. Organized groups like labor unions, consumer advocates, and government bureaucracies rarely monitor and resist a small company's moves as they might a big company's. Finally, new companies do not face the psychological pain and the economic costs of laying off employees, shutting down plants and even communities, and displacing supplier relationships built with years of mutual commitment and effort. Such barriers to change in large organizations are real, important, and legitimate.

The complex products and systems that society expects large companies to undertake further compound the risks. Only big companies can develop new ships or locomotives; telecommunication networks; or systems for space, defense, air traffic control, hospital care, mass foods delivery, or nationwide computer interactions. These large-scale projects always carry more risk than single-product introductions. A billion-dollar development aircraft, for example, can fail if one inexpensive part in its 100,000 components fails.

Clearly, a single enterprise cannot by itself develop or produce all the parts needed by such large new systems. And communications among the various groups making design and production decisions on components are always incomplete. The probability of error increases exponentially with complexity, while the system innovator's control over decisions decreases significantly—further escalating potential error costs and risks. Such forces inhibit innovation in large organizations. But proper management can lessen these effects.

Of Inventors and Entrepreneurs

A close look at innovative small enterprises reveals much about the successful management of innovation. Of course, not all innovations follow a single pattern. But my research—and other studies in combination—suggest that the following factors are crucial to the success of innovative small companies:

NEED ORIENTATION

Inventor-entrepreneurs tend to be "need or achievement oriented." They believe that if they "do the job better," rewards will follow. They may at first focus on their own view of market needs. But lacking resources, successful small entrepreneurs soon find that it pays to approach potential customers early, test their solutions in users' hands, learn from these interactions, and adapt designs rapidly. Many studies suggest that effective technological innovation develops hand-in-hand with customer demand (Von Hippel, 1982:117).

EXPERTS AND FANATICS

Company founders tend to be pioneers in their technologies and fanatics when it comes to solving problems. They are often described as "possessed" or "obsessed," working toward their objectives to the exclusion even of family or personal relationships. As both experts and fanatics, they perceive probabilities of success as higher than others do. And their commitment allows them to persevere despite the frustrations, ambiguities, and setbacks that always accompany major innovations.

LONG TIME HORIZONS

Their fanaticism may cause inventor-entrepreneurs to underestimate the obstacles and length of time to success. Time horizons for radical innovations make them essentially "irrational" from a present value viewpoint. In my sample, delays between invention and commercial production ranged from 3 to 25 years.* In the late 1930s, for example, industrial chemist Russell Marker was working on steroids called sapogenins when he discovered a technique that would degrade one of these, diosgenin, into the female sex hormone progesterone. By processing some ten tons of Mexican yams in rented and borrowed lab space, Marker finally extracted about four pounds of diosgenin and started a tiny business to produce steroids for the laboratory market. But it was not until 1962, over 23 years later, that Syntex, the company Marker founded, obtained FDA approval for its oral contraceptive.

For both psychological and practical reasons, inventor-entrepreneurs generally avoid early formal plans, proceed step-by-step, and sustain themselves by other income and the momentum of the small advances they achieve as they go along.

LOW EARLY COSTS

Innovators tend to work in homes, basements, warehouses, or low-rent facilities whenever possible. They incur few overhead costs; their limited resources go directly into their projects. They pour nights, weekends, and "sweat capital" into their endeavors. They borrow whatever they can. They invent cheap equipment and prototype processes, often improving on what is available in the marketplace. If one approach fails, few people know; little time or money is lost. All this decreases the costs and risks facing a small operation and improves the present value of its potential success.

MULTIPLE APPROACHES

Technology tends to advance through a series of random—often highly intuitive—insights frequently triggered by gratuitous interactions between the discoverer and the outside world. Only highly committed entrepreneurs can tolerate (and even enjoy) this chaos. They adopt solutions wherever they can be found, unencumbered by formal plans or PERT charts that would limit the range of their imaginations. When the odds of success are low, the participation and interaction of many motivated players increase the chance that one will succeed.

A recent study of initial public offerings made in 1962 shows that only 2 percent survived and still looked like worthwhile investments 20 years later (Business Economics Group, 1983). Small-scale entrepreneurship looks efficient in part because history only records the survivors.

FLEXIBILITY AND QUICKNESS

Undeterred by committees, board approvals, and other bureaucratic delays, the inventor-entrepreneur can experiment, test, recycle, and try again with little time lost. Because technological progress depends largely on the number of successful experiments accomplished per unit of time, fast-moving small entrepreneurs can gain both timing and performance advantages over clumsier competitors. This responsiveness is often crucial in finding early markets for radical innovations where neither innovators, market researchers, nor users can quite visualize a product's real potential. For example, Edison's lights first appeared on ships and in baseball parks; Astroturf was intended to convert the flat roofs and asphalt playgrounds of city schools into more humane environments; and graphite and boron compos-

---

*A study at Battelle found an average of 19.2 years between invention and commercial production. Battelle Memorial Laboratories, "Science, Technology, and Innovation," Report to the National Science Foundation, 1973; also Dean (1974:13).

ites designed for aerospace unexpectedly found their largest markets in sporting goods. Entrepreneurs quickly adjusted their entry strategies to market feedback.

INCENTIVES

Inventor-entrepreneurs can foresee tangible personal rewards if they are successful. Individuals often want to achieve a technical contribution, recognition, power, or sheer independence, as much as money. For the original, driven personalities who create significant innovations, few other paths offer such clear opportunities to fulfill all their economic, psychological, and career goals at once. Consequently, they do not panic or quit when others with solely monetary goals might.

AVAILABILITY OF CAPITAL

One of America's great competitive advantages is its rich variety of sources to finance small, low-probability ventures. If entrepreneurs are turned down by one source, other sources can be sought in myriads of creative combinations.

Professionals involved in such financings have developed a characteristic approach to deal with the chaos and uncertainty of innovation. First, they evaluate a proposal's conceptual validity: If the technical problems can be solved, is there a real business there for someone and does it have a large upside potential? Next, they concentrate on people: Is the team thoroughly committed and expert? Is it the best available? Only then do these financiers analyze specific financial estimates in depth. Even then, they recognize that actual outcomes generally depend on subjective factors, not numbers (Pence, 1982).

Timeliness, aggressiveness, commitment, quality of people, and the flexibility to attack opportunities not at first perceived are crucial. Downside risks are minimized, not by detailed controls, but by spreading risks among multiple projects, keeping early costs low, and gauging the tenacity, flexibility, and capability of the founders.

Large-Company Barriers to Innovation

Less innovative companies and, unfortunately, most large corporations operate in a very different fashion. The most notable and common constraints on innovation in larger companies include the following:

TOP MANAGEMENT ISOLATION

Many senior executives in big companies have little contact with conditions on the factory floor or with customers who might influence their thinking about technological innovation. Since risk perception is inversely related to familiarity and experience, financially oriented top managers are likely to perceive technological innovations as more problematic than acquisitions that may be just as risky but that will appear more familiar (Hayes and Garvin, 1982:70; Hayes and Abernathy, 1980:67).

INTOLERANCE OF FANATICS

Big companies often view entrepreneurial fanatics as embarrassments or troublemakers. Many major cities are now ringed by companies founded by these "nonteam" players—often to the regret of their former employers.

SHORT TIME HORIZONS

The perceived corporate need to report a continuous stream of quarterly profits conflicts with the long time spans that major innovations normally require. Such pressures often make publicly owned companies favor quick marketing fixes, cost cutting, and acquisition strategies over process, product, or quality innovations that would yield much more in the long run.

ACCOUNTING PRACTICES

By assessing all its direct, indirect, overhead, overtime, and service costs against a project, large corporations have much higher development expenses compared with entrepreneurs working in garages. A project in a big company can quickly become an exposed political target, its potential net present value may sink unacceptably, and an entry into small markets may not justify its sunk costs. An otherwise viable project may soon founder and disappear.

EXCESSIVE RATIONALISM

Managers in big companies often seek orderly advance through early market research studies or PERT planning. Rather than managing the inevitable chaos of innovation productively, these managers soon drive out the very things that lead to innovation in order to prove their announced plans.

EXCESSIVE BUREAUCRACY

In the name of efficiency, bureaucratic structures require many approvals and cause delays at every turn. Experiments that a small company can perform in hours may take days or weeks in large organizations. The interactive feedback that fosters innovation is lost, important time windows can be missed, and real costs and risks rise for the corporation.

INAPPROPRIATE INCENTIVES

Reward and control systems in most big companies are designed to minimize surprises. Yet innovation, by definition, is full of surprises. It often disrupts well-laid plans, accepted power patterns, and entrenched organizational behavior at high costs to many. Few large companies make millionaires of those who create such disruptions, however profitable the innovations may turn out to be. When control systems neither penalize opportunities missed nor reward risks taken, the results are predictable.

How Large Innovative Companies Do It

Yet some big companies are continuously innovative. Although each such enterprise is distinctive, the successful big innovators I studied have developed techniques that emulate or improve on their smaller counterparts' practices. What are the most important patterns?

ATMOSPHERE AND VISION

Continuous innovation occurs largely because top executives appreciate innovation and manage their company's value system and atmosphere to support it. For example, Sony's founder, Masaru Ibuka, stated in the company's "Purposes of Incorporation" the goal of a "free, dynamic, and pleasant factory . . . where sincerely motivated personnel can exercise their technological skills to the highest level." Ibuka and Sony's chairman, Akio Morita, inculcated the "Sony spirit" through a series of unusual policies: hiring brilliant people with nontraditional skills (like an opera singer) for high management positions, promoting young people over their elders, designing a new type of living accommodation for workers, and providing visible awards for outstanding technical achievements.

Because familiarity can foster understanding and psychological comfort, engineering and scientific leaders are often those who create atmospheres supportive of innovation, especially in a company's early life. Executive vision is more important than a particular management background—as IBM, Genentech, AT&T, Merck, Elf Aquitaine, Pilkington, and others in my sample illustrate. CEOs of these companies value technology and include technical experts in their highest decisions circles.

Innovative managements—whether technical or not—project clear long-term visions for their organizations that go beyond simple economic measures. . . . Genentech's original plan expresses [such a] vision: "We expect to be the first company to commercialize the [rDNA] technology, and we plan to build a major profitable corporation by manufacturing and marketing needed products that benefit mankind. The future uses of genetic engineering are far reaching and many. Any product produced by a living organism is eventually within the company's reach."

Such visions, vigorously supported, are not "management fluff," but have many practical implications.* They attract quality people to the company and give focus to their creative and entrepreneurial drives. When combined with sound internal operations, they help channel growth by concentrating attention on the actions that lead to profitability, rather than on profitability itself. Finally, these visions recognize a realistic time frame for innovation and attract the kind of investors who will support it.

ORIENTATION TO THE MARKET

Innovative companies tie their visions to the practical realities of the marketplace. Although each company uses techniques adapted to its own style and strategy, two elements are always present: a strong market orientation at the very top of the company and mechanisms to ensure interactions between technical and marketing people at lower levels. At Sony, for example, soon after technical people are hired, the company runs them through weeks of retail selling. Sony engineers become sensitive to the ways retail sales practices, product displays, and nonquantifiable customer preferences affect success. . . .

From top to bench levels in my sample's most innovative companies, managers focus primarily on seeking to anticipate and solve customers' emerging problems.

SMALL, FLAT ORGANIZATIONS

The most innovative large companies in my sample try to keep the total organization flat and project teams small. Development teams normally include only 6 or 7 key people. This number seems to constitute a critical mass of skills while fostering maximum communication and commitment among members. According to research done by my colleague, Victor McGee, the number of channels of communication increases as $n(2^{n-1}-1)$. Therefore:

For team size	=	1	2	3	4	5	6	7	8	9	10	11
Channels	=	1	2	9	28	75	186	441	1016	2295	5110	11253

Innovative companies also try to keep their operating divisions and total technical units small—below 400 people. Up to this number, only two layers of management are required to maintain a span of control over 7 people. In units much larger than 400, people quickly lose touch with the concept of their product or process, staffs and bureaucracies tend to grow, and

---

*Thomas J. Allen (1977) illustrates the enormous leverage provided such technology accessors (called "gatekeepers") in R&D organizations.

projects may go through too many formal screens to survive. Since it takes a chain of yesses and only one no to kill a project, jeopardy multiplies as management layers increase.

MULTIPLE APPROACHES

At first one cannot be sure which of several technical approaches will dominate a field. The history of technology is replete with accidents, mishaps, and chance meetings that allowed one approach or group to emerge rapidly over others. Leo Baekelund was looking for a synthetic shellac when he found Bakelite and started the modern plastics industry. At Syntex, researchers were not looking for an oral contraceptive when they created 19-norprogesterone, the precursor to the active ingredient in half of all contraceptive pills. And the microcomputer was born because Intel's Ted Hoff "happened" to work on a complex calculator just when Digital Equipment Corporation's PDP8 architecture was fresh in his mind.

Such "accidents" are involved in almost all major technological advances. When theory can predict everything, a company has moved to a new stage, from development to production. Murphy's law works because engineers design for what they can foresee: hence what fails is what theory could not predict. And it is rare that the interactions of components and subsystems can be predicted over the lifetime of operations. For example, despite careful theoretical design work, the first high performance jet engine literally tore itself to pieces on its test stand, while others failed in unanticipated operating conditions (like an Iranian sandstorm).

Recognizing the inadequacies of theory, innovative enterprises seem to move faster from paper studios to physical testing than do noninnovative enterprises. When possible, they encourage several prototype programs to proceed in parallel. . . . Such redundancy helps the company cope with uncertainties in development, motivates people through competition, and improves the amount and quality of information available for making final choices on scale-ups or introductions.

DEVELOPMENTAL SHOOT-OUTS

Many companies structure shoot-outs among competing approaches only after they reach the prototype stages. They find this practice provides more objective information for making decisions, decreases risk by making choices that best reflect marketplace needs, and helps ensure that the winning option will move ahead with a committed team behind it. Although many managers worry that competing approaches may be inefficient, greater effectiveness in choosing the right solution easily outweighs duplication costs when the market rewards higher performance or when large volumes justify increased sophistication. Under these conditions, parallel development may prove less costly because it both improves the probability of success and reduces development time.

Perhaps the most difficult problem in managing competing projects lies in reintegrating the members of the losing team. If the company is expanding rapidly or if the successful project creates a growth opportunity, losing team members can work on another interesting program or sign on with the winning team as the project moves toward the marketplace. For the shoot-out system to work continuously, however, executives must create a climate that honors high-quality performance whether a project wins or loses, reinvolves people quickly in their technical specialties or in other projects, and accepts and expects rotation among tasks and groups. . . .

SKUNKWORKS

Every highly innovative enterprise in my research sample emulated small company practices by using groups that functioned in a skunkworks style. Small teams of engineers, technicians, designers, and model makers were placed together with no intervening organizational or physical barriers to developing a new product from idea to commercial prototype stages. In innovative Japanese companies, top managers often worked hand in hand on projects with young engineers. Surprisingly, *ringi* decision making was not evident in these situations. Soichiro Honda was known for working directly on technical problems and emphasizing his technical points by shouting at his engineers or occasionally even hitting them with wrenches!

The skunkworks approach eliminates bureaucracies, allows fast, unfettered communications, permits rapid turnaround times for experiments, and instills a high level of group identity and loyalty. Interestingly, few successful groups in my research were structured in the classic "venture group" form, with a careful balancing of engineering, production, and marketing talents. Instead they acted on an old truism: introducing a new product or process to the world is like raising a healthy child—it needs a mother (champion) who loves it, a father (authority figure with resources) to support it, and pediatricians (specialists) to get it through difficult times. It may survive solely in the hands of specialists, but its chances of success are remote.

INTERACTIVE LEARNING

Skunkworks are as close as most big companies can come to emulating the highly interactive and motivating learning environment that characterizes successful small ventures. But the best big innovators have gone even farther. Recognizing that the random, chaotic nature of technological change cuts across organizational and even institutional lines, these companies tap into multiple outside sources of technology as well as their customers' capabilities. Enormous external leverages are possible. No company can spend more than a small share of the world's $200 billion devoted to R&D. But like small entrepreneurs, big companies can have much of that total effort cheaply if they try.

In industries such as electronics, customers provide much of the innovation on new products. In other industries, such as textiles, materials or equipment suppliers provide the innovation. In still others, such as biotechnology, universities are dominant, while foreign sources strongly supplement industries such as controlled fusion. Many R&D units have strategies to develop information for trading with outside groups and have teams to cultivate these sources. Large Japanese companies have been notably effective at this. So have U.S. companies as diverse as DuPont, AT&T, Apple Computer, and Genentech.

An increasing variety of creative relationships exist in which big companies participate-as joint venturers, consortium members, limited partners, guarantors of first markets, major academic funding sources, venture capitalists, spin-off equity holders, and so on. These rival the variety of inventive financing and networking structures that individual entrepreneurs have created.

Indeed, the innovative practices of small and large companies look ever more alike. This resemblance is especially striking in the interactions between companies and customers during development. Many experienced big companies are relying less on early market research and more on interactive development with lead customers. Hewlett-Packard, 3M, Sony, and Raychem frequently introduce radically new products through small teams that work closely with lead customers. These teams learn from their customers' needs and innovations, and rapidly modify designs and entry strategies based on this information.

Formal market analyses continue to be useful for extending product lines, but they are often misleading when applied to radical innovations. Market studies predicted that Haloid would never sell more than 5,000 xerographic machines, that Intel's microprocessor would never sell more than 10% as many units as there were minicomputers, and that Sony's transistor radios and miniature television sets would fail in the marketplace. At the same time, many eventual failures such as Ford's Edsel, IBM's FS system, and the supersonic transport were studied and planned exhaustively on paper, but lost contact with customers' real needs.

The flexible management practices needed for major innovations often pose problems for established cultures in big companies. Yet there are reasonable steps managers in these companies can take. Innovation can be bred in a surprising variety of organizations, as many examples show. What are its key elements?

AN OPPORTUNITY ORIENTATION

In the 1981-1983 recession, many large companies cut back or closed plants as their "only available solution." Yet I repeatedly found that top managers in these companies took these actions without determining firsthand why their customers were buying from competitors, discerning what niches in their markets were growing, or tapping the innovations their own people had to solve problems. These managers foreclosed innumerable options by defining the issue as cost cutting rather than opportunity seeking. As one frustrated division manager in a manufacturing conglomerate put it: "If management doesn't actively seek or welcome technical opportunities, it sure won't hear about them."

By contrast, Intel met the challenge of the last recession with its "20% solution." The professional staff agreed to work one extra day a week to bring innovations to the marketplace earlier than planned. Despite the difficult times, Intel came out of the recession with several important new products ready to go—and it avoided layoffs.

Entrepreneurial companies recognize that they have almost unlimited access to capital and they structure their practices accordingly. They let it be known that if their people come up with good ideas, they can find the necessary capital—just as private venture capitalists or investment bankers find resources for small entrepreneurs.

STRUCTURING FOR INNOVATION

Managers need to think carefully about how innovation fits into their strategy and structure their technology, skills, resources, and organizational commitments accordingly. A few examples suggest the variety of strategies and alignments possible:

Hewlett-Packard and 3M develop product lines around a series of small, discrete, freestanding products. These companies form units that look like entrepreneurial start-ups. Each has a small team, led by a champion, in low-cost facilities. These companies allow many different proposals to come forward and test them as early as possible in the marketplace. They design control systems to spot significant losses on any single entry quickly. They look for high gains on a few winners and blend less successful, smaller entries into prosperous product lines.

Other companies (like AT&T or the oil majors) have had to make large system investments to last for decades. These companies tend to make longterm needs forecasts. They often start several programs in parallel to be sure of selecting the right technologies. They then extensively test new technologies in use before making systemwide commitments. Often they sacrifice speed of entry for long-term low cost and reliability.

Intel and Dewey & Almy, suppliers of highly technical specialties to EOMs, develop strong technical sales networks to discover and understand customer needs in depth. These companies try to have technical solutions designed into customers' products. Such companies have flexible applied technology groups working close to the marketplace. They also have quickly expandable plant facilities and a cutting edge technology (not necessarily basic research) group that allows rapid selection of currently available technologies.

Dominant producers like IBM or Matsushita are often not the first to introduce new technologies. They do not want to disturb their successful product lines any sooner than necessary. As market demands become clear, these companies establish precise price-performance windows and form overlapping project teams to come up with the best answer for the marketplace. To decrease market risks, they use product shoot-outs as close to the market as possible. They develop extreme depth in production technologies to keep unit costs low from the outset.

Finally, depending on the scale of the market entry, they have project teams report as close to the top as necessary to secure needed management attention and resources.

Merck and Hoffman-LaRoche, basic research companies, maintain laboratories with better facilities, higher pay, and more freedom than most universities can afford. These companies leverage their internal spending through research grants, clinical grants, and research relationships with universities throughout the world. Before they invest $20 million to $50 million to clear a new drug, they must have reasonable assurance that they will be first in the marketplace. They take elaborate precautions to ensure that the new entry is safe and effective, and that it cannot be easily duplicated by others. Their structures are designed to be on the cutting edge of science, but conservative in animal testing, clinical evaluation, and production control.

These examples suggest some ways of linking innovation to strategy. Many other examples, of course, exist. Within a single company, individual divisions may have different strategic needs and hence different structures and practices. No single approach works well for all situations.

COMPLEX PORTFOLIO PLANNING

Perhaps the most difficult task for top managers is to balance the needs of existing lines against the needs of potential lines. This problem requires a portfolio strategy much more complex than the popular four-box Boston Consulting Group matrix found in most strategy texts. To allocate resources for innovation strategically, managers need to define the broad, long-term actions within and across divisions necessary to achieve their visions. They should determine which positions to hold at all costs, where to fall back, and where to expand initially and in the more distant future.

A company's strategy may often require investing more resources in current lines. But sufficient resources should also be invested in patterns that ensure intermediate and long-term growth; provide defenses against possible government, labor, competitive, or activist challenges; and generate needed organizational, technical, and external relations flexibilities to handle unforeseen opportunities or threats. Sophisticated portfolio planning within and among divisions can protect both current returns and future prospects—the two critical bases for that most cherished goal, high price/earnings ratios.

An Incrementalist Approach

Such managerial techniques can provide a strategic focus for innovation and help solve many of the timing, coordination, and motivation problems that plague large, bureaucratic organizations. Even more detailed planning techniques may help in guiding the development of the many small innovations that characterize any successful business. My research reveals, however, that few, if any, major innovations result from highly structured planning systems. [Why?] . . .

The innovative process is inherently incremental. As Thomas Hughes says, "Technological systems evolve through relatively small steps marked by an occasional stubborn obstacle and by constant random breakthroughs interacting across laboratories and borders" (Hughes, 1984:83). A forgotten hypothesis of Einstein's became the laser in Charles Townes's mind as he contemplated azaleas in Franklin Square. The structure of DNA followed a circuitous route through research in biology, organic chemistry. x-ray crystallography, and mathematics toward its Nobel prize-winning conception as a spiral staircase of [base pairs]. Such rambling trails are characteristic of virtually all major technological advances.

At the outset of the attack on a technical problem, an innovator often does not know whether his problem is tractable, what approach will prove best, and what concrete characteristic the solution will have if achieved. The logical route, therefore, is to follow several paths—though perhaps with varying degrees of intensity—until more information becomes available. Not knowing precisely where the solution will occur, wise managers establish the widest feasible network for finding and assessing alternative solutions. They keep many options open until one of them seems sure to win. Then they back it heavily.

Managing innovation is like a stud poker game, where one can play several hands. A player has some idea of the likely size of the pot at the beginning, knows the general but not the sure route to winning, buys one card (a project) at a time to gain information about probabilities and the size of the pot, closes hands as they become discouraging, and risks more only late in the hand as knowledge increases. . . .

CHAOS WITHIN GUIDELINES

Effective managers of innovation channel and control its main directions. Like venture capitalists, they administer primarily by setting goals, selecting key people, and establishing a few critical limits and decision points for intervention rather than by implementing elaborate planning or control systems. As technology leads or market needs emerge, these managers set a few—most crucial—performance targets and limits. They allow their technical units to decide how to achieve these, subject to defined constraints and reviews at critical junctures.

Early bench-scale project managers may pursue various options, making little attempt at first to integrate each into a total program. Only after key variables are understood—and perhaps measured and demonstrated in lab models—can more precise planning be meaningful. Even then, many factors may remain unknown; chaos and competition can continue to thrive in the pursuit of the solution. At defined review points, however, only those options that can clear performance milestones may continue. . . .

Even after selecting the approaches to emphasize, innovative managers tend to continue a few others as smaller scale "side bets" or options. In a surprising number of cases, these alternatives prove winners when the planned option fails.

Recognizing the many demands entailed by successful programs, innovative companies find special ways to reward innovators. Sony gives "a small but significant" percentage of a new product's sales to its innovating teams. Pilkington, IBM, and 3M's top executives are often chosen from those who have headed successful new product entries. Intel lets its Magnetic Memory Group operate like a small company, with special performance rewards and simulated stock options. GE, Syntex, and United Technologies help internal innovators establish new companies and take equity positions in "nonrelated" product innovations.

Large companies do not have to make their innovators millionaires, but reward should be visible and significant. Fortunately, most engineers are happy with the incentives that Tracy Kidder (1981) calls "playing pinball"—giving widespread recognition to a job well done and the right to play in the next exciting game. Most innovative companies provide both. . . .

Match Management to the Process

. . . Executives need to understand and accept the tumultuous realities of innovation, learn from the experiences of other companies, and adapt the most relevant features of these others to their own management practices and cultures. Many features of small company innovators are also applicable in big companies. With top-level understanding, vision, a commitment to customers and solutions, a genuine portfolio strategy, a flexible entrepreneurial atmosphere, and proper incentives for innovative champions, many more large companies can innovate to meet the severe demands of global competition.

THE DIVERSIFIED CONTEXT

A good deal of evidence has accumulated on the relationship between diversification and divisionalization. Once organizations diversify their product or service lines, they tend to create distinct structural divisions to deal with each business. This relationship was perhaps first carefully documented in the classic historical study by Alfred D. Chandler, *Strategy and Structure: Chapters in the History of the Great American Enterprise.* Chandler traced the origins of diversification and divisionalization in Du Pont and General Motors in the 1920s, which were followed later by other major firms. A number of other studies elaborated on Chandler's conclusions; these are discussed in the readings of this chapter.

The first reading, drawn from Mintzberg's work on structuring, probes the structure of divisionalization—how it works, what brings it about, what intermediate variations of it exist, and what problems it poses for organizations that use it and for society at large. It concludes on a rather pessimistic note about conglomerate diversification and about the purer forms of divisionalization. A follow-up reading by Mintzberg describes the generic "corporate" strategies pursued by diversified organizations—that is, those of the group of businesses, as opposed to the "business" strategies pursued by individual divisions or self-standing businesses (as discussed in his reading in Chapter 4).

Across the world, diversified corporations take many different forms. That is why we have included the next reading, by Philippe Lasserre of INSEAD in France. Lasserre describes three forms that such organizations take in the West, which he labels industrial group, industrial holdings, and financial conglomerates. Then he describes three that are common in Asia, labeled entrepreneurial conglomerates, keiretsus, and national holdings. When he compares them, an interesting result emerges: While we in the West tend to control impersonally (or analytically), and yet in some ways more loosely (or less synergistically), the Asians favor softer and more personalized forms of control, yet often achieve tighter connections. (Harking back to Pitcher's three styles of Chapter 8, the technocrats are more common in the West apparently; the artists and craftsmen easier to find in the East.) Lasserre warns, however, that you cannot just adopt an approach because it looks good; beware of the limitations of your own culture!

Aspects of the diversified organization, particularly in its more conglomerate form, come in for some heavy criticism in this chapter, as in the next reading, too. But it quickly turns to the more constructive questions of how to use strategy to combine a cluster of different businesses into an effective corporate entity. This is Michael Porter's award-winning *Harvard Business Review* article "From Competitive Advantage to Corporate Strategy." Porter discusses in a most insightful way various types of overall corporate strategies, including portfolio management, restructuring, transferring skills, and sharing activities (the last two referred to in his 1985 book *Competitive Advantage* as "horizontal strategies"), the former dealing with "intangible," the latter "tangible" interrelationships among business units and conceived in terms of his value chain.

by Henry Mintzberg

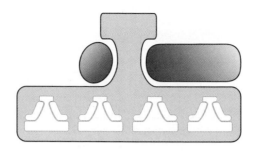

....
The Basic Divisionalized Structure

The diversified organization is not so much an integrated entity as a set of semiautonomous units coupled together by a central administrative structure. The units are generally called *divisions*, and the central administration, the *headquarters*. This is a widely used configuration in the private sector of the industrialized economy; the vast majority of the *Fortune* 500, America's largest corporations, use this structure or a variant of it. But, as we shall see, it is also found in other sectors as well.

In what is commonly called the "divisionalized" form of structure, units, called "divisions," are created to serve distinct markets and are given control over the operating functions necessary to do so, as shown in Figure 1. Each is therefore relatively free of direct control by headquarters or even of the need to coordinate activities with other divisions. Each, in other words, appears to be a self-standing business. Of course, none is. There *is* a headquarters, and it has a series of roles that distinguish this overall configuration from a collection of independent businesses providing the same set of products and services.

ROLES OF THE HEADQUARTERS

Above all, the headquarters exercises performance control. It sets standards of achievement, generally in quantitative terms (such as return on investment or growth in sales), and then monitors the results. Coordination between headquarters and the divisions thus reduces largely to the standardization of outputs. Of course, there is some direct supervision—headquarters' managers have to have personal contact with and knowledge of the divisions. But that is largely circumscribed by the key assumption in this configuration that if the division managers are to be responsible for the performance of their divisions, they

*Adapted from *The Structuring of Organizations* (Prentice Hall, 1979), Chap. 20 on "The Divisionalized Form." A chapter similar to this appeared in *Mintzberg on Management: Inside Our Strange World of Organizations* (Free Press, 1989).

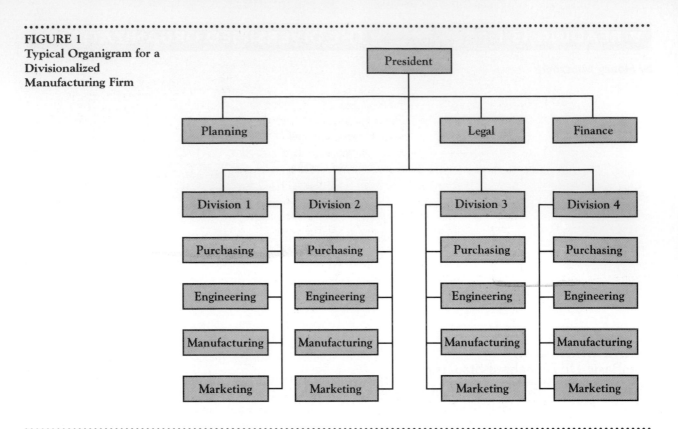

FIGURE 1
Typical Organigram for a
Divisionalized
Manufacturing Firm

must have considerable autonomy to manage them as they see fit. Hence there is extensive delegation of authority from headquarters to the level of division manager.

Certain important tasks do, however, remain for the headquarters. One is to develop the overall *corporate* strategy, meaning to establish the portfolio of businesses in which the organization will operate. The headquarters establishes, acquires, divests, and closes down divisions in order to change its portfolio. Popular in the 1970s in this regard was the Boston Consulting Group's "growth share matrix," where corporate managers were supposed to allocate funds to divisions on the basis of their falling into the categories of dogs, cash cows, wildcats, and stars. But enthusiasm for that technique waned, perhaps mindful of Pope's warning that a little learning can be a dangerous thing.

Second, the headquarters manages the movement of funds between the divisions, taking the excess profits of some to support the greater growth potential of others. Third, of course, the headquarters, through its own technostructure, designs and operates the performance control system. Fourth, it appoints and therefore retains the right to replace the division managers. For a headquarters that does not directly manage any division, its most tangible power when the performance of a division lags—short of riding out an industry downturn or divesting the division—is to replace its leader. Finally, the headquarters provides certain support services that are common to all the divisions—a corporate public relations office or legal counsel, for example.

STRUCTURE OF THE DIVISIONS

It has been common to label divisionalized organizations "decentralized." That is a reflection of how *certain* of them came to be, most notably Du Pont early in this century. When organizations that were structured functionally (for example, in departments of marketing, manufacturing, and engineering, etc.) diversified, they found that coordination of their different product lines across the functions became increasingly complicated. The central managers had to spend great amounts of time intervening to resolve disputes. But once these corporations switched to a divisionalized form of structure, where all the functions for a given business could be contained in a single unit dedicated to that business, management became much simpler. In effect, their structures became *more* decentralized, power over distinct businesses being delegated to the division managers.

But more decentralized does not mean *decentralized*. That word refers to the dispersal of decision-making power in an organization, and in many of the diversified corporations much of the power tended to remain with the few managers who ran the businesses. Indeed, the most famous case of divisionalization was one of relative *centralization*: Alfred P. Sloan introduced the divisionalized structure to General Motors in the 1920s to *reduce* the power of its autonomous business units, to impose systems of financial controls on what had been a largely unmanaged agglomeration of different automobile businesses.

In fact, I would argue that it is the *centralization* of power within the divisions that is most compatible with the divisionalized form of structure. In other words, the effect of having a headquarters over the divisions is to drive them toward the machine configuration, namely a structure of centralized bureaucracy. That is the structure most compatible with headquarters control, in my opinion. If true, this would seem to be an important point, because it means that the proliferation of the diversified configuration in many spheres—business, government, and the rest—has the effect of driving many suborganizations toward machine bureaucracy, even where that configuration may be inappropriate (school systems, for example, or government departments charged with innovative project work).

The explanation for this lies in the standardization of outputs, the key to the functioning of the divisionalized structure. Bear in mind the headquarters' dilemma: to respect divisional autonomy while exercising control over performance. This it seeks to resolve by after-the-fact monitoring of divisional results, based on clearly defined performance standards. But two main assumptions underlie such standards.

First, each division must be treated as a single integrated system with a single, consistent set of goals. In other words, although the divisions may be loosely coupled with each other, the assumption is that each is tightly coupled internally.*

Second, these goals must be operational ones, in other words, lend themselves to quantitative measurement. But in the less formal configurations—entrepreneurial and innovative—which are less stable, such performance standards are difficult to establish, while in the professional configuration, the complexity of the work makes it difficult to establish such standards. Moreover, while the entrepreneurial configuration may lend itself to being integrated around a single set of goals, the innovative and professional configurations do not. Thus, only the machine configuration of the major types fits comfortably into the conventional divisionalized structure, by virtue of its integration and its operational goals.

In fact, when organizations with another configuration are drawn under the umbrella of a divisionalized structure, they tend to be forced toward the machine bureaucratic form, to make them conform with *its* needs. How often have we heard stories of entrepreneurial firms recently acquired by conglomerates being descended upon by hordes of headquarters technocrats bemoaning the loose controls, the absence of organigrams, the informality of the systems? In many cases, of course, the very purpose of the acquisition was to do just this, tighten up the organization so that its strategies can be pursued more pervasively and systematically. But other times, the effect is to destroy the organization's basic strengths, sometimes

---

*Unless, of course, there is a second layer of divisionalization, which simply takes this conclusion down another level in the hierarchy.

including its flexibility and responsiveness. Similarly, how many times have we heard tell of government administrators complaining about being unable to control public hospitals or universities through conventional (meaning machine bureaucratic) planning systems?

This conclusion is, in fact, a prime manifestation of the hypothesis [discussed in Chapter 6] that concentrated external control of an organization has the effect of formalizing and centralizing its structure, in other words, of driving it toward the machine configuration. Headquarters' control of divisions is, of course, concentrated; indeed, when the diversified organization is itself a *closed system*, as I shall argue later many tend to be, then it is a most concentrated form of control. And, the effect of that control is to render the divisions its *instruments*.

There is, in fact, an interesting irony in this, in that the less society controls the overall diversified organization, the more the organization itself controls its individual units. The result is increased autonomy for the largest organizations coupled with decreased autonomy for their many activities.

To conclude this discussion of the basic structure, the diversified configuration is represented in the opening figure, symbolically in terms of our logo, as follows. Headquarters has three parts: a small strategic apex of top managers, a small technostructure to the left concerned with the design and operation of the performance control system, and a slightly larger staff support group to the right to provide support services common to all the divisions. Each of the divisions is shown below the headquarters as a machine configuration.

Conditions of the Diversified Organization

While the diversified configuration may arise from the federation of different organizations, which come together under a common headquarters umbrella, more often it appears to be the structural response to a machine organization that has diversified its range of product or service offerings. In either case, it is the diversity of markets above all that drives an organization to use this configuration. An organization faced with a single integrated market simply cannot split itself into autonomous divisions; the one with distinct markets, however, has an incentive to create a unit to deal with each.

There are three main kinds of market diversity—product and service, client, and region. In theory, all three can lead to divisionalization. But when diversification is based on variations in clients or regions as opposed to products or services, divisionalization often turns out to be incomplete. With identical products or services in each region or for each group of clients, the headquarters is encouraged to maintain central control of certain critical functions, to ensure common operating standards for all the divisions. And that seriously reduces divisional autonomy, and so leads to a less than complete form of divisionalization.

Thus, one study found that insurance companies concentrate at headquarters the critical function of investment, and retailers concentrate that of purchasing, also controlling product range, pricing, and volume (Channon, 1975). One need only look at the individual outlets of a typical retail chain to recognize the absence of divisional autonomy: usually they all look alike. The same conclusion tends to hold for other businesses organized by regions, such as bakeries, breweries, cement producers, and soft drink bottlers: Their "divisions," distinguished only by geographical location, lack the autonomy normally associated with ones that produce distinct products or services.

What about the conditions of size? Although large size itself does not bring on divisionalization, surely it is not coincidental that most of America's largest corporations use some variant of this configuration. The fact is that as organizations grow large, they become inclined to diversify and then to divisionalize. One reason is protection: large organizations tend to be risk averse—they have too much to lose—and diversification spreads the risk. Another is that as firms grow large, they come to dominate their traditional market, and so must often find growth opportunities elsewhere, through diversification. Moreover, diversification feeds on itself. It creates a cadre of aggressive general managers, each running his or her own division, who push for further diversification and further growth. Thus, most of the giant corporations—with the exception of the "heavies," those with enormously high fixed-cost operating systems, such as the oil or aluminum producers—not only were able to reach their status by diversifying but also feel great pressures to continue to do so.

Age is another factor associated with this configuration, much like size. In larger organizations, the management runs out of places to expand in its traditional markets; in older ones, the managers sometimes get bored with the traditional markets and find diversion through diversification. Also, time brings new competitors into old markets, forcing the management to look elsewhere for growth opportunities.

As governments grow large, they too tend to adopt a kind of divisionalized structure. The central administrators, unable to control all the agencies and departments directly, settle for granting their managers considerable autonomy and then trying to control their results through planning and performance controls. Indeed the "accountability" buzzword so often heard in governments these days reflects just this trend—to move closer to a divisionalized structure.

One can, in fact, view the entire government as a giant diversified configuration (admittedly an oversimplification, since all kinds of links exist among the departments), with its three main coordinating agencies corresponding to the three main forms of control used by the headquarters of the large corporation. The budgetary agency, technocratic in nature, concerns itself with performance control of the departments; the public service commission, also partly technocratic, concerns itself with the recruiting and training of government managers; and the executive office, top management in nature, reviews the principal proposals and initiatives of the departments.

In the preceding chapter, the communist state was described as a closed-system machine bureaucracy. But it may also be characterized as the ultimate closed system diversified configuration, with the various state enterprises and agencies its instruments, machine bureaucracies tightly regulated by the planning and control systems of the central government.

Stages in the Transition to the Diversified Organization

There has been a good deal of research on the transition of the corporation from the functional to the diversified form. Figure 2 and the discussion that follows borrow from this research to describe four stages in that transition.

At the top of Figure 2 is the pure *functional* structure, used by the corporation whose operating activities form one integrated, unbroken chain from purchasing through production to marketing and sales. Only the final output is sold to the customers.* Autonomy cannot, therefore, be granted to the units, so the organization tends to take on the form of one overall machine configuration.

---

*It should be noted that this is in fact the definition of a functional structure: Each activity contributes just one step in a chain toward the creation of the final product. Thus, for example, engineering is a functionally organized unit in the firm that produces and markets its own designs, while it would be a market organized unit in a consulting firm that sells its design services, among other, directly to clients.

FIGURE 2
Stages in the Transition to
the Pure Diversified Form

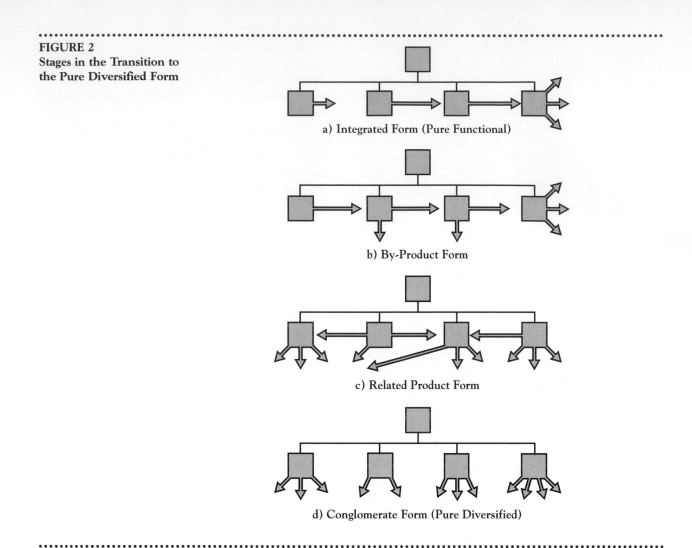

a) Integrated Form (Pure Functional)

b) By-Product Form

c) Related Product Form

d) Conglomerate Form (Pure Diversified)

As an integrated firm seeks wider markets, it may introduce a variety of new end products and so shift all the way to the pure diversified form. A less risky alternative, however, is to start by marketing its intermediate products on the open market. This introduces small breaks in its processing chain, which in turn calls for a measure of divisionalization in its structure, giving rise to the *by-product* form. But because the processing chain remains more or less intact, central coordination must largely remain. Organizations that fall into this category tend to be vertically integrated, basing their operations on a single raw material, such as wood, oil, or aluminum, which they process to a variety of consumable end products. The example of Alcoa is shown in Figure 3.

Some corporations further diversify their by-product markets, breaking down their processing chain until what the divisions sell on the open market becomes more important than what they supply to each other. The organization then moves to the *related-product* form. For example, a firm manufacturing washing machines may set up a division to produce the motors. When the motor division sells more motors to outside customers than to its own sister division, a more serious form of divisionalization is called for. What typically holds the divisions of these firms together is some common thread among their products, perhaps a core skill or technology, perhaps a central market theme, as in a corporation such as 3M that likes to describe itself as being in the coating and bonding business. A good deal

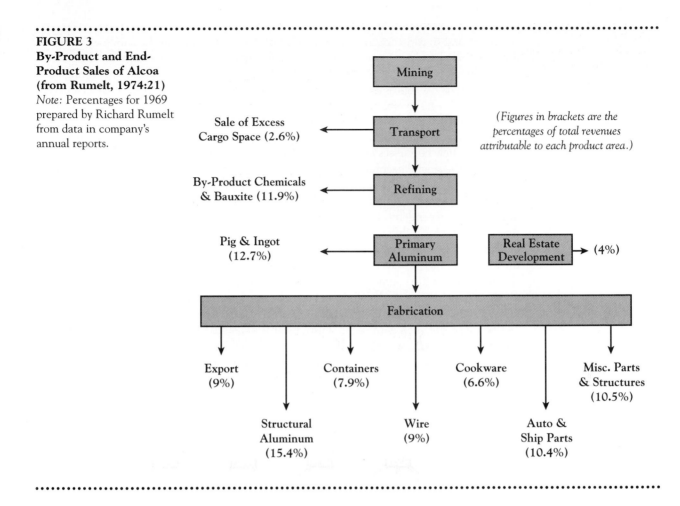

FIGURE 3
By-Product and End-Product Sales of Alcoa (from Rumelt, 1974:21)
Note: Percentages for 1969 prepared by Richard Rumelt from data in company's annual reports.

(Figures in brackets are the percentages of total revenues attributable to each product area.)

Mining

Transport ← Sale of Excess Cargo Space (2.6%)

Refining ← By-Product Chemicals & Bauxite (11.9%)

Primary Aluminum ← Pig & Ingot (12.7%)

Real Estate Development → (4%)

Fabrication

Export (9%)

Structural Aluminum (15.4%)

Containers (7.9%)

Wire (9%)

Cookware (6.6%)

Auto & Ship Parts (10.4%)

Misc. Parts & Structures (10.5%)

of the control over the specific product-market strategies can now revert to the divisions, such as research and development.

As a related-product firm expands into new markets or acquires other firms with less regard to a central strategic theme, the organization moves to the *conglomerate* form and so adopts a pure diversified configuration, the one described at the beginning of this reading. Each division serves its own markets, producing products unrelated to those of the other divisions—chinaware in one, steam shovels in a second, and so on.* The result is that the headquarters planning and control system becomes simply a vehicle for regulating performance, and the headquarters staff can diminish to almost nothing—a few general and group managers supported by a few financial analysts with a minimum of support services.

Some Issues Associated with the Diversified Organization

THE ECONOMIC ADVANTAGES OF DIVERSIFICATION?

It has been argued that the diversified configuration offers four basic advantages over the functional structure with integrated operations, namely an overall machine configuration. First, it encourages the efficient allocation of capital. Headquarters can choose where to put

---

*I wrote this example here somewhat whimsically before I encountered a firm in Finland with divisions that actually produce, among other things, the world's largest icebreaker ships and fine pottery!

its money and so can concentrate on its strongest markets, milking the surpluses of some divisions to help others grow. Second, by opening up opportunities to run individual businesses, the diversified configuration helps to train general managers. Third, this configuration spreads its risk across different markets, whereas the focused machine bureaucracy has all its strategic eggs in one market basket, so to speak. Fourth, and perhaps most important, the diversified configuration is strategically responsive. The divisions can fine-tune their bureaucratic machines while the headquarters can concentrate on the strategic portfolio. It can acquire new businesses and divest itself of old, unproductive ones.

But is the single machine organization the correct basis of comparison? Is not the real alternative, at least from society's perspective, the taking of a further step along the same path, to the point of eliminating the headquarters altogether and allowing the divisions to function as independent organization? Beatrice Foods, described in a 1976 *Fortune* magazine article, had 397 different divisions (Martin, 1976). The issue is whether this arrangement was more efficient than 397 separate corporations.* In this regard, let us reconsider the four advantages discussed earlier.

In the diversified corporation, headquarters allocates the capital resources among the divisions. In the case of 397 independent corporations, the capital markets do that job instead. Which does it better? Studies suggest that the answer is not simple.

Some people, such as the economist Oliver Williamson (1975, 1985), have argued that the diversified organization may do a better job of allocating money because the capital markets are inefficient. Managers at headquarters who know their divisions can move the money around faster and more effectively. But others find that arrangement more costly and, in some ways, less flexible. Moyer (1970), for example, argued early on that conglomerates pay a premium above stock market prices to acquire businesses, whereas the independent investor need pay only small brokerage fees to diversify his or her own portfolio, and can do so easier and more flexibly. Moreover, that provides the investor with full information on all the businesses owned, whereas the diversified corporation provides only limited information to stockholders on the details inside its portfolio.

On the issue of management development, the question becomes whether the division managers receive better training and experience than they would as company presidents. The diversified organization is able to put on training courses and to rotate its managers to vary their experience; the independent firm is limited in those respects. But if, as the proponents of diversification claim, autonomy is the key to management development, then presumably the more autonomy the better. The division managers have a headquarters to lean on—and to be leaned on by. Company presidents, in contrast, are on their own to make their own mistakes and to learn from them.

On the third issue, risk, the argument from the diversified perspective is that the independent organization is vulnerable during periods of internal crisis or economic slump; conglomeration offers support to see individual businesses through such periods. The counterargument, however, is that diversification may conceal bankruptcies, that ailing divisions are sometimes supported longer than necessary, whereas the market bankrupts the independent firm and is done with it. Moreover, just as diversification spreads the risk, so too does it spread the consequences of that risk. A single division cannot go bankrupt; the whole organization is legally responsible for its debts. So a massive enough problem in one division can pull down the whole organization. Loose coupling may turn out to be riskier than no coupling!

Finally, there is the issue of strategic responsiveness. Loosely coupled divisions may be more responsive than tightly coupled functions. But how responsive do they really prove to

---

*The example of Beatrice was first written as presented here in the 1970s, when the company was the subject of a good deal of attention and praise in the business press. At the time of our first revision, in 1988, the company was being disassembled. It seemed appropriate to leave the example as first presented, among other reasons to question the tendency to favor fashion over investigation in the business press.

be? The answer appears to be negative: this configuration appears to inhibit, not encourage, the taking of strategic initiatives. The problem seems to lie, again, in its control system. It is designed to keep the carrot just the right distance in front of the divisional managers, encouraging them to strive for better and better financial performance. At the same time, however, it seems to dampen their inclination to innovate. It is that famous "bottom line" that creates the problem, encouraging short-term thinking and shortsightedness; attention is focused on the carrot just in front instead of the fields of vegetables beyond. As Bower has noted,

> [T]he risk to the division manager of a major innovation can be considerable if he is measured on short-run, year-to-year, earnings performance. The result is a tendency to avoid big risk bets, and the concomitant phenomenon that major new developments are, with few exceptions, made outside the major firms in the industry. Those exceptions tend to be single-product companies whose top managements are committed to true product leadership. . . . Instead the diversified companies give us a steady diet of small incremental change. (1970:194)

Innovation requires entrepreneurship, or intrapreneurship, and these, as we have already argued, do not thrive under the diversified configuration. The entrepreneur takes his or her own risks to earn his or her own rewards; the intrapreneur (as we shall see) functions best in the loose structure of the innovative adhocracy. Indeed, many diversified corporations depend on those configurations for their strategic responsiveness, since they diversify not by innovating themselves but by acquiring the innovative results of independent firms. Of course, that may be their role—to exploit rather than create those innovations—but we should not, as a result, justify diversification on the basis of its innovative capacity.

THE CONTRIBUTION OF HEADQUARTERS

To assess the effectiveness of conglomeration, it is necessary to assess what actual contribution the headquarters makes to the divisions. Since what the headquarters does in a diversified organization is otherwise performed by the various boards of directors of a set of independent firms, the question then becomes, what does a headquarters offer to the divisions that the independent board of directors of the autonomous organization does not?

One thing that neither can offer is the management of the individual business. Both are involved with it only on a part-time basis. The management is, therefore, logically left to the full-time managers, who have the required time and information. Among the functions a headquarters *does* perform, as noted earlier, are the establishment of objectives for the divisions, the monitoring of their performance in terms of these objectives, and the maintenance of limited personal contacts with division managers, for example to approve large capital expenditures. Interestingly, those are also the responsibilities of the directors of the individual firm, at least in theory.

In practice, however, many boards of directors—notably, those of widely held corporations—do those things rather ineffectively, leaving business managements carte blanche to do what they like. Here, then, we seem to have a major advantage to the diversified configuration. It exists as an administrative mechanism to overcome another prominent weakness of the free-market system, the ineffective board.

There is a catch in this argument, however, for diversification by enhancing an organization's size and expanding its number of markets, renders the corporation more difficult to understand and so to control by its board of part-time directors. Moreover, as Moyer has noted, one common effect of conglomerate acquisition is to increase the number of shareholders, and so to make the corporation more widely held, and therefore less amenable to director control. Thus, the diversified configuration in some sense resolves a problem of its own making—it offers the control that its own existence has rendered difficult. Had the corporation remained in one business, it might have been more narrowly held and easier to understand, and so its directors might have been able to perform their functions more effectively. Diversification thus helped to create the problem that divisionalization is said to solve. Indeed, it is ironic that many a diversified corporation that does such a vigorous job of monitoring the performance of its own divisions is itself so poorly monitored by its own board of directors!

All of this suggests that large diversified organizations tend to be classic closed systems, powerful enough to seal themselves off from much external influence while able to exercise a good deal of control over not only their own divisions, as instruments, but also their external environments. For example, one study of all 5,995 directors of the *Fortune* 500 found that only 1.6 percent of them represented major shareholder interests (Smith, 1978) while another survey of 855 corporations found that 84 percent of them did not even formally require their directors to hold any stock at all! (Bacon, 1973:40).

What does happen when problems arise in a division? What can a headquarters do that various boards of directors cannot? The chairman of one major conglomerate told a meeting of the New York Society of Security Analysts, in reference to the headquarters vice presidents who oversee the divisions, that "it is not too difficult to coordinate five companies that are well run" (in Wrigley, 1970:V78). True enough. But what about five that are badly run? What could the small staff of administrators at a corporation's headquarters really do to correct problems in that firm's thirty operating divisions or in Beatrice's 397? The natural tendency to tighten the control screws does not usually help once the problem has manifested itself, nor does exercising close surveillance. As noted earlier, the headquarters managers cannot manage the divisions. Essentially, that leaves them with two choices. They can either replace the division manager, or they can divest the corporation of the division. Of course, a board of directors can also replace the management. Indeed, that seems to be its only real prerogative; the management does everything else.

On balance, then, the economic case for one headquarters versus a set of separate boards of directors appears to be mixed. It should, therefore, come as no surprise that one important study found that corporations with "controlled diversity" had better profits than those with conglomerate diversity (Rumelt, 1974). Overall, the pure diversified configuration (the conglomerate) may offer some advantages over a weak system of separate boards of directors and inefficient capital markets, but most of those advantages would probably disappear if certain problems in capital markets and boards of directors were rectified. And there is reason to argue, from a social no less than an economic standpoint, that society would be better off trying to correct fundamental inefficiencies in its economic system rather than encourage private administrative arrangements to circumvent them, as we shall now see.

THE SOCIAL PERFORMANCE OF THE PERFORMANCE CONTROL SYSTEM

This configuration requires that headquarters control the divisions primarily by quantitative performance criteria, and that typically means financial ones—profit, sales growth, return on investment, and the like. The problem is that these performance measures often become virtual obsessions in the diversified organization, driving out goals that cannot be measured—product quality, pride in work, customers well served. In effect, the economic goals drive out the social ones. As the chief of a famous conglomerate once remarked, "We, in Textron, worship the god of Net Worth" (in Wrigley, 1970:V86).

That would pose no problem if the social and economic consequences of decisions could easily be separated. Governments would look after the former, corporations the latter. But the fact is that the two are intertwined; every strategic decision of every large corporation involves both, largely inseparable. As a result, its control systems, by focusing on economic measures, drive the diversified organization to act in ways that are, at best, socially unresponsive, at worst, socially irresponsible. Forced to concentrate on the economic consequences of decisions, the division manager is driven to ignore their social consequences. (Indeed, that manager is also driven to ignore the intangible economic consequences as well, such as product quality or research effort, another manifestation of the problem of the short-term, bottom-line thinking mentioned earlier.) Thus, Bower found that "the best records in the race relations area are those of single-product companies whose strong top managements are deeply involved in the business" (1970:193).

Robert Ackerman, in a study carried out at the Harvard Business School, investigated this point. He found that social benefits such as "a rosier public image . . . pride among managers . . . an attractive posture for recruiting on campus" could not easily be measured and so could not be plugged into the performance control system. The result was that

> . . . the financial reporting system may actually inhibit social responsiveness. By focusing on economic performance, even with appropriate safeguards to protect against sacrificing long-term benefits, such a system directs energy and resources to achieving results measured in financial terms. It is the only game in town, so to speak, at least the only one with an official scoreboard. (1975:55, 56)

Headquarters managers who are concerned about legal liabilities or the public relations effects of decisions, or even ones personally interested in broader social issues, may be tempted to intervene directly in the divisions' decision-making process to ensure proper attention to social matters. But they are discouraged from doing so by this configuration's strict division of labor: divisional autonomy requires no meddling by the headquarters in specific business decisions.

As long as the screws of the performance control system are not turned too tight, the division managers may retain enough discretion to consider the social consequences of their actions, if they so choose. But when those screws are turned tight, as they often are in the diversified corporation with a bottom-line orientation, then the division managers wishing to keep their jobs may have no choice but to act socially unresponsively, if not actually irresponsibly. As Bower has noted of the General Electric price-fixing scandal of the 1960s, "a very severely managed system of reward and punishment that demanded yearly improvements in earnings, return and market share, applied indiscriminately to all divisions, yielded a situation which was—at the very least—conducive to collusion in the oligopolistic and mature electric equipment markets" (1970:193).

THE DIVERSIFIED ORGANIZATION IN THE PUBLIC SPHERE

Ironically, for a government intent on dealing with these social problems, solutions are indicated in the very arguments used to support the diversified configuration. Or so it would appear.

For example, if the administrative arrangements are efficient while the capital markets are not, then why should a government hesitate to interfere with the capital markets? And why shouldn't it use those same administrative arrangements to deal with the problems? If Beatrice Foods really can control those 397 divisions, then what is to stop Washington from believing it can control 397 Beatrices? After all, the capital markets don't much matter. In his book on "countervailing power," John Kenneth Galbraith (1952) argued that bigness in one sector, such as business, promotes bigness in other sectors, such as unions and government. That has already happened. How long before government pursues the logical next step and exercises direct controls?

While such steps may prove irresistible to some governments, the fact is that they will not resolve the problems of power concentration and social irresponsibility but rather will aggravate them, but not just in the ways usually assumed in Western economics. All the existing problems would simply be bumped up to another level, and there increase. By making use of the diversified configuration, government would magnify the problems of size. Moreover, government, like the corporation, would be driven to favor measurable economic goals over intangible social ones, and that would add to the problems of social irresponsibility—a phenomenon of which we have already seen a good deal in the public sector.

In fact, these problems would be worse in government, because its sphere is social, and so its goals are largely ill suited to performance control systems. In other words, many of the goals most important for the public sector—and this applies to not-for-profit organizations in spheres such as health and education as well—simply do not lend themselves to measurement, no matter how long and how hard public officials continue to try. And without measurement, the conventional diversified configuration cannot work.

There are, of course, other problems with the application of this form of organization in the public sphere. For example, government cannot divest itself of subunits quite so easily as can corporations. And public service regulations on appointments and the like, as well as a host of other rules, preclude the degree of division manager autonomy available in the private sector. (It is, in fact, these central rules and regulations that make governments resemble integrated machine configurations as much as loosely coupled diversified ones, and that undermine their efforts at "accountability.")

Thus, we conclude that, appearances and even trends notwithstanding, the diversified configuration is generally not suited to the public and not-for-profit sectors of society. Governments and other public-type institutions that wish to divisionalize to avoid centralized machine bureaucracy may often find the imposition of performance standards an artificial exercise. They may thus be better off trying to exercise control of their units in a different way. For example, they can select unit managers who reflect their desired values, or indoctrinate them in those values, and then let them manage freely, the control in effect being normative rather than quantitative. But managing ideology, even creating it in the first place, is no simple matter, especially in a highly diversified organization.

IN CONCLUSION: A STRUCTURE ON THE EDGE OF A CLIFF

Our discussion has led to a "damned if you do, damned if you don't" conclusion. The pure (conglomerate) diversified configuration emerges as an organization perched symbolically on the edge of the cliff, at the end of a long path. Ahead, it is one step away from disintegration—breaking up into separate organizations on the rocks below. Behind it is the way back to a more stable integration, in the form of the machine configuration at the start of that path. And ever hovering above is the eagle, representing the broader social control of the state, attracted by the organization's position on the edge of the cliff and waiting for the chance to pull it up to a higher cliff, perhaps more dangerous still. The edge of the cliff is an uncomfortable place to be, perhaps even a temporary one that must inevitably lead to disintegration on the rocks below, a trip to that cliff above, or a return to a safer resting place somewhere on that path behind.

by Henry Mintzberg

In Chapter 3 we examined three sets of strategies—for locating, then distinguishing and elaborating the core business. These are appropriate for the business level. After locating the core business in a given industry, the strategist answers the business-level question of "How do we compete successfully in this industry?" by distinguishing and elaborating the core business.

Next comes the question of what strategies of a generic nature are available to extend and reconceive that core business. These are approaches designed to answer the corporate-level question, "What business should we be in?"

Extending the Core Business

Strategies designed to take organizations beyond their core business can be pursued in so-called vertical or horizontal ways, as well as combinations of the two. "Vertical" means backward or forward in the operating chain, the strategy being known formally as "vertical integration," although why this has been designated vertical is difficult to understand, especially since the flow of product and the chain itself are almost always drawn horizontally! Hence this will here be labeled chain integration. "Horizontal" diversification (its own geometry no more evident), which will be called here just plain diversification, refers to encompassing within the organization other, parallel businesses, not in the same chain of operations.

CHAIN INTEGRATION STRATEGIES

Organizations can extend their operating chains downstream or upstream, encompassing within their own operations the activities of their customers on the delivery end or their suppliers on the sourcing end. In effect, they choose to "make" rather than to "buy" or sell. *Impartation* (Barreyre, 1984; Barreyre and Carle, 1983) is a label that has been proposed to describe the opposite strategy, where the organization chooses to buy what it previously made (also called "outsourcing"), or sell what it previously transferred.

DIVERSIFICATION STRATEGIES

Diversification refers to the entry into some business not in the same chain of operation. It may be *related* to some distinctive competence or asset of the core business itself (also called *concentric* diversification); otherwise, it is referred to as *unrelated* or *conglomerate* diversification. In related diversification, there is evident potential synergy between the new business and the core one, based on a common facility, asset, channel, skill, even opportunity. Porter (1985: 323–4) makes the distinction here between "intangible" and "tangible" relatedness. The former is based on some functional or managerial skill considered common across the businesses, as in a Philip Morris using its marketing capabilities in Kraft. The latter refers to businesses that actually "share activities in the value chain" (p. 323), for example, different products sold by the same sales force. It should be emphasized here that no matter what its basis, every related diversification is also fundamentally an unrelated one, as many diversifying organizations have discovered to their regret. That is, no matter what is common between two different businesses, many other things are not.

---

*Abbreviated version, prepared for this book, of an article by Henry Mintzberg, "Generic Strategies: Toward a Comprehensive Framework," originally published in *Advances in Strategic Management*, Vol. 5 (Greenwich, CT: JAI Press, 1988), pp. 1–67.

STRATEGIES OF ENTRY AND CONTROL

Chain integration or diversification may be achieved by *internal development* or *acquisition*. In other words, an organization can enter a new business by developing it itself or by buying an organization already in business. Both internal development and acquisition involve complete ownership and formal control of the diversified business. But there are a host of other possible strategies, as follows:

STRATEGIES OF ENTRY AND CONTROL

Full ownership and control	• Internal development
	• Acquisition
Partial ownership and control	• Majority, minority
	• Partnership, including
	–Joint venture
	–Turnkey (temporary control)
Partial control without ownership	• Licensing
	• Franchising
	• Long-term contracting

COMBINED INTEGRATION-DIVERSIFICATION STRATEGIES

Among the most interesting are those strategies that combine chain integration with business diversification, sometimes leading organizations into whole networks of new businesses. *By-product diversification* involves selling off the by-products of the operating chain in separate markets, as when an airline offers its maintenance services to other carriers. The new activity amounts to a form of market development at some intermediate point in the operating chain. *Linked diversification* extends by-product diversification: one business simply leads to another, whether integrated "vertically" or diversified "horizontally." The organization pursues its operating chain upstream, downstream, sidestream; it exploits pre-products, end-products, and by-products of its core products as well as of each other, ending up with a network of businesses, as illustrated in the case of a supermarket chain in Figure 1. *Crystalline diversification* pushes the previous strategy to the limit, so that it becomes difficult and perhaps irrelevant to distinguish integration from diversification, core activities from peripheral activities, closely related businesses from distantly related ones. What were once clear links in a few chains now metamorphose into what looks like a form of crystalline growth, as business after business gets added literally right and left as well as up and down. Here businesses tend to be related, at least initially, through internal development of core competencies, as in the "coating and bonding technologies" that are common to so many of 3M's products.

WITHDRAWAL STRATEGIES

Finally there are strategies that reverse all those of diversification: organizations cut back on the businesses they are in. "Exit" has a been one popular label for this, withdrawal is another. Sometimes organizations *shrink* their activities, canceling long-term licenses, ceasing to sell by-products, reducing their crystalline networks. Other times they abandon or *liquidate* businesses (the opposite of internal development), or else they *divest* them (the opposite of acquisition).

FIGURE 1

Linked Diversification on a Time Scale—
The Case of the Steinberg Chain
Source: From Mintzberg and Waters (1982: 490)

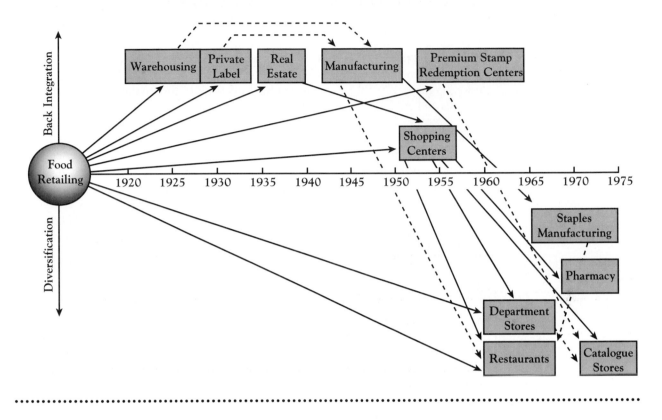

Reconceiving the Core Business(es)

It may seem strange to end a discussion of strategies of ever more elaborate development of a business with ones involving reconception of the business. But in one important sense, there is a logic to this: after a core business has been identified, distinguished, elaborated and extended, there often follows the need not just to consolidate it but also to redefine it and reconfigure it—in essence, to reconceive it. As they develop, through all the waves of expansion, integration, diversification, and so on, some organizations lose a sense of themselves. Then reconception becomes the ultimate form of consolidation: rationalizing not just excesses in product offerings or markets segments or even new businesses, but all of these things together and more—the essence of the entire strategy itself. We can identify three basic reconception strategies.

BUSINESS REDEFINITION STRATEGY

A business, as Abell (1980) has pointed out, may be defined in a variety of ways—by the function it performs, the market it serves, the product it produces. All businesses have popular conceptions. Some are narrow and tangible, such as the canoe business, others broader and vague, such as the financial services business. All such definitions, no matter how tangible, are ultimately concepts that exist in the minds of actors and observers. It therefore becomes possible, with a little effort and imagination, to *redefine* a particular business—

reconceive the "recipe" for how that business is conducted (Grinyer and Spender, 1979; Spender, 1989)—as Edwin Land did when he developed the Polaroid camera.*

BUSINESS RECOMBINATION STRATEGIES

As Porter notes, through the waves of diversification that swept American business in the 1960s and 1970s, "the concept of synergy has become widely regarded as passe"—a "nice idea" but "one that rarely occurred in practice" (1985: 317–18). Businesses were elements in a portfolio to be bought and sold, or, at best, grown and harvested. Deploring that conclusion, Porter devoted three chapters of his 1985 book to "horizontal strategy," which we shall refer to here (given our problems with the geometry of this field) as *business recombination strategies*—efforts to recombine different businesses in some way, at the limit to reconceive various businesses as one. Businesses can be recombined tangibly or only conceptually. The latter was encouraged by Levitt's "Marketing Myopia" (1960) article. By a stroke of the pen, railroads could be in the transportation business, ball-bearing manufacturers in the friction reduction business. Realizing some practical change in behavior often proved much more difficult, however. But when some substantial basis exists for combining different activities, a strategy of business recombination can be very effective. There may never have been a transportation business, but 3M was able to draw on common technological capabilities to create a coating and bonding business.** Business recombination can also be more tangible, based on shared activities in the value chain, as in a strategy of *bundling*, where complementary products are sold together for a single price (e.g., automobile service with the new car). Of course, *unbundling* can be an equally viable strategy, such as selling "term" insurance free of any investment obligation. Carried to their logical extreme, the more tangible recombination strategies lead to a "systems view" of the business, where all products and services are conceived to be tightly interrelated.

CORE RELOCATION STRATEGIES

Finally we come full circle by closing the discussion where we began, on the location of the core business. An organization, in addition to having one or more strategic positions in a marketplace, tends to have what Jay Galbraith (1983) calls a single "center of gravity," some conceptual place where is concentrated not only its core skills but also its cultural heart, as in a Procter & Gamble focusing its efforts on "branded consumer products," each "sold primarily by advertising to the homemaker and managed by a brand manager" (p. 13). But as changes in strategic position take place, shifts can also take place in this center of gravity, in various ways. First, the organization can move *along the operating chain*, upstream or downstream, as did General Mills "from a flour miller to a related diversified provider of products for the homemaker"; eventually the company sold off its flour milling operation altogether (p. 76). Second, there can be a shift *between dominant functions*, say from production to marketing. Third is the shift *to a new business*, whether or not at the same stage of the operating chain. Such shifts can be awfully demanding, simply because each industry is a culture with its own ways of thinking and acting. Finally, is the shift *to a new core theme*, as in the reorientation from a single function or product to a broader concept, for example, when Procter & Gamble changed from being a soap company to being in the personal care business.

This brings us to the end of our discussion of generic strategies—our loop from locating a business to distinguishing it, elaborating it, extending it and finally reconceiving it.

---

* MacMillan refers to the business redefinition strategy as "reshaping the industry infrastructure" (1983:18), while Porter calls it "reconfiguration" (1985:519–523), although his notion of product *substitution* (273–314) could sometimes also constitute a form of business redefinition.

** Our suspicion, we should note, is that such labels often emerge after the fact, as the organization seeks a way to rationalize the diversification that has already taken place. In effect, the strategy is emergent. (See Chapter 1 on "Five Ps for Strategy.")

We should close with a warning that while a framework of generic strategies may help to think about positioning an organization, use of it as a pat list may put that organization at a disadvantage against competitors that develop their strategies in more creative ways.

by Philippe Lasserre

. . . there is no one single best method for managing groups of businesses, and the globalization of markets and competition has revealed the emergence of organizational forms of business, particularly in the Asia Pacific region, which differs significantly from the one adopted in Europe and North America. The purpose of this article is to underline some of the salient differences between corporations in Asia and in Europe, to analyze the basis of those differences and finally to draw some recommendations.

In the first and second parts one will identify some prominent types of corporations in Europe and in Asia Pacific. In a third part, their organizational forms and their corporate control styles will be compared. Finally, some recommendations. . . will be proposed.

European Corporate Archtypes

European groups can be broadly classified into three major types: industrial groups, industrial holdings, and financial conglomerates.

A first type of corporation is characterized by a portfolio of business activities which share a common set of competences and in which a high degree of synergy is achieved by managing key interdependencies at corporate level. Andrew Campbell and Michael Goold at the Ashridge Strategic Management Center in the UK, in their study of British corporations, have named this type "Strategic Planning" groups (Campbell and Goold, 1987), because of the strong input from corporate headquarters in those groups into the strategy formulation of business units. Here, those groups are identified as *industrial groups*. Examples of industrial groups in Europe are British Petroleum or Glaxo in the UK, Daimler Benz or Henkel in Germany, Philips in the Netherlands, or l'Air Liquide and Michelin in France.

Industrial holdings are corporations in which the business units are clustered into subgroups or sectors. In this type of corporate grouping, synergies are strong within subgroups and weak between subgroups. In industrial holdings, the task of value creation through synergies is delegated to the subgroup level of management, while the corporate role is to impose management discipline through the implementation of planning and control systems, to manage acquisitions and leverage and allocate human and financial resources. Campbell and Goold call these groups "Strategic Control" groups, because of their intensive use of planning and control systems to regulate the relationships between business units and corporate headquarters. Examples of industrial holdings are: ICI or Courtaulds in the UK, BSN or Alsthom-Alcatel in France, Siemens or BASF in Germany.

Financial conglomerates are characterized by a constellation of business units which do not necessarily share any common source of synergies and whose corporate value is essentially created by the imposition of management discipline, financial leverage, and the management of acquisitions and restructuring. Heavy reliance on financial control systems as the major mechanisms of corporate governance have led Campbell and Goold to call these "Financial Control" groups. Hanson Trust or BTR in the UK are examples of financial con-

*Originally published as "The Management of Large Groups: Asia and Europe Compared," in *European Management Journal*, Vol. 10, No. 2, June 1992, 157–162. Reprinted with deletions with permission of the Journal, Elsciver Science Ltd., Pergamon Imprint, Oxford, England.

glomerates. A more recent and extreme version of financial conglomerates has appeared in the USA under the form of what Professor Michael Jensen at the Harvard Business School has identified as "LBO Partnerships," in which value is extracted through corporate restructuring and financial discipline imposed on business units under the form of heavy debts, as in the case of Kolberg, Kravis and Roberts (Jensen, 1989).

In Europe one can find examples of the three types of groups in a variety of corporate ownership arrangements, whether private or government-owned. In France one can find in the public sector industrial groups such as Renault, SNECMA, or Aerospatiale or, in the private sector, Peugeot, Dassault, or Michelin. Similarly Rhone Poulenc, a government-owned group, is managed as an industrial holding like BSN, which is a privately-owned group. . . .

Asian Corporate Archetypes

In the Asia Pacific region, where in the past three decades local corporations have emerged as strong competitors, one can possibly identify three major types: the entrepreneurial conglomerates, the Japanese Keiretsus, and the national holdings.

The *entrepreneurial conglomerate* is a prevailing form of corporate organization in South East Asia, Korea, Taiwan and Hong Kong. Entrepreneurial conglomerates are widely diversified into a large number of unrelated activities ranging from banking, trading, real estate, manufacturing, and services. These groups are usually under the leadership of a father figure who exercises control over the strategic decisions of business units and is the driving force behind any strategic move. Very little attempt is made in Asian entrepreneurial conglomerates to manage synergies. The major source of value in those groups emanates from the ability of the entrepreneur to leverage financial and human resources, to establish political connections, to conclude deals with governments and business partners, and to impose loyalty and discipline upon business units. One can distinguish three major types of entrepreneurial conglomerates in Asia: the large Korean groups or Chaebols such as Samsung, Daewoo, or Hyundai; the Overseas Chinese groups such as Liem Sioe Liong or Astra International in Indonesia, Formosa Plastics in Taiwan, Charoen Pokphand in Thailand or Li Ka Shing in Hong Kong; and the colonial "Hongs" such as Swire or Jardine Matheson in Hong Kong.

The *Keiretsus* are a unique feature of Japanese corporate organization. They constitute super groups, or clusters of groups in which businesses are either vertically integrated as in the case of Honda, NEC, Toyota, or Matsushita, or horizontally connected as in the case of Mitsubishi, Mitsui, or Sumitomo. Although some companies in the groups exercise greater "power" than others, Keiretsus are not hierarchically organized. They are like a club of organizations which share common interests. Linkages across companies are made through cross shareholdings, the regular meeting of a "Presidential council" in which chairmen of leading companies exchange views. Transfer of staff and, in some cases, long-term supplier-client relationships are also mechanisms used among the vertical Keiretsus. Value is added in Keiretsus through their ability to coordinate informally a certain number of key activities (R&D, export contracts), to transfer expertise through personnel rotation, and to build strong supplier-distributor chains.

The Asian *national holdings* groups have been formed more recently as an expression of industrial independence in order to capitalize on domestic markets and public endowment. Some of these are government-owned like Petronas in Malaysia, Singapore Airlines, Singapore Technology, Gresik in Indonesia, or private like Siam Cement in Thailand or San Miguel in the Philippines. Their business portfolios tend to be less diversified than the ones of the entrepreneurial conglomerates, and their value creation capabilities stem from their "nationality." . . .

Group Management: A Comparison

In order to proceed to a comparison of the ways groups organize themselves to control and coordinate their activities, one needs to define the key dimensions which capture the most significant differences. In the management literature, various parameters have been proposed to study organizational differences, and the objective of this article is not to review previous research, but to propose what seem to be the most salient measures of differences. Two dimensions are considered as the most important ones:

a. First, the way corporations organize the respective roles of headquarters, the "center," and business units, whether those are divisions or subsidiaries. This dimension is referred to as *Organizational Setting.*

b. Second, the way headquarters ensure that business units' performances and behavior are in line with corporate expectations. This is referred to as *Corporate Control.*

ORGANIZATIONAL SETTING

Corporations around the world appear to cluster themselves around four types of corporate organizational settings.

In the first type of organization, the center plays an important role in managing synergies. Strategic and operational integration and coordination of business units are considered to be the major sources of competitive advantage. Interdependencies are achieved through a variety of mechanisms, including centralized functions, top-down strategic plans, strong corporate identity and socialization of personnel. Given this high role assigned to the center of this form of organization, it can be qualified as a *federation*. This form prevails in the first type of European groups identified above: the industrial groups, and in certain of national holdings in the Asia Pacific region.

In a second type, the center functions as both resource allocator, guardian of the corporate identity, and source of strategic renewal. Business units enjoy a large degree of strategic autonomy provided that their strategies are "negotiated" and fit with the overall "corporate strategic framework" inspired by the center. Bottom-up planning, negotiated strategies, operational autonomy, and central mechanisms of financial and human resources allocation are key characteristics of this type of organizational setting. It differs from the federate organization by the more balanced power sharing between the center and the operating units; for that reason it is referred to, here, as a *confederation*. This form is most often characteristic of the European industrial holdings as well as Asian national holdings.

In a third category, one can find groups organized as a multitude of uncoordinated business units, each of them linked directly or indirectly to the center. The role of the center in those groups can be either "hands on," as in the case of Asian entrepreneurial conglomerates, or "hands off," as in the case of European financial conglomerates. What characterizes these groups is the fact that the relationships between business units and corporate headquarters are composed of a series of one to one "contractual" agreements. This form resembles a *constellation* and, as said earlier, is predominantly adopted by Asian and European conglomerates.

Finally, in a fourth type of organizational setting, one can find groups in which there is no center or, on the contrary, there are several centers. Some coordination mechanisms are loose, as in the case of informal meetings, while some are more tightly controlled, as in the case of long-term suppliers' contracts. Japanese Keiretsus are representative of this organizational type. Because it is structured as a network, it is called here the *connexion* type of organization.

CORPORATE CONTROL

Corporate control describes how groups ensure that business units' performances and behaviors are in line with corporate expectations. One can distinguish five major methods of exercising control: control by financial performance only, control by systems, control by strategy, direct subjective control of the persons, and control by ideology.

In groups which rely primarily on *financial controls*, headquarters assign financial goals based on financial standards (return on assets, shareholder value). Performances are monitored and evaluated according to achievement of these financial goals. Rewards and punishments of managers are based on those achievements and, for the group, the strategic value of businesses is assessed on their capacities to produce the "figures." This method of control prevails in European financial conglomerates.

The exercise of *control by systems* is based on the implementation of planning and control mechanisms such as interactive strategic planning sessions, investments decisions using capital budgeting techniques, control reviews, etc. Systems use financial as well as nonfinancial information (strategic, marketing). This mode of control predominates in the European industrial holdings and the European industrial groups.

In the *control by strategy* mode, the emphasis is neither on the financial measurement of performance nor on "systems," but on the appreciation of the strategic trajectory of business units and on their degree of fit with the whole corporation. This is done through task forces, corporate conferences, informal meetings, temporary assignments of key executives to business units, etc. European industrial groups and, to some extent, Japanese Keiretsus are practicing this form of control, whose purpose is not to measure or enforce, but to make sure that there is a coherent corporate strategic fit.

Personalized control is exercised through a direct interface between the group chairman and business units' key managers. Subjective, holistic forms of assessment are in use. Although some form of measurement and use of systems can be found in these groups, the main concern for unit managers is to behave according to the norms and beliefs of the chairman. Asian entrepreneurial conglomerates are practicing, nearly exclusively, this form of control.

Finally, with *ideological control* the focus is to make sure that managers have internalized the values of the group and are behaving accordingly. Systems, financial measurements, special relationships with the chairman, if used at all, do not play a dominant role here. What does matter is the development of strong beliefs, norms, values across the organization. Recruitments, socialization, training, rotation of staff are all kinds of process which build and maintain an ideology. This type of control prevails in the Asian national holdings in which strong national and corporate identities constitute the essential glue of group performance. Vertical Keiretsus are also well-known to use extensively this form of control.

Comparing European and Asian Groups

Those two dimensions combined give the opportunity to contrast the Asian groups with their European counterparts in the chart represented in Figure 1. As it appears in this figure, Asian and European large corporations live in a different organizational world. While they share some similarities in the way they control their operations, they differ in the way they design their organizational settings, and vice versa. What is interesting to observe in Figure 1 is that Asian corporations introduce, in any case, an interpersonal feature in their management system.

The Keiretsus are built around the ability of group members to connect to each other in one way or another through personal contacts. In the entrepreneurial conglomerate, the entrepreneur is in direct contact with business units and all relationships are personalized. In the case of national holdings, the personification of rapport is established through ideological means, sense of belonging, and nationalistic stand.

FIGURE 1
Asian and European
Groups

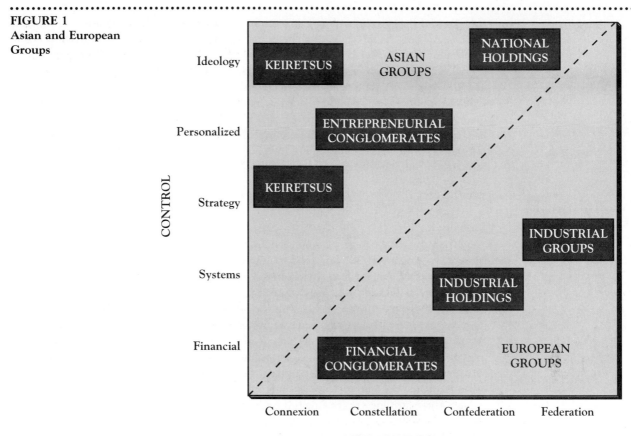

The European groups, by contrast, tend to prefer systematic or administrative features in their corporate management. Financial conglomerates are driven by "numbers," industrial holdings favor complex planning and control mechanisms, while industrial groups adopt structural and regulatory means of coordination. When confronted by a problem of change the typical reaction of a Western corporation will be to find a new "structure" or a new "system." . . .

Western corporate designers adopt an "engineering" approach to building and regulating organizational life. Although over the past 50 years behavioral sciences have brought an immense contribution to the art of management, this has been, most of the time, translated into practice with an instrumental perspective. Motivation theories have given birth to "management by objectives," experimental psychology using conditioning techniques has been used for the design of rewards and bonus systems, information theory is applied in the setting up of computer systems, etc. The rationale underlying this effort is probably the belief that human behavior can be influenced by the *manipulation* of organizational mechanisms. The main concern of Western managers confronted with a situation of strategic change is to install a new "organization" or a new "management system" which is supposed to align behavior with the new realities.

This instrumental engineering approach is challenged by Asian corporate architects who conceive enterprises as living entities where various individuals and groups obtain mutual benefit through cooperation. Organizations are not seen as independent of the people who compose them and, most of the time, enterprises are compared to "families." In 1984, Chairman Kim Woo Choong, founder of Daewoo, was participating in a session at the Harvard Business School with a group of US senior executives. He was asked by one participant how he could coordinate some 40 subsidiaries without controlling them. Chairman Kim answered that coordination was achieved through *"spiritual linkages"!* (Aguilar, 1984.) That does not mean that Asian firms do not use systems for their management, but that personification of interrelationships are given priorities over formal systems. One major underlying assumption of Asian managers is that organizational mechanisms are not set up to "manipulate" people but rather to give a structure to social interactions. In fact, most of the time, people are not rewarded for their performance, as measured in terms of results, but in terms of conformity to behavior. Organizations are not seen as machines (an engineering view) but as a set of "codified" relationships (a biological view).

Decoding Asian Firms

. . . When the competitive pressure from Asian firms becomes too intense, Western managers try to emulate them. One good example is provided by an article published in 1990 in the *Harvard Business Review* by Charles Ferguson (1990) in which the author proposes the creation of Western Keiretsus between US and European countries in the computer industry! This proposition reflects an engineering view of the organizational world: the machine "works" in Japan, why don't we import the machine? It is as if we asked US society to renounce individualism. What an ambition! Instead of trying to "import the machine," Western managers should be inspired to gain an understanding of the way the relationships function or don't function in these groups, what social roles do they play, in other terms to "decode" and not to "imitate" Asian organizations. This decoding ability requires three attitudes: (a) getting rid of *a priori* judgments, (b) making the necessary effort to study the social and cultural background of Asian societies, and (c) resisting the temptation of easy translations.

A. GET RID OF *A PRIORI* JUDGMENTS

More often than not, when presented with Asian cases, particularly successful ones, Western managers give ready-made explanations: Japan Inc. exploited manpower, "workaholism," nationalism, sacrificed generation, etc. Those views are meaningless because they are based on a simplistic engineering causality leading to defeatism or stubborn protectionism. Understanding the functionality of a social structure is the first necessary step in the analysis of organization, while the deciphering of causal links comes second. A rushed application of ready-made causal schemes based on superficial facts does not help to understand Asian partners and competitors.

B. INVEST IN THE STUDY OF CULTURES AND SOCIETIES

One of the dangers of "instrumental" thinking is that it bypasses what is not considered of immediate relevance. Cultural and social knowledge are all too frequently considered to be a waste of time or, at best, as subjects of "executive summaries." Organizations and business behavior are part of an historical and cultural heritage which, in the case of Asian societies, is very rich, complex, and heterogeneous. The manager who does not make the necessary efforts to enlighten him or herself with such knowledge is condemned to go from surprise to surprise if not from disillusion to disillusion.

C. RESIST THE TEMPTATION OF "EASY TRANSLATIONS"

Some managers fall into the trap of adopting, naively, a so-called "Asian" way of doing things. In the early 1980s, a European bank set up a regional office in Singapore, its first commitment in the region. The newly appointed general manager, a very enthusiastic person, decided that he would work "the Chinese way": handshakes, networking, personal trust, etc. He found himself trapped two years later with a portfolio of bad debts amounting to several million US$! Such horror stories can only fuel the resistance of corporate boards to commit resources for developing strategies in the Asia Pacific region. . . .

▼ READING 13.4 FROM COMPETITIVE ADVANTAGE TO CORPORATE STRATEGY*

by Michael E. Porter

Corporate strategy, the overall plan for a diversified company, is both the darling and the stepchild of contemporary management practice—the darling because CEOs have been obsessed with diversification since the early 1960s, the stepchild because almost no consensus exists about what corporate strategy is, much less about how a company should formulate it.

A diversified company has two levels of strategy: business unit (or competitive) strategy and corporate (or companywide) strategy. Competitive strategy concerns how to create competitive advantage in each of the businesses in which a company competes. Corporate strategy concerns two different questions: what businesses the corporation should be in and how the corporate office should manage the array of business units.

Corporate strategy is what makes the corporate whole add up to more than the sum of its business unit parts.

The track record of corporate strategies has been dismal. I studied the diversification records of 33 large, prestigious U.S. companies over the 1950–1986 period and found that most of them had divested many more acquisitions than they had kept. The corporate strategies of most companies have dissipated instead of created shareholder value.

The need to rethink corporate strategy could hardly be more urgent. By taking over companies and breaking them up, corporate raiders thrive on failed corporate strategy. Fueled by junk bond financing and growing acceptability, raiders can expose any company to takeover, no matter how large or blue chip. . . .

A Sober Picture

. . . My study of 33 companies, many of which have reputations for good management, is a unique look at the track record of major corporations. . . . Each company entered an average of 80 new industries and 27 new fields. Just over 70% of the new entries were acquisitions, 22% were start-ups, and 8% were joint ventures. IBM, Exxon, Du Pont, and 3M, for example, focused on startups, while ALCO Standard, Beatrice, and Sara Lee diversified almost solely through acquisitions. . . .

My data paint a sobering picture of the success ratio of these moves. . . . I found that on average corporations divested more than half their acquisitions in new industries and more than 60% of their acquisitions in entirely new fields. Fourteen companies left more than 70% of all the acquisitions they had made in new fields. The track record in unrelated acquisitions is even worse—the average divestment rate is startling 74%. Even a highly

respected company like General Electric divested a very high percentage of its acquisitions, particularly those in new fields. . . . Some [companies] bear witness to the success of well-thought-out corporate strategies. Others, however, enjoy a lower rate simply because they have not faced up to their problem units and divested them. . . .

I would like to make one comment on the use of shareholder value to judge performance. Linking shareholder value quantitatively to diversification performance only works if you compare the shareholder value that is with the shareholder value that might have been without diversification. Because such a comparison is virtually impossible to make, my own measure of diversification success—the number of units retained by the company—seems to be as good an indicator as any of the contribution of diversification to corporate performance.

My data give a stark indication of the failure of corporate strategies.* Of the 33 companies, 6 had been taken over as my study was being completed. . . . Only the lawyers, investment bankers, and original sellers have prospered in most of these acquisitions, not the shareholders.

Premises of Corporate Strategy

Any successful corporate strategy builds on a number of premises. These are facts of life about diversification. They cannot be altered, and when ignored, they explain in part why so many corporate strategies fail.

COMPETITION OCCURS AT THE BUSINESS UNIT LEVEL

Diversified companies do not compete; only their business units do. Unless a corporate strategy places primary attention on nurturing the success of each unit, the strategy will fail, no matter how elegantly constructed. Successful corporate strategy must grow out of and reinforce competitive strategy.

DIVERSIFICATION INEVITABLY ADDS COSTS AND CONSTRAINTS TO BUSINESS UNITS

Obvious costs such as the corporate overhead allocated to a unit may not be as important or subtle as the hidden costs and constraints. A business unit must explain its decisions to top management, spend time complying with planning and other corporate systems, live with parent company guidelines and personnel policies, and forgo the opportunity to motivate employees with direct equity ownership. These costs and constraints can be reduced but not entirely eliminated.

SHAREHOLDERS CAN READILY DIVERSIFY THEMSELVES

Shareholders can diversify their own portfolios of stocks by selecting those that best match their preferences and risk profiles (Salter and Weinhold, 1979). Shareholders can often diversify more cheaply than a corporation because they can buy shares at the market price and avoid hefty acquisition premiums.

These premises mean that corporate strategy cannot succeed unless it truly adds value—to business units by providing tangible benefits that offset the inherent costs of lost independence and to shareholders by diversifying in a way they could not replicate.

---

* Some recent evidence also supports the conclusion that acquired companies often suffer eroding performance after acquisition. See Frederick M. Scherer, "Mergers, Sell-Offs and Managerial Behavior," in *The Economics of Strategic Planning*, ed. Lacy Glenn Thomas (Lexington, MA: Lexington Books, 1986), p. 143, and David A. Ravenscraft and Frederick M. Scherer, "Mergers and Managerial Performance," paper presented at the Conference on Takeovers and Contests for Corporate Control, Columbia Law School, 1985.

To understand how to formulate corporate strategy, it is necessary to specify the conditions under which diversification will truly create shareholder value. These conditions can be summarized in three essential tests:

1. *The attractiveness test.* The industries chosen for diversification must be structurally attractive or capable of being made attractive.
2. *The cost-of-entry test.* The cost of entry must not capitalize all the future profits.
3. *The better-off test.* Either the new unit must gain competitive advantage from its link with the corporation or vice versa.

Of course, most companies will make certain that their proposed strategies pass some of these tests. But my study clearly shows that when companies ignored one or two of them, the strategic results were disastrous.

HOW ATTRACTIVE IS THE INDUSTRY?

In the long run, the rate of return available from competing in an industry is a function of its underlying structure [see Porter reading in Chapter 4]. An attractive industry with a high average return on investment will be difficult to enter because entry barriers are high, suppliers and buyers have only modest bargaining power, substitute products or services are few, and the rivalry among competitors is stable. An unattractive industry like steel will have structural flaws, including a plethora of substitute materials, powerful and price-sensitive buyers, and excessive rivalry caused by high fixed costs and a large group of competitors, many of whom are state supported.

Diversification cannot create shareholder value unless new industries have favorable structures that support returns exceeding the cost of capital. If the industry doesn't have such returns, the company must be able to restructure the industry or gain a sustainable competitive advantage that leads to returns well above the industry average. An industry need not be attractive before diversification. In fact, a company might benefit from entering before the industry shows its full potential. The diversification can then transform the industry's structure.

In my research, I often found companies had suspended the attractiveness test because they had a vague belief that the industry "fit" very closely with their own businesses. In the hope that the corporate "comfort" they felt would lead to a happy outcome, the companies ignored fundamentally poor industry structures. Unless the close fit allows substantial competitive advantage, however, such comfort will turn into pain when diversification results in poor returns. Royal Dutch Shell and other leading oil companies have had this unhappy experience in a number of chemicals businesses, where poor industry structures overcame the benefits of vertical integration and skills in process technology.

Another common reason for ignoring the attractiveness test is a low entry cost. Sometimes the buyer has an inside track or the owner is anxious to sell. Even if the price is actually low, however, a one-shot gain will not offset a perpetually poor business. Almost always, the company finds it must reinvest in the newly acquired unit, if only to replace fixed assets and fund working capital.

Diversifying companies are also prone to use rapid growth or other simple indicators as a proxy for a target industry's attractiveness. Many that rushed into fast-growing industries (personal computers, video games, and robotics, for example) were burned because they mistook early growth for long-term profit potential. Industries are profitable not because they are sexy or high tech; they are profitable only if their structures are attractive.

WHAT IS THE COST OF ENTRY?

Diversification cannot build shareholder value if the cost of entry into a new business eats up its expected returns. Strong market forces, however, are working to do just that. A company can enter new industries by acquisition or start-up. Acquisitions expose it to an increasingly efficient merger market. An acquirer beats the market if it pays a price not fully reflecting the prospects of the new unit. Yet multiple bidders are commonplace, information flows rapidly, and investment bankers and other intermediaries work aggressively to make the market as efficient as possible. In recent years, new financial instruments such as junk bonds have brought new buyers into the market and made even large companies vulnerable to takeover. Acquisition premiums are high and reflect the acquired company's future prospects—sometimes too well. Philip Morris paid more than four times book value for Seven-Up Company, for example. Simple arithmetic meant that profits had to more than quadruple to sustain the preacquisition ROI. Since there proved to be little Philip Morris could add in marketing prowess to the sophisticated marketing wars in the soft drink industry, the result was the unsatisfactory financial performance of Seven-Up and ultimately the decision to divest.

In a start-up, the company must overcome entry barriers. It's a real catch-22 situation, however, since attractive industries are attractive because their entry barriers are high. Bearing the full cost of the entry barriers might well dissipate any potential profits. Otherwise, other entrants to the industry would have already eroded its profitability.

In the excitement of finding an appealing new business, companies sometimes forget to apply the cost-of-entry test. The more attractive a new industry, the more expensive it is to get into.

WILL THE BUSINESS BE BETTER OFF?

A corporation must bring some significant competitive advantage to the new unit, or the new unit must offer potential for significant advantage to the corporation. Sometimes, the benefits to the new unit accrue only once, near the time of entry, when the parent instigates a major overhaul of its strategy or installs a first-rate management team. Other diversification yields ongoing competitive advantage if the new unit can market its product, through the well-developed distribution system of its sister units, for instance. This is one of the important underpinnings of the merger of Baxter Travenol and American Hospital Supply.

When the benefit to the new unit comes only once, the parent company has no rationale for holding the new unit in its portfolio over the long term. Once the results of the one-time improvement are clear, the diversified company no longer adds value to offset the inevitable costs imposed on the unit. It is best to sell the unit and free up corporate resources.

The better-off test does not imply that diversifying corporate risk creates shareholder value in and of itself. Doing something for shareholders that they can do themselves is not a basis for corporate strategy. (Only in the case of a privately held company, in which the company's and the shareholder's risk are the same, is diversification to reduce risk valuable for its own sake.) Diversification of risk should only be a by-product of corporate strategy, not a prime motivator.

Executives ignore the better-off test most of all or deal with it through arm waving or trumped-up logic rather than hard strategic analysis. One reason is that they confuse company size with shareholder value. In the drive to run a bigger company, they lose sight of their real job. They may justify the suspension of the better-off test by pointing to the way they manage diversity. By cutting corporate staff to the bone and giving business units nearly complete autonomy, they believe they avoid the pitfalls. Such thinking misses the whole point of diversification, which is to create shareholder value rather than to avoid destroying it.

The three tests for successful diversification set the standards that any corporate strategy must meet; meeting them is so difficult that most diversification fails. Many companies lack a clear concept of corporate strategy to guide their diversification or pursue a concept that does not address the tests. Others fail because they implement a strategy poorly.

My study has helped me identify four concepts of corporate strategy that have been put into practice—portfolio management, restructuring, transferring skills, and sharing activities. While the concepts are not always mutually exclusive, each rests on a different mechanism by which the corporation creates shareholder value and each requires the diversified company to manage and organize itself in a different way. The first two require no connections among business units; the second two depend on them. . . . While all four concepts of strategy have succeeded under the right circumstances, today some make more sense than others. Ignoring any of the concepts is perhaps the quickest road to failure.

PORTFOLIO MANAGEMENT

The concept of corporate strategy most in use is portfolio management, which is based primarily on diversification through acquisition. The corporation acquires sound, attractive companies with competent managers who agree to stay on. While acquired units do not have to be in the same industries as existing units, the best portfolio managers generally limit their range of businesses in some way, in part to limit the specific expertise needed by top management.

The acquired units are autonomous, and the teams that run them are compensated according to unit results. The corporation supplies capital and works with each to infuse it with professional management techniques. At the same time, top management provides objective and dispassionate review of business unit results. Portfolio managers categorize units by potential and regularly transfer resources from units that generate cash to those with high potential and cash needs. . . .

In most countries, the days when portfolio management was a valid concept of corporate strategy are past. In the face of increasingly well-developed capital markets, attractive companies with good managements show up on everyone's computer screen and attract top dollar in terms of acquisition premium. Simply contributing capital isn't contributing much. A sound strategy can easily be funded; small to medium-size companies don't need a munificent parent.

Other benefits have also eroded. Large companies no longer corner the market for professional management skills; in fact, more and more observers believe managers cannot necessarily run anything in the absence of industry-specific knowledge and experience. . . .

But it is the sheer complexity of the management task that has ultimately defeated even the best portfolio managers. As the size of the company grows, portfolio managers need to find more and more deals just to maintain growth. Supervising dozens or even hundreds of disparate units and under chain-letter pressures to add more, management begins to make mistakes. At the same time, the inevitable costs of being part of a diversified company take their toll and unit performance slides while the whole company's ROI turns downward. Eventually, a new management team is installed that initiates wholesale divestments and pares down the company to its core businesses. . . .

In developing countries, where large companies are few, capital markets are undeveloped, and professional management is scarce, portfolio management still works. But it is no longer a valid model for corporate strategy in advanced economies. . . . Portfolio management is no way to conduct corporate strategy.

RESTRUCTURING

Unlike its passive role as a portfolio manager, when it serves as banker and reviewer, a company that bases its strategy on restructuring becomes an active restructurer of business units. The new businesses are not necessarily related to existing units. All that is necessary is unrealized potential.

The restructuring strategy seeks out undeveloped, sick, or threatened organizations or industries on the threshold of significant change. The parent intervenes, frequently changing the unit management team, shifting strategy, or infusing the company with new technology. Then it may make follow-up acquisitions to build a critical mass and sell off unneeded or unconnected parts and thereby reduce the effective acquisition cost. The result is a strengthened company or a transformed industry. As a coda, the parent sells off the stronger unit once results are clear because the parent is no longer adding value, and top management decides that its attention should be directed elsewhere. . . .

When well implemented, the restructuring concept is sound, for it passes the three tests of successful diversification. The restructurer meets the cost-of-entry test through the types of company it acquires. It limits acquisition premiums by buying companies with problems and lackluster images or by buying into industries with as yet unforeseen potential. Intervention by the corporation clearly meets the better-off test. Provided that the target industries are structurally attractive, the restructuring model can create enormous shareholder value. . . . Ironically, many of today's restructurers are profiting from yesterday's portfolio management strategies.

To work, the restructuring strategy requires a corporate management team with the insight to spot undervalued companies or positions in industries ripe for transformation. The same insight is necessary to actually turn the units around even though they are in new and unfamiliar businesses. . . .

Perhaps the greatest pitfall . . . is that companies find it very hard to dispose of business units once they are restructured and performing well. . . .

TRANSFERRING SKILLS

The purpose of the first two concepts of corporate strategy is to create value through a company's relationship with each autonomous unit. The corporation's role is to be a selector, a banker, and an intervenor.

The last two concepts exploit the interrelationships between businesses. In articulating them, however, one comes face-to-face with the often ill-defined concept of synergy. If you believe the text of the countless corporate annual reports, just about anything is related to just about anything else! But imagined synergy is much more common than real synergy. GM's purchase of Hughes Aircraft simply because cars were going electronic and Hughes was an electronics concern demonstrates the folly of paper synergy. Such corporate relatedness is an ex post facto rationalization of a diversification undertaken for other reasons.

Even synergy that is clearly defined often fails to materialize. Instead of cooperating, business units often compete. A company that can define the synergies it is pursuing still faces significant organizational impediments in achieving them.

But the need to capture the benefits of relationships between businesses has never been more important. Technological and competitive developments already link many businesses and are creating new possibilities for competitive advantage. In such sectors as financial services, computing, office equipment, entertainment, and health care, interrelationships among previously distinct businesses are perhaps the central concern of strategy.

To understand the role of relatedness in corporate strategy, we must give new meaning to this often ill-defined idea. I have identified a good way to start—the value chain. [See

Readings 4–1 and 4–2.] Every business unit is a collection of discrete activities ranging from sales to accounting that allow it to compete. I call them value activities. It is at this level, not in the company as a whole, that the unit achieves competitive advantage.

I group these activities in nine categories. *Primary* activities create the product or service, deliver and market it, and provide after-sale support. The categories of primary activities are inbound logistics, operations, outbound logistics, marketing and sales, and service. *Support* activities provide the input and infrastructure that allow the primary activities to take place. The categories are company infrastructure, human resource management, technology development, and procurement.

The value chain defines the two types of interrelationships that may create synergy. The first is a company's ability to transfer skills or expertise among similar value chains. The second is the ability to share activities. Two business units, for example, can share the same sales force or logistics network.

The value chain helps expose the last two (and most important) concepts of corporate strategy. The transfer of skills among business units in the diversified company is the basis for one concept. While each business unit has a separate value chain, knowledge about how to perform activities is transferred among the units. For example, a toiletries business unit, expert in the marketing of convenience products, transmits ideas on new positioning concepts, promotional techniques, and packaging possibilities to a newly acquired unit that sells cough syrup. Newly entered industries can benefit from the expertise of existing units, and vice versa.

These opportunities arise when business units have similar buyers or channels, similar value activities like government relations or procurement, similarities in the broad configuration of the value chain (for example, managing a multisite service organization), or the same strategic concept (for example, low cost). Even though the units operate separately, such similarities allow the sharing of knowledge. . . .

Transferring skills leads to competitive advantage only if the similarities among businesses meet three conditions:

1. The activities involved in the businesses are similar enough that sharing expertise is meaningful. Broad similarities (marketing intensiveness, for example, or a common core process technology such as bending metal) are not a sufficient basis for diversification. The resulting ability to transfer skills is likely to have little impact on competitive advantage.
2. The transfer of skills involves activities important to competitive advantage. Transferring skills in peripheral activities such as government relations or real estate in consumer goods units may be beneficial but is not a basis for diversification.
3. The skills transferred represent a significant source of competitive advantage for the receiving unit. The expertise or skills to be transferred are both advanced and proprietary enough to be beyond the capabilities of competitors. . . .

Transferring skills meets the tests of diversification if the company truly mobilizes proprietary expertise across units. This makes certain the company can offset the acquisition premium or lower the cost of overcoming entry barriers.

The industries the company chooses for diversification must pass the attractiveness test. Even a close fit that reflects opportunities to transfer skills may not overcome poor industry structure. Opportunities to transfer skills, however, may help the company transform the structures of newly entered industries and send them in favorable directions.

The transfer of skills can be one time or ongoing. If the company exhausts opportunities to infuse new expertise into a unit after the initial post-acquisition period, the unit should ultimately be sold. . . .

By using both acquisitions and internal development, companies can build a transfer-of-skills strategy. The presence of a strong base of skills sometimes creates the possibility for internal entry instead of the acquisition of a going concern. Successful diversifiers that employ the concept of skills transfer may, however, often acquire a company in the target industry as a beachhead and then build on it with their internal expertise. By doing so, they can reduce some of the risks of internal entry and speed up the process. Two companies that have diversified using the transfer-of-skills concept are 3M and PepsiCo.

SHARING ACTIVITIES

The fourth concept of corporate strategy is based on sharing activities in the value chains among business units. Procter & Gamble, for example, employs a common physical distribution system and sales force in both paper towels and disposable diapers. McKesson, a leading distribution company, will handle such diverse lines as pharmaceuticals and liquor through superwarehouses.

The ability to share activities is a potent basis for corporate strategy because sharing often enhances competitive advantage by lowering cost or raising differentiation. . . .

Sharing activities inevitably involves costs that the benefits must outweigh. One cost is the greater coordination required to manage a shared activity. More important is the need to compromise the design or performance of an activity so that it can be shared. A salesperson handling the products of two business units, for example, must operate in a way that is usually not what either unit would choose were it independent. And if compromise greatly erodes the unit's effectiveness, then sharing may reduce rather than enhance competitive advantage. . . .

Despite . . . pitfalls, opportunities to gain advantage from sharing activities have proliferated because of momentous developments in technology, deregulation, and competition. The infusion of electronics and information systems into many industries creates new opportunities to link businesses. . . .

Following the shared-activities model requires an organizational context in which business unit collaboration is encouraged and reinforced. Highly autonomous business units are inimical to such collaboration. The company must put into place a variety of what I call horizontal mechanisms—a strong sense of corporate identity, a clear corporate mission statement that emphasizes the importance of integrating business unit strategies, an incentive system that rewards more than just business unit results, cross-business-unit task forces, and other methods of integrating.

A corporate strategy based on shared activities clearly meets the better-off test because business units gain ongoing tangible advantages from others within the corporation. It also meets the cost-of-entry test by reducing the expense of surmounting the barriers to internal entry. Other bids for acquisitions that do not share opportunities will have lower reservation prices. Even widespread opportunities for sharing activities do not allow a company to suspend the attractiveness test, however. Many diversifiers have made the critical mistake of equating the close fit of a target industry with attractive diversification. Target industries must pass the strict requirement test of having an attractive structure as well as a close fit in opportunities if diversification is to ultimately succeed.

Choosing a Corporate Strategy

. . . Both the strategic logic and the experience of the companies I studied over the last decade suggest that a company will create shareholder value through diversification to a greater and greater extent as its strategy moves from portfolio management toward sharing activities. . . .

Each concept of corporate strategy is not mutually exclusive of those that come before, a potent advantage of the third and fourth concepts. A company can employ a restructuring strategy at the same time it transfers skills or shares activities. A strategy based on shared activities becomes more powerful if business units can also exchange skills. . . .

My study supports the soundness of basing a corporate strategy on the transfer of skills or shared activities. The data on the sample companies' diversification programs illustrate some important characteristics of successful diversifiers. They have made a disproportionately low percentage of unrelated acquisitions, *unrelated* being defined as having no clear opportunity to transfer skills or share important activities. . . . Even successful diversifiers such as 3M, IBM, and TRW have terrible records when they strayed into unrelated acquisitions. Successful acquirers diversify into fields, each of which is related to many others. Procter & Gamble and IBM, for example, operate in 18 and 19 interrelated fields respectively and so enjoy numerous opportunities to transfer skills and share activities.

Companies with the best acquisition records tend to make heavier-than-average use of start-ups and joint ventures. Most companies shy away from modes of entry besides acquisition. My results cast doubt on the conventional wisdom regarding start-ups. . . . successful companies often have very good records with start-up units, as 3M, P&G, Johnson & Johnson, IBM, and United Technologies illustrate. When a company has the internal strength to start up a unit, it can be safer and less costly to launch a company than to rely solely on an acquisition and then have to deal with the problem of integration. Japanese diversification histories support the soundness of start-up as an entry alternative.

My data also illustrate that none of the concepts of corporate strategy works when industry structure is poor or implementation is bad, no matter how related the industries are. Xerox acquired companies in related industries, but the businesses had poor structures and its skills were insufficient to provide enough competitive advantage to offset implementation problems.

AN ACTION PROGRAM

. . . A company can choose a corporate strategy by:

1. Identifying the interrelationships among already existing business units. . . .
2. Selecting the core businesses that will be the foundation of the corporate strategy. . . .
3. Creating horizontal organizational mechanisms to facilitate interrelationships among the core businesses and lay the groundwork for future related diversification. . . .
4. Pursuing diversification opportunities that allow shared activities. . . .
5. Pursuing diversification through the transfer of skills if opportunities for sharing activities are limited or exhausted. . . .
6. Pursuing a strategy of restructuring if this fits the skills of management or no good opportunities exist for forging corporate interrelationships. . . .
7. Paying dividends so that the shareholders can be the portfolio managers. . . .

CREATING A CORPORATE THEME

Defining a corporate theme is a good way to ensure that the corporation will create shareholder value. Having the right theme helps unite the efforts of business units and reinforces the ways they interrelate as well as guides the choice of new businesses to enter. NEC Corporation, with its "C&C" theme, provides a good example. NEC integrates its computer, semiconductor, telecommunications, and consumer electronics businesses by merging computers and communication.

It is all too easy to create a shallow corporate theme. CBS wants to be an "entertainment company," for example, and built a group of businesses related to leisure time. It entered such industries as toys, crafts, musical instruments, sports teams, and hi-fi retailing. While this corporate theme sounded good, close listening revealed its hollow ring. None of these businesses had any significant opportunity to share activities or transfer skills among themselves or with CBS's traditional broadcasting and record businesses. They were all sold, often at significant losses, except for a few of CBS's publishing-related units. Saddled with the worst acquisition record in my study, CBS has eroded the shareholder value created through its strong performance in broadcasting and records.

Moving from competitive strategy to corporate strategy is the business equivalent of passing through the Bermuda Triangle. The failure of corporate strategy reflects the fact that most diversified companies have failed to think in terms of how they really add value. A corporate strategy that truly enhances the competitive advantage of each business unit is the best defense against the corporate raider. With a sharper focus on the tests of diversification and the explicit choice of a clear concept of corporate strategy, companies diversification track records from now on can look a lot different.

THE INTERNATIONAL CONTEXT

While the "international context" is hardly a situation like the others in this section of the book, there has been increasing attention to this dimension in recent years, most often under the label "global" (although few corporations in fact cover the globe, let alone significant parts of it). In a sense, the international context is diversified too, but in a particular respect—as to geography.

Operating in an international rather than a domestic arena presents managers with many new opportunities. Having worldwide operations not only gives a company access to new markets and specialized resources, it also opens up new sources of information to stimulate future product development. And it broadens the options of strategic moves and countermoves the company might make in competing with its domestic or more narrowly international rivals. However, with all these new opportunities comes the challenge of managing strategy, organization, and operations that are innately more complex, diverse, and uncertain. We include two readings on the international context.

The first, by George Yip, who teaches at the University of California in Los Angeles, focuses on the strategic aspects of managing in an international context. Yip's views on "global strategy" reflect the same orientation of industrial organization economics that influenced Porter's work: In deciding on markets to participate in, products and services to offer, and location of specific activities and tasks, managers must analyze the "globalization drivers" in their industries and find the right strategic fit.

In the second reading, Christopher Bartlett and Sumantra Ghoshal of the Harvard and London Business Schools, respectively, deal with the organizational aspects of managing in the international context. To operate effectively on a worldwide basis, Bartlett and Ghoshal suggest, companies must learn to differentiate how they manage different businesses, countries, and functions, create interdependence among units instead of either dependence or independence, and focus on coordination and co-option rather than control. The key to such organizational capability lies in the same elements of shared vision and values that they described in their article in Chapter 7, as essential for "building a matrix in managers' minds."

by George S. Yip

Whether to globalize, and how to globalize, have become two of the most burning strategy issues for managers around the world. Many forces are driving companies around the world to globalize by expanding their participation in foreign markets. Almost every product market in the major world economies—computers, fast food, nuts and bolts—has foreign competitors. Trade barriers are also falling; the recent United States/Canada trade agreement and the impending 1992 harmonization in the European Community are the two most dramatic examples. Japan is gradually opening up its long barricaded markets. Maturity in domestic markets is also driving companies to seek international expansion. This is particularly true of U.S. companies that, nourished by the huge domestic market, have typically lagged behind their European and Japanese rivals in internationalization.

Companies are also seeking to globalize by integrating their worldwide strategy. Such global integration contrasts with the multinational approach whereby companies set up country subsidiaries that design, produce, and market products or services tailored to local needs. This multinational model (also described as a "multidomestic strategy") is now in question (Hout et al., 1982). Several changes seem to increase the likelihood that, in some industries, a global strategy will be more successful than a multidomestic one. One of these changes, as argued forcefully and controversially by Levitt (1983) is the growing similarity of what citizens of different countries want to buy. Other changes include the reduction of tariff and nontariff barriers, technology investments that are becoming too expensive to amortize in one market only, and competitors that are globalizing the rules of the game.

Companies want to know how to globalize—in other words, expand market participation—and how to develop an integrated worldwide strategy. As depicted in Figure 1, three steps are essential in developing a total worldwide strategy:

▼ Developing the core strategy—the basis of sustainable competitive advantage. It is usually developed for the home country first.
▼ Internationalizing the core strategy through international expansion of activities and through adaptation.
▼ Globalizing the international strategy by integrating the strategy across countries.

Multinational companies know the first two steps well. They know the third step less well since globalization runs counter to the accepted wisdom of tailoring for national markets (Douglas and Wind, 1987).

This article makes a case for how a global strategy might work and directs managers toward opportunities to exploit globalization. It also presents the drawbacks and costs of globalization. Figure 2 lays out a framework for thinking through globalization issues.

*My framework, developed in this article, is based in part on M. E. Porter's (1986) pioneering work on global strategy. Bartlett and Ghoshal (1987) define a "transnational industry" that is somewhat similar to Porter's "global industry."

Originally published in the *Sloan Management Review* (Fall 1989). Copyright © *Sloan Management Review* Association 1989; all rights reserved; reprinted with deletions by permission of the publisher.

FIGURE 1
Total Global Strategy

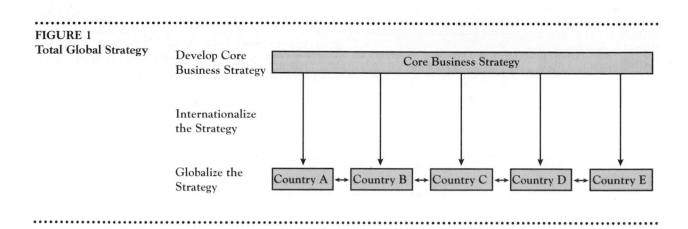

Develop Core
Business Strategy

Internationalize
the Strategy

Globalize the
Strategy

Industry globalization drivers (underlying market, cost, and other industry conditions) are externally determined, while global strategy levers are choices available to the worldwide business. Drivers create the potential for a multinational business to achieve the benefits of global strategy. To achieve these benefits, a multinational business needs to set its *global strategy levers* (e.g., use of product standardization) appropriately to industry drivers, and to the position and resources of the business and its parent company. The organization's ability to implement the strategy affects how well the benefits can be achieved.

What Is Global Strategy?

Setting strategy for a worldwide business requires making choices along a number of strategic dimensions. Table 1 lists five such dimensions or "global strategy levels" and their respective positions under a pure multidomestic strategy and a pure global strategy. Intermediate positions are, of course, feasible. For each dimension, a multidomestic strategy seeks to maximize worldwide performance by maximizing local competitive advantage, revenues, or profits; a global strategy seeks to maximize worldwide performance through sharing and integration.

**FIGURE 2
Framework of Global
Strategy Forces**

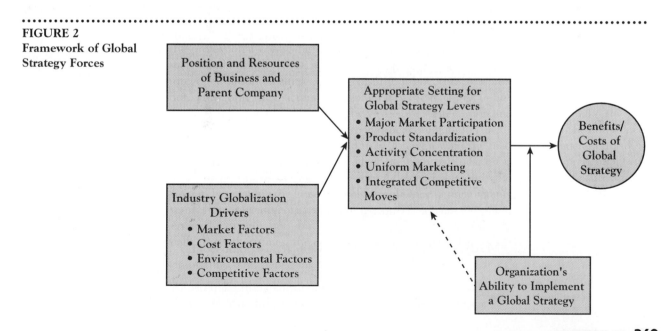

TABLE 1
Globalization Dimensions/
Global Strategy Levers

DIMENSION	SETTING FOR PURE MULTIDOMESTIC STRATEGY	SETTING FOR PURE GLOBAL STRATEGY
Market Participation	No particular pattern	Significant share in major markets
Product Offering	Fully customized in each country	Fully standardized worldwide
Location of Value-Added Activities	All activities in each country	Concentrated—one activity in each (different) country
Marketing Approach	Local	Uniform worldwide
Competitive Moves	Stand-alone by country	Integrated across countries

MARKET PARTICIPATION

In a multidomestic strategy, countries are selected on the basis of their stand-alone potential for revenues and profits. In a global strategy, countries need to be selected for their potential contribution to globalization benefits. This may mean entering a market that is unattractive in its own right, but has global strategic significance, such as the home market of a global competitor. Or it may mean building share in a limited number of key markets rather than undertaking more widespread coverage. . . . The Electrolux Group, the Swedish appliance giant, is pursuing a strategy of building significant share in major world markets. The company aims to be the first global appliance maker. . . .

PRODUCT OFFERING

In a multidomestic strategy, the products offered in each country are tailored to local needs. In a global strategy, the ideal is a standardized core product that requires minimal local adaptation. Cost reduction is usually the most important benefit of product standardization. . . . Differing worldwide needs can be met by adapting a standardized core product. In the early 1970s, sales of the Boeing 737 began to level off. Boeing turned to developing countries as an attractive new market, but found initially that its product did not fit the new environments. Because of the shortness of runways, their greater softness, and the lower technical expertise of their pilots, the planes tended to bounce a great deal. When the planes bounced on landing, the brakes failed. To fix this problem, Boeing modified the design by adding thrust to the engines, redesigning the wings and landing gear, and installing tires with lower pressure. These adaptations to a standardized core product enabled the 737 to become the best selling plane in history.

LOCATION OF VALUE ADDED ACTIVITIES

In a multidomestic strategy, all or most of the value chain is reproduced in every country. In another type of international strategy—exporting—most of the value chain is kept in one country. In a global strategy, costs are reduced by breaking up the value chain so each activity may be conducted in a different country. . . .

MARKETING APPROACH

In a multidomestic strategy, marketing is fully tailored for each country, being developed locally. In a global strategy, a uniform marketing approach is applied around the world, although not all elements of the marketing mix need be uniform. Unilever achieved great success with a fabric softener that used a globally common positioning, advertising theme, and symbol (a teddy bear), but a brand name that varied by country. Similarly, a product that serves a common need can be geographically expanded with a uniform marketing program, despite differences in marketing environments.

COMPETITIVE MOVES

In a multidomestic strategy, the managers in each country make competitive moves without regard for what happens in other countries. In a global strategy, competitive moves are integrated across countries at the same time or in a systematic sequence: a competitor is attacked in one country in order to drain its resources for another country, or a competitive attack in one country is countered in a different country. Perhaps the best example is the counterattack in a competitor's home market as a parry to an attack on one's own home market. Integration of competitive strategy is rarely practiced, except perhaps by some Japanese companies.

Bridgestone Corporation, the Japanese tire manufacturer, tried to integrate its competitive moves in response to global consolidation by its major competitors. . . . These competitive actions forced Bridgestone to establish a presence in the major U.S. market in order to maintain its position in the world tire market. To this end, Bridgestone formed a joint venture to own and manage Firestone Corporation's worldwide tire business. This joint venture also allowed Bridgestone to gain access to Firestone's European plants.

Benefits of a Global Strategy

Companies that use global strategy levers can achieve one or more of these benefits. . . .

▼ cost reductions
▼ improved quality of products and programs
▼ enhanced customer preference
▼ increased competitive leverage

COST REDUCTIONS

An integrated global strategy can reduce worldwide costs in several ways. A company can increase the benefits from economies of scale by *pooling production or other activities* for two or more countries. Understanding the potential benefit of these economies of scale, Sony Corporation has concentrated its compact disc production in Terre Haute, Indiana, and Salzburg, Austria.

A second way to cut costs is by *exploiting lower factor costs* by moving manufacturing or other activities to low-cost countries. This approach has, of course, motivated the recent surge of offshore manufacturing, particularly by U.S. firms. For example, the Mexican side of the U.S.-Mexico border is now crowded with "maquiladoras"—manufacturing plants set up and run by U.S. companies using Mexican labor.

Global strategy can also cut costs by *exploiting flexibility*. A company with manufacturing locations in several countries can move production from location to location on short notice to take advantage of the lowest costs at a given time. Dow Chemical takes this approach to minimize the cost of producing chemicals. Dow uses a linear programming model that takes account of international differences in exchange rates, tax rates, and transportation and labor costs. The model comes up with the best mix of production volume by location for each planning period.

An integrated global strategy can also reduce costs by *enhancing bargaining power*. A company whose strategy allows for switching production among different countries greatly increases its bargaining power with suppliers, workers, and host governments. . . .

IMPROVED QUALITY OF PRODUCTS AND PROGRAMS

Under a global strategy, companies focus on a smaller number of products and programs than under a multidomestic strategy. This concentration can improve both product and program quality. Global focus is one reason for Japanese success in automobiles. Toyota markets a far smaller number of models around the world than does General Motors, even allowing for its unit sales being half that of General Motors's. . . .

ENHANCED CUSTOMER PREFERENCE

Global availability, serviceability, and recognition can enhance customer preference through reinforcement. Soft drink and fast food companies are, of course, leading exponents of this strategy. Many suppliers of financial services, such as credit cards, must have a global presence because their service is travel related. . . .

INCREASED COMPETITIVE LEVERAGE

A global strategy provides more points from which to attack and counterattack competitors. In an effort to prevent the Japanese from becoming a competitive nuisance in disposable syringes, Becton Dickinson, a major U.S. medical products company, decided to enter three markets in Japan's backyard. Becton entered the Hong Kong, Singapore, and Philippine markets to prevent further Japanese expansion (Var, 1986).

Drawbacks of Global Strategy

Globalization can incur significant management costs through increased coordination, reporting requirements, and even added staff. It can also reduce the firm's effectiveness in individual countries if overcentralization hurts local motivation and morale. In addition, each global strategy lever has particular drawbacks.

A global strategy approach to *market participation* can incur an earlier or greater commitment to a market than is warranted on its own merits. Many American companies, such as Motorola, are struggling to penetrate Japanese markets, more in order to enhance their global competitive position than to make money in Japan for its own sake.

Product standardization can result in a product that does not entirely satisfy *any* customers. When companies first internationalize, they often offer their standard domestic product without adapting it for other countries, and suffer the consequences. . . .

A globally standardized product is designed for the global market but can seldom satisfy all needs in all countries. For instance, Canon, a Japanese company, sacrificed the ability to copy certain Japanese paper sizes when it first designed a photocopier for the global market.

Activity concentration distances customers and can result in lower responsiveness and flexibility. It also increases currency risk by incurring costs and revenues in different countries. Recently volatile exchange rates have required companies that concentrate their production to hedge their currency exposure.

Uniform marketing can reduce adaptation to local customer behavior. For example, the head office of British Airways mandated that every country use the "Manhattan Landing" television commercial developed by advertising agency Saatchi and Saatchi. While the commercial did win many awards, it has been criticized for using a visual image (New York City) that was not widely recognized in many countries.

Integrated competitive moves can mean sacrificing revenues, profits, or competitive position in individual countries, particularly when the subsidiary in one country is asked to attack a global competitor in order to send a signal or to divert that competitor's resources from another country.

Finding the Balance

The most successful worldwide strategies find a balance between overglobalizing and underglobalizing. The ideal strategy matches the level of strategy globalization to the globalization potential of the industry. . . .

Industry Globalization Drivers

To achieve the benefits of globalization, the managers of a worldwide business need to recognize when industry globalization drivers (industry conditions) provide the opportunity to use global strategy levers. These drivers can be grouped in four categories: market, cost, governmental, and competitive. Each industry globalization driver affects the potential use of global strategy levers. . . .

MARKET DRIVERS

Market globalization drivers depend on customer behavior and the structure of distribution channels. These drivers affect the use of all five global strategy levers.

HOMOGENEOUS CUSTOMER NEEDS
When customers in different countries want essentially the same type of product or service (or can be so persuaded), opportunities arise to market a standardized product. Understanding which aspects of the product can be standardized and which should be customized is key. In addition, homogeneous needs make participation in a large number of markets easier because fewer different product offerings need to be developed and supported.

GLOBAL CUSTOMERS
Global customers buy on a centralized or coordinated basis for decentralized use. The existence of global customers both allows and requires a uniform marketing program. There are two types of global customers: national and multinational. A national global customer searches the world for suppliers but uses the purchased product or service in one country. National defense agencies are a good example. A multinational global customer also searches the world for suppliers, but uses the purchased product or service in many countries. The World Health Organization's purchase of medical products is an example. Multinational global customers are particularly challenging to serve and often require a global account management program.. . . .

GLOBAL CHANNELS
Analogous to global customers, channels of distribution may buy on a global or at least a regional basis. Global channels or middlemen are also important in exploiting differences in prices by buying at a lower price in one country and selling at a higher price in another

country. Their presence makes it more necessary for a business to rationalize its worldwide pricing. Global channels are rare, but regionwide channels are increasing in number, particularly in European grocery distribution and retailing.

TRANSFERABLE MARKETING

The buying decision may be such that marketing elements, such as brand names and advertising, require little local adaptation. Such transferability enables firms to use uniform marketing strategies and facilitates expanded participation in markets. A worldwide business can also adapt its brand names and advertising campaigns to make them more transferable, or, even better, design global ones to start with. Offsetting risks include the blandness of uniformly acceptable brand names or advertising, and the vulnerability of relying on a single brand franchise.

COST DRIVERS

Cost drivers depend on the economics of the business; they particularly affect activity concentration.

ECONOMIES OF SCALE AND SCOPE

A single-country market may not be large enough for the local business to achieve all possible economies of scale or scope. Scale at a given location can be increased through participation in multiple markets combined with product standardization or concentration of selected value activities. Corresponding risks include rigidity and vulnerability to disruption. . . .

LEARNING AND EXPERIENCE

Even if economies of scope and scale are exhausted, expanded market participation and activity concentration can accelerate the accumulation of learning and experience. The steeper the learning and experience curves, the greater the potential benefit will be. Managers should beware, though, of the usual danger in pursuing experience curve strategies—overaggressive pricing that destroyed not just the competition but the market as well. Prices get so low that profit is insufficient to sustain any competitor.

SOURCING EFFICIENCIES

Centralized purchasing of new materials can significantly lower costs. . . .

FAVORABLE LOGISTICS

A favorable ratio of sales value to transportation cost enhances the company's ability to concentrate production. Other logistical factors include nonperishability, the absence of time urgency, and little need for location close to customer facilities. . . .

DIFFERENCES IN COUNTRY COSTS AND SKILLS

Factor costs generally vary across countries; this is particularly true in certain industries. The availability of particular skills also varies. Concentration of activities in low-cost or high-skill countries can increase productivity and reduce costs, but managers need to anticipate the danger of training future offshore competitors. . . .

PRODUCT DEVELOPMENT COSTS

Product development costs can be reduced by developing a few global or regional products rather than many national products. The automobile industry is characterized by long product development periods and high product development costs. One reason for the high costs is duplication of effort across countries. The Ford Motor Company's "Centers of Excellence" program aims to reduce these duplicating efforts and to exploit the differing expertise of Ford specialists worldwide. As part of the concentrated effort, Ford of Europe is designing a common platform for all compacts, while Ford of North America is developing platforms for the replacement of the mid-sized Taurus and Sable. This concentration of design is estimated to save "hundreds of millions of dollars per model by eliminating duplicative efforts and saving on retooling factories" (*Business Week*, 1987).

GOVERNMENTAL DRIVERS

Government globalization drivers depend on the rules set by national governments and affect the use of all global strategy levers.

FAVORABLE TRADE POLICIES

Host governments affect globalization potential through import tariffs and quotas, nontariff barriers, export subsidies, local content requirements, currency and capital flow restrictions, and requirements on technology transfer. Host government policies can make it difficult to use the global levers of major market participation, product standardization, activity concentration, and uniform marketing; they also affect the integrated-competitive moves lever. . . .

COMPATIBLE TECHNICAL STANDARDS

Differences in technical standards, especially government-imposed standards, limit the extent to which products can be standardized. Often, standards are set with protectionism in mind. Motorola found that many of their electronics products were excluded from the Japanese market because these products operated at a higher frequency than was permitted in Japan.

COMMON MARKETING REGULATIONS

The marketing environment of individual countries affects the extent to which uniform global marketing approaches can be used. Certain types of media may be prohibited or restricted. For example, the United States is far more liberal than Europe about the kinds of advertising claims that can be made on television. The British authorities even veto the depiction of socially undesirable behavior. For example, British television authorities do not allow scenes of children pestering their parents to buy a product. . . .

COMPETITIVE DRIVERS

Market, cost, and governmental globalization drivers are essentially fixed for an industry at any given time. Competitors can play only a limited role in affecting these factors (although a sustained effort can bring about change, particularly in the case of consumer preferences). In contrast, competitive drivers are entirely in the realm of competitor choice. Competitors can raise the globalization potential of their industry and spur the need for a response on the global strategy levers.

INTERDEPENDENCE OF COUNTRIES

A competitor may create competitive interdependence among countries by pursuing a global strategy. The basic mechanism is through sharing of activities. When activities such as production are shared among countries, a competitor's market share in one country affects its scale and overall cost position in the shared activities. Changes in that scale and cost will affect its competitive position in all countries dependent on the shared activities. Less directly, customers may view market position in a lead country as an indicator of overall quality. Companies frequently promote a product as, for example. "the leading brand in the United States." Other competitors then need to respond via increased market participation, uniform marketing, or integrated competitive strategy to avoid a downward spiral of sequentially weakened positions in individual countries.

In the automobile industry, where economies of scale are significant and where sharing activities can lower costs, markets have significant competitive interdependence. As companies like Ford and Volkswagen concentrate production and become more cost competitive with the Japanese manufacturers, the Japanese are pressured to enter more markets so that increased production volume will lower costs. Whether conscious of this or not, Toyota has begun a concerted effort to penetrate the German market: between 1984 and 1987, Toyota doubled the number of cars produced for the German market.

GLOBALIZED COMPETITORS

More specifically, matching or preempting individual competitor moves may be necessary. These moves include expanding into or within major markets, being the first to introduce a standardized product, or being the first to use a uniform marketing program.

The need to preempt a global competitor can spur increased market participation. In 1986, Unilever, the European consumer products company, sought to increase its participation in the U.S. market by launching a hostile takeover bid for Richardson-Vicks Inc. Unilever's global archrival, Procter & Gamble, saw the threat to its home turf and outbid Unilever to capture Richardson-Vicks. With Richardson-Vicks's European system, P&G was able to greatly strengthen its European positioning. So Unilever's attempt to expand participation in a rival's home market backfired to allow the rival to expand participation in Unilever's home markets.

In summary, industry globalization drivers provide opportunities to use global strategy levers in many ways. Some industries, such as civil aircraft, can score high on most dimensions of globalization (Yoshino, 1986). Others, such as the cement industry, seem to be inherently local. But more and more industries are developing globalization potential. Even the food industry in Europe, renowned for its diversity of taste, is now a globalization target for major food multinationals.

CHANGES OVER TIME

Finally, industry evolution plays a role. As each of the industry globalization drivers changes over time, so too will the appropriate global strategy change. For example, in the European major appliance industry, globalization forces seem to have reversed. In the late 1960s and early 1970s, a regional standardization strategy was successful for some key competitors (Levitt, 1983). But in the 1980s the situation appears to have turned around, and the most successful strategies seem to be national (Badenfuller et al., 1987).

In some cases, the actions of individual competitors can affect the direction and pace of change; competitors positioned to take advantage of globalization forces will want to hasten them. . . .

More Than One Strategy Is Viable

Although they are powerful, industry globalization drivers do not dictate one formula for success. More than one type of international strategy can be viable in a given industry.

INDUSTRIES VARY ACROSS DRIVERS

No industry is high on every one of the many globalization drivers. A particular competitor may be in a strong position to exploit a driver that scores low on globalization. . . . The hotel industry provides examples both of successful global and successful local competitors.

GLOBAL EFFECTS ARE INCREMENTAL

Globalization drivers are not deterministic for a second reason: the appropriate use of strategy levers adds competitive advantage to existing sources. These other sources may allow individual competitors to thrive with international strategies that are mismatched with industry globalization drivers. For example, superior technology is a major source of competitive advantage in most industries, but can be quite independent of globalization drivers. A competitor with sufficiently superior technology can use it to offset globalization disadvantages.

BUSINESS AND PARENT COMPANY POSITION AND RESOURCES ARE CRUCIAL

The third reason that drivers are not deterministic is related to resources. A worldwide business may face industry drivers that strongly favor a global strategy. But global strategies are typically expensive to implement initially even though great cost savings and revenue gains should follow. High initial investments may be needed to expand within or into major markets, to develop standardized products, to relocate value activities, to create global brands, to create new organization units or coordination processes, and to implement other aspects of a global strategy. The strategic position of the business is also relevant. Even though a global strategy may improve the business's long-term strategic position, its immediate position may be so weak that resources should be devoted to short-term, country-by-country improvements. Despite the automobile industry's very strong globalization drivers, Chrysler Corporation had to deglobalize by selling off most of its international automotive businesses to avoid bankruptcy. Lastly, investing in nonglobal sources of competitive advantage, such as superior technology, may yield greater returns than global ones, such as centralized manufacturing.

ORGANIZATIONS HAVE LIMITATIONS

Finally, factors such as organization structure, management processes, people, and culture affect how well a desired global strategy can be implemented. Organizational differences among companies in the same industry can, or should, constrain the companies' pursuit of the same global strategy. . . .

by Christopher A.
Bartlett and
Sumantra Ghoshal

. . . Recent changes in the international operating environment have forced companies to optimize *efficiency*, *responsiveness*, and *learning* simultaneously in their worldwide operations (Bartlett and Ghoshal, 1987). To companies that previously concentrated on developing and managing one of these capabilities, this new challenge implies not only a total strategic reorientation but a major change in organizational capability, as well.

Implementing such a complex, three-pronged strategic objective would be difficult under any circumstances, but in a worldwide company the task is complicated even further. The very act of "going international" multiplies a company's organizational complexity. Typically, doing so requires adding a third dimension to the existing business- and function-oriented management structure. It is difficult enough balancing product divisions that bring efficiency and focus to domestic product-market strategies with corporate staffs whose functional expertise allows them to play an important counterbalance and control role. The thought of adding capable, geographically oriented management—and maintaining a three-way balance of organizational perspectives and capabilities among product, function, and area—is intimidating to most managers. The difficulty is increased because the resolution of tensions among product, function, and area managers must be accomplished in an organization whose operating units are often divided by distance and time and whose key members are separated by culture and language.

FROM UNIDIMENSIONAL TO MULTIDIMENSIONAL CAPABILITIES

Faced with the task of building multiple strategic capabilities in highly complex organizations, managers in almost every company we studied** made the simplifying assumption that they were faced with a series of dichotomous choices. They discussed the relative merits of pursuing a strategy of national responsiveness as opposed to one based on global integration; they considered whether key assets and resources should be centralized or decentralized; and they debated the need for strong central control versus greater subsidiary autonomy. How a company resolved these dilemmas typically reflected influences exerted and choices made during its historical development. In telecommunications, ITT's need to develop an organization responsive to national political demands and local specification differences was as important to its survival in the pre– and post–World War II era as was NEC's need to build its highly centralized technological manufacturing and marketing skills and resources in order to expand abroad in the same industry in the 1960s and 1970s.

When new competitive challenges emerged, however, such unidimensional biases became strategically limiting. As ITT demonstrated by its outstanding historic success and NEC showed by its more delayed international expansion, strong *geographic management* is essential for development of dispersed responsiveness. Geographic management allows worldwide companies to sense, analyze, and respond to the needs of different national markets.

Effective competitors also need to build strong *business management* with global product responsibilities if they are to achieve global efficiency and integration. These managers act as champions of manufacturing rationalization, product standardization, and low-cost

**The findings presented in this article are based on a three-year research project on the organization and management of multinational corporations. Extensive discussions were held with 250 managers in nine of the world's largest multinational companies, in the United States, Europe, and Japan. Complete findings are presented in *Managing across Borders: The Transnational Solution* (Boston: Harvard Business School Press, 1988).

global sourcing. (As the telecommunications switching industry globalized, NEC's organizational capability in this area gave it a major competitive advantage.) Unencumbered by either territorial or functional loyalties, central product groups remain sensitive to overall competitive issues and become agents to facilitate changes that, though painful, are necessary for competitive viability.

Finally, a strong, worldwide *functional management* allows an organization to build and transfer its core competencies—a capability vital to worldwide learning. Links between functional managers allow the company to accumulate specialized knowledge and skills and to apply them wherever they are required in the worldwide operations. Functional management acts as the repository of organizational learning and as the prime mover for its consolidation and circulation within the company. It was for want of a strongly linked research and technical function across subsidiaries that ITT failed in its attempt to coordinate the development and diffusion of its System 12 digital switch.

Thus, to respond to the needs for efficiency, responsiveness, and learning *simultaneously*, the company must develop a multidimensional organization in which the effectiveness of each management group is maintained *and* in which each group is prevented from dominating the others. As we saw in company after company, the most difficult challenge for managers trying to respond to broad, emerging strategic demands was to develop the new elements of multidimensional organization without eroding the effectiveness of their current unidimensional capability.

OVERCOMING SIMPLIFYING ASSUMPTIONS

For all nine companies at the core of our study, the challenge of breaking down biases and building a truly multidimensional organization proved difficult. Behind the pervasive either/or mentality that led to the development of unidimensional capabilities, we identified three simplifying assumptions that blocked the necessary organizational development. The need to reduce organizational and strategic complexity has made these assumptions almost universal in worldwide companies, regardless of industry, national origin, or management culture.

▼ There is a widespread, often implicit assumption that roles of different organizational units are uniform and symmetrical; different businesses should be managed in the same way, as should different functions and national operations.

▼ Most companies, some consciously, most unconsciously, create internal interunit relationships on clear patterns of dependence or independence, on the assumption that such relationships *should* be clear and unambiguous.

▼ Finally, there is the assumption that one of corporate management's principal tasks is to institutionalize clearly understood mechanisms for decision making and to implement simple means of exercising control.

Those companies most successful in developing truly multidimensional organizations were the ones that challenged these assumptions and replaced them with some very different attitudes and norms. Instead of treating different business functions, and subsidiaries similarly, they systematically *differentiated* tasks and responsibilities. Instead of seeking organizational clarity by basing relationships on dependence or independence, they built and managed *interdependence* among the different units of the companies. And instead of considering control their key task, corporate managers searched for complex mechanisms to *coordinate and coopt* the differentiated and interdependent organizational units into sharing a vision of the company's strategic tasks. These are the central organizational characteristics of what we described in an earlier article as transnational corporations—those most effective in managing across borders in today's environment of intense competition and rapid, often discontinuous change.

FROM SYMMETRY TO DIFFERENTIATION

. . . Just as they saw the need to change symmetrical structures and homogeneous processes imposed on different businesses and functions, most companies we observed eventually recognized the importance of differentiating the management of diverse geographic operations. Despite the fact that various national subsidiaries operated with very different external environments and internal constraints, they all traditionally reported through the same channels, operated under similar planning and control systems, and worked under a set of common generalized mandates.

Increasingly, however, managers recognized that such symmetrical treatment can constrain strategic capabilities. At Unilever, for example, it became clear that Europe's highly competitive markets and closely linked economies meant that its operating companies in that region required more coordination and control than those in, say, Latin America. Little by little, management increased the product-coordination groups' role in Europe until they had the direct line responsibility for all operating companies in their businesses. Elsewhere, however, national management maintained its historic line management role, and product coordinators acted only as advisers. Unilever has thus moved in sequence from a symmetrical organization to a much more differentiated one: differentiating by product, then by function, and finally by geography. . . .

But Unilever is far from unique. In all of the companies we studied, senior management was working to differentiate its organizational structure and processes in increasingly sophisticated ways. . . . For example, Procter & Gamble is differentiating the roles of its subsidiaries by giving some of them responsibilities as "lead countries" in product strategy development, then rotating that leadership role from product to product. . . . Thus, instead of deciding the overall roles of product, functional, and geographic management on the basis of simplistic dichotomies such as global versus domestic businesses or centralized versus decentralized organizations, many companies are creating different levels of influence for different groups as they perform different activities. Doing this allows the relatively underdeveloped management perspectives to be built in a gradual, complementary manner rather than in the sudden, adversarial environment often associated with either/or choices. Internal heterogeneity has made the change from unidimensional to multidimensional organization easier by breaking the problem up into many small, differentiated parts and by allowing for a step-by-step process of organizational change.

FROM DEPENDENCE OR INDEPENDENCE

. . . New strategic demands make organizational models of simple interunit dependence *or* independence inappropriate. The reality of today's worldwide competitive environment demands collaborative information sharing and problem solving, cooperative support and resource sharing, and collective action and implementation. Independent units risk being picked off one-by-one by competitors whose coordinated global approach gives them two important strategic advantages—the ability to integrate research, manufacturing, and other scale-efficient operations, and the opportunity to cross-subsidize the losses from battles in one market with funds generated by profitable operations in home markets or protected environments. . . .

On the other hand, foreign operations totally dependent on a central unit must deal with problems reaching beyond the loss of local market responsiveness. . . . They also risk being unable to respond effectively to strong national competitors or to sense potentially important local market or technical intelligence. This was the problem Procter & Gamble's

Japan subsidiary faced in an environment where local competitors began challenging P&G's previously secure position with successive, innovative product changes and novel market strategies, particularly in the disposable diapers business. After suffering major losses in market share, management recognized that a local operation focused primarily on implementing the company's classic marketing strategy was no longer sufficient; the Japanese subsidiary needed the freedom and incentive to be more innovative. Not only to ensure the viability of the Japanese subsidiary, but also to protect its global strategic position, P&G realized it had to expand the role of the local unit and change its relationship with the parent company to enhance two-way learning and mutual support.

But it is not easy to change relationships of dependence or independence that have been built up over a long history. Many companies have tried to address the increasing need for interunit collaboration by adding layer upon layer of administrative mechanisms to foster greater cooperation. Top managers have extolled the virtues of teamwork and have even created special departments to audit management response to this need. In most cases these efforts to obtain cooperation by fiat or by administrative mechanisms have been disappointing. The independent units have feigned compliance while fiercely protecting their independence. The dependent units have found that the new cooperative spirit implies little more than the right to agree with those on whom they depend.

Yet some companies have gradually developed the capability to achieve such cooperation and to build what Rosabeth Kanter (1983) calls an "integrative organization." Of the companies we studied, the most successful did so not by creating new units, but by changing the basis of the relationships among product, functional, and geographic management groups. From relations based on dependence or independence, they moved to relations based on formidable levels of explicit, genuine interdependence. In essence, they made integration and collaboration self-enforcing by making it necessary for each group to cooperate in order to achieve its own interests.

Procter & Gamble . . . in Europe, for example, has formed a number of Eurobrand teams for developing product-market strategies for different product lines.* Each team is headed by the general manager of a subsidiary that has a particularly well-developed competence in that business. It also includes the appropriate product and advertising managers from the other subsidiaries and relevant functional managers from the company's European headquarters. . . .

In observing many such examples of companies building and extending interdependence among units, we were able to identify three important flows that seem to be at the center of the emerging organizational relationships. Most fundamental was the product interdependence that most companies were building as they specialized and integrated their worldwide manufacturing operations to achieve greater efficiency, while retaining sourcing flexibility and sensitivity to host country interests. The resulting *flow of parts, components, and finished goods* increased the interdependence of the worldwide operations in an obvious and fundamental manner.

We also observed companies developing a resource interdependence that often contrasted sharply with earlier policies that had either encouraged local self-sufficiency or required the centralization of all surplus resources. . . .

Finally, the worldwide diffusion of technology, the development of international markets, and the globalization of competitive strategies have meant that vital strategic information now exists in many different locations worldwide. Furthermore, the growing dispersion of assets and delegation of responsibilities to foreign operations have resulted in the development of local knowledge and expertise that has implications for the broader orga-

---

*For a full description of the development of Eurobrand in P&G, see C.A. Bartlett, "Procter & Gamble Europe: Vizir Launch," Harvard Business School, Case Services #9-384-139.

nization. With these changes, the need to manage the *flow of intelligence, ideas, and knowledge* has become central to the learning process and has reinforced the growing interdependence of worldwide operations, as P&G's Eurobrand teams illustrate.

It is important to emphasize that the relationships we are highlighting are different from the interdependencies commonly observed in multiunit organizations. Traditionally, MNC managers have attempted to highlight what has been called "pooled interdependence" to make subunit managers responsive to global rather than local interests. (Before the Euroteam approach, for instance, P&G's European vice president often tried to convince independent-minded subsidiary managers to transfer surplus generated funds to other more needy subsidiaries, in the overall corporate interest, arguing that, "Someday when you're in need they might be able to fund a major product launch for you.")

As the example illustrates, pooled interdependence is often too broad and amorphous to affect day-to-day management behavior. The interdependencies we described earlier are more clearly reciprocal, and each unit's ability to achieve its goals is made conditional upon its willingness to help other units achieve their own goals. Such interdependencies more effectively promote the organization's ability to share the perspectives and link the resources of different components, and thereby to expand its organizational capabilities.*

FROM CONTROL TO COORDINATION AND COOPTION

The simplifying assumptions of organizational symmetry and dependence (or independence) had allowed the management processes in many companies to be dominated by simple controls—tight operational controls in subsidiaries dependent on the center, and a looser system of administrative or financial controls in decentralized units. When companies began to challenge the assumptions underlying organizational relationships, however, they found they also had to adapt their management processes. The growing interdependence of organizational units strained the simple control-dominated systems and underlined the need to supplement existing processes with more sophisticated ones. Furthermore, the differentiation of organizational tasks and roles amplified the diversity of management perspectives and capabilities and forced management to differentiate management processes.

As organizations became, at the same time, more diverse and more interdependent, there was an explosion in the number of issues that had to be linked, reconciled, or integrated. The rapidly increasing flows of goods, resources, and information among organizational units increased the need for *coordination* as a central management function. But the costs of coordination are high, both in financial and human terms, and coordinating capabilities are always limited. Most companies, though, tended to concentrate on a primary means of coordination and control—"the company's way of doing things." . . .

In a number of companies, we saw a . . . broadening of administrative processes as managers learned to operate with previously underutilized means of coordination. Unilever's heavy reliance on the socialization of managers to provide the coordination "glue" was supplemented by the growing role of the central product-coordination departments. In contrast, NEC reduced central management's coordination role by developing formal systems and social processes in a way that created a more robust and flexible coordinative capability.

Having developed diverse new means of coordination, management's main task is to carefully ration their usage and application. . . . It is important to distinguish where tasks can be formalized and managed through systems, where social linkages can be fostered to encourage informal agreements and cooperation, and where the coordination task is so vital or sensitive that it must use the scarce resource of central management arbitration. . . .

---

*The distinction among sequential, reciprocal, and pooled interdependencies has been made in J. D. Thompson, *Organizations in Action* (New York: McGraw-Hill, 1967).

We have described briefly how companies began to . . . differentiate roles and responsibilities within the organization. Depending on their internal capabilities and on the strategic importance of their external environments, organizational units might be asked to take on roles ranging from that of strategic leader with primary corporatewide responsibility for a particular business or function, to simple implementer responsible only for executing strategies and decisions developed elsewhere.

Clearly, these roles must be managed in quite different ways. The unit with strategic leadership responsibility must be given freedom to develop responsibility in an entrepreneurial fashion, yet must also be strongly supported by headquarters. For this unit, operating controls may be light and quite routine, but coordination of information and resource flows to and from the unit will probably require intensive involvement from senior management. In contrast, units with implementation responsibility might be managed through tight operating controls, with standardized systems used to handle much of the coordination—primarily of goods flows. Because the tasks are more routine, the use of scarce coordinating resources could be minimized.

Differentiating organizational roles and management processes can have a fragmenting and sometimes demotivating effect, however. Nowhere was this more clearly illustrated than in the many companies that unquestioningly assigned units the "dog" and "cash cow" roles defined by the Boston Consulting Group's growth-share matrix in the 1970s (see Haspeslagh, 1982). Their experience showed that there is another equally important corporate management task that complements and facilitates coordination effectiveness. We call this task *cooption*: the process of uniting the organization with a common understanding of, identification with, and commitment to the corporation's objectives, priorities, and values.

A clear example of the importance of cooption was provided by the contrast between ITT and NEC managers. At ITT, corporate objectives were communicated more in financial than in strategic terms, and the company's national entities identified almost exclusively with their local environment. When corporate management tried to superimpose a more unified and integrated global strategy, its local subsidiaries neither understood nor accepted the need to do so. For years they resisted giving up their autonomy, and management was unable to replace the interunit rivalry with a more cooperative and collaborative process.

In contrast, NEC developed an explicitly defined and clearly communicated global strategy enshrined in the company's "C&C" motto—a corporatewide dedication to building business and basing competitive strategy on the strong link between computers and communications. For over a decade, the C&C philosophy was constantly interpreted, refined, elaborated, and eventually institutionalized in organizational units dedicated to various C&C missions (e.g., the C&C Systems Research Laboratories, the C&C Corporate Planning Committee, and eventually the C&C Systems Division). Top management recognized that one of its major tasks was to inculcate the worldwide organization with an understanding of the C&C strategy and philosophy and to raise managers' consciousness about the global implications of competing in these converging businesses. By the mid-1980s, the company was confident that every NEC employee in every operating unit had a clear understanding of NEC's global strategy as well as of his or her role in it. Indeed, it was this homogeneity that allowed the company to begin the successful decentralization of its strategic tasks and the differentiation of its management processes.

Thus the management process that distinguished transnational organizations from simpler unidimensional forms was one in which control was made less dominant by the increased importance of interunit integration and collaboration. These new processes required corporate management to supplement its control role with the more subtle tasks of coordination and cooption, giving rise to a much more complex and sophisticated management process.

SUSTAINING A DYNAMIC BALANCE: ROLE OF THE "MIND MATRIX"

Developing multidimensional perspectives and capabilities does not mean that product, functional, and geographic management must have the same level of influence on all key decisions. Quite the contrary. It means that the organization must possess a differentiated influence structure—one in which different groups have different roles for different activities. These roles cannot be fixed but must change continually to respond to new environmental demands and evolving industry characteristics. Not only is it necessary to prevent any one perspective from dominating the others, it is equally important not to be locked into a mode of operation that prevents reassignment of responsibilities, realignment of relationships, and rebalancing of power distribution. This ability to manage the multidimensional organization capability in a flexible manner is the hallmark of a transnational company.

In the change process we have described, managers were clearly employing some powerful organizational tools to create and control the desired flexible management process. They used the classic tool of formal structure to strengthen, weaken, or shift roles and responsibilities over time, and they employed management systems effectively to redirect corporate resources and to channel information in a way that shifted the balance of power. By controlling the ebb and flow of responsibilities, and by rebalancing power relationships, they were able to prevent any of the multidimensional perspectives from atrophying. Simultaneously, they prevented the establishment of entrenched power bases.

But the most successful companies had an additional element at the core of their management processes. We were always conscious that a substantial amount of senior management attention focused on the *individual* members of the organization. NEC's continual efforts to inculcate all corporate members with a common vision of goals and priorities; P&G's careful assignment of managers to teams and task forces to broaden their perspectives; Philips's frequent use of conferences and meetings as forums to reconcile differences; and Unilever's extensive use of training as a powerful socialization process and its well-planned career path management that provided diverse experience across businesses, functions, and geographic locations—all are examples of companies trying to develop multidimensional perspectives and flexible approaches at the level of the individual manager.

What is critical, then, is not just the structure, but also the mentality of those who constitute the structure. The common thread that holds together the diverse tasks we have described is a managerial mindset that understands the need for multiple strategic capabilities, that is able to view problems from both local and global perspectives, and that accepts the importance of a flexible approach. This pattern suggests that managers should resist the temptation to view their task in the traditional terms of building a formal global matrix structure—an organizational form that in practice has proven extraordinarily difficult to manage in the international environment. They might be better guided by the perspective of one top manager who described the challenge as "creating a matrix in the minds of managers."

Our study has led us to conclude that a company's ability to develop transnational organizational capability and management mentality will be the key factor that separates the winners from the mere survivors in the emerging international environment.

15

MANAGING CHANGE

Strategy is technically about continuity, not change: After all, it is concerned with imposing structured patterns of behavior on an organization, whether these take the form of intentions in advance that become deliberate strategies or actions after the fact that fall into the consistent patterns of emergent strategies. But today to manage strategy is frequently to manage change—to recognize when a shift of a strategic nature is possible, desirable, necessary, and then to act—possibly putting into place mechanisms for continuous change.

Managing major change is generally far more difficult than it may at first appear. The need for reorientation occurs rather infrequently, and when it does, it means moving from a familiar domain into a less well-defined future where many of the old rules no longer apply. People must often abandon the roots of their past successes and develop entirely new skills and attitudes. This is clearly a frightening situation—and often, therefore, the most difficult challenge facing a manager.

The causes of such change also vary, from an ignored steady decline in performance which ultimately demands a "turnaround" to a sudden radical shift in a base technology that requires a reconceptualization of everything the organization does; from the gradual shift into the next stage of an organization's "life cycle"; to the appearance of a new chief executive who wishes to put his or her particular stamp on the organization. The resulting strategic alignments may also take a variety of forms, from a shift of strategic position within the same industry to a whole new perspective in a new industry. Some changes require rapid transitions from one structural configuration to another, as in a machine organization that has diversified into new businesses and so must switch to a divisionalized form of structure. Other changes are accompanied by slower structural shifts, as when a small entrepreneurial firm grows steadily into a larger mature company. Each transition has its own management prerequisites and problems.

This chapter covers a number of these aspects of organizational change, presenting material on what evokes them in the first place, what forms they can take, and how they can and should be managed in differing situations. These readings appropriately cap the earlier chapters of this book: on strategy and its formation, structure and systems, power and culture, and the various contexts in which these come together. Major changes typically involve them all. Configuration, so carefully nurtured in earlier chapters, turns out to be a double-edged sword, promoting consistency on the one hand but sometimes discouraging change on the other.

The first reading seeks to bring some closure to our discussion of the different configurations of structure presented in Section III. Called "Beyond Configuration," it is, in a sense, Mintzberg's final chapter of his book on structure, except that it was written more recently and edited down to its essence for this edition of the text. The reading seeks to do just what its title says: make the point that while the different structural forms (configurations) of the last chapters can help us to make sense of and to manage in a complex world, there is also a need to go beyond configuration, to consider the nuanced linkages among these various forms. Mintzberg proposes that this be done by treating all the forms as a framework of forces that act on every organization and whose contradictions need to be reconciled. By so doing, we can begin to see the weaknesses in each form as well as the times when an organization is better off to design itself as a combination of two or more forms. Some organizations, to use a metaphor introduced in this reading, achieve greater effectiveness by playing "organizational LEGO"—creating their own form rather than letting themselves be put together like a jigsaw puzzle into a standard form. Finally, this reading discusses how the forces of ideology (representing cooperation—pulling together) and of politics (representing competition—pulling apart) work both to promote change and also to impede it, and how the contradictions among these two must also be reconciled if an organization is to remain effective in the long run.

Our second reading on managing the context of change considers the "unsteady pace of organizational evolution" in terms of distinct periods of "convergence" and "upheaval." Related to the literature on organizational life cycles, its three authors, Michael Tushman and William Newman of Columbia University's Graduate School of Business and Elaine Romanelli of the Georgetown business school, argue for what has also been referred to as a "quantum theory" of organizational change (Miller and Freisen, 1984). The essence of the argument is that organizations prefer to stay on course most of the time, accepting incremental changes to improve their strategies, processes, and structures. But periodically, they must submit to dramatic shifts in these—"strategic revolutions" of a sort—to realign their overall orientation.

This argument is obviously compatible with the earlier notion of configuration, which represents a form of alignment of strategy, structure, and processes that dictate a certain stability in an organization. But note that it differs from Quinn's concept of "logical incrementalism," introduced in Reading 5.1, which argues for more of a gradual shift in strategic thinking as a way to achieve major change in an organization. There appears to be merit in both approaches. But how can we reconcile them? Perhaps they are not as contradictory as they may seem. Consider three dimensions: (1) the specific aspects of the strategy change process that each considers, (2) the time frames of the two viewpoints, and (3) the types of organizations involved. Quinn's incrementalist view focuses on the processes going on in senior managers' minds as they help create new strategies. Because of the complexities involved, effective strategic thinking requires an incremental, interactive, learning process for all key players. The quantum approach, in contrast, focuses not on the strategists' intentions so much as on the strategies actually pursued by the organization (referred to in Reading 1.2 as the realized strategies of the organization). It is these that often seem to change in quantum fashion. It may be, therefore, that managers conceive and promote their intended strategies incrementally, but once that is accomplished they change their organizations in rapid, integrated leaps, quantum fashion.

The last reading of this book, by Charles Baden-Fuller of the University of Bath and John Stopford of the London Business School, presents a specific model of how a company can rejuvenate itself. The key challenge, these authors believe, lies in rebuilding corporate entrepreneurship, and they describe a four-step process of renewal, which starts with galvanizing the top team to create a commitment to change. In the next phase, the company must simplify both its businesses and its organization so as to create the base for the third step of building new skills, knowledge, and resources. Then, in the final step, the company can restart the growth engine by leveraging the new sources of advantage it has created. Overall, this model of change builds directly on the concept of core competencies, and is quite consistent with Quinn's views on strategies for change with which we started on this journey of mapping the strategy process.

▼ READING 15.1   BEYOND CONFIGURATION*

by Henry Mintzberg

"Lumpers" are people who categorize, who synthesize. "Splitters" are people who analyze, who see all the nuances. From the standpoint of organization, both are right and both are wrong. Without categories, it would be impossible to practice management. With only categories, it could not be practiced effectively.

The author was mostly a lumper until a colleague asked him if he wanted to play "jigsaw puzzle" or "LEGO" with his concepts. In other words, do all these concepts fit together in set ways and known images (puzzle), or were they to be used creatively to create new images? The remainder of this reading is presented in the spirit of playing "organizational LEGO." It tries to show how we can use splitting as well as lumping to understand what makes organizations effective as well as what causes many of their fundamental problems.

Forms and Forces

The configurations described in the chapters of this section of the book are *forms*, and they are laid out at the nodes of a pentagon in Figure 1. Many organizations seem to fit naturally into one of the original five, but some do not fit, to the lumpers' chagrin. To respond to this, five *forces* have been added, each associated with one of the original forms:

▼ *Direction* for the entrepreneurial form, for some sense of where the organization must go. This is often called "strategic vision." Without direction the various activities of an organization cannot easily work together to achieve common purpose.

▼ *Efficiency* for the machine form. This ensures a viable ratio of benefits gained to costs incurred. Lack of concern for efficiency would cause all but the most protected organization to fade.

▼ *Proficiency* for the professional form. Organizations need this to carry out tasks with high levels of knowledge and skill. The difficult work of organizations would otherwise simply not get done.

*Adapted from a chapter of this title in *Mintzberg on Management: Inside Our Strange World of Organizations* (Free Press, 1989); an article similar to this chapter was published in the *Sloan Management Review*.

FIGURE 1
An Integrating Pentagon of Forces and Forms

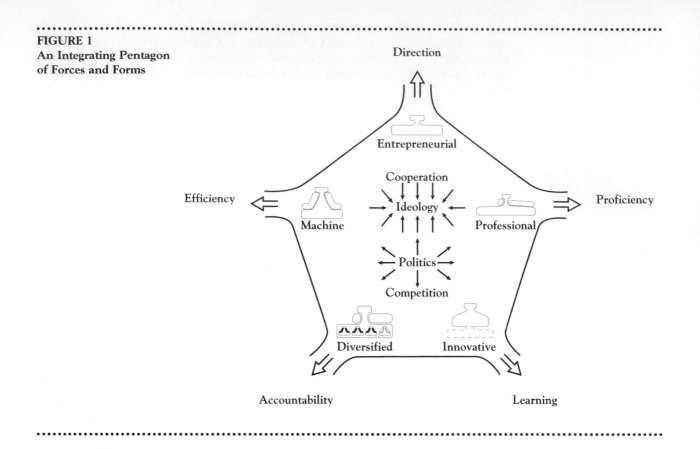

▼ *Accountability* for the diversified form. If individual units in an organization are not accountable for their efforts in particular markets, it becomes almost impossible to manage a diversified organization.

▼ *Learning* for the innovative or adhocracy form. Organizations need to be able to learn, to discover new things for their customers and themselves—to adapt and to innovate.

Two other forces exist that are not necessarily associated with a particular form:

▼ *Cooperation*, represented by ideology. This is the force for pulling together.

▼ *Competition*, represented by politics. This is the force for pulling apart.

For the lumpers we now have a *portfolio of forms*, and for the splitters we now have a *system of forces*. Both views are critical for the practice of management. One represents the most fundamental forces that act on organizations. All serious organizations experience all seven of them, at one time or another, if not all the time. The other represents the fundamental forms that organizations can take, which some of them do some of the time. Together, these forces and forms appear to constitute a powerful diagnostic framework by which to understand what goes on in organizations and to prescribe effective change in them.

When one force dominates an organization, it is drawn toward the associated *configuration*, but must deal with *contamination*. When no force dominates, the organization is a balanced *combination* of forces, including periods of *conversion* from one form to another. But then there is a problem of *cleavage*. Contamination and cleavage require the management of *contradiction*, which is where ideology and politics come in. We shall discuss each of these notions shortly.

Dominant forces drive an organization to one of the pure forms discussed earlier—entrepreneurial, machine, professional, diversified, innovative. These are not "real," but are abstract models designed to capture some reality. Some organizations *do* match the pure forms closely. If the form fits, the organization should wear it. Configuration has benefits: the organization achieves a sense of order, or integration. Configuration also helps outsiders understand an organization. The consistency of configuration keeps workers from being confused. For classification, for comprehension, for diagnosis, and for design, configuration seems to be effective. But only so long as everything holds still. Introduce the dynamics of evolutionary change and, sooner or later, configuration becomes ineffective.

CONTAMINATION BY CONFIGURATION

The harmony, consistency, and fit that is configuration's greatest strength is also its greatest weakness. The dominant force can become so strong that it drives out everything else. For example, control in machine organizations may contaminate the innovators in research. Machine organizations recognize this when they put their research and development facilities away from the head office, to avoid the contaminating effects of the central efficiency experts. The opposite case is also well known—the "looseness" in adhocracies may contaminate the efforts of the accountants concerned with efficiency. This contamination may be a small price to pay for being coherently organized, until things go out of control.

CONFIGURATION OUT OF CONTROL

When the need arises for change, the dominating forces may act to hold the organization in place. The other forces may have atrophied, and so the organization goes out of control. For instance, the machine organization in need of a new strategy may have no entrepreneurs and no innovators left to give it its new direction. Miller and Kets de Vries (1987) have developed five organizational "neuroses" that correspond roughly to what can happen in extreme cases of contamination in the five forms. Each is an example of a system that may once have been healthy but has run out of control.

▼ *Dramatic*: the entrepreneur, freed from other forces, may take the organization on an ego trip. This can even occur in large diversified organizations that are dominated by strong CEOs.
▼ *Compulsive*: this happens when there is completeness of control in machine organizations. This is the classic overbearing bureaucracy.
▼ *Paranoid*: paranoia is often a collective tendency in some professional organizations like universities and hospitals. Professors and doctors are always suspicious that their peers, or worse, the "administration," are planning to undermine their efforts.
▼ *Depressive*: this can be the result of an obsession with the bottom line in diversified organizations. Being a cash cow that is constantly being "milked" is very bad for morale.
▼ *Schizoid*: the need to innovate, and to get the commercial benefits from innovation, means that adhocracies can be in constant oscillation between divergent and convergent thinking.

In other words, behaviors that were once functional become dysfunctional when pursued to excess.

CONTAINMENT OF CONFIGURATION

Truly effective organizations thus do not exist in pure form. What keeps a configuration effective is not only the dominance of a single force but also the constraining effects of other forces. This is *containment*. To manage configuration effectively is to exploit one form but also to reconcile the different forces. Machine organizations must exploit their efficiency but must still allow for innovation. Innovative forms must exploit their power to create, but must find a way to remain somewhat efficient.

Combination

Configuration is nice if you can have it. But some organizations all of the time, and all organizations some of the time, are unable to have it. They must instead balance competing forces. Organizations like this can be called *combinations*; instead of being a node in the pentagon, they are somewhere within it.

KINDS OF COMBINATIONS

When only two of the five forces meet in rough balance, that is a *hybrid*. A symphony orchestra is an example, being a rough balance of entrepreneurial and professional forms. Some organizations experience *multiple combinations*. Apple Computer in Canada was once described as a combination of adhocracy (a legacy of its founder, Steve Jobs), machine (for efficiency in production and distribution), entrepreneurial (in the person of a dynamic sales manager), and professional (in marketing and training).

CLEAVAGE IN COMBINATIONS

If configuration encourages contamination, sometimes combination encourages *cleavage*. Instead of one force dominating, two or more confront each other to the point of paralyzing the organization. A common example from business organizations is the innovative drive of R&D against the machine-like drive of production.

Despite the problems created by having to balance forces, combination of one kind or another is probably necessary in most organizations. Effective organizations usually balance many forces. Configuration merely means a tilt toward one force; combination is more balanced.

Conversion

The preceding discussions of configuration and combination implied stability. But few organizations stay in one form or combination; they undergo *conversion* from one configuration or combination to another. Often these result from external changes. For example, an innovative organization decides to settle down as a machine to exploit an innovation. Or a suddenly unstable market makes a machine become more innovative. Conversions are often temporary, as in the machine organization that becomes an entrepreneurial organization during a crisis.

CYCLES OF CONVERSION

The forces that may destroy the organization may instead drive it to another, perhaps more viable, configuration. For example, the entrepreneurial form is inherently vulnerable, because of its reliance on a single leader. It may work well for the young organization, but with aging and growth a dominant need for direction may be displaced by that for efficiency. Then conversion to the machine form becomes necessary—the power of one leader must be replaced by that of administrators.

The implication is that organizations go through stages as they develop, sequenced into so-called life cycles. The most common life cycle is the one mentioned above. It begins with

the entrepreneurial form and moves down along the left edge of the pentagon. Growth leads to the machine form, and even greater growth leads ultimately to the diversified form. Another life cycle, depicted along the right edge of the pentagon, occurs for firms dependent on expertise. They move from the entrepreneurial form to either the professional form (if they can standardize their services) or the innovative form (if their services are more creative). Another common conversion is when an innovative form decides to exploit and perfect the skills it has developed and settles into a professional form, a common conversion in consulting.

Ideology and politics play a role in conversion. Ideology is a more important form in young organizations. That is because cultures can develop more easily there, especially with charismatic leadership in the entrepreneurial stage. By comparison, it is extremely difficult to build a strong and lasting culture in a mature organization. Politics, by contrast, typically spreads as the energy of the young organization dissipates and its activities become more diffuse. As the organization becomes more formalized, its culture is blunted, and politics becomes a more important force.

CLEAVAGE IN CONVERSION

Some conversions are easy because they are so overdue. But most are more difficult and conflictual, requiring periods of transition, prolonged and agonizing. As the organization in transition sits between its old and new forms, it becomes a kind of combination. The forces that create the conversion also create the possibility of cleavage. How does the organization deal with these contradictions?

Contradiction

Organizations that have to reconcile contradictory forces, especially in dealing with change, often turn to the cooperative force of ideology or the competitive force of politics. Indeed, these two forces themselves represent a contradiction that must be managed if an organization is not to run out of control.

While it is true that each can dominate an organization, and so draw it toward a missionary or political form, more commonly they act differently, as *catalysts*. Ideology tends to draw behavior inwards toward a common core; politics drives behavior away from any central place. One force is centripetal, the other centrifugal. Both can act to promote change or also to prevent it. Either way, they sometimes render an organization more effective, sometimes less.

COOPERATION THROUGH IDEOLOGY

Ideology (or strong culture) represents the force for cooperation in an organization, for collegiality and consensus. It encourages members to look inward, to take their lead from the imperatives of the organization's own vision. One important implication is that infusion of ideology renders any particular configuration more effective. People get fired up to pursue efficiency or proficiency or whatever else drives the organization. When this happens to a machine organization—as in a McDonald's, very responsive to its customers and very sensitive to its employees—we have a "snappy bureaucracy." Bureaucratic machines are not supposed to be snappy, but ideology changes the nature of their quest for efficiency.

Another implication is that ideology helps an organization manage contradiction and so to deal with change. The innovative machine and the tightly controlled innovative organization are inherent contradictions. These organizations handle their contradictions by having strong cultures. Such organizations can more easily reconcile their opposing forces because what matters to their people ultimately is the organization itself, more than any of its particular parts, like efficient manufacturing or innovative R&D. This is how Toyota gets efficiency and high quality at the same time.

LIMITS TO COOPERATION

Ideologies sound wonderful, but they are difficult to build and sustain. And established ideologies can get in the way of organizational effectiveness. They may discourage change by forcing everyone to work within the same set of beliefs. This has implications for strategy. Change *within* strategic perspective, to a new position, is facilitated by a strong ideology. But change *of* perspective—fundamental change—is discouraged by it.

COMPETITION THROUGH POLITICS

Politics represents the force for competition in an organization, for conflict and confrontation. It too can infuse any of the configurations or combinations, in this case aggravating contamination and cleavage. In a configuration, the representative of the dominant force "lord it" over others. This could lead to contamination. In a combination, representatives of the various forces relish opportunities to do battle with each other, aggravating the cleavage.

One problem facing strategic managers is that politics may be a more "natural" force than ideology. Left to themselves, organizations seem to pull apart rather easily. Keeping them together requires considerable and constant effort.

BENEFITS OF COMPETITION

If the pulling together of culture discourages people from addressing fundamental change, then the pulling apart of politics may become the only way to ensure that happens. Change requires challenging the status quo. Politics may facilitate this; if there are no entrepreneurial or innovative forces stimulating strategic change, it may be the *only* available force for change.

Both politics and ideology can promote organizational effectiveness as well as undermine it. Ideology can be a force for revitalization, energizing the organization and making its people more responsive. But it can also hinder fundamental change. Likewise, politics often impedes necessary change and wastes valuable resources. But it can also promote important change that may be available in no other way. It can enable those who realize the need for change to challenge those who do not.

COMBINING COOPERATION AND COMPETITION

The last remaining contradiction is the one between ideology and politics themselves. Ideology and politics themselves have to be reconciled. Pulling together ideologically infuses life; splitting apart politically challenges the status quo. Only by encouraging both can an organization sustain its viability. Ideology helps secondary forces to contain a dominant one; politics encourages them to challenge it.

The balance between ideology and politics should be a dynamic equilibrium. Most of the time ideology should be pulling things together, contained by healthy internal competition. When fundamental change becomes necessary, however, politics should help pull the organization apart temporarily.

Competence

What makes an organization effective? The "Peterian" view (named after Tom Peters of *In Search of Excellence* fame) is that organizations should be "hands on, value driven." The

"Porterian" view (named after Michael Porter) says that organizations should use competitive analysis. To Porter, effectiveness resides in strategy, while to Peters it is the operations that count. One says do the right things, the other says do things right. But we need to understand what takes an organization to a viable strategy in the first place, what makes it excellent there, and how some organizations are able to sustain viability and excellence in the face of change.

Here are five views to guide us in our search for organizational effectiveness:

CONVERGENCE

First is the *convergence* hypothesis. Its motto is that there is "one best way" to design an organization. This is usually associated with the machine form. A good structure is one with a rigid hierarchy of authority, with spans of control no greater than six, with heavy use of strategic planning, MIS, and whatever else happens to be in the current fashion of the rationalizers. In *In Search of Excellence*, by contrast, Peters and Waterman argued that ideology was the key to an organization's success. We cannot dismiss this hypothesis—sometimes there *are* proper things to do in most, perhaps all, organizations. But we must take issue with its general thrust. Society has paid an enormous price for "one best way" thinking over the course of this century, on the part of all its organizations that have been drawn into using what is fashionable rather than functional. We need to look beyond the obvious, beyond the convergence hypothesis.

CONGRUENCE

Beyond convergence is the *congruence* or "it all depends" approach. Introduced into organization theory in the 1960s, it suggests that running an organization is like choosing dinner from a buffet table—a little bit of this, a little bit of that, all selected according to specific needs. Organizational effectiveness thus becomes a question of matching a given set of internal attributes, treated as a kind of portfolio, with various situational factors. The congruence hypothesis has certainly been an improvement, but like a dinner plate stacked with an old assortment of foods, it has not been good enough.

CONFIGURATION

The motto of the *configuration* hypothesis is "getting it all together." Design your organization as you would a jigsaw puzzle, fitting the organizational pieces together to create a coherent, harmonious picture. There is reason to believe that organizations succeed in good part because they are consistent in what they do; they are certainly easier to manage that way. But, as we have seen, configuration has its limits, too.

CONTRADICTION

While the lumpers may like the configuration hypothesis, splitters prefer the *contradiction* hypothesis. Their call is to manage the dynamic tension between contradictory forces. They point to the common occurrence of combinations and conversions, where organizations are forced to manage contradictory forces. This is an important hypothesis—together with that of configuration (which are in their own dynamic tension) it is an important clue to organizational effectiveness. But still it is not sufficient.

CREATION

The truly great organization transcends all of the foregoing while building on it to achieve something more. It respects the *creation* hypothesis. Creativity is its forte, "understand your inner nature" is its motto, LEGO its image. The most interesting organizations live at the edges, far from the logic of conventional organizations, where as Raphael (1976:5–6) has pointed out in biology (for example, between the sea and the land, or at the forest's edge), the richest, most varied, and most interesting forms of life can be found. This might be called the "Prahaladian" view (after C. K. Prahalad, and his ideas of "strategic intent" discussed in Chapter 2). Don't just do the right things right, but keep doing them! Such organizations keep inventing novel approaches that solve festering problems and so provide all of us with new ways to deal with our world of organizations.

▼ READING 15.2   CONVERGENCE AND UPHEAVAL: MANAGING THE UNSTEADY PACE OF ORGANIZATIONAL EVOLUTION*

by Michael L. Tushman, William H. Newman, and Elaine Romanelli

A snug fit of external opportunity, company strategy, and internal structure is a hallmark of successful companies. The real test of executive leadership, however, is in maintaining this alignment in the race of changing competitive conditions.

Consider the Polaroid or Caterpillar corporations. Both firms virtually dominated their respective industries for decades, only to be caught off guard by major environmental changes. The same strategic and organizational factors which were so effective for decades became the seeds of complacency and organization decline.

Recent studies of companies over long periods show that the most successful firms maintain a workable equilibrium for several years (or decades), but are also able to initiate and carry out sharp, widespread changes (referred to here as reorientations) when their environments shift. Such upheaval may bring renewed vigor to the enterprise. Less successful firms, on the other hand, get stuck in a particular pattern. The leaders of these firms either do not see the need for reorientation or they are unable to carry through the necessary frame-breaking changes. While not all reorientations succeed, those organizations which do not initiate reorientations as environments shift underperform.

This reading focuses on reasons why for long periods most companies make only incremental changes, and why they then need to make painful, discontinuous, system-wide shifts. We are particularly concerned with the role of executive leadership in managing this pattern of convergence punctuated by upheaval. . . .

The task of managing incremental change, or convergence, differs sharply from managing frame-breaking change. Incremental change is compatible with the existing structure of a company and is reinforced over a period of years. In contrast, frame-breaking change is abrupt, painful to participants, and often resisted by the old guard. Forging these new strategy-structure-people-process consistencies and laying the basis for the next period of incremental change calls for distinctive skills.

Because the future health, and even survival, of a company or business unit is at stake, we need to take a closer look at the nature and consequences of convergent change and of differences imposed by frame-breaking change. We need to explore when and why these painful and risky revolutions interrupt previously successful patterns, and whether these discontinuities can be avoided and/or initiated prior to crisis. Finally, we need to examine what managers can and should do to guide their organizations through periods of convergence and upheaval over time. . . .

The following discussion is based on the history of companies in many different industries, different countries, both large and small organizations, and organizations in various stages of their product class's life-cycle. We are dealing with a widespread phenomenon—not just a few dramatic sequences. Our research strongly suggests that the convergence/upheaval

*Originally published in the *California Management Review* (Fall 1986). Copyright © 1986 by The Regents of the University of California. Reprinted with deletions by permission of the *Review*.

pattern occurs within departments at the business-unit level . . . and at the corporate level of analysis. . . . The problem of managing both convergent periods and upheaval is not just for the CEO, but necessarily involves general managers as well as functional managers.

Patterns in Organizational Evolution: Convergence and Upheaval

BUILDING ON STRENGTH: PERIODS OF CONVERGENCE

Successful companies wisely stick to what works well. . . .

. . . convergence starts out with an effective dovetailing of strategy, structure, people, and processes. . . . The formal system includes decisions about grouping and linking resources as well as planning and control systems, rewards and evaluation procedures, and human resource management systems. The informal system includes core values, beliefs, norms, communication patterns, and actual decision-making and conflict resolution patterns. It is the whole fabric of structure, systems, people, and processes which must be suited to company strategy (Nadler and Tuchman, 1986).

As the fit between strategy, structure, people, and processes is never perfect, convergence is an ongoing process characterized by incremental change. Over time, in all companies studied, two types of converging changes were common: fine-tuning and incremental adaptations.

▼ *Converging change: Fine-tuning*—Even with good strategy-structure-process fits, well-run companies seek even better ways of exploiting (and defending) their missions. Such effort typically deals with one or more of the following:
  ▼ *Refining* policies, methods, and procedures.
  ▼ Creating *specialized units and linking mechanisms* to permit increased volume and increased attention to unit quality and cost.
  ▼ *Developing personnel* especially suited to the present strategy—through improved selection and training, and tailoring reward systems to match strategic thrusts.
  ▼ Fostering individual and group *commitments* to the company mission and to the excellence of one's own department.
  ▼ Promoting *confidence* in the accepted norms, beliefs, and myths.
  ▼ *Clarifying* established roles, power, status, dependencies, and allocation mechanism.

The fine-tuning fills out and elaborates the consistencies between strategy, structure, people, and processes. These incremental changes lead to an ever more interconnected (and therefore more stable) social system. Convergent periods fit the happy, stick-with-a-winner situations romanticized by Peters and Waterman (1982).

▼ *Converging change: Incremental adjustments to environmental shifts*—In addition to fine-tuning changes, minor shifts in the environment will call for some organizational response. Even the most conservative of organizations expect, even welcome, small changes which do not make too many waves.

A popular expression is that almost any organization can tolerate a "ten percent change." At any one time, only a few changes are being made; but these changes are still compatible with the prevailing structures, systems, and processes. Examples of such adjustments are an expansion in sales territory, a shift in emphasis among products in the product line, or improved processing technology in production.

The usual process of making changes of this sort is well known: wide acceptance of the need for change, openness to possible alternatives, objective examination of the pros and cons of each plausible alternative, participation of those directly affected in the preceding analysis, a market test or pilot operation where feasible, time to learn the new activities, established role models, known rewards for positive success, evaluation, and refinement.

The role of executive leadership during convergent periods is to reemphasize mission and core values and to delegate incremental decisions to middle-level managers. Note that the uncertainty created for people affected by such changes is well within tolerable limits. Opportunity is provided to anticipate and learn what is new, while most features of the structure remain unchanged.

The overall system adapts, but it is not transformed.

CONVERGING CHANGE: SOME CONSEQUENCES

For those companies whose strategies fit environmental conditions, convergence brings about better and better effectiveness. Incremental change is relatively easy to implement and ever more optimizes the consistencies between strategy, structure, people, and processes. At AT&T, for example, the period between 1913 and 1980 was one of ever more incremental change to further bolster the "Ma Bell" culture, systems, and structure all in service of developing the telephone network.

Convergent periods are, however, a double-edged sword. As organizations grow and become more successful, they develop internal forces for stability. Organizational structures and systems become so interlinked that they only allow compatible changes. Further, over time, employees develop habits, patterned behaviors begin to take on values (e.g., "service is good"), and employees develop a sense of competence in knowing how to get work done within the system. These self-reinforcing patterns of behavior, norms, and values contribute to increased organizational momentum and complacency and, over time, to a sense of organizational history. This organizational history—epitomized by common stories, heroes, and standards—specifies "how we work here" and "what we hold important here."

This organizational momentum is profoundly functional as long as the organization's strategy is appropriate. The Ma Bell . . . culture, structure, and systems—and associated internal momentum—were critical to [the] organization's success. However, if (and when) strategy must change, this momentum cuts the other way. Organizational history is a source of tradition, precedent, and pride which are, in turn, anchors to the past. A proud history often restricts vigilant problem solving and may be a source of resistance to change.

When faced with environmental threat, organizations with strong momentum

▼   may not register the threat due to organization complacency and/or stunted external vigilance (e.g., the automobile or steel industries), or

▼   if the threat is recognized, the response is frequently heightened conformity to the status quo and/or increased commitment to "what we do best."

For example, the response of dominant firms to technological threat is frequently increased commitment to the obsolete technology (e.g., telegraph/telephone; vacuum tube/transistor; core/semiconductor memory). A paradoxical result of long periods of success may be heightened organizational complacency, decreased organizational flexibility, and a stunted ability to learn.

Converging change is a double-edged sword. Those very social and technical consistencies which are key sources of success may also be the seeds of failure if environments change. The longer the convergent periods, the greater these internal forces for stability. This momentum seems to be particularly accentuated in those most successful firms in a product class . . . in historically regulated organizations . . . or in organizations that have been traditionally shielded from competition. . . .

ON FRAME-BREAKING CHANGE

FORCES LEADING TO FRAME-BREAKING CHANGE

What, then, leads to frame-breaking change? Why defy tradition? Simply stated, frame-breaking change occurs in response to or, better yet, in anticipation of major environmental changes—changes which require more than incremental adjustments. The need for discontinuous change springs from one or a combination of the following:

▼ *Industry discontinuities*—Sharp changes in legal, political, or technological conditions shift the basis of competition within industries. *Deregulation* has dramatically transformed the financial services and airlines industries. *Substitute product technologies* . . . or *substitute process technologies* . . . may transform the bases of competition within industries. Similarly, the emergence of industry standards, or *dominant designs* (such as the DC-3, IBM 360, or PDP-8) signal a shift in competition away from product innovation and towards increased process innovation. Finally, *major economic changes* (e.g., oil crises) and *legal shifts* (e.g., patent protection in biotechnology or trade/regulator barriers in pharmaceuticals or cigarettes) also directly affect bases of competition.

▼ *Product life-cycle shifts*—Over the course of a product class life cycle, different strategies are appropriate. In the emergence phase of a product class, competition is based on product innovation and performance, where in the maturity stage, competition centers on cost, volume, and efficiency. Shifts in patterns of demand alter key factors for success. For example, the demand and nature of competition for mini-computers, cellular telephones, wide-body aircraft, and bowling alley equipment was transformed as these products gained acceptance and their product classes evolved. Powerful international competition may compound these forces.

▼ *Internal company dynamics*—Entwined with these external forces are breaking points within the firm. Sheer size may require a basically new management design. For example, few inventor-entrepreneurs can tolerate the formality that is linked with large volume. . . . Key people die. Family investors may become more concerned with their inheritance taxes than with company development. Revised corporate portfolio strategy may sharply alter the role and resources assigned to business units or functional areas. Such pressures, especially when coupled with external changes, may trigger frame-breaking change.

SCOPE OF FRAME-BREAKING CHANGE

Frame-breaking change is driven by shifts in business strategy. As strategy shifts so too must structure, people, and organizational processes. Quite unlike convergent change, frame-breaking reforms involve discontinuous changes throughout the organization. These bursts of change do not reinforce the existing system and are implemented rapidly. . . . Frame-breaking changes are revolutionary changes *of* the system as opposed to incremental changes *in* the system.

The following features are usually involved in frame-breaking change:

▼ *Reformed mission and core values*—A strategy shift involves a new definition of company mission. Entering or withdrawing from an industry may be involved; at least the way the company expects to be outstanding is altered. . . .

▼ *Altered power and status*—Frame-breaking change always alters the distribution of power. Some groups lose in the shift while others gain. . . . These dramatically altered power distributions reflect shifts in bases of competition and resource allocation. A new strategy must be backed up with a shift in the balance of power and status.

- ▼ *Reorganization*—A new strategy requires a modification in structure, systems, and procedures. As strategic requirements shift, so too must the choice of organization form. A new direction calls for added activity in some areas and less in others. Changes in structure and systems are means to ensure that this reallocation of effort takes place. New structures and revised roles deliberately break business-as-usual behavior.
- ▼ *Revised interaction patterns*—The way people in the organization work together has to adapt during frame-breaking change. As strategy is different, new procedures, work flows, communication networks, and decision-making patterns must be established. With these changes in work flows and procedures must also come revised norms, informal decision-making/conflict-resolution procedures, and informal roles.
- ▼ *New executives*—Frame-breaking change also involves new executives, usually brought in from outside the organization (or business unit) and placed in key managerial positions. Commitment to the new mission, energy to overcome prevailing inertia, and freedom from prior obligations are all needed to refocus the organization. A few exceptional members of the old guard may attempt to make this shift, but habits and expectations of their associations are difficult to break. New executives are most likely to provide both the necessary drive and an enhanced set of skills more appropriate for the new strategy. While the overall number of executive changes is usually relatively small, these new executives have substantial symbolic and substantive effects on the organization. . . .

WHY ALL AT ONCE?

Frame-breaking change is revolutionary in that the shifts reshape the entire nature of the organization. Those more effective examples of frame-breaking change were implemented rapidly. . . . It appears that a piecemeal approach to frame-breaking changes gets bogged down in politics, individual resistance to change, and organizational inertia. . . . Frame-breaking change requires discontinuous shifts in strategy, structure, people, and processes concurrently—or at least in a short period of time. Reasons for rapid, simultaneous implementation include:

- ▼ *Synergy* within the new structure can be a powerful aid. New executives with a fresh mission, working in a redesigned organization with revised norms and values, backed up with power and status, provide strong reinforcement. The pieces of the revitalized organization pull together, as opposed to piecemeal change where one part of the new organization is out of synch with the old organization.
- ▼ *Pockets of resistance* have a chance to grow and develop when frame-breaking change is implemented slowly. The new mission, shifts in organization, and other frame-breaking changes upset the comfortable routines and precedent. Resistance to such fundamental change is natural. If frame-breaking change is implemented slowly, then individuals have a greater opportunity to undermine the changes and organizational inertia works to further stifle fundamental change.
- ▼ Typically, there is a *pent-up need for change*. During convergent periods, basic adjustments are postponed. Boat rocking is discouraged. Once constraints are relaxed, a variety of desirable improvements press for attention. The exhilaration and momentum of a fresh effort (and new team) make difficult moves more acceptable. Change is in fashion.
- ▼ Frame-breaking change is an inherently *risky and uncertain venture*. The longer the implementation period, the greater the period of uncertainty and instability. The most effective frame-breaking changes initiate the new strategy, structure, processes, and systems rapidly and begin the next period of stability and convergent change. The sooner fundamental uncertainty is removed, the better the chances of organizational survival and growth. While the pacing of change is important, the overall time to implement frame-breaking change will be contingent on the size and age of the organization.

PATTERNS IN ORGANIZATION EVOLUTION

This historical approach to organization evolution focuses on convergent periods punctuated by reorientation—discontinuous, organizationwide upheavals. The most effective firms take advantage of relatively long convergent periods. These periods of incremental change build on and take advantage of organization inertia. Frame-breaking change is quite dysfunctional if the organization is successful and the environment is stable. If, however, the organization is performing poorly and/or if the environment changes substantially, frame-breaking change is the only way to realign the organization with its competitive environment. Not all reorientations will be successful. . . . However, inaction in the face of performance crisis and/or environmental shifts is a certain recipe for failure.

Because reorientations are so disruptive and fraught with uncertainty, the more rapidly they are implemented, the more quickly the organization can reap the benefits of the following convergent period. High-performing firms initiate reorientations when environmental conditions shift and implement these reorientations rapidly. . . . Low-performing organizations either do not reorient or reorient all the time as they root around to find an effective alignment with environmental conditions. . . .

Executive Leadership and Organization Evolution

Executive leadership plays a key role in reinforcing systemwide momentum during convergent periods and in initiating and implementing bursts of change that characterize strategic reorientations. The nature of the leadership task differs sharply during these contrasting periods of organization evolution.

During convergent periods, the executive team focuses on *maintaining* congruence and fit within the organization. Because strategy, structure, processes, and systems are fundamentally sound, the myriad of incremental substantive decisions can be delegated to middle-level management, where direct expertise and information resides. The key role for executive leadership during convergent periods is to reemphasize strategy, mission, and core values and to keep a vigilant eye on external opportunities and/or threats.

Frame-breaking change, however, requires direct executive involvement in all aspects of the change. Given the enormity of the change and inherent internal forces for stability, executive leadership must be involved in the specification of strategy, structure, people, and organizational processes *and* in the development of implementation plans. . . .

The most effective executives in our studies foresaw the need for major change. They recognized the external threats and opportunities, and took bold steps to deal with them. . . . Indeed, by acting before being forced to do so, they had more time to plan their transitions.

Such visionary executive teams are the exceptions. Most frame-breaking change is postponed until a financial crisis forces drastic action. The momentum, and frequently the success, of convergent periods breeds reluctance to change. . . .

. . . most frame-breaking upheavals are managed by executives brought in from outside the company. The Columbia research program finds that externally recruited executives are more than three times more likely to initiate frame-breaking change than existing executive teams. Frame-breaking change was coupled with CEO succession in more than 80% of the cases. . . .

There are several reasons why a fresh set of executives are typically used in company transformations. The new executive team brings different skills and a fresh perspective. Often they arrive with a strong belief in the new mission. Moreover, they are unfettered by prior commitments linked to the status quo; instead, this new top team symbolizes the need for change. Excitement of a new challenge adds to the energy devoted to it.

We should note that many of the executives who could not, or would not, implement frame-breaking change went on to be quite successful in other organizations. . . . The stimulation of a fresh start and of jobs matched to personal competence applies to individuals as well as to organizations.

Although typical patterns for the when and who of frame-breaking change are clear—wait for a financial crisis and then bring in an outsider, along with a revised executive team, to revamp the company—this is clearly less than satisfactory for a particular organization. Clearly, some companies benefit from transforming themselves before a crisis forces them to do so, and a few exceptional executives have the vision and drive to reorient a business which they nurtured during its preceding period of convergence. The vital tasks are to manage incremental change during convergent periods; to have the vision to initiate and implement frame-breaking change prior to the competition; and to mobilize an executive team which can initiate and implement both kinds of change.

Conclusion

. . . Managers should anticipate that when environments change sharply:

▼ Frame-breaking change cannot be avoided. These discontinuous organizational changes will either be made proactively or initiated under crisis/turnaround conditions.
▼ Discontinuous changes need to be made in strategy, structure, people, and processes concurrently. Tentative change runs the risk of being smothered by individual, group, and organizational inertia.
▼ Frame-breaking change requires direct executive involvement in all aspects of the change, usually bolstered with new executives from outside the organization.
▼ There are no patterns in the sequence of frame-breaking changes, and not all strategies will be effective. Strategy and, in turn, structure, systems, and processes must meet industry-specific competitive issues.

Finally, our historical analysis of organizations highlights the following issues for executive leadership:

▼ Need to manage for balance, consistency, or fit during convergent period.
▼ Need to be vigilant for environmental shifts in order to anticipate the need for frame-breaking change.
▼ Need to manage effectively incremental as well as frame-breaking change.
▼ Need to build (or rebuild) a top team to help initiate and implement frame-breaking change.
▼ Need to develop core values which can be used as an anchor as organizations evolve through frame-breaking changes (e.g., IBM, Hewlett-Packard).
▼ Need to develop and use organizational history as a way to infuse pride in an organization's past and for its future.
▼ Need to bolster technical, social, and conceptual skills with visionary skills. Visionary skills add energy, direction, and excitement so critical during frame-breaking change. . . .

by Charles Baden-Fuller and John M. Stopford

Is rejuvenation really possible? How does a business paralyzed by years of turmoil and failure and constrained by limited resources create a vibrant organization committed to entrepreneurship? Unless the organization is frugal and produces some short-term results, it risks losing support from its many stakeholders. But short-term results alone are not enough; longer-term survival must be sought. A start must be made to initiate a form of entrepreneurial behavior that increases the chances of durable recovery. As one chairman said, "We have put in new controls and financial disciplines that have stanched the hemorrhaging, cut costs, and returned us, temporarily, to profit. That's the easy part. Getting some momentum going is much harder." . . .

The Crescendo Model

We regard building corporate entrepreneurship as the essential ingredient for lasting rejuvenation. . . . The task is difficult and often subtle. To ensure that all the attributes of entrepreneurship are diffused throughout an organization, the business must avoid the "quick fixes" so beloved by many. . . . Massive capital investment programs, aggressive but shallow attempts to force total quality management, or reengineering, or "cultural immersion" are usually ineffective if undertaken with insufficient attention to the issues we raised. The quick fix rarely delivers any long-term sustainable reward for, like the Tower of Babel, it falls if its foundations are insecure. The way forward must carry the whole organization to be self-sustaining.

Rebuilding a mature organization takes time; it cannot be done with a leap. It is, for example, seldom clear at the outset, because of information gaps, just where the business should be headed. Even when the direction has become clear, the details of the twists and turns in the road ahead can remain fogbound. Experimentation is necessary to test the feasibility of ideas. Too early commitment to a new direction can be unduly risky. A way has to be found to build consistently and to link newfound strengths before real and lasting transformation can be achieved.

While there are many routes mature businesses might take, the experience of firms can be distilled to identify one path that we feel is more sure than many others. It is a four-stage renewal process, an orchestrated crescendo. Crescendo is musical term meaning "a gradual increase in volume." Our renewal process is also gradual, requiring many steps over many years. The crescendo has to be managed and momentum for change established to allow businesses to reach for ever more challenging targets.

. . . We address the question of how businesses can get started and shrug off the stasis that has plagued so many mature firms. To place that start in context and show where we are headed, we begin with a brief summary of the overall model. . . .

BOX 1

FOUR STAGES FOR REJUVENATION

1. Galvanize: create a top team dedicated to renewal.
2. Simplify: cut unnecessary and confusing complexity.
3. Build: develop new capabilities.
4. Leverage: maintain momentum and stretch the advantages.

*Reprinted from *Rejuvenating the Mature Business* (Chapter 6), published by the Harvard Business School Press, Boston, 1994. Copyright © 1994 by the President and Fellows of Harvard College; all rights reserved. Reprinted with deletions by permission of the Harvard Business School Press.

GALVANIZE

Although it seems obvious to begin by creating a top team dedicated to renewal, this vital stage is often overlooked. Rejuvenation is not the fixing up of a few activities or functions that have gone awry; it is the process of changing every part of an organization and the way its functions, territories, and various groups interact. No individual, not even the chief executive, can alone achieve this magnitude of change, but at the start it requires leadership from the top team. Such commitment carries important positive messages to the whole organization, for without that commitment those who labor in the firm become demoralized or frustrated.

To galvanize the top team, the agenda for action needs to be drawn up carefully. At the start, detailed plans of action are neither necessary nor wise. Instead there must be a broad understanding of the issues and a belief that progress will be achieved only by many small steps. There is serious danger in the early stages that top management will either try to buy its way out of difficulties with overgrandiose schemes, such as investing in expensive state-of-the-art technology that few in the organization understand, or spend too much time chasing culture change programs and not enough time initiating action.

SIMPLIFY

Simplifying the business helps change managers and workers' perceptions of what has been wrong and what new actions are required. Like clearing the rubbish from an overgrown garden, cutting some activities is a necessary precursor to building something new. Removing outdated control systems and incorrect data helps eliminate the causes of resistance to change. Simplifying the business concentrates scarce resources on a smaller agenda and so increases the chances of gaining positive results in the short to medium term. Simplification also signals to outside stakeholders—owners, suppliers, customers, bankers, and employers alike—that something positive is being attempted.

Actions to simplify the task and provide focus for the effort are no more than temporary measures. They must be regarded as work to provide a "beachhead" in complex industry structures that can be defended while work to build new strengths can proceed.

BUILD

In the third stage, which overlaps the second, the organization must set about building new advantages for later deployment as the business breaks out of the beachhead. It is at this stage that corporate rather than individual entrepreneurship must be developed. Beginning with raised aspirations to do better and resolve old problems, in the course of time new challenges need to be articulated, which will help all to work to a common purpose. That purpose, expressed in terms of visions and a direction for progress, is typically phrased in terms that all can understand. Making progress along the chosen path requires managers to experiment and to discover what can work and what fails.

Experiments, of necessity have to be small at the start: resources are limited, knowledge about possibilities uncertain, and the risks seem immense. As some experiments pay off, momentum should increase to the point where major investments in new technology for delivering the product or service may be required. Learning may also start slowly, though ordinarily some parts of the organization progress more quickly than others. Over time the organization must invest in deepening existing skills and acquiring new ones, developing new systems, data bases, and knowledge. Alongside these initiatives, teamwork must be developed, first on a small scale to deal with essential tasks but then growing across the whole organization and extending along the supply chain. The momentum created helps build the values that underpin the crucial ingredient of the will to win.

LEVERAGE

The final stage is leveraging advantages and maintaining momentum. As the organization grows in competitive strength, it can expand the sphere of its operations into new markets, new products, and new parts of the value chain. Leveraging capabilities can be by acquisition, alliances, or internal moves so that the business can extend its newfound advantages to a much wider sphere of activities. Pressures for expansion must be balanced against the danger of too much complexity slowing down the pace of innovation and forcing the organization to a standstill.

We label the rejuvenation process a *crescendo* to emphasize that the four stages are not discrete steps but rather activities which merge into each other as the magnitude of change increases over time. The reality of all organizations is messy, confusing, and complex. In the building of corporate entrepreneurship, activities in one department or at one level of the organization may proceed faster and more effectively than others. Moreover, organizations do not rejuvenate only once: they may need to do so repetitively. The challenges of one period may be resolved, but those of the next may again require organizational change.

The rejuvenation steps are summarized in Figure 1. The arrows are drawn as lines, though in practice progress is usually made in loops of learning. The dance to the crescendo of music is the samba. *One step back to take two steps forward* describes how organizations proceed—and it is exactly what happens with simplification and building. Let us use an analogy: renovators of old buildings know full well that the plaster has to come off the walls if a rotten structure is to be repaired. It is rarely possible to fix it without spoiling the decorations. . . .

We emphasize that in the early simplifying stage of renewal, cutting may have to be radical. The contraction can be tangible, for example, cutting out parts of the product range, geographic territory, or stages of the value chain; it can also be less tangible, for example, eliminating systems and procedures. Even profitable activities may have to be dropped if they distract attention and deflect resources from building the new "core."

In building, progress is best achieved by many small initiatives, because resources are limited. Small steps spread the risks and prevent the organization from betting everything on one initiative. As rejuvenation proceeds, the risks become better understood and progress more secure, allowing the steps to get bigger. Small steps also allow the organization to encourage initiatives from below and help build an entrepreneurial culture. Whereas

FIGURE 1
Critical Path for
Corporate Renewal

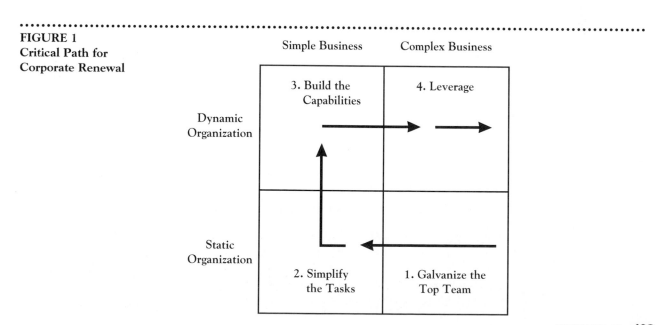

instructions for surgery are imposed from the top, it is the bottom-up flow of ideas and actions that accelerates the convalescence and return to fighting fitness.

We stress that organizations need a long time to rejuvenate. It takes years to build a truly entrepreneurial company. Like builders of houses, who spend almost two-thirds of the cost and time below ground digging foundations and preparing the site, effective organizations that aim to become entrepreneurial also have to sink deep foundations; rushing for the quick-fix solution is unlikely to result in long-term rewards. . . .

Galvanizing the Top Team

Rejuvenating a mature organization is impossible without commitment from the top. As we pointed out, . . . many mature organizations show signs of life with innovative actions being taken in parts, and include many able individuals who are committed to change. Entrepreneurial individuals generally labor in isolated groups. They are unable to make the connections essential to altering the path of the organization, for that requires linkages across functions and territories, which cannot be achieved without the backing of top management.

Initial moves are often made by a new chief executive, and in all the firms we studied, the CEO played a vital and decisive role. The effective ones, however, did not act alone; they all realized the importance of teams. . . .

Building a top team dedicated to change provides continuity and reduces the risks that the process will falter if one person leaves. In several of our organizations the chief executive changed without loss of momentum. . . .

Effective top teams span all the key functions. Rejuvenation involves changing the way in which the functions work and the way in which they relate. An effective top team must have a real understanding of the functions so that it understands what is technically possible, what is required by customers, suppliers, the work force, and other stakeholders. Without shared knowledge within the team, there can be no intuition, which is vital for the business.

The need to involve the key functions also ensures the involvement of the vital power brokers of the organization. Functional or territorial heads carry weight in getting things done. They can influence the perceptions and actions of their group, perhaps because of their position but often because of their background and skills. Unless they are involved in the early stages, the power brokers may sabotage or slow down the process through misunderstanding and lack of appreciation.

For rejuvenation, all members of the top team must share an understanding of the problem. An effective top team avoids vacillation, does not seek outsiders to resolve its problems (although they may help), does not look for a quick fix or shirk dealing with immediate issues. In short, many rocks and whirlpools have to be avoided. To sidestep these hazards, the team must believe that there is a crisis, that action has to be taken, and that the action must extend throughout the organization. Only where there is real common acceptance of these three priorities does the top team feel empowered to start the process of rejuvenation. Achieving consensus is not easy, so we examine the issues. (See Table 1.)

SENSING THE NEED TO START

What triggers actions that can lead to rejuvenation? Why is correct sensing so critical to generating a sense of urgency? Earlier we discussed the difficulty of recognizing crises in a form that can lead to action and the even more serious problem of using the recognition of an opportunity as a way of focusing energies to change behavior. It is one thing to bring together a top team, quite another to have it share, collectively, a sense that change is imperative.

TABLE 1
Galvanizing the Top Team

LIMITING PERCEPTIONS	GALVANIZING PERCEPTIONS
The problem we face is temporary.	There is a crisis and the issues are major and fundamental.
We must move slowly to avoid upsetting the existing order.	There is a sense of urgency. Change must must be set into motion even if we do not know exactly where we are going.
It is someone else's fault that we are in trouble.	We must understand why we are in the mess, so that we, the top team, can lead the way forward.
The problems lie in specific areas of the organization; they are not widespread.	Firmwide change is needed across functions, territories, and hierarchy.
The financial figures tell us what is wrong.	We have to look behind the figures to find out where the markets are going and the needed capabilities.

We use the word sense advisedly, because at the earliest stages only rarely does hard data indicate a clear direction; information by itself seldom "proves" or "disproves" any action.

Consider what can happen when managers sense the signals for change. They may seem so vague that they are effectively ignored. They may point to solutions that are beyond current capabilities, they can provoke responses of general concern, but the actions are little more than tinkering with the symptoms. More precise signals can also be ignored, even when the solutions are within capabilities, because the team has yet to share a common will to respond. The issue of the urgency is also embodied in the message. Managers may feel that they have plenty of time and allow other agendas to preoccupy them. Alternatively, an urgent message may seem to be so complex that appropriate responses are hard to calculate.

We found that all the top teams of rejuvenating firms had experienced many of these difficulties before they could commit themselves to collective internal action. Often, we found top teams working to exhaust all the "obvious" actions before they could perceive the need to consider more radical approaches to transform the business as a whole. Rational calculations of partial response to complex challenges can be used, perhaps unwittingly, to perpetuate the inertia of maturity. The problem is exacerbated when the agenda is so complex that team members cannot agree on priorities. . . .

It is important to appreciate that the data in signals for change need to be interpreted for others, particularly when they are weak. Consider the assessment of competitors, so commonly undertaken by top management. Measures of competition may cover profitability, productivity, reliability, or customer acceptance. Generally, a few competitors are doing better on some if not all the measures, but many may be similar to a given organization and some may be doing worse. Should this fact be seen as a trigger for action or a signal for complacency? Unless someone has high aspirations and a sense of danger, complacency prevails. . . . There are always those who believe that poor performance, be it in profits or some other measure, can be excused: "It is not our fault." Worse yet, competitor benchmarking studies can be used to justify the status quo. One mature firm that later went out of business went so far as to reject a study that indicated the need for a fundamental change of approach. In the words of one director, it was "obviously fallacious. If this was possible, we would be doing it already."

There are many other reasons why managers may fail to react to changing circumstance. Mature organizations can become trapped in an illusion bred of undue focus on accounting profits. Of necessity, accounting figures can register only what has happened, not what is about to happen; when confronted by "satisfactory" profits, many top groups ignored other signals indicating declining competitiveness. . . .

Only a few of our rejuvenators did the obvious thing at the start, that is, establish measures that heighten the sense of urgency to deal with emergent problems before they become serious. Wise and successful organizations broaden their measures of performance to include specific indicators of relative achievement of financial and nonfinancial goals. A broader and more balanced scorecard helps top teams in general, and chief executives in particular, to anticipate where trouble might strike. It amplifies the weak signals that forewarn of danger and diminishes those signals which encourage complacency. If the top team does not anticipate it, the organization may be submerged and unable to retrieve itself when the real crisis arrives.

TRIGGERS FOR ACTION

Sensing impending doom is not always sufficient to induce action. Although it comes late in the day, falling profitability seems to be the most common trigger for inducing a sufficient enough sense of urgency and crisis that actions to cure the roots of the problem can be instituted. . . .

Must firms wait for a financial crisis before top managers do more than tinker with some of the parts? Though harder to do, it is possible for individuals to anticipate a looming crisis and initiate corrective action before it is too late or too expensive to try. It is relatively easier for that to happen when an individual has the power to act. The awareness may come first to shareholders, who appoint a new chief executive to carry the message, or the chief executive may be prescient. It is more difficult when the messages come from outside and are heard by individual managers without power. Dealings with suppliers, customers, bankers, and innumerable others can highlight the problem and stir up action within isolated groups. But when that happens, action to change business fundamentally usually has to wait until. . . there is a chief executive who listens and buys into the possibilities.

. . . It is possible to anticipate a real crisis. Those who have done so have been able to take positive action at less cost than would have been incurred had they procrastinated. In such instances, hindsight seems to show repetitively that the actions taken were less risky than a policy of standing still. But before the event, the risks may have appeared large.

EMPOWERING MANAGEMENT

Bringing together a top team and making its members realize that there is a crisis is not enough to start rejuvenation: the team must believe that it has the power and the responsibility to do something. It is necessary that certain aspects of the problem are appreciated by the top team: that the problem is not limited to a single part of the organization, that the quick fix does not work. The top team must also appreciate that it does not have to know all the answers before it can act. Its job is to chart the direction ahead and enlist the aid of others in finding durable solutions. It is tempting to suggest that the realization comes quickly, but the truth is that appreciation comes gradually.

. . . Managers of mature organizations are often keen to fasten blame on others. Sometimes they blame the environment, poor demand, overfussy customers, adverse exchange rates, even the weather. Sometimes they blame the decisions of previous top management and sometimes the failure of current middle management to implement decisions made by the top team. While an element of blame may rightly be attached to these groups, in all cases top management showed insufficient appreciation of the issues at stake. Progress can take place only when team members appreciate the extent of a problem and realize that they, and only they, are ultimately responsible for [their] organization's failures. More important, only the top team can lead the organization out of its mess.

It is also common for senior managers to perceive that the problems (and hence the solutions) lie in a single function or part of their organization. Blaming particular functions, territories, or groups is often unhelpful, as the crisis reflects failures of the whole organization. For example, when high-cost products are also poor quality, the production department is usually blamed. Such finger-pointing is naive, for rarely is production alone to blame for poor quality. It may be that production, not being told by the service department which failures occur most frequently, is trying to improve the wrong elements. Distribution may be at fault, damaging goods in transit. Purchasing may be paying insufficient attention to ensuring that suppliers provide quality components, and marketing may insist on designs that are difficult and expensive to produce. Quality at low cost can be achieved only when all functions work closely together. . . .

The dawning realization that the problems are serious and that the causes extend beyond a single function to all parts of the organization is one step on the road toward taking necessary corrective actions. But before effective action can be initiated, hard choices among many alternatives must be made. Here the chief executive has the central role of holding the ring as people test their intuition against always imperfect data. Lacking hard evidence, a top team always has members with competing senses of priority. And lacking anything more than a common will to be positive, the debates can all too readily become unproductive without firm leadership.

Choosing Effective Action

Some top teams choose to manage their way forward by exhaustive analysis of the alternatives they can perceive at the time of crisis. Others feel their way by trying solutions and discovering what does and does not work. Still others examine the experience of other organizations. And often all these approaches are combined. However choices are made, there are many false paths and blind alleys, which can seduce and lull management into thinking that it is effectively dealing with the issues at hand.

The steps that we suggest mark out the most effective path of action are in stark contrast to other actions we observed. Simplification involves cutting to conserve resources, revealing a new core, and pointing the way forward. The subsequent building, later described in detail, lays new foundations for the entrepreneurial organization and requires an extended time perspective. These measured steps contrast with the following alternatives, which many have taken and which fail to address key issues effectively: scrapping everything and starting afresh—rather than saving what is of value, looking to outsiders to alleviate a problem—as a substitute for internal action; vacillation among extreme directives issued by top management—paralyzed uncomprehending top management; large-scale investments in state-of-the-art technology and systems at the initial stages—quick fix or big hit; and culture change programs without parallel actions—denying that there is an immediate crisis. These issues. . . are discussed more fully below.

SCRAP EVERYTHING AND START AFRESH

Consider first the problem of those Cassandras who argue that it is hopeless to try to rejuvenate—better to give up without a struggle and go elsewhere. Their pessimistic views can be justified if *all* the alternatives are more costly and more risky. Only if all else fails must an organization be extinguished.

One U.S. company considered seeking the rejuvenation of an existing operation a waste of time. Instead of tackling the deep-seated problems in its Midwest plants, it moved the whole operation to the South, leaving its past behind. In so doing, the company abandoned many skilled and loyal workers who might have been capable of adapting to new working methods faster than it took to train a brand new workforce and at less cost. The Japanese experience of buying U.S. facilities and doubling or trebling productivity within less than a year illustrates that the possibility of rejuvenation often exists. Their experience also confirms that faster returns may come from renewal rather than greenfield initiatives, a point often overlooked by those in a hurry to "get something going."*

Sometimes, to be sure, troubled organizations do not have the option of a clean start elsewhere. Even though they might wish to walk away, the owners may not be able to afford the exit costs. They may also face severe union opposition and the resistance of politicians and local government officials. In such cases, management is obliged to try to find a middle way, regardless of how many Cassandras argue that the effort will be in vain.

SEEKING OUTSIDE SUPPORT

For years, many major European chemical companies, particularly the Italian giants, the French and Belgians, and even the British ICI, perceived the problems of their industry as being caused by government's failure to manage demand in the economy and allowing the Middle Eastern countries power over oil prices. In these firms, top management consistently lobbied governments for support to resolve their problems and failed to take internal initiatives. ICI, one of the bigger culprits, was also one of the first to break out of the vicious circle and realize that internal action was necessary. A galvanized top management led the way, and ten years later, in better shape than many of its European counterparts, it is still trying to pull its organization around. . . .

Lest we be accused of ignoring politics and reality, we fully recognize that all organizations have a role to lobby and put their case to government, and all need to watch and influence events. However, we draw a distinction between this approach and those failing organizations which do nothing for themselves while waiting to be rescued by the white knight of outside support. The first puts the role of public policy in perspective, while the second fails in the duties of management.

TOP-DOWN DIRECTIVES THAT ADDRESS SYMPTOMS, NOT CAUSES

Many top managers seem to believe that issuing orders from the top and expecting immediate responses is the best way to start things going. . . . This is unlikely to instill corporate entrepreneurship. As a sense of crisis looms, if statements from the top become hysterical, they can be met by inaction or lack of results from below. Vacillation is usually another sign that top management is not really in control and does not understand either the causes of a problem or how to respond effectively. Seldom can top-down directives do more than preserve yesterday's "formula.". . .

GOING FOR THE BIG HIT

The recognition that an organization is far behind in its capabilities can drive top management to seek a quick fix. At the beginning of the renewal process there is a temptation to spend money on modern capital by buying state-of-the-art factories, service delivery systems, or other forms of technology. Typically, consultants or other outsiders have suggested

---

*The West German approach to rebuilding East Germany also has the appearance of trying to start afresh: old factories are demolished, workers dismissed, and the new owners act as if they are setting up greenfield sites. For an academic view of when it is best to start afresh, see M. T. Hannan and J. Freeman, "Structural Inertia and Organizational Change," in K. S. Cameron, R. I. Sutton, and D. A Whetten, eds., *Readings in Organizational Decline* (Cambridge, Mass.: Ballinger, 1988).

that such investments permit a firm to catch up with its industry leaders. Usually the investments are large, take several years to build, and commit the organization to a single unchangeable route for the future. There is often an absence of understanding in the organization of how the new technology works, and certainly a lack of appreciation for all the issues it involves. At the early stages of rejuvenation, big programs are dangerous, not least because most of the organization's resources are bet on a single course.

For the mature organization in crisis, the arrival of massive amounts of new capital, new computers, or new systems without a corresponding building of a skill base risks disasters. All our rejuvenators discovered, if they did not already know, that skills have to be built in tandem with investment in hardware. Without the proper skills and awareness throughout the whole organization, the investments are misused or underused. Little progress is made in delivering either financial results or building a competitive edge. Worse, the spirit of entrepreneurial enthusiasm with its characteristics of learning and experimentation may be repressed.

We should make it clear that large investment programs can pay off handsomely when undertaken by firms that have gained entrepreneurial capabilities. When organizations have built their internal skills and processes, they can leverage new investments effectively.

CULTURE CHANGE PROGRAMS WITHOUT CORRESPONDING ACTION

If the big hit is dangerous because it squanders resources, takes unnecessary risks, and does not build a new organization, the culture change program goes to the opposite extreme. It is certainly true that mature organizations need to change their culture if they are to become entrepreneurial, but many mistakenly believe that the culture has to be changed before actions for improvement can be taken, or that culture change is sufficient in itself. A culture change program without action is very risky because it denies the existence of a crisis and takes the organization's attention away from the necessity for immediate action. Moreover, it fails to appreciate the most obvious fact that organizations change only through actions because actions reflect and alter beliefs.

Our finding echoes the observations of Tom Peters and Robert Waterman, [1982], who noted that effective organizations had a bias for action. Their point was that unless action is taken, progress cannot be made. Their message is highly appropriate for rejuvenating organizations. We found a surprising number of firms investing heavily in changing the culture of their organizations without ensuring that deliberate progress was made in the specification of the actual tasks. . . .

Rejuvenating a business does require a culture change, but change must be linked to action. Our research suggests that effective culture change requires managers to deal with tasks. Thus, abolishing the executive dining room at one firm did help, but only because it reinforced other important initiatives dealing with productivity and quality. In many organizations, quality circles and the like are introduced, and it seems that those which work well are those which have short-term tangible goals as well as long-term ones. Grand schemes for change without action seldom work. . . .

THE QUICK FIX: TQM OR PROCESS REENGINEERING

All our rejuvenators subscribed in one way or another to aspects of total quality management (TQM) and all have reengineered their processes, occasionally several times over. But what they did. . . bore little relation to those peddlers of snake oil who claim instant results.

A few less careful proponents of TQM or process engineering (or the equivalent) portray complex philosophies as quick-fix solutions. They understate the investment in the time, energy, and effort required to yield results. In their desire for speed, they fail to stress the need to teach the organization the skills to ensure that the process can be continued and typically do not build a proper foundation for lasting success. Not surprisingly, recent surveys of organizations that took up the TQM fad in the 1980s show that many have been disappointed and stopped earlier initiatives.* To be sure, there have been successes, but we suggest that they have probably been organizations which were either far down the rejuvenation road or, like our mature firms, patient and persistent ones. We forecast the same for process reengineering.

Claims by consultants that process reengineering can deliver a ten-fold improvement come as no surprise. . . . But boasts that such progress is achieved quickly do not ring true. Long before the recent fad, we observed mature firms attempting such rapid engineering without preparation and failing. . . .

The Way Forward

To go forward, the mature firm aspiring to rejuvenate must galvanize and build a top team committed to action. Crucial choices need to be made about the scope of the firm and how and where it will compete. In addition, action must be taken to start the building of entrepreneurship, which we assert is necessary for renewal and any higher aspirations. Some businesses have found that outside stakeholders can play a role. One such group is the top team of a business that is part of a holding company or parent organization. . . .

There may be a gap in cultural perceptions on these matters about what is and is not effective. Where many U.S. managers espouse the value of directives from the very top and point to the benefits of the resulting focus and speed of change, many we spoke to across Europe adopted a different perspective. Those whose job it was to look after a whole portfolio often preferred to work on encouraging managers to embrace the values of creativity, innovation, and challenge to conventions without specifying the actions or processes. Many set challenging targets, but some who regarded their approach as slower and harder to control, bet that the end results would be much more durable.

There is no way we know to resolve the issue of which is the superior approach. Both have good and bad points and both are dependent on the climate of attitudes into which such initiatives are introduced. The difference of opinion, however, serves to reinforce the point we made at the start: . . . real transformation of a business cannot begin in earnest without the recognition by its top managers that a new direction must be found.

---

*See, for instance, the studies by Arthur D. Little in the United States and A. T. Kearney in the United Kingdom as reported in *The Economist*, April 18, 1992.

▼ BIBLIOGRAPHY FOR READINGS

ABELL, D. F., *Defining The Business: The Starting Point of Strategic Planning*. Englewood Cliffs, N.J.: Prentice Hall, 1980.

ABERNATHY, W. J., & K. WAYNE, "Limits On the Learning Curve," *Harvard Business Review*, September–October 1974: 109–119.

ACKERMAN, R. W., *The Social Challenge to Business*. Cambridge, Mass.: Harvard University Press, 1975.

ADVISORY COMMITTEE ON INDUSTRIAL INNOVATION: FINAL REPORT. Washington, D.C.: U.S. Government Printing Office, 1979.

AGUILAR, F. J., *Scanning the Business Environment*. New York: Macmillan, 1967.

———, Interview With Kim Woo Chong, Harvard Business School, 1984.

ALLEN, M. P., "The Structure of Interorganizational Elite Cooptation: Interlocking Corporate Directorates," *American Sociological Review*, 1974: 393–406.

ALLEN, S. A., "Organizational Choices and General Management Influence Networks In Divisionalized Companies," *Academy Of Management Journal*, 1978: 341–365.

ALLISON, G. T., *Essence of Decision: Explaining the Cuban Missile Crisis*. Boston: Little, Brown, 1971.

ANSOFF, H. I., *Corporate Strategy: An Analytic Approach to Business Policy for Growth and Expansion*. New York: McGraw-Hill, 1965.

ARGYRIS, C., "Double Loop Learning In Organizations," *Harvard Business Review*, September–October 1977: 115–125.

———, & D. A. SCHON, *Organizational Learning: A Theory of Action Perspective*. Reading, Mass.: Addison-Wesley, 1978.

ASHBY, W. R., *Design for a Brain*. London: Chapman & Hall, 1954.

ASTLEY G., & C. J. FOMBRUN, "Collective Strategy: Social Ecology of Organizational Environments," *Academy of Management Review*, 1983: 576–587.

BACON, J., *Corporate Directorship Practices: Membership and Committees of The Board*. Conference Board and American Society Of Corporate Secretaries. Inc., 1973.

———, & J. K. BROWN, *Corporate Directorship Practices: Role, Selection and Legal Status of The Board*. New York: The Conference Board, 1975.

BADEN FULLER, C., ET AL., "National Or Global? The Study of Company Strategies and the European Market for Major Appliances," London Business School Centre for Business Strategy, Working Paper Series No. 28 (June 1987).

BARNARD, C. I., *The Functions of the Executive*. Cambridge, Mass.: Harvard University Press, 1938.

BARREYRE, P. Y., "The Concept of 'Impartition' Policy In High Speed Strategic Management." Working Paper, Institut d'Administration Des Entreprises, Grenoble, 1984.

———, "The Concept of Impartition Policies: A Different Approach to Vertical Integrating Strategies," *Strategic Management Journal*, 1988(9): 507–520.

———, & M. CARLE, "Impartition Policies: Growing Importance in Corporate Strategies and Applications to Production Sharing in Some World-Wide Industries." Paper Presented at Strategic Management Society Conference, Paris, 1983.

BARRIER, M., "Walton's Mountain," *Nation's Business*, April 1988: 18–26.

BARTLETT, C. A., "Proctor & Gamble Europe: Vizir Launch." Boston: Harvard Business School, Case Services #9-384-139.

———, & S. GHOSHAL, "Managing Across Borders: New Strategic Requirements," *Sloan Management Review*, Summer 1987: 7–17.

BATY, G. B., W. M. EVAN, & T. W. ROTHERMEL, "Personnel Flows As Interorganizational Relations," *Administrative Science Quarterly*, 1971: 430–443.

BAUER, R. A., 1. POOL, & L. A. DEXTER, *American Business and Public Policy*. New York: Atherton Press, 1968.

BAUMBACK, C., & J. MANCUSO, *Entrepreneurship and Venture Management*. Englewood Cliffs, N.J.: Prentice Hall, 1975.

BECKER, G., *Human Capital*. New York: National Bureau of Economic Research, 1964.

BEER, S., *Designing Freedom*. Toronto: CBC Publications, 1974.

BENNIS, W. G., & P. L. SLATER, *The Temporary Society*. New York: Harper & Row, 1968.

BERLEW, D. E. & D. T. HALL, "The Management of Tension in Organization: Some Preliminary Findings," *Industrial Management Review*, Fall 1964: 31–40.

BERNSTEIN, L., "Joint Ventures In the Light of Recent Antitrust Developments," *The Antitrust Bulletin*, 1965: 25–29.

BETTIS, R. A., "Performance Differences In Related and Unrelated Diversified Firms," *Strategic Management Journal*, 1981: 379–394.

BHIDE, A. "Hustle As Strategy," *Harvard Business Review*, September–October 1986.

BLOCK, Z, & I. C. MACMILLAN, *Corporate Venturing: Creating New Businesses Within the Firm*. Boston, Mass.: Harvard Business School Press, 1993.

BOSTON CONSULTING GROUP, *Perspective on Experience*. Boston, 1972.

———, *Strategy Alternatives for the British Motorcycle Industry*. London: Her Majesty's Stationery Office, 1975.

BOULDING, K. E., "The Ethics of Rational Decision," *Management Science,* 1966: 161–169.

BOWER, J. L., "Planning Within the Firm," *The American Economic Review,* 1970: 186–194.

BOWMAN, E. H., "Epistemology, Corporate Strategy, and Academe," *Sloan Management Review,* Winter 1974: 35–50.

BRAYBROOKE, D., "Skepticism of Wants, and Certain Subversive Effects of Corporations on American Values," in S. Hook, Ed., *Human Values and Economic Policy.* New York: New York University Press, 1967.

———, & C. E. LINDBLOM, *A Strategy of Decision: Policy Evaluation as a Social Process.* New York: Free Press, 1963.

BRENNER, S. N., & E. A. MOLANDER, "Is the Ethic of Business Changing?" *Harvard Business Review,* January–February 1977: 57–71.

BROOK, P., *The Empty Space.* Harmondsworth, Middlesex: Penguin Books, 1968.

BROOM, H. N., J. G. LONGNECKER & C. W. MOORE, *Small Business Management.* Cincinnati, Ohio: Southwest, 1983.

BRUNSSON, N., "The Irrationality of Action and Action Rationality: Decisions, Ideologies, and Organizational Actions," *Journal Of Management Studies,* 1982(1): 29–44.

BUCHELE, R. B., *Business Policy In Growing Firms.* San Francisco, Calif.: Chandler, 1967.

BURNS, T., "Micropolitics: Mechanisms of Institutional Change," *Administrative Science Quarterly.* December 1961: 257–281.

———, & G. M. STALKER, *The Management of Innovation,* 2d Ed. London: Tavistock, 1966.

BUSINESS ECONOMICS GROUP, W. R. Grace & Co., 1983.

BUSINESS WEEK, "Japan's Strategy for the '80s," December 14, 1981: 39–120.

———, "The Hollow Corporation," March 3, 1986: Supplement.

BUZZELL, R. D., B. T. GALE, & R. G. M. SULTAN, "Market Share—A Key to Profitability," *Harvard Business Review,* January–February 1975: 97–106.

BYRNE, J. A. "The Horizontal Corporation," Business Week, December 20, 1993: 76–81.

CAMPBELL, A. & M. GOOLD, *Strategy and Style: The Role of the Centre in Managing Diversified Corporations.* Oxford: Basil Blackwell, 1987.

CARLZON, J., *Moments of Truth.* New York: Ballinger Press, 1987.

CHANDLER, A. D., *Strategy and Structure: Chapters in the History of the Industrial Enterprise.* Cambridge, Mass.: M.I.T. Press, 1962.

CHANNON, D. F., "The Strategy, Structure and Financial Performance of the Service Industries," Working Paper, Manchester Business School, 1975.

CHEIT, E. F., "The New Place of Business: Why Managers Cultivate Social Responsibility," in E. F. Cheit, Ed., *The Business Establishment.* New York: John Wiley, 1964.

CHRISTENSON, C. R., K. R. ANDREWS, & J. L. BOWER, *Business Policy: Text and Cases.* Homewood, Ill.: Richard D. Irwin, 1978.

CLARK, B. R., *The Distinctive College: Antioch, Reed and Swarthmore.* Chicago: Aldine, 1970.

———, "The Organizational Saga In Higher Education,"*Administrative Science Quarterly,* 1972: 178–184.

CLARK, R. C., *The Japanese Company.* New Haven: Yale University Press, 1979.

COHEN, K. J, & R. M. CYERT, "Strategy: Formulation, Implementation and Monitoring," *The Journal of Business,* 1973: 349–367.

———, & J. P. OLSEN, "A Garbage Can Model of Organizational Choice," *Administrative Science Quarterly,* 1972: 1–25.

COHN, T., & R. A. LINDBERG, *How Management Is Different in Small Companies.* New York: American Management Association, 1972.

COLE, A. H., *Business Enterprise in Its Social Setting.* Cambridge, Mass.: Harvard University Press, 1959.

COLE, R. E., *Japanese Blue Collar: The Changing Tradition.* Berkeley: University of California Press, 1971.

———, *Work, Mobility and Participation.* Berkeley: University of California Press, 1979.

COPEMAN, G. H., *The Role of the Managing Director.* London: Business Publications, 1963.

COYNE, K. P., "Sustainable Competitive Advantage," *Business Horizons,* January–February 1986: 54–61.

CROZIER, M., *The Bureaucratic Phenomenon.* Chicago: University of Chicago Press, 1964.

CVAR, M. R., "Case Studies in Global Competition," in M. E. Porter, Ed., *Competition in Global Industries.* Boston: Harvard Business School Press, 1986.

CYERT, R. M., W. R. DILL, & J. G. MARCH, "The Role of Expectations In Business Decision Making." *Administrative Science Quarterly,* 1958: 307–340.

CYERT, R. M., & J. G. MARCH, *A Behavioral Theory of the Firm.* Englewood Cliffs, N.J.: Prentice Hall, 1963.

D'AVENI, R. A., *Hypercompetition.* New York: Free Press, 1994.

———, & A. ILLINICH, "Complex Patterns of Vertical Integration in the Forest Products Industry," *Academy of Management Journal,* 1992(35): 596–625.

D'AVENI, R. A., & D. RAVENSCRAFT, "Economics of Integration vs. Bureaucracy Costs: Does Vertical Integration Improve Performance?" *Academy of Management Journal,* 1994 (37): 1167–1206.

DAVIS, R.T., *Performance and Development of Field Sales Managers.* Boston: Harvard Business School, 1957.

DE GEUS, A. P., "Planning as Learning," *Harvard Business Review*, March–April 1988: 70–74.

DE PREE, M., *Leadership Is an Art*. New York: Doubleday, 1989.

DELBECQ, A. & A. C. FILLEY, *Program and Project Management in a Matrix Organization: A Case Study*. Madison, Wis.: University of Wisconsin, 1974.

DOERINGER, P., & M. PIORE, *Internal Labor Market and Manpower Analysis*. Lexington, Mass.: Lexington Books, 1971.

DOUGLAS, S. P., & Y. WIND, "The Myth of Globalization," *Columbia Journal of World Business*, Winter 1987: 19–29.

DRUCKER, P. F., *The Practice of Management*. New York: Harper & Row, 1954.

———, *Management: Tasks, Responsibilities, Practices*. New York: Harper & Row, 1974.

———, "Clouds Forming Across the Japanese Sun," *The Wall Street Journal*, July 13, 1982.

———, "The Coming of the New Organization," *Harvard Business Review*, Vol. 66, No. 1: 1988: 45–53.

EDWARDS, J. P., "Strategy Formulation as a Stylistic Process," *International Studies of Management and Organization*, Summer 1977: 13–27.

ELECTRONIC BUSINESS, "Services Get the Job Done," September 15, 1988: 87–90.

EPSTEIN, E. M., *The Corporation in American Politics*. Englewood Cliffs, N.J.: Prentice Hall, 1969.

———, "The Social Role of Business Enterprise in Britain: An American Perspective; Part II," *The Journal of Management Studies*, 1977: 281–316.

ESSAME, H., *Patton: A Study in Command*. New York: Charles Scribner's Sons, 1974.

EVERED, R., *So What Is Strategy?* Working Paper, Naval Postgraduate School, Monterey, 1980.

FARAGO, L., *Patton: Ordeal and Triumph*. New York: I. Obolensky, 1964.

FERGUSON, C., "Computers and the Coming of US Keiretsus," *Harvard Business Review*, July–August 1990.

FIRSIROTU, M. Y. S., "Strategic Turnaround as Cultural Revolution: The Case of Canadian National Express," Doctoral Dissertation, Faculty of Management, 1985.

FLEISHMANN, E. A., E. F. HARRIS, & H. E. BURT, *Leadership and Supervision in Industry: An Evaluation of Supervisory Training Program*. Columbus, Ohio: The Ohio State University, 1955.

FOCH, F., *Principles of War,* Translated By J. Demorinni. New York: AMS Press, 1970. First Published London: Chapman & Hall, 1918.

FORRESTER, J. W., "A New Corporate Design," *Sloan Management Review*, Fall 1965: 5–17.

———, "Counterintuitive Behavior of Social Systems," *Technology Review*, January 1971: 52–68.

FRANKLIN, B., *Poor Richard's Almanac*. New York: Ballantine Books, 1977. First Published, Century Company,1898.

FRIEDMAN, M., *Capitalism and Freedom*. Chicago: University of Chicago Press, 1962.

———, "A Friedman Doctrine: The Social Responsibility of Business Is to Increase Its Profits," *The New York Times Magazine,* September 13, 1970.

FRITZ, R., *The Path of Least Resistance*. New York: Ballantine, 1989.

———, *Creating*. New York: Ballantine, 1990.

GALBRAITH, J. K., *American Capitalism: The Concept of Countervailing Power*. Boston: Houghton Mifflin, 1952.

———, *The New Industrial State*. Boston: Houghton Mifflin, 1967.

GALBRAITH, J. R., *Organization Design*. Reading, Mass.: Addison-Wesley, 1977.

———, "Strategy and Organization Planning," *Human Resource Management*, 1983: 63–77.

———, & D. NATHANSON, *Strategy Implementation*. St. Paul, Minn.: West Publishing, 1978.

GARDNER, J. W., "The Anti-Leadership Vaccine," In *Carnegie Corporation of New York Annual Report*, 1965.

GARSON, G. D., "The Codetermination Model of Worker's Participation: Where Is It Leading?" *Sloan Management Review*, Spring 1977: 63–78.

GERTH, H. H., & C. WRIGHT MILLS, eds. *From Max Webber: Essays in Sociology*. New York: Oxford University Press, 1958.

GHISELLI, E. E., "Managerial Talent," In D. Wolfe, Ed., *The Discovery of Talent*. Cambridge, Mass.: Harvard University Press, 1969.

GILDER, G., *Wealth and Poverty*. New York: Basic Books, 1981.

GILMORE, F. F., "Overcoming the Perils of Advocacy in Corporate Planning," *California Management Review,* Spring 1973: 127–137.

GLUECK, W. F., *Business Policy and Strategic Management*. New York: McGraw Hill, 1980.

GOSSELIN, R., A *Study of the Interdependence of Medical Specialists in Quebec Teaching Hospitals*. Ph.D. thesis, McGill University, 1978.

GREEN, P., *Alexander the Great*. New York: Frederick A. Praeger, 1970.

GREENLEAF, R. K., *Servant Leadership: A Journey Into the Nature of Legitimate Power and Greatness*. New York: Paulist Press, 1977.

GREINER, L. E., "Evolution and Revolution As Organizations Grow," *Harvard Business Review*, July–August 1972: 37–46.

———, "Senior Executives As Strategic Actors," *New Management*, vol. 1, no. 2, Summer 1983.

GRINYER, P. H., & J. C. SPENDER, *Turnaround—Management Recipes For Strategic Success*. New York: Associated Business Press, 1979.

GROSS, W., "Coping with Radical Competition," in A. Gross & W. Gross, Eds., *Business Policy: Selected Readings and Editorial Commentaries*. New York: Ronald Press, 1967.

GROVE, A., *High Output Management*. New York: Random House, 1983.

GUEST, R. H., "Of Time and the Foreman," *Personnel*, May 1956: 478–486.

HAITANI, K., "Changing Characteristics of the Japanese Employment System," *Asian Survey*, 1978: 1029–1045.

HAMERMESH, R. G., M. J. ANDERSON, JR. & J. E. HARRIS, "Strategies for Low Market Share Business," *Harvard Business Review*, May–June 1978: 95–102.

HART, B. H. L., *Strategy*. New York: Frederick A. Praeger, 1954.

HASPESLAGH, P., "Portfolio Planning: Uses and Limits," *Harvard Business Review*, January–February 1982: 58–73.

HATTORI, I., "A Proposition on Efficient Decision-Making in Japanese Corporation," *Management Japan*, Autumn 1977: 14–20.

HAYES, R. H. & W. J. ABERNATHY, "Managing Our Way to Economic Decline," *Harvard Business Review*, July–August 1980: 67–77.

——, & D. A. GARVIN, "Managing As If Tomorrow Mattered," *Harvard Business Review*, May–June 1982: 70–79.

HAZAMA, H., "Characteristics of Japanese-Style Management," *Japanese Economic Studies*, Spring–Summer 1978: 110–173.

HEDBERG, B. L. T., "How Organizations Learn and Unlearn," in P. C. Nystrom and W. H. Starbuck, Eds., *Handbook of Organizational Design*, Volume 1. New York: Oxford University Press, 1981.

——, & S.A. JÖNSSON, "Designing Semi-Confusing Information Systems for Organizations in Changing Environments," *Accounting Organizations and Society*, 1978: 47–64.

——, P. C. NYSTROM, & W. H. STARBUCK, "Camping on Seesaws: Prescriptions for a Self-Designing Organization," *Administrative Science Quarterly*, 1976: 41–65.

HENDERSON, B., *Henderson on Corporate Strategy*. Cambridge, Ma.: Abt Books, 1979.

HICKSON, D. J., C. A. LEE, R. E. SCHNECK & J. M. PENNINGS, "A Strategic Contingencies' Theory of Intraorganizational Power," *Administrative Science Quarterly*, 1971: 216–229.

HIRSCH, P. M., "Organizational Effectiveness and the Institutional Environment," *Administrative Science Quarterly*, 1975: 327–344.

HOFER, C. W., & D. SCHENDEL, *Strategy Formulation: Analytical Concepts*. St. Paul, Minn.: West Publishing, 1978.

HOSMER, A., "Small Manufacturing Enterprises," *Harvard Business Review*, November–December 1957: 111–122.

HOUSE OF REPRESENTATIVES, Staff Report to the Antitrust Subcommittee of the Committee on the Judiciary, *Interlocks In Corporate Management*. Washington, D.C.: U.S. Government Printing Office, 1965.

HOUT, T., M. E. PORTER, & E. RUDDEN, "How Global Companies Win Out," *Harvard Business Review*, September–October 1982: 98–108.

HUGHES, T., "The Inventive Continuum," *Science 84*, November 1984.

HUNT, R. G., "Technology and Organization," *Academy of Management Journal*, 1970: 235–252.

IACOCCA, L., WITH W. NOVAK, *Iacocca: An Autobiography*. New York: Bantam Books, 1984.

IMAI, K., I. NONAKA, & H. TAKEUCHI, "Managing the New Product Development Process: How Japanese Companies Learn and Unlearn," In K. B. Clark, R. H. Hayes, and C. Lorenz, Eds., *The Uneasy Alliance*. Boston: Harvard Business School Press, 1985.

IRVING, D., *The Trail of the Fox*. New York: E. P. Dutton, 1977.

ITAMI, H., *Mobilizing Invisible Assets*. Cambridge, Ma.: Harvard University Press, 1987.

JACOBS, D., "Dependency and Vulnerability: An Exchange Approach to the Control of Organizations," *Administrative Science Quarterly*, 1974: 45–59.

JAMES, D. C., *The Years of MacArthur, 1941–1945*. Boston: Houghton Mifflin, 1970.

JANIS, I., *Victims of Group Think*. Boston: Houghton Mifflin, 1972.

JAY, A., *Management and Machiavelli*. New York: Penguin Books, 1970.

JENKINS, C., *Power at the Top*. Westport, Conn.: Greenwood Press, 1976.

JENNINGS, E. E., *The Mobile Manager*. Ann Arbor: University Of Michigan, 1967.

Jensen, M., "The Eclipse of the Public Corporation," *Harvard Business Review*, September–October 1989.

JOHNSON, S. C., & C. JONES, "How to Organize for New Products," *Harvard Business Review*, May–June 1957:49–62.

JOMINI, A. H., *Art of War*, Translated by G. H. Mendell and W. P. Craighill. Westport, Conn.: Greenwood Press, 1971. Original Philadelphia: J. B. Lippincott, 1862.

JÖNSSON, S. A. & R. A. LUNDIN, "Myths and Wishful Thinking as Management Tools," in P. C. Nystrom and W. H. Starbuck Eds., *Prescriptive Models of Organizations*. Amsterdam: North-Holland, 1977.

JORDAN, W. A., "Producer Protection Prior Market Structure and the Effects of Government Regulation," *Journal of Law and Economics*, 1972.

KAGONO, T., I. NONAKA, K. SAKAKIBARA, & A. OKUMURA, *Strategic vs. Evolutionary Management: A U.S.-Japan Comparison of Strategy and Organization*. Amsterdam: North-Holland, 1985.

KAHN, R. L., D. M. WOLFE, R. P. QUINN, J. D. SNOEK, & R. A. ROSENTHAL, *Organizational Stress*. New York: John Wiley, 1964.

KAMI, M. J. & J. E. ROSS, *Corporate Management In Crisis: Why the Mighty Fall*. Englewood Cliffs, N.J.: Prentice Hall, 1973.

KANO, T., "Comparative Study of Strategy, Structure and Long-Range Planning in Japan and in the United States," *Management Japan*, 1980(1): 20–34.

KANTER, R. M. *The Change Masters*. New York: Simon & Schuster, 1983.

KATZ, R. L., *Cases and Concepts in Corporate Strategy*. Englewood Cliffs, N.J.: Prentice Hall, 1970.

———, "Time and Work: Towards an Integrative Perspective," in B. M. Staw and L. L. Cummings, Eds., *Research In Organizational Behavior*, Vol. 1. Greenwich, Conn.: JAI Press, 1980.

KIDDER, T., *The Soul of a New Machine*. Boston: Little, Brown, 1981.

KIECHEL, W., III, "Sniping At Strategic Planning (interview with himself)," *Planning Review*, May 1984: 8–11.

KONO, T., "Comparative Study of Strategy, Structure and Long-Range Planning in Japan and in the United States," *Management Japan*, Spring 1980: 20–34.

KOTLER, P., & R. SINGH, "Marketing Warfare in the 1980s," *Journal of Business Strategy*, Winter 1981: 30–41.

KOTTER, J. P., & L. A. SCHLESINGER, "Choosing Strategies for Change," *Harvard Business Review*, March–April 1979: 106–114.

KUHN, T., *The Structure of Scientific Revolutions*. Chicago: University of Chicago Press, 1970.

LAND, E., "People Should Want More From Life . . ." *Forbes*, June 1, 1975.

LAPIERRE, L., "Le Changement Stratégique: Un Rêve En Quête De Réel." Ph.D. Management Policy Course Paper, McGill University, Canada, 1980.

LEARNED, E. P., C. R. CHRISTIANSEN, K. R. ANDREWS & W. D. GUTH, *Business Policy: Text and Cases*. Homewood, Ill.: Richard D. Irwin, 1965.

———, D. N. ULRICH, & D. R. BOOZ, *Executive Action*. Boston: Harvard Business School, 1951.

LENIN, V. I., *Collected Works of V.I. Lenin*, Edited and Annotated. New York: International Publishers, 1927.

LEVINSON, H., "On Becoming a Middle-Aged Manager," *Harvard Business Review*, July–August 1969: 51–60.

———, *Executive Stress*. New York: Harper & Row, 1970.

LEVITT, T., "Marketing Myopia," *Harvard Business Review*, July–August 1960: 45–56.

———, "Why Business Always Loses," *Harvard Business Review*, March–April 1968: 81–89.

———, "Industrialization of Service," *Harvard Business Review*, September–October 1976: 63–74.

———, "Marketing Success Through Differentiation—Of Anything," *Harvard Business Review*, January–February 1980: 83–91.

———, "The Globalization of Markets," *Harvard Business Review*, May–June 1983: 92–102.

———, *The Marketing Imagination*. New York: Free Press, 1983.

LEWIN, K., *Field Theory In Social Science*. New York: Harper & Row, 1951.

LIKERT, R., *New Patterns of Management*. New York: McGraw-Hill, 1969.

LINDBLOM, C. E., "The Science of 'Muddling Through,'" *Public Administration Review*, 1959: 79–88.

———, *The Policy-Making Process*. Englewood Cliffs, N.J.: Prentice Hall, 1968.

LITTLE, A. D., INC., "Transportation Planning In the District of Columbia, 1955–65: A Review and Critique," Report to the Policy Advisory Committee to the District Commissioners. Washington, D.C.: U.S. Government Printing Office, 1966.

LODGE, G. C., *The New American Ideology*. New York: Alfred A. Knopf, 1975.

LOHR, S., "Japan Struggling with Itself," *The New York Times*, June 13, 1982.

MACAVOY, P. W., *The Economic Effects of Regulation*. Cambridge, Mass.: M.I.T. Press, 1965.

MACMILLAN, I.C., "Seizing Competitive Initiative," *Journal of Business Strategy*, Spring 1982: 43–57.

———, "Preemptive Strategies," *Journal of Business Strategy*, Fall 1983: 16–26.

———, & P. E. JONES, "Designing Organizations to Compete," *Journal of Business Strategy*, Spring 1984: 11–26.

———, M. MCCAFFERY & G. VAN WIJK, "Competitors' Responses to Easily Imitated New Products—Exploring Commercial Banking Product Introductions," *Strategic Management Journal*, 1985: 75–86.

MACE, M. L. & G. G. MONTGOMERY, *Management Problems of Corporate Acquisitions*. Boston: Harvard Business School, 1962.

MACHIAVELLI, N., *The Prince, and the Discourses*. New York: Modern Library, 1950.

MACKWORTH, N. H., "Originality," in D. Wolfe, ed., *The Discovery of Talent*. Cambridge, Mass.: Harvard University Press, 1969.

MAETERLINCK, M., *The Life of the Bee*. New York: Dodd, Mead, 1918.

MAGEE, J. F., "Decision Trees for Decision Making," *Harvard Business Review*, July–August, 1964: 126–138.

———, *Desirable Characteristics of Models in Planning*, a paper delivered at the Symposium on the Role of Economic Models in Policy Formulation, sponsored by the Department Of Housing and Urban Development, Office of Emergency Planning, National Resource Evaluation Center, Washington, D.C., October, 1966.

MAJONE, G., "The Use of Policy Analysis," in *The Future and the Past: Essays on Programs*, Russell Sage Foundation Annual Report, 1976–1977.

MALINEY, G. J., "The Choice of Organizational Form . . ." *Strategic Management Journal*, 1992(13): 559–584.

MAO TSE-TUNG, *Selected Military Writings, 1928–1949*. San Francisco: China Books, 1967.

MARCH, J. G., & J. P. OLSEN, *Ambiguity and Choice in Organizations*. Bergen, Norway: Universitetsforlaget, 1976.

———, & H. A. SIMON, *Organizations*. New York: John Wiley, 1958.

MARSHALL, G. L., *Predicting Executive Achievement*. Ph.D. thesis, Harvard Business School, 1964.

MARTIN, L. C. "How Beatrice Foods Sneaked Up on $5 Billion," *Fortune*, April 1976: 119–129.

MASON, R. & I. MITROFF, *Challenging Strategic Planning Assumptions*. New York: John Wiley, 1981.

MATLOFF, M. & E. M. SNELL, *Strategic Planning for Coalition Warfare (1941–42)*. Washington, D. C.: Office of Chief of Military History, Department of the Army, 1953.

MAYO, E., *The Social Problems of an Industrial Civilization*. Boston: Harvard Business School, 1945.

McCLELLAND, D.C., "The Two Faces of Power," *Journal of International Affairs*, 1970: 29–47.

McDONALD, J., *Strategy in Poker, Business and War*. New York: W.W. Norton, 1950.

McINTYRE, S. H., "Obstacles to Corporate Innovation," *Business Horizons*, January–February 1982: 23–28.

MECHANIC, D., "Sources of Power of Lower Participants In Complex Organizations," *Administrative Science Quarterly*, 1962: 349–364.

MILES, R. & C. SNOW, "Organizations, New Concepts and New Forms," *California Management Review*, Spring 1986: 62–73.

———, & H. J. COLEMAN, JR., "Managing 21st Century Network Organizations," *Organization Dynamics*, 1992.

MILLER, D., & P. H. FRIESEN, "Archetypes of Strategy Formulation," *Management Science*, May 1978: 921–933.

———, *Organizations: A Quantum View*. Englewood Cliffs, N.J.: Prentice Hall, 1984.

———, & M. KETS DE VRIES, *The Neurotic Organization*. San Francisco: Jossey-Bass, 1984.

———, *Unstable at the Top*. New York: New American Library, 1987.

———, & H. MINTZBERG, *Strategy Formulation in Context: Some Tentative Models*. Working Paper, McGill University, 1974.

MILLER, L., *American Spirit: Visions of a New Corporate Culture*. New York: William Morrow, 1984.

MILLS, D. Q., *Rebirth of the Corporation*. New York: John Wiley, 1991.

MINTZBERG, H., "Research on Strategy-Making," *Academy of Management Proceedings*, 1972: 90–94.

———, *The Nature of Managerial Work*. New York: Harper & Row, 1973.

———, "Strategy Making in Three Modes," *California Management Review*, Winter 1973b: 44–53.

———, "The Manager's Job: Folklore and Fact," *Harvard Business Review*, July–August 1975: 49–61.

———, "Generic Strategies: Toward a Comprehensive Framework," *Advances in Strategic Management*, Vol. 5, pp. 1–67. Greenwich, Conn.: JAI Press, 1988.

———, "Crafting Strategy," *Harvard Business Review*, July–August 1987: 66–75.

———, D. RAÌSINGNANÌ, & A. THÉORÉT, "The Structure of 'Unstructured' Decision Processes," *Administrative Science Quarterly*, 1976: 246–275.

———, & J. A. WATERS, "Tracking Strategy in an Entrepreneurial Firm," *Academy of Management Journal*, 1982: 465–499.

———, "Of Strategies, Deliberate and Emergent," *Strategic Management Journal*, 1985: 257–272.

MITROFF, I., *Break-Away Thinking*. New York: John Wiley, 1988.

MONTGOMERY, B. L., *The Memoirs of Field-Marshal The Viscount Montgomery of Alamein*. Cleveland: World Publishing, 1958.

MORITANI, M., *Japanese Technology: Getting the Best for the Least*. Tokyo: Simul Press, 1981.

MOYER, R. C., "Berle and Means Revisited: The Conglomerate Merger," *Business and Society*, Spring 1970: 20–29.

NADLER, D. A. & E. E. LAWLER, III, "Motivation—A Diagnostic Approach," in J. R. Hackman, E. E. Lawler, III, & L. W. Porter, Eds., *Perspective on Behavior in Organizations*. New York: McGraw-Hill. 1977.

NADLER, D., & M. L. TUSHMAN, *Strategic Organization Design*. Homewood, Ill.: Scott Foresman, 1986.

NAISBITT, J., *Megatrends*. New York: Warner Books, 1982.

NAPOLEON, I., "Maximes de Guerre," in T. R. Phillips, Ed., *Roots of Strategy*. Harrisburg, Pa.: Military Service Publishing, 1940.

NATHANSON, D., & J. CASSANO, "Organization Diversity and Performance," *The Wharton Magazine,* Summer 1982: 18–26.

NEUSTADT, R. E., *Presidential Power: The Politics of Leadership.* New York: John Wiley, 1960.

NOËL, A., "Strategic Cores and Magnificent Obsessions: Discovering Strategy Formation through Daily Activities of CEOs," *Strategic Management Journal* 1989(10): 33–49.

NONAKA, I., "Creating Organizational Order Out of Chaos: Self-Renewal in Japanese Firms," *California Management Review,* Spring 1988: 57–73.

NORMANN, R., *Management for Growth,* translated by N. Adler. New York: John Wiley, 1977.

NYSTROM, P. C., B. L. T. HEDBERG, & W. H. STARBUCK, "Interacting Processes as Organization Designs," in R. H. Kiltmann, L. R. Pondy, & D. P. Slevin, eds., *The Management of Organization Design,* Vol. 1. New York: Elsevier North-Holland, 1976.

OGILVY, D., *Ogilvy on Advertising.* New York: Crown, 1983.

OHMAE, K., *The Mind of the Strategist.* New York: McGraw-Hill, 1982.

ONO, H., "Nihonteki Keiei Shisutemu to Jinji Kettei Shisutemu" ("Japanese Management System and Personnel Decisions"), *Soshiki Kagaku,* 1976: 22–32.

OUCHI, W. G., "Market, Bureaucracies and Clans," *Administrative Science Quarterly,* 1980: 129–140.

———, *Theory Z.* Reading, Mass.: Addison-Wesley, 1981.

———, & A. M. JAEGER, "Type Z Organization: Stability in the Midst of Mobility," *Academy of Management Review,* 1978: 305–314.

———, & B. JOHNSON, "Types of Organizational Control and Their Relationship to Emotional Well Being," *Administrative Science Quarterly,* 1978: 293–317.

PARSONS, T., *Structure and Process in Modern Societies.* Glencoe, Ill.: Free Press, 1960.

PASCALE, R. T., "Perspectives on Strategy: The Real Story Behind Honda's Success," *California Management Review,* Spring 1984: 47–72.

PAUL, N. L., "The Use of Empathy in the Resolution of Grief," in *Perspective in Biology and Medicine.* Chicago: University of Chicago Press, 1967.

PENCE, C. C., *How Venture Capitalists Make Venture Decisions.* Ann Arbor, Mich.: UMI Research Press, 1982.

PERROW, C., "The Analysis of Goals in Complex Organizations," *American Sociological Review,* 1961: 854–866.

———, *Organizational Analysis: A Sociological Review.* Belmont, Calif.: Wadsworth, 1970.

———, *Complex Organizations: A Critical Essay,* New York: Scott, Foresman, 1972.

PETERS, T. J., "A Style for All Seasons," *Executive,* Summer 1980: 12–16.

———, & R. H. WATERMAN, *In Search of Excellence: Lessons from America's Best Run Companies.* New York: Harper & Row, 1982.

PFEFFER, J., "Size and Composition of Corporate Boards of Directors: The Organization and Its Environment," *Administrative Science Quarterly,* 1972a: 218–228.

———, "Merger as a Response to Organizational Interdependence," *Administrative Science Quarterly,* 1972b: 382–394.

———, "Size, Composition and Function of Hospital Boards of Directors: A Study of Organization-Environment Linkage," *Administrative Science Quarterly,* 1973: 349–364.

———, "Administrative Regulation and Licensing: Social Problem or Solution?" *Social Problems,* 1974: 468–479.

———, *Management as Symbolic Action: The Creation and Maintenance of Organizational Paradigms.* Working Paper, Stanford University, 1979.

———, & H. LEBLEBICI, "Executive Recruitment and the Development of Interfirm Organizations," *Administrative Science Quarterly,* 1973: 449–461.

———, & P. NOWAK, "Patterns of Joint Venture Activity: Implication for Antitrust Policy," *The Antitrust Bulletin,* 1976: 315–339.

———, "Joint Ventures and Interorganizational Interdependence," *Administrative Science Quarterly,* 1976b: 398–418.

———, *Organizational Context and Interorganizational Linkages Among Corporations.* Working Paper, University of California at Berkeley, no date.

———, & H. LEBLEBICI, "The Effect of Uncertainty on the Use of Social Influence in Organizational Decision-Making," *Administrative Science Quarterly,* 1976: 227–245.

PFIFFNER, J. M., "Administrative Rationality," *Public Administration Review,* 1960: 125–132.

PHILLIPS, T. R. ed., *Roots of Strategy.* Harrisburg, Pa.: Military Service Publishing, 1940.

PORTER, M. E., *Competitive Strategy: Techniques for Analyzing Industries and Competitors.* New York: Free Press, 1980.

———, *Competitive Advantage: Creating and Sustaining Superior Performance.* New York: Free Press, 1985.

———, "Generic Competitive Strategies," in M. E. Porter, *Competitive Advantage,* pp. 34–46. New York: Free Press, 1985.

———, "Competition in Global Industries: A Conceptual Framework," in M. E. Porter, ed., *Competition in Global Industries.* Boston: Harvard Business School Press, 1986.

———, "From Competitive Advantage to Corporate Strategy," *Harvard Business Review,* May–June 1987: 43–59.

POSNER, B., & B. BURLINGHAM, "The Hottest Entrepreneur in America," *Inc.,* January 1988, 44–58.

POSNER, R. A., "Theories of Economic Regulation," *Bell Journal of Economics and Management Science*, 1974: 335–358.

PRAHALAD, C., & G. HAMEL, "The Core Competence of the Corporation," *Harvard Business Review*, May–June 1990: 79–91.

PRICE, J. L., "The Impact of Governing Boards on Organizational Effectiveness and Morale," *Administrative Science Quarterly*, 1963: 361–378.

PUCIK, V., "Getting Ahead In Japan," *The Japanese Economic Journal*, 1981: 970–971.

———, "Promotions and Intra-Organizational Status Differentiation among Japanese Managers," *The Academy of Management Proceedings*, 1981: 59–63.

PURKAYASTHA, D., *"Note on the Motorcycle Industry 1975."* Copyrighted Case, Harvard Business School, 1981.

QUINN, J. B., "Strategic Goals: Process and Politics," *Sloan Management Review*, Fall 1977: 21–37.

———, *Strategies for Change: Logical Incrementalism.* Homewood, Ill.: Richard D. Irwin, 1980.

———, *Intelligent Enterprise.* New York: Free Press, 1992.

———, "Leveraging Knowledge and Service Based Strategies Through Strategic Outsourcing," In *Intelligent Enterprise.* New York: Free Press. 1992.

———, T. DOORLEY, & P. C. PAQUETTE, "Technology In Services: Rethinking Strategic Focus," *Sloan Management Review*, January 1990.

RAPHAEL, R., *Edges.* New York: Alfred A. Knopf, 1976.

REESER, C., "Some Potential Human Problems in the Project Form of Organization," *Academy of Management Journal*, 1969: 459–467.

REID, S. R., *Mergers, Managers, and the Economy.* New York: McGraw-Hill, 1968.

RHENMAN, E., *Organization Theory for Long-Range Planning.* New York: John Wiley, 1973.

ROHLEN, T. P., *For Harmony and Strength: Japanese White-Collar Organization in Anthropological Perspective.* Berkeley: University Of California Press, 1974.

ROSNER, M., *Principle Types and Problems of Direct Democracy in the Kibbutz.* Working Paper, Social Research Center on the Kibbutz, Givat Haviva, Israel, 1969.

ROSS, I., "How Lawless Are the Big Companies?" *Fortune*, December 1, 1980: 56–64.

ROSSOTTI, C. O., *Two Concepts of Long-Range Planning.* Boston: The Management Consulting Group, The Boston Safe Deposit & Trust Company, no date.

RUMELT, R. P., *Strategy, Structure and Economic Performance.* Boston: Harvard Business School Press, 1974.

———, "A Teaching Plan for Strategy Alternatives for the British Motorcycle Industry," in *Japanese Business: Business Policy.* New York: The Japan Society, 1980.

———, "Diversification Strategy and Profitability," *Strategic Management Journal*, 1982: 359–370.

———, Strategic Management Society Conference, Montreal, October 1982.

SAHLMAN, W. A., & H. H. STEVENSON, "Capital Market Myopia," *Journal of Business Venturing*, Winter 1985: 7–30.

SAKIYA, T., "The Story of Honda's Founders," *Asahi Evening News*, June–August, 1979.

———, *Honda Motor: The Men, The Management, The Machines.* Tokyo, Japan: Kadonsha International, 1982.

SALTER, M. S., & W. A. WEINHOLD, *Diversification Through Acquisition.* New York: Free Press, 1979.

SAYLES, L. R., *Managerial Behavior: Administration In Complex Organizations.* New York: McGraw-Hill, 1964.

———, "How Graduates Scare Bosses," *Careers Today*, January 1969.

———, *The Working Leader*, New York: Free Press, 1993.

SCHEIN, E., *Organizational Culture and Leadership.* San Francisco: Jossey-Bass, 1985.

SCHELLING, T. C., *The Strategy of Conflict*, 2d ed. Cambridge, Mass.: Harvard University Press, 1980.

SCHENDEL, D. G., R. PATTON, & J. RIGGS, "Corporate Turnaround Strategies: A Study of Profit Decline and Recovery," *Journal of General Management*, Spring 1976: 3–11.

SCOTT, W. E., "Activation Theory and Task Design," *Organizational Behavior and Human Performance.* September 1966: 3–30.

SELZNICK, P., *TVA and the Grass Roots.* Berkeley: University Of California Press, 1949.

———, *Leadership in Administration: A Sociological Interpretation.* New York: Harper & Row, 1957

SENGE, P. *The Fifth Discipline: The Art and Practice of the Learning Organization.* New York: Doubleday/Currency, 1990.

SHUBIK, M., *Games for Society, Business, and War: Towards a Theory of Gaming.* New York: Elsevier, 1975.

SIMON, H. A., "The Architecture of Complexity," *Proceedings of the American Philosophical Society*, 1962(106): 122–137.

SIMON, M. A., "On the Concept of Organizational Goals," *Administrative Science Quarterly*, 1964–1965: 1–22.

SIMONS, R., "The Role of Management Control Systems in Creating Competitive Advantage: New Perspectives," *Accounting, Organizations and Society*, 1990(15): 127–143.

———, "Strategic Orientation and Top Management Attention to Control Systems," *Strategic Management Journal*, 1991(12): 49–62.

SMITH, L., "The Boardroom Is Becoming a Different Scene," *Fortune*, May 8, 1978: 150–88.

SMITH, W. R., "Product Differentiation and Market Segmentation as Alternative Marketing Strategies," *Journal of Marketing*, July 1956: 3–8.

SOLZHENITSYN, A., "Why the West Has Succumbed to Cowardice," *The Montreal Star: News and Review*, June 10, 1978.

SPEER, A., *Inside the Third Reich*. New York: Macmillan, 1970.

SPENCER, F. C., "Deductive Reasoning in the Lifelong Continuing Education of a Cardiovascular Surgeon," *Archives of Surgery*, 1976: 1177–1183.

SPENDER, J. C., *Industry Recipes: The Nature and Sources of Managerial Judgement*. London: Basil Blackwell, 1989.

STALK, G., JR., "Time: The Next Source of Competitive Advantage," *Harvard Business Review*, July–August 1988: 41–51.

STARBUCK, W. H., "Organizations and Their Environments," in M. D. Dunnette, ed., *Handbook of Industrial and Organizational Psychology*. Chicago: Rand McNally, 1976.

STARBUCK, W. H. & B. L. T. HEDBERG, "Saving an Organization from a Stagnating Environment," in H. B. Thorelli, ed., *Strategy + Structure = Performance*. Bloomington: Indiana University Press, 1977.

THE STATE OF SMALL BUSINESS, A REPORT TO THE PRESIDENT. Washington, D.C.: U.S. Government Printing Office, 1984.

STERN, L. W., B. STERNTHAL, & C. S. CRAIG, "Managing Conflict in Distribution Channels: A Laboratory Study," *Journal of Marketing Research*, 1973: 169–179.

STEVENSON, "Defining Corporate Strengths and Weaknesses," *Sloan Management Review*, Spring 1976: 51–68.

STEVENSON, W., *A Man Called Intrepid: The Secret War*. New York: Harcourt Brace Jovanovich, 1976.

STEWART, R., *Managers and Their Jobs*. London: Macmillan, 1967.

STIGLER, C. J., "The Theory of Economic Regulation," *Bell Journal of Economics and Management Science*, 1971: 3–21.

SUN TZU, *The Art of War*, translated by S. B. Griffith. New York: Oxford University Press, 1963. Original 500 B.C.

TAKEUCHI, H., & I. NONAKA, "The New New Product Development Game," *Harvard Business Review*, January–February 1986: 137–146.

TAYLOR, W. H., "The Nature of Policy Making In Universities," *The Canadian Journal of Higher Education*, 1983: 17–32.

TECHNOLOGICAL INNOVATION: ITS ENVIRONMENT AND MANAGEMENT. Washington, D.C.: U.S. Government Printing Office, 1967.

THOMPSON, J. D., *Organizations in Action*. New York: McGraw-Hill, 1967.

THOMPSON, V. A., *Modern Organizations*. New York: Alfred A. Knopf, 1961.

TILLES, S., "How to Evaluate Corporate Strategy," *Harvard Business Review*, July–August 1963: 111–121.

TIME, "The Most Basic Form of Creativity," June 26, 1972.

TOFFLER, A., *Future Shock*. New York: Bantam Books, 1970.

TREGOE, B., & I. ZIMMERMAN, *Top Management Strategy*. New York: Simon & Schuster, 1980.

TSUJI, K., "Decision-Making in the Japanese Government: A Study of Ringisei," in R. E. Wards, ed., *Political Development in Modern Japan*, Princeton: Princeton University Press, 1968.

TSURUMI, Y., *Multinational Management: Business Strategy and Government Policy*. Cambridge, Mass.: Ballinger, 1977.

TUCHMAN, B. W., *The Guns of August*. New York: Macmillan, 1962.

TURNER, D., & M. CRAWFORD, "Managing Current and Future Competitive Performance: The Role of Competence." Kensington, Australia, University of New South Wales, Australian Graduate School of Management, Center for Corporate Change, 1992.

URBAN, G. L., R. CARTER, S. GASKIN, & Z. MUCHA, "Market Share Rewards to Pioneering Brands," *Management Science*, June 1986(6): 645–659.

VANCIL, R. F., "Strategy Formulation in Complex Organizations," *Sloan Management Review*, Winter 1976: 1–18.

————, & P. LORANGE, "Strategic Planning in Diversified Companies," *Harvard Business Review*, January–February 1975: 81–90.

VAN DOREN, M., *Liberal Education*, Boston: Beacon Press, 1967.

VARNER, V. J. & J. I. ALGER, eds., *History of the Military Art: Notes for the Course*. West Point, N.Y.: U.S. Military Academy, 1978.

VICKERS, G., "Is Adaptability Enough?" *Behavioral Science*, 1959: 219–234.

VOGEL, E., *Japan As Number One*. Cambridge, Mass.: Harvard University Press, 1979.

VON BÜLOW, D. F., *The Spirit of the Modern System of War*, translated by C. M. DeMartemont. London: C. Mercier, 1806.

VON CLAUSEWITZ, C., *On War*, translated by M. Howard and P. Paret. Princeton, N.J.: Princeton University Press, 1976.

VON HIPPEL, E., "Get New Products from Customers," *Harvard Business Review*, March–April 1982: 117–122.

VON NEUMANN, J. & O. MORGENSTERN, *Theory of Games and Economic Behavior*. Princeton, N.J.: Princeton University Press, 1944.

WACK, P. "Scenarios: Uncharted Waters Ahead," *Harvard Business Review*, September–October 1985: 73–89.

WARD, L. B., *Analysis of 1969 Alumni Questionnaire Returns.* Unpublished Report, Harvard Business School, 1970.

WATERMAN, R. H., JR., T. J. PETERS & J. R. PHILLIPS, "Structure Is Not Organization," *Business Horizons,* June 1980: 14–26.

WEBER, M., "The Three Types of Legitimate Rule," translated by H. Gerth, in A. Etzioni, ed., *A Sociological Reader on Complex Organizations.* New York: Holt, Rinehart and Winston, 1969.

WEICK, K. E., "Educational Organizations As Loosely Coupled Systems," *Administrative Science Quarterly,* 1976: 1–19.

———, *The Social Psychology of Organizing.* Reading, Mass: Addison -Wesley, 1979.

WESTLEY, F., & H. MINTZBERG, "Visionary Leadership and Strategic Management," *Strategic Management Journal,* 1989: 11–32.

WHEELWRIGHT, S. C., "Japan—Where Operations Really Are Strategic," *Harvard Business Review,* July–August 1981: 67–74.

WHITE, T. H., *In Search of History: A Personal Adventure.* New York: Warner Books, 1978.

WHITEHEAD, A. N., *Aims of Education and Other Essays.* New York: Macmillan, 1929.

WHYTE, W. F., *Street Corner Society.* Chicago: University of Chicago Press, 1955.

WILLIAMSON, O. E., *Markets and Hierarchies: Analysis and Antitrust Implications.* New York: Free Press, 1975.

———, *The Economic Institutions of Capitalism.* New York: Free Press, 1985.

WISE, D., "Apple's New Crusade," *Business Week,* November 26, 1984.

WITTE, E., "Field Research on Complex Decision-Making Processes—The Phase Theorem," *International Studies of Management and Organization,* Summer 1972: 156–182.

WODARSKI, J. S., R. L. HAMBLIN, D. R. BUCKHOLDT, & D. E. FERRITOR, "Individual Consequences versus Different Shared Consequences Contingent on the Performance of Low-Achieving Group Members," *Journal of Applied Social Psychology,* 1973: 276–290.

WOO, C., & A. COOPER, "Strategies of Effective Low Share Businesses," *Strategic Management Journal,* 1981: 301–318.

WORTHY, J. C., "Organizational Structure and Employee Morale," *American Sociological Review,* 1950: 169–179.

———, *Big Business and Free Men.* New York: Harper & Row, 1959.

WRAPP, H. E., "Good Managers Don't Make Policy Decisions," *Harvard Business Review,* September–October 1967: 91–99.

WRIGLEY, L., "Diversification and Divisional Autonomy," DBA dissertation, Graduate School of Business Administration, Harvard University, 1970.

YOSHINO, M., *Japan's Managerial System.* Cambridge, Mass.: M.I.T. Press, 1968.

YOSHINO, M. Y., "Global Competition in a Salient Industry: The Case of Civil Aircraft," in M. E. Porter, ed., *Competition in Global Industries.* Boston: Harvard Business School Press, 1986.

YOUNG, D., *Rommel: The Desert Fox.* New York: Harper & Row, 1974.

ZALD, M. N., "Urban Differentiation, Characteristics of Boards of Directors and Organizational Effectiveness," *American Journal of Sociology,* 1967: 261–272.

———, & M. A. BERGER, "Social Movements in Organizations: Coup D'etat, Insurgency, and Mass Movements," *American Journal of Sociology,* 1978.

ZALEZNIK, A., "Power and Politics in Organizational Life," *Harvard Business Review,* May–June 1970: 47–60